Preface

This guide to Scandinavia is one of the new generation of Baedeker guides.

These guides, illustrated throughout in colour, are designed to meet the needs of the modern traveller. They are quick and easy to consult, with the principal places of interest described in alphabetical order, and the information is presented in a format that is both attractive and easy to follow.

This guide covers Norway, Sweden and Finland, the Scandinavian countries in the north of Europe, which offer a range of interesting towns and magnificent scenery, including the fjords and mountains in the west, the skerries off the coasts and the Finnish Lakeland in the east. Also included are Lapland and various islands and island groups, like Spitzbergen (Svalbard) in the far north.

Angling a popular pastime: Tivedon National Park in Sweden

The guide is in three parts. The first part gives a general account of the three countries, their topography and geology, climate, flora and fauna, population, government and society, economy, history, famous people, art and culture. A selection of literary quotations and a number of suggested routes lead in to the second part, in which places of tourist interest are described. The third part contains a variety of practical information. Both the sights and the practical information are listed in alphabetical order.

The new Baedeker guides are noted for their concentration on essentials and their convenience of use. They contain numerous specially drawn plans and colour illustrations; and at the end of the book is a large map making it easy to locate the various places described in the "A to Z" section of the guide with the help of the co-ordinates given at the head of each entry.

Contents

$\mathcal{B}aedeker$

SCANDINAVIA

NORWAY
SWEDEN
FINLAND

Hints for using the Guide

Following the tradition established by Karl Baedeker in 1844, buildings and works of art, places of natural beauty and sights of particular interest, as well as hotels and restaurants of especially high quality, are distinguished by one ★ or two ★★ stars.

To make it easier to locate the various places listed in the "A to Z" section of the Guide, their co-ordinates are shown in red at the head of each entry: e.g., Helsinki F/G 5.

Coloured lines down the right-hand side of the page are an aid to finding the main heading in the Guide: blue stands for the Introduction (Nature, Culture, History, etc.), red for the "A to Z" section, and yellow indicates Practical Information.

Only a selection of hotels and restaurants can be given; no reflection is implied therefore on establishments not included.

In a time of rapid change it is difficult to ensure that all the information given is entirely accurate and up-to-date, and the possibility of error can never be entirely eliminated.

Although the publishers can accept no responsibility for inaccuracies and omissions, they are constantly endeavouring to improve the quality of their Guides and are therefore always grateful for criticisms, corrections and suggestions for improvement.

Fjords, forests and

. . . are some of the features that we all associate with Scandinavia. Can there be anyone who has not seen a photograph showing a part of Norway lit up by the midnight sun or the never-to-be-forgotten fjords on the Norwegian coast? Similar regions are also to be found further inland – in the south of Sweden, for example, or on Lake Saimaa in Finland. Scandinavia particularly attracts those who are interested in nature in all its guises and who also like peace and quiet. All that is necessary is to rent a holiday cottage, relax and explore the surrounding countryside.

Because of the large numbers of forests, timber plays a special role in the lives of the Scandinavian peoples and has been a major factor in the economy since time immemorial. It is now used in paper making, while in days gone by it was the chief material used in building, for example, the typical stave churches and farmsteads which can be seen and admired in the many open-air museums. Ships, such as the Viking ships to be seen on the Bygdøy Peninsula near Oslo, were also made of wood.

In Lapland. the northern part of Scandanivia which incorporates parts of Norway, Sweden and Finland, live the Sami (Lapps). They are easily recognisable in summer by their costumes of blue material with red or yellow trimming, and together with their reindeer are a

At the North Cape
Sunrise at midnight

South Sweden
Typical of Skåne are farmsteads surrounded by fields and meadows

Finland
With its lakes and rivers Finland is an Eldorado for lovers of water sports. A boat trip is very relaxing and enjoyable

the midnight sun

popular tourist attraction. Carved reindeer horn is a favourite souvenir.

Anyone visiting cities such as Bergen, Oslo, Stockholm or Helsinki will see some impressive buildings. These may be castles or churches with their memorials to well-known historical figures, such as the Riddarholm church in Stockholm, which contains the tomb of King Gustavus Adolphus as well as those of other Swedish rulers, or later buildings which display the Scandinavians' flair for modern architecture. There are also many interesting museums such as the Munch Museum in Oslo; the Old Town quarters, fountains and parks in the major cities all possess their own particular magic.

The island of Öland

The characteristic windmills on Öland are all listed buildings

Historically, there have been many political links between the three countries of Norway, Sweden and Finland, some of which – such as the Union of Kalmar in 1397 – involved Denmark as well. In the 19th century Norway was united with Sweden. For many centuries Finland belonged to Sweden and then to Russia. The "land of the sixty thousand lakes" formed the point where East and West met, as is clearly witnesed by the gilded domes of the Uspenski Cathedral in Helsinki. Today these northern countries are actively seeking economic alliances with central Europe. When travelling in these northern countries the visitor will discover much about the peoples and their social problems.

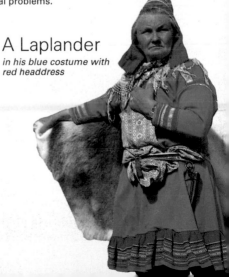

A Laplander

in his blue costume with red headdress

Market scene

Much fish is caught and eaten in Scandinavian countries. This picture shows a fisherwoman's stall on Helsinki market

Facts and Figures

General

Scandinavia consists of a central core formed by the two countries of Norway and Sweden, together with Denmark to the west and Finland to the east. Since there is a separate AA/Baedeker guide to Denmark (along with the Faroes and Greenland), the present guide covers only the three countries of Norway, Sweden and Finland.

Scandinavia in the narrower sense consists of the Scandinavian Peninsula, the largest peninsula in Europe, with an area of some 750,000sq.km/290,000sq. miles. It extends for some 1800km/1120 miles from Skåne in the south to the North Cape, separating the Baltic from the North Sea. On this peninsula are Norway and Sweden. Finland, which borders on both Norway and Sweden in the north and is bounded on the west by the Gulf of Bothnia and on the south by the Gulf of Finland, belongs geographically to Eastern Europe and is bordered on the east by Russia (Karelia).

Situation and territory

Finland was shaped by the same natural forces as Sweden, and in many ways it shows the topographical forms moulded by the last Ice Age more markedly than its neighbour. Its coastal regions bear a strong Swedish historical and cultural imprint, and the busy shipping traffic in the Gulf of Bothnia has bound the two countries closely together.

If account is also taken of Denmark, with which for centuries Skåne was politically associated, Scandinavia in the wider sense coincides with the geographical conception of Northern Europe, a region of clearly marked individuality. If we disregard Eastern Europe, there is no other part of the European continent with such a uniform topographical structure. It lacks the fragmented pattern of uplands and mountains found in Central and particularly in Southern Europe; and although the coasts of Scandinavia are much indented they follow a generally straight line, while there is easy passage from end to end of Sweden, impeded by rivers but without any mountain barriers. Though much broken up by geological action, the Scandinavian mountains form a unified and self-contained complex.

Northern Europe

The total population of this large area, however, is only some 23,000,000, and the population of its northern parts is particularly sparse: although the regions north of the 61st parallel account for two-thirds of the total area of Scandinavia they are occupied by only a fifth of its population, at a density of about 5 to the sq. kilometre (13 to the sq. mile). This relative concentration of population in the southern parts of Scandinavia is primarily due to climatic conditions; but the northern regions could undoubtedly support a larger population than any other part of the world in the same latitude.

More significant, however, than the inhospitable climate – though this, thanks to the Gulf Stream, is milder than in similar territories

◄ *Runic Stone on the island of Öland (Sweden)*

elsewhere – is the fact of the long winter nights, with their inevitably depressing psychological effect. The variation in the length of the day over the course of a year increases towards the north, so that beyond the Arctic Circle (66°33') the sun is above the horizon in summer and below it in winter for an increasing number of days (at Kiruna about 45 days, at Hammerfest 72). At the North Pole it appears above the horizon on March 21st and does not set until September 21st, so that in spring it climbs above the horizon in an apparently spiral course and in autumn spirals down again.

Topography and Geology

Topography

High plateaux

The topographical structure of Scandinavia appears remarkably simple. Throughout the whole length of Norway and along the Norwegian–Swedish frontier the Scandinavian mountain chain extends for a distance of some 1700km/1050 miles (compared with barely 1000km/620 miles for the Alps). Its characteristic features are the great expanses of high plateau, partly consisting of peat-bogs and dotted with small lakes, which lie at a fairly uniform altitude between 1000 and 1500m (3300 and 4900ft). Above the plateau, particularly round the Sognefjord and in northern Sweden, rear numerous sharply pointed and much glaciated peaks which reach heights of 2468m/8098ft in central Norway (Galdhøpiggen) and 2117m/6946ft in northern Sweden (Kebnekaise). Here and there, too, isolated massifs rise to heights of some 1800m/5900ft.

Fjords and skerries in Norway

On the Norwegian side of the chain the high plateaux are slashed by numerous valleys, the lower reaches of which are frequently filled by the ends of fjords which cut deeply into the land, and the upper parts by long narrow lakes. The valleys have the typical U-shaped profile gouged out by mighty Ice Age glaciers, extending right down to the Atlantic. Along the west side of the mountains is a relatively flat coastal strip, beyond which the tops of rocky hills worn by glacial action emerge from the sea in the form of skerries. Where the coastal strip is wider and stands higher above the sea, as at the mouth of the Hardangerfjord, there are expanses of attractive green countryside.

Uplands and isolated hills in Sweden

On the Swedish side the valleys tend to be wider and the plateaux more broken up into separate massifs. Along the eastern fringe of the mountains in northern Sweden runs a broad swathe of uplands ranging in width between 150 and 250km (95 and 155 miles), falling from about 600m/2000ft to 200m/650ft near the Gulf of Bothnia. In this region are numerous isolated hills known to geologists as monadnocks (local name *klack*), but these rise barely above 800m/2600ft. In Norrland (the name given to northern Sweden) the coastal strip and the girdle of skerries are very narrow indeed.

Finnish Lakeland

From the Finnish coast, lying opposite Sweden across the Gulf of Bothnia, the land rises much more gradually to the Finnish Lakeland, an immense tangle of lakes, inlets, islands and peninsulas such as is found in Sweden, on a smaller scale, only in some areas round Lake Mälar. This region – the inland counterpart of the fjords and skerries of the Scandinavian west coast – is brought to an abrupt end by the Salpausselkä ridge of hills, to the south of which the land slopes regularly and gradually down, with only a few small lakes, to the Gulf of Finland.

Skerries off the Finnish and Swedish coasts

Off the south-west coast of Finland is the largest belt of skerries. Between Turku and the Åland Islands are swarms of these rocky islets, with rounded tops formed by glacial action, those near the coast being

Fjell country in the Lofotens in autumn

Skerries, Stockholm

higrer and wooded, while farther out they are completely bare. There is a similar fringe of skerries off Stockholm in which no fewer than 24,000 islands and islets have been counted.

Central Swedish depression

From Stockholm a stretch of lowlands extends by way of Lake Mälar into the central Swedish depression, with Lake Vänern, a relic of the sea which once covered this region. To the south is Småland, with hills rising to barely 400m/1300ft; and beyond this, to the south-west, are Bohuslän and Halland, their coasts fringed by skerries.

Geology

Skåne

Skåne, at the southernmost tip of the Scandinavian peninsula, has a quite different geological structure from the rest of Scandinavia. A narrow ridge of ancient rocks does, it is true, emerge from more recent deposits, pointing towards Bornholm; but for the rest the basement rocks match those of the Danish islands, and the coastal forms of Skåne are quite different from those found elsewhere on the Scandinavian peninsula. Here there are no fjords or skerries instead there are projecting spits of land and fringes of dunes.

Southern and central Sweden

Everywhere in Scandinavia north of Skåne very ancient rocks predominate in the landscape, though in many places they are overlaid by the most recent geological formations, the morainic deposits of the Ice Age Mesozoic strata are entirely absent. The western parts of southern and central Sweden are mainly built up of gneiss, while to the east of a line running south through Lake Vättern granites predominate, overlaid in some areas by flows of porphyry. Horizontally bedded Cambrian and Silurian sediments are found only in remnants of varying size, the Silurian deposits frequently providing the basis for expanses of fertile arable land. At various points, too, volcanic eruptions in the Palaeozoic era have yielded diabases − producing, for example, the prominent Kinnekulle range and the plateau-like hills of Västergötland with their striking rock walls.

Öland and Gotland

The islands of Öland and Gotland consist almost entirely of Silurian limestones. The Silurian period, which began some 440 million years ago and ended some 400 million years ago, was formerly also known as the Gotlandium, after the Swedish island of Gotland.

Scandinavian mountains

In Silurian times the ancient rocks of the Scandinavian mountains were subjected to the Caledonian folding movement and thrust over the horizontally bedded rocks to the east. The south-western continuation of the range, which is some twenty times older than the Alps, emerges again in Scotland and northern Ireland.

Geological processes of the last Ice Age

The geological processes of the last Ice Age played a much greater part in shaping the present topography of the Scandinavian countries than those of earlier periods. Even where the morainic formations, so common everywhere, and other glacial deposits are lacking, the work of the ice has so radically transformed the earth's surface that all older forms can be only dimly perceived below the surface: only the massive Scandinavian mountain chain has survived For tens of thousands of years the whole of northern Europe and North Germany was covered with great masses of ice, only the highest peaks of the Scandinavian mountains emerging in the form of "nunataks"; but while North Germany became ice-free some 20,000 years ago northern Scandinavia was still covered with ice 10,000 years ago. As a result of the gradual retreat of the ice the Baltic, originally only a large lake along the fringes of the ice, had a constantly changing coastline. Only in what is known as the Yoldia phase did it connect up with the open sea − not through the Øresund, as it does now, since that was not yet open, but by way of the "Billingen Gate" in central Sweden when this was opened up by the retreat of the ice. At the same time the Baltic was connected with the White Sea by a channel running north-east along the edge of the ice mass, so that the whole of northern Scandinavia now became an island.

The large lakes of central Sweden are relics of the sea which once covered that area; but the abundant flow of water from many rivers has long removed any trace of salt.

The great masses of ice, 2km/1¼ miles thick, bore down heavily on the underlying land, and when this pressure was relieved with the melting of the ice the land rose, most markedly in the middle of the area previously covered by ice. Some 8500 years ago, therefore, the channels traversing central Sweden and Finland were raised above sea level and drained of water; and the Baltic again became a lake, known as Lake Ancylus, which with the continuing retreat of the ice included what is now the Gulf of Bothnia. Finally, some 7000 years ago, the present channels between the Danish islands opened up and provided a link with the North Sea. Thus there came into being the Litorina Sea, the forerunner of the Baltic as we know it today.

Lake Ancylus
Litorina Sea

Geologists have been able to establish an absolute time scale for these events with the help of the "varve" deposits, which are particularly well exposed at Uppsala. Just as tree-rings can be dated by the varying pattern they form from year to year, so these deposits of clay, varying in colour and grain size, form a pattern which can be dated, and the thickness and quality of each annual layer yield information about meteorological conditions year by year in the post-glacial period.

Varve deposits

The land is continuing to rise in Scandinavia, at a rate which round the Gulf of Bothnia amounts to about 1 metre (40 inches) in a century,

Rise in the land

Glacier stream in southern Norway

so that towns like Luleå and Oulu have had to move their harbours steadily farther out to follow the retreating sea. In the Stockholm area the rise is still at the rate of some 40 centimetres (16 inches) in a century; and within historical times new skerries have regularly emerged from the sea and inlets of the sea have become dry land.

Variety of topography

The action of the glaciers produced a very varied topographical pattern. In the Scandinavian mountains they ground their way over the high plateaux, leaving only the prominent "nunataks" which had always stood out above the mass of the ice. The separate arms of the glaciers gouged out mighty U-shaped valleys, forming vertical rock faces over which waterfalls now tumble. The valleys often had deeper basins scooped out by the ice or were blocked by moraines, leading to the formation of the lakes so commonly found in them. The fjords, too, were carved out to very great depths: the Sognefjord, for example, is very much deeper (1245m/4085ft) than the North Sea, which barely attains a tenth of that depth.

Lakes

On the east side of the Scandinavian mountains the great fringe of lakes in the Norrland came into being because the last remnants of the ice cover lay not within the mountains but farther east, thus blocking any outflow to the Gulf of Bothnia. In consequence the lakes found a lower overflow westward to the North Atlantic, so carving out the deep valleys through the mountains which now form convenient passages between the Norwegian coast and the interior. After the disappearance of the last great ice masses these lakes all found an easier outflow to the Baltic, so that the old valleys through the mountains were left high and dry.

Terminal moraines

The terminal moraines marking the different stages in the melting of the ice now extend across Sweden and Finland in gigantic ribbons of debris. The traveller constantly encounters these great accumulations of boulders, which have been cleared only in a few places. In southern Finland some of these moraines were deposited under the sea and then evenly distributed by the action of the waves, producing the regularly shaped Salpausselkä ranges of hills.

Roches moutonnées, eskers

The grinding action of the glaciers is also seen in the lowland areas, for example in the *roches moutonnées* (rocks rounded and smoothed by glacial action) found in the skerries and also inland, where even the hardest rocks have been eroded into a characteristic "whale-backed" shape. Particularly striking are the eskers (*åser*, singular *ås;* Swedish *ås*): long stratified gravel ridges which may extend for several hundred kilometres and sometimes enclose lakes of some size. These were originally sediments deposited in the channels carved out by rivers under the ice, and when the ice melted were left as natural causeways which provided convenient traffic routes for man. Stockholm is situated where it is largely because of an esker which helped to close off Lake Mälar and offered a convenient means of passage.

Kettleholes

Among the numerous other glacial forms is the "kettlehole", a shallow depression found particularly in arable land, formed where a mass of ice was covered by drift and, being thus protected from the sun, was slower to melt; then when it did melt the covering of soil fell in and formed a funnel-shaped depression.

Fjords

The most characteristic features of the coastal regions formerly covered by ice are the fjords which are found in Scandinavia in every variety of form. In northern Norway they cut deep into the land, broad and funnel-shaped. The rugged Lofoten Islands are dissected by a labyrinthine network of fjords. The Trondheimfjord, in a drowned longitudinal valley, is broad and has many inlets opening off it. The much

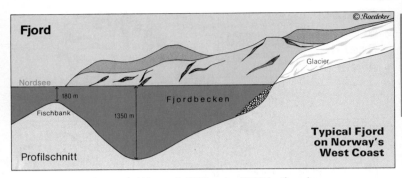

Fjord

© *Baedeker*

Glacier

Nordsee

180 m

Fischbank

1350 m

Fjordbecken

**Typical Fjord
on Norway's
West Coast**

Profilschnitt

ramified fjords in the area of Norway's 2000-metre (6500-foot) peaks have the appearance of flooded Alpine valleys. In southern Norway and Bohuslän, where the mountains slope down more gently towards the coast and the ice cover was not so thick, the fjords are shorter; only the Oslofjord, in a tectonic rift valley, reaches far inland.

In Sweden and Finland the fjords are more intimately intermeshed with the fringe of skerries, with their heads reaching in between the low rounded contours of the roches moutonnées.

During the last Ice Age, some 100,000 years ago, the whole of Scandinavia was covered by a massive ice sheet, reducing in thickness towards the coast. The existing river valleys were gouged out by the ice to ever greater depths – often as deep as the rocks rearing above the valley were high. Since along the coast the ice was thinner, the fjords were carved out to a lesser depth at their mouths. The bank at the mouth of a fjord may be only some 180m/590ft below the surface, while farther inland depths of up to 1350m/4430ft have been measured. When the ice retreated the huge fjord basins were filled with sea-water. Thanks to the salt content of the water and the warming influence of the Gulf Stream the fjords remain ice-free throughout the year except in their innermost reaches.

The great ice-fields in the mountain regions are remains of the Ice Age glaciers. The melt-water from these surviving glaciers, pouring into the valleys in innumerable waterfalls, is now harnessed in many places to produce hydro-electric power.

Formation of
the fjords

Climate

The climate of Scandinavia is determined by its situation between Central Europe in the south and the Arctic to the north, by the North Atlantic to the west and the great expanses of the Euro-Asiatic continent to the east.

While in Central Europe, particularly in the North German plain and the Baltic area, air currents can move eastward unimpeded, in Scandinavia they come up against the barrier of the Scandinavian mountains, which run down the length of the peninsula under various names. This chain of mountains separates a narrow coastal strip to the west with a maritime climate – the heartland of Norway – from a larger region of continental climate to the east, in the lee of the mountains, in the centre of which are the Baltic and its northern extension the Gulf of Bothnia. Only in the south, where Sweden is faced to the west by the low-lying country of Denmark and the straits of Skagerrak and Kattegat, can currents of maritime air advance eastward with less hindrance. Thus, going from west to east, the Norwegian coastal strip, the Scandinavian

Climate in Scandinavia

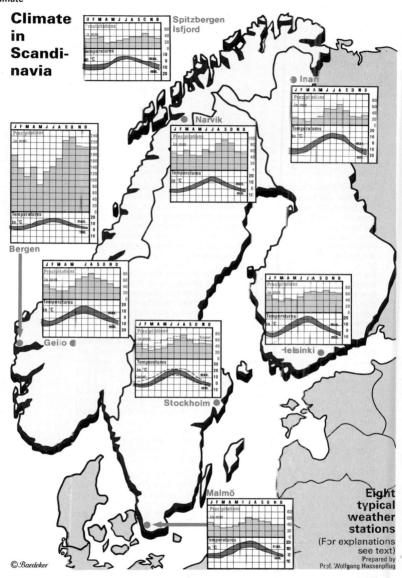

Eight typical weather stations
(For explanations see text)

Prepared by Prof. Wolfgang Hassenpflug

© Baedeker

The diagrams are based on climatic data typical of Scandinavia. On the Norwegian coast, thanks to the Gulf Stream, the climate is relatively mild and in some fjords fruit-trees flourish; but in Finnish Lapland the temperature can fall as low as −20°C/−4°F in winter.

mountain zone and the Swedish-Finnish area are the main climatic regions of Scandinavia, with clearly defined boundaries. Since they extend over very considerable areas from north to south, however, they are divided in this direction into a series of climatic units with fluid boundaries.

A distinctive characteristic of the climate of Scandinavia is its pattern of daylight and darkness, the result of its situation in high northern latitudes. In no other part of the world has man extended his habitat so far towards the Pole, and nowhere else can travellers so easily reach polar latitudes.

The most southerly point in Scandinavia, in southern Sweden, is in the same latitude as the icy region of Labrador in North America; and it corresponds in the southern hemisphere to storm-ridden Cape Horn, at the farthest tip of South America.

The nearer a place is to the Pole the shorter are its days in winter and the longer its days in summer; and the longer, too, the period of half-light in the morning and twilight in the evening, since in the higher latitudes the course of the sun appears lower. A visitor to Scandinavia from farther south will notice a difference at the 55th parallel.

The capitals of the Scandinavian countries – Oslo, Stockholm and Helsinki – lie approximately in latitude 60° north; the Arctic Circle is at 66°33' north, the North Cape a little south of 70° north.

At the spring and autumn equinoxes (March 21st and September 23rd) day and night are of almost equal length in all latitudes. Between March and June the length of the day increases rapidly towards the north. In latitude 65° north there is no darkness at night from May 20th to July 25th, and the evening twilight merges into the half-light of morning. In latitude 70° north there is no darkness between May 1st and August 20th, and from May 20th to July 25th the sun is permanently above the horizon (the "midnight sun"). Kiruna has 45 days with the midnight sun, Tromsø 64, Hammerfest 72, the North Cape 78 and Spitzbergen 127.

In winter, on the other hand, there are long hours of darkness. Visitors who go to Scandinavia to ski should bear in mind that at Christmas the days are much shorter than in Central Europe. In latitude 70° north, between November 22nd and January 20th, the half-light of morning merges immediately into the twilight of evening, and instead of the day there is only a two-hour twilight (the polar night).

The climatic characteristics of different regions in Scandinavia are shown in the climatic diagrams on page 16, which give the monthly average temperatures and precipitations (rainfall and snow) at eight typical weather stations. The blue columns show precipitations in millimetres, in accordance with the scale in the right-hand margin, while the orange band shows temperatures in °C, the upper edge giving the average maximum day temperature and the lower edge the average minimum night temperature, in accordance with the red scale in the margin.

On the basis of these diagrams it is possible to estimate climatic conditions for places between the weather stations shown, bearing in mind that temperatures fall with increasing height and towards the north and that precipitations decrease towards the east.

Midnight sun

Climatic diagrams

Southern Sweden: an Area of Transition

Southern Sweden (Skåne, Småland, Götaland) is an area of transition between Scandinavian and Central European climate. Within this relatively small area can be seen the west-to-east transition from a maritime to a continental climate which is a dominant feature farther north. Halmstad on the west coast has annual precipitations of 736mm/ 29in., Kalmar on the east coast only 471mm/18½in. In general the east

Malmö
weather station

17

coast has warm summers with settled weather, while or the hills and on the west side of the southern Swedish uplands annual precipitations of over 1000mm/40in. are not uncommon.

The south end of the Swedish west coast, on the lee side of the Danish island of Zealand, is still drier than the more northerly sections of the coast, along which the western currents of air coming in from the sea are compelled to rise and discharge their moisture in the form of rain (Malmö 553mm/22in., Göteborg 670mm/26in.).

West Coast of Norway

Bergen and Narvik weather stations

The cool, moist oceanic climate of the Norwegian west coast is unique in the world: nowhere else does a temperate climate reach so far towards the Pole. The reason for this lies in the offshoots of the Gulf Stream, which carry relatively warm water from more southerly latitudes far north up the Norwegian coast: even in Spitzbergen this influence is still perceptible. The surface temperature of the water in winter (January) remains almost constant at 5°C/41°F from southern Norway to Hammerfest. On an average of the months from December to March the water here is 2°C/3.6°F warmer than in the warmest parts of the North Sea (Heligoland Bay) and the southern Baltic. Accordingly there is no ice in winter as far north as Murmansk. The moderating influence of the sea is particularly evident when streams of cold air move into the area.

With the prevailing west winds the warmth of the sea is carried on to the land. At the same time the moisture absorbed by the air is discharged in the form of rain on the slopes of the hills. Thus the Norwegian west coast is characterised by relatively high temperatures, fairly regular over the year, and by high precipitations. The leve of precipitations falls from south to north, but there may be sharp local variations depending on the situation of a particular place on this much indented coast with its fjords, inlets, islands, peninsulas and skerries and on its altitude. In the lee of hills and islands and in fjords precipitations are much lower than in the outlying parts of the coast and in the hills.

The Bergen weather station is representative of climatic conditions in the southern section of the west coast. Annual precipitations here rise to almost 2000mm/80in., or sometimes even higher, and are never below 1000mm/40in. (e.g. Stavanger 1130mm/44½in.). The pattern over the year shows a marked minimum in May and a maximum in autumn. Given the equable temperature conditions, average minimum night temperatures rarely fall below freezing point even in winter, while in summer average maximum day temperatures do not rise above 20°C/68°F.

The south coast of Norway to the east of Kristiansand, sheltered from wind and weather, has correspondingly lower precipitations and the highest duration of sunshine in Norway (Kristiansand 1850 hours of sunshine a year, Bergen 1233), with warmer water in sheltered inlets as a result.

In the northern section of the west coast (Narvik weather station) precipitations decrease, both within the fjords (Narvik 755mm/30in.) and off the coast in the Lofoten Islands (Skrova 893mm/35in.). The pattern over the year, however, shows the same maximum in autumn as in the southern sections of the coast.

Temperatures are closely dependent on the situation of a particular place, whether in the open sea (Lofotens) or within a fjord (Narvik). Winter temperatures in the Lofotens, and daily maxima and minima, are some 4°C/7.2°F higher, summer temperatures 0.5–1°C (0.9–1.8°F) lower, than at Narvik.

Still farther north winter temperatures are almost unchanged, while summer temperatures fall markedly below a monthly average of

10°C/50°F. At Vardø, 200km/125 miles east of the North Cape, average minima and maxima in July are 7.1°C/44.8°F and 11.5°C/52.7°F, compared with 10.7°C/51.3°F and 16.1°C/61°F at Narvik. Annual precipitations fall to 544mm/21½in.; even in August and October, the periods of maximum rainfall, the monthly figure rarely exceeds 60mm/2½in.

In northern Scandinavia there can be a sudden change in the weather at any time, even in summer; and while in western Europe this would merely be a nuisance, in these regions it could be dangerous for travellers who are not properly equipped (with suitable clothing, supplies of food, maps, etc.).

Spitzbergen

Spitzbergen has a polar climate, with ice, changeable weather and frequent fog on the west coast, where the influence of the Gulf Stream is still felt and encourages the movement of shipping from May to October. Summers are usually short and cool (average July temperature 4.5°C/40.1°F), sufficient only to thaw the permanently frozen soil to a depth of around a metre (40in.).

Precipitations are low (an annual 378mm/15in.), but with low temperatures and little evaporation this is sufficient to form extensive glaciers, frequently reaching down to the sea and "calving" there.

The midnight sun shines from April 20th to August 23rd; the polar night lasts from October 23rd to February 19th.

Isfjord
weather station

Scandinavian Mountains

The Scandinavian peninsula is traversed throughout its length by long ranges of rolling hills which on the west side fall steeply down to the fjords but slope down more gradually to the east, with ranges of mountains rearing above them. This is the *fjell* (fell) region, which because of its altitude and low temperatures can support no trees apart from scrub birches.

The air masses driving in from the North Atlantic come up against the west side of the mountains, producing heavy cloud formation and abundant precipitations (3000mm/120in. or more). Since temperatures fall by an average of 0.6°C/1.1°F for every additional 100m/330ft of altitude, the height is soon reached – between 1000m/3300ft and 2000m/6600ft, depending on the time of year and air temperature – where the precipitations fall in the form of snow, which lies, providing a basis for the formation of glaciers.

The farther north one goes, with steadily falling temperatures, the tree-line and the snow-line also fall lower. In the Hardangervidda (southern Norway) the tree-line is at 1000m/3300ft, in Finnmark (northern Scandinavia) at 200m/650ft.

The snow-line, which in the Alps is at 3000m/9850ft, is at 2000m/6500ft in the Jotunheim, at 1200m/3950ft on the Svartisen glacier (in the latitude of the Arctic Circle) and at sea level on Spitzbergen.

Any continuing fall in temperatures leads to a further extension of the glaciers, any rise to a melting of the ice. Falls of only a few degrees in the last Ice Age were sufficient to cause glaciers to advance from the Scandinavian mountains into North Germany – a process during which large quantities of rock detritus were transported to Germany.

Geilo
weather station
(alt. 795m/2608ft)

Continental Sweden and Finland

Sheltered from the North Atlantic and exposed to continental air masses coming from the east, the regions to the east of the Scandinavian mountains – Sweden and, beyond the Baltic, Finland – have a climate which shows markedly continental features. Precipitations and cloud cover are much reduced as compared with the west coast, and in

Stockholm,
Helsinki
and Inari
weather stations

some areas like the upper Gudbrandsdal artificial irrigation is necessary. Summer temperatures are distinctly higher than in the west, winter temperatures distinctly lower, and the range of temperature over the year lies between 20° and 30°C (68° and 86°F)

The Baltic does little to moderate the continental climate. Although in summer it is colder than the land, which quickly warms up, and, like Finland's numerous lakes, has a cooling effect on the surrounding country, in winter it regularly freezes over, remaining frozen in the northern stretches of the Gulf of Bothnia for anything up to six months, and then has the same effect – of hardening the frost – as the snow lying on the land. In the south of the region the ground is snow-covered for around 20 days in the year, in the far north for up to 250 days.

Since the Gulf of Bothnia is ice-covered and closed to shipping during the winter, Swedish ore from the mines at Kiruna is shipped throughout the year from the Norwegian port of Narvik.

Comparison of the climatic diagrams for Stockholm, Helsinki and Inari shows the differences in climate between different parts of the Swedish-Finnish region of continental climate

The climatic diagram for Stockholm is representative of the climate of the south-western part of the region. Thanks to Stockholm's sheltered situation in the lee of the rain-bringing west winds annual precipitations, at 555mm/22in., are particularly low.

To the south, along the coast, precipitations fall still lower (Kalmar 471mm/18½in.); to the west they increase slightly (Karlstad 648mm/25½in., Oslo 740mm/29in.).

The temperature band for Stockholm shows a steeper "hump" than the Norwegian coastal stations, reflecting the wider range of variation over the year characteristic of a continental climate

The continental character of the climate becomes more marked towards the east, as can be seen by comparing the climatic diagrams for Stockholm and Helsinki. It is still more marked beyond Helsinki in eastern Finland (annual range of temperature at Helsinki 23.3°C/41.9°F, at Punkaharju, 300km/190 miles north-east, 27.1°C/30.8°F).

To the north, towards Lapland, the climate also becomes more continental (the influence of the Baltic being still further reduced in this area); still farther north, towards the Pole, it also becomes colder. This can be seen in the climatic diagram for Inari, which has the most continental climate in Scandinavia. The annual range of temperature, at 26.7°C/80.1°F, is greater than at Stockholm and precipitations (405mm/16in.) are lower. The growing period for vegetation (days with average temperatures over 5°C/41°F) is 120 days, compared with 175 in the south. The area is thus beyond the northern boundary for the growing of corn.

Farther north, towards the coast of the Barents Sea, the continental character of the climate falls a little. At Vardø the range of temperature over the year is only 24.4°C/43.9°F, and the daily range of variation is only half the figure for Inari, while annual precipitations rise to 544mm/21½in.

Flora and Fauna

Flora

Vegetation zones

In spite of the climatic differences between the Atlantic coast and the interior, the boundaries between different vegetation zones for the most part cut right across Scandinavia; for the growing period, which is determined by temperatures in spring and autumn, is less affected by differences between east and west and tends rather to become shorter in stages from south to north, while the light conditions which

Liverwort (Anemone hepatica)   *Wood anemone (Anemone nemorosa)*

play such an important part in plant growth also vary with latitude. In addition, of course, the vegetation of the mountain regions is affected by differences in altitude.

The beech is still found in Skåne, Halland and Blekinge but does not grow in Småland. In Norway it grows as far north as the latitude of Bergen. Oaks – a relic of an earlier forest cover – are found as far north as Trondheim in Norway and Gävle in Sweden, and also in the southwestern coastal region of Finland and on the Åland Islands. The deciduous forests are often of mixed type. Most of Sweden, in particular Norrland, belongs to the northern coniferous forest zone, as do the interior regions of Norway and Finland. The predominant forest tree, usually growing on morainic soils, is the Norway spruce (*Picea excelsa*), but pines are also found. The pine forests of northern Scandinavia have a sparser appearance than elsewhere: a well-grown pine in the mountain regions may be three times the age of a similar tree in more southerly latitudes. Here and there can be found birches and – particularly in Finland – goat willows. Pure pine forests cover a considerably larger area in northern Finland than in Sweden. In northern Sweden pine and birch forests growing on sandy soil form a transition to the northern Swedish tundra zone. The upper limit of the conifers falls from 900m/2950ft in the Hardangerfjord area and Telemark to 450m/1475ft in Finnmark, these heights being reached only by spruces of notably slender growth and a few scattered pines.

Deciduous and coniferous trees

A feature typical of Scandinavia and not found anywhere else is the birch zone which extends for some 200m/650ft above the coniferous zone. The mountain valleys are green with birch forest and scrub willows, sometimes forming impenetrable thickets. The upper limit of the birch forest ranges between 500 and 800m (1650 and 2625ft). The ground cover in the northern forests consists of berry-bearing shrubs

Birch zone

and, in drier situations, lichens. The extensive forest regions of Scandi-navia are interrupted by numerous lakes and expanses of peat-bog.

Heathland

Areas of mountain pasture are found only in southern Norway. Farther north the upper slopes of the mountains are covered with a heath vegetation of dwarf shrubs and low-growing plants extending up to the snow-line. The vegetation of the mountain heathland is particularly rich on chalky south-facing slopes, ranging from orchids to dry scrub, with junipers, willows and heather.

Forests

In spite of the intensive timber-working industry of northern Sweden and Finland the forests – apart from the scattered areas which have been brought into cultivation – have suffered little thinning-out and the natural vegetation has largely been preserved, though in some areas much timber has been consumed by the busy ironworking industry of past centuries. The situation is very different in extensive areas in Norway, where the character of the mountains has largely confined the forests to the sheltered valleys – which, however, have been fre-quented and developed by man since very ancient times. The Norwe-gian Atlantic coast is by nature sparsely forested, while the outer skerries consist of bare rock and, with the high rainfall in this region, suffer heavy erosion of the soil.

Forest and arable land

Central Sweden is predominantly a region of arable farming, though numerous *roches moutonnées* shaped by Ice Age glaciers emerge like inland skerries from the clayey alluvial plain. The distribution of arable land and forest – here confined to areas of rocky and morainic soil – is mainly determined by this natural mosaic. Only in the Silurian basins are there large continuous expanses of land suitable for arable farm-ing. The crops grown in Norway, southern and central Sweden and Finland are similar to those found in Germany. Rye and oats grow up to

Cranberries   *Bilberries*

latitude 67° north, barley to 68°. Potatoes grow well even in Lapland. In addition there are apple, pear and cherry trees and various shrubs – though not in the far north. The most favourable conditions for agriculture are in the lower-lying parts of Skåne.

Also common in some areas are wood anemones, liverworts and cowslips. There are many kinds of berry plants, including bilberries, cranberries and cloudberries, and many species of mushrooms.

Berries

Fauna

The animal life of the Scandinavian countries is conditioned by two climatic and vegetation zones. The forests in the southern regions are within the Central European temperate zone and are inhabited by much the same species as are – or were – the forests of Germany (red deer, roe-deer, foxes, hares, badgers, etc.). Thanks to the lower population density and to a lesser degree of human intrusion or interference with natural conditions Scandinavia has preserved a greater variety of species, including animals which in Central Europe have become extinct or have been much reduced in numbers.

Southern regions

The rugged cliffs on the Norwegian coast provide sheltered nesting-places not only for countless seabirds – mainly auks and guillemots – but also for species which have become rare or have died out elsewhere in Europe, like the white-tailed eagle and the golden eagle (both species which breed only in natural conditions). In Norway's coastal waters are found seals and various species of whale. The rivers and lakes of the north, still largely preserved from harmful environmental influences, are well stocked with salmon, trout, carp, perch and char. In the coastal waters of the Baltic is found a local species of herring.

Seabirds and fishes

Arctic fox in winter coat

Elks on grazing grounds (Sweden)

Northern regions
(Lapland)

The northern regions of Scandinavia, in particular Lapland, lie within the Arctic alpine zone. Their fauna is more restricted than that of the other regions, but excellently adapted to living in the most rigorous conditions. The commonest animals are the reindeer which roam in huge herds over the inhospitable tundra and are of supreme economic importance to the native population as suppliers of milk, meat and skins. As a result of strict conservation measures there has been a considerable increase in the stock of elks. Other species characteristic of these regions are the ptarmigan, the blue hare, the glutton, the arctic fox and the lemming (*Lemmus lemmus*), a small vole-like rodent known for the long migrations in which countless numbers die.

Three Countries: Sweden, Finland, Norway

General

The topographical pattern of Scandinavia has been produced by a great variety of factors – geological structure, mountain formation, ice action, climate, vegetation. The boundaries between the different countries and regions, however, are not always clearly defined by nature: much sharper is the distinction between the rocky and morainic hills on the one hand and the lower land with its lakes and rivers on the other, and it is the intricate intermingling of these different elements that gives the landscape of Scandinavia its pattern. A further element is contributed by the farmsteads, mostly still timber-built, which are scattered about in the countryside, coming together to form villages only in the area round Lake Siljan – though the farms themselves, with their numerous separate buildings serving a variety of functions, look from a distance like little hamlets on their own. In Sweden a characteristic note is given to the landscape by the rust-red Falu paint which is used on most of the houses. In a progressively-minded country like Sweden, however, the old traditions of the countryside are much less vigorously preserved than in Norway, where the countryfolk are by nature more conservative and the old "log cabin" type of house, often with carved decoration and a turf roof, is still preserved and cherished. Norway, too, has a more austere natural landscape, with its great expanses of high plateau, its glacier-hewn valleys with their lakes and fjords and its fringe of islands, from the swarms of tiny skerries to the great rock masses of the Lofotens, towering up as if built by a giant's hand.

Sweden

Skåne, the most southerly region in southern Sweden (Götaland), is wooded only in the north and has fertile morainic soils. It has a number of considerable ports, chief among them Malmö, with an agricultural hinterland mainly devoted to the growing of sugar-beet and wheat. In the centre of this agricultural area is the quiet little university town of Lund with its Romanesque cathedral, Sweden's finest church.

Southern Sweden

Skåne

A more distinctively Swedish region begins at the low ridge of hills which runs south-east across Skåne from the steep and sharply pointed Cape Kullen and re-emerges on the Danish island of Bornholm. The landscape of Småland, still in the latitude of Jutland though it is, has an authentically northern stamp. Its rump of gneisses and granites, worn down by Ice Age glaciers and now rising to barely 400m/1300ft, is still largely a sparsely inhabited expanse of forest and moorland. In earlier times the abundance of timber in this region led to the establishment of a busy glass-making industry; the industrial towns of the present day have developed round the junctions of the extensive railway network.

Småland

From the north Lake Vättern thrusts into the Småland hills like a wedge, its straight shorelines reflecting its situation in a tectonic rift valley. At its southern tip are Jönköping and the smaller town of Huskvarna, at the geographical midpoint of Sweden. To the south of Jönköping is the Taberg, from which high-grade iron ore was formerly extracted by opencast working; the hill is now a nature reserve which attracts many visitors.

Lake Vättern

Of the coastal regions flanking Småland, Halland, to the west, has profited economically from the important railway line from Skåne to Göteborg which runs through its territory. Blekinge to the south and the Kalmar region to the east have extensive morainic deposits, so that the forests mostly reach right down to the coast, which is much indented by fjords.

Halland
Blekinge

Central Sweden (Svealand) is a much more open and hospitable territory, with a milder climate. Its coasts, however, are less welcoming: Göteborg, on the west coast, has an excellent natural harbour on the funnel-shaped estuary of the Götaälv, but the coastal strip on the Kattegat is narrow and rocky, so that the town has been compelled to expand on to the surrounding hills and to build its industrial suburbs in narrow side valleys.

Central Sweden

Göteborg

On the east side of central Sweden is Stockholm, sheltered by an almost impenetrable girdle of skerries and accessible from the sea only through a labyrinth of hidden channels. The intricate landscape pattern is continued on the city's landward side by Lake Mälar with its thousand inlets and islands, and it is further protected by a dense ring of forest. Farther inland the peasant population of ancient Svealand found an abundance of open country; and this situation, cut off from

Lake Mälar

Scandinavia

Norway
Sweden
Finland

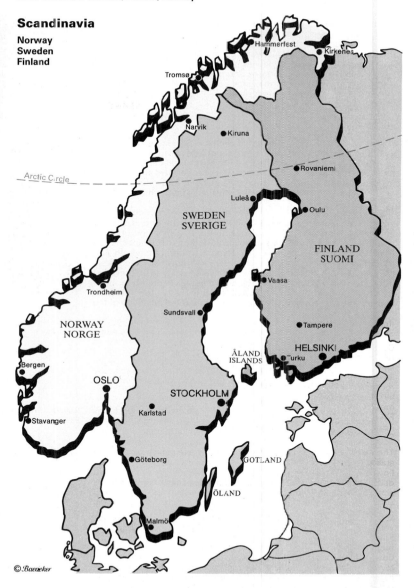

© Baedeker

The land area north of the Artic Circle – in Norway, Sweden and Finland as well as in Russia – is known in Scandinavia as the "Nordic Cap" (Nordkalotten). On the northern Norwegian coast it is bounded by the Arctic Ocean.

Coastal scenery, Smögen (western Sweden)

the coasts, may have helped to develop the continental outlook of the Swedes.

Central Sweden is very far from being a uniform region, and it has no real centre: no other part of Sweden is so sharply compartmented into small separate units. Stretches of level arable land on the Silurian limestones alternate constantly with densely wooded horsts of ancient rock and bleak moorland plateaux formed of volcanic rocks (particularly diabases) of the Palaeozoic era. Nature thus determined the rigid medieval subdivisions of the land; and until modern times people of Finnish stock from the north continued to make their way through the impassable stretches of forest between these areas into central Sweden.

The variety of landscape pattern is reflected most clearly in the constantly changing shoreline of Lake Vänern: now following a straight line along a fault, now fringed by clusters of skerries, now shaped into deltas by alluvial deposits, now extending in wide bays formed by the action of wind and water. Lake Vänern

The towns of central Sweden each have their special functions: Norrköping is a textile town; Linköping manufactures machinery and motor vehicles; Örebro is a centre of the leather industry; and in and around Karlstad numerous sawmills and large cellulose factories process the huge quantities of timber from northern Värmland which are floated down the great rivers or transported by land. The smaller country towns handle the agricultural produce of their immediate surroundings; their function as market centres brought them early prosperity, reflected in imposing secular buildings and old religious houses. Towns

Although Göteborg, situated in western Sweden in convenient proximity to the open sea, has developed into the country's leading international port and its second largest city, Stockholm, on the east side Stockholm

27

of the country, is not only the geographical centre of Sweden but the focal point of all traffic in the Baltic. It has thus taken over the role once played by Visby (Gotland) in the heyday of the Hanseatic League. The intricate landscape of forests and lakes does not at first sight seem a favourable area for the establishment of a capital city; but the situation had one decisive advantage, since it was only at this point that a road running up the east side of Sweden from south to north could find a means of passage along an esker between the much indented Lake Mälar and the tangle of skerries off the Baltic coast. Moreover in the middle of the waterway that had to be crossed here there lay an island which provided not only a defensible situation for a medieval town but a means of watching over traffic both by water and by land.

In the layout of present-day Stockholm the port and industrial installations are agreeably unobtrusive, while the city's extensive new residential districts thrust outwards in all directions into the hilly and wooded surrounding countryside; and out in the Skärgård, the endless scatter of skerries, the people of the modern capital city of Sweden have a magnificent holiday and recreation area where they can find peace and relaxation in the intricately ramified waterways and on a host of lonely little islets.

Bergslagen

Immediately north of central Sweden is Bergslagen, a region of rather mixed character, still preserving many relics of the busy mining industry which once brought it prosperity. Elsewhere there are great concentrations of modern heavy industry, like the steelworks of Sandviken, Domnarvet and Kvarnsveden. Similar contrasts are found in the two neighbouring towns of Falun and Borlänge.

Dalarna

Not far from this region, in Dalarna, is an oasis of traditionally minded, prosperous farming country, the area round Lake Siljan, whose beauty attracts many visitors.

Northern Sweden

Lake Siljan is less than half way up the total length of Sweden. The more northerly regions beyond this, Norrland and Lapland, are immense territories with much less differentiation of character than southern Sweden. They are regions of endless forests, traversed by untamed rivers coming down from the mountains which were formerly used to float down huge quantities of spruce logs. Nowadays extensive areas of forest are served by good roads, so that most of the timber – still felled on a considerable scale – is now transported to the numerous sawmills by truck. The sawmills, formerly all situated on the estuaries of the great rivers, are now also to be found inland, away from the rivers. Large quantities of timber are also used by cellulose factories.

Norrland

Norrland is a remote and austere region with unspoiled lakes which in winter are concealed for many months under a thick armour-plating of ice. Far to the north, beyond the Arctic Circle, are numerous large hydro-electric stations – at Porjus, Harsprånget and many other places – and more are under construction.

Kiruna

Still farther north, in the zone of birch forest, is Kiruna, founded only in the early years of the 20th century, which in terms of area if not of population is one of the largest towns in Sweden. In the immediate vicinity of the town are two hills ("monadnocks") of ore with an iron content of 70%. The ore is transported on the "ore railway" to Narvik in Norway and shipped from there. In summer, when the Gulf of Bothnia is ice-free, the neighbouring double town of Gällivare-Malmberget ships its ore from Luleå.

Lapland

These ore towns lie in the heart of Lapland. Here the coniferous forests have given place to expanses of open birch forest and great stretches

Lake Torneträsk (Swedish Lapland)

of moorland and bog, with sluggish streams pursuing an uncertain course through the debris left by the last Ice Age. Until quite recently this was the domain of the Lapps' great herds of reindeer, but their possession of the territory is increasingly being disputed by modern developments. In the summer of 1986 the reindeer grazing grounds were badly polluted by radioactive fallout from the Chernobyl nuclear reactor.

Finland

Immediately east is northern Finland. Like Norrland, this is a region of sublime austerity, and from any hill rising above the surrounding forest there is an immense prospect of unspoiled natural beauty. The continually repeated but continually varied pattern of woodland and water, now clamorous with the sound of the wind and the rivers, now hushed to silence, reduces man to insignificance and humility and then lifts his heart with the radiance of the sun and the white splendour of the clouds pursuing one another across the sky.

Finland is called the "land of a thousand lakes", but in reality there are many more than that; and surely nowhere else on earth are woodland and water so intimately interwoven. The Finnish Lakeland slopes gradually down in a north-westerly direction to the Gulf of Bothnia; but there too the ground is stony and the rivers tumble their way down over outcrops of rock. The lakeland region, which seems to extend endlessly northward, is much more sharply bounded on the south by the Salpausselkä ridge.

Finnish Lakeland

To the south of the Salpausselkä hills is the most densely populated part of Finland, mainly devoted to arable and stock farming; and in the

Helsinki

29

Birch forest, Finland

centre of this area, on a rocky promontory projecting into the Gulf of Finland, is the country's capital, Helsink . From the sea there is an impressive view of the city, dominated by the dome of its cathedral. Offshore are numerous islands.

Lost territories

After the Second World War Finland was compelled to cede considerable areas of its territory to the Soviet Union. In the south-east it lost Viipuri (Viborg) and the north-western shore of Lake Ladoga, and in the north the important port of Petsamo on the Arctic Ocean, which in spite of its northerly situation was, thanks to an offshoot of the Gulf Stream, the only port in Finland which was ice-free throughout the year; and most of Karelia, a region of typically Finnish landscape, also passed to the Soviet Union.

Åland Islands

The Åland Islands, at the entrance to the Gulf of Bothnia, belong to Finland but have a Swedish-speaking population. There has always been a considerable Swedish element in the Finnish coastal towns, leading on occasion in the past to conflicts between the two population groups.

Inland Finland

In spite of the obstacles created by nature the interior of Finland is served by railways and roads, for the industry and hard work of the Finns have opened up these inhospitable regions for the activities of man. Some 70% of the area of Finland is covered by forest, in which pine, spruce and birch predominate, and just under 12% by lakes, while more than 1440 rapids have been counted on the country's rivers. The wealth of Finland lies in its forests and its never failing supply of water power. Only some 9% of its area can be used for agriculture (arable farming), with crops similar to those grown in Central Europe. Wild berries also feature prominent y in the landscape.

Norway

In spite of its long land frontiers Norway stands, as it were, back to back with the other Scandinavian countries. Its capital, Oslo, has a sheltered situation at the head of the Oslofjord, which cuts deeply into the land and has the country's largest rivers flowing into it. The long valleys of these rivers lead road traffic to the capital, which lies in rolling, well cultivated country – a double advantage giving it a privileged situation among the northern capitals.

Oslo

Round Oslo is a region of varied and attractive scenery, occupied by an active and industrious population which, particularly on the southern and south-eastern slopes of the mountains, can look back on long farming and mining traditions. The Setesdal in particular is famed for its trim farmhouses and its traditional costumes. The prosperity of the agricultural population of Telemark is now based on highly developed stock farming, in which the Alpine pastures in the higher areas of the region play an important part.

Setesdal
Telemark

Some 400km/250 miles north of Oslo is the old town of Trondheim, surrounded by an area brought into cultivation by peasant farmers. High up in the hinterland of Trondheim is the little mining town of Røros, with rich deposits of ore which over the past 300 years have yielded over 100,000 tons of pure copper.

Trondheim

The Norwegian west coast with its succession of fjords extends for some 2000km/1250 miles from Stavanger to Kirkenes, offering scenery of breathtaking magnificence. On this coast is Bergen, the largest town in western Norway; but it has remained a purely coastal town, with little in the way of hinterland. Its main sources of income are fishing, the fish-processing industry and the fish trade. West of Bergen, in the Norwegian part of the North Sea, are oilfields producing large

West coast:
Bergen

Farmhouse and granary (stabbur) in Telemark

quantities of oil and natural gas. Bergen is linked with Oslo by a boldly engineered railway which crosses the high plateaux at a height of 1300m/4265ft. In recent years industry has been successfully established at a number of points on the west coast: thus the abundant supplies of water power on the steep flanks of the Sognefjord (Høyanger) and the Hardangerfjord (Odda) have been harnessed for the manufacture of aluminium, and an active smelting industry has grown up round the copper and pyrite mines in the Sulitjelma area in northern Norway.

Stavanger

In southern Norway the developing port town of Stavanger has specialised in the fish canning industry. Its shipyards build drilling rigs and platforms for the North Sea oilfields, and refineries have been established to handle North Sea oil.

Ålesund
Kristiansund

Farther north, in the skerries, are Ålesund and Kristiansund, which have remained fishing towns. Off the coast, still farther north, are the Lofoten Islands, where the life of the fishermen is at its hardest and most strenuous.

Lofoten Islands

Northern Norway begins in the latitude of the Lofotens, a region of magnificently imposing scenery, with its numerous islands emerging from the sea like the peaks of a submerged mountain range and alarmingly narrow passages between them. Ensconced in a fjord on the mainland is Narvik, an ice-free port which ships the iron ore of Swedish Lapland, brought from the mines on the important "ore railway" over a pass only 593m/1945ft high.

Hammerfes

In the most northerly part of Norway the fjords, flanked by the sheer rock faces which terminate the featureless mountain plateaux, are rather broader. Hammerfest, long famed as the most northerly town in Europe, is still 100km/60 miles short of the North Cape. One of the most interesting places in this area is Bossekop, on the Altafjord, almost the only place where the twin elements in the economy of the most northerly part of Europe, fishing and reindeer-herding, are found together.

Scandinavian
mountains

Behind the much indented west coast of Scandinavia rear up the high Scandinavian mountains, which extend along the whole length of the peninsula from the Skagerrak to the North Cape. Particularly towards the north they are only of medium height. Although there are a number of convenient routes through the mountains there are relatively few contacts between the west coast of Norway and the interior of Sweden. Northern Norway is too exclusively turned towards the North Sea, and the economically unproductive swathe of mountain country (parts of which, to the north, are still used by the Lapps as grazing for their reindeer) is too broad to encourage communication between the two regions.

External
possessions

To Norway belong the Spitzbergen island group and Bear Island in the Arctic Ocean, which together form the administrative district of Svalbard, and the volcanic island of Jan Mayen, as well as some territories in the Antarctic.

Population

Norway

Population
density

The kingdom of Norway has an area of 323,878sq.km/125,049sq. miles and a population of 4.2 million. The low population density of 13 to the sq. kilometre (34 to the sq. mile) reflects the country's geological structure: only about 3% of its area is suitable for agriculture, and the inhospitable terrain, the climate and the scope for trade with other countries have led to a heavy concentration of population in and around Oslo. Some 2 million people – almost half the population – live in the south-east of the country. Relations between the centre and the periphery are a major problem for Norway. The thinly populated regions of inland western Norway and the whole of northern Norway depend for their survival on a good infrastructure and a sound regional policy involving large subsidies.

The undramatic and peaceful development of this country on the periphery of Europe, which until it achieved independence in 1814 was ruled by the Danes, has produced a strongly homogeneous society. The transition from an agrarian to an industrial society which began at the end of the 19th century was for the most part achieved painlessly and without creating any marked distinction of social classes in the usual definition of the term. The most notable change in the population structure was the flight from the land, which is still continuing.

Norway's largest minority, the Sami (Lapps), living mainly in the northern part of the country, now have their own parliament to regulate their own affairs. All Norwegians must know the country's two official languages, the Bokmål which closely resembles Danish and the Nynorsk which was developed in the 19th century on the basis of Norwegian dialects; but the Lapps can also study their own Sami language in their schools.

Minorities

90% of the population belong to the national Lutheran church, of which the king is the formal head. When an infant is baptised it becomes a member of the church.

In addition to the established church there are a total of ten other recognised denominations, which, like the Lutheran church, receive contributions from the national exchequer related to the number of members.

Religion

Norway has traditionally sent out large numbers of immigrants: in the second half of the 19th century, for example, almost a million Norwegians emigrated to America. The number of immigrants is relatively small: only some 3.2% of the population come from other countries, most of them from Denmark, Sweden and Britain. Since 1975 there has been a standstill on immigration, except for Scandinavian citizens, refugees and the spouses and children of Norwegian nationals. Immigrants, particularly those from the Third World, are offered instruction in their mother tongue and in Norwegian; in dealings with public authorities they are entitled to the services of an interpreter.

Immigration and emigration

Norway's movement for the emancipation of women and its effective family policy are the consequence of the country's Scandinavian-style social democracy, its comfortably small population and its high educational level. The equality of women in public life has been demonstrated by the fact that the Social Democratic governments since the mid-eighties have had more female than male members and have been headed by a woman.

Norway was one of the first countries to give women the vote, in 1913. Nowadays an equal rights law provides preference for women in employment, qualifications in other respects being equal, and the operation of the law is monitored by a public official.

Position of women

School attendance is compulsory from the age of seven for a period of nine years. Thereafter some 90% of all young people take a further three-year course either in a general or a vocational school.

Norway has four universities and numerous other institutions of higher education. Over the last twenty years the educational standard and the degree of specialisation have risen considerably.

Education

School orchestra, Lillehammer

Children

The Children's Service (Ombud) is responsible for creating the conditions for children's safety and welfare, e.g. for improving the circumstances of families with children and guaranteeing children's rights at school and in public playgrounds. Children have their established place in Norwegian society – demonstrated, for example, on National Day (May 17th), when thousands of singing children march past the royal family on the balcony of the palace.

Sweden

Population density

The kingdom of Sweden has an area of some 450,000sq.km/ 173,750sq. miles (including 38,885sq.km/15 015sq. miles of inland waters), making it the fourth largest country in Europe (almost twice the size of the United Kingdom). Of this area 65,000sq.km/ 25,100sq. miles lie north of the Arctic Circle. Sweden has a total population of 8.6 million, some 85% of whom live in the southern half of the country, while the density of population in Norrbotten is only 3 to the sq.km (7.8 to the sq. mile).

Minorities

For many centuries Sweden was an ethnically homogeneous country. The only ethnic minority of any size was the Sami (Lapps), a nomadic people in the extreme north of the country who lived by herding reindeer. Nowadays the Sami living in Sweden – numbering some 17,000 out of a total of 50,000–60,000 – are a minority even in their own territory. In the early 20th century the official policy on the Sami was directed towards their assimilation: it was only at the end of the sixties, when many groups of immigrants began to demand concessions from the state, that the right of the Sami to their own culture and their own language became an important national issue

Immigration and emigration

Around the turn of the century more than a million people (roughly a quarter of the then population), driven by want and poverty, emigrated from Sweden; until after the Second World War, however, there was practically no immigration. During the war the first wave of immigrants – refugees from Finland, Denmark, Norway and the Baltic states – came to Sweden, to be followed later by immigrants from more distant countries. Now something like 10% of the population consists of immigrants, either themselves born abroad or with at least one parent of foreign origin. Most of them are Finnish citizens with Swedish as their mother tongue. Sweden thus has the largest proportion of foreigners in its population of any Western European country.

The large numbers of immigrants have naturally influenced the way of life of the Swedes. This is a very slow process, but in the long run it will inevitably alter the typically Swedish behaviour pattern. A delaying factor is that many first generation immigrants, socially and linguistically, live apart from the native Swedish population. The street scene is no longer dominated by people with fair hair – a characteristic formerly very common but nowadays no longer so prominent that it can be described as typically Swedish.

Swedish, like Danish, Faroese, Icelandic and Norwegian, belongs to the North Germanic family of languages. In Sweden, unlike Norway and Finland, there is only one official language, Swedish. Swedes in general tend to speak English – partly at least because foreign films on television are not dubbed in Swedish but are shown in the original version with subtitles. As a result of the immigration from Finland which has been going on for many centuries the Finnish language is spoken by some 300,000 inhabitants of Sweden. Sami (Lapp), a Finno-Ugric language with a number of different dialects, is the mother tongue of Sweden's 17,000 Lapps. *Languages*

Every Swedish child is born a member of the national Lutheran church if at least one of its parents is a member of that church. There is at *Religion*

Folk dancing in Dalarna

35

present much discussion about a possible separation of church and state. In spite of the frequent assertion that Sweden is a secularised country the fact is that 90% of the population belong to the established church – though statistics show that only 5% of the population are regular churchgoers.

There are many other religious denominations in Sweden. The largest is the Roman Catholic church, with 130,000 members, while the Orthodox and other eastern churches have 100,000 members. In addition there are a number of "free churches" (Protestant denominations outside the established church). The largest non-Christian group is the Muslims (50,000). Jews (now numbering some 16,000) have been represented in Sweden for 200 years.

Position
of women

Since the early seventies Swedish women have been increasing their share of the labour market: a change which results from both social and political developments. In the seventies women were needed in the rapidly expanding public sector, and to encourage their employment new tax laws were introduced and day nurseries were established. Now 85% of mothers with children under seven have jobs. This massive change was promoted by the provision made in the reforms for encouraging part-time work.

In comparison with other countries women are strongly represented in Parliament and other elected bodies. There are few women in key positions in business and the trade unions, but they are well represented in middle management.

Education

School attendance is compulsory for nine years from the age of seven. Education is free, and uniform throughout the country. Marks are given only from the eighth year onward. Over 90% of pupils leaving this first school at the age of sixteen go on to the gymnasium (secondary school), which provides both vocational training (combined with practical work) and general education; the course usually lasts three years. All schools are run by the communes (local authorities), which also have extensive programmes of adult education.

35% of school leavers go on to one of the thirty state universities and colleges of higher education, most university courses being vocationally oriented. University education is free; students pay only for books and other requirements and for board and lodging. The state provides financial subsidies and loans, so that no one is deprived of university education on financial grounds; parents are required to maintain their children only up to the age of eighteen or until they leave secondary school.

Finland

Population
density

Finland, the country with the largest expanses of inland water in the world (33,500sq.km/12,900sq. miles), has a total area of 338,000sq.km/130,500sq. miles – considerably more than that of the whole British Isles – but has a population of just under 5 million: i.e. some 15 inhabitants to the sq. kilometre (38 to the sq. mile). A sixth of the population live in the Helsinki region.

Swedish-speaking
Finns

The Finns are a very homogeneous people, but are not entirely uniform in character. They are predominantly fair-haired, but not to such an extent that fair hair can be regarded as a typically Finnish characteristic. Some 6% of the total population are of Swedish stock. In this group the tall slender physical type is commoner than in the Finnish-speaking population. Over all, however, the ethnic differences are slight.

Languages

Finnish belongs to the group of Finno-Ugric languages, which are spoken by only 23 million people; but though quantitatively small, qualitatively it stands on a level with the Indo-European languages. Other members of the Finno-Ugric group are Estonian and Hungarian. Finnish is closely related to Estonian but has a much remoter affinity to Hungarian.

The Swedish language came to Finland by two routes. In the first place it was the language of the conquerors, colonisers and evangelisers of the country, and later the official language of the Swedish principality of Finland; and it was also brought in when the Swedish kings settled a farming and fishing population from Sweden on the east coat of the Gulf of Bothnia and the south coast of the Gulf of Finland. Under the Finnish constitution of 1919 Swedish was given the privileged position of a second national language, a status which it still retains. The Åland Islands, where Finnish speakers account for less than 5% of the population, enjoy extensive rights of self-government.

Of Finland's two marginal population groups the Roma (gipsies), who Minorities live mainly in the southern part of the country, are the larger, numbering around 5500. Many of them speak a language of their own as well as Finnish and/or Swedish. While the dress of the men differs only in minor respects (usually in the wearing of light brown leather boots) from that of other Finns, the women still hold to their traditional dress.

In northern Finland there are some 2000 Sami (Lapps). In spite of the impression created by tourist literature, the Sami – men, women and children – only rarely wear their colourful traditional costume of felt coats, reindeer-skin boots and the "cap of the four winds" with its four floppy points. Ethnologists believe that the Sami developed out of a Finno-Ugric tribe who came into the country before the Finns and were later driven north. Finnish and the Sami language, which has three main dialects, are closely related.

The number of foreigners in Finland is low (around 20,000). The Finnish authorities admit mainly asylum-seeking refugees assigned to Finland by the United Nations Commissioner for Refugees, and accept other individual immigrants only after very careful scrutiny of their reasons for entry.

Christianity reached Finland in the 12th century, coming both from the Religion east and from the west. The Swedish conquerors brought Roman Catholicism, Greek monks the Greek Orthodox faith. The Reformation came to the duchy of Finland at the same time as to Sweden, and the Protestant church of Finland, with over 4½ million members in almost 600 communities, is now the third largest in the world. Nine out of ten Finns belong to the national Lutheran church. The second largest group is the Orthodox, with some 55,000 members. The Orthodox population is culturally very active and maintains close connections with the Finnish population of Karelia over the country's eastern frontier. During recent developments in the former Soviet Union the Orthodox Finns have been ready to help their brethren in Karelia. One of the major tasks being undertaken in common is the restoration of the Orthodox monastery of Valamo (Valaam; founded 992) on Lake Ladoga.

There are few members of other religious denominations in Finland. They include 13,000 Jehovah's Witnesses and fewer than 4000 Catholics. There are some 1300 Jews.

Finnish women are proud of the fact that they were the first women in Emancipation of women Europe to get the vote and that women are well represented in the Finnish Parliament, with between 60 and 80 members. Practically no government posts are closed to women, as was shown in 1990 when Elisabeth Ren became minister of defence. It is likely that in 1994 there will for the first time be a woman candidate for the highly respected and powerful office of President.

There is a historical explanation for the strong position of Finnish women. The men were often away at the wars for years at a time, and the women were obliged to carry on their work, always facing the possibility that they might, as widows, have to bear the whole responsibility of bringing up their children. After the Second World War the emancipation of women continued at an increasing pace. Women held on to the positions as members of the working population which they had occupied while the men were at the front, and their increased self-confidence led to a kind of educational explosion among women.

Education

School attendance is obligatory from the age of seven. Six years of primary and junior school are followed by three years in the secondary stage, after which pupils can stay on at school for a further three years to obtain the certificate qualifying them for admission to universities and colleges of higher education. Half of all young people – 60% of them girls – gain this certificate. Thereafter they must sit a university entrance examination. Finland has 21 universities and colleges of higher education with some 80,000 students; but the government has been unable to keep pace with the demand, with only some 10,000 student places available for 30,000 applicants.

The Finns set themselves high targets in the educational field. A government commission recommended in 1990 that the aim should be to make the Finns the best educated people in Europe by the year 2010, though adding the warning that this would call for considerably increased financial resources.

Government and Society

Norway

A constitutional monarchy

The Norwegian constitution drafted at Eidsvoll in 1814 provided the basis for the establishment of Norway's hereditary constitutional monarchy. Legislative power rests with the Storting (Parliament), subject to the king's right of veto. The king (since 1991 Harald V) holds the executive power, which he exercises through his ministers. Ministers are not members of the Storting but have the right to speak in it. The 165 members of the Storting are elected by voters in the country's 19 counties (fylker; singular fylke). The three largest counties are also the most thinly populated – Finnmark, Troms and Nordland in the far north

Political parties

The development of Norway into a typically Scandinavian "social state" has been directed since the 1920s – apart from short periods and the years of German occupation between 1940 and 1945 – by the Norwegian Labour Party. Six parties are represented in the present Storting: the two largest, the Labour Party and the conservative Høyre (Right), together with the Christian Popular Party, the Centre Party, the left-wing Socialist Party and the Progressive Party. Since the eighties the Labour Party has been dependent on the support of the Socialists and one other party.

Control of the economy

Many large firms are wholly or partly state-owned. The enormously important energy industry is controlled by the state, and the importance of this branch of the economy is emphasised by the existence of a ministry of oil and energy. The government's monopoly of services vital to the life of the country and the massive subsidies to agriculture and fisheries have led to a further concentration of power in the hands of the state. Responsibility for the social insurance of the population also rests with the state, and this is one of the main reasons for the high level of taxation in Norway.

International organisations

Norway's international commitment is centred on the United Nations, the first secretary general of which was a Norwegian, Trygve Lie. After

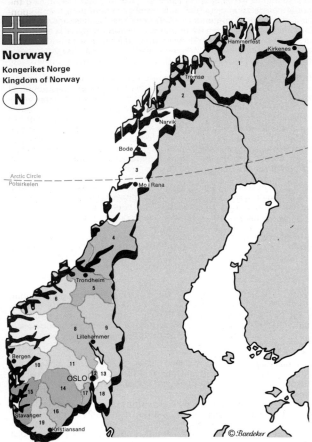

Norway

Kongeriket Norge
Kingdom of Norway

The Norwegian Counties

County (fylke)	Area in sq.km (sq. miles)		Population
1 Finnmark	48,637	(18,779)	75,000
2 Troms	25,954	(10,021)	147,000
3 Nordland	38,327	(14,798)	239,000
4 Nord-Trøndelag	22,463	(8673)	127,000
5 Sør-Trøndelag	18,831	(7271)	251,000
6 Møre og Romsdal	15,104	(5832)	238,000
7 Sogn og Fjordane	18,634	(7195)	107,000
8 Oppland	25,260	(9753)	182,000
9 Hedmark	27,388	(10,575)	187,000
10 Hordaland	15,634	(6036)	411,000
11 Buskerud	14,927	(5763)	225,000

County (fylke)	Area in sq.km (sq. miles)		Population
12 Oslo	454	(175)	461,000
13 Akershus	4917	(1898)	418,000
14 Telemark	15,315	(5913)	163,000
15 Rogaland	9141	(3529)	338,000
16 Aust-Agder	9212	(3557)	97,000
17 Vestfold	2216	(856)	198,000
18 Østfold	4183	(1615)	238,000
19 Vest-Agder	7281	(2811)	145,000
Kingdom of Norway	323,878	(125,050)	4,249,000

(excluding Svalbard, Jan Mayen and Antarctic territories)

39

its experience in the Second World War Norway abandoned its traditional neutrality and in 1949 was one of the founding members of NATO. A national referendum in 1972 and 1994 decided against membership of the European Community. At present Norway is a member of the European Free Trade Association (EFTA), and in international affairs has traditionally followed policies agreed with the other members of the Nordic Council.

Administration

Norway's administrative structure is regulated by the constitution and a law on administration. The basis of the system is the separation of legislative, executive and judicial powers. Associated with the 19 ministries are various directorates, which together form the country's central administration. A number of control bodies watch over the functioning and the budgets of the various state institutions, and in addition there are five commissions (*ombud*) responsible for monitoring the observance of the rights of different population groups. The "civil ombudsmann" deals with complaints by citizens against the administration.

Local government

Norway is not a federal state, and the responsibilities of the 19 counties are confined to limited areas – infrastructure, energy supply, further education and medical aftercare. The county council (*fylkesting*) decides on the allocation of financial resources for the various services. Its chief official, the *fylkesmann,* is also responsible for co-ordinating government projects at county level. The lower level of local government is formed by the 448 communes, which are responsible for social and health services and for local cultural and technical matters. The leading political representative of the commune is the *borgermester* or mayor.

Svalbard

Svalbard, in the Arctic Ocean, is an administrative anomaly. Although Norway has since 1920 had sovereignty over this group of islands, most of the inhabitants have Russian citizenship. A *sysselmann* appointed by the king is head of the island's administration and police. In recognition of the difficult living conditions in this Arctic possession the inhabitants enjoy lower rates of tax.

Law and
law enforcement

The third power in the state is the judiciary. Political and civil rights are guaranteed by the constitution. The judiciary is headed by the Supreme Court, consisting of five judges. In addition there are communal and municipal courts.

The age of majority is 18, when young Norwegians acquire all civil rights except that of buying strong drink. Young people are subject to the criminal law from the age of 16, but the present trend in relation to young criminals is towards substituting social service for custodial sentences.

Drug-dealing, murder and treason are treated as the most serious crimes in Norway, with maximum penalties of 15 (in exceptional cases up to 21) years' imprisonment. For lesser offences a fine is a much used alternative penalty. Under Norwegian road traffic laws the boundary between a fine and a prison sentence is fluid, and even minor offences may attract a relatively heavy penalty. The lowest fine is around £50, and exceeding the speed limit by 25km/15 miles an hour may lead to a ban on driving for a specified period. Visitors to Norway will be well advised not to drive after drinking alcohol and not to drive too fast.

Sweden

In the words of the 19th century Swedish historian and poet Erik Gustav Geijer, "the history of Sweden is the history of her kings". Nowadays, however, social, economic and political developments are of more account than dramatic historical events.

During the 18th century a strong opposition developed to autocratic rule by kings, and during the so-called "period of freedom" the Riksdag (Parliament) became the centre of political power. The four estates of Parliament developed into political groups which took the most important decisions on domestic and foreign affairs. During the last "years of freedom" the conflict between the nobility and the unprivileged classes became steadily fiercer, and for many years the kings were unable to assert their authority against the power of the estates.

After the Napoleonic wars, which ended for Sweden with the treaty of Kiel in 1814, the Swedish people lived in peace. This led to a long period of political stability in Sweden, with little in the way of serious religious, ethnic or social conflicts.

In 1865 the old Riksdag with its four estates (the nobility, the clergy, the burghers and the peasants) gave place to a two-chamber Parliament. In 1921 a democratic system with universal and equal suffrage was established, and in parallel with this the modern party system developed. Since then there have been only minor modifications of the political spectrum, which centres on the five main parties – the Conservatives, the Liberals and the Centre Party (formerly the Agrarian Party) on the one hand and the Social Democrats and Socialists on the other. *Parliament*

The Riksdag now consists of a single chamber of 329 members elected for a three-year term. It has the legislative power, while executive power lies with the government, which consists of the prime minister and his cabinet.

In parallel with the development of the parties there came into being popular movements like trade unions, temperance associations, etc. The Swedish trade union organisation (LO) and the Social Democratic Party work closely together. The LO, with over 2 million members (90% of the working population), plays an important part in Swedish politics.

Sweden is still a monarchy, but the political power of the king is now much reduced. Under the constitution which came into force on January 1st 1975 Sweden is a constitutional monarchy on a democratic and parliamentary basis. The king (since 1973 Carl XVI Gustaf) has only ceremonial and representative functions. There is, however, no public debate about abolishing the monarchy: the Swedes are proud of "their" royal family. *A constitutional monarchy*

Sweden remained neutral during the First and Second World Wars, and the success of this policy of neutrality became the basis of the Swedish conviction of their own excellence, the most prominent representative of which was the Social Democrat Olof Palme (prime minister 1969–76 and 1982–86), assassinated in 1986 by an assailant who has never been identified. *Neutrality*

In 1990 the Social Democratic government adopted a policy of closer association with Europe; then in the autumn of 1991 it suffered an electoral defeat which marked the irrevocable end of Sweden's "splendid isolation" in Europe. The new conservative government declared the policy of neutrality which had been followed since 1814 to be obsolete, and set their sights on Sweden's admission to the European Community. (It joined the European Union, as it is now known, on January 1st 1955.) Sweden's business concerns supported the country's entry to the EU on the grounds that by not joining it would risk an economic catastrophe. On the other hand, there were many who opposed entry. *Sweden and Europe*

A closer association with the European Community is likely to present no problems for Sweden's efficient industry. There will of course be some difficulties of adaptation, and these will undoubtedly condition the country's development in both domestic and foreign affairs until the year 2000.

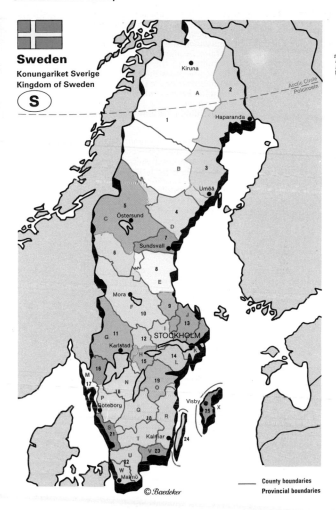

Sweden

Konungariket Sverige
Kingdom of Sweden

(S)

The Swedish Counties

1 Lapland
  (North Lapland,
  South Lapland)
2 Norrbotten
3 Västerbotten
4 Ångermanland
5 Jämtland
6 Härjedalen
7 Medolpad

8 Hälsingland
9 Gästrikland
10 Dalarna
11 Värmland
12 Västmanland
13 Uppland
14 Södermanland
15 Närke
16 Dalsland

17 Bohuslän
18 Västergötland
19 Östergötland
20 Småland
21 Halland
22 Skåne
23 Blekinge
24 Öland
25 Gotland

Sweden is divided into 24 counties (*län*), which coincide for the most part with the country's old historical provinces. Each county authority is headed by a governor (*landshövding*) appointed by the central government. Within the counties there are smaller local government units, the communes.

Swedish civil law is laid down in separate enactments, including laws on marriage and on parenthood. New criminal legislation was introduced in 1965. As in Norway, the trend is toward humane penal practice.

Finland

Finland's declaration of independence on December 6th 1917 did not mark a sudden leap into independent status, but was merely the last short stage in a long journey.

In the 18th century the Swedish duchy of Finland suffered heavily under the ambitious Ostpolitik of the kings in Stockholm. In 1788 there was an unsuccessful conspiracy by officers against the Swedish king; then in 1808 Russia declared war on Sweden and rapidly advanced through the whole of Finland into northern Sweden, after which Sweden was compelled to cede Finland to Russia. The Tsar then declared Finland an autonomous Grand Duchy, with himself as Grand Duke. In 1906 the Diet of the four estates was converted into a Parliament of 200 members, elected every four years by universal, equal and secret vote.

In 1908 there was a fresh wave of Russification in Finland, and the idea began to gain ground that the only alternative to capitulation to foreign domination was complete independence. Thus the Finns had had more than a hundred years in which to gain experience in self-government, and when they became independent in 1917 they had merely to graft on a ministry of defence and a foreign ministry to the existing system of government.

The Finnish constitution, based on Swedish and other western models, came into force in 1919. Finland is now a democratic parliamentary republic headed by a President. The President, who is elected for a six-year term and has wide powers and responsibilities, and Parliament together form the legislature.

After achieving independence Finland continued to develop its democratic infrastructure and to build up a social structure similar to that of the other Scandinavian countries. The members of the single-chamber Parliament (Eduskunta or Riksdag) are elected for a four-year term.

The Swedish Provinces

		Area in sq.km (sq. miles)		Population			Area in sq.km (sq. miles)		Population
A	Norrbotten	98,911	(38,190)	264,000	N	Skaraborg	7938	(3065)	277,000
B	Västerbotten	55,401	(21,390)	252,000	O	Östergötland	10,562	(4078)	403,000
C	Jämtland	49,443	(19,090)	136,000	P	Älvsborg	11,395	(4400)	441,000
D	Västernorrland	21,678	(8370)	261,000	Q	Jönköping	9944	(3839)	308,000
E	Gävleborg	18,191	(7024)	289,000	R	Kalmar			
F	Kopparberg	28,194	(10,886)	289,000		(including Öland)	11,170	(4313)	241,000
G	Värmland	17,583	(6789)	283,000	S	Halland	5454	(2106)	255,000
H	Örebro	8519	(3289)	273,000	T	Kronoberg	8458	(3266)	178,000
I	Västmanland	6302	(2433)	258,000	U	Kristianstad	6089	(2351)	289,000
J	Uppsala	6986	(2697)	269,000	V	Blekinge	2941	(1136)	151,000
K	Stockholm	6488	(2505)	1,642,000	W	Malmöhus	4938	(1907)	779,000
L	Södermanland	6060	(2340)	256,000	X	Gotland	3140	(1212)	57,000
M	Göteborg och								
	Bohus	5141	(1985)	740,000		**Kingdom of Sweden**	410,929	(158,660)	8,590,000

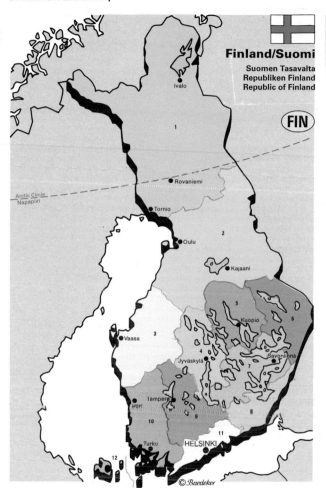

Finland/Suomi

Suomen Tasavalta
Republiken Finland
Republic of Finland

FIN

The Finnish Provinces

Province (lääni)	Area in sq.km (sq. miles)		Population
1 Lappi	93,057	(35,929)	200,000
2 Oulu	56,866	(21,956)	435,000
3 Vaasa	26,447	(10,211)	444,000
4 Keski-Suomi	16,230	(6266)	250,000
5 Kuopio	16,511	(8375)	256,000
6 Pohjois-Karjala	17,782	(6866)	176,000
7 Mikkeli	16,342	(6310)	208,000
8 Kymi	10,783	(4163)	336,000
9 Häme	17,010	(6568)	684,000
10 Turku ja Pori	22,170	(8560)	716,000
11 Uudenmaa	9898	(3822)	1,226,000
12 Åland Islands	1527	(590)	24,000
Republic of Finland	304,623	(117,615)	4,954,000

There are at present up to ten parties represented in Parliament, the largest being the Social Democrats, the Conservatives and the Centre Party (formerly the Agrarian Party). Many Finns are floating voters, owing no permanent allegiance to any one party, and only the small Swedish People's Party can rely on the loyalty of its electorate. The successor party to the left-wing People's Democratic Union, which in 1958 won 50 of the 200 seats in Parliament, has now shrunk into insignificance.

Government is by coalition, usually consisting of two of the three largest parties together with one or more of the smaller parties. Since predominance alternates between the three large parties and the small ones claim about a third of the seats, coalition governments of three or even more parties are inevitable. In 1991 a coalition of Conservatives and Social Democrats was succeeded by a coalition of Conservatives and the Centre Party.

Coalition government

Finland is a member of the United Nations and the Nordic Council, one of whose objectives is the removal of trade barriers between member states. Looking forward to the European single market due to come into force in 1993, the Finnish Parliament decided in March 1992, after long debate, to apply for admission to the European Community. A referendum held in 1994 found the majority of the population in favour of joining the EU, as it was now known, and Finland became a member with effect from January 1st 1995.

International organisations

Finland is divided into 12 provinces (*lääni*), each headed by a prefect. Local government functions, including regional planning, transport, health and education, are in the hands of rural and municipal communes. The self-governing Åland Islands have their own parliament (Landsting).

Local government

The highest Finnish courts are the Supreme Court and the Supreme Administrative Court in Helsinki. There are also appeal courts in Turku, Vaasa, Kuopio, Helsinki, Kouvola and Rovaniemi and municipal courts consisting of the mayor and two assessors. An ombudsman appointed by Parliament deals with complaints by citizens against government departments.

Law and law enforcement

Economy

Agriculture

The northern European countries have very different agricultural patterns. Some 9% of the territory of Sweden and Finland and 3% of that of Norway is suitable for agriculture. In all three countries the agricultural land is mainly in the southern areas of marine transgression, in which fertile sediments were deposited towards the end of the Ice Age. It consists principally of coastal strips, wide valleys in the lower courses of rivers and tectonic depressions like the central Swedish depression. This concentration of agriculture in the southern parts of the countries is also due to the unfavourable climatic conditions in higher latitudes. The growing period in the north is exceedingly short – in Lapland, for example, only about 140 days in the year. Arable farming, therefore, steadily gives place to stock farming towards the north, and even potatoes and barley cannot be grown beyond the 60th parallel, which indeed marks the northern limit of any cultivation. And so north of the Arctic Circle the herding of reindeer remains of economic importance.

    Favourable conditions for agriculture are also promoted by the intense light conditions in summer and the warmth brought by the Gulf

General

Mountain pasture in Norway (Leirdal, Jotunheim)

Stream. In the far north, where agriculture is no longer possible, the sun remains permanently above the horizon for more than 70 days (Hammerfest); at Kiruna it still shines continuously for 40 days. This increases the growth rate of plants adapted to the northern climate, but does not permit the cultivation of useful plants, since the growing period is so short.

Norway

The fertile loam and clay soils of southern Norway, central Sweden and southern Finland provide a basis for intensive cultivation and much stock-farming. The unfavourable pattern of relief, however, limits the scope for agricultural development, particularly in Norway. In western Norway, for example, agriculture is concentrated in an area along the coast ranging in width between 40 and 60km (25 and 40 miles) and narrow strips of land along the lower reaches of the fjords. In view of the large proportion of Norwegian territory occupied by hills and mountains rising above the altitude at which cultivation is possible the scope for agriculture is reduced to under half the total area; and transport and marketing conditions mean that the cultivation of useful crops in Norway is increasingly being concentrated in the favoured areas round the Oslofjord, the Trondheimfjord and Lake Mjøsa and to the south of Stavanger. Fruit-growing and cultivation under glass have been particularly successful in these areas. Given the move towards the rationalisation of production, the best prospects for survival lie with holdings of over 20 hectares (50 acres). In the vicinity of towns, where there are other forms of employment, agriculture is increasingly becoming a second occupation.

In northern Norway the best economic prospects are sheep-farming and the breeding of animals for their fur. Towards the north, too, farming is increasingly combined with fishing or forestry, and agricultural crops are grown mainly for personal consumption. 80% of Norway's foodstuffs now have to be imported.

Sweden offers much more favourable conditions for agriculture than Norway. The climate and particularly the fertile soils of Skåne and the central Swedish depression make possible a productive agriculture. In corn, dairy products and meat Sweden meets its own needs. In Sweden as in Norway, too, a process of concentration has been at work. Whereas at the turn of the century some 73% of all Swedes were employed in agriculture, the proportion has now fallen to 5%. There has been a corresponding change in the structure of farm holdings, promoted in recent years particularly by the mechanisation and specialisation of cultivation. The largest group of farm holdings is that of farms between 50 and 100 hectares (125 and 250 acres); and whereas in 1950 some 34% of holdings were of only 2–5 hectares (5–12½ acres) the percentage of farms in this group is now only 2%. In southern Sweden a quarter of total agricultural production comes from 2% of total area. This is true particularly of wheat and sugar-beet, but also of dairy products.

Towards the north there is a steady transition to the growing of fodder plants and the rearing of fat stock. Accordingly in Norrland arable farming accounts for only a very small proportion of agricultural land and stock-farming predominates. In the country's most northerly province, Norrbotten, the herding of reindeer by the Sami is the dominant feature. As in Norway, the amount of woodland owned by farmers increases towards the north. State subsidies by themselves are insufficient to maintain the traditional farming pattern: income from timber-working plays an important part in the economy of the farms.

In comparison with Norway and Sweden Finland has a much higher proportion of small and medium-sized farm holdings. Of the total of 208,000 farms 58% have under 10 hectares (25 acres). The most important form of production is stock-farming (cattle and pigs); and in

Cornfield with poppies on Öland (Sweden)

consequence three-quarters of the total area of arable land is devoted to the growing of corn for animal feed, with barley and oats showing yields of up to 60 metric hundredweight per hectare (24 cwt per acre). Like Sweden, Finland supplies a high proportion of its own domestic consumption of agricultural produce, and indeed produces small surpluses of corn, dairy products and meat for export. In the more northern latitudes, as in Norway and Sweden, deteriorating climatic conditions result increasingly in farming being supplemented by forestry.

Forestry

Finland

Timber is a raw material of great economic importance, particularly to Finland and Sweden. In the three countries of Norway, Sweden and Denmark there are 50 million hectares (125 million acres) of forest, and the annual production of timber is some 100 million cu.m/130 million cu.yd. Finland is the most heavily wooded country in Europe, over two-thirds of its area being covered with pine, spruce and birch forests, with the conifers accounting for 82% of the total. In central and eastern Finland forests cover up to nine-tenths of the total area. Between 40 and 50 million cu.m (52 and 65 million cu.yd) of solid timber are felled annually in Finland. 63% of the Finnish forests belong to 800,000 private owners; the state forests are mainly in the north and east of the country.

Sweden

57% of the area of Sweden is covered by forest, with deciduous forest predominating in the south. Over the country as a whole, however, the percentage of coniferous forest (85%) is higher than in Finland. The pattern of ownership in Sweden is very different: half the forests are owned by individuals or farming families, a quarter by large companies and the remaining quarter by the state. The amount of timber

Timber rafts on a Finnish river

Sawmill on the Arctic Circle (Sweden)

felled annually (60 million cu.m/78 million cu.yd) is even higher than in Finland. As in Finland, most of the timber goes to the cellulose and paper-making industries; only some 10 million cu.m/13 million cu.yd are exported as timber or in the form of wood products.

Forestry is of less importance to the economy of Norway than to Finland and Sweden. Only 26% of the total area of the country is forest-covered, and efforts are being made to increase the area under forest in the longer term: some 25,000 hectares (62,500 acres) are at present reafforested annually, with the aid of large subsidies from the state.

Norway

The traditional forestry methods of Scandinavia are in process of major change. Within a decade the number of man-hours per cubic metre of timber felled was reduced by two-thirds as a result of the introduction of machinery. In Sweden, thanks to the use of modern methods, only some 50,000 workers are employed in the production of timber and the management of the forests. The rational organisation of timber production is more difficult in the disadvantaged northern regions of the Scandinavian countries than in the central and southern regions: the determining factors are the rate of natural growth and the transport facilities available. As a result the management of forests by small farmers, particularly in Finland, falls still further behind.

Changes in forestry methods

Fisheries

Norway, with a long fishing tradition behind it, is dominant among the Scandinavian countries in this field. In terms of annual catch it is Europe's leading fishing nation, particularly in the deep-sea fisheries, landing 1.8 million tons of fish annually. The main species of fish caught are now the lodde or capelin (a fish of the salmon family), cod,

49

mackerel, haddock and sea trout. Norway's fish-processing industries are of international importance, producing fish meal, fish oil and canned fish. In the coastal areas fishing is often combined with farming, enabling many small farmers to supplement their income. The coastal fisheries are now declining, particularly in the Lofoten area. In the deep-sea fisheries herring and cod are now of much less importance, accounting in 1989 for only 15% and 11% of the total catch. Whaling has also declined and indeed, under the pressure of international publicity, almost died out. Against this, catches of mackerel have increased considerably, with foreign boats contributing to the total; and in 1990 Norway's quota of 150,000 tons of mackerel was substantially exceeded. The breeding of salmon and trout in large fish farms is of steadily increasing importance in Norway. At present there are almost 600 such farms, producing 150,000 tons of salmon in 1990.

In Sweden fishing is of little importance except on the west coast, where two-thirds of the total catch is landed. The yield of Finland's fisheries is still smaller, some four-fifths of the total catch consisting of sea fish from the Baltic and the Gulfs of Bothnia and Finland.

Minerals

Mineral ores

The ancient basement rocks of the Fenno-Scandian shield and the Caledonian mountains contain numerous seams of valuable minerals, particularly iron and copper ores. The working of iron ore began as early as the beginning of the 14th century at Bergslagen in central Sweden, and in the 19th century the iron ores of Kiruna and Gällivare-Malmberget in Swedish Lapland were of major economic importance in the world market. With the help of the Thomas process these ores with their high phosphorus content are still successfully worked. More than 80% of the ore produced in Sweden comes from this area. There are still extensive reserves (just under 3 billion tons) of high grade ore (iron content 60%), but it is now increasingly facing competition in world markets from ore from Brazil, Labrador and Australia. Since the beginning of the 1970s exports of iron ore have fallen by more than half.

Finland also produces a variety of ores, but exports consist almost exclusively of copper, zinc and nickel. Outukumpu in central Finland has one of the largest copper mines in Europe.

Coal, oil and natural gas

Energy-producing raw materials are very unevenly distributed in northern Europe. Finland has neither coal nor oil, and the only fuel it produces, on a small scale, is peat. Sweden has 80% of the known reserves of uranium. Coal is found in any significant quantity only in the outlying Norwegian possession of Spitzbergen. Oil and natural gas are of great economic importance in the Norwegian sector of the North Sea, where exploration began in 1963 and the first Norwegian oil was extracted in the Cod field in 1968. Of major importance is the Ekofisk field 240km/150 miles off Stavanger, where large reserves were found at a depth of 3000m/9900ft. The high costs of extracting the oil became economic sooner than expected when oil prices increased sharply during the first energy crisis of 1973–74. At that time one of the more than thirty drillings cost 12 million US dollars. From the mid seventies Norway developed into one of the world's leading oil-producing countries and a net exporter of oil.

Activity in exploration and extraction is now moving steadily farther north. Two fields of great economic importance are the Frigg field to the west of Bergen and the Statford field west of the mouth of the Sognefjord. In 1990 Norwegian oil production amounted to 81 million tons. The production of natural gas has also increased considerably, reaching 28 billion cu.m/37 billion cu.yd in 1990. In spite of Norway's extensive reserves of fossil fuel, however, thermal power stations play only a small part in Norwegian energy production. With the country's mountainous topography 99% of its electricity requirements are met by hydro-electric power stations.

Industry

As a result of the rapid structural changes that have taken place in Norway, Sweden and Finland, particularly since the Second World War, the natural resources of these countries are now being exported in crude form on a much smaller scale than in the past and instead are being processed and refined, using increasingly specialised facilities, in the countries themselves. In consequence employment in this secondary sector has increased sharply, and now amounts in Norway to 26%, in Sweden to 30% and in Finland to 31%. Here too, however, the maximum has been reached, and as a result of rationalisation (particularly automation) employment in the services sector has in recent years become increasingly predominant. Technological advances and changed conditions in world markets have led to a sharp decline in once important branches of industry. This is seen, for example, in the Swedish metal-smelting industry, formerly with some 200 plants smelting iron and non-ferrous metals, which has now shrunk to a tenth of its former size. There has been a similar decline in large parts of the shipbuilding, sawmilling, glass-manufacturing and foodstuffs industries. The decline in particular industries has also been accompanied by a regional concentration on efficient and conveniently situated processing plants. Amalgamations of existing firms promoted the development of large companies and multi-nationals.

General

Norway's situation on the sea meant that its early economic development was concentrated on fishing, shipping and shipbuilding. This provided a starting-point for industrialisation in the production of fishing boats, small coastal vessels and large freighters. The traditional use of timber in shipbuilding was soon displaced by steel, produced from Scandinavian ore. The leading shipbuilding centres are now Stavanger, Bergen and Trondheim, where this traditional branch of industry was given a boost by the oil boom of the early 1970s. The great demand for offshore equipment like drilling rigs and tanker facilities led to a dynamic development of industry, and the increase in the production of oil and natural gas promoted the growth of the Norwegian chemical industry.

Norway

Recent developments have included a petro-chemical complex north of Narvik and a large oil refinery near Bergen. The interrelated investment of capital by large concerns like Statoil and Norsk Hydro has led to industrial integrations extending beyond the frontiers of Norway, particularly with Sweden. Norway's abundant supply of energy, particularly hydro-electric power, also promoted the development of energy-intensive branches like the aluminium industry. The availability of cheap hydro-electric power has been a decisive factor in the metal-smelting industries, which use aluminium and other imported raw materials to produce high-grade alloys. Metalworking is thus, after the oil industry, Norway's most important earner of foreign currency. After these come the papermaking and cardboard packaging industries, shipbuilding and electrical engineering. During the last decade the textile and clothing industry has declined sharply, as have the foodstuffs industries.

The metal-processing industries are also an important element in the Swedish economy, accounting for just under half the total value of industrial output. The main centres of engineering and motor vehicle manufacture are Stockholm and Göteborg. In recent years industry has been internationalised in Sweden to an even greater extent than in

Sweden

Oil rig, Stavanger

Norway. This is true also of the electrical, chemical and woodworking industries; examples of this are firms like Volvo, Electrolux, ASEA and LM Ericsson.

Finland

After the Second World War industrialisation made great strides in Finland. Woodworking, metalworking, metal-processing and ship-building benefited from Finland's connections with the Soviet Union, on which some 200,000 jobs depended. The timber and woodworking industries made the main contributions to Finnish export earnings; but since 1960, when they accounted for 75% of exports, their share has fallen sharply to 35%. Finland is now a modern industrial nation which has increasingly concentrated its industrial production on high-value technology-oriented products like computer-controlled mechanical engineering and special types of vehicles and shipping.

Tourism

Sweden, Finland and Norway are now becoming increasingly popular holiday countries. In 1988 visitors accounted for 20 million "bed-nights" in hotels, etc., in Sweden, 8.9 million in Finland and 5.2 million in Norway; and if holiday houses and cabins were included the figures would be much higher. According to the Swedish tourist authorities the total number of bed-nights in 1991 was 34 million, including 6.5 million foreign visitors. Tourism creates additional jobs, especially in the northern regions with their limited infrastructure. This is true particularly of Sweden and Finland. In Sweden 235,000 people are employed in the tourist trade, with a total turnover of some 35 billion crowns, 6 billion of them spent by foreign visitors. In Norway tourism is still a very minor element in the economy, providing only 4% of total employment in 1990.

The development of tourism is held back by the short summer season and uncertain weather conditions. Hitherto the main tourist areas have been the lakes of central Sweden and the Finnish Lakeland, while Norway has been particularly favoured for cruising holidays. With the development of winter sports areas attractive to an international public increasing numbers of visitors are going to Scandinavia – particularly to central Sweden and Lapland – in winter.

Problems and Prospects

The countries of northern Europe are at present in a phase of radical change. The image of the Swedish welfare state, is now beginning to crumble, and this is having an influence on the neighbouring countries. High taxes and above all high pay increases have severely affected the competitiveness of export-oriented industries. Since 1991 the Swedish government has been trying to reduce the predominance of the public sector and to ease a tax burden which by European standards is extremely high. To date, however, the problems – which include putting the country's finances on a sound basis and reducing the number of unemployed – have not been satisfactorily resolved.

Norway has not yet been able to reduce its heavy economic dependence on oil and on metalworking, shipping and fishing and to diversify its industry. Finland for its part has been faced with much greater problems; in particular it has been badly hit by the political changes in the East. Trade with the Soviet Union, which in the past had accounted for up to a quarter of the country's total foreign trade, almost completely collapsed in 1991. Now, however, the new political constellation in the East offers the prospect of a fresh impetus to the economy. The enlarged Baltic area has a population of some 40 million, and it also has 50 or so large towns, over 70 ports, an excellent network of ferry services and six international airports. Economic relations betwen Helsinki and Tallinn are now very close, and many Estonians travel to work in Finland during the week.

In spite of these new possibilities in the East the Scandinavian countries are seeking a closer integration with the European Community. Since January 1st 1994 the European Economic Area, a combination of the EFTA countries and the EU states, has been in existence. While the number of EU member states has increased since January 1st 1995 that of the EFTA countries has decreased, and the disbandment of EFTA seems a probability. Even before they joined the European Union Finnish and Swedish firms had invested in EU countries. Following Sweden and Finland, Norway also expressed a wish to join the EU, but a public referendum held in October 1994 again decided against entry. Finnish and above all Swedish firms are now investing less in their own country and more in the European Community: between 1985 and 1988 alone Swedish investments in the Community multiplied sevenfold, Finnish investments fourfold. The reduction in capital gains tax and income tax by the Swedish government will undoubtedly encourage investors from Community countries to play an increased part in the planned privatisation of state-owned undertakings, and this will promote the closer integration of Scandinavia with the rest of Europe. Modern means of communication and the hoped-for improvement in transport facilities by the construction of a bridge over the Great Belt can only speed up this development.

History

Prehistory and Protohistory of Scandinavia

It is only in quite recent years that detailed studies have been published on the settlement of northern Europe (Denmark, Norway, Sweden and Finland) in prehistoric and early historical times. This section outlines the history of Norway, Sweden and Finland, the three countries with which this guide is concerned.

Stone Age
(c. 7000 to
1800 B.C.)

In the Stone Age there are settlements in the western Baltic region (southern Sweden and Denmark). Hunters and fishermen move into Sweden as far as the Dalälv and up the Norwegian coast to the Trondheim area. The inhabitants of the coastal regions live by fishing and gathering shellfish, leaving evidence of their presence in the shells and kitchen refuse found on their "kitchen middens" (køkkenmøddinger) in southern Norway and elsewhere.

It is only in the middle of the 3rd millennium B.C., in the Neolithic period, that we find evidence of the first farming culture (the Trichterbecher or TRB culture, with the first pottery), but this is confined by climatic conditions to a very meagre level. During this period Eastern European tribes from Finland push into central Scandinavia but are later driven back.

Nordic
Bronze Age
(c. 1800–500 B.C.)

The Nordic Bronze Age appears mainly in Denmark and southern Sweden, but material belonging to this period has also been found in southern and western Norway. The bronze was obtained by barter from regions farther south, though what it was exchanged for – perhaps amber – is not clear. From this period date the rock carvings found particularly at Tanum (in Bohuslän, north of Göteborg), on the east coast of Sweden in the area north of Lake Mälar, on the west side of the Oslofjord and in a band of territory extending eastwards from Trondheim into Sweden, as well as the chambered tomb at Kivik on the south-east coast of Sweden and various solar wheels or solar discs reflecting a cult of the sun.

Nordic
Iron Age
(c. 500 B.C.
to A.D. 500)

The Nordic Iron Age, of which only scanty evidence has been found on the Swedish islands of Gotland and Öland as well as in Denmark, is represented by domestic equipment, jewellery and above all improved weaponry. The area of Germanic settlement extends up to the Arctic Circle. Runic inscriptions are found on jewellery and implements from the 2nd century A.D. onwards, and from about the end of the 4th century runes begin to be carved on stone (rock faces, standing stones, gravestones).

Scandinavia

The name Scandinavia occurs for the first time in Pliny the Elder (c. A.D. 75), and is found also in the name of the Swedish province of Skåne. There are references in Tacitus to Swedes (Suiones) and Finns (Fenni).

Southern Sweden and the Danish islands are originally occupied by the Heruli, but during the age of the Great Migrations they and the tribes on the Jutland peninsula are compelled to withdraw in face of the Danes pushing forward from the east and north. During these troubled times numerous fortified settlements and ring forts are built. To the north of these various peoples, on the Scandinavian peninsula, are the Goths, separated by dense forests from the Swedes settled still farther to the north. Forests and mountains, together with Lake Vänern and the Götaälv to the south-west, bound the territory of the Norwegians, for whom the older songs have no common name: the later term Norvegr or Nordmenn is probably no more than a reference to the fact that they lived farther to the north. Internal conflicts and struggles for power seen to have lain at the origin of the expeditions of these Norsemen, named Vikings after the fjords and inlets (*vikr*) from which they sailed, who ravaged the whole of Europe and are believed to have been the first Europeans to reach America.

Norway

In the Bronze Age Norway is occupied by Germanic peoples. The mountainous nature of the country hampers communications between the different valleys and fjords and leads to the formation of kinship groups ruled by petty kings. By the time of the Viking expeditions, however, there is a form of loose association into four large communities called "tings".

Early history

Harald Hårfager (Fairhair).
    Harald, scion of an old ruling family in the Oslofjord, defeats the other petty kings, after bitter fighting, and unifies a large part of the country under his rule. Many freedom-loving peasants leave the country (first settlers in Iceland, 874).

872–930

Some of the petty kingdoms are re-established, and after Harald's death there is no overall royal authority. During this period the Vikings set out on their raiding expeditions to the coastal regions of Europe. On returning from their campaigns the warriors for the most part go back to tilling the soil.

9th–11th c.

Olav Tryggvason (Tryggvessøn).
    Olav Tryggvason, Harald's great-grandson, continues to fight for the unity of the country, enlisting in his cause the missionary spirit of Christianity. He builds a royal palace in Trondheim. He is killed in a naval battle off Rügen against a combined force of Danes, Swedes and Trondheimers.

995–1000

In the early medieval period royal authority and the Christian faith are gradually established in Norway. Among the most stubborn opponents are the pagan jarls (petty kings) of Trondheim. For a time the country is subject to Denmark.

11th c.

St Olav.
    Consolidation of the unified kingdom and the Christian church, often by methods of extreme severity. Olav fights the Danes and the men of Trondheim; he is driven out in 1028, tries to return and is killed in the battle of Stiklestad in 1030. He soon comes to be regarded as a martyr, is declared a saint by popular acclaim and becomes Norway's national hero.

1015–30

The kings fight for power.
    In the 11th century there are several conflicts with the Danes. Bergen is founded in 1070. In the 12th century the power of the church grows; it claims the power to grant the crown as an ecclesiastical fief.

11th and 12th c.

Olav Kyrre.
    Denmark abandons its claims to Norway. Internal consolidation; growth in the strength of the towns. Establishment of Norwegian bishoprics at Nidaros (Trondheim), Bergen and Oslo.

1066–93

King Sverre.
    Sverre, leader of the Trondheim party, the Birkebeiners (named after their birch-bark leggings), defeats the Baglers ("Crosier-Men") who support the cause of the Danish Church and are powerful in southern Norway.

1177–1202

History

1217–63	**Håkon Håkonsson.**
	The great days of chivalry. Håkon, Sverre's grandson, ends the conflict between the parties. Iceland is incorporated into Norway.
1263–80	**Magnus Lagaboetir ("Reformer of the Law").**
	Further constitutional reforms; national system of law; abolition of the old "tings".
12th and 13th c.	**Building of stave churches.**
	The native timber architecture of Norway reaches its peak in these old wooden churches, several of which have survived (including Heddal, Borgund, Fantoft near Bergen and Gol, now in the National Museum in Oslo).
1387	Margaret of Denmark, daughter of King Valdemar IV Atterdag of Denmark and wife of King Håkon VI Magnusson of Norway and Sweden, is elected queen in both Denmark and Norway after the death of her son Olaf.
1397	Under the Union of Kalmar Denmark, Norway and Sweden are united. Eric of Pomerania, Margaret's grand-nephew, is crowned king of the three kingdoms. Norway remains united with Denmark until 1814; Sweden wins its independence between 1433 and 1523.
1387–1814	Norway united with Denmark in a personal union.
	The old nobility has been destroyed in the conflict with the monarchy. The economy, which is thriving, is mainly in the hands of the Hanseatic League. The Reformation is introduced in 1536, and at the same time Norway becomes a Danish province ruled by a governor. Danish becomes the language of government, the church and the schools, and Old Norwegian survives only in local dialects. In its wars with Denmark Sweden also attacks Norway, and this arouses Norwegian national feeling, which had been almost extinguished. The development of maritime trade brings new ideas into the country and provides a powerful new intellectual stimulus.
1556–60	Decline of Hanseatic power. In 1559 the power of the Hanseatic League, which had almost completely dominated Norwegian trade in the 15th and 16th centuries, is broken in Bergen.
1624	Mining increases in importance: silver at Kongsberg (1624), copper at Røros (1644).
1807	The continental blockade.
	Denmark's alliance with France and its involvement in Napoleon's "colonial system" leads to a British blockade of the Norwegian coast. Shipping is brought to a standstill and the country suffers acute shortages. Norway seeks to break free from Denmark.
1814	Norway united with Sweden.
	After Napoleon's defeat Denmark is compelled, under the treaty of Kiel, to cede Norway to Sweden. The Norwegians do not recognise the treaty, declare their country independent and adopt a liberal constitution at Eidsvoll (May 17th: now Norway's National Day). They are compelled by the arrival of Swedish troops under Bernadotte and pressure from the great powers to accept a personal union with Sweden, but are allowed to have their own constitution.
1853	Beginning of the "language movement".
	Ivar Aasen publishes samples of Landsmål, a written language diverging from Danish which he has developed out of local dialects. It is widely adopted.

Oscar II (d. 1907).   1872–1905
   The last king of both Norway and Sweden. Conflicts between the
Storting and the Crown which arise after the electoral victory of the Left
(1882) are settled by the formation of a cabinet.

A national referendum decides in favour of dissolving the union of   1905
Norway and Sweden, and is confirmed by the treaty of Karlstad on
October 26th.

King Håkon VII (b. 1872).   1905–57
   Prince Karl of Denmark is elected king of Norway and takes the name
of Håkon.
   The constitution is further democratised. Women get the vote in
1913.

First World War.   1914–18
   Norway remains neutral. Half its merchant fleet, which carries cargo
for the Allies, is sunk by German submarines. Popular feeling is hostile
to Germany.

Norway joins the League of Nations. It is granted sovereignty over   1920
Spitzbergen (Svalbard), which is finally incorporated in Norway in
1925.

Prohibition (a complete ban on alcohol).   1920–27

Norway occupies the island of Jan Mayen.   1929

Second World War.   1939–45
   In 1940 German troops invade and occupy Norway, anticipating a
British landing. There is fierce fighting for the possession of Narvik.
The king and government flee to London. Norway is ruled by a German
commissioner, who is supported by a former Norwegian minister,
Vidkun Quisling.
   After the German surrender in May 1945 the Norwegian government
in exile returns from Britain.

The Labour Party wins a general election.   1945
   Norway becomes a founding member of the United Nations.

Treaty with the Soviet Union regulating the northern frontier between   1949
the two countries. Norway joins NATO.

Norway is a founding member of the Nordic Council (economic and   1951
cultural co-operation between the Nordic states).

Crown Prince Olav (b. 1903), only son of Håkon VII, succeeds his father. 1957

Nordic Passport and Customs Union.   1958

Norway becomes a founding member of the European Free Trade   1960
Association (EFTA).

The right-wing parties win a majority in a general election.   1965

Free trade agreement with the European Economic Community, after a 1973
national referendum in 1972 which decides against full membership of
the Community.

Drilling for oil and natural gas begins in the North Sea.   1974

An oil pipeline, 450km/280 miles long, from the Ekofisk oilfield, north- 1977
west of Stavanger, to Emden in Germany is brought into operation.
   General election: the Labour Party wins 76 seats in the Storting.

History

1979   A huge field of natural gas is discovered 130km/80 miles north-west of Bergen.

The Social Democrats fare badly in local government elections.

1980   The Alexander Kielland supply platform in the Ekofisk oilfield in the North Sea capsizes in a storm (123 dead and missing).

Agreement on the deployment of US troops in Norway for defensive purposes.

1981   Prime Minister Odvar Nordli (Labour) resigns of health grounds (January 30th) and is succeeded by Gro Harlem Brundtland, Norway's first woman prime minister.

Complete price freeze until the end of 1981; cut in income tax.
General election in September, won by the Conservatives. Their leader, Kaare Willoch, forms a minority government (October).

1982   Parliament decides by a majority of one to carry out NATO's "twin-track" resolution (on nuclear arms modernisation and the pursuit of arms limitation), which the Social Democrats in particular oppose (November).

1983   Prime Minister Kaare Willoch persuades the Christian Popular Party and the Centre Party to join the government. The coalition government has only a bare majority.

1984   The security police arrest Arne Treholt, a senior official in the Ministry of Trade and Maritime Law; he confesses that he has been an agent of the Soviet KGB.

1985   Arne Treholt is given a life sentence by an Oslo court.

In a general election Kaare Willoch's coalition government wins a narrow majority (September).

1986   Kaare Willoch resigns as prime minister. Gro Harlem Brundtland forms a minority Social Democratic government (May).

Further controversy over Norway's relationship to the European Community and the possibility of joining the Community.

1987   Conflict between Norway and the Soviet Union over the frontier line in the Barents Sea (April). Incident between a Norwegian reconnaissance aircraft and a Soviet interceptor in international air space over the Barents Sea (September).

In local government elections in September the right-wing Progressive Party wins increased votes; the Conservatives and the ruling Labour Party lose votes.

1988   Prime Minister Gro Harlem Brundtland and the Soviet prime minister, Ryzhkov, discuss the problem of the Barents Sea frontier line but fail to reach agreement (January).

1989   In a general election in September the ruling Social Democrats suffer heavy losses. This leads to a right-wing minority government, a three-party coalition (Conservative Party, Christian Popular Party, Centre Party) headed by Jan P. Syse, a Conservative.

1990   The Syse government resigns following disagreement over policy on EFTA and the European Community; the Centre Party, which represents agricultural interests, is against any closer co-operation with the Community. In November Gro Harlem Brundtland, prime minister for the third time, forms a minority Social Democratic government. By making compromises in economic matters she hopes to be able to continue negotiations on membership of the Community and an agreement on a "European Economic Area".

King Olav V dies in January at the age of 87 and is succeeded by his son Harald as Harald V (b. 1937). The new king takes the oath in the Storting to uphold the constitution.   1991

In parliamentary elections, at which the main theme is Norway's membership of the EU, the former head of government Gro Harlem Brundtland is victorious. The Centre (Agrarian) Party is against joining the EU.   1993

In a public referendum Norwegians vote against joining the EU.   1994

Sweden

Settlement of the country.   1st–5th c. A.D.
The earliest inhabitants of Sweden are probably ancestors of the Finns. Germanic tribes coming from the west and south push northwards as far as the coast of Finland.

Skåne in southern Sweden is occupied by Danes. To the north of   c. 500
Skåne, in Götaland, are the Götar, who have become wealthy through their trade with the south but have lost much of their population by movement to other regions. Round Lake Mälar and in Uppland are the Svear, who have a strict tribal discipline.

Struggle for predominance.   6th–8th c.
The Svear overcome the Götar; the final battle is fought about 750. The Svear give their name to the whole country (Svearike, the land of the Svear: hence the modern name of Sweden, Sverige).

The Viking age.   8th–11th c.
Swedish Vikings ravage the Baltic coasts and in their light ships penetrate far into the lowlands of eastern Europe, where they found a number of states, beginning with one on Lake Ilmen centred on Holmgard (later Novgorod) and another round Kiev.

Christianisation of Sweden.   9th–12th c.
Around 830 St Ansgar preaches Christianity at Birka (then Sweden's largest trading town) on the little island of Björkö in Lake Mälar. In 1000 King Olaf Eriksson is baptised. In 1164 an archbishop is appointed in Sweden.

The early monarchy.   10th–12th c.
The king is elected in Upper Sweden and must then receive homage throughout the country. Alongside the king, however, there is still a powerful and ambitious nobility.

King Eric IX (St Eric) rules the country from Uppsala.   1150–60
In order to beat back Finnish incursions Eric launches a "crusade" into south-western Finland, the first step towards the establishment of Swedish rule in that area.

The Folkungs.   1250–1363
Kings and regents of the Folkung dynasty consolidate Sweden's power and complete the conquest of Finland.

Birger Jarl as Regent.   1250–66
He strengthens internal security by the so-called "peace laws", founds Stockholm in 1255 as a stronghold against Finnish raids and promotes trade by the grant of privileges to Hanseatic merchants.

History

1275–90	**Magnus I Ladulås.** Magnus protects townspeople and peasants against oppression by the nobility. Around 1280 mining begins at Falun with the help of miners from Germany. The privileges granted to the Germans arouse hostility among Swedes.
14th–16th c.	Between 1319 and 1523 Sweden is linked at various times with Norway and Denmark in personal unions. Union with Denmark, however, is usually seen as foreign domination, and on several occasions Sweden fights for, and obtains, de facto independence.
1319–63	**Magnus II Eriksson.** Magnus, a Folkung, is also king of Norway until 1343. In 1350 a national code of law replaces the various regional systems of law. In 1360 Skåne and in 1361 Öland and Gotland are annexed by Denmark. Magnus is deposed.
1363–89	**Albert III.** The nobility gain considerable power.
1389–1412	Margaret, daughter of Valdemar IV of Denmark, becomes Regent of Sweden (Union of Kalmar, 1397: see under Norway). Margaret is a strong ruler; she restricts the power of the nobility.
1433–1523	Swedish resistance to the Union. There are constant risings in Sweden against the kings and the royal governors, who are concerned only with the interests of Denmark. On several occasions Sweden gains virtual independence as a result of these risings.
1433–36	Peasant rising led by the mine-owner Engelbrekt Engelbrektsson.
1448–70	Charles VIII Knutsson "anti-king" of Sweden.
1470–1503	Sten Sture the Elder, "Guardian of the Realm". In 1471 he defeats the Danish king Christian I in a battle on the Brunkeberg.
1520	The "Stockholm Massacre". Christian II of Denmark defeats Sten Sture the Younger, Guardian of the Realm, and has 82 leading Swedes executed in Stockholm.
1523–60	**Gustavus I Vasa.** Gustavus Vasa, leader of a rising which starts in Dalarna in 1521, drives out the Danes and is elected king of Sweden in 1523. He brings in the Reformation in 1527, helps to break the commercial predominance of Lübeck by his participation in the "Count's War" (1534–36) and in 1544 makes Sweden a hereditary monarchy.
1560–1611	Under Gustavus's sons Sweden finds itself in grave difficulties on a number of occasions, until finally his youngest son Charles IX (1599–1611) re-establishes settled government and enhances the standing of the kingdom.
1611–32	**Gustavus II Adolphus.** Gustavus brings to a successful end the wars which his father had begun against Russia, which is compelled to cede Ingermanland in 1617, and Poland, which cedes Livonia in 1629. He reorganises the administration and promotes trade and industry.
1630	At the request of the German Protestant princes Gustavus intervenes in the Thirty Years' War. He is killed after the victorious battle of Lützen in 1632.

Queen Christina, daughter of Gustavus Adolphus.   1632–54
    Her chief minister is Axel Oxenstjerna. The Swedish army, led by
Gustav Horn, Johann Banér and Lennart Torstensson, successfully
continues the war. In 1645 Denmark is forced to give up Jämtland and
later Gotland and other territories. In 1648 Sweden gains the princi-
palities of Bremen and Verden, western Pomerania, Stettin and the
island of Rügen.

Charles X Gustavus of the Palatinate and Zweibrücken.   1654–60
    A cousin of Queen Christina, he becomes king after her abdication.
He wages war against Poland and Denmark, which in 1658 is obliged to
give up Halland and Skåne. Charles's principal aim is to establish the
sole authority of Sweden over the Baltic and its coastal regions.

Charles XI.   1660–97
    He succeeds his father, Charles X, at the age of four. Under the treaty
of Oliva (1660), which ends the Northern War (1655–60), the Polish king
renounces all claims to the Swedish throne.
    Charles joins in Louis XIV's war against Holland, Britain and Bran-
denburg. The Swedish army is defeated by Brandenburg in the battle
of Fehrbellin (1675), but Sweden is not compelled to surrender any
territory. The king takes advantage of the general discontent with the
maladministration of the nobility to recover Crown fiefs which had
fallen into the hands of nobles and to introduce legislation giving the
Crown almost unlimited powers.

Charles XII.   1697–1718
    This gifted and energetic king beats back attacks by Denmark, Poland
and Russia (battle of Narva, 1700) and carries the war into the enemy's
territory. During a daring campaign in Ukraine, however, he is deci-
sively defeated at Poltava in 1709 and flees to Turkey. In 1714, with two
companions, he rides to Stralsund in sixteen days. He is killed in 1718
under the walls of the Norwegian fortress of Fredrikssten. This ends
the brief period of absolutism in Sweden.

The "Era of Liberty".   1719–72
    After this collapse Sweden is compelled, between 1719 and 1721, to
give up the Baltic provinces, Bremen, Verden and western Pomerania,
and ceases to be a European great power. Nevertheless the country
makes a rapid economic recovery. The Estates limit the power of the
kings (who from 1751 to 1818 belong to the House of Holstein-Gottorp).
The war party, known as the Hattar ("Hats"), drive Sweden into the
Seven Years' War.

Gustavus III.   1771–92
    The king recovers control of the government from the Estates by a
coup d'état in 1772 and reigns under a system of enlightened absolutism. He abolishes the use of torture, introduces the freedom of the
press and stabilises the coinage. In 1792 he is assassinated at a masked
ball in a conspiracy by the nobility.

Gustavus IV Adolphus.   1792–1809
    Gustavus joins the coalition against Napoleon, and loses Pomerania
(1807) and Finland (1809). He is deposed in 1809.

Charles XIII.   1809–18
    Since Gustavus's uncle, Charles, is old and childless the Riksdag in
1810 elects the French marshal Jean-Baptiste Bernadotte as heir to the
throne; he is adopted by the king and takes the name of Charles John
(Karl Johan). In 1813 he leads Swedish forces against Napoleon, and in
the treaty of Kiel (1814) compels Denmark to give up Norway; in return
Denmark receives Swedish Pomerania.

History

1814–1905

Union with Norway.

Kings: Carl XIV Johan (Bernadotte; 1818–44), Oscar I (1844–59), Carl XV (1859–72), Oscar II (1872–1907).

Sweden keeps out of the European wars. In 1865 a new constitution comes into force. This is a period of economic and cultural advance, and Swedish industry develops rapidly. Changes in social structure. The first laws for the protection of workers are passed in 1889. Foundation of the Social Democratic Party.

Norway's increasing national awareness leads to a revival of old hostilities. In 1905 King Oscar gives up the Norwegian crown and thus dissolves the union.

20th c.

Swedish neutrality.

Kings: Gustaf V (1907–50), Gustaf VI Adolf (1950–73), Carl XVI Gustaf (from 1973).

Sweden preserves its neutrality in the two world wars in spite of considerable difficulties. The Swedish Red Cross serves the cause of humanity (Count Folke Bernadotte, 1895–1948).

The constitution is still further democratised. The continued improvement of social conditions and social services involves the heavy financial burden of the welfare state.

1946

Sweden becomes a member of the United Nations.

1949

Sweden joins the Council of Europe.

1951

Sweden and the other Scandinavian countries establish the Nordic Council (see under Norway).

1958

Nordic Passport and Customs Union.

1960

Sweden becomes a founding member of the European Free Trade Association (EFTA).

1973

King Gustaf VI Adolf is succeeded by his grandson as Carl XVI Gustaf.

Free trade agreement with the European Community.

1974

New constitution. The king's powers are drastically reduced from January 1st 1975.

1976

Law providing for workers' participation in industrial management.

The right-wing parties win a general election after 44 years of Social Democratic government.

1977

Birth of Princess Victoria Ingrid Alice Désirée.

Amendment of the law on succession to the throne (since 1810 confined to males).

1979

General election: the right-wing parties again win a narrow majority. Thorbjörn Fälldin, leader of the Centre Party, forms a right-wing coalition government.

The Riksdag passes a law on succession to the throne by the first-born child, male or female.

1980

Princess Victoria, as heiress to the throne, is granted the title of Duchess of Västergötland.

The Riksdag, by a majority of 59%, decides on a further programme of nuclear power production (maximum of 12 reactors).

Serious labour conflict (strike by 100,000 workers).

1981

The Conservative Party withdraws from the coalition. Thorbjörn Fälldin forms a new minority government of the Centre Party and Liberals.

The economic crisis and inflation continue.

A Soviet submarine runs aground in the skerries off the Swedish naval base of Karlskrona (May); diplomatic row with the Soviet Union.

In a general election in September the left-wing parties (Social Democrats and Communists) win a majority. Olof Palme forms a minority Social Democratic government with Communist support, promising to expand the economy and calling for a nuclear-weapon-free zone in northern Europe (October). 1982

Foreign submarines again detected in Swedish waters.

Law directed against tax evasion by "moonlighting" workers (January). 1983

Establishment of regional "Wage-Earner Funds" (Löntagarfondar), financed by a levy on company profits and wages and designed to provide capital for investment in private firms (December).

Conference on Confidence- and Security-Building Measures and Disarmament in Europe — a follow-up to the Conference on Security and Cooperation in Europe (CSCE) — attended by 35 foreign ministers, opens in Stockholm (January). 1984

Labour troubles, with strike and lockout (May). 1985

A general election in September is won by the Social Democrats, led by Olof Palme.

Opening of the ninth round of negotiations on Confidence- and Security-Building Measures and Disarmament in Stockholm (January). 1986

Prime Minister Olof Palme is murdered (February).

The Social Democrat Ingvar Carlsson becomes prime minister (March).

Following the Chernobyl nuclear disaster the government bans all imports of food from the Soviet Union and Eastern Europe (April).

The government imposes a trade boycott of South Africa (July). 1987

In the light of the controversy over nuclear energy the ruling Social Democrats decide on a programme for closing down atomic power stations, beginning in 1993 (March).

The minister of justice, Sten Wickborn, resigns after the escape of a Soviet spy serving a life sentence (October).

In January Prime Minister Carlsson and the Soviet prime minister, N. I. Ryzhkov, sign an agreement on sovereignty over an area of 13,500sq.km/5200sq. miles east of the island of Gotland (75% to Sweden, 25% to the Soviet Union). 1988

The minister of energy, Dahl, declares in March that the government will close down two atomic reactors in the mid-nineties and thereafter will give up the use of nuclear energy altogether.

Severe criticism of the police, the public prosecutor's department and the minister of justice over the failure to clear up the murder of Olof Palme.

An election in September confirms Ingvar Carlsson's government in power. The Greens win seats in the Riksdag for the first time.

Sweden reaches an agreement with Poland on the line of their common frontier in the Baltic to the south of Gotland. Agreement with the Soviet Union on environmental matters in the Baltic area. 1989

The head of the secret service, Sune Sanderström, who is held responsible for deficiencies in its work, resigns.

The Social Democratic minority government reaches an agreement with the opposition Centre Party on a programme for relieving the economic crisis (May).

Christer Pettersson, serving a life sentence for the murder of Olof Palme, is released on appeal.

1990

In January Rune Molin joins the government as minister for industry and energy and advocates the retention of existing nuclear power stations and the continued use of nuclear energy (a departure from the policy previously declared of closing all the country's twelve nuclear power stations by the year 2002).

The Social Democratic minority resigns after losing a vote in the Riksdag on its proposal for a wage and price freeze in view of the country's economic problems. Ingvar Carlsson again becomes prime minister (February).

Faced with continuing economic difficulties, the government puts forward a crisis programme (October). In December the Riksdag votes by a large majority in favour of joining the European Community. The ruling Social Democrats, the Centre Party, Conservatives and Liberals are all in favour; only the Communists and the Greens vote against the proposal.

1991

On July 1st, in The Hague, Prime Minister Carlsson submits Sweden's application to join the European Community.

In an election in September the Social Democrats are defeated and Carlsson resigns as prime minister. He is succeeded by Carl Bildt, leader of the Conservatives, who forms a coalition government of four right-wing parties.

1993

Increasing unemployment; the Swedish krone suffers losses on the foreign exchange market.

1994

The ferry-ship "Estonia" sinks en route from Estonia to Stockholm and more than 800 people lose their lives.

The Social Democrats win the September parliamentary elections. A minority government is formed under Ingvar Carlsson.

A public referendum decides in favour of Sweden joining the EU.

1995

Sweden becomes a member of the European Union from January 1st 1995. The Social Democrats are defeated in the European Parliament elections held in September.

Finland

Early history

Around the beginning of the Christian era the Finns arrive in what is now Finland, coming from the east and also by sea from the south into territories which are already inhabited.

1st millennium

The main occupations are farming and stock-rearing. The settlers first establish themselves along the coast and then move inland.

6th–10th c.

Finland is occupied by three ethnic groups – in the south-west the true Finns, in the southern lake region the people of Häme or Tavaste, in the east the Karelians.

The fur trade, carried on by sea with the countries to the west and south, brings a measure of economic well-being. There is still, however, no move towards a unified state.

9th–13th c.

Sweden gains control of Finland.

There is evidence of a Christian population on the south-west coast about the year 1000. In a series of "crusades" in 1154, 1249 and 1293 Sweden extends its authority over the country and drives back the influence of Novgorod and the Orthodox church, which had reached into central Finland.

Finland becomes a Swedish province, with the same rights as other parts of the country.

    In 1362 Finland is given the right to vote in the election of the Swedish king, and later sends representatives to the Riksdag.

    During the period of Swedish rule Finnish national traditions are not suppressed, but neither are they fostered. Swedish is the language of government and of culture. Finland experiences both the advantages and the disadvantages of being part of a powerful foreign state.

14th c.

Russian incursions. The areas exposed to invasion are devastated, and the coastal towns suffer damage to their trade with the Hanseatic towns.

1495–1595

The Reformation comes to Finland.

    Mikael Agricola's translation of the New Testament (1548) becomes the basis of the Finnish written language.

    Beginning of education for all children.

1523

A peasant rising against the nobility, the "Cudgel War", is ruthlessly repressed.

1596–97

Gustavus II Adolphus king of Sweden.

    1611–17, war with Russia. Gustavus Adolphus gains territory on the shores of Lake Ladoga.

    Finnish troops in the Swedish army fight in Germany during the Thirty Years' War.

1611–32

Count Per Brahe is Swedish governor of Finland.

    1640, foundation of the Academy (University) of Åbo (Turku), then capital of Finland; teaching is in Swedish.

1637–40
and 1648–54

More than 100,000 people die of hunger and epidemics.

1696–97

Wars between Sweden and Russia.
Finland is repeatedly devastated. The idea of separation from Sweden comes to the fore from time to time (1788–90, Anjala conspiracy), but is always repressed.

    Russian troops conquer the whole of Finland in 1808.

1700–1808

Finland becomes a Russian Grand Duchy. In March Tsar Alexander I promises at the Diet of Borgå (Porvoo) to maintain Finnish rights and privileges and receives homage as Grand Duke of Finland. Under the treaty of Fredrikshamn (Hamina), signed in September, Sweden cedes the whole of Finland and the Åland Islands to Russia.

1809

The territories lost in 1721 and 1743, including Viipuri, are reunited with Finland. Helsingfors (Helsinki) becomes capital.

1811–12

Elias Lönnrot publishes the Finnish national epic "Kalevala".

1835

Suppression of Finnish self-government. In 1891 postal services, customs and the currency are taken over by Russia. In 1900 Russian becomes the language of government. In 1903 the Finnish army is abolished. In 1912 Finnish citizenship is granted to Russians.

1880–1912

Declaration of independence (December 6th).

    P. E. Svinhufvud becomes head of the new government.

1917

War of Liberation.
n January Finnish Communists and Russian Bolsheviks occupy Helsinki and advance farther into Finland. Finnish government forces led by General C. G. E. Mannerheim, supported by German troops,

1918

defeat the Communists in southern Finland (April and May). General Mannerheim becomes Regent of Finland.

1919   Republican constitution.
K. J. Ståhlberg becomes the first President of Finland.

1920   Treaty of Dorpat: Finland is recognised as an independent state and receives the area round Petsamo on the Arctic Ocean.

1919–21   The Åland Islands seek reunion with Sweden but are assigned by the League of Nations to Finland. The islands are given self-government and are demilitarised.

1922   Land reform.

1930–38   Finland's foreign policy is directed towards avoiding involvement in German or Soviet policies.

1939–40   The "Winter War" with the Soviet Union. The Soviet Union demands bases in southern Finland and gives notice of termination of a non-aggression pact signed in 1932. War begins at the end of November 1939.
Under the treaty of Moscow Finland is obliged to cede important territories to the Soviet Union (including Viipuri and part of Karelia; Hanko is leased to the Soviet Union).

1941–44   Renewal of war with the Soviet Union. Under the armistice agreement Finland loses the Petsamo area and leases Porkkala to the Soviet Union in place of Hanko. This involves the resettlement of 480,000 Finns.

1944–46   Marshal Mannerheim President of Finland.

1946–56   J. K. Paasikivi President. Right-wing government.

1947   The treaty of Paris confirms the agreements reached in the armistice.

1948   Treaty of friendship and mutual assistance with the Soviet Union.

1955   Finland joins the Nordic Council (see under Norway) and becomes a member of the United Nations.

1956   The Soviet naval base at Porkkala is returned to Finland.
Urho Kaleva Kekkonen becomes President.

1958   Nordic Passport and Customs Union.

1961   Finland becomes an associate member of the European Free Trade Association (EFTA).

1970   The treaty of friendship between Finland and the Soviet Union is extended for another 20 years.

1973   Free trade agreement with the European Community.

1975   Final summit meeting of the Conference on Security and Cooperation in Europe (CSCE) in Helsinki.

1978   New government of Social Democrats, the Centre Party, Liberals and Communists, without the Swedish People's Party, which had been in the previous government.

1979   General election (March). The new government consists of Social Democrats, Communists, the Centre Party and the Swedish People's Party.

In local government elections in October the Social Democrats have 25.6% of the votes, the opposition Conservative National Union Party 23.1% and the Centre Party 18.8%. The Communists suffer losses.   1980

The adoption of a "social package" obviates a government crisis.   1981
    Urho Kaleva Kekkonen (now aged 81) resigns as President in October. Pending the election of a successor Prime Minister Mauno Koivisto (Social Democratic Party) takes over the office of President.

Mauno Koivisto is elected President (January).   1982
    In February Kalevi Sorsa, leader of the Social Democratic Party, forms a four-party coalition government. After a clash with the Communists over the defence budget the cabinet is reshuffled (December).

Following a general election in March a new four-party coalition is formed in June, again headed by Kalevi Sorsa.   1983
    The treaty of friendship and mutual assistance between Finland and the Soviet Union (which has not yet expired) is extended for a further period.

Local government elections in October make only minor changes in party representation. The strongest political force is still the Social Democratic Party.   1984

Meeting of the foreign ministers of the 35 CSCE countries on the 10th anniversary of the signing of the Final Act (July–August).   1985

In spring several thousand civil servants strike in support of their claim for higher pay.   1986
    The veteran statesman Urho Kaleva Kekkonen (prime minister in five post-war governments, President 1956–81) dies in Helsinki (August).

In an election in March the Conservatives gain votes, while the Social Democrats lose one seat. A new coalition government of Conservatives, Social Democrats, the Swedish People's Party and the Country Party is formed in April, led by Harri Holkeri (Social Democrat).   1987

Mauno Koivisto is re-elected President for a further six-year term (February).   1988

Kalevi Sorsa (foreign minister since 1987) resigns on January 24th and is elected President of the Riksdag on February 1st. Pertti Paasio (Social Democrat) becomes foreign minister.   1989
    On May 4th, the 40th anniversary of the establishment of the Council of Europe, Finland becomes the 23rd member of the Council.
    On October 25th the Soviet head of state, Mikhail Gorbachev, arrives in Helsinki on a state visit. He and President Koivisto sign a Finnish-Soviet declaration in which Finland's status as a neutral country is recognised for the first time without reservation. They also sign agreements on economic and cultural co-operation and on the protection of the environment.

A strike by bank employees in February ends on March 6th when trade unions and employers accept a settlement proposed by a state arbitrator.   1990
    The former Communist and Socialist parties establish a "Union of the Left" (May).
    Pope John Paul II visits Helsinki in June.
    In the course of the discussion of the possible entry of the Scandinavian countries into the European Community Prime Minister Holkeri declares that membership of the Community would be incompatible with the maintenance of Finland's neutrality (November).

History

1991   In an election in March the government coalition (Conservatives and Social Democrats) loses seats, while the Centre (Agrarian) Party increases its representation. The new prime minister, Esko Aho (Centre Party), forms his cabinet and puts forward the government's programme at the end of April.

1992   In view of the changed situation in Central and Eastern Europe Finland and Russia sign a new treaty in Helsinki (January). It contains no provision for consultation and mutual assistance as in the 1948 treaty between Finland and the Soviet Union.

         The Finnish Parliament approves the government's proposal to apply for membership of the European Community (March 18th), and the application is submitted by Finnish diplomats in Brussels on the afternoon of the same day.

1993   As high unemployment and the national debt have caused a crisis drastic economic measures are announced in the autumn. The guarding of the Fino–Russian border is to be strengthened.

1994   On March 1st the Social Democrat Martti Ahtisaari succeeds Mauno Loivistos as prime minister.

         In a public referendum the majority of the Finnish people vote in favour of Finland joining the European Union.

1995   Finland becomes a member of the EU from January 1st 1995.

         The Social Democrats win the parliamentary elections (March). The new prime minister is Paavo Lipponen, leader of the Social Democrat party.

Famous People

This section contains brief biographies, in alphabetical order, of interesting people who were born, lived or died in the Scandinavian countries – Sweden, Norway and Finland – and are of more than local importance. A number of other notable figures are referred to in the chapter on Art and Culture.

The Finnish architect Alvar Aalto, acclaimed by architects all over the world, ranks as the Nestor of the great architects of our century: a status granted in virtue of his thoughtful personality rather than by the number of buildings designed by him throughout the world.

Hugo Alvar
Henrik Aalto
(1898–1976)

After completing his training, in 1923, Aalto set up in practice in Jyväskylä, then a small town. Over the years, as his reputation grew, a strong affinity developed between the architect and the town: a connection which has continued since his death, with its visible manifestation in the Municipal Theatre of Jyväskylä.

For a layman perhaps the best description of Aalto's style is functionalism in process of change. His first two purely functional buildings were a sanatorium in Paimio (south-western Finland) and the Public Library (now much dilapidated) in Viipuri/Viborg, which was ceded to the Soviet Union in 1944. His best known building is the Finlandia Hall in Helsinki, an unfortunate demonstration of the fact that even Nestors can err. Aalto chose Carrara marble for its outer cladding, and when asked why he had not used Finnish granite, replied laconically, "Italian marble is the best. Basta!"; but after less than two decades of extreme Finnish temperatures the marble slabs were beginning to warp.

Aalto's most notable utterance can equally well be applied to architecture and to any other field of human activity. When Swiss journalists asked him during an interview whether he was a cosmopolitan he replied, "Yes; but you can only be a cosmopolitan if you have local roots".

The great polar expeditions of the 19th century were motivated by scientific enquiry, and the Norwegian polar explorer Roald Amundsen was involved in travel and research in both the north and south polar zones. In 1897–99 he joined a Belgian expedition to the Antarctic. Then, after a period of study in Germany during which he was particularly concerned with the technique of measuring the earth's magnetism, he investigated the north magnetic pole. In 1903–06, in the smack "Gjöa", he became the first man to navigate the North-West Passage, the sea route between the Atlantic and the Pacific in northern North America. In January 1911 he landed on the coast of the Antarctic continent (the Ross Barrier) and, travelling with dog sledges over the shelf and inland ice, became the first man to reach the South Pole, arriving there on December 14th 1911, four weeks before his British rival Captain Scott. On the way back he discovered the Queen Maud mountain range. In 1918–20 he became the second man (after Adolf Erik von Nordenskiöld) to make the North-East Passage between the Atlantic and Pacific to the north of Europe and Asia, by way of the Barents Sea and the Barents Strait; he did not, however, reach the drift ice over the North Pole, which was his real objective. In May 1926, after the failure of two previous attempts to reach the North Pole by air, he flew over the Pole in the airship "Norge". In 1928 he was lost at sea in a flight to Spitzbergen.

Roald Amundsen
(1872–1928)

The Swedish film and theatre director Ingmar Bergman was born in Uppsala, the son of a pastor. He took up the study of literature in 1937

Ingmar Bergman
(b. 1918)

Alvar Aalto

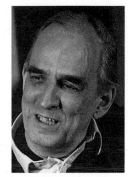

Ingmar Bergman

Edvard Grieg

but soon gave abandoned it. Thereafter he directed a number of amateur theatrical productions, worked in a student theatre and finally turned to the cinema. His films soon earned him a reputation in Sweden. He formulated his aim in these words: "I try to tell the truth about the human condition – the truth as I see it." In his work the emphasis is not on experiments with form, but he has shown that it is possible to achieve new effects with existing means. Originally his films were concerned with young people – the sceptical young of the postwar period; later he dealt with the problems of adults in the family setting and in their work. In the 1950s he turned to intellectual and religious themes: the existence of God, the meaning of life, men's understanding of themselves. After becoming involved in a dispute with the Swedish tax authorities Bergman worked for a time mainly in Germany.

Bergman attracted particular attention with his film "Wild Strawberries" (1957), a nostalgic depiction of an elderly man looking back on his life. Other notable films were "Scenes from a Marriage" (1973), with Liv Ullman, his companion for many years, "The Serpent's Egg" (1976), "Autumn Sonata" (1977), "From the Life of a Puppet" (1979–80) and "Fanny and Alexander" (1981–82), a largely autobiographical work. Bergman also directed a film of Mozart's "Magic Flute" (1974) and various documentary films, including one on the island of Fårö (1979). In 1987 he published his autobiography under the title "My Life".

Minna Canth
(1844–97)

Minna Canth was the greatest Finnish woman writer of the 19th century. Her husband, a schoolmaster by profession, was also a journalist and was thus able to ensure that her articles on such questions as alcohol abuse and the situation of working class women achieved wide publicity. After his death she moved to the small town of Kuopio in eastern Finland, where she took over her father's business, enabling her to provide for her seven children.

She came from a Swedish-Finnish family and went to a Swedish-speaking school, but her literary work was mainly in Finnish. She ranks along with Aleksis Kivi (see below) as one of the pioneers of naturalism in Finland. Her first play, with which she reached a wide public, was "Työmiehen Vaimo" ("The Worker's Wife"), which appeared in 1885 in the little town of Porvoo in southern Finland. The play had its première in the first professional Finnish-language theatre.

This first work now seems weak, melodramatic and crude in its depiction of character: its importance lies in the fact that it is the first example of social criticism in the theatre. The central characters are the drunkard Risto and his downtrodden wife Johanna. Risto squanders all her money on drink after spending all his own. (In those days a husband had sole control of his wife's property.)

Minna Canth's story "Kauppa-Lopo", published in 1910, is also a work of social criticism, but with much sharper characterisation than her first work. It established her position as the leading figure in Finnish literature after the death of Aleksis Kivi.

King Carl XVI Gustaf was the fifth child and only son of Duke Gustaf Adolf and his wife Sibylla of Saxe-Coburg-Gotha. Carl Gustaf never knew his father, who was killed in an aircraft accident six months after the boy's birth. On the death of Gustaf VI Adolf at the age of 91 in September 1973 his grandson, then aged 27, became king, taking as his watchword "For Sweden – Moving with the Times". After twenty years on the throne this popular king has lived up to his motto. His love of nature and animals and his commitment to the environment are qualities that appeal to the Swedish people. The Swedes are also delighted when their sport-loving king takes part in the Vasa ski race.

Carl XVI Gustaf (b. 1946)

Under the new constitution which came into force in 1975 the king remained head of state but had no political power. Among his duties is the ceremonial opening of Parliament in September each year. He is also chairman of the Committee on Foreign Affairs and presides over the Cabinet during a change of government, though he is not permitted to influence its decisions.

In 1976 Carl Gustaf married the German-born Silvia Sommerlath (b. 1943). The charming and popular queen, who was chief hostess of the 1972 Olympic Games, frequently appears on television with her family: a practice which contributes to the popularity of the royal house. She quickly mastered the Swedish language, though not completely flawlessly. She took up the cause of the disabled, which had the effect of increasing public awareness of their problems.

The king and queen have three children – Crown Princess Victoria (1977), Carl Philip (1979) and Madeleine (1982) – and the royal family are seen as a model of domestic harmony.

Queen Christina of Sweden, daughter of Gustavus II Adolphus (see below), was born in Stockholm and died in Rome. When Gustavus Adolphus was killed in the battle of Lützen in 1632 Christina, his only daughter, succeeded him (female accession to the throne having been permitted in Sweden since 1590), but since she was still under age the country was at first ruled by a Regency Council headed by Chancellor Axel Oxenstjerna. From 1644 Christina ruled as queen but refused to marry on dynastic grounds. In 1649 she contrived that her cousin Charles Gustavus of the Palatinate and Zweibrücken should be elected by the Riksdag as her successor, and in 1654 she abdicated and was succeeded by him.

Queen Christina (1626–89)

A keen horsewoman, Christina was more interested in science and art than in politics. She attracted foreign scholars to her court, among them the philosopher René Descartes (who died in Stockholm in 1650). After her abdication she left Sweden and lived abroad, and in 1655 became a Catholic. She spent the last years of her life in Rome, where she died in 1689. Christina's enigmatic personality has engaged the interest of historians and artists, and she was portrayed in a well-known film by Greta Garbo, herself a Swede.

Between the 8th and 11th centuries the Vikings or Norsemen sailed from Scandinavia to all the coasts of Europe as pirates, merchants or conquerors. Eric the Red, a Viking from Norway, sailed to Iceland and in 982 reached the island to which he gave the name of Greenland. In 985, in the south-west of the island, he established the first settlement. (In 1261 Greenland became subject to the king of Norway; it is now an autonomous region of Denmark.) Eric's son Leif Eriksson (see below) discovered the coast of the North American continent.

Eric the Red (c. 950–1007)

Famous People

Edvard Grieg
(1843–1907)

The Norwegian composer Edvard Grieg, a native of Bergen, studied at the Leipzig Conservatoire and continued his studies in Copenhagen with Niels Gade, then the leading Norwegian composer. He was also much influenced by Richard Nordraak, who introduced him to the folk music of the Nordic countries. In 1866 Grieg gave the first concert of his own compositions (piano and violin sonatas, lieder) in Christiania (Oslo). He travelled to Italy and made the acquaintance of Franz Liszt in Rome. Later he lived in Christiania and from 1885 until his death in his house of Troldhaugen near Bergen.

After his return from Rome Grieg joined a group of young musicians and writers who were striving to establish a national art in Norway. Grieg brought Norwegian music to international attention with his treatments of folk songs combining the native Norwegian idiom with the compositional forms of his century. He wrote piano music ("Wedding Day at Troldhaugen", "Norwegian Dances and Folk Tunes", "Lyric Pieces"), chamber music (violin sonatas, string quartets, etc.), orchestral works ("Holberg Suite"; music celebrating the 200th anniversary of the birth of the playwright Ludwig Holberg) and a piano concerto in A minor (1868). Particularly notable are the music he wrote for Bjørnstjerne Bjørnson's "Sigurd Jorsalfar" (1870) and the music for Ibsen's "Peer Gynt", composed at the author's request in 1874–76 (the most effective pieces later being brought together in two suites). The "Peer Gynt" music mirrors the atmosphere of the mountains, the anger of the wedding guests at the abduction of the bride and finally Peer Gynt's dramatic homecoming and the peace of life with Solvejg, who has waited for him ("Solvejg's Song").

Gustavus II
Adolphus
(1594–1632)

Gustavus II Adolphus, son of Charles IX and grandson of Gustavus I Vasa, is the outstanding figure among the kings of Sweden. In 1611, after the death of his father, the 17-year-old Gustavus Adolphus was declared of full age by the Riksdag in return for a guarantee of extensive rights, including the "constitutional involvement of the nobility in the government of Sweden". Thereafter he made good his claim to the throne against his nephew Sigismund III Vasa of Poland, a son of John III. A series of domestic reforms, carried through with the help of the Chancellor, Count Axel Oxenstjerna, paved the way for Swedish power politics in the Baltic area. Of particular importance were the reform of the army and the energetic development of the national economy. In peace treaties signed at Knäred in 1613 and Stolbovo in 1617 Gustavus Adolphus ended the wars with Denmark and Poland which had been begun by Charles IX. The acquisition of Ingermanland (a Russian territory to the south of the Gulf of Finland) and eastern Karelia enabled the Swedish king to launch an attack on Sigismund, who was compelled under an armistice agreement in 1629 to cede Livonia to Sweden.

Europe was then involved in the Thirty Years' War, and since Gustavus Adolphus was alarmed by the advance of Habsburg power into the Baltic region he resolved to enter the war. In 1630 he landed on the island of Usedom in Pomerania in order to aid the Protestant cause. Advancing into central Germany, he defeated the imperial general, Tilly, and continued through Thuringia and Franconia to Mainz, on the Rhine. After a further victory over Tilly the Swedish army encountered the imperial forces, commanded by Wallenstein, at Lützen, a town south-west of Leipzig, in November 1632. The Swedes were victorious, but Gustavus Adolphus had been killed. The king's motives for entering the Thirty Years' War have been variously judged by historians.

Knut Hamsun
(1859–1952)

The Norwegian novelist Knut Hamsun (originally Pedersen) was the son of a poor tailor of peasant origin. In 1862 the family moved to Hamarøy, opposite the Lofotens on the Hamsund, from which the writer took his name. In his early days Hamsun led a restless wandering life, earning his living as a labourer and occasional teacher. In

1883–85 and 1886–88 he lived in North America, where he acquired a pessimistic view of the mechanised American way of life. After further travels he lived from 1918 onwards on the property of Nørholm, near Grimstad in southern Norway. His wife was the actress Anna Marie Anderson. He received the Nobel Prize for literature in 1920.

Hamsun first caused a stir with his novel "Hunger" (1890), depicting a young writer's struggle to achieve success and the extreme deprivations which reduce him to physical and spiritual exhaustion. Among other important works are "Pan" (1894), the trilogy "Wanderers" ("Autumn", 1906; "With Muted Strings", 1909; "Look Back on Happiness", 1912), the Segelfoss novels ("Children of their Time", 1913; "The Town of Segelfoss", 1915), "The Growth of the Soil" (1917), "The Last Chapter" (1923) and the trilogy "Landstrykere" ("Vagabonds", 1927; "August", 1930; "The Road Leads On", 1933). The central figures of the novels are frequently wanderers and adventurers or people who live a lonely life in the forest or as peasants. The Segelfoss novels depict the transition from peasant society to modern civilisation, which the writer regards with scepticism. Hamsun's works reflect a strong feeling for nature and a belief in an all-pervading vital force. He frequently brings out the irrational element in the behaviour of his characters. His literary work can be seen as going beyond and displacing naturalism.

Hamsun supported the German occupation of Norway in 1940 and published articles in newspapers published by Quisling's pro-Nazi party. After the end of the war he was arrested and condemned to pay a fine.

The Swede Sven Hedin (ennobled in 1902), the last of the great travellers and explorers and a pioneer of Asian studies, was born in Stockholm. He studied in Berlin under Ferdinand von Richthofen (1833–1905), the geographer and sinologist. Between 1894 and 1935 Hedin undertook four expeditions to Central Asia, each lasting several years, which took him to Tibet and Lhasa and the Karakorum. He also explored remote regions like the Tarim basin, a depression at an altitude of 700–1400m (2300–4600ft) between the Tien Shan, Pamir and Kunlun Mountains with an expanse of desert in the centre. He visited the source region of the Brahmaputra and Indus on the northern slopes of the Himalayas and explored the Transhimalaya, a mountain in southern Tibet which is also known as Mount Hedin. On his last expedition he led an international, inter-disciplinary research group which worked in the Gobi region and in Turkestan.

Sven Hedin (1865–1952)

In addition to scientific reports on his travels Hedin wrote popular travel books and adventure stories for young people, including "From Pole to Pole" (1911–12), "The Silk Road" (1936) and "The Wandering Lake" (1937), and was also a talented draughtsman and cartographer.

The Norwegian zoologist and ethnologist Thor Heyerdahl set out to demonstrate the possibility of early transoceanic contacts between peoples. For this purpose he crossed various oceans in the simplest of boats, with the help only of the wind and marine currents. In 1947 he sailed in the balsa raft "Kon-Tiki" from the Pacific coast of South America to Tahiti in Polynesia; in 1969–70 he crossed the Atlantic from Morocco to Barbados in the "Ra"; and in 1977–78 he made his way from Basra through the Gulf to Jibuti in the reed boat "Tigris", based on Sumerian models. In 1955–56 he studied the culture of Easter Island and in 1983 he discovered remains of an advanced culture in the Maldives. He described his various enterprises in a number of successful books.

Thor Heyerdahl (b. 1914)

Henrik Ibsen, the greatest Scandinavian dramatist, was born at Skien in southern Norway and died in Christiania (now Oslo). He attended the secondary school in his home town, and when his father fell into

Henrik Ibsen (1828–1906)

Gustavus Adolphus

Thor Heyerdahl

Urho Kekkonen

poverty became an apprentice pharmacist in Grimstad; then in 1850 he took up the study of medicine in Christiania. From 1851 he was stage-manager of the municipal theatre in Bergen, and then moved to Christiania as artistic director of the theatre there. In 1864, after various disagreements and disputes, he left Norway and lived abroad – in Rome, Dresden, Munich and other places – for many years. Thereafter he returned to Christiania, where he died in 1906.

Ibsen wrote his first plays at an early age, beginning with the Roman drama "Catiline" in 1849. In subsequent years his works were written under the influence of the national romantic movement, to the conservative features of which he was opposed. After historical dramas and dramas of ideas Ibsen created the new genre of the "social play", which with its radical criticism of social conditions marked the beginning of the modern theatre. In "Pillars of Society" (1877) and later works on everyday themes he revealed the shams of life, the hidden fragility of human relations. With "A Doll's House" (1879), in which the wife asserts her equality with her husband, he achieved world fame. Like his later play "Ghosts" (1881), it aroused much discussion in the Nordic countries. "An Enemy of the People" (1882) was a vehicle for sharp satire on Ibsen's opponents. Other important works are "The Wild Duck" (1884), "Rosmersholm" (1886), "The Lady from the Sea" (1888), "The Master Builder" (1892) and "When We Dead Awaken" (1899). In "Hedda Gabler" (1890) a woman is again the central figure in a conflict.

Ibsen's work exerted a powerful influence on the drama of the late 19th and early 20th century. His play "Peer Gynt" (1867), set in the Gudbrandsdal and the mountains, was written in Italy, and music to accompany it was composed by Edvard Grieg (see above).

Urho Kaleva Kekkonen (1900–86)

Urho Kaleva Kekkonen, President of Finland from 1956 to 1981, was undoubtedly the most outstanding politician and statesman of his time in northern Europe, though the rather autocratic regime of his later years cast a shadow on his reputation.

Kekkonen grew up in north-eastern Finland in modest circumstances. During the war of liberation and civil war in 1918 he served as a dispatch rider. Thereafter he studied law and entered politics, becoming a member of the Agrarian Union party.

In 1941, after the beginning of the Russian campaign, he opposed Finland's entry into the war, and in 1943 he advocated its withdrawal from the war, though he found few supporters. After the war he was several times prime minister, and in 1956 he stood for the office of President, a post which in Finland carries considerable powers, particularly in the field of foreign policy. He was elected with the smallest possible majority of 151 to 149, and at first had most of the Conservatives and many of the Social Democrats against him. He could rely for support only on the Agrarian Union (now the Centre Party) and the People's Democratic Union, which welcomed his policy of seeking an understanding with the Soviet Union. This situation led to the development of his authoritarian style of government, which became more evident with increasing age.

Kekkonen was more successful than his predecessor Paasikivi in persuading the leaders of the two super-powers of the genuineness of Finland's policy of neutrality. Incontestably his greatest success was the establishment of the Conference on Security and Cooperation in Europe, the preparatory phase of which began in November 1972. The Final Act of the Conference was signed in Helsinki in the summer of 1975 by representatives of 35 nations, including the Soviet Union and the German Democratic Republic. The obligations on the observance of human rights which it imposed led to the formation of numerous "Helsinki groups" throughout Eastern Europe, the most prominent representative of which was Vaclav Havel. The demand for human rights was a major motive force in the growing resistance movement in the Eastern Bloc during the 1980s.

Kekkonen was a man of wide culture, frequently quoting Goethe in his conversation and Bismarck in his speeches. With his increasingly gruff manner he ended up as the disciplinarian of the nation.

After a fishing accident in 1981 Kekkonen became incapable of carrying out the duties of his office and resigned. His last years were spent in a state of mental confusion.

The Finnish writer Aleksis Kivi (originally A. Stenvall), was born at Nurmijärvi in southern Finland, the son of a poor tailor. After learning Swedish he became a student in Helsinki, living a life of great deprivation. He attended lectures by Elias Lönnrot (see below) on the "Kalevala", studied history and literature and read the classics of world literature. After a life of poverty and illness Kivi died at the age of 38, mentally deranged.

Aleksis Kivi
(1834–72)

He founded modern Finnish literature and now ranks as Finland's great classic writer. Notable among his works are the tragedy "Kullervo" (1860), a dramatisation of the Kullervo episode in the "Kalevala", and a comedy of character, "The Cobblers on the Heath" (1864). His imaginative power and descriptive skill are demonstrated particularly in his principal work, the novel "Seven Brothers" (1870), which incorporates old legends, fairytales and ancient Finnish poetry. His poems in blank verse are remarkable for their vigour and expressive force.

"Seven Brothers" is set in the landscape of southern Finland in the early 19th century. After disputes with the villagers of Toukola the seven brothers leave their farm at Jukola and take refuge in the forest, where they live in a charcoal-burner's hut, fish and shoot, and fight a bear. Then, after consuming great quantities of brandy, they return from the wilderness, reoccupy their farm and celebrate their reconciliation with the villagers. The change in the brothers exemplifies the development of mankind.

The Swedish novelist and story-writer Selma Lagerlöf was born on the estate of Mårbacka (Värmland), where she spent much of her life. After working as a teacher for some years she travelled in Italy in 1895–96, and, following a journey to Egypt and Palestine in 1899–1900, wrote a religious novel, "Jerusalem" (1901–02). Her reputation was mainly due, however, to her novels with a Swedish setting, like "Gösta Berling's Saga" (1891), "The Wonderful Adventures of Nils" (1906–07), "Liljecrona's Home" (1911), the story of her grandfather's youth, and the Löwensköld trilogy, written in the tone of the sagas. Selma Lagerlöf received the Nobel Prize for literature in 1909. "The Adventures of Nils"

Selma Lagerlöf
(1858–1940)

was originally commissioned as a school book for the teaching of geography. Nils, a badly behaved little boy, is changed by a gnome into a dwarf and is carried off into the air on the back of a wild goose. On the journey with the wild geese through Sweden and into Lapland the boy learns about the geography, economy, animals and plants of his native land. After enjoying the summer in Lapland with the wild geese Nils returns home with the geese and is restored to his normal size.

Selma Lagerlöf also wrote "Legends of Christ" (1904), some of which are based on the Bible and old Christian traditions, while others are imagined by the author and written in traditional fairytale style.

Carl Larsson (1853–1919)

The Swedish painter Carl Larsson was born in Stockholm and died at Sundborn, near Falun. He began his career in 1882 as an open-air painter in the Scandinavian artists' colony at Grez, near Fontainebleau. Later he became the chief exponent of Art Nouveau in Sweden, painting six large frescos in the National Museum in Stockholm depicting events in the history of art in Sweden. Larsson was a brilliant draughtsman and a prolific book illustrator. He became particularly renowned for numerous series of water colours depicting his home and family life in Sundborn. His book "The House in the Sun" was published in 1909. He also painted portraits of many of his distinguished contemporaries, including August Strindberg and Selma Lagerlöf.

Leif Eriksson (c. 975–c. 1020)

The Norwegian seafarer Leif Eriksson, son of Eric the Red (see above), diverged from the true course on a voyage to Greenland around the year 1000 and reached the coast of North America, probably in Nova Scotia. He thus anticipated Columbus as the discoverer of America. He called the country on the east coast of North America Vinland ("fertile meadowland").

Astrid Lindgren (b. 1907)

The Swedish author of children's books Astrid Lindgren, the daughter of a farmer, began her working life in a publishing firm; then in 1944 she became known as a writer with the publication of a book for girls and a detective play. Thereafter she wrote "Pippi Longstocking" (1945) and numerous other successful children's books, many of them sequels to earlier books. "The Six Children of Bullerby", "Karlson on the Roof", "Mardie", "Rasmus and the Tramp", "Simon Small Moves In", "The Brothers Lionheart", "The Mischievous Martens", "The Runaway Sleigh Ride" and other books are widely popular.

Astrid Lindgren's books show remarkable inventiveness, and the children on whom the stories centre are independent and resourceful characters. Thus Pippi Longstocking refuses to submit to the ideas of grown-ups and follows her own nature, while the "master detective" Blomquist helps in catching thieves and even prevents a murder.

Lindgren also wrote a number of plays for children. Altogether she has published more than 70 books, which have been translated into 40 languages; some have been made into films. In 1978 she was awarded the Peace Prize of the German book trade.

Carl von Linné (1707–78)

The Swedish botanist Carl von Linné, perhaps better known by the Latin form of his name, Linnaeus, was born in Råshult (Småland) and died in Uppsala. After studying medicine and the natural sciences he travelled to Lapland, the Low Countries, Britain and France. Thereafter he practised as a doctor in Stockholm. In 1739 he became President of the Swedish Academy of Sciences, which had been established on his initiative. From 1741 he was professor of anatomy in Uppsala University, from 1742 also professor of botany.

Linnaeus laid down the foundations of botanical nomenclature: the binomial system of naming plants by two Latin names, the first indicating the genus and the second the species. The abbreviation "L" after the Latin name of a plant indicates that Linnaeus was the first to describe and name the species. The "Linnaean system" published in

1735 was based on differences in the sexual organs of plants. Linnaeus also established zoological and mineralogical systems of nomenclature. His son Carl von Linné (1741–83) wrote a work on grasses and mosses (1781).

The Finnish folklorist and writer Elias Lönnrot originally practised as a doctor. From 1853 to 1862 he was professor of Finnish language and literature in Helsinki. He created the epic poem " Kalevala" (1835; final version 1849) on the basis of orally transmitted folk poetry which he had recorded on his travels through Finland and eastern Karelia. He also published "Kanteletar" (1840–41), a collection of songs and ballads, as well as proverbs and spells and a Finnish–Swedish dictionary.

Elias Lönnrot
(1802–84)

"Kalevala" (meaning "land of Kaleva": in Lönnrot's view Old Finland) is the national epic of the Finns. Its 50 cantos, with a total of over 22,000 lines, against the background of the rivalry between Kaleva (the land of the Finns) and Pohjola (the "Northland"), relate the adventures of the divine heroes of Kaleva. The poem contains pagan, Christian and historical (Viking age) features, as well as evidence of a farming way of life. Before Lönnrot put the old songs together to form the epic they had been sung by folk singers for hundreds of years. The collecting of old songs continued in the 19th and 20th centuries, resulting in the publication of a 33-volume work, "The Old Songs of the Finnish People" (1908–48).

Mannerheim – or "Marski", as he was known in his later years – showed himself in three wars and four campaigns a soldier of outstanding quality. As President of Finland from the autumn of 1944, after the armistice with the Soviet Union, he guided the country through one of the most difficult periods in its modern history; then in 1946, stricken by illness, he was succeeded by J. K. Paasakivi. He spent his last years abroad, seeking treatment for his illness.

Carl Gustaf Emil
Mannerheim
(1867–1951)

He got his military training in the Russian army, and commanded a cavalry division in the war with Germany. After the October Revolution he returned to Finland, where the provisional independent government gave him the task of building up the country's armed forces. In a three-month-long war he defeated an attempt by the Finnish Socialists, supported locally by Russian units, to seize power. During the defensive war with the Soviet Union in 1939–40 (the "Winter War") he succeeded in holding up the Soviet advance long enough to allow the government to negotiate a tolerable armistice agreement with the Soviet Union. The German attack on the Soviet Union brought Finland into the war, willy-nilly, on the German side. Mannerheim held strictly to Finnish war aims (the recovery of the territory lost in 1940), and Finnish forces took no part in the siege of Leningrad. After the Finnish–Soviet armistice of autumn 1944 it was left to Mannerheim to drive German forces out of northern Finland.

Mannerheim's achievements, including his efforts to reconcile White and Reds after the war of liberation and the civil war, are now recognised on almost all sides as having been directed towards the survival of Finnish democracy.

Edvard Munch, the greatest Scandinavian painter, was born at Løten, near Hamar (southern Norway) and died at Ekely, near Oslo. His childhood was spent in Christiania (as Oslo was then known); his mother died of tuberculosis when he was five. From 1885, with some interruptions, he lived in Paris, where he was influenced by Van Gogh and Gauguin. Later he spent a good deal of time in Germany, particularly in Munich. After a nervous breakdown in 1908 he returned to Norway in 1909. In 1916 he painted a series of murals for Oslo University. During the last years of his life, over which eye trouble cast a shadow, he spent much of his time in Åsgårstrand and other places on the Oslofjord. The coast and the sea are the setting of many of his pictures.

Edvard Munch
(1863–1944)

Famous People

Marshal Mannerheim

Edvard Munch

Fridtjof Nansen

Munch produced paintings, drawings, lithographs and woodcuts, often showing the influence of Art Nouveau and Symbolism. His landscapes, giving intense expression to personal experiences in simplified, darkly gleaming areas of colour, are forerunners of Expressionism. His human figures, usually in dark tones, are involved in basic human experiences – anguish, death, erotic feelings. Many of the themes are treated in several versions. In 1893 Munch began the "Frieze of Life" cycle for Max Reinhardt's theatre in Berlin, which consists of a total of twelve pictures ("Dance on the Beach"; other subjects are "The Voice", "Madonna", "Vampire", "Ashes", "Woman in Three Stages", "Melancholy" and "Death in the Sickroom"). Other well known pictures by Munch are "The Sick Child" (1885–86), "The Scream" (1893), "Dance of Life" (1800–1900) and "The Girl on the Bridge" (1900). Munch also painted numerous self-portraits and portraits of other artists; he presented a portrait of Strindberg (1892) to the National Museum in Stockholm.

In his will Munch left his collection of work – 1000 pictures, 15,400 sheets of printed graphic art, 5400 watercolours and drawings and six works of sculpture – to the city of Oslo. Most of these are now to be seen in the Munch Museum and the National Gallery in Oslo. Some 80 works by Munch in German private collections were designated by the Nazis in 1937 as "degenerate art" and confiscated.

Fridtjof Nansen
(1861–1930)

The Norwegian polar explorer Fridtjof Nansen, born on a farm near Christiania (now Oslo), became the first man, along with another Norwegian, Otto Sverdrup (1854–1930), to cross from the east to the west coast of Greenland (1888) – on skis and with sledges on ski runners. In 1893, in the "Fram" ("Forward"), he sailed from Novaya Zemlya and drifted in the current through the pack-ice into the Arctic Ocean. In 1895, starting out from the "Fram" in an attempt to travel to the North Pole by sledge, he reached latitude 86°14' north, and in the following year returned to Norway by way of Franz Josef Land. He then became professor of zoology (1896) and oceanography (1897). Between 1900 and 1914 he undertook a number of research expeditions in the North Atlantic. He wrote a number of books about his researches and travels ("On Snowshoes through Greenland", "Eskimo Life", "In Darkness and Ice", "Spitzbergen", "Among Seals and Polar Bears", etc.). The "Fram" is now housed in the Fram House on the south-east side of the Bygdøy peninsula, where there is also an open-air museum.

Nansen later occupied various political offices. In 1906–08 he was Norwegian ambassador in London. In 1920 he was in charge of the repatriation of prisoners of war from Russia, and in 1921–23, as high commissioner of the League of Nations, he organised relief work in the famine areas of the Soviet Union. On his initiative a special travel document for Russian refugees, replacing a passport, was introduced, and later, as the "Nansen passport", this was made available to other groups. In 1922 Nansen was awarded the Nobel Peace Prize.

The Swedish chemist Alfred Nobel was born in Stockholm and died in San Remo. His working life began in his father's engineering factory in St Petersburg. From 1859, in Stockholm, he was engaged in the manufacture of explosives, and in 1867 he invented dynamite, which became the foundation of his fortune. Other important advances were the development of blasting gelatine and smokeless powder. Nobel's inventions led to the establishment of explosives factories in many industrial countries.

Alfred Nobel
(1833–96)

Nobel left his fortune (some 31 million Swedish crowns) to a foundation, specifying in his will that the interest on the capital was to be divided annually into five equal parts and awarded to men and women whose work had "in the past year been of the greatest benefit to mankind" in five fields – physics, chemistry, physiology and medicine, literature and peace between the nations.

In 1968 the Swedish National Bank, after discussion with the Nobel Foundation, founded an Economics Prize in honour of Alfred Nobel, which has been awarded since 1969 by the Royal Swedish Academy of Sciences. The Nobel Prizes for the sciences, medicine, economics and literature are presented in Stockholm by the king of Sweden on December 10th, the anniversary of Alfred Nobel's death. The winner of the Peace Prize is nominated by the Nobel Committee of the Norwegian Storting and the prize is presented in Oslo. The awards are made after consultation with the Nobel Institutes in Stockholm and Oslo. The prizes can be awarded to an individual, to two individuals in equal parts, to a number of persons in common or to an institution or society.

In the 1912 Olympic Games, held in Stockholm, Finland gained nine gold medals, three of them won by the long-distance runner Hannes Kolehmainen. Even more remarkable was the achievement of the long-distance runner Paavo Nurmi, who during the 1920s and 1930s set numerous world records in the Summer Olympics at distances between 1500 and 20,000 metres. Competing in both individual and team events, he won twelve Olympic medals for Finland, nine golds and three silvers. At the 1924 Olympics in Paris he created a sensation by establishing two world records, for 5000 and 1500 metres.

Paavo Nurmi
(1897–1973)

The Swedish politician Sven Olof Palme, a lawyer by training, was a member of the Swedish Social Democratic Party and for several years a member of the board of the Social Democratic youth organisation. He was elected to the Riksdag in 1958, and during the 1960s occupied various ministerial posts. In 1969 he succeeded Tage Erlander as leader of the Social Democratic Party and became prime minister. He continued the reforming socialist policies of his predecessor with increased vigour and promoted the development of Sweden into a welfare state. He was strongly critical of the United States involvement in Vietnam. After the victory of a right-wing coalition in 1976 he ceased to be prime minister and thereafter led the Social Democratic opposition. After a Social Democratic success in an election in 1982 he formed a minority government with Communist support. As prime minister his main concern was to pull Sweden out of recession, and he argued in favour of a nuclear-weapon-free zone in northern Europe. He won a further election in 1985.

Olof Palme
(1927–86)

On the evening of February 28th 1986 Palme was shot at close range when leaving a cinema and died during the night. It was at first thought that the murderer was a Kurd belonging to the extremist Workers' Party of Kurdistan, of which there were a number of members in Sweden, and the security police were blamed for not doing enough to protect the prime minister. A report by the parliamentary commission appointed by the government to investigate the circumstances of the murder, published in April 1988, severely criticised the police and the state prosecution service. When bugging devices (prohibited in Sweden) were found in a policeman's car in June 1988, pointing to a semi-official search for the murderer, there was a public outcry, and a few days later the minister of justice resigned. One Christer Pettersson was arrested in December 1988 and accused of the murder; in July 1989 he was found guilty and sentenced to life imprisonment, but in the following October, on appeal, he was released for lack of sufficient evidence.

Jean Sibelius
(1866 1957)

The Finnish composer Jean Sibelius was born in Tavastehus (now Hämeenlinna) and died at Järvenpää, near Helsinki. After studying music in Helsinki, Berlin and Vionna he lived in Finland from 1893. In 1897 the Finnish government made him an annual grant for life so that he might be free for composition.

Sibelius was the founder of Finnish music and Finland's most important symphonic composer. Stylistically his compositions show the influence of the German romantic and late romantic schools. He found much of his inspiration in the landscapes of Finland, and the real domain of his music – sometimes of epic breadth, sometimes lyrical – is the representation of the great moods of nature. The main characteristics of the music in harmony, rhythm and tempo are derived from Finnish folk music. His programme music takes its themes from Finnish myths and sagas, in particular from the Finnish national epic "Kalevala" (see Lönnrot, above).

Among Sibelius's principal works are seven symphonies (1899 to 1924) and several symphonic compositions, among them "The Swan of Tuonela" (1893–96), "Finlandia" (1899) and "Tapiola" (1925), an orchestral work which conjures up Finland's endless forests and the figure of Tapio, the god of the forest. Sibelius also composed a violin concerto in D minor (1903), two serenades for violin and orchestra (1912–13), chamber music, choral works, lieder and piano pieces. Helsinki's great concert hall bears the name Finlandia, and there is a modern memorial to the composer in the Sibelius Park.

Frans Emil
Sillanpaa
(1888–1964)

Frans Emil Sillanpää is the only Finn to have been awarded the Nobel Prize for literature. He received the prize in December 1939, and many Finns still claim that the Swedes made the award because they had a bad conscience over their non-involvement in the Finnish-Soviet "Winter War" of 1939 40.

Sillanpää grew up in poor circumstances but in spite of this was able to go to university. Like Minna Canth, he learned the discipline of writing by contributing articles and stories to newspapers and magazines. His first novel, "Elämä ja Aurinko" ("Sun of Life") was published in 1916, at a turbulent time in Finland's history, and attracted considerable attention. The subject is one which has been treated by many Scandinavian writers – a man torn between two types of women, the sweet wife and mother and the seductive beauty.

Sillanpää won the Nobel Prize at a time when most Europeans were concerned with the possibility of military service and had little time for literature. Largely because of this, the prize did not bring him the international fame which goes with a Nobel Prize in normal times. In view of the international competition and the fact that the prize can be awarded only to living writers, there seems little prospect of another award to a Finnish writer in the foreseeable future.

Thereafter Sillanpää published a number of other works which attracted little attention outside Scandinavia. The only exception was "Nuorena Nukkunut" ("Fallen Asleep While Young"; published in English in 1931 as "The Maid Silja"), his most important novel, which was translated into many languages and was the subject of two Finnish

Olof Palme *F. E. Sillanpää* *August Strindberg*

films. The maid Silja, the daughter of a landless peasant who dies of consumption at the age of 22, "fulfilling her destiny with a smile", ranks as the most moving figure of a woman in Finnish literature.

The Swedish writer Johan August Strindberg came from an impoverished family which had lived in Stockholm for generations. After an unhappy childhood he went to Uppsala University. His first ambition was to become an actor, but when this project fell through he turned to literature. From 1872 he worked as a reporter in Stockholm, where he came in contact with the ideas of socialism. In 1883 he went to Paris, in 1884 to Switzerland and thereafter to Berlin and Denmark. After suffering a nervous breakdown he returned in 1899 to Stockholm, where he became one of the founders of the Intimate Theatre. After the bitter "Strindberg feud", carried on in two newspapers in 1910–12 – Strindberg's final struggle against conservative literary Establishment – he died a lonely death; married three times, each marriage came to grief.

August Strindberg
(1849–1912)

Strindberg wrote plays, novels and poetry. Particularly concerned as a writer with the psychology of the war of the sexes, he began with naturalistic works under the influence of Ibsen (see above). Among his naturalistic dramas is "The Father" (1887), a tragedy showing an almost clinical dissection of the characters' psychology. As a result of his contacts with occultist circles and his reading of the Swedish theosophist Swedenborg (1688–1772) Strindberg developed a mystical religious feeling of Catholic inspiration, reflected, for example, in his three-part Drama "The Road to Damascus" (1898–1904), which depicts the various stages of conversion. This work, the characters in which are symbols of psychological states, anticipates some of the features of Expressionism and Surrealism. In "A Dream Play" (1901) Strindberg sought to imitate the incoherent but seemingly logical form of a dream. Other notable plays are "Miss Julie" (1888), "The Dance of Death" (1901) and "The Ghost Sonata" (1907). Strindberg also wrote a number of plays centred on Swedish historical figures, including Gustavus Adolphus and Queen Christina.

Strindberg made his name as a novelist with "The Red Room" (1879), a work of social criticism dealing with a group of bohemian artists and academics who meet in the "red room" of a Stockholm club. Other novels of social criticism are "The Gothic Rooms" (1904) and "Black Banners" (1907). "The Son of a Servant" (1886), "Confession of a Fool" (1897), "Inferno" (1897), "Legends" (1898), "The Convent" (1898) and "Loneliness" (1903) are partly autobiographical. Strindberg planned his books as a stocktaking of his life, transformed by his artistic skill into works which transcended the purely private element in his confessions.

Art and Culture

Art and Architecture

Norway and Sweden

Neolithic
(to *c.* 1800 B.C.)

The Neolithic period, during which the transition from a hunting culture to a settled farming culture took place and the pre-Indo-European peoples were steadily thrust back by the advancing Germanic tribes, lasted in Scandinavia until about 1800 B.C. The Nordic culture, which later spread into Central Europe, is known to us only through its pottery, of various types and in various styles. The two main groups, Megalithic ware and Single Grave or Corded ware, are found in many local variations. In the Megalithic ware, for example, two broad trends can be distinguished, a Danish and a Swedish style. There are various types of decoration – ribs and scratched vertical lines; a framework of horizontal and vertical lines formed by deep incisions; and a type of framework decoration, sometimes with overall patterns.

To the Neolithic period belong also the realistic (earlier) or schematic (later) rock carvings of the Arctic culture, found particularly in Norway, which are attributed to the pre-Indo-European population (the Arcto-Baltic culture). These carvings, mostly of the animals which were the hunters' prey, more rarely of human figures, were no doubt of magical significance, designed to bring luck in the chase.

Germanic art

Germanic art covers a period of almost 3000 years, divided between the Bronze Age, the Iron Age and the art of the protohistorical period of the 1st millennium A.D.

Bronze Age
(1800–600 B.C.)

The Bronze Age, which lasted in Scandinavia from about 1800 to 600 B.C., offered fresh scope for technical and artistic development through the introduction of a new material, bronze (nine parts copper, one part tin). Weapons, implements and ornaments were now cast in stone and clay moulds, and in the Middle Bronze Age the *cire perdue* method came into use. The decoration was either cast in the mould or applied by the use of punches, engraving or hammering. As in the earlier period, pottery was made without the potter's wheel. The Nordic culture of the Bronze Age was undoubtedly developed by Germanic peoples, whose work in bronze was of a high technical and artistic standard. Four stylistic phases can be distinguished:

Proto-Bronze Age: rectilinear designs following the Neolithic traditions of Nordic culture.
Early Bronze Age: transition to spiral geometric ornament.
Middle Bronze Age: the spiral ornament running round the vessel gives place to central star patterns.
Late Bronze Age: the star patterns in turn are replaced by spiral whorls and bands of wavy lines; the decoration becomes less rigidly geometric and begins to incorporate vegetable forms (tendrils and foliage). Rich assemblages of grave goods have been found in burial mounds, particularly at Uppsala and Seddin. The existence of a solar cult is reflected in numerous representations of the solar disc.

Rock carvings

The representational art of the Bronze Age is known to us only in the rock carvings of southern Sweden and Norway – schematic figures of cultic significance, ceremonial processions, ritual contests, trains of sledges, ships, pilgrims. Although the detailed interpretation of these

Rock carving in southern Sweden: man with boat

carvings is still the subject of dispute, they are undoubtedly connected with fertility rites. The Scandinavian carvings are among the finest of the kind to be found anywhere. There are also a number of figural representations on funerary monuments, like the Early Bronze Age cist grave at Kivik on the Skåne peninsula. The stone slabs of the cist have carved representations of solar wheels, weapons and schematically drawn cloaked and fettered human figures, the significance of which is a matter of controversy.

During the Iron Age, which lasts in Scandinavia from about 600 B.C. to A.D. 400, the decorative art of the Bronze Age disappears and is replaced by only the most modest attempts at ornament.

Iron Age (from 600 B.C.)

The second main period of Germanic art, the protohistorical period of the 1st millennium A.D., saw a great flowering of artistic achievement, with a development from the simple filigree ornament of the early part of the period through a phase of decoration using inlaid coloured stones to the organic vigour of the animal style of ornament. From the 6th century figural representations become commoner. Four stages of development can be distinguished:

Protohistorical period (beginning of Christian era to 1200)

The filigree style (from the beginning of the Christian era to about 350): ornaments, particularly fibulas, decorated with gold or silver wire by the techniques of "flushing" or granulation.

The "coloured" style, using chip-carved ornament (350–550). The Goths adopted decorative techniques of Iranian origin – inlays of precious stones (frequently garnets) and cloisonné enamel work. Chip-carving is a form of decoration in which small chips of triangular profile, meeting at an angle, are cut in the surface of the object. In Scandinavia the chips are usually cut in the body of the metal with a burin. Originally no doubt taken over from wood-carving, the technique is still used in folk art.

Abstract animal ornament and interlace patterns (550–800). The earliest form, Animal Style I, is characterised by animal figures so fantastically articulated that they sometimes disintegrate altogether. The heads, often consisting only of semicircular eye apertures, are juxtaposed to form mosaic-like patterns. A later form of the style, Animal Style II, incorporating interlace ornament of southern Germanic type, became the main type of animal ornament on the European continent. In Animal Style III, which developed in Scandinavia about 700, highly abstract animal figures are used to form elaborate ornamental compositions, producing for example animal whorls or mirror-image pairs. Here again the burin was used.

The Viking style or late animal style (800–1100). The great Viking expansion was made possible by their keeled boats with strengthened bottoms to take the mast and keel, like those found in a bog at Nydam in Slesvig (three sea-going boats dating from the 4th century, the largest being an open oared boat 25m/82ft long which could accommodate a crew of forty) and at Kvalsund.

The Oseberg Ship

An impressive example of the new type of keeled boat is the Oseberg Ship, the ship tomb of a Norwegian princess (now in the Norwegian Folk Museum, Bygdøy, Oslo). This vessel, 22m/72ft long, with carved animal ornament on the prow and stern, contains a timber burial chamber, beside which were found a wagon, several sledges, furniture and remains of clothing and woven carpets. A magnificent animal-head post is decorated with two superimposed systems of ornament in the "gripping beast" style, also known as the Oseberg style. The burial is dated to about 850.

The Gokstad Ship

A further example of the type is the Gokstad Ship from the Kongshaugen area (also in the Folk Museum at Bygdøy). This 24m/79ft long vessel, clinker-built of oak, contained the body of a man lying fully clad on a splendid funeral couch, with rich grave goods.

In contrast to the Oseberg style, which was probably influenced by Carolingian art, is the more abstract Jelling style (900–1100), which shows the influence of the Celtic animal ornament of Ireland and later of Anglo-Saxon art. The style takes its name from the runic stone of Harald Bluetooth (c. 985) at Jelling in Denmark, the finest surviving example of Viking sculpture. Of rather later date are the runic stones of Stenkyrka on Gotland (c. 1000), Lundagård (Lund) and Tulstorp (Skåne). The characteristic animal is the "great beast", a beast of prey with spiral limbs and a massive mane.

With the final victory of Christianity the animal style disappears: the last examples date from around 1100 (stave church at Urnes in Norway, c. 1090; Swedish runic stones). Figural decoration is relatively rare, and the gold bracteates (ornamental discs, usually pendants, often decorated only on one side, with figural representations) of the 6th century are an isolated phenomenon. Then in the 7th century we find small figural representations, in severe style, on helmet mountings (Vendel and Torskinda, Sweden) depicting deities and cultic scenes, like the figure of Wotan as a horseman carrying a lance (helmet from Vendel).

Romanesque
(11th–12th c.)

Until the beginning of the Christian period in Scandinavia, however, there is little artistic progress to record. The adoption of Christianity about the year 1000 marked the terminal point of Viking art. Around 1160 the technique of building in brick came in, and the building of stone churches displayed the power of the new faith. These churches, the best preserved monuments of the Romanesque period, were originally simple buildings in calc-tufa, later in granite. The finest – three-aisled basilicas with two towers at the west end showing the influence of the imperial cathedrals of the Rhineland – are the cathedrals of Lund

Romanesque relief in Heda church (Östergötland)

(now in Sweden but in the area of Danish architectural tradition), Viborg and Ribe (both in Denmark). The village churches were influenced by the great cathedrals, as can be seen for example in the churches of Tveje Merløse (with beehive-shaped steeples) and Fjenneslev (*c.* 1140). The Swedish churches of the 12th and 13th centuries are usually simpler. There are also a number of round churches, particularly on Gotland (Church of the Holy Ghost and St Lars' Church, Visby; both about 1260), and hall-churches influenced by those of Westphalia. Another notable church is that of Varnhem (*c.* 1200).

The stave churches (see page 92), found mainly in Norway, are timber-built structures on a framework of vertical posts which show the influence of shipbuilding techniques. They are not merely an imitation of masonry construction in wood but a deliberately developed architectural form, with a large internal space which may derive from the old royal hall of the Scandinavian kings. The gables with their dragons' heads recall the prows of the Viking ships.

The architectural style of the Gothic churches in southern Scandinavia is often based on French and Spanish models, with some churches showing the influence of German brick-built Gothic. Only a few secular buildings of this period have been preserved.

Gothic
(13th–15th c.)

In Sweden the churches of the Gothic period tend to be rather low and squat. For large-scale buildings foreign masons were brought in, as in the construction of the Gothic choir of Linköping Cathedral (by Master Gerlach of Cologne). The second important building of the Gothic period is Uppsala Cathedral (begun about 1250). Considerably later in date are St Birgitta's Church at Vadstena (1388–1430) and St Peter's, Malmö (*c.* 1400).

In Norway the stone churches of both the Romanesque period (Stavanger Cathedral, *c.* 1130; Lyse Cathedral, begun 1146) and the

Gothic period (Trondheim Cathedral, rebuilding begun 1152) follow English models.

The medieval painting of Scandinavia achieves no very distinctive character of its own (altar frontals at Hitterdal, Kinsarvik, Nes, Dåle and Årdal; all c. 1250–1350). It is preserved chiefly in wall and ceiling paintings in churches (e.g. the cathedrals of Vä and Vidtskofte, Sträng-näs and Härkeberga in Sweden).

Norwegian sculpture of this period is also of no particular distinction. The carving on the stave churches is a survival of older Germanic traditions, and in the later medieval period Norwegian work was modelled on sculpture imported from the Netherlands and the Lübeck area (winged altars) and from England. Danish sculpture of this period, however, showed great variety.

Gothic sculpture now increasingly finds expression in wood and ivory rather than stone, and it is often difficult to decide whether a particular item is of French or Danish workmanship. Later Danish sculpture of the Gothic period shows strong German influence, the most notable examples of this being the work of the German sculptors Bernt Notke (c. 1440–1509) and Claus Berg (c. 1470 to after 1532).

Sweden too showed great interest in Lübeck sculpture from the end of the 14th century, when English and French influence began to give place to influences from Germany and the Netherlands. The fine St George and the Dragon in the north aisle of the Storkyrka in Stockholm is attributed to Bernt Notke, who lived in Stockholm from 1483 to 1489. Sculpture from Lübeck and the Netherlands and alabaster reliefs from England also found their way to Norway.

Renaissance and Baroque (16th–18th c.)

While the Renaissance and Baroque periods are represented by little work of any significance in Norway – with gifted artists like the architect L. van Haven and the sculptor M. Berg going to the Danish court – in post-Reformation Sweden church building took second place to the

Wooden bowl with rose pattern (Norway)

building of castles (Gripsholm, 1573; Vadstena, mainly 17th c.). In the 16th century German architects brought the Lombard Renaissance style to Sweden. The finest castle of the 17th century, mainly following models in the Netherlands, is Drottningholm on Lake Mälar, the summer palace of the Swedish kings, begun in 1662 by the Swedish architect Nicodemus Tessin the Elder (1616 to after 1685).

Other notable buildings of this period are the Royal Palace in Stockholm, in Roman High Baroque style, begun by Nicodemus Tessin the Younger (1654–88), with an 18th century interior; Kalmar Cathedral (by the two Tessins); and Skokloster Castle near Uppsala (1654–65).

In Sweden and Denmark sculptors from the Netherlands were at first predominant, followed in the 18th century by the French. Particularly notable are funerary monuments like those of Gustavus Vasa in Uppsala Cathedral (1580) and Gabriel Gustafson Oxenstierna in the church at Tyresö (1641) and a number of statues, including particularly the equestrian statue of Gustavus Adolphus (1796) in Stockholm.

Swedish painting of this period is seen at its best in the interior decoration of Kalmar Castle and the Royal Palace in Stockholm (by J. B. van Uther, c. 1562) and the work of Master Holger Hansson (fl. 1586–1619), Ottomar Elliger the Elder (1633–79), Johan Sylvius (d. 1695), the Hamburg artist David Klöcker von Ehrenstrahl (1629–98), the Flemish artistic dynasty of the van Meytens or Mytens, Alexander Roslin (1718–93), Gustaf Lundberg (1695–1786) and C. G. Pilo (1711–93).

With the work of the Swedish sculptor Johan Tobias Sergel (1740–1814) – who was also an excellent draughtsman – the Classical style established itself in Sweden; his best works can be seen in the National Museum in Stockholm. Other practitioners of this style were J. N. Byström (1783–1848), B. E. Fogelberg (1786–1854) and Per Hasselberg (1850–94).

18th and 19th centuries
Classicism

Notable examples of Swedish architecture are the Old Opera House (by F. Adelcrantz, 1716–96), the Exchange by E. Palmstedt, 1741–1803) and the interior of the Royal Palace (by C. Hårlemann, 1700–53), all in Stockholm.

Norway has produced much notable work, with a distinctive character of its own, in the field of folk art, as indeed have the other Scandinavian countries, particularly in the "rose painting" by peasant artists. The heyday of the peasant painting of southern Sweden was between 1750 and 1850 (Dalarna, Gästrikland, Helsingland). The painted wall hangings produced mainly for festive occasions are mostly on cloth or paper; in the north the walls and ceilings are painted.

Folk art

In the 19th century many Swedish painters went to Düsseldorf and later to Paris for training. Notable artists of this period were the landscapist C. J. Fahlcrantz (1774–1861), Peter Krafft the Younger (1777–1863), a German, C. Wahlbom (1810–58), A. Wahlberg (1834–1906) and above all the greatest of modern Swedish painters, Anders Zorn (1860–1920), who was also an etcher.

Sweden has played a prominent role in the architecture of the 20th century. Particularly during the 1920s and 1930s a "close to the earth" style of building was popular – detached family houses, terraced houses, the *backehus* ("hill houses") of the Danish architect Ivar Bentsen (1876–1943). The international Functionalism of Gunnar Asplund (1885–1940) also made increasing headway, with such creations as the exhibition halls for the Werkbund exhibition in Stockholm in 1930 (light airy buildings of glass and steel), Stockholm Municipal Library (1924–27) and the extension to Göteborg Town Hall (1934–37). Sven Markehus built the Concert Hall in Helsingborg (1936). The ideas of the Swedish Arts and Crafts Association (Werkbund) on modern design

20th century
Architecture

Sculpture by Carl Milles in Millesgården (Stockholm)

were the starting-point of a distinctive Scandinavian school of interior decoration and the design of everyday articles and utensils.

New housing types developed in Sweden included various types of high-rise block (star-shaped, slab-shaped, etc.), like those at Örebro (1948–50) and Danviksklippen (by S. Backström and L. Reinius, 1945).

Sculpture

A leading Swedish sculptor was Carl Milles (1875–1955). Others were Carl Johan Eld (1873–1954) and Johannes Collin (1873–1951). The latest generation of Scandinavian artists often break through the traditional boundaries between sculpture and painting. Notable Norwegian sculptors are Stephan Sinding (1846–1922) and Gustaf Vigeland (1869–1943; fountains in Frogner Park, Oslo), both trained in France.

Painting

Norwegian painters also have impressive achievements to their credit. In the 19th century there were the Romantic painter Johan Christian Dahl (1788–1857) and his pupil Thomas Fearnley (1802–42). J. F. Eckersberg and Hans Gude (1825–1903) were associated with the Düsseldorf school, while Gerhard Munthe (1849–1929), Erik Werenskiold (1855–1938) and Christian Krogh followed French models.

Edvard Munch

A Norwegian painter of international standing was Edvard Munch (1863–1944), who is regarded as one of the founders of Expressionism, though he did not carry it through to its final conclusion. In his later works he turned away from the gloomier sides of life (*angst*, illness, death, the battle between the sexes) to more positive themes. He also achieved remarkable effects in his graphic work.

In addition to Anders Zorn, who was concerned to preserve the old peasant culture of Dalarna, Swedish painters of the late 19th and early 20th century include Carl Larsson (1853–1919), noted for his charming children's books, the animal painter Bruno Liljefors (1860–1939), L. Engström (1886–1927), O. Baertling and C. O. Hultén. Around 1930

Edvard Munch: "Åsgårdstrand"

O. G. Carlsund brought abstract art to Sweden; and in the 1950s the Hungarian-born E. Nemes was the leader of the Valand school.

The younger generation of artists, who are no longer bound by the laws of traditional art, include Olle Kåks (b. 1941); J. Franzén (b. 1942) and Ola Billgren (b. 1940), who belong to the Photorealist school; and Curt Hillfon (b. 1943). Lars Englund (b. 1933) creates "volumes" of rubber and plastic; Hans Nordenström (b. 1927) does collages; and Arne Jones (b. 1914) works with mobiles and "light sculpture".

Finland

Although the Finns are not of Germanic stock but moved into Finland from the Baltic area in the early years of the Christian era, the development of their art in the early and medieval periods was closely associated with that of the other northern European countries. The churches, apart from the stave churches, were mostly built of undressed stone, with a steeply pitched saddle roof and a separate belfry; the interior, usually with aisles flanking the nave, was decorated in the late medieval period with wall and ceiling paintings, frequently with plant ornament. Examples are the 15th century church at Lohja, near Helsinki, and the cathedral of Turku (Åbo), begun in the 13th century and enlarged in the 15th.

Artists from the Hanseatic towns worked in Finland as in the other Scandinavian countries; examples of their work are the 15th century brasses on St Henry's tomb at Nousiainen and the St Barbara altar by Master Francke (c. 1410; National Museum, Helsinki). The Finnish fortified castles are of imposing monumental effect (Viipuri, now in Russia; Olavinlinna, in Savonlinna, c. 1475).

After the Reformation there was only a very limited amount of church building, mostly wooden churches which either imitated the medieval churches with a nave or had a cruciform plan with arms of equal length and a central dome. The interior was decorated in popular style by local artists, as at Salvinen (1632), Padasjoki (1675) and Kanhava (1756).

Early period and Middle Ages

Art and Architecture

Edvard Munch: "Winter Landscape"

Modern times

During the 18th century there developed alongside this folk art an art of a more "middle-class" character. Manor-houses and burghers' houses were built; portrait-painting came into fashion.

Helsinki, capital of Finland from 1812, was given a Neo-Classical aspect from 1825 onwards by the Berlin architect C. L. Engel (1778–1840). The present townscape, however, is predominantly the work of Finnish architects of the modern school.

Painting

Finnish painting also began to develop in the 18th century, at first under German influence (Ekman, 1808–73; Holmberg, 1830–60) and later under French influence (Edelfelt, 1853–1905). Around 1900 a distinctive national style began to emerge, particularly in the work of Akseli Gallén-Kallela (1865–1931; Illustrations for the Finnish national epic "Kalevala") and Tyko Constantin Sallinen (c. 1900). A sculptor of notable quality was Väinö Aaltonen (1894–1966; statue of Aleksis Kivi in Helsinki, 1939).

Architecture

After the romantic "national" architecture of around 1900 (National Museum, Helsinki) Finnish architecture developed the clear, calm forms which have established its international reputation. In spite of its uncompromisingly progressive approach, however, it has remained in tune with the harshness and austerity of the northern landscape. The pioneer of modern Finnish architecture was Eliel Saarinen (1873–1950; Central Station, Helsinki, designed 1904), who, like other Finnish architects, later worked in the United States. No less important was the work of his son Eero Saarinen (1910–61), who designed the General Motors Technical Centre in Warren, Michigan (1950), the MIT Auditorium in Cambridge, Massachusetts (1955), Yale University Hockey Rink in New Haven, Connecticut (1958), the TWA Terminal at J. F. Kennedy Airport, New York (1962) and the Gateway Arch in St Louis, Missouri (1965).

Alvar Aalto

Also of international reputation is Alvar Aalto (1898–1976), who was particularly concerned with the effect of colour ("red" and "white" periods). His work in Finland includes a sanatorium at Paimio (1930),

Carl Larsson: "Lisbeth Fishing" (detail)

Sculpture by the Finnish sculptor Olavi Lanu (near Retretti Art Centre)

Carved chair in Heddal stave church

the Municipal Library in Viipuri (1927–34; now in Russia), the Mairea housing development in Norrmark (1938–39), the Palace of Culture in Helsinki (1955–58) and the Town Hall of Säynätsalo (1951–52). He also designed the Finnish pavilion at the New York International Exposition of 1939.

Among other well-known 20th century architects are the husband and wife Kaija and Heikki Sirén (Forest Church, Otaniemi, 1956–57), Aarne Ervi (b. 1910; Community Centre of Tapiola, a modern district of Espoo), Jorma Järvi (secondary school, Tapiola) and Viljo Revell (1910–64; nursery school, Tapiola, 1954; Toronto City Hall).

Lapland

The Sami (Lapps), whose ethnic origins are the subject of dispute, live in northern Norway, Sweden and Finland and in Karelia, most of which at present belongs to Russia. Their semi-nomadic way of life, now gradually being abandoned, is mainly centred on reindeer herding. The Sami have a rich and distinctive tradition of folk art, but this, like folk traditions in other countries, is threatened by the pressures of modern life.

Stave Churches in Norway

The wooden stave churches (*stavkirker*) of Norway are the most famous and most characteristic achievements of medieval Norwegian architecture. The distinguishing feature of their construction – in contrast to the "log-cabin" technique in which the timber is laid horizon-

Borgund stave church (Lærdal) ▶

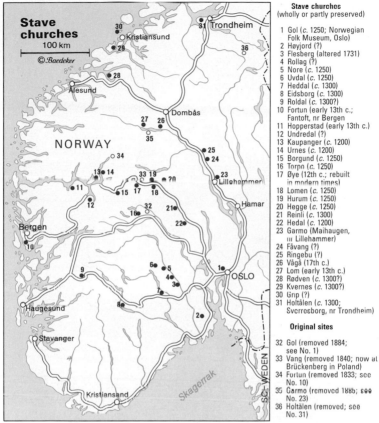

Stave churches
100 km
©Baedeker

NORWAY

Stave churches
(wholly or partly preserved)

1 Gol (c. 1250; Norwegian Folk Museum, Oslo)
2 Høyjord (?)
3 Flesberg (altered 1731)
4 Rollag (?)
5 Nore (c. 1250)
6 Uvdal (c. 1250)
7 Heddal (c. 1300)
8 Eidsborg (c. 1300)
9 Roldal (c. 1300?)
10 Fortun (early 13th c.; Fantoft, nr Bergen)
11 Hopperstad (early 13th c.)
12 Undredal (?)
13 Kaupanger (c. 1200)
14 Urnes (c. 1200)
15 Borgund (c. 1250)
16 Torpo (c. 1250)
17 Øye (12th c.; rebuilt in modern times)
18 Lomen (c. 1250)
19 Hurum (c. 1250)
20 Hegge (c. 1250)
21 Reinli (c. 1300)
22 Hedal (c. 1200)
23 Garmo (Maihaugen, in Lillehammer)
24 Fåvang (?)
25 Ringebu (?)
26 Vågå (17th c.)
27 Lom (early 13th c.)
28 Rødven (c. 1300?)
29 Kvernes (c. 1300?)
30 Grip (?)
31 Holtålen (c. 1300; Sverresborg, nr Trondheim)

Original sites

32 Gol (removed 1884; see No. 1)
33 Vang (removed 1840; now at Brückenberg in Poland)
34 Fortun (removed 1833; see No. 10)
35 Garmo (removed 1885; see No. 23)
36 Holtålen (removed; see No. 31)

Of the 31 stave churches in Norway which still survive, 27 are on their original site and four have been taken down and re-erected elsewhere as "museum churches". In addition one church was removed in the 19th century to a site in Germany (now Poland).

tally – is the use of vertical planks or "staves", either anchored in the ground or to horizontal sills, to support the saddle roof.

As in the Viking ships, the structure is so solidly bound together by its timber framing, struts and scissors trusses that it is well able to stand up to the northern storms. Massive round corner buttresses stabilise the outer walls, which stand free of the interior. The outer gallery has a shed-roof, the lowest stage in the stepped roof structure. Between the posts and pillars in the interior of the church, which is built without the use of a single iron nail, are round-headed arches which give the structure the necessary elasticity.

There is evidence of the building of stave churches in the 9th century, but their heyday was in the 12th and 13th centuries – at a time when, with the spread of Christianity, the technique of building in stone came to Scandinavia. Romanesque forms were now assimilated into the ancient technique of timber building, though at first the ornament remained wholly in the Viking tradition, which remained vigorously alive into the 12th century. From this period dates the highly stylised animal and interlace carving which with its decorative compositions and motifs taken from the pre-Christian Edda poetry creates a fantastic and almost uncanny effect.

With the coming of Christianity, however, this figural ornament, regarded as pagan, fell into disfavour and in the Norman period gave place to more restrained forms of decoration which had their proto-types in the stone buildings of the period. At the same time the bas-ilican type of church with a raised nave separated from the lateral aisles by mast-like timber columns appeared alongside the older aisleless ground-plan. The Roman type of basilica became predominant at a time when the first regular episcopal sees were being established in Norway, where previously there had been only itinerant evangelising bishops. The figural decoration now grew richer, and there was a renaissance of the Viking formal tradition; the pagan ornament of earlier times, however, was replaced by Christian themes showing European influence. This gave rise to the famous "dragon style", named after the terrifying dragons' heads which crowned each section of roof.

In the 13th century the scissors truss came into use, and was some-times inserted also in older churches. Arcading, apses and ridge turrets now appeared for the first time.

In view of the dim light in the interior wall paintings of any size were rare, though Gothic and Byzantine work is occasionally found on the vaulting.

Around the year 1300 there are believed to have been more than 850 stave churches in Norway. When more than half the country's popu-lation was carried off by plague most of them fell into disrepair; then between the 17th and 19th centuries many churches were demolished because they were too small for the growing congregations. As a result there are now only 32 surviving stave churches (31 in Norway and one in Poland), some much altered from their original form. Of these 27 are still on their original site and five have been moved to a new site and rebuilt as museum churches.

In the mid 19th century there was a revival of interest in the stave churches, thanks to the efforts of the Norwegian painter J. C. C. Dahl, who became a professor at the Academy of Art in Dresden in 1824 and on his frequent visits to Norway campaigned for the preservation of these unique monuments. Unfortunately the restoration work which now began frequently distorted the original effect: thus new windows were often inserted, though the original churches had been only dimly lit by small openings high up on the walls.

The surviving stave churches are all in southern Norway, extending as far north as Trondheim.

Quotations

John Story
"Travels through
Sweden"
(1632)

Next in order follows Finland, which some think to be so called in comparison of Sweden, as tho' it did in fruitfulness far exceed it, (who are foully deceived; for it is more probable that it was first called Fiendland by reason of the great hostility those Finlanders exercised against this nation, so long as they were commanded by a king of their own). The country abounds in corn, pasture, fish and fowl, and finally in such things as are most necessary for the life of man. The people are very laborious, and able to endure hardship. Of old they were esteemed the mildest among all the Scanzian people; howbeit, at this day they are somewhat harsher; and their valour in war was well witnessed in the memorable battle fought near Leipsick in Misnia. They have a peculiar language of their own . . .

Queen Christina
of Sweden
(1626–89)
"Memoirs and
Aphorisms"

I will attempt to describe the men who then occupied the five offices of state:
. . . The fourth was Chancellor Axel Oxenstierna, the great man of whom I have already spoken, and of whom one can never say enough. He was a learned man who had studied widely in his youth; and he continued his studies even when he was dealing with the most important business. He possessed great abilities and a profound knowledge of the world. He knew the strengths and weaknesses of all the countries of Europe. He was distinguished by his wisdom, his great foresight, his many talents and his great generosity. He was indefatigable, a man of unexampled diligence and energy. Work occupied his whole time and was his only pleasure; even his leisure was spent in useful occupations. He was moderate in eating and drinking, and he slept well: he used to say that only two events had disturbed his rest, the news of the death of the late king [Gustavus Adolphus] and the news of the defeat at Nördlingen [a battle in 1634 in which the Swedes were defeated by the Emperor and his allies]. He has often told me that when he went to bed at night he stripped off his cares along with his clothes, forgetting about them until the following morning. For the rest he was ambitious, but loyal; incorruptible, but somewhat slow and phlegmatic. He became Chancellor in the reign of Charles IX at the age of 20 — a thing without example in Sweden. He served four monarchs in that office, and died six months after my abdication, which affected him so strongly that at his advanced age he was unable to survive the blow.

William Coxe
"Travels Into
Poland,
Russia, Sweden,
etc."
(1792)

I have seen no town with whose situation I was so much struck as that of Stockholm, for its singular and romantic scenery. This capital, which is very long and irregular, occupies, beside two peninsulas, seven small rocky islands, scattered in the Maeler, in the streams which issue from that lake, and in a bay of the Baltic. A variety of contrasting and enchanting views are formed by numberless rocks of granite rising boldly from the surface of the water, partly bare and craggy, partly dotted with houses, or feathered with wood. The harbour is an inlet of the Baltic: the water is of such depth that ships of the largest burthen can approach the quay, which is of considerable breadth, and lined with spacious buildings and warehouses. At the extremity of the harbour several streets rise one above another in the form of an amphitheatre; and the palace, a magnificent building, crowns the summit. Towards the sea, about two or three miles from the town, the harbour is contracted into a narrow strait, and, winding among high rocks, disappears from sight; and the prospect is terminated by distant hills overspread with forest. It is far beyond the power of words, or of the pencil, to delineate these singular views.

... Half a mile from this spot we finally came on the Lapp, who had changed his lodging yesterday. I was much relieved.

9th July. Tired after my last journey, I stayed indoors; in my exhaustion I did not venture on to the ice. Also this was a *dies sanctus.* The lake on the glacier mountain is covered with ice a fathom deep.

... The reindeer or *rhenones,* countless in number, were driven home morning and evening for milking. I saw how they were to be driven home and how they would not go in the direction the dogs were manoeuvring them and the girl who was driving them wanted them to go. I saw also how, when they were being taken back again (there was a strong east wind), what trouble they were causing, for the girl did not want to go where they wanted to go and they did not want to go where she wanted. The reindeer ran back, round about and then forward again, with the dog rushing round them. I was told that the reindeer always want to go into the wind and, if they are not allowed to, spring ahead with great rapidity, hoping thus to get cool. A little later I saw the reindeer standing in the shade behind a high hill, huddled together on a patch of snow, for the sun was warm. When it is hot they do not eat. The midges were very troublesome.

Carl von Linné (Linnaeus) (1707–78) "Journey in Lapland" (published 1811)

I soon became good friends with this first Hälsinger. He served as an omen for all Norrlanders and for the pleasure of my travels in Norrland; and I must confess that this omen did not deceive me ...

He then began to talk about the trolls. This term is not a very precise one: as a rule it means the little spirits of the forests and the mountains, known in our own popular belief as the underground people, but it also extends to the whole host of forest, lake and house spirits in their various disguises and appearances. "Here," he said, "the mountains are full of trolls. They live in houses of crystal and gold. My father saw them one night, when on a holy festival on St John's night the mountains opened up. They were dancing and drinking, and seemed to be waving to him to join them; but his horse snorted and, try as he might to control it, bolted. In the Guldberg (a hill in the neighbourhood) there are many of them; they have carried down there the gold and silver which people hid in the ground during the Russian war ..."

Ernst Moritz Arndt (1769–1860) "Journey through Sweden in 1804" (1806)

The atmosphere [in Åland] was so clear and dry that, being well clothed, the effect of it was charming. An intensity of general cheerfulness seemed to keep pace with the intensity of the season. Brilliant skies; horses neighing and dancing; peasants laughing and singing – "Fine snow! Brave winter!" Merry making in all the villages. Festival days, with unclouded suns; nights of inconceivable splendour and ineffable brightness; the glorious firmament displaying one uninterrupted flood of light, heightened by an *aurora borealis,* while boundless fields of snow reflected every ray.

Edward Clarke "Travels in Various Countries ..." (1819)

Väinämöinen, old and steadfast,
On his kantele was playing;
Long he played, and long was singing,
And was ever full of gladness.
In the moon's house heard they playing,
Came delight to the sun's window,
And the moon came from his dwelling,
Standing on a crooked birch-tree,
And the sun came from his castle,
Sitting on a fir-tree's summit,
To the kantele to listen,
Filled with wonder and rejoicing.
Louhi, Pohjola's old Mistress,
Old and gap-toothed dame of Pohja,

"Kalevala" (Finnish national epic, published by Elias Lönnrot, 1835 and 1849)

Set to work the sun to capture,
In her hands the moon seized likewise.
From the birch the moon she captured,
And the sun from fir-tree's summit;
Straightway to her home she brought them,
To the gloomy land of Pohja.
Then she hid the moon from shining,
In the mottled rocks she hid him,
Sang the sun to shine no longer,
Hidden in a steel-hard mountain;
And she spoke the words which follow:
"Never more again in freedom
Shall the moon arise for shining,
Nor the sun be free for shining,
If I come not to release them,
If I do not go to fetch them,
When I bring nine stallions with me,
Which a single mare has littered."
When the moon away was carried,
And the sun had been imprisoned
Deep in Pohjola's stone mountain,
In the rocks as hard as iron,
Then she stole away the brightness,
And from Väinölä the fires,
And she left the houses fireless,
And the rooms no flame illumined.
(Translation by W. F. Kirby)

Samuel Laing
(1812–97)
"A Tour in
Sweden
in 1838"
(1839)

Visby:
This ancient city is the most extraordinary place in the north of Europe. It is a city of the middle ages, – existing unbroken, and unchanged in a great measure to the present day; – it appears to have undergone less alteration from time, devastation, or improvement, than any place of the same antiquity. The appearance from the sea of this mother of the Hanseatic cities is very striking, from the numerous remains of churches and ancient structures within a small space. I counted thirty-five towers, spires, or prominent ruins. On landing, the aspect is equally novel. Ancient streets, well paved, cross each other in all directions; and the causeway work, with two or three parallel bands, or stripes of larger paving stones, running lengthwise through the streets, looks ornamental, or at least regular. I have seen such paving about some cathedral in England. The houses on each side of these ancient streets are in general poor cabins, with gardens, potato-ground, and corn crops, all huddled together, among ruins of churches of very extraordinary beauty and workmanship, and, as ruins, in very picturesque preservation. The whole city is surrounded by its ancient wall, with towers – square, octagonal, and round – as they stood in the 13th century, and with very little demolition. The wall is entire, and above thirty feet high for the greater part, and is in no place demolished. Of forty-five towers upon it, the greater part are entire: some are roofed-in, and used as magazines, a prison, storehouses, or workshops.

James D. Forbes
"Norway and
its Glaciers"
(1853)

Oslo:
Christiania itself is seen to advantage from the fjord, as well as from many places in its environs. It is built on an agreeable slope, facing the south. Its suburbs are intermingled with wood. The old castle of Aggershuus, picturesque in form, adorned with fine trees, and standing on a bold promontory, commanding at once the fjord and the greater part of the town, has a striking effect. The city graduates into the country by means of innumerable villas, built usually in commanding situations, which remind one of the environs of Geneva. Indeed,

there is something in the entire aspect of the town and surrounding scenery, which is exceedingly pleasing and peculiar. The traveller who is acquainted with the aspects of middle and southern Europe finds himself at a loss to draw a comparison. The clearness of the air, the warmth of the sun, and a certain intensity of colour which clothes the landscape, involuntarily recall southern latitudes, and even the shores of the Mediterranean. But the impression is counteracted by the background of pine forest, which reminds him of some of the higher and well-wooded cantons of Switzerland, to which the varied outline of the fjord – which may compare in irregularity with the lake of the four cantons [Lake Lucerne] – lends an additional resemblance; yet again we miss the background of alpine peaks and perpetual snows.

And now it is Christmas Eve. The weather is mild, the sky is hung with grey clouds and freshly fallen snow covers the hills and valleys. A gentle rustling comes from the forest; the black grouse are feeding on the tiny birch buds, the waxwings on the rowan berries, while the raven, the lustful virgin of the pine forest, gathers twigs for her future nest. Joy and peace reign in cottages and manor-houses; so too in the brothers' cabin in the cleared forest land on the Impivaara. Outside the door is a load of straw which Valko has brought from the Viertola estate to lay on the floors of the rooms in honour of Christmas. The brothers cannot forget the crackling of the Christmas straw, the finest memory of their childhood.

Aleksis Kivi
Finnish writer
(1834–72)
"Seven Brothers"
(1870)

From the house there sounded the hissing of the steam on the hot stones of the oven and the swishing of the bunches of twigs in the bath. The brothers were having a good Christmas bath; then, when at last the scalding-hot steam bath was over they came down, dressed and sat on the beams round the walls which served in place of benches. There they sat, recovering their breath and sweating. The room was lit by a flickering pine spill. Valko was grinding oats in his own corner, for this had to be thought of at Christmas too. The cock was dozing and yawning on its roof-beam. The dogs Killi and Kiiski lay close to the stove with their heads resting on their paws; and the old grey cat which they had brought from Jukola was purring on Juhani's knees.

The voyage [from Christiansand to Stavanger] by the large steamers presents few attractions, as the coast is imperfectly seen from the steam-boat; but the entrance to the Flekkefjord and some other points are striking. The vessel's course is at places protected by islands (*Skjær),* but is often entirely in the open sea, particularly off Cape Lindesnæs, on the coast of Listerland, and near Jæderen. The small local steamers are much slower and call at many unimportant stations, but they afford a good view of the interesting formations of the coast. The fjords are continued inland by narrow and deep valleys, gradually rising towards the bleak and barren tablelands (*Fjeldvidder)* of the interior. These valleys are usually watered by rivers which frequently expand into lakes, and their inhabitants, the *Oplandsfolk,* are mostly engaged in cattle-rearing. Each valley forms a little world of its own, with its own peculiar character, dialect, and customs. The *Kystfolk,* or dwellers on the coast, are much engaged in the export of mackerel and lobsters to England.

Baedeker's
"Norway and
Sweden"
(6th edition, 1895)

There are old streets without any atmosphere of their own and streets which are full of atmosphere, even though they are new. The newest part of Riddargatan is full of romance, not to say mysticism. In this street there are no human beings, no shops, to interrupt the walls; it is genteel, closed, desolate, although the large houses enclose so many human destinies. The names of the side streets, which commemorate great figures of the Thirty Years' War, enhance the feeling of history created by an agreeable mingling of past and present. If you turn the corner into Banérgatan you see to the west a hill in Grev-Magnigatan,

Johan August
Strindberg
Swedish writer
(1849–1912)
"Loneliness"
(1903)

which bears right and forms a myste rious termination of the vista in an area of shadow concealing who knows what.

But if you come from the west, up the old Riddargatan, and look down Grev-Magnigatan the view is very different. The palatial houses, dark-coloured, with their doorways and long oriels, speak of loftier destinies. These are the homes of magnates and statesmen who exert influence on nations and dynasties. But immediately above this, up Grev-Magnigatan, an old house dating from the beginning of last century has been preserved. I like to walk past this house, for I lived there in my turbulent youth. There I planned campaigns which were later carried out and were successful; and there I wrote my first works of any consequence. The recollection is not a bright one, for poverty, humiliation, negligence and conflict spread their dirt over everything.

Knut Hamsun
Norwegian writer
(1859–1952)
"The Growth of
the Soil" (1917)

The long, long path over the moor into the forest: who trod it out? The first man, the first human being who was here. There was no path when he came here. Later some animal or other followed the faint track over marsh and moor, making it clearer, and later still some Lapp or other found the path and followed it as he travelled from hill to hill looking after his reindeer. Thus there came into being the road through the wide Allmende, which belonged to no one, the land without an owner.

The man comes along the road, going north. He carries a bag containing food and a few tools. The man is strong and tough, he has a rosy beard and small scars on his face and hands – did he get them at work or in a fight? Perhaps he is just out of prison and is trying to hide; perhaps he is a philosopher in search of peace. At any rate here he is, a man walking by himself in this immense solitude. He keeps walking on: it is quiet all round him, with not a bird or animal to be heard. Now and then he mutters a few words. When he comes to an area of moorland and better ground, or a clearing in the forest, he puts down his bag and walks round examining the soil; then he takes his bag up again and continues on his way. This goes on all day; then he sees from the sun what time it is; night falls, and he throws himself down in the heather and sleeps on his arm.

Selma Lagerlöf
Swedish writer
(1858–1940)
"The Wonderful
Adventures of
Nils"
(1906–07)

The boy was so bewildered that for a long time he didn't known what was happening to him. The air whistled towards him, the wings beside him flapped up and down, and a storm seemed to be blowing through the feathers. Thirteen geese were flying round him, all beating their wings and gabbling. The wind was blowing in his face and roaring in his ears. He had no idea whether they were flying high or low, or where he was being taken.

. . . When at last the boy looked down he saw what looked like a large cloth spread out below him, divided into innumerable squares, large and small.

. . . Then the boy realised that the large check cloth over which he was flying was the flat landscape of Skåne, and he began to understand why it was so broken up and had such different colours. He recognised first the light green squares: they were the fields of rye which had been sown in the previous autumn and had remained green under the snow. The yellowish-grey squares were the stubble-fields which had borne crops last summer; the brownish ones were old clover-fields and the black ones areas of empty grazing or unploughed fallow. The brown squares with a yellow edge must be the beechwoods, with the tall trees in the centre, leafless in winter, and round the edges the young trees which preserve their yellowed leaves until spring. There were also dark-coloured squares with a grey patch in the middle: these were the large square farmsteads with their blackened thatched roofs surrounding a paved court. And there were also squares which were green in the middle and had brown borders: these were gardens in which the grass was already green, while the shrubs and trees round the edges were still in their naked brown bark.

The essence of a journey to Finland lies in the general impression of the innumerable dark-coloured lakes with their many islets, the abundantly flowing rivers and the much indented coasts with their fringes of skerries. There are few outstanding features of individual interest. Visitors travelling to Finland usually arrive in Helsingfors, the country's young capital. The city has a number of notable new monumental buildings and a fine National Museum which offers an excellent survey of Finnish culture from prehistoric times to the present day. There are attractive excursions to the islands in the surrounding area. Particularly to be recommended is a steamer trip through the skerries to Borgå, which is visited mainly for its associations with the poet Runeberg.

Baedeker's "Sweden and Finland" (14th edition, 1929)

[The Finnish-Swedish poet Johan Ludvig Runeberg, 1804–77, made a major contribution to the development of Finnish national awareness.]

I see for the first time a phenomenon of literary history: how could our folk poetry have survived were it not for the farms of Karelia? They are real homesteads, like those of the Old Testament. In these closed communities the old folk poems are cherished and preserved. The main living room, the bedrooms, the stables, the barns and sometimes the well are all under one roof. In winter, when the snow beats against the grey log walls, the daily business of the household can be done without setting a foot out of doors.

Olavi Paavolainen Finnish writer (1904–64) "Gloomy Talks with Myself" (a wartime diary)

Just as they (Tommy and Annika) were wondering what they should do today and whether something interesting would happen or whether it would be a dull day when they couldn't think what to do, the gate to Villekulla Cottage opened and a little girl came out. She was the funniest girl Tommy and Annika had ever seen: it was Pippi Longstocking coming out for her morning walk.

Astrid Lindgren Swedish author of children's books (b. 1907) "Pippi Longstocking" (1945)

This was what she was like. She had carrot-coloured hair plaited into two pigtails which stood out from her head. Her nose was the shape of a very small potato and was covered all over with freckles. Under the nose was a very large mouth with healthy white teeth. Her dress was funny too. Pippi had made it herself. It was a beautiful yellow colour, but there hadn't been enough cloth and it was too short, and so her blue knickers with white spots peeped out from under it. On her long thin legs she had a pair of long stockings, one brown and the other black. She had black shoes which were twice the size of her feet. Her father had bought the shoes in South America, with the idea that she would grow into them, and Pippa wouldn't wear any others.

Tommy and Annika's eyes opened even wider at the sight of the monkey which sat on her shoulder. It was a little long-tailed monkey wearing blue trousers, a yellow jacket and a white straw hat . . .

Galajärvi Lake:

It was approaching the end of August, and the brief Lapland summer was disappearing as rapidly as it had come. The leaves of the birches turned yellow and then red. The Galajärvi hills were clad in a blood-flecked mantle. The lake, however, still preserved its eternally green colouring: only on the leaves of the water plants had a few drops of blood fallen. It was the time when the eyes of the water-lilies were open to the sky. The two fishermen remained even longer motionless in the middle of the lake, and their heads dropped even lower over the edge of the boat until their ears almost touched the water.

The first rays of the morning sun found it increasingly difficult to pierce the darkness, now growing ever denser. The nearer came

Robert Crottet Journalist (1908–87) "Magical Forests and Legends from Lapland" (1955)

autumn and the time of perpetual night the less was the lake able to shake off the shadows. It almost seemed to enjoy the darkness and to hold out longer than other lakes against the light of morning . . .

William Sansom
English writer
"Blue Skies,
Brown Studies"
(1961)

Sognefjord:
More or less everywhere along the fjord there is one consistent picture, representative of all mountain-fjords in summertime. It is a vertical one: one views it up and down. In the centre, and taking up most of the picture, rises the immediate massed cliffside, furred with dark green fir-trees, one or two thousand feet or more of rock. At the top, patches of snow – and glimpses above of higher mountains bellying up snow and dark granite against the distant sky like the giant black and white rump of a celestial panda. Now whizz the eye down to the bottom where a very small patch of bright yellow-green or emerald shines out – the fields of the lonely village with their dicing of painted houses. In the immediate foreground, the bottle-green glass of the tree-reflecting fjord-water.

Suppose this up-and-down strip of a picture to be two foot high – sky, snowline, tall mountain-side, farm, water – then only about one small inch will be represented by the yellow-green glint of human life. It is awe-inspiring, pathetic, and warming. It is like watching, and feeling for, the odyssey of a small green insect trying to climb a window-pane. Proportions viewed from the boat-deck, or from another farmer's eye from the opposite side of the fjord, are somersaulted – the village becomes a toy and only the vertiginous mountain-side of real size.

A. O. Schwede
German
journalist
(1973)

Mora, on Lake Siljan:
Mora is the town of the red horses of Dalarna. I did not see a single living horse in the town, but I did see hundreds of red wooden horses, from the smallest size to half the height of a pony. The little Dalarna horse is a simple but very attractive creation of peasant art. I have been unable to find out anything about its origins. Does it go back to a remote antiquity, or has it come into being to bring the wood-carvers of Dalarna a little extra money? The village of Nusnäs, near Mora, is said to be its original home, but you do not need to go there, for in Utmeland you are invited to visit a workshop where the horses are made. The carvers, who work at home, are always glad to see a visitor: it makes a change, and always leads to a small sale. The horses are carved from blocks of wood in a very placid – one might almost say "un-horse-like" pose, as a small child paints a horse, with all four feet planted on the ground, without a tail and with only a single ear stretching right across its head. They are painted a glossy red and equipped with harness and saddlecloth, painted in bluish-white, and are then ready for sale.

Liv Ullmann
Norwegian actress
(b. 1938)
"Changes" (1976)

We are on a tour with the "Doll's House". This time we are competing with the midnight sun in northern Norway. I have been unable to sleep for a week, so beautiful it is here.

What a country it is, my homeland! Snow-covered hills and a smell of heath and moorland. A fresh breeze blowing towards us over crystal-clear water from fjords which wind their way into the remotest corners. Where in summer the sun never disappears, merely touching the horizon before rising again and pursuing its course across the sky. People who express their feelings spontaneously and speak animatedly in a sing-song tone, as if they cannot restrain their joy at escaping from the eternal darkness of winter.

. . . I have travelled the whole world, and I know that I have never received stronger impressions than here. Here the contrasts are so enormous. The sea is so unfathomable when I lean over the rail of the boat and imagine the extraordinary world deep down in the water. And the hills which rear up all round me, jagged and bare, are nearer the sky than I could have imagined.

To feel the wind and the sun on your face and the smell of the trees, the rocks and the earth on your skin: this too is one of the things that change my life.

Tromsø:

The huge arched concrete bridge over the sound separates the long island on which Tromsø is built from the hilly islands which lie all around. Latitude 70° north, just below the Arctic Circle. Greenland and Alaska, which lie in the same latitude, offer their jagged and icy coasts to the midnight sun; but in Tromsø this blood-red dispenser of light, scarcely hidden even behind the hills, brings it about that night ceases to exist. The few moments when a rosy shadow falls over the land does nothing to halt the bustle of activity in the streets. On summer nights sleep becomes a siesta. We are constantly exposed to a searchlight which varies its intensity from time to time, and I am sure that the flowers cannot make out what is happening in this climate in which their colours glow more joyously than anywhere else. Could it be the influence of the Gulf Stream which flows along the Norwegian coast? For a brief moment everything takes on a flesh-pink colouring − the fronts of the houses, the silver birches . . .

Julien Green
French writer
(b. 1900)
"My Cities"
(1986)

Suggested Routes

The routes suggested in this section are designed to help visitors travelling by car to plan their trips in the Scandinavian countries, leaving them free to vary the routes according to their particular interests and the time available.

The suggested routes take in the main places of interest described in this guide, though some of them involve side trips off the main route. In addition there are many suggestions for excursions and round trips in the entries for particular places in the A to Z section of the guide, including in particular the trip round Lake Vänern, which is not, therefore, included among the routes suggested here.

The routes can be followed on the map at the end of the book, which will facilitate the detailed planning of trips.

In the description of the routes places for which there is a separate entry in the A to Z section are shown in **bold** type.

Most of the towns, villages, regions, rivers, lakes and other sights mentioned in the main section of the guide, whether the subject of a separate entry or not, are listed in the Index at the end of the volume, making it easy to find the description of a particular place.

The distances shown in brackets at the head of each route are in round figures and relate to the main route. Where side trips or detours of any length are suggested the additional distance involved is indicated.

Sweden

1. Helsingborg via Jönköping and Norrköping to Stockholm
(about 600km/375 miles)

This route (E 4; partly motorway) runs north-east from the Öresund through Skåne and Småland and then through Östergötland and Södermanland to the Swedish capital, passing through areas of agricultural land as well as expanses of forest.

Main route

From **Helsingborg**, situated on the Öresund opposite the Danish town of Helsingør (Elsinore), take E 4 (from which a motorway branches off and heads south to **Malmö**), running through western **Skåne**. 4.5km/3 miles south of Åstorp is the castle of Vrams Gunnarstorp (1633), in Dutch Renaissance style. The road continues through wooded country, varied by rounded hills. Beyond Örkelljunga it enters **Småland** and comes to Markaryd, set amid five lakes. It then continues for another 50km/31 miles, passing a prehistoric burial area, to Ljungby, on the right bank of the river Laga. Beyond this is a beautiful stretch along the wooded shores of Lake Vidöster to the industrial and commercial town of Värnamo, from which the route continues by way of Vaggeryd through forest country to Jönköping.

Side trip

Shortly before Jönköping a country road goes off on the left and runs 9km/ 6 miles south-west, via the industrial town of Norrahammer, to the Taberg (343m/1125ft), a hill consisting almost entirely of magnetite. From the foot of the hill a road (1.5km/1 mile) runs up to a car park;

on top of the hill are a restaurant and a monument commemorating a visit by King Oscar II.

E 4 continues to **Jönköping**, at the south end of **Lake Vättern**, perhaps Main route the most beautiful lake in southern Sweden, occupying a rift valley. It then runs along the shores of the lake by way of the garden city of Huskvarna to Gränna, a pretty little town at the foot of the Grännaberg, with the impressive ruins of Brahehus Castle. To the west is the island of Visingsö, with the ruins of Visingsborg Castle and the old church of Kumlaby. From Ödeshög there are alternative routes. A road goes off on the left and runs up the shores of the lake to reach Linköping by way of Vadstena and Motala (Göta Canal), while E 4 continues north-east via Rök and Mjölby to **Linköping**, chief town of Östergötland, on the west bank of the Stångå. Just before Norsholm the road crosses the Göta Canal and then continues to **Norrköping**, a large industrial town at the west end of an inlet on the Baltic. Beyond this it runs up into the forest-covered uplands of Kolmården, which extend from west to east along the border between Östergötland and Södermanland, and then down through the wooded region of Södermanland, with its many lakes, to **Nyköping**, chief town of Södermanland, situated on the Nyköpingså. 7km/4½ miles beyond this a side road runs north to the burial mound of Uppsa-Kulle (15km/9 miles). E 4 then continues via Vagenhärad and Södertälje, on the Södertälje Canal, which links Lake Mälar with the Baltic, to **Stockholm**.

2. Göteborg via Karlstad and Örebro to Stockholm
(about 580km/360 miles)

This route runs through south-western and central Sweden, traversing the provinces, partly forest-covered and partly lake country, of Västergötland, Dalsland, Värmland, Närke, Västermanland and Södermanland. From Karlstad a road runs north to Lake Siljan.

From **Göteborg** Road 45 runs up the left bank of the Götaälv, which Main route here marks the boundary between Bohuslän and Västergötland; to the left, in the river, can be seen the ruins of Bohus Castle. After passing through Nödinge (church with wall paintings) and Älvängen the road comes to Lilla Enget, a dam on the river, with a hydro-electric station, locks and a large papermaking factory. Beyond this the road turns away from the river and comes in 5km/3 miles to a junction where Road 45 continues straight ahead to the industrial town of Trollhättan, on the Götaälv, with the once famous Trollhättan Falls, which now power a hydro-electric station. From Trollhättan the route continues north to **Lake Vänern** and the town of Vänersborg, situated at the north end of an island in the lake. Beyond Vänersborg it follows the shore of the lake, crosses the border into Dalsland and then turns away from the lake, running north, passing on the left the forest-covered Kroppenfjäll, to Mellerud and Köpmannebro on the west side of Lake Vänern. Köpmannebro is the starting-point of the Dalsland Canal (constructed by Nils Erikson in the 19th century), which links Lake Vänern with a number of other lakes in Upper Dalsland. 13km/8 miles beyond Köpmannebro by way of Ånimskog is Åmål, a charmingly situated little port town with a leisure park, the Örnäspark. Beyond Åmål the road turns away from the lake and enters the southern part of **Värmland**, the setting of Selma Lagerlöf's "Gösta Berling's Saga", the northern part of which borders the Swedish Norrland. The road then continues to Säffle and 17km/10½ miles beyond this joins E 18, which runs west to the Norwegian frontier and east to **Karlstad**.

An attractive excursion from Karlstad is to Lake Siljan. The route runs Side trip up the right bank of the Klarälven but soon turns into a road on the left which follows the shores of the beautiful Fryken Lakes. At Osebol it returns briefly to the Klarälv valley and then follows Road 45, which runs via Johannisholm to the tourist centre of Mora on **Lake Siljan**.

Main route

Beyond Karlstad E 18 runs east along the shores of Lake Vänern. In 3km/2 miles, to the right, is the former manor-house of Alster (good bathing station on the lake). 40km/25 miles farther on is Kristinehamn, a port and commercial town at the outflow of the river Varna into an inlet on Lake Vänern. Beyond this the road finally leaves the lake and runs through forest country to Karlskoga, beautifully situated at the north end of Lake Möckeln, with an old wooden church (wall paintings); to the north is Rävåsan (good views). The road then continues through a forest-covered region with many lakes, traversing the southern part of the Kilsberge range (279m/915ft). It leaves Värmland and enters the province of Närke, which extends south to **Lake Vättern**. 5km/3 miles before Örebro E 18 runs into E 20, coming from the south. From **Örebro** it is possible to reach **Stockholm** either by going along the north side of **Lake Mälar** via **Västerås** and Enköping (E 18) or along the south side via Strängnäs and Södertälje (E 20).

3. Stockholm via Kalmar to Malmö and Helsingborg
(about 500km/310 miles)

The route, most of it on excellent roads, follows E 4, E 22 and then a main road round the coast, passing through the provinces of Södermanland, Östergötland, Småland, Blekinge and Skåne.

Main route

Leave **Stockholm** on E 4 (first section motorway), which runs through Södermanland to **Norrköping**. From there E 22 heads south through the hilly coastal part of Östergötland, crossing the **Göta Canal** on a bridge at Söderköping. From there it continues through hills covered with forest and pastureland. A side road goes off on the left to the port of **Västervik**. Beyond Oskarshamn the road runs at some distance from the coast, off which, beyond the Kalmarsund, is the island of **Öland**. It then continues via Mönsterås, Ålem (good bathing at the fishing village of Timmernabben) and Ryssby to **Kalmar**, on the Kalmarsund, with its imposing castle.

South of Kalmar E 22 runs through south-eastern **Småland** and then through Blekinge. After passing Hagby, with an old round church, it continues through the park-like landscape of Blekinge to Lyckeby and **Karlskrona**, which is built on a number of islands linked by bridges. Then via Ronneby and Karlshamn, an industrial town at the outflow of the Mieå into the Karlshamnfjord, to Sölvesborg (church with medieval wall paintings). Beyond Sölvesborg the road enters **Skåne**, the most southerly and most densely populated province in Sweden. It is worth making a side trip to Bäckaskog Castle. Then on to **Kristianstad**.

The coast road from Kristianstad to Malmö (No. 9) runs through a fertile region which is particularly beautiful when the fruit trees are in blossom. By way of Kivik (Bronze Age tomb, reconstructed), the little coastal town of Simrishamn and Glimmingehus Castle it comes to **Ystad**, a town with old half-timbered houses. The road then continues, running close to the coast, to the port of **Trelleborg**. Soon after this it turns away from the coast and runs north (side road on left to the seaside resort of Falsterbo) to the port and industrial town of **Malmö**, from which there is a ferry service to Copenhagen. It then continues north via Landskrona to **Helsingborg**, at the narrowest point on the Öresund.

Variants

From Kristianstad there is a more northerly route to Helsingborg via Hässleholm (No. 21). It begins by running north-west through wooded country. Just before Hässleholm a road goes off on the left to Tykarps-grottan, a limestone cave some 140m/153yd long. At Åstorp Road 21 runs into E 4, the main road to Helsingborg.

The road from Kristianstad via the old university town of **Lund** to Malmö runs over the forest-covered Linderödsåsan, on which are a number of castles, including particularly Maltesholm and Skarhult.

4. Göteborg to Oslo (about 320km/200 miles)

This route, the "Highway of the Sun", follows E 6, an important link between the busy port of Göteborg and the Norwegian capital. The Swedish section of the route runs through the province of Bohuslän.

Leave **Göteborg** by the Tingstad Tunnel under the Götaälv on the motorway to the north. In 20km/12½ miles, crossing the Nordre Älv, a branch of the Götaälv, it enters Kungälv, the oldest town in Bohuslän, from which there is a ferry to Marstrand, a popular seaside resort situated on an island. At the road junction at St Höga there is a choice between taking a side road to the left which runs via the islands of Tjörn and Orust (bathing resorts) and continuing on E 6. From the bathing resort of Ljungskile E 6 runs at some distance from the coast. Then on to Uddevalla, where a road goes off on the right to Vänersborg on **Lake Vänern**. From the road heading north for Oslo there are fine views of the coastal waters and fjords. The route continues to Munkedal and Gläborg, from which it is worth while making a side trip to the popular seaside resort of Lysekil, 30km/19 miles south-west. E 6 now runs along the western edge of an area containing many prehistoric rock carvings and comes to Tanum, from which it continues through areas of forest and cultivated land, passing the estate of Blomsholm (prehistoric stone-setting in the form of a ship, off the road to the right). The road then continues to the Swedish frontier post of Svinesund and crosses the Svinesund, a narrow inlet which here marks the Swedish-Norwegian frontier, on a reinforced concrete bridge 420m/460yd long.

The route continues on E 6. Some 10km/6 miles beyond a road going off to **Fredrikstad** E 6 skirts the town of Sarpsborg on a road and rail bridge over the Glåma, the longest river in the Scandinavian peninsula. Beyond Karlshus the motorway runs through a patchwork of forest and fields along the Ryggeræt, a large terminal moraine. It then runs through a tunnel into the pleasant little town of Moss on the Mossesund. Soon afterwards a road goes off on the left to the bathing resort of Son. Beyond Korsegården the road begins to run down towards Oslo, with wide views ahead. Some 4km/2½ miles farther on is a junction where Road 156 goes off on the left and runs up to the north end of the Nesodden peninsula, which lies between the **Oslofjord** and the Bunnefjord; the main route continues north to Oslo on a beautiful stretch of road. At Vinterbru E 18, coming from the Swedish frontier, runs into E 6. The road then gradually climbs to the Bunnefjord, the innermost branch of the Oslofjord, with a succession of fine views of the fjord, runs along the western slopes of the Ekeberg, crosses the railway and continues past the port installations (on left) to the East Station of **Oslo**.

5. Trondheim via Östersund to Lake Siljan and Stockholm
(about 960km/600 miles)

This route, beginning in Norway on the Trondheimfjord, runs south-east through the Swedish provinces of Jämtland, Hälsingland, Dalarna, Västmanland and Uppland.

Main route

Suggested Routes

Main route

Leave **Trondheim** on E 6, which runs along the south side of the Trondheimfjord to Stjørdalshalsen, where E 14 goes off on the right and winds its way up the valley of the Stjørdalselv, passing the imposing fortress of Hegra. 20km/12½ miles beyond Meråker it comes to the Norwegian–Swedish frontier (alt. 523m/1716ft). E 14 now runs through the eastern part of Jämtland and comes to Ånn, at the north end of the Ånnsjö, a popular resort both in summer and for winter sports. At Sta a road goes off on the left and runs north to the Tännfors, an impressive waterfall. E 14 then continues via Åre, on the north side of a wider stretch of the Indalsälv known as the Åresjö, to Järpen. On this stretch of road it is possible to make side trips to various mountain villages. Beyond Järpen E 14 runs along the north side of the Litensjö, passes Mattmar church and continues through forest country. Just before Trångsviken it crosses a northern arm of the Storsjö, passes through Ytterån and comes to Krokom-Hissmofors, where it crosses the Indalsälv on a 160m/175yd long bridge; then along the east side of the Storsjö and through the village of Ås; in the lake, to the south-east, is the large island of Frösö (runic stone). Just beyond this is **Östersund**, the chief town of **Jämtland**.

From Östersund the route continues on E 14 along the east side of an offshoot of the Storsjö. At Brunflo it branches off E 14, which runs on to **Sundsvall**, and continues south-west on Road 45 to Hackås on the Storsjö (old church with interesting wall paintings) and then along the eastern shore of the Storsjö to Svenstavik at the south end of the lake.

Variant

From the church at Mattmar a provincial road (No. 321) runs south through beautiful scenery near the west side of the Storsjö, which is surrounded by dark forests and expanses of arable land, to Svenstavik. A side road runs west to Bydalen, a good base for fell walking.

Main route

At a road junction just before the bridge which crosses the Ljunga at Åsarna, to the south of Svenstavik, the main road (No. 45) bears left to cross the Ljunga. From another junction at Rätansbyn it continues south-east through forest-covered uplands in the valley of the Vitälv. At Kvarnen the valley of the Haå comes in on the right, and the river is now followed downstream into Hälsingland. Then via Ytterhogdal to Kårböle, from which a side trip can be made to the 25m/80ft high waterfall of Løfors. From Kårhöle the route continues on Road 296 via Los to Orsa and Mora, the well-known resort at the north end of **Lake Siljan**. From Rättvik, at the eastern tip of the lake, Road 70 runs south and south-east to Börlänge (which can also be reached on a detour via **Falun**). The road to Börlänge, the largest industrial town in Dalarna, runs through the wooded valley of the Österdalälv and then through that of the Dalälv to Säter, to the north of which is the beautiful Säterdal. Beyond this are Hedemora, the oldest town in Dalarna, beautifully situated amid lakes, and Avesta, on the Dalälv (two waterfalls, hydro-electric station). Beyond Avesta the main road to Stockholm (No. 70) follows the right bank of the Dalälv, passing through Västmanland and through forest country to Sala on the Sagå, noted for the silver-mine south-west of the town. The road now runs through fairly level country, mostly forest-covered, to Enköping and from there on E 18, running east along the north side of **Lake Mälar**, to **Stockholm**.

6. Rovaniemi via Luleå to Sundsvall (about 840km/520 miles)

The route, beginning in northern Finland (Finnish Lapland), crosses into Sweden and runs down the west side of the Gulf of Bothnia through the Swedish provinces of Norrbotten, Västerbotten, Ångermanland and Medelpad, on E 4 for most of the way.

From **Rovaniemi** E 75 (in Finland Road 4) runs south, parallel to the Kemijoki, and in 114km/71 miles runs into E 4, which leads east to Kemi and west to Tornio. At the Finnish frontier town of **Tornio** the road crosses the Tornionjoki (Swedish Torneälv); to the south of the town is the island of Röyttä, where larger vessels anchor. On the west side of Tornio the road crosses a marshy arm of the Tornio, here marking the Finnish–Swedish frontier, on a causeway. On the far side, to the left, is the Swedish customs post. Immediately beyond this is the Swedish town of Haparanda. E 4 continues through southern Norrbotten, running at some distance from the coast, through forest country and past a number of lakes, to Kalix, where the Kalixälv flows into the Gulf of Bothnia. It then crosses the river and soon afterwards runs through a military area, in which foreigners are subject to certain restrictions, and comes to the port of Töre.

Main route

From Töre an excursion can be made to Gällivare and Kiruna. Take E 10, which runs north, crosses the Arctic Circle and comes to **Gällivare** (off the main road to the left) in Swedish Lapland. From a hill to the south of the town, Dundret (823m/2700ft), there are wide views. E 10 continues through forest country, with many lakes, to the iron-mining town of **Kiruna**, the starting-point for the ascent of Kebnekaise (2117m/6946ft).

Side trip

From Töre E 4 runs close to the north-western corner of the Gulf of Bothnia to **Luleå**, an old port town at the mouth of the Luleälv, which is crossed on a bridge. The route continues via Gäddvik and Öjebyn to Piteå (reached on a side road to the left), a port town built partly on an island and partly on the mainland. E 4, running at some distance from the coast, now enters Västerbotten and comes to the industrial town of **Skellefteå**, on the north bank of the Skellefteälv; to the north of the town, at Boliden, are large copper-mines. Beyond Skellefteå the road runs through flat and mostly forest-covered country to the town of **Umeå** and then through the province of Ångermanland, which is watered by a large river, the Ångermanälv. After passing Örnsköldsvik, on the skerry-fringed bay of that name, and a number of other coastal towns and crossing the Ångermanälv on Sandö Bridge it comes to **Härnösand**, with the old part of the town on the island of Härnö, which is linked with the mainland by a bridge. Beyond Härnösand E 4 turns away from the coast again and after a short stretch of motorway reaches **Sundsvall**, a port and commercial town at the mouth of the Selångerå. (Thereafter it continues south to **Stockholm**; about 400km/250 miles.)

Main route

Norway

7. Oslo via Larvik and Kristiansand to Stavanger
(about 600km/375 miles)

The route, following E 18 for most of the way, keeps close to the coast of the Skagerrak and then the North Sea through southern Norway, running south-west as far as Cape Lindesnes and then north-west, at some distance from the coast, to Stavanger.

Leave **Oslo** on E 18, which runs west and then round Frognerkilen, an inlet on the **Oslofjord**. After passing through a number of small places it comes to Drammen, where the Dramselv flows into the Dramsfjord. From here a road runs up through a tunnel to Bragernesås (293m/961ft; wide views). The route continues by way of Sande to Holmestrand, the port of Horten and Tønsberg, which until 1951, when whaling was stopped on conservation grounds, was a whaling station; then bears west to Sem to rejoin E 18, which crosses the Lågen, a river

Main route

340km/210 miles long, on the Brommestadbru. The road bypasses **Larvik**, at the head of the Larviksfjord, and then begins to climb gently, running through the coastal regions of **Telemark** with its numerous fjords and crossing the Frierfjord on a bridge. After passing through the seaside resort of Kragerø it comes to Arendal, a port and ship-building town. Beyond this is Grimstad, where Henrik Ibsen lived for a time. The road continues close to the coast and after crossing a suspension bridge comes to **Kristiansand**, chief town of Sørland ("Southland"), from which the Haukeli Road (see route 8) runs north through the **Setesdal** to Bergen. Farther south is Mandal, Norway's most southerly town, lying on both sides of the Mandalselv just above its outflow into the open Mannefjord. E 18 then turns north-west to Vigeland, 28km/17 miles south-west of which is Lindesnes, at the southern tip of Norway (lighthouse), crosses the river Lynga just beyond Lyngdal, runs up the Møskedal to its highest point at Kvinsheia and then descends the valley of the Kvina, with wide views extending down to the sea, and comes to the little town of Flekkefjord, on the North Sea coast of Norway.

From Flekkefjord E 18 runs inland to Stavanger. A more rewarding route, however, is on the coast road (No. 44), which winds its way up and down to the little town of Egersund on the fjord of the same name, between the island of Egerø and the mainland. The road then continues over the coastal plain of Jæren, with expanses of moorland, to **Stavanger** on the Stavangerfjord, whose Cathedral is the finest church in Norway after Trondheim Cathedral.

8. Oslo to the Hardangerfjord and Bergen on the Haukeli Road
(about 500km/310 miles)

This interesting route, which links Norway's two largest towns, runs through the forest country of **Telemark** and follows the Haukeli Road, which heads north from Haukeligrend through magnificent mountain scenery; first E 18, then Roads 11 and 13.

Main route

Leave **Oslo** on E 18, and at Drammen continue west on Road 11, running up the north bank of the Dramselv, which is crossed at Hokksund; then on by way of Darbu (Fiskum church) to **Kongsberg**, on the Låge (old silver-mines). From Kongsberg Road 11 follows the Låge valley and in 5km/3 miles turns off to the right, runs past old silver-mines, crosses the Kobberbergselv and continues through forest-covered hills to Notodden, the chief town in eastern Telemark. 6km/4 miles beyond this, at Heddal, is the largest of Norway's stave churches (restored). The road continues, with some gentle ups and downs, to Ørvella and Sauland, from which a road runs north to Mt Gausta (1883m/6178ft; view), a skiing area. From Sauland Road 11 follows the valley of the Hjortdøla, climbs and then descends, with many bends (view of the Lifjell to the rear), to Brunkeberg. It then follows the Morgedal (off the road to the left, the stave church of Eidsborg) and continues via Åmont to Haukeligrend, starting-point of the interesting Haukeli Road (many tunnels; toll). This leads to Haukeliseter, in a lonely mountain setting at the east end of the Ståvann (view of the fjell). Beyond this is the Dyrskar pass (1148m/3767ft), which is bypassed by a tunnel. The road then comes to Horda, at an important junction.

Side trip

From Horda Road 13 runs south through the steep and narrow Bratlandsdal to Nesflatn, on the northern shore of the Suldalsvann, and then through a tunnel under the Suldalsport defile and down the valley of the Suldalslåge to Sand, a little port on the Sandfjord, from which there is a hydrofoil service to **Stavanger** (about 1½ hours).

From Horda the road to Bergen (No. 13) winds its way north-westward
up the slopes of the Hordabrekkene and then runs through the Røldal
Tunnel (4700m/5140yd long), the Seljestad Tunnel (1284m/1404yd
long) and the Seljestad Gorge. From the Steinaberg Bridge Road 11
runs south-west to the port of Haugesund (a rewarding side trip). The
Bergen road (No. 13) runs north through a gorge and then along the
east side of the Sandvenvann to Odda, an industrial town at the south
end of the Sørfjord, an arm of the Hardangerfjord; to the west is the
Folgefonn glacier. The road then continues along the east side of the
40km/25 mile long Sørfjord, with a mild climate in which cherry and
apple trees flourish. Then via Tyssedal and Lofthus to Kinsarvik, at the
mouth of the Sørfjord, from which there is a ferry to Kvanndal. The
road continues along the **Hardangerfjord** and crosses the Fykesund on
a suspension bridge. The last section of the route runs from Norheimsund through the Togkagjelet gorge to Ådland and Indre Arna, near a
side arm of the Sørfjord, and then via Nesttum to **Bergen**, Norway's
second largest city.

9. Oslo via Hamar and Lillehammer to the Sognefjord
(about 550km/340 miles)

This route runs through magnificent scenery along Lake Mjøsa and
through the Gudbrandsdal to the west coast of Norway. It begins by
following E 6, which runs north to Kirkenes; then at Otta turns west on
Roads 15 and 55.

Leave **Oslo** on E 6, which runs north-east through the city's extensive
suburbs. The motorway continues to Kløfta, where a road goes off on
the right to Kongsvinger, with an old fortress (view). Beyond Kløfta E 6
runs through rolling country and beyond Minnesund crosses the river
Vorma, which here flows out of Lake Mjøsa. It then follows the east side
of **Lake Mjøsa**, but beyond Espa turns away from the lake and comes to
Hamar, on the northern shore of the Akersvik, an inlet opening off the
lake, at the mouth of the Furnesfjord. From Hamar there is a ferry to
Gjøvik, on the west side of Lake Mjøsa. E 6 then continues, passing
Ringsaker church, to Moelv and **Lillehammer**, beautifully situated near
the northern arm of Lake Mjøsa, with an interesting open-air museum.
Beyond Lillehammer E 6 follows the **Gudbrandsdal**, through which
flows the river Låge. The route continues north to Tretten (off the road
to the right, the stave church of Ringebu), Vinstra and Otta, at an
important road junction, where it turns west on Road 15. This runs up
the valley of the Otta to Vågåmo, crosses the Vågåvann and comes to
Lom. From there the road to the Sognefjord (No. 55; open from mid
June to the beginning of October) runs south-west along the north-
west side of the **Jotunheim**, with impressive views of snow-covered
mountains and glaciers. Galdesand is a good base for a trip into the
mountains and the ascent of Galdhøpiggen (2468m/8098ft), to the east
of which is Glittertind (2452m/8045ft). From Galdesand the road runs
up to the Sognefjell, a passage through the mountains, and after
reaching the highest point (1440m/4725ft) runs down in sharp bends to
the hotel at Turtagrö. At Skjolden it comes to the north end of the
Lusterfjord and from there runs south-west to Sogndal and Slinde,
where it reaches the **Sognefjord** proper. It then continues to Hella, from
which there is a ferry to Balestrand, the largest tourist centre on the
Sognefjord. From Balestrand there are boat services to other places on
the Sognefjord, and Road 5 runs north from the town to Moskog.

From Lom it is possible to continue on Road 15 to the Nordfjord and
Geirangerfjord. It runs along the shores of the Ottavann and the banks
of the Otta to Grotli, at a road junction in the mountains. At Stryn Road
15 reaches the **Nordfjord**, continuing west from there to Måløy. From

the Nordfjord there is a road link to the **Sognefjord** to the south (Road 1; from Moskog Road 5).

From Grotli Road 60 runs north through impressive mountain scenery to Geiranger, a busy little port at the east end of the **Geiranger-fjord**, which runs into the Sunnylvsfjord. From Geiranger there is an attractive trip northward to Åndalsnes, on the beautiful Romsdalsfjord.

10. Trondheim to Narvik (about 930km/580 miles)

This route follows the middle section of E 6, which runs through the whole length of Norway to Kirkenes (the northern section of the "Arctic Highway"). For much of the way it runs close to the coasts of central and northern Norway, which with their innumerable fjords offer constantly changing scenery. The road is kept open in winter as far as Mosjøen.

Main route

From **Trondheim** E 6 runs along the south side of the Trondheimfjord, passing a side road on the right to the Selbusjö. Beyond Alstadhaug (church with wall paintings) it continues to Levanger, an angling centre on the Trondheimfjord, and the little town of Steinkjer, situated on both banks of the Steinkjerelv. It then runs up to Asp, through hilly and partly forest-covered country and along the north-western shore of the long Snåsavann (to the right of the road, the white wooden church of Kvam). From there it continues (with various roads going off eastward into Sweden) to Grong, and then along the banks of the Namsenelv, passing numerous waterfalls, to Majavatn (with a small church frequented by Lapps), in southern Nordland; to the east is the Børgefjell National Park. Then on through the Svenningdal to Mosjøen, a pleasant little town at the outflow of the Vefsenelv into the Vefsenfjord. Passing the Stabbfoss, a waterfall 42m/140ft high, E 6 comes to the industrial and commercial town of **Mo i Rana**, crosses the river Rana and continues up the valley (possible side trip to the Grønli Cave). To the north-west can be seen the Svartisen ("Black Ice") glacier. The road continues up the Dunderlandsdal, beyond Messingsletten crosses the **Arctic Circle** and runs down the Lønsdal and Saltdal to Rognan, a little port at the south end of the Saltdalfjord. Then on to Fauske, from which a road runs west to **Bodø** (boat services to the **Lofoten Islands**). From Fauske E 6 continues north along the east side of the Sørfoldafjord to Sommerset (ferry to Bonnåsjøen), Ulvsvåg, on an inlet in the Vestfjord, and Bognes, from which there are ferries over the Tysfjord and to the **Vesterålen**. The last section of the route (bridges, tunnels) runs north and along the south-east side of the Ofotfjord to **Narvik**, from which it is possible to continue to **Tromsø**, **Hammerfest** and **Kirkenes**.

11. Narvik to Tromsø and Hammerfest
(about 260km/160 miles and 700km/435 miles)

This route, mostly on E 6, runs past magnificent fjords and snow-covered mountains, through the county of Nordland and the two northernmost counties of Troms and Finnmark, mostly inhabited by Sami.

Main route

From **Narvik** E 6 runs along the Rombaksfjord and then turns north to Bjerkvik, from which a road runs west to the **Vesterålen**. It then winds its way up the Mølndal, through which flows the Prestjordelv, and comes to the tourist resort of Gratangen, with fine views of the Gratangenfjord and the surrounding hills. After reaching its highest point (428m/1404ft) it runs down through birch forests, with many bends; a road on the left (No. 851) runs west to the head of the impressive Salangen fjord. The road now follows the valley of the Barduelv, partly forest-covered, and comes to Andselv, south-east of which is the Bardufoss waterfall. Then through the Takelvdal, with many stretches of birch forest, to Storsteinnes and over a boggy plateau to Nordkjosbotn, where the road to Tromsø branches off the Hammerfest road.

From Nordkjosbotn the Tromsø road (E 8; 73km/45 miles) runs along the east side of the Balsfjord and then turns away from it to reach Fagernes, where it bears south-west and then runs north to Tromsdalen, at the mouth of the Tromsdal, which here debouches into the Tromsøsund. It then crosses the Tromsøsund on a bridge 1036m/ 1133yd long and comes to the port of **Tromsø**, on the small island of that name.

From Nordkjosbotn the Hammerfest road (E 6 and E 8) runs up the valley of the Nordkjoselv to Øvergård. Ahead can be seen the magnificent **Lyngenfjord**, along the south-east side of which the road continues. It then crosses the Skibotnelv and comes to a road junction at Olderbakken, where E 6 continues north, while E 8 runs south-east.

E 8 runs up the valley of the Skibotnelv to the Norwegian summer customs post, crosses the Norwegian–Finnish frontier and in 5km/ 3 miles comes to the Finnish frontier post. It then continues close to the shores of the Kilpisjärvi, a lake well stocked with fish where the frontiers of Norway, Sweden and Finland meet; to the left is Saanatunturi (1024m/3360ft), the sacred mountain of the Lapps, from which there are wide panoramic views.

Side trip

From the junction at Olderbakken E 6 continues to Skibotn and then along the east side of the Kåfjord to Olderdal and, through magnificent scenery, along the Lyngenfjord. Beyond Sørkos it crosses the Reisaelv and comes to Storslett; then along the east side of the Straumfjord and the Kvænangsfjord to the Altafjord, which is broken up into a number of arms. On its southern shore is the market town of **Alta**, from which a road runs south to Kautokeino, a town mainly inhabited by Sami. E 6 continues north-east to Skaidi, from which Road 94 runs west to Kvalsund. From Kvalsund there is a ferry to the large island of Kvaløy, on the west side of which is the port of **Hammerfest** (boat services to Honningsvåg, near the **North Cape**).

Main route

Finland

12. Hammerfest via Karasjok and Ivalo to Rovaniemi
(about 680km/425 miles)

This route (open only from May, in Finnish Lapland only from mid June) begins in northern Norway and runs south through Finnish Lapland to Rovaniemi. In Norway it follows Road 94 and then E 6, in Finland Road 4 (E 75). The road between Ivalo and Rovaniemi was part of the old Arctic Highway which until 1944 ran north to the Arctic port of Petsamo, then Finnish but now Russian (Pechenga).

From **Hammerfest** the route follows Road 94 as far as Skaidi and then E 6, which runs along the west side of the Porsangerfjord to Lakselv, at the head of the fjord, and then continues up the wide valley of the Lakselv through low-growing birch forest, skirts a large lake, the Nattvann, and comes to **Karasjok**, a town on the Karasjokka inhabited mainly by Sami. 19km/12 miles beyond this is the Norwegian–Finnish frontier. From there Road 4, passing the Finnish frontier post, runs

Main route

through pine and birch forests, with expanses of bog, and past numerous small lakes. It then crosses the foaming Kaamasjoki and comes to Kaamanen. The route, now on E 75, continues through a boggy region with many lakes and past the holiday resort of Lapponia to Inari, on the west side of **Lake Inari**; 7.5km/4½ miles north-east is the old Lapp church of Pielppajärvi. It then runs along the shores of the lake, some stretches of which are rocky, to Ivalo, where it joins the old Arctic Highway, which now ends at Virtaniemi, on the Finnish-Russian frontier. From Ivalo the section of the Arctic Highway which remains Finnish (E 75) runs south through forest country. To the right is the wide Ivalojoki, which accompanies the road as far as Törmänen. In another 30km/19 miles a road goes off on the left to the summit of Kaunispää (438m/1437ft; view). The road then continues south through a region in which gold was found at some points in the bed of the river during the 19th century to Vuotso, a village of wooden houses. 37km/23 miles beyond this the road crosses the Kitinen and follows it to Sodankylä, from which Road 4 (E 75) continues south.

Side trip

Beyond the village of Vikajärvi Road 00 goes off on the left to Kemijärvi 60km/37 miles east on the north side of Lake Kemijärvi. From there a road runs north to the eastern slopes of Pyhätunturi (the "holy mountain"), from the highest peak of which (539m/1768ft) there are wide views of southern Lapland.

Main route

From Vikajärvi the road to Rovaniemi skirts Lake Olkkajärvi, crosses the **Arctic Circle** (Finnish Napapiiri), runs down through forest country and crosses the Ounasjoki near its junction with the Kemijoki, the longest and most abundantly flowing river in Finland. To the south of the confluence are the Ounaskoski rapids; to the east is Ounasvaara (204m/669ft; view). The road then comes to **Rovaniemi**, the administrative centre of Finnish Lapland, from which it is possible to continue to **Kemi**, on the Gulf of Bothnia.

13. Rovaniemi via Kemi to Oulu (about 230km/145 miles)

This route runs south from Rovaniemi on Road 4 (E 75), which beyond Kemi follows the coast of the Gulf of Bothnia fairly closely. The landscape of Finnish Lapland gives place to the flat wooded country in the north-west of the Finnish province of Oulu.

Main route

From **Rovaniemi** E 75 runs south-west along the banks of the Kemijoki via Hirvas (glacial pot-holes) and then through beautiful scenery to Muurola.

Variant

28km/17 miles beyond Muurola a road goes off on the left, crosses the Kemijoki and runs down the east bank by way of the village of Tervola to Kemi.

Main route

E 75 continues along the west bank of the Kemijoki. 16km/10 miles downstream, separated from the road by forest, are the Taivalkoski rapids.

Side trip

Just before E 75 runs into the Kemi–Tornio road a side road on the left leads in 3.5km/2 miles to the old parish church of Kemi, by the roadside beyond the railway. Built of undressed stone, it has ceiling paintings of scenes from Christ's Passion. From the embankment behind the church there are fine views of the Kemijoki and the town of Kemi.

Main route

E 75 now passes under the railway and comes to a T junction at which the road to the right (E 4) leads to the frontier town of **Tornio**, while E 75 turns left for Kemi and Oulu. This road goes over a dam on the Kemi-joki, which here flows into the Gulf of Bothnia, and comes to **Kemi**, a port on the Gulf of Bothnia (woodworking industry). Beyond Kemi E 75 runs close to the flat, wooded coast of the Gulf, of which, however, there are only occasional views. Beyond Simo the road runs past the wooden church of Haukipudas and the little town of Kello (timber stores), crosses the estuary of the Oulujoki on a number of bridges, and comes to **Oulu** (Swedish Uleåborg), chief town of the province of that name.

14. Oulu via Kuopio and Mikkeli to Helsinki
(about 700km/435 miles)

This route, on Roads 4 (E 75), 19 and 5 (partly E 63), runs south from Oulu through great expanses of forest and the Finnish Lakeland, crosses the Salpausselkä ridge, which bounds the lake district on the south, and continues to Helsinki, on the Gulf of Finland.

From **Oulu** E 75 runs south to a road junction at Pulkkila, where Road 19 goes off on the left and follows a winding course through the forests. At Pippola, on the right of the road, is a church with a free-standing belfry. Beyond this are occasional farms in clearings in the forest. 20km/12½ miles from the road junction is the lake of Pyhännänjärvi. The road continues to the village of Vieremä, which has a church with a deco-rated timber roof. Beyond this is a beautiful stretch of road, passing several lakes, after which Road 19 runs into Road 5 (E 63). *Main route*

From the junction with Road 5 a side trip can be made on this road (to left) to **Kajaani**, on the south bank of the Kajaanijoki near its outflow into the Oulujärvi (Lake Oulu). Elias Lönnrot, editor of the Finnish national epic "Kalevala", was district doctor in the town from 1833. North of Kajaani is Pöllyvaara (201m/659ft), from which there are wide panoramic views. *Side trip*

From the junction with Road 19 E 63 runs past the old wooden parish church of Iisalmi to the little town of that name. It then continues through an area of forest and past a number of lakes, and comes, via Lapinlahti and Siilinjärvi, to **Kuopio**, on a peninsula in the Kallavesi. Beyond this is the **Finnish Lakeland**. From Kuopio E 63 runs south-east to the industrial town of Varkaus and then, running through forest for much of the way, to **Mikkeli**, on a western arm of **Lake Saimaa**. Round Mikkeli is a popular skiing area. Some 100km/65 miles farther on is the attractive holiday resort of Heinola; north-west of the town is the large lake of Ruotsalainen. At the south end of Heinola the road crosses the Kyminjoki, which drains a large area of the Finnish Lakeland, the largest lake in which is Päijänne. The road then climbs gently up the Salpausselkä ridge. From **Lahti**, at the south end of the Vesijärvi, E 75 (motorway) runs south via Kerava to **Helsinki**, where a number of important roads meet. *Main route*

15. Helsinki via Turku and Vaasa to Oulu
(about 860km/535 miles)

This route (E 18, then Road 8 and finally R 75) begins by running west along the shores of the Gulf of Finland. From Turku it runs north-west and then north, close to the Gulf of Bothnia, to Oulu in northern Finland. Soon after leaving Helsinki it crosses the south-western out-liers of the Salpausselkä ridge.

Suggested Routes

Main route

From Helsinki the motorway runs west past the city's modern suburbs (possible side trips to the Gallén-Kallela Museum and to Espoo and the garden city of Tapiola). E 18 then runs through an area with numerous lakes to Salo, on the Uskelanjoki, and comes to a junction where a road goes off on the right to the village of Halikko, with an old stone church. The main road continues to Piikkiö and Kaarina.

Side trip

From Kaarina a country road runs south to Parainen by way of the island of Kuusisto (Swedish Kustö), at the east end of which are the remains of Kuusisto Castle. South of Parainen, amid a cluster of skerries, is the island of Stormälö, a popular bathing resort. Offshore is the island of Korpo (church with wood sculpture).

Main route

From Kaarina E 18 continues north-west to **Turku** (Swedish Åbo), the oldest town in Finland, at the outflow of the Aurajoki into the Gulf of Bothnia. From Turku Road 8 runs through an area of great historical interest, by way of Raisio (side road to the little town of Naantali, a popular bathing resort), Mynämäki and Laitila, from which a road runs south-west to the port of Uusikaupunki (Swedish Nystad) on the Gulf of Bothnia, where the peace ending the Northern War was signed in 1721. Beyond Laitila the road runs past a number of lakes to Rauma and **Pori** (Swedish Björneborg), near the mouth of the Kokemäenjoki. It then continues, at some distance from the coast, to Lapväärtti and (now E 12) **Vaasa** (Swedish Vasa).

Variant

Beyond Lapväärtti a road goes off on the left and crosses a bridge to reach Kristiinankaupunki (Swedish Kristinestad), a port situated on a peninsula in the Gulf of Bothnia. On Sundays and holidays the local women sometimes wear the old traditional costumes. From here a road runs north to Närpio (Swedish Närpes), from which there is a country road up the coast to Vaasa.

Main route

From Vaasa Road 8 continues north, running close to the much indented coast through farming country. To the west of the junction with Road 67 is Uusikaarlepyy (Swedish Nykarleby), with a fine wooden church. Farther north another side road runs west to Pietarsaari (Swedish Jakobstad), birthplace of the Finnish-Swedish poet Johan Ludvig Runeberg (1804–77). The main road continues past an inlet formed by skerries to **Kokkola** (Swedish Karleby), and then, hugging the coast, through a more thinly populated area to Kalajoki (beautiful sand-dunes). Farther up the coast is Raahe (Swedish Brahestad), with a statue of Per Brahe, who founded the town in 1649. North-east of Raahe Road 8 joins E 75, which runs through low-lying country to **Oulu** (Swedish Uleåborg).

Helsinki Cathedral and statue of Tsar Alexander II in Senate Square ▶

Sights from A to Z

**N.B.

Place-names in Norway and Sweden may be found either with or without the suffixed definite article -(e)n, -a or -(e)t.
In Norway, Sweden and Finland words such as "street", "river", etc., are usually suffixed to the name and do not appear as separate words. The Glossary of Geographical Terms on page 540 of this guide will be found useful in interpreting place-names of this kind.

Abisko   E 2

Country: **Sweden**
Province: Lapland
Altitude: 395m/1296ft
Post code: S–98024   Telephone code: 0980

Situation and
characteristics

Abisko lies in northern Sweden on Lake Torneträsk, a mountain lake 71km/44 miles long, up to 9km/6 miles wide and 164m/538ft deep. It is reached on the Lapland Railway, which runs from Kiruna to Narvik, or on a road running parallel to the railway. Abisko, situated on the northern edge of the Abisko National Park, is the starting-point of the Kungsleden (Royal Trail: see Lapland). The midnight sun is visible here from June 13th to July 4th.

★Torneträsk

Abisko depends almost entirely on the tourist trade. From the tourist hotel, situated on a 15m/50ft deep canyon-like gorge on the Abiskojokk, there are wide views of Lake Torneträsk and the mountains. There are motorboat trips on the lake.

Surroundings

Njula

A cableway 1958m/2140yd long and a marked footpath run up Mt Njula or Nuolja (1199m/3934ft). From the summit of the hill the midnight sun can be seen from May 31st to July 18th.

Pallemtjåkko
Nissontjårre

15km/9 miles south of Abisko are two other mountains, Pallemtjåkko (1740m/5709ft) and Nissontjårre (1745m/5725ft), which offer rewarding climbs. Between Nissontjårre and Tjuonjatjåkko (1582m/5191ft), to the east, is the saddle known as the Lapporten ("Lapps' Gate").

Abisko to Narvik by Rail

A trip on the Lapland Railway (known beyond the Norwegian frontier as the Ofot Line) to Narvik (see entry) is an experience not to be missed: for the best views, sit on the right. The line runs under Mt Njula in the longest tunnel in Sweden (1100m/1200yd) and crosses the Rakkasjokk on a high viaduct.

Björkliden

The train then comes to the little town of Björkliden (alt. 420m/1378ft), in a beautiful setting. 20 minutes' walk to the south-east is the picturesque Rakkaskårtje waterfall, formed by the Rakkasjokk at its entry into Lake Torneträsk. The line follows the shores of the lake for another 5km/3 miles and then turns west.

After passing through the Tornehamn Tunnel (536m/580yd long) the train comes to Kopparåsen station, beyond which the landscape shows the typical scouring effect of glaciers. It then continues to Vassijaure and the frontier station, Riksgränsen (alt. 520m/1706m), in a popular skiing area. The mountains here are almost completely treeless. 2km/1¼ miles beyond the Riksgränsen station is the Norwegian frontier, beyond which the line continues to Narvik.

Åland Islands (Ahvenanmaa)

E 5

Country: **Finland**
Autonomous region: Landskapet Åland
  (Ahvenanmaan maakunta)
Area: 1505sq.km/580sq. miles
Population: 24,000
Post code: FIN–22100
Telephone code: 928

Car ferries: from Stockholm, Grisslehamn and Kapellskår (Sweden); from Turku and Naantali (Finland).
  Air services: from Stockholm and from Helsinki and Turku.

Transportation

The Åland Islands (Finnish Ahvenanmaa) lie between Finland and Sweden at the south end of the Gulf of Bothnia, separating it from the Baltic. To the west of the islands, extending between them and Sweden, is the Åland Sea, some 40km/25 miles across; to the east is the arm of the sea known as Skiftet. The group consists of no fewer than 6554 islands and stacks, only 80 of which are inhabited.
  The islands are a popular holiday area, particularly with Swedes.

Situation and characteristics

The Åland Islands, off the south-west coast of Finland

Kastelholm Castle

Panoramic view of Ålesund

The Åland Islands, along with the whole of Finland, passed into Russian hands in 1809. After the First World War there was a movement for union with Sweden, but in 1921 the islands were assigned by the League of Nations to Finland, the population being granted full self-government, permanent demilitarisation and the exclusive use of the Swedish language. Finland has always recognised the islands' autonomy and indeed has extended it: for example the Åland Islands now issue their own stamps. The islanders are proud of their independence and do not like to be called Finns.

The main sources of income are shipping (second largest tonnage in Finland), agriculture and tourism.

Sights

On the main island of Åland is the only town in the group, Mariehamn (Finnish Maarianhamina; pop. 11,000). Situated on a promontory at the south end of the island, it is a very popular seaside resort. In the centre of the town, in Norra Esplanadsgatan, stands the church of St Göran (1927; stained glass). In Storagatan is the Åland Museum (archaeology and cultural history), and in the West Harbour are the Maritime Museum and an old sailing ship, the four-masted barque "Pommern", which is also a museum.

Mariehamn

3km/2 miles west of Mariehamn lies the beautiful Ramsholmen nature reserve, with a landscape of meadows and woodland very typical of the islands.

Ramsholmen

23km/14 miles north-east of Mariehamn by way of Jomala (church with Romanesque frescos) is the 14th century stronghold of Kastelholm, which until 1634 was the residence of the governor of Åland. In the mid 18th century it was badly damaged by fire. One wing which survived the fire now houses the Åland Museum of Cultural History. Nearby are the Jan Karlsgården open-air museum and a historic old prison known as the Vita

Kastelholm
Transportation

Ålesund

Björn (White Bear). A few kilometres north of Kastelholm is the stone-built church of Sund (13th c.), with notable sculptural decoration.

Bomarsund

11km/7 miles east of Kastelholm is the fort of Bomarsund, built by the Russians about 1830 and destroyed by British and French forces in 1854, during the Crimean War.

Saltvik

23km/14 miles north of Mariehamn (via Jomala, then road on left before Kastelholm) we come to Saltvik, with a church which is one of the oldest on the island. It has a font of Gotland limestone, a triumphal cross and a 15th century reredos. There are a number of prehistoric sites in the area.

Orrdalsklint

North-east of Saltvik is the Orrdalsklint (132m/433ft), the highest point on the island. Another good viewpoint is the Kasberg (116m/381ft), to the north of Saltvik.

Finström
Geta

20km/12½ miles north of Mariehamn (road on left beyond Jomala) is Finström, with a church containing medieval wall paintings (signs of the Zodiac). 21km/13 miles farther north is Geta, the most northerly parish on the island; fine view from Sottuna Hill.

Hammarland and Eckerö

21km/13 miles north-west of Mariehamn is the red granite church of Hammarland, which may date from the 12th century. In nearby Eckerö, housed in an old post office (designed by C. L. Engel), is a Postal Museum.

Every summer (June) a traditional mailboat race to Grisslehamn in Sweden is held.

Lemland

On an island 15km/9 miles south-east of Mariehamn is the village of Lemland. Near the ruins of the Lemböte Chapel can be seen a Viking cemetery, one of the largest on Åland. Skerry garden.

Kökar

Reached by ferry from Korpo (74km/46 miles south-west of Turku) or Långnäs (28km/17 miles east of Mariehamn) is the sailing enthusiasts' paradise of Kökar (pop. 300; Sandvik and Hellsö boating harbours), far out in the skerries. It has a fine church of grey stone, built on the ruins of a Franciscan friary. Hotel, restaurant, camping site.

Ålesund   B 4

Country: **Norway**
Region: Central Norway
Population: 40,000   Post code: N–6000

Situation and characteristics

The busy port and commercial town of Ålesund in western Norway lies on the islands of Nørvøy, Aspøy and Hessa, far out in the coastal fringe of skerries. It is Norway's principal fishing port, with fish-processing plants, as well as shipyards and clothing factories. After a great fire in 1904 which destroyed almost all the town's old timber houses it was rebuilt in stone, and has many Art Nouveau houses fronts dating from that period.

Town

Aspøy
Nørvøy

The two main islands on which the town is built, Aspøy and Nørvøy, are linked by a bridge. Features of interest on Aspøy are the church (1909) with fine frescos and stained glass. Not far from the church is an aquarium with fish and sea creatures from the North Sea. On Nørvøy is the town centre, with hotels, the Post Office and the Municipal Museum.

Harbour

The harbour lies between the two islands, facing north and sheltered by the Skansen peninsula which projects from Nørvøy. On Skansenkai is the landing-stage used by vessels of the Hurtigrute (fast coastal service: see entry).

Park

On the east side of the town in a beautiful park is a 7m/23ft high standing stone carved with a likeness of Kaiser Wilhelm II – commemorating the help given by Germany after the 1904 fire. Also in the park is a statue of Rollo (Rolf the Ganger), the conqueror of Normandy, who came from the Ålesund area; the statue was presented by the city of Rouen in 1911.

To the east of the park is Aksla, a hill 189m/620ft high with a steep path running up to the top. On the nearer summit is a *fjellstue* (mountain inn) from which there are fine views of the town, the sea, the islands and the hills of Sunnmøre to the south-east. The fjellstue can also be reached on a road which branches off Borgundvei.

Aksla

★★View

Surroundings

There are numerous motor vessels sailing to the outer islands and the small fjords to the south of the town. The islands of Ellingsøy and Valderøy (with the Vigra airstrip) are reached by a long tunnel under the sea.

On the west side of Valderøy (10 min.) is Skjonghelleren cave (130m/140yd long), which was inhabited in Neolithic times.

Valderøy

On the island of Giske (20 min.) stands a chapel, partly built of white marble, which is thought to date from the 12th century.

Giske

South-west of Ålesund, on the island of Runde, is the most southerly seabird cliff in Norway, the nesting-place of some 700,000 birds of 40 different species.

Runde

It is worth taking the ferry across the Storfjord from Solevågen to Festøy (Road 1) for the sake of the magnificent view into the Hjørundfjord.

Hjørundfjord

On a peninsula 4km/2½ miles east of Ålesund town centre lies the village of Borgund, with an 11th century church rebuilt in its original form after its destruction in the 1904 fire. Also of interest is the open-air Sunnmøre Museum, with old houses and boats and a section devoted to the fishing industry.

Borgund

Alingsås

D 6

Country: **Sweden**
Province: Västergötland
Population: 32,000
Post code: S–441.. Telephone code: 0322

Alingsås, the Swedish "potato town" (Potato Festival, annually in June), lies on the north side of Lake Mjörn. The town received its municipal charter in 1619. An industrial centre (weaving, etc.) and the seat of lawcourts, it acquired a considerable reputation when Jonas Alströmer and Christoffer Polhem established a textile mill in the town.

Situation and characteristics

Alingsås has preserved its small-town charm. It is famed for its attractive timber houses and its numerous inviting cafés and cake-shops. In the market square can be seen a bust of Jonas Alströmer (1685–1761). Here too are the old Arsenal (1631), now a museum, and the Storken craft centre, with a potter's workshop, a weaving room, a carpenter's shop, a knitwear workshop and a café. In the park of Nolhaga Castle Alströmer grew potatoes and tobacco for the first time in Sweden.

Town

Surroundings

South-west of the town on the Göteborg road (E 3), at Floda, stands Nääs Castle (19th c.). Situated in a beautiful park on a peninsula, it now houses a college of arts and crafts and a craft museum. The 19th century interior is well preserved.

Nääs Castle

Alta

Lerum	Lerum, in a beautiful setting on the shores of Lake Aspen, has a church with ceiling paintings. Nearby is the Härskogen nature reserve. At Jonsered the road enters the province of Bohuslän.
Anten Gräsnäs	North-west of Alingsås (Road 180), at Brobacka, the river linking Lakes Anten and Mörn flows between steep rock walls. During the summer an old-world railway (with an engine and coaches dating from the turn of the century) runs from Anten to Gräsnäs (12km/7½ miles). The ruined castle of Gräsnäs (recorded in the 14th century under the name of Loo) stands in a park laid out in the English style.

Alta   E 2

	Country: **Norway** Region: Northern Norway Population: 10,000 Post code: N–9500
Situation and characteristics	Alta, the largest town in the thinly populated county of Finnmark, lies at the head of the Altafjord on the banks of the Alta, the best known salmon river in Norway. It has direct air connections with Oslo and is on the main coast road (E 6). Its economic importance lies in fishing and fish-processing and mining and, in the educational field, it has two technical colleges. Although the town lies in latitude 70° north it has a mild inland climate which offers excellent conditions for agriculture and forestry. The midnight sun can be seen here from May 16th to July 26th, and between November 24th and January 18th the sun is not visible at all. Alta is served by the coastal ships of the Hurtigrute (see entry). There are bus services from here to the North Cape and Hammerfest (see entries) and to the Lapp towns of Karasjok (see entry) and Kautokeino. For information about services enquire locally.
Sights ★★ Rock carvings	Excavations have brought to light traces of human settlement dating back 9000 years – though how men could survive here during the Ice Age is unexplained. In the 1970s seven areas with some 3000 rock carvings were discovered here. They date from between 6200 and 2500 years ago and show a wide range of subject. The carvings at Hjemmeluft were added to the UNESCO list of specially protected world heritage monuments in 1985.
Alta Museum	The Alta Museum (open: daily in summer) is responsible for the Hjemmeluft excavations and has an interesting collection of material on the local slate-mining industry, the river and fjord fisheries and the domestic art of the Lapps. At Peska (15km/9 miles south of the town centre) visitors can get a first-hand view of slate-mining methods and the life and work of the local population.
River Alta Sausto Canyon	The main attraction of Alta is the river Alta with its varied facilities for recreation and excursions. The Sausto Canyon offers a fascinating view of the forces of nature; it can be traversed either on foot or by boat (with guide).
Salmon fishing	The most popular sporting activity on the river Alta is salmon fishing (from June 22nd onwards). Anglers from all over the world come here to try their skill (special permit required).

Surroundings

Haldde	At Haldde (alt 1000m/3300ft), west of Alta, is the oldest observatory for watching the aurora borealis (in operation from 1899 to 1927; restored).
Kåfjord	On the road to Haldde, in the commune of Kåfjord, is an old copper-mine, now closed down. In the middle of the 19th century Kåfjord was the largest

Rock carving: men on a ship

Rock carving: ornaments

commune in the province of Finnmark. The village church, built in 1837 by a British mining company, was completely restored in 1969. During the Second World War the German battleship "Tirpitz" hid in the Kåfjord, where it was attacked by British mini-submarines in 1943.

Ängelholm   D 7

Country: **Sweden**
Province: Skåne
Population: 33,000
Post code: S–262..   Telephone code: 0431

Situation and characteristics	Ängelholm, lying north of Helsingborg at the head of the inlet of Skäldervik in the Skagerrak, was founded in 1516 by King Christian II of Denmark, but its origins go farther back to the medieval town of Luntertun, near Rönne Bro, on Skäldervik, of which there now remains only a ruined church. Christian moved the site of the town farther inland for defensive reasons. Strategically situated near the mouth of the Rönneå, it was until the beginning of the 18th century a bone of contention between Denmark and Sweden.

Since the 16th century Ängelholm has been a favourite haunt of salmon fishers. Now an industrial town, it has a military airfield, the base of a squadron of the Swedish air force, as well as a civil airfield.

Town
Ängelholm has preserved its small-town aspect, with narrow little streets and low houses. In the market square (Stortorget) are the old Town Hall (1775; renovated) and the church (originally 1516; altered in the 19th century). To the south-east, on the Rönneå, are the new Town Hall (1975) and the landing-stage used by the tourist boat "Laxen" ("Salmon"). In Tingstorget, housed in Sweden's oldest state prison (1780), is the Craft Museum, with a potter's workshop.

Hembygdspark
Beach
North-west of the town centre lies the Hembygdspark, with a museum and a small zoo. On Skälderviken is a long sandy beach.

Surroundings

Vegeholm
6km/4 miles south of the town, set in a large park on an island in the Vegeå, is Vegeholm Castle (16th c.), with two square towers. From here Road 112 runs west to Höganas and Mölle (see Helsingborg, Surroundings).

Torekov
A road goes north along the coast to Barkåkra (12th c. church) and Torekov, at the tip of the Bjäre peninsula. This little fishing village is now a popular seaside resort. Features of interest are the Maritime Museum, housed in an old sailing ship, and the Rosa Ljung ceramic factory (ornaments).

Väderö
From Torekov there are boat services to the island of Väderö (area 3sq.km/1sq. mile). The whole island is a nature reserve, the haunt of large numbers of birds.

Hovs Hallar
nature reserve
From Torekov Road 115 runs east to Hov. A rewarding side trip from this road is to the Hovs Hallar nature reserve, where the Hallandsåsen range of hills ends abruptly on the coast, with striking rock formations. From here the "Italian Road" winds its way eastward to a beautiful park, Norrvikens Trädgårdar.

Båstad
Båstad (pop. 2500), 4km/2½ miles east, is one of Sweden's most modern and most fashionable seaside resorts. St Mary's Church dates from the 15th century. International tennis tournaments are held here.

Arctic Circle (Polsirkelen/Polcirkeln/Napapiiri)

Countries: **Norway, Sweden** and **Finland**

The Arctic and Antarctic Circles are imaginary lines round the earth in latitudes 66.5° north and 66.5° south. The Arctic Circle, which is the one concerning Scandinavia, is the latitude beyond which the length of the day so increases in summer that the sun never sinks below the horizon, producing the phenomenon known as the midnight sun. In climatic terms it separates the northern temperate zone from the polar zone.

In northern Norway the Arctic Circle (Polsirkelen) runs just north of Mo i Rana, in Sweden (Polcirkeln) near Jokkmokk in Lapland, in Finland (Napapiiri) a little to the north of Rovaniemi.

The different lengths of day and night in all latitudes except on the Equator are due to the angle of 23°5' between the earth's equatorial plane and the plane of its orbit.

At the summer solstice (June 22nd) the apparent course of the sun on the Arctic Circle reaches its greatest northern declination (i.e. its greatest angular distance north of the celestial equator), so that at midnight the sun is still in the sky. In a clear sky this midnight sun is an impressive sight, but even when the sun is obscured by mist or clouds its glowing red ball in the night sky is a memorable spectacle.

★Midnight sun

Exactly on the Arctic Circle this phenomenon of the polar day is visible only on one night in the year, but its duration increases steadily towards the north. At the North Pole the polar day should in theory last exactly half a

Polar day

On the Arctic Circle in northern Norway

year, but the refraction of the sun's rays in the earth's atmosphere makes it slightly longer than this.

Moreover the altitude from which it is observed also affects the length of time during which the midnight sun can be seen, since the published data are calculated for sea level. Thus an observer on a hill can see the midnight sun some distance south of the Arctic Circle.

"Nordic Cap"

The parts of Norway, Sweden and Finland north of the Arctic Circle – the "Land of the Midnight Sun" – are also known in Scandinavia as the "Nordic Cap" (Nordkalotten, Finnish Pohjoiskalotti).

★Northern Lights

The Arctic Circle also marks the approximate southern boundary of the Northern Lights or Aurora Borealis which can be observed on clear winter nights. This phenomenon is caused when electrically charged particles emitted by the sun are caught up in the earth's magnetic field. They then produce striking light effects in the thin ionised upper atmosphere at heights of between 70 and 1000km (40 and 620 miles). The sky is lit up by bluish arcs of light, glowing coronas and shimmering curtains of radiance flaring over the sky in constant movement, offering the fortunate spectator an unforgettable experience.

Atlantic Highway/Atlanterhavsveien   B 4

Country: Norway
Region: Central Norway

Between the towns of Molde (see entry) and Kristiansund (see Sunndal), along the notorious Hustadvika channel, lie innumerable islands which until quite recently could be reached only by ferry. The construction of the

The Atlantic Highway on the west coast of Norway

Atlantic Highway, exactly 8474m/9268yd long, has been not only a vital improvement in the infrastructure in this maze of skerries but also a great attraction for anglers, diving enthusiasts and visitors who want to get as close as possible to the sea. This new road, one of the most fascinating coast roads in the whole of Europe, with eight bridges of varying length, has opened up a paradise whose particular charms lie below the surface of the sea. On a windless day there are magnificent views of the open sea, while when a strong north-west wind is blowing there is an awe-inspiring display of the wild forces of nature.

On either side of the Atlantic Highway are *fiskevær* (fishing villages) in which visitors can rent houses. At the turn of the century the countless little islands supported a population of around 120 living solely from fishing, but now the life of the islands is dominated from spring to autumn by hosts of holidaymakers and anglers. Within easy reach of the Atlantic Highway are excellent facilities for camping, bathing and walking.

Fishing villages

In the commune of Fræna, on the south side of the Atlantic Highway, is the little fishing village of Bud, where in 1553 Norway's last archbishop called together the Norwegian Diet of peasants and burghers in order to liberate Norway from its dependence on Denmark. The attempt failed, and four years later the archbishop was forced to flee from Norway. The wooden village church dates from 1717.

Bud

The island of Bjørnsund, north-west of Bud, can be reached in summer by motorboat. As late as 1950 it was still an important centre of the fish trade: it is now inhabited only in summer.

Bjørnsund

On the mainland north of Molde is the Trollkirka ("Trolls' Church"), the largest and most impressive of the many limestone caves in this area: 70m/230ft long and up to 7m/23ft high, with a waterfall. Visitors should have stout footwear and a torch.

★Trollkirka

Bergen   B 5

Country: **Norway**
Region: Southern Norway
Population: 210,000   Post code: N–5000

Visitors travelling by car should note that in the city centre cars are admitted only on payment of a toll and that parking is permitted only in marked parking places.

N.B.

Bergen, Norway's second largest city, lies in the inner reaches of the Byfjord. It is the largest port on the west coast of Norway, with a considerable merchant fleet and several large shipyards, the administrative centre of the Bergen district and the county of Hordaland, the seat of the Lutheran bishop of Bjørgvin and an educational centre, with a university and a commercial college. Surrounded by a ring of hills (up to 643m/2110ft), partly forest-covered, with its houses reaching up the lower slopes, Bergen is one of the most attractive towns in Norway. In spite of its northern latitude (60°24' – rather farther north than the southern tip of Greenland) its humid and unusually mild climate enables all the usual deciduous trees of Europe to flourish and gives it a rich and varied growth of vegetation. It is noted for its high rainfall (over 80in./2000mm annually, compared with Oslo's 30in./750mm), the result of its maritime climate and the surrounding hills. The Hurtigrute (see entry) and the mounntain railway to Oslo also start from Bergen.

Situation and characteristics

The oldest parts of the town lie in a semicircle round the busy harbour, Vågen, and extend up the slopes of the Fløyfjell to the north-east. Like most

The town

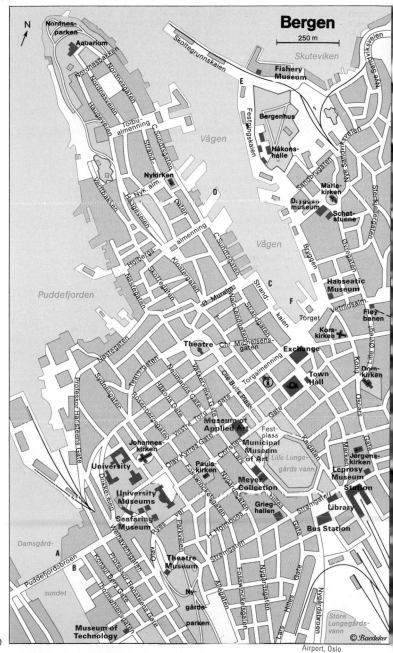

Bergen

250 m

Nordnes-
parken

Aquarium

Skoltegrunnskaien

Skuteviken

Fishery
Museum

E

Vågen

Bergenhus

Håkons-
halle

Nykirken

D

Maria-
kirken

Bryggen
museum

Schøt-
stuene

Vågen

Puddefjorden

Hanseatic
Museum

C

F

Torget

Fløy-
banen

Korskirken

Theatre

Exchange

Dom-
kirken

Town
Hall

Museum of
Applied Art

Johannes-
kirken

University

Municipal
Museum
of Art

Lille Lunge-
gårds vann

Jørgens-
kirken

Leprosy
Museum

Pauls-
kirken

Meyer
Collection

Station

University
Museums

Grieg-
hallen

Library

Seafaring
Museum

Bus Station

Damsgård-

A

B

Theatre
Museum

sundet

Puddefjordsbroen

Ny-
gårds-
parken

Store
Lungegårds
vann

Museum of
Technology

© Baedeker

Airport, Oslo

Scandinavian towns, Bergen has suffered repeatedly from devastating fires, the most serious being those of 1702 and 1916; in the 1916 fire several hundred houses in the timber-built commercial district to the south of Vågen were destroyed. These frequent destructions have left little of the old Bergen, and the pattern of the town centre is now set by its wide streets and stone buildings. The Nordnes and Fløyfjell districts, however, have preserved something of the atmosphere of the past, with their wooden houses and the narrow lanes known to the local people as *smug*. Only in the northern districts of Skuteviken and Sandviken are there still a few of the old seafront warehouses (*søgårder*) once so characteristic of Bergen – large timber buildings with a crane on the harbour front. Unfortunately many of the old warehouses which still survived were destroyed in great fires in 1955 and 1958.

About the year 1070 Olav Kyrre granted a municipal charter to the port settlement of Bjørgvin ("hill pasture") on the east side of Vågen, which was already a place of some consequence. Thereafter the town developed rapidly, becoming an occasional residence of the king. In 1233 Håkon Håkonsson's hereditary right to the throne was recognised at a national Diet held here.

History

As early as 1236 there were permanent German trading establishments in Bergen. The town's real rise to prosperity, however, began with the establishment of a Hanseatic counting-house, first recorded in 1343. In virtue of a privilege granted by the Danish kings, under which the fishermen of the northern territories were required to bring their catches to Bergen and to no other port, the German merchants soon gained control of all Norwegian trade. Their employees lived in a special quarter of the town on the "German Bridge" (Tyskebryggen), with sixteen long narrow houses which served also as warehouses. Each house was headed by a *bygherre* and was divided into several *stuer* ("rooms"), each belonging to a particular owner.

In 1559 the power of the Hanseatic merchants was destroyed by the feudal lord, Kristoffer Valkendorf, but the counting-house remained in existence for another 200 years, until in 1764 the last *stue* was sold to a Norwegian.

During the Second World War Bergen suffered considerable damage; among the buildings destroyed was the old Theatre in Sverresgate – Norway's first theatre, founded in 1851 by the celebrated fiddler Ole Bull, of which Ibsen (1851–57) and Bjørnson (1858–60) were managers.

Throughout its history the prosperity of Bergen has been based on fishing and on commerce, particularly the trade in fish and fish products. In the 17th century Bergen was still of much greater importance as a commercial centre than Copenhagen, and at the beginning of the 19th century it had a larger population than the capital, Christiania (now Oslo).

Shipping and commerce

Until the 20th century Bergen remained the leading centre of the Norwegian fish trade, and fish and fish products are still important to its economy. In more recent years the establishment of large shipping companies and numerous canning and preserving plants near the fishing grounds has fostered the development of other centres of the fish trade. Nevertheless Bergen's outgoing trade (steel, machinery, etc.) is second only to that of Oslo.

LEGEND FOR THE TOWN PLAN (opposite)

A Express coastal ships to Northern Norway (Hurtigrute)

B Ships to Sognefjord and Nordfjord

C High speed catamarans to Sognefjord and Nordfjord

D High speed catamarans to Haugesund and Stavanger to the Hardangerfjord and Sunnhordland

E Ferries to Newcastle, Iceland, Faroes and the Shetland Islands

F Excursion boats

View of Bergen harbour

Harbour Area

Market Square

At the south-east end of the main harbour, Vågen, is the Market Square (Torget), with the quays where the fishermen land their catches in the early morning. The picturesque fish market is a fascinating spectacle (weekdays 8am–3pm). On the south-east side of the square is a statue (by John Børjeson) of the writer Ludvig Holberg, creator of the Danish-Norwegian comedy (b. Bergen 1684, d. Copenhagen 1754). Behind it is the Exchange. At the upper end of the Vetrlidsalmenning, which runs north-east from the square, is the lower station of the funicular (Fløybanen) up the Fløyfjell.

★Bryggen

Along the east side of the harbour runs Bryggen (formerly Tyskebryggen, the "German Bridge"). Here once stood the houses of the German merchants, later increasingly replaced by stone-built warehouses in a style modelled on that of the Hanseatic period.

★Hanseatic Museum

Of the old merchants' houses only the one at the south end of Bryggen, the early 18th century Finnegård, has been preserved in its original condition. Since 1872 it has housed the Hanseatic Museum, which gives an excellent impression of the interior of a Hanseatic merchant's establishment, with displays of weapons, domestic furnishings and equipment, mostly dating from the last days of the counting-house. The ground floor was used for the storage of goods; on the first floor were the merchant's office, dining room and bedroom, and on the second the sleeping quarters of the apprentices and clerks.

Bryggen Museum

The Bryggen Museum displays material recovered in excavations carried out between 1955 and 1968.

St Mary's Church

North-west of the Bryggen Museum stands the twin-towered Romanesque and Gothic St Mary's Church (Maria Kirke; 12th and 13th c., pulpit and altar 17th c.). This was the church of the Hanseatic merchants from 1408 to 1766, and services were still held in German until 1868. In the churchyard are a number of German graves.

Bryggen, the old merchants' quarter

Opposite the church, at Øvregate 50, are the Schøtstuene, the assembly rooms of the Hanseatic merchants, which were heated in winter.

Schøtstuene

Bryggen is continued to the north-west by the Festningskai, on the north side of which is the old fortress of Bergenhus, formerly commanding the entrance to the harbour. At the south end of the fortress, on the quay, is the Rosenkrantz Tower, built by Erik Rosenkrantz in 1562–67 round an earlier 13th century structure; it was severely damaged by the explosion of a German munition ship in 1944 but later rebuilt. Behind it is the Håkonshalle, begun in English Gothic style by King Håkon Håkonsson in 1247; thereafter it fell into disrepair and was restored in 1880–95 and again in 1957–61. Above the Bergenhus fortress are the walls of the Sverresborg, built about 1660 on the remains of a castle of King Sverre.

Bergenhus

To the north of the fortress are the old districts of Skuteviken and Sandviken. In Sandviken is the Open-Air Museum of Old Bergen (Gamle Bergen), with old Bergen houses.

Old Bergen Open-Air Museum

On the Bontelabo, near the quay used by the ferries to Iceland and the Faroes, can be found the interesting Fishery Museum (Fiskerimuseet), which tells the story of the Norwegian fishing industry.

Fishery Museum

In the north-west of the town, at the tip of the peninsula between Vågen and the Puddefjord, is Nordnespark (view), with the fine Bergen Aquarium, one of the largest in northern Europe.

★ Aquarium

South-west of the market square are Bergen's main shopping streets, with a well designed modern shopping centre, Galleriet.

City Centre

From the north end of the market square Kong Oscarsgate runs south-east past the Korskirke (Holy Cross Church, founded 1170; present building 1593) to the Cathedral (Domkirke), originally a monastic church built in

Cathedral

133

Fishmarket, with flowers for sale

1248, rebuilt in 1537 and restored in 1870; notable features are the doorway in the tower and the beautiful Gothic windows.

Leprosy Museum

At the lower end of Kong Oscarsgate is the interesting Leprosy Museum, on the site of a medieval leper hospital, which illustrates Norway's contribution to international leprosy research.

Kong Oscarsgate ends a little way east of the railway station at an old town gate (1628). Outside the gate, to the right, is an old cemetery with the grave of the fiddler Ole Bull, marked by a large black urn.

Grieg Hall

South-west of the Cathedral, in Rådstuplass, stands the Old Town Hall, a small 16th century building. To the south of this is the Lille Lungegårdsvann (lake), near the east end of which, adjoining the station, is the Municipal Library. Farther south-west, in Strømgate, is the Grieg Hall (Grieghallen), an impressive example of modern architecture world-famed for its excellent acoustics (concerts, opera and ballet).

Rasmus Meyer Collection

On the south side of the lake, at Rasmus Meyers Allé 7, is the Rasmus Meyer Collection, which was bequeathed to the city in 1923 by the businessman of that name. The collection includes pictures by Norwegian artists from 1814 to 1914 (J. C. Dahl, H. Gude, E. Munch, G. Munthe).

Municipal Museum of Art

Close by, at Rasmus Meyers Allé 3, is the Municipal Museum of Art, with a collection of Norwegian art of the last 150 years (including J. C. Dahl and Edvard Munch) as well as European art.

In the same building are the Bergen Art Union (periodic exhibitions of contemporary art) and the Sterner Collection, which includes works by well known modern artists including Munch, Picasso and Klee.

Museum of Applied Art

Some 200m/220yd north-west, at the south end of the Municipal Park, is the Vestlandske Kunstindustrimuseum (known as "Permanenten"), with rare porcelain and pottery, Bergen goldsmith's work and modern Norwegian applied and decorative art. The museum is at present closed for reconstruction.

From here Christiesgate runs south, passing St Paul's Church (Paulskirken; R.C.), to the hill of Sydneshaugen, on which are the University, the Botanic Garden and the University museums: in the old building the Natural History Museum, in the new building the Historical Museum; also a Seafaring Museum.

University (museums)

South-east of the University campus lies the beautiful Nygårdspark, near the south end of which is the Unicorn Fountain (by Gustav Vigeland).

Nygårdsparken

From the University museums the Puddefjord Bridge (Puddefjordsbroen) leads to the southern districts of the city. South-east of the bridge, in Thormøhlensgate, is the Museum of Technology (old vehicles, ship models, etc.).

Museum of Technology

To the north of the Museum of Applied Art extends the small Municipal Park, near the north end of which is a statue (by J. Vik, 1917) of the Bergen-born composer Edvard Grieg (1843–1907). West of the park is the long, narrow Ole Bulls Plass, with a monument (by Stephan Sinding, 1901) to another native of Bergen, the "king of fiddlers", Ole Bull (1810–80). At the west end of the square is the handsome National Theatre (Nasjonale Scene; 1906–09); in the gardens is a bronze statue (by G. Vigeland, 1917) of the dramatist Bjørnstjerne Bjørnson (1832–1910).

Monuments Theatre

Surroundings

North-east of the town rises the Fløyfjell (319m/1047ft), from which there are magnificent views of Bergen and the surrounding area, particularly in the early morning or when the sun is setting. The hill can be climbed either on foot (about 3km/2 miles) or by means of the funicular (Fløybanen) from the Vetrlidsalmenning (10 minutes; the line runs up through a 150m/160yd long tunnel and, after the Fjellveien station, another tunnel 75m/80yd long). From the upper station of the funicular, Fløyen (313m/1027ft), there are superb views of the city and the coastal scenery, extending beyond the islands of Askøy and Sotra to the open sea.

Fløyfjell

★★ Views

From the Fløyen station a road (30 minutes' walk) runs north-east over the plateau, which becomes steadily barer, to the foot of the Blåmann (551m/1808ft). There is a footpath to the top of the hill, from which there are fine panoramic views, particularly by evening light. The somewhat higher peak to the rear is not worth the climb. The road continues to the radio station on the Rundemann (556m/1824ft; 30 minutes' climb). From the Fjellvei, which runs round the slopes of the Fløyfjell, there are fine views; at its south-eastern end, some 25 minutes' walk from the funicular station, is the Bellevue Restaurant.

Blåmann

South-east of Bergen is another hill, Ulriken (643m/2110ft), offering far-ranging views. It is reached by cableway (lower station at Haukeland), or can be climbed in about 2 hours.

Ulriken

Some 6km/4 miles from the city centre is the Fantoft stave church, brought here from its original site at Fortun in 1884. The church was destroyed by fire in 1992 but is being rebuilt in its original form (completion expected 1994).

Fantoft stave church

To the south of the town are some of the attractions which have contributed to Bergen's reputation as the cultural capital of Norway. Among them is Troldhaugen, home of Edvard Grieg (see Introduction, Famous People), which gives some feeling of the life and work of the world-famous Norwegian composer.

★ Troldhaugen

Troldhaugen, once the home of Edvard Grieg

Lysøy

On Lysøy, an island in the suburb of Fana, is the villa (built 1872–73) of the famous Norwegian fiddler Ole Bull, a medley of different architectural styles.

★Lyse Abbey

Close by are the ruins of Lyse Abbey, the first Cistercian house in Norway, founded in 1146 by monks from York. Excavations were carried out here in 1822 and 1838, and the remains give a vivid impression of monastic life in the Middle Ages.

See also Sognefjord, Hardangerfjord, Nordfjord, Hardangervidda.

Bodø   D 3

Country: **Norway**
Region: Central Norway. Population: 35,000
Post code: N–8000

Situation and characteristics

The Norwegian port of Bodø, chief town of Nordland county, lies in the Saltfjord, north of the Arctic Circle. From the beginning of June to the middle of July the sun never sets here. The town received its municipal charter in 1816, but its development was slow until the second half of the 19th century, when the herring fisheries gave it a boost.

During the Second World War Bodø suffered heavy damage in the fighting of May 1940, when almost the whole town centre was destroyed by fire. Rebuilt in modern style, it is now a lively commercial town, with a number of factories, a shipyard and several technical colleges.

In addition to its commercial harbour, which is busy throughout the year, Bodø has a large pleasure harbour which has contributed to the international atmosphere of the town. It also prides itself on being the musical capital of northern Norway.

Bodø harbour

Bodø is linked with the important European highway E 6 by a road to Fauske; there are two trains daily from Trondheim on the Nordland line, which was extended to Bodø in 1962; the fast ships of the Hurtigrute (see entry) from Bergen to Kirkenes call in here; and there is now an airstrip linking the town with the network of Scandinavian air services. There are air and ferry services from Bodø to the Lofoten Islands (see entry).

Communications

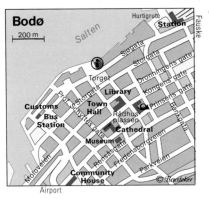

In Rådhusplassen is the Town Hall (1959), with a tower from which there are extensive views. Close by is the Cathedral (1956; fine stained glass by Aagen Storstein), with a separate belfry. To the south of the Cathedral is the Nordland County Museum (Nordlandfylkesmuseum), with sections devoted to agriculture, local crafts and fisheries, together with a collection of prehistoric and medieval material.

Town

Surroundings

3km/2 miles east of the town centre stands the old stone-built church of Bodin (12th c.), which has a fine Baroque altarpiece of 1670. Louis-Philippe,

Bodin church

Bohuslän

Duke of Orleans and later king of France (1830–48), stayed in the pastor's house on a journey to the North Cape.

Rønvikfjell

4km/2½ miles north of Bodø is the Rønvikfjell (155m/509ft; mountain hut), from which there are panoramic views. From here it is a 2 hours' walk on a waymarked path to the summit of the Løpsfjell (603m/1978ft), with a view extending to the Lofotens, 100m/60 miles away; to the east can be seen the glacier-covered Sulitjelma (1913m/6277ft), 90km/55 miles away on the Swedish frontier, and to the left of this the Blåmannsis, with its snowfields rising to 1571m/5154ft.

Geitvågen

From Bodø Road 834 runs north to Geitvågen, the finest sandy beach north of the Arctic Circle. A visit to Geitvågen on midsummer night is one of the high spots of the year for many inhabitants of Bodø.

★Kjerringøy

40km/25 miles north of Bodø is Kjerringøy, an old trading town which until the 19th century was one of the most important in northern Norway. Its open-air museum, with 15 old buildings, gives a fascinating picture of life and trade in a Norwegian coastal settlement.

★Saltstraumen

35km/22 miles south of Bodø is Saltstraumen, a strait 2.5km/1½ miles long, 150m/160yd wide and up to 50m/165ft deep between the islands of Straumen and Straumøy which links the Saltfjord with the Skjerstadfjord. The ebb and flow of the tide force some 370 million cu. metres (485 million cu. yards) of water through this narrow passage, creating whirlpools and eddies. Good fishing.

Bohuslän   C 6

Country: **Sweden**

Situation and characteristics

Bohuslän, extending along the coast of the Skagerrak from Göteborg to the Norwegian frontier, is the most westerly province of Sweden, to which it has belonged since the treaty of Roskilde in 1658. The traditional fisheries, for long the region's only significant source of income, have been supplemented in recent years by a growing tourist and holiday trade, with the result that in summer Bohuslän sometimes tends to be overcrowded.

The much indented coastal regions with their innumerable skerries, worn smooth by wind and water, and their clean, salty water have been a popular holiday area for more than a century. In addition Bohuslän is rich in remains of the past, particularly rock carvings of the Stone and Bronze Ages and Viking stone-settings.

Through Bohuslän

The main traffic artery of Bohuslän is the E 6, which runs north from Göteborg to the Swedish–Norwegian frontier at Svinesund (continuing to Oslo). Numerous attractive side trips, going west towards the coast, can be made from this road, particularly in its southern section.
From Göteborg (see entry) the road runs north below the Götaälv and then follows the valley of the river (here canalised),

Kungälv

Kungälv (pop. 32,000), known in medieval times as Kongahälla, is Sweden's oldest town. It has a wooden church (1679) with fine ceiling paintings.

Bohus Castle

On the southern outskirts of the town E 20 crosses the Nordreälv, on an island in which (to right) can be seen the large ruined castle of Bohus, built by King Håkon of Norway in 1310, from which the region takes its name. For centuries this stood on the frontier between Sweden and Norway.

Arvidsvik
Marstrand

From Kungälv a country road runs west to the coast (18km/11 miles), from which bridges and a ferry lead to the seaside resort of Arvidsvik on Koön

(Cow Island). From here there is a ferry to the resort of Marstrand, situated on a small island (motor vehicles prohibited) and dominated by the 17th century Carlsten Castle. St Mary's Church dates from the 13th century (rebuilt 1804). The island is an internationally known sailing centre.

Beyond Kungälv E 6 leaves the canalised river, runs past the medieval church of Kareby and soon afterwards passes the Ingetorpssjö (on right), with an Iron Age cemetery.

From St Höga an attractive side trip can be made on Road 160, which runs **Tjörn** north to Uddevalla by way of the islands of Tjörn and Orust, through a beautiful skerry region with many prehistoric remains. The Stenasund is spanned by a massive suspension bridge 600m/660yd long, opened in November 1981, the successor to an earlier bridge which collapsed in January 1980 when a ship crashed into it. On the west coast of Tjörn is Skärhamn, a fishing town and a port for the export of motor vehicles.

Road 160 continues over another bridge to the island of Orust, the third **Orust** largest in Sweden (336sq.km/130sq. miles), with many fishing villages and seaside resorts. Off Orust is the little island of Gullholmen, with the oldest fishing village in Bohuslän (13th c.).

The road returns to the mainland on the 603m/660yd long Nötesund Bridge; then either left for Fiskebäckskil or right for Uddevalla.

From St Höga E 6 leads a little way inland to the seaside resort of Lyckorna **Ljungskile** (founded 1876) and the commercial town and resort of Ljungskile, on an inlet opening off the Havstensfjord, with the ruins of a 12th century church. 5km/3 miles farther on, off the road to the left, is Resteröd church, one of the oldest in Bohuslän (partly 12th c., restored 1919–20).

Skärhamn, on the island of Tjörn

Bohuslän

Uddevalla

Uddevalla (pop. 47,000), a busy industrial town with large shipyards, lies near the outflow of the Bäveå into the Byfjord. In Kungstorg can be seen an equestrian statue of Charles X Gustavus (1908), and to the east of this an early 19th century church, with a belfry of 1751 on higher ground beside it. The Bohuslän Museum has interesting displays of material on the history, natural history and landscape of the province, together with an art collection. To the south of the town is Gustavsberg, one of the oldest seaside resorts in Sweden (18th c.).

From Uddevalla Road 44 runs east to Lake Vänern (see entry). 2.5km/1½ miles along this road, at Bräcke, are the Skalgrusbänkar, banks of gravel deposited by the sea.

Skaftö

From Uddevalla E 6 continues north-west. At Torp Road 161 branches off on the left and runs via Bokenäs (12th c. church) to the old fishing village and seaside resort of Fiskebäckskil on the island of Skaftö, situated in the beautiful Gullmarsfjord, the only real fjord in Sweden.

Lysekil

Road 161 continues by way of a ferry to the attractive seaside resort of Lysekil (pop. 15,000), at the southern tip of the Stångenäs peninsula (fish preserving). Near the handsome Gothic church is the rocky Flaggberg, from which there are extensive views.

Railway Museum

In Småröd, to the south of Munkedal on E 6, is a Railway Museum, with model railway layouts and a narrow-gauge line with steam engines running between Åstorpsherrgård and Munkedal Harbour.

The rocky stretch of coast extending north to Strömstad, almost on the Norwegian frontier, is fringed by skerries and islands, old-established seaside resorts and spas; also fish-preserving industry. There are many large and well preserved prehistoric remains in this area.

Hunnebostrand Kungshamn Smögen

At Dingle Road 174 branches off E 6, cuts across the coast road and comes to the seaside resorts of Hunnebostrand (with Hunneboklyfta, two large rock formations with a gorge between them carved out in the Ice Age, and Bronze Age burial mounds) and Kungshamn (ABBA fish-preserving plant, world-famed for Kalles caviar) and the island of Smögen, with one of the best known fishing villages and summer holiday resorts on the Swedish west coast (fish and prawn auctions).

Fjällbacka

Fjällbacka, a fishing village which is now also a seaside resort, can be reached from the same road. In the market square is a bust of the actress Ingrid Bergman, a very frequent holiday visitor.

Greby cemetery area

Farther up E 6, between Tanumshede and the fishing village of Grebbestad, is the Greby cemetery area, with some 200 burial mounds and many standing stones ("bauta" stones), probably dating from the 4th century but associated in popular tradition with the defeat of a Scottish invading force.

Tanum

E 6 now skirts the western edge of the parish of Tanum, which contains numerous rock carvings (hällristningar), and comes to Tanum, with one of the largest churches in Bohuslän. Opposite the church are a runic stone and an orientation table. Rock Carving Institute and Museum.

★Rock carvings

2km/1¼ miles south, at Vitlycke, are large rock carvings depicting ships, warriors and lur-players. There are other carvings at Litsleby and Fossum. North of Tanumshede is Tanums Sommarland, an amusement park.

Road 163 goes off E 6 on the right, leading to the 29km/18 mile long Bullaresjö, the largest inland lake in Bohuslän. Good walking and canoeing.

Strömstad

From Vik a road branches off E 6 and runs west to Strömstad (pop. 10,500), the oldest seaside and health resort in Sweden (established 1781), with an Art Nouveau Town Hall and an open-air museum. 6km/4 miles west is Skee church, with a Romanesque doorway.

Rock carvings at Vitlycke . . .   *. . . and Aspeberget*

10km/6 miles south-west (boat trips from Strömstad) are the Koster Islands, Sweden's most westerly island group, notable for their rich flora.

Koster Islands

North of Strömstad, on E 6, is a large prehistoric stone-setting in the form of a ship, the Blomsholmsskep (42m/138ft long, 9m/30ft across). Nearby are an old place of judgment (eleven stone blocks) and several burial mounds.

★Stone-setting

E 6 continues through wooded and rocky country. At Svinesund is the Swedish customs post. Beyond this the Svinesund, the narrow inlet which here marks the frontier between Sweden and Norway, is spanned by a reinforced concrete bridge 420m/450yd long and 60m/200ft high (magnificent views). Among the hills around the Svinesund is Björnerödspiggen, the highest point in Bohuslän (222m/728ft).

★Svinesund Bridge

E 6 now runs along the Oslofjord to Oslo.

Borås   D 6

Country: Sweden
Province: Västergötland
Altitude: 120m/395ft
Population: 100,000
Post code: S–50...   Telephone code: 033

This textile town straddling the river Viska was founded by Gustavus Adolphus in 1622. It developed into a place of some commercial importance only after the railway, the cotton trade and mechanical weaving looms came to Västergötland. Thereafter it became a leading centre of the clothing industry and the mail order business.

Situation and characteristics

141

Svinesund Bridge

Town	In the market square (Stora Torget) is the massive Town Hall (*c.* 1910), with a carillon. In front of it is the beautiful Sjuhärad Fountain (by Nils Sjögren, 1941). A little way north stands the Charles Church (1660; restored 1941), with a fine interior. The House of Culture (1975) houses the Museum of Art, the Municipal Theatre and a library. In the Municipal Park is a swimming pool.
Borås Museum	In Ramna Park is the Borås Museum, an open-air museum with old farmhouses and a 16th century church.
Borås Park	In the north of the town is Knalleland, the main centre of the mail order business in the north. Nearby is Borås Park, with a Zoo and an open-air swimming pool.

Surroundings

Seglora	South-west of Borås on Road 41 is Seglora, with a stone recording the removal of the village church to the Skansen open-air museum, Stockholm. At Rydal are Sweden's oldest surviving spinning-mill and the first Swedish factory to be lit by electricity. Fristla has two fine old stone bridges over the Häggå.
Hedared	North-west of Borås on the Alingsås road (No. 180) is Hedared, with Sweden's only surviving medieval stave church.
Sundholmen Torpa	North-east of Borås stands Brämhult (church with 18th c. paintings). At Dalsjöfors gold and silver articles can be bought. Farther east, on a small island in Lake Tolken, is the ruined castle of Sundholmen (16th c.). In Torpa, to the south of the Valdbrosjö, are a 14th century house where Gustavus Adolphus is said to have found his third wife and a former frontier stronghold between Denmark and Sweden.

The lake country between Borås and the little town of Ulricehamn offers plenty of scope for walking and fishing. The town grew up in the Middle Ages in the valley of the river Ätran. The church (1688) has fine 17th and 18th century ceiling paintings. The Town Hall is built in the style of a manor-house.

Ulricehamn

North of Ulricehamn, on Lake Tolken, is the church of Södra Vings, the oldest parts of which date from the 12th century; notable pictures (15th c.) and sculpture.

Södra Vings

Dalarna

D 5

Country: Sweden

Dalarna (also known in English as Dalecarlia) lies in central Sweden north-west of Stockholm, extending to the Norwegian frontier. From Stockholm to Lake Siljan is about 260km/160 miles. It is one of the most popular tourist areas in Sweden, with its colourful little wooden horses providing favourite souvenirs.

Situation and characteristics

This wooded upland region watered by the Västerdalälv and the Österda-lälv is one of the most attractive parts of Sweden, with its fertile valleys, the beautiful Lake Siljan and the rugged hills to the north-west.
  Dalarna began to attract visitors in the mid 19th century. It offers good walking and fishing, facilities for various water sports and, in winter, skiing. Midsummer night is celebrated with particular enthusiasm on Lake Siljan, the "heart of Sweden", though the occasion has lost much of its original charm; visitors are likely to see the celebrations at their best in the smaller towns and villages.

★★Topography

The people of Dalarna are noted for their bravery and love of freedom. In 1434 Engelbrekt Engelbrektsson led a peasant rising against the then ruler of the area, Eric of Pomerania; then in 1520 Gustav Eriksson called on his countrymen to rise against the Danish king Christian II, and in 1523 was crowned as king of Sweden under the style of Gustavus I Vasa. In the early days of the rising Gustavus was compelled to flee to Norway: an event still commemorated in the Vasa Run (Vasaloppet), a cross-country ski run of 85.8km/53¼ miles between Sälen and Mora held every year at the beginning of March (first run in 1922).

History

The land rises towards the Norwegian frontier to a height of some 1200m/4000ft, and around 20,050sq.km/7740sq. miles (72% of the total area of Dalarna) are covered by forest. In addition to agriculture and forestry (woodworking industry) there is mining (iron smelting; steel-works) in the south-west of the region. In the old mining town of Falun the red Falu paint with which so many Swedish houses are now painted was originally merely a by-product of copper-mining.

Economy

Visitors coming from the south can reach Dalarna either on Road 60 from Örebro or on Road 70 from Stockholm. The starting-point of this tour is the town of Avesta, 170km/105 miles north-west of Stockholm.

★Through Dalarna

Avesta (alt. 84m/276ft, pop. 25,000), on the Dalälv (two waterfalls), has been an industrial town since the 14th century. The largest copper coin in the world, weighing almost 20kg/44lb, was minted here in 1644, and the town now has a large steelworks producing high-grade steel. The Gamla By (Old Town) of Avesta still preserves the atmosphere of the 17th century.

Avesta

6km/4 miles south-east of Avesta is Karlbo, with the house (Tolvmannagår-den) in which the poet Erik Axel Karlfeldt (1864–1931) was born. His grave is in the Folkärna cemetery (11km/7 miles north-east).

Karlbo

One of the little wooden horses of Dalarna

Hedemora

20km/12½ miles beyond Avesta on Road 70 lies Hedemora (alt. 107m/351ft, pop. 17,000), the oldest town in Dalarna (chartered 1446). In the main square, Stora Torget, are the Town Hall (1761) and a red-painted timber-built pharmacy of 1779. The Theatre (1820) was once used as a granary. North of the town, on a small lake, is Hedemora Gammelgård, an open-air museum with a collection of old houses.

Husbyring (round trip)

12km/7½ miles north-east (Road 270), on the Dalälv, is the village of Näsgård, starting-point of the round trip (35km/22 miles) known as the Husbyring: Husby Kungsgården, where the first mining rights in the Falu mines (see Falun) were granted in 1347. – Stjärnsund, on Lake Grycken. There was an iron foundry in operation here until 1942. Manufacture of the Stjärnsund clocks, originally made by Christoffer Polhem (1661–1751); museum. – Sylvhytteå, with an old iron foundry (restored). – Högsta-Weg: stone-settings. – Kloster: ruins of the Cistercian abbey of Gudsberga (1477–1538). – Then back to Näsgård.

Säter

From Hedemora Road 70 continues to Säter (alt. 157m/515ft, pop. 11,500), with the interesting Åsgårdarnas Hof (old houses, workshop for making tiled stoves). To the north extends the Säterdal, a beautiful valley some 6km/4 miles long. From the old mining settlement of Bispberg, 3km/2 miles north-east, a path runs up Bispbergs Klack (314m/1030ft; view).

Beyond Säter there is a distant view of the 86m/282ft high church tower of Stora Tuna. The church dates from 1486 (paintings, crucifix 6m/20ft high).

Borlänge

Road 70 continues to Borlänge (alt. 139m/456ft, pop. 46,000), a considerable industrial town, with iron and steel works and rolling mills. Geological Museum, with a special section on Dalarna. From the Forssa Klack, 2km/1¼ miles north, there are extensive views. 20km/12½ miles north-east of Borlänge is Falun (see entry); 45km/28 miles south is Ludvika.

At Djurås the Öster- and Västerdalälv join to form the Dalälv, which Road 70 | Djurås
now follows. From Djurås it runs north to the old village of Gagnef (alt.
183m/600ft; 16th c. church with beautiful stained glass), which is famed for
its fine lace, and the industrial town of Insjön (alt. 183m/600ft), to the north
of which is the 15th century church of Ål, with a local museum adjoining the
church. The road then comes to Leksand (26km/16 miles), on the south side
of Lake Siljan (see entry).

Immediately north of Lake Siljan is a rather smaller lake, the Orsasjö, at the | Orsa
north end of which is the town of Orsa (alt. 171m/561ft, pop. 7000), the
industrial and commercial centre of northern Dalarna. The church (originally 14th c.) has 16th century frescos and a fine font with a wooden base.

12km/7½ miles north-west of Orsa is the Fryksåsen leisure centre (winter | Fryksåsen
sports), from which there are far-ranging views over Lakes Orsa and Siljan. | leisure centre

17km/11 miles north-east of Orsa, situated some 100m/330ft above the | Skattungbyn
Oreälv, is the village of Skattungbyn, at the west end of which is a birch-tree
("Skattungsbjörken") which retains its leaves until the new shoots appear
in spring.

20km/12½ miles farther east the tourist resort of Furudal (alt. 205m/673ft), | Furudal
between the Skattungsjö to the north-west and the Oresjö to the south-
east, is popular with anglers in summer and skiers in winter (ski-tow). The
church has some medieval wood sculpture.
  12km/7½ miles north of Furudal are the summer grazings of Ärteråsen
(alt. 468m/1535ft). Some 20km/12½ miles south (Road 300), near Boda, is
the Styggfors, a waterfall 36m/120ft high.

From Orsa Road 45 leads north into an inhospitable forest region, the Orsa | Orsa Finnmark
Finnmark, which was settled by Finnish immigrants in the 17th century and
still has many villages and hills with Finnish names, such as Pilkalampi-
noppi (644m/2113ft; view) and Korpimäki (706m/2316ft). Both of these
hills, together with the Fågelsjö, lie within the Hamra National Park (27
hectares/70 acres), a heavily wooded area resembling a primeval forest.

Djurås to Särna (about 260km/160 miles)

This route runs from Djurås through south-western and western Dalarna to
Särna, near the Norwegian frontier.

Leave Djurås on Road 71, which runs west, parallel to the course of the
Västerdalälv. At Dala-Floda is the oldest and longest timber suspension
bridge in Sweden. From here trips can be made to the surrounding mountain grazings (views).

From Björbo Road 247 leads south, passing an expanse of protected | Side trip
natural forest at Skärlacken, and comes in 27km/17 miles to the old mining | from Björbo
town of Nyhammar. 5km/3 miles north-west of the little town is the Gasen-
berg (417m/1368ft); 8km/5 miles north-east is Grangärde-Hästberg, with
rock carvings and the Hästbergsklack (419m/1375ft). 3km/2 miles beyond
Nyhammar, between two lakes, lies the village of Grangärde (alt.
160m/525ft).

The road continues, skirting the Västmansjø at some points, to Ludvika | Ludvika
(21km/13 miles; alt. 157m/515ft; pop. 29,000), once an important mining
town (first ironworks 1555) but now dominated by the electrical industry
(transformer testing plant of the ASEA Brown Boveri corporation). To the
west of the town is a good example of a 16th century mining settlement, the
Gammelgård (houses with old furnishings); Mining Museum.

Dalarna

Särna, on the Österdalälv

Grängesberg	16km/10 miles south-west of Ludvika on Road 60, near the border between Dalarna and Västmanland, is the little mining town of Grängesberg (alt. 273m/896ft), which has given its name to the large Grängesberg iron and steel corporation. In this area are the largest reserves of iron ore in Sweden outside Lapland, which have been mined since the 16th century and are now worked to a depth of 600m/2000ft (conducted tours). From here a trip can be made to the Fjällberg (469m/1539ft), 5km/3 miles north-west.
Main route	From Björbo Road 71 continues west to Nås (17km/11 miles), probably the oldest parish in Dalarna. Here Selma Lagerlöf found the theme of her novel "Jerusalem", and a play by Rune Lindström based on the novel is performed here every year at the beginning of July. 17km/11 miles south of Nås is the old iron foundry of Lindesnäs, now closed down.
Vansbro	In another 28km/17 miles Road 71 reaches Vansbro, a typical railway town with an imposing station, where a "Vasa Run for swimmers" (5km/3 miles) is held in the Västerdalälv at the beginning of July, when the water is still quite cold.
Malung	45km/28 miles farther on is Malung (alt. 302m/990ft, pop. 12,000), chief town of a district, an industrial town and the centre of the Swedish leather industry (midsummer celebrations in which leather features prominently). The church (13th c.) has a 15th century effigy of St Olof. Open-air museum (Malungs Gammelgård), with old houses.
Sälen	From Malung Road 297 runs north through the valley of the Västerdalälv by way of the villages of Lima and Transtrand and comes in 65km/40 miles to Sälen, a tourist centre under the south side of the Transtrandsfjäll, the most southerly of Sweden's higher hills, in magnificent walking country. On the banks of the river is a monument to Gustavus Vasa, who reached this point

in his flight from the Danes. Sälen is now the starting-point of the Vasa Run
to Mora.

69km/43 miles farther north, on the Österdalälv (here dammed to form the   Särna
Trängsletsjö, a lake 70km/44 miles long), lies the village of Särna (alt.
440m/1445ft), with a wooden church of 1690 (renovated 1766). The village
was Norwegian until 1644.

3km/2 miles south of Särna stands Mickeltemplet (624m/2047ft; lookout   ★Njupeskärsfall
tower), from which there is a superb view of the Fulufjäll (1044m/3425ft;
nature reserve) to the south-west. On the north side of the fjäll is the
Njupeskärsfall, the highest waterfall in Sweden (125m/410ft, with a sheer
drop of 70m/230ft). The falls can be reached on a footpath (3km/2 miles)
from the village of Mörkret, 26km/16 miles west of Särna.

32km/20 miles from Särna on Road 295, which continues to the Norwegian   Idre
frontier (customs post at Flötningen; 70km/43 miles), is Idre, a tourist
centre on the Österdalälv (which is dammed at this point). From Idre a road
– the highest motorable road in Sweden – climbs north up the Nipfjäll
(1191m/3908ft; nature reserve; parking place at about 1000m/3300ft), and
another road runs north-west (about 45km/28 miles) to the Grövelsjö
tourist station, on the western slopes of the Långfjäll, which rises to over
1200m/3900ft.

Eskilstuna   E 6

Country: **Sweden**
Province: Södermanland. Population: 89,000
Post code: S–632.. Telephone code: 016

Eskilstuna lies on the Eskilstunaå, which links Lake Mälar with Lake Hjälmar   Situation and
to the south-west. Here the two little trading settlements of Tuna and Fors   characteristics
grew up at an early stage. Legend has it that St Eskil, the apostle of
Södermanland, was buried in Tuna.

The beginnings of the ironworking industry in this area go back to the 16th   Industry
century, and in 1654, at the behest of Charles X Gustavus, a large iron
foundry was established at Fors by a Livonian named Reinhold Rademacher. The foundry was designed by Jean de la Vallée, an architect who
was also responsible for planning the layout of Eskilstuna. Thereafter
numerous steelworks were established.

In the centre of the town is the Fristadstorg, with the Town Hall (1897), a   **Town**
fountain ("The Honour and Joy of Labour") by Ivar Johnson and a piece of
sculpture ("The Smiths") by Allan Ebeling. The monastic church on the
other side of the square was designed by Otar Hökerberg (1929). Nearby is
the Fors Church, which dates from the 12th century, with later alterations
and restorations; notable features of the interior are the unusual wood
sculpture and the coats of arms.

The six best preserved of Reinhold Rademacher's forges are at Rade-   Old forges
machergatan 50. Two are now museums; the others are occupied by
various craftsmen. There are also displays illustrating the town's modern
industries, particularly cutlery, for which Eskilstuna is renowned.

Also worth seeing is the Museum of Technology (Faktorimuseet), which   Museums
illustrates the history of technology (coining press). The Museum of Art
displays modern Swedish art.

147

Eskilstuna

Parken-Zoo   South west of the town centre is the Parken-Zoo, a zoo and leisure park, with magnificent banks of flowers, a "Waterland" and a "Phantomland" for children.

Surroundings

South of Eskilstuna, on the shores of Lake Hjälmar, lies Hedlandet, a nature reserve in good walking country. In Malmköping, to the south-east, is an unusual Tramway Museum.

Strängnäs
★Cathedral

East of Eskilstuna on E 3 is the little town of Strängnäs (pop. 26,000), founded in the 13th century. Here in 1523 Gustavus Vasa was chosen as king. The building of the Cathedral extended from the end of the 13th century to the end of the 15th, when it was finally completed by Bishop Rogge. The ceiling paintings in the nave date from the 14th century, the paintings in the choir from the 15th. The reredos on the high altar (1490), depicting the Annunciation and the Last Judgment, with a profusion of figures, was carved in Brussels. In front of the altar, to the left, is the magnificent gilded armour of Charles IX, whose tomb is in the cathedral. Among other monuments is that of Isabella, daughter of John III. On the walls of the cathedral and in front of it can be seen runic stones from the surrounding area.

Near the cathedral are the medieval Consistory House and the Paulinska Hus, built for Laurentius Paulinus Gothus, bishop of Strängnäs from 1609 to 1637. The 17th century printing press which once belonged to the cathedral is now in the Municipal Museum (Strängnäs Museum). It is also worth looking in at the Grassagård, an old craftsman's workshop (open in summer).

Strängnäs

Although Strängnäs is now mainly the administrative and cultural centre of the surrounding area, it has preserved an old-world charm with its narrow streets and red-painted wooden houses.

Falkenberg   D 6

Country: **Sweden**
Province: Halland
Population: 37,000
Post code: S–311..   Telephone code: 0346

Falkenberg, situated at the outflow of the Ätra, a river well stocked with salmon, into the Kattegat, has a history going back to medieval times. It takes its name from a trap for catching falcons, which in earlier days were exported from Halland.
    This typical summer resort on the Swedish west coast has an 8km/5 mile long beach and is noted for its salmon fisheries.

Situation and characteristics

In the charming older part of the town is the Gåsatorg (Goose Market), surrounded by low wooden houses of the 18th and 19th centuries. St Lawrence's Church, which dates in part from the 14th century, has fine wall and ceiling paintings of the 17th and 18th centuries.
    To the east of the church, in an old merchant's house, is the Municipal Museum. In Krukmakaregatan are the Töngren pottery workshops, which have been run by the same family since 1786.
    Storgatan runs north to the town centre, with the Town Hall (1830) to the left. To the right is the old toll bridge (1756), which is Falkenberg's principal tourist attraction. The Town House was built in 1959. There are only scanty remains of the old castle, which was destroyed by Engelbrekt Engelbrektsson and his peasant forces in 1434; originally it was similar to the stronghold of Kärnan in Helsingborg (see entry).

Town

Surroundings

In a wooded region to the south of the town are the bathing beaches of Skreanäs, Ugglarp (Motor and Aircraft Museum, open in summer) and Steninge. E 6 runs past the manor-house of Fröllinge (main building 1623) and Kvibille church (partly 17th c.). On the road south to Halmstad are the Haverdalsstrand nature reserve and the seaside resort of Tylösand (see Halmstad, Surroundings).

Beaches

Abild (Road 150) and Asige, to the east of Falkenberg, are surrounded by beautiful beech forests. There are many Bronze Age tombs and standing stones in this area.

Abild, Asige

North-west of Falkenberg is Morups Tånge (from *tång*, "seaweed"), a staging point for migratory birds, with a 28m/92ft high lighthouse. From Stafsinge church, 2km/1¼ miles north of Falkenberg town centre, there is a fine view of the town.

Morups Tånge

Falun   D 5

Country: **Sweden**
Province: Dalarna. Altitude: 113m/371ft
Population: 52,000   Post code: S–791..
Telephone code: 023

Falun

The old mining town of Falun, now the administrative centre of Kopparberg county, lies on both banks of the river Falun between the Varpasjö and the Runnsjö.

Although Falun's deposits of copper, discovered before the year 1000, were of great economic importance to Sweden for many centuries, the town received its municipal charter only in 1614, when its great days were coming to an end. It is now a considerable industrial town, and also attracts many winter sports enthusiasts.

Town

In the town centre old and new buildings rub shoulders. In the main square (Stora Torget), which has a monument to Engelbrekt Engelbrektsson, leader of the 15th century peasant rising (see Dalarna), are the Old Town Hall (1764), the new local government offices (1968) and the Kristine Church (17th c.; tower 1865), in Renaissance style, with a fine interior. Also in the square are the headquarters of the Stora Kopparberg mining corporation (see below). Here too is the house in which Selma Lagerlöf lived while writing "The Wonderful Adventures of Nils" and other works.

At the North Station (Norra Station) stands the 14th century Kopparberg Church, Falun's oldest building.

There are numbers of old wooden houses (17th–19th c.) in the Östanfors, Gamla Herrgården and Elsborg districts.

On the east side of the town is the Lugnet Ski Stadium (1973), with ski-jump towers up to 52m/171ft high (lift; fine views). Nearby is a large sports hall.

Dalarna Museum

To the west of the town, across the river, is the Dalarna Museum (opened 1962), with a hall used for art exhibitions. The museum displays local costumes, paintings by local artists, craft products and other material illustrating the folk traditions of Dalarna.

Falu Mine

On the south-west side of the town is the Falu Mine (Falu Gruva), which is reached by way of Gruvgatan. The opencast workings extend over an area 400m/440yd by 350m/380yd and are up to 95m/310ft deep; below this the underground workings go down to a depth of 450m/1475ft. In the middle of

Carl Larsson: "Winter Scene"

the 17th century the mine produced some 3000 tons of crude copper annually, or about two-thirds of total world output at that time; its total output to date amounts to some 500,000 tons. The collapse of underground galleries in 1687, 1833 and 1876 led to the decline of this "treasurehouse of the realm" and to the development of the present opencast workings (Stora Stöten), which yield mainly iron pyrites, zinc and lead (annual output of ore about 150,000 tons).

The mine belongs to Stora Kopparberget, probably the oldest industrial corporation in the world (its predecessor being mentioned in an episcopal letter of 1288 and a royal charter of 1347). In 1888 Stora Kopparberget became a limited company, and it is now one of the largest industrial concerns in Sweden, its main interests being in metals and woodworking.

Stora Kopparberget

There are conducted tours of the mine from May to the end of August. Adjoining the workings is the Stora Kopparberg Museum, housed in the 18th century mine offices, with models of the mine, displays of minerals and a collection of copper coins.

Museum

Surroundings

4km/2½ miles north-east of Falun, on the southern shore of the Toftasjö, is Sundborn. The Swedish painter Carl Larsson (1853–1919) lived here from 1901 until his death and was buried beside the red chapel (1755), which has a number of his pictures; there are others in the local government offices.

Sundborn

Carl Larsson's house, preserved as it was in his lifetime, is now a museum (conducted visits from May to September). The interior of the house, depicted in a series of watercolours as the "House in the Sun", provided a model which was followed by many Swedes and attracted interest in other countries as well.

★Museum

Carl Larsson's house

Filipstad   D 5

Country: **Sweden**
Province: Värmland. Population: 13,000
Post code: S–682.. Telephone code: 0590

Situation and characteristics

Filipstad lies at the north end of Lake Daglösen, surrounded by forests and lakes, with a background of hills – an area which attracts many skiers in winter. The town is named after Karl Filip, son of Charles IX.

For centuries the economy of the town depended on its iron-mines. Before receiving its municipal charter in 1611 Filipstad was a trading town where iron was exchanged for corn and beef cattle, since the agriculture of the area contributed little to the feeding of the population. In recent years old industries have been modernised and new ones established. Among the most important undertakings are Wasabröd, which makes crispbread, and Rosendahls Fabrikker, Sweden's largest producer of ink and carbon paper.

Town

On a promontory in Lake Daglösen stands the church (by Nicodemus Tessin the Younger, 1785), on a cruciform plan.

In Östra Kyrkogården is the mausoleum of the engineer and inventor John Ericsson, who was responsible for the construction of Sweden's railway system. In the markot square is an unusual statue (by Bejemark) of Nils Ferlin, a well known local character (actor, singer and composer of popular and satirical songs), who is depicted sitting on a park bench.

Visitors to the town in the first half of September should not miss the traditional Öxhälja market.

Surroundings

Storbrohytta

To the north of Filipstad is the Storbrohytta, a 16th century hammer-mill which remained in operation until 1920.

Hagfors

North-west of Filipstad, on Lake Vermullen (good fishing, canoeing), lies the little town of Hagfors. The Railway and Industrial Museum illustrates the history of ironworking in the area. The Dalkarlstorp local museum depicts the way of life of a working class family at the end of the 19th century.

Finnish Lakeland/Järvi-Suomi   F/G 4/5

Country: **Finland**
Region: Central Finland

Situation and characteristics

The Finnish Lakeland, with its intricately patterned lakes and thousands of islands, covers almost a third of Finland's total area, earning it the name of the "land of 60,000 lakes": in fact the latest count makes the total more than 180,000. To the east the lakes extend to the Russian frontier, on the south they are bounded by the massive terminal moraines of the Salpausselkä and on the north by the Suomenselkä ridge, which forms the watershed between the Gulfs of Bothnia and Finland. The harmonious mingling of woodland and water makes this a paradise for nature-lovers and sailing enthusiasts.

★Finnish Lakeland

Within this extensive area in southern Finland are three main lake systems. To the west, north of Tampere, is Näsijärvi, the smallest of the three; in the centre the long, straggling Lake Päijänne; and to the east the large Lake Saimaa (see entry), which is drained by the river Vuoksen, flowing south-east into Russia. All these lake systems lie between 76 and 78m (250 and 255ft) above sea level.

The Finnish Lakeland is traversed from south to north by three important roads, linked by a number of transverse roads. E 75 runs along the western edge of the lake region from Lahti by way of Jyväskylä and Kärsämäki to Oulu; Road 5 runs through the centre of the area from Lahti via Mikkeli and Kuopio; and Roads 6 and 18 extend in a wide arc round the eastern edge of the lake region by way of Lappeenranta and Joensuu to Kajaani and Oulu.

Lahti via Jyväskylä to Oulu (E 75)

The town of Lahti (see entry) lies at the southern tip of Vesijärvi (area 113sq.km/44sq. miles), which forms the south end of Lake Päijänne. In the northern outskirts of the town Road 5 branches off E 75 on the right and runs north-east to Mikkeli on Lake Saimaa (see entry), while E 75 continues through hilly and wooded country to the little town of Vääksy (Tallukka Museum of Veteran Cars). Here there is a swing bridge over the Vääksy Canal, constructed in 1871 to link the Vesijärvi with Lake Päijänne (4m/13ft lower; lock). The road now follows the western shore of Päijänne.

Vääksy

Lake Päijänne, lying 78m/255ft above sea level, is 140km/87 miles long and up to 28km/17 miles wide, with an area of some 1111sq.km/430sq. miles. Its shores are wooded and for much of the way rocky and rugged. Immediately beyond the bridge Road 314 goes off on the right to Asikkala (pop. 7600), continuing over the narrow isthmus of Pulkkiilanharju, 8km/5 miles long, to the eastern shore of Lake Päijänne, along which it runs north to Sysmä (pop. 7000), with a fine stone-built 15th century church and a Doll Museum and dolls' house (Onkiniemi).

Lake Päijänne

20km/12½ miles beyond the turning for Asikkala E 75 comes to the village of Padasjoki (pop. 4800), and then continues by way of Kuhmoinen (side trip to Mt Linnavuori; fine views) to Jämsä (pop. 12,000), an industrial town (papermaking) at a road junction where Road 9 (E 80) goes off to Tampere (see entry). Jämsä has an interesting Troll Park.

Padasjoki
Jämsä

38km/24 miles north-east is Mänttä, another town whose economy depends on woodworking. Here, in Joenniemi, a country house designed by Jarl Eklund (1935), is displayed the fine art collection (including Flemish and Italian masters) of the industrialist Gösta Suerlachius. The road from Jämsä to Mänttä traverses the impressive Synninluko gorge.

Side trip
to Mänttä

E 75 continues by way of the beautifully situated village of Korpilahti to Muurame, with a church designed by Alvar Aalto. Beyond this, off the road to the right, is the village of Säynätsalo, with a parish house also designed by Alvar Aalto.

Muurame

E 75 then comes to Jyväskylä (see entry), finely situated on the northern shore of the Jyväsjärvi. Here Road 9 branches off on the right to Kuopio. E 75 continues north, past a side road (No. 13) to the beautifully situated village of Saarijärvi (Kolkanlahti manor-house museum; park with aquatic animals).

Jyväskylä
Saarijärvi

From the turning for Saarijärvi E 75 continues to Äänekoski (pop. 11,000), 1.5km/1 mile off the road to the right, a woodworking town (museum of the papermaking firm Metsä-Serla). At the outflow of Lake Keitele is a hydro-electric power station. 8km/5 miles south-east is the busy little industrial town of Suolahti (pop. 6200).

Äänekoski

E 75 continues via Konginkangas (off the road to the right) to Viitasaari, on an island at the north end of the long and much ramified Lake Keitele. To the

Viitasaari

north of the village, which is reached on a causeway, is a lookout tower. Pleasant boat trips on the lake; good fishing. A Festival of New Music (part of the Finland Festival) is held at Viitasaari in summer.

Pihtipudas

Pihtipudas lies at the north-western end of the Kolimajärvi, on the northern border of central Finland. On the shores of the Pyhäjärvi (alt. 141m/463ft) is the mining town of Pyhäsalmi (iron ore, precious metals). Here E 76 leaves the Finnish Lakeland and continues via Kärsämäki and Leskelä to Oulu (see entry) on the Gulf of Bothnia.

Lahti via Mikkeli and Kuopio to Kajaani (Road 5 and E 63)

This route through the centre of the Finnish Lakeland also starts from Lahti. From the north end of the town Road 5 runs north-east. Off the road to the right, in a beautiful setting, is Vierumäki, with the National Sports College (main building 1937; can be visited). The road then crosses the Kyminjoki, which flows from Lake Päijänne into the Gulf of Finland, on an arched bridge (fine views).

Heinola

Heinola (pop. 16,000), on the north side of the Jyrängönvirta, a stretch of rapids on the Kyminjoki, is a popular holiday resort as well as an industrial town and an educational centre. The town received its charter in 1776. Beside the finely situated wooden church (1811) is a belfry (1843) by the Berlin architect C. L. Engel.

Lusi

From Lusi Road 59 runs north to Jyväskylä (see entry), while Road 5 continues north-east through great expanses of forest and past numerous lakes to Mikkeli on Lake Saimaa.

Mikkeli

40km/25 miles north-east of Mikkeli (see entry) Road 14 goes off on the right to Savonlinna. Road 5 continues through forest country to the village of Joroinen.

Varkaus

Beyond this is Varkaus (pop. 25,000), an important industrial town, with sawmills, a paper and cellulose factory, an engineering plant and large shipyards where boats for service on inland waters are built. An interesting feature is a nine-storey water-tower (1954; fine views) which also houses an art museum on the ground floor and flats on the upper floors. In Pelimannikatu is a Museum of Mechanical Music, with 170 mechanical instruments.

From Varkaus there are boat services to Kuopio and Savonlinna (see entries). Savonlinna can also be reached on a charming minor road which runs along the east side of the Haukivesi.

Excursion:
★ Lintula Convent and ★ Uusi Valamo Monastery

From Varkaus a rewarding excursion can be made to the only two Orthodox religious houses in Finland. Take Road 23, which runs north-east to Karvio (55km/35 miles); then turn into a road on the left which leads to the nunnery of Lintula, in the commune of Palokki (open to visitors, café, overnight accommodation). 8km/5 miles farther along Road 23 another side road on the left leads to the monastery of Uusi Valamo (overnight accommodation), in the commune of Papinniemi, at the southern tip of the Juojärvi. A community of Orthodox monks found a new home here when they were compelled by the Soviet advance in the winter of 1940 to leave their old monastery of Valamo on an island in Lake Ladoga. They were able to bring with them many icons and valuable church furnishings. The church of Uusi Valamo, consecrated in 1976, is believed to be the largest Russian Orthodox church outside Russia.

Leppävirta

From Varkaus Road 5 continues to the village of Leppävirta (fine stone-built church, 1846), on the northern shore of Lake Unnukka, which is dotted with islands.

Uusi Valamo monastery

Farther north is Vehmasmäki, with a farmyard zoo which appeals particularly to children.

A few kilometres before Kuopio a road goes off on the left to Kartula (36km/22 miles). At Riuttala, to the north of this road, is a large Farmhouse Museum, with displays of implements and machinery, a farm steading and livestock kept in 19th century fashion. The farm is still operational.   Farmhouse Museum

At Tervo, 14km/8½ miles from Kartula, is the large angling centre of Lohimaa ("Salmon Land").

The town of Kuopio (see entry) lies on a peninsula in Kallavesi, which the road crosses to the north of the town on a causeway with several bridges. On the far side, to the left, is a monument commemorating General Sandel, who resisted the Russians in 1808.   Kuopio Kallavesi

2.5km/1½ miles beyond this Road 17 branches off on the right to Joensuu. Road 5 (E 63) continues via Siilinjärvi to Lapinlahti (museum and art centre in the house of the painter Emil Halonen).

Beyond this is the industrial town of Iisalmi (pop. 22,000), on the northern shore of Porovesi. This was the birthplace of the poet Juhani Aho (1861–1921), who founded the Realist school of literature in Finland at a time when the country was in the throes of industrialisation. To the north of the town is the old wooden parish church of Iisalmi.   Iisalmi

4km/2½ miles beyond Iisalmi Road 19 bears left for Oulu, while Road 5 (E 63) continues north to Kajaani (see entry), from which Road 22 runs along the northern shores of the Oulujärvi to Oulu (see entry).

Helsinki via Lappeenranta and Joensuu to Kajaani

This route traverses the eastern part of the Finnish Lakeland. In the southern part of the route the road in places runs close to the Russian frontier.

For the first section of the route, from Helsinki to Lappeenranta, there are alternative possibilities:

1. The first alternative is on E 75 from Helsinki to Lahti, then on Road 12, which runs east to Kouvola, and from there on Road 6.

Kouvola

Kouvola (pop. 30,000) is the administrative centre of Kymi province, with an Academy of Music. The Tykkimäki family amusement park is worth a visit.

6.5km/4 miles north-west, on the Kymenjoki, is the industrial town of Kuusankoski (large paper-mills). 12km/7½ miles north is Jaala, with the old Verla pulp and paper factory, closed down in 1964 and now a museum.

Orilampi leisure centre

47km/29 miles north of Kouvola is the Orilampi leisure centre on Vuohinjärvi (water sports, tennis).

At Kouvola Road 15, coming from Kotka on the Gulf of Finland, joins Road 6, which is now followed to Lappeenranta.

2. The other route from Helsinki to Lappeenranta runs farther south. It leaves Helsinki on Road 7, which skirts the Gulf of Finland at some distance from the coast. It then continues by way of Porvoo (see entry), Loviisa (remains of town walls) and Kotka (see Hamina, Surroundings) and comes to the junction with Road 15, which is followed to Kouvola.

Anjala

The village of Anjala has a manor-house of 1790, now a museum, and a fine wooden church of 1756. From here the road continues via Myllykoski (paper-mill) to Kouvola.

Lappeenranta

From Kouvola Road 6 leads east along the north edge of the Salpausselkä ridge to Lappeenranta (see entry), at the south end of Lake Saimaa (see entry), and 7km/4½ miles beyond this crosses the Salmaa Canal at Lauritsala.

Imatra

Imatra (see Lappeenranta, Surroundings), only 6.5km/4 miles from the Russian frontier, has large timber-processing plants. Farther north-west, at Särkisalmi, Road 14 branches off on the left, offering an attractive side trip to Savonlinna (see entry).

★Punkaharju

The road to Savonlinna passes through Punkaniemi, on the Punkasalmi, which links the Puruvesi, to the north, with the Väistönselkä. It then continues alongside the railway on a narrow causeway and along the Punkaharju ridge (7km/4½ miles long and up to 25m/80ft high; nature reserve). The ridge, deposited by the melt-waters of the last Ice Age, falls steeply down on both sides and is covered with pine, larch and birch forest (marked footpaths). A tourist attraction for families with children is the "Summerland" leisure park at Punkaharju.

★Retretti

Close by is the Retretti Art Centre (opened 1983), which puts on exhibitions of Finnish and international art in summer. Part of the centre was blasted out of the rock.

Kerimäki

At Antola the route turns off Road 14 and follows Road 71, which goes off on the right to Kerimäki, on the west bank of the Puruvesi. Kerimäki is famed for its large wooden church (designed by A. F. Granstedt; consecrated 1847), which was built at the expense of a local man who had emigrated to the United States. The large size of the church is said to be due to the fact that the measurements on the plan, in feet, were interpreted as metres. Some of the events in the Savonlinna Festival of Opera are staged in the church.

At Puhos the route rejoins Road 6, which runs north up the east side of the Puruvesi.

Punkaharju nature reserve

Church, Kerimäki

Joensuu | The road goes through Onkamo and Pyhäselkä and comes to Joensuu (see entry), chief town of northern Karelia. From here Road 17 runs west to Kuopio.

The route continues on Road 18 to a junction at Uuro.

Lake Pielinen | Road 73 to the right, via Eno, comes to Uimaharju at the south end of Lake Pielinen (area 1095sq.km/423sq. miles), and continues along the east side of the lake, through beautiful scenery.

From the south end of Lake Pielinen the Pielisjoki (with several locks) provides a link with Lake Saimaa (see entry).

Lieksa | Lieksa has an open-air museum, with some 60 old buildings, and a modern church (1982), replacing an earlier one which was burned down in 1979. This is a popular water sports centre.

A possible excursion from here is to the Ruunaa rapids (25km/15 miles north-east).

Nurmes | Continuing along the shores of Lake Pielinen, Road 73 comes in 56m/35 miles to the little town of Nurmes (pop. 7000), laid out on a regular grid on the slopes of a hill, with beautiful avenues of birch-trees. Features of interest are the old part of the town, with wooden houses dating from the turn of the century, and the small Municipal Museum which occupies the Ikola House in the northern district of Porokylä. On the main road from the south is a reconstruction of the Karelian village of Bomba, with holiday chalets, leisure facilities, restaurants and an open-air theatre (festival in summer).

In another 5km/3 miles Road 73 rejoins Road 18.

Karjajanselkä | From the road junction at Uuro Road 18 runs north to the Karjajanselkä ridge, which follows the south-west side of Lake Pielinen. At Ahmovaara a road goes off on the right to the Koli Hills (see entry).

Juuka | Juuka, a straggling village on the west side of Lake Pielinen, has a wooden church with a free-standing tower.

Suomenselkä | Road 18 continues north-west, crossing the Suomenselkä ridge, and at Kajaani (see entry) joins Road 22, which leads to Oulu (see entry).

Fredrikstad   C 6

Country: **Norway**
Region: Southern Norway. Population: 26,500
Post code: N–1601

Situation and characteristics | Frederikstad lies near the Oslofjord (see entry) amid a group of towns with a total population of 70,000, mainly employed in industry. Norway's longest river, the Glåma, flows into the Skagerrak here and divides the town into two – the historic old town, still surrounded by its walls, on the east bank and the modern port and industrial town on the west.

King Frederick II of Denmark ordered the building of the town in 1567, but three years later it was burned down by the Swedes. After several repetitions of this the town was surrounded by strong fortifications in the 17th century, and in 1685 Fredrikstad, with a total of 130 cannon, was the strongest fortress in the whole of Norway. The old town is now the only surviving fortified town in Scandinavia. In 1903 the army ceased to man the fortifications. These were restored in 1994 and now 60 cannons can be seen on the walls.

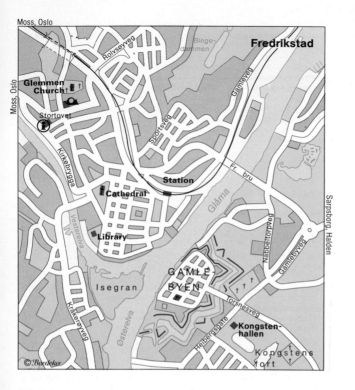

Within its protecting walls and bastions lies the Old Town (Gamlebyen) of Fredrikstad, with its quiet Renaissance quarters and roughly cobbled streets. The Victuals Store dates from 1687, the Prison (Slaveriet), now housing the Municipal Museum, from 1731. The church (1779), unlike its five predecessors, survived the fires which ravaged the town from time to time. The Town Hall was built in 1784.

Town

★ Old Town

Fort Kongsten (1685) was one of the outer defences of the stronghold. The underground chambers and passages illustrate the military engineering techniques of the early modern period.

★ Fort Kongsten

Another outwork of the stronghold lies opposite it on the island of Isegran, on which, about the year 1280, the last Jarl of Norway had his castle.

Isegran

On the west side of the Glåma are Fredrikstad Cathedral (1880), which has one of the finest organs in Norway (4000 pipes) and stained glass by Emanuel Vigeland, and the medieval Glemmen Old Church, spanning the long and eventful history of the town.

Cathedral

Glemmen Church

Surroundings

Road 110, which runs between Fredrikstad and Skjeberg, is known – not only to local people – as Oldtidsveien, the Old Road.

★ Oldtidsveien

The 3000-year-old rock carvings at Begby on agricultural and seafaring motifs show that the Old Road was already in use in Bronze Age times.

Begby

Borge   The church at Borge, also on the Old Road, dates only from 1861, but there are remains of walls belonging to a predecessor of the early medieval period.

Hunn   At Hunn traces of ploughing have been found which show that there was a settlement here 4000 years ago. The burial mounds in this area date from between the beginning of the Christian era and the Viking age.

A walk along the Old Road is a walk through several thousand years of European history. The features likely to be of most interest to the ordinary visitor are the rock carvings.

Gällivare   E 3

Country: **Sweden**
Province: Norrbotten
Altitude: 359m/1178ft
Population: 23,000
Post code: S–97200   Telephone code: 0970

Situation and characteristics   The town of Gällivare in northern Sweden owes its existence to the local deposits of iron ore. It lies close to the twin town of Malmberget, 70km/ 44 miles north of the Arctic Circle. The midnight sun shines here from June 2nd to July 12th. Gällivare has a wooden church of 1881, known as the "one öre church" because every taxpayer was obliged to make an offering of one öre towards its cost.
    There is a boarding school for Sami children which in summer is used as a youth hostel.

Iron-Mines   The deposits of iron ore around Gällivare have been known since the 18th century. A British company began to work them in 1869 and built a railway line to Luleå (1884), but six years later sold out to the Swedish government, which in 1957 took over another private company, Luossavaara-Kiiruna-vaara AB (LKAB). The reserves of ore, with an iron content of 62–70%, are estimated at 400 million tons. The ore is mostly exported during the summer from Luleå; only a small proportion is processed in Luleå by the state-owned Svenska Stål company or in other Swedish steelworks.

Surroundings

★Dundret   5km/3 miles south-west of Gällivare is the hill of Dundret, with the Dundret leisure centre. From the summit of the hill (893m/2930ft; mountain hut), which can be climbed in 1½–1¾ hours (or with less effort by cableway), there are superb views. This is a popular skiing area.

Malmberget   6km/4 miles north of Gällivare is another ore mountain, the Malmberg, with three peaks: Välkomman (617m/2024ft), Kungsryggen (580m/1903ft) and Kaptenshöjden (518m/1700ft). At the foot of the hill is the mining settlement of Malmberget (fine view of Dundret). All Saints Church, built in 1944, had to be moved to a new site some years ago because it was in danger of sinking into the underground workings; the altar is a block of Malmberg ore. In the LKAB offices is an informative Mining Museum. Conducted tours of the workings (some 250km/155 miles of underground galleries and passages).

Koskullskulle   4km/2½ miles north-east of Malmberget are the iron-mines of Koskullskulle.

Gävle

Country: **Sweden**
Province: Gästrikland
Population: 88,000
Post code: S–80...   Telephone code: 026

The busy industrial and commercial town of Gävle, between Stockholm and Sundsvall, is the administrative centre of the county of Gävleborg, which takes in the provinces of Gästrikland and Hälsingland. It lies on both banks of the Gävleå, which here flows into the Gulf of Bothnia.

Situation and characteristics

Gävle is the largest and oldest town in Norrland (founded 1446), and with its modern port installations plays an important part in the export of timber and metal ores. The town was rebuilt after a fire in 1869 which destroyed the districts north of the river.

In Rådhustorget (Town Hall Square) are the 18th century Town Hall and the Town House (Stadshuset, 1803–05). From here two broad parallel streets, Norra Rådmansgatan and Norra Kungsgatan, lead to the finely situated Theatre (1878).

Town

Town Hall

From Town Hall Square Drottninggatan runs south-west to Trinity Church, the oldest building in the town after the Castle (built 1654, restored 1936–38 and 1954). Farther along the north bank of the river is the beautiful Municipal Park (Stadsträdgården).

Trinity Church

A little way south of Town Hall Square, on the other bank of the river, stands the Castle, built in 1583–93 by King John III and rebuilt in the 18th century after a fire. It is now the seat of the provincial government.

Castle

To the east of the Castle, in Södra Strandgatan, is the County Museum (Länsmuseet), with material on the history of the town, pictures and sculpture, and a collection of antiquities, including a boat of about A.D. 100, of a type described by Tacitus in his "Germania", which was excavated at Björke in 1948, and a Persian lamp brought here by Vikings.

County Museum

South of the Provincial Museum, in Södra Centralgatan, can be found the Folkets Hus (People's House, 1946). To the west is the carefully renovated district of Gamla Gävle (Old Gävle), with many 18th century wooden houses now occupied by artists and craftsmen.

Gamla Gävle

1km/³⁄₄ mile west of the Castle is the Museum Silvanum (Forestry Museum; exhibitions on the woodworking industry, etc.), in a park containing over 400 species of trees and shrubs which grow in Sweden.

Forestry Museum

On the south side of the town, on E 4, is the Railway Museum of the Swedish State Railways (SJ), documenting over a hundred years of railway history in Sweden.

Railway Museum

Surroundings

3km/2 miles south-east of Gävle lies the Järvsta cemetery area, with a runic stone. To the east of this, on Gävle Bay, is the little seaside resort of Furuvik, with a sandy and rocky beach; zoo and amusement park.

Järvsta
Furuvik

From Furuvik the road continues south to the port and industrial town of Skutskär (timber-processing), on the boundary between Gästrikland and Uppland, and crosses the Dalälv. Straddling the three arms of the river is Älvkarleby (pop. 10,000), which has a 15th century church with fine wall paintings and a salmon hatchery. The once imposing falls on the river have

Älvkarleby

lost their charm since the construction of a hydro-electric power station. Above this, opposite the island of Flakö, is a hydraulic research laboratory, with models of hydro-electric installations.

8km/5 miles north-east is Sweden's first wind-operated power station, an experimental unit with a 23m/95ft high tower.

Sandviken

From Gävle Road 80 runs west to Falun (see entry). 3km/2 miles along this road is Valbo, with a 14th century church and a runic stone of about A.D. 100. Beyond this are Mackmyra (iron foundry of 1885, now closed down) and the industrial town of Sandviken (alt. 71m/233ft, pop. 40,000), on the northern shore of the Storsjö. The town is dominated by a large steelworks established in 1862, with the oldest Bessemer converter in Sweden.

Årsunda

On the south side of the Storsjö stands Årsunda church (c. 1450), with a medieval altar of Flemish workmanship and wall paintings.

Ockelbo

North-west of Gävle the little town of Ockelbo (formerly a railway junction) has many turn-of-the-century wooden houses with attractive details. The church (1793) was destroyed by fire in 1904. Beside the church is a reproduction of the Ockelbo Stone (Ockelbostenen), one of the most richly decorated runic stones in Sweden; the original was destroyed in the fire.

Strömsbro
Hamrånge

North of Gävle, at Strömsbro, are cemeteries of the Viking period. To the east of E 4 are the old fishing villages of Bönan (lighthouse of 1840, 16.4m/54ft high, with museum) and Utvalnäs. Hamrånge (35km/22 miles north of Gävle on E 4) has a notable church (1854) with a font and ten figures of saints from the medieval church. Bergby has a beautifully situated community centre.

Geirangerfjord   B 5

Country: **Norway**
Region: Central Norway

Situation

The Geirangerfjord and surrounding area offer some of the finest scenery in the whole of Norway. It is the eastward continuation of the Sunnylvsfjord, a branch of the Storfjord. From the shores of the Geirangerfjord, with its numerous waterfalls, there is a succession of magnificent views.

Access

The narrow and winding road to the village of Geiranger, at the east end of the fjord, turns north off Road 15 (Gudbrandsdal to the Nordfjord) to the west of Grotli.

Grotli

Grotli (alt. 870m/2854ft), an important road junction, is frequently snowbound well into the summer. Some 15km/9 miles west of the town the Geiranger road (No. 58) turns off. The first stretch of the road runs through bare mountain country on the northern shore of the Breidalsvann (alt. 880m/2887ft), which is caught between the Breidalsegga to the north and the Vassvendegga to the south, and then skirts two smaller lakes (on left). In 18km/11 miles the road passes, also on the left, the Djupvann (1004m/3294ft), which is frequently frozen until August, and in another 2km/1¼ miles comes to the highest point on the road (1038m/3406ft), which is open for traffic from June 1st to October 15th. On the south side of the lake are the sheer rock faces of the Grasdalsegga (1570m/5151ft). At the west end of the lake is the Djupvasshytta hotel (alt. 1020m/3347ft), which is frequented by summer skiers (ski race at end of June).

Dalsnibba
★★Views

Here the road known as the Nibbevej (normally open June 1st to October 1st; toll) branches off and climbs 5km/3 miles, with gradients of up to 12.5%

Mountain grazings near Grotli

and ten hairpin bends, to the summit of the Dalsnibba (1495m/4905ft), from which there are superb views of the mountains and the Geirangerfjord far below.

Soon after Djupvasshytta, beyond the watershed between the Skagerrak and the Atlantic, an impressive stretch of mountain road begins. The Geiranger road (opened in 1885) descends some 1000m/3280ft, with gradients of up to 8% and twenty sharp bends (some of them very tight indeed) and several bridges, to reach Geiranger in 17km/10 miles (distance as the crow flies only 7km/4½ miles). On this road there is a sudden transition from the severe climate of the mountain regions to the warmer and milder air of the sheltered valley. 2km/1¼ miles along the road, on the left, is the Blåfjell, with the Jettegryte ("Giant's Cauldron"), a cavity 2.2m/7ft across and 9.5m/30ft deep gouged out by glacial action.

★Geiranger road

Beyond the Øvre Blåfjellbro (bridge) there is a magnificent view: to the left the Flydalshorn, to the right the Vindåshorn and beyond it the Såthorn (1779m/5837ft) and the Grindalshorn (1534m/5033ft), and straight ahead the "Eagles' Road" which winds its way up from Geiranger to Eidsdal (see below). The road then crosses the Nedre Blåfjellbro, with the falls on the Kvandalselv to the right, and descends into the next "step" in the valley, the Flydal. To the left we reach the Flydalshorn, to the right the Blåhorn (1738m/5702ft).

Flydal

Beyond Ørjeseter is the Flydalsjuv (alt. 300m/1000ft; car park), a gorge offering a superb view. From Hole, a short distance beyond this, a rewarding trip can be made to Vesterås and from there on a marked footpath to the Storseterfoss, a waterfall 30m/100ft high.

From Hole the main road continues to the Utsikten Bellevue Hotel. Beyond this (on left, before a bridge) is a standing stone commemorating the adoption of the Norwegian constitution of 1814.

★Flydalsjuv
★Storseterfoss

Geirangerfjord

Autumn in the Geirangerfjord

Geiranger ★★Geirangerfjord	The road then continues to Geiranger, a little port and tourist resort at the east end of the Geirangerfjord.
Sightseeing cruises	During the season very attractive sightseeing cruises by motor-ship (2 hours) are run several times daily – a good way of seeing the impressive scenery of the fjord, with its sheer rock walls and numerous waterfalls. High up on the left can be seen the abandoned farm of Skageflå; then on the right the Syv Søstre (Seven Sisters) waterfall, which forms seven separate falls when swollen by melt-water in spring. To the left of this is another waterfall, Friaren (the Suitor), to the right Brudesløret (the Bridal Veil).
★Sunnylvstjord	To the west the Geirangerfjord runs into the Sunnylvsfjord. At the south end of this fjord is the village of Hellesylt; at its north end, to the west, Stranda. From Hellesylt there is a ferry to Geiranger. From Geiranger Road 60 follows the north side of the Geirangerfjord, coming in 3km/2 miles to Møllgårdene, a group of houses over 200 years old, the starting-point of the "Eagles' Road".

★Eagles' Road

The Eagles' Road (Ørneveien) links the Geirangerfjord with the Norddalsfjord. It climbs in eleven hairpin bends, with fine views of the Geirangerfjord and its waterfalls, to Korsmyra (alt. 624m/2047ft), where it reaches its highest point, and then descends, passing the Eidsvann, to Eidsdal.

Eidsdal	Eidsdal, on the Norddalsfjord, has some industry (woodworking, clothing manufacture) and a fine octagonal church of 1782. There is a ferry to Linge on the north side of the fjord, from which Road 63 runs east to Åndalsnes (see Romsdal) and west to Ålesund (see entry).

Göta Canal

Country: **Sweden**
Region: Southern Sweden
Provinces: Bohuslän, Västergötland, Östergötland, Södermanland, Uppland

The four-day trip in one of the old passenger boats on the Göta Canal from Göteborg to Stockholm (or vice versa) is one of the most memorable tourist experiences Sweden can offer. The total distance by water is 560km/350 miles, of which 87km/55 miles are in canals. To overcome a difference in height of 91.5m/300ft there are 65 locks on the route. The service operates from mid May to the beginning of September.

The four boats which ply on the Göta Canal are old, but have been brought up to modern standards. They do not carry cars, but the shipping company can arrange for the transport of passengers' cars by land. These trips are very popular, and early booking is therefore advisable. It is possible to return by train if desired.

The construction of a waterway between Stockholm and Göteborg so as to link the Kattegat with the Baltic was contemplated by Gustavus Vasa, but the first steps towards realising the project were not taken until the time of Charles XII (1716). Two engineers, Swedenborg and Polhem, sought to bypass the Trollhättan falls by the construction of locks, but the protective embankment was destroyed by drifting logs in 1755, and thereafter the

History

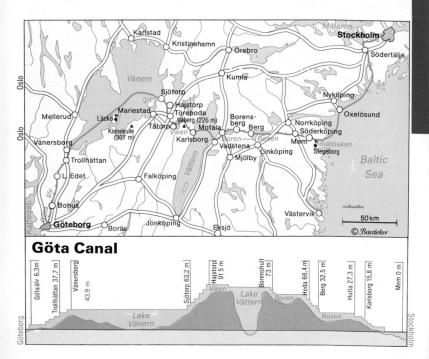

165

Passenger ship on the Göta Canal

project hung fire until 1793. In 1810 work began on the section of the canal between Lakes Vänern and Vättern, in Västergötland (61.5km/38 miles long, with 21 locks). The Östergötland section, between Motala and the Baltic, is 92.5km/57 miles long, with 37 locks. The construction of the canal is particularly associated with the names of Baron Baltzar Bogislaus von Platen and Daniel Thunberg. By 1832 the whole length of the canal from Göteborg to Mem on the Baltic (385km/239 miles) was open for traffic. In those days the canal was an important industrial transport route: nowadays it is used almost exclusively by tourist traffic.

★Along the Göta Canal

Trollhättan

Starting from Gøteborg (see entry), the boat sails up the Götaälv, passing the ruins of Bohus Castle, and comes in some 5 hours to Trollhättan (alt. 38m/125ft). While the boat is passing through the locks (height difference 32m/105ft) there is time to look round the power station.

Lake Vänern

By the time (about 6pm) the boat enters Lake Vänern (see entry) at Vänersborg (alt. 44m/144ft) is has passed through six locks. The size of the locks varies considerably; some operate automatically.

Läckö Castle

In the lake the boat passes (on right) Läckö Castle, on the Kållandsö peninsula, built in 1298 by the bishop of Skara. Opposite it is the wooded hill of Kinnekulle (307m/1007ft).

Sjötorp
Lake Viken

On the east side of Lake Vänern, at Sjötorp, is the beginning of the Östergötland section of the canal, where during the night and early morning the boat climbs 47m/154ft over a distance of 36km/22 miles, with the help of 20 locks, to reach Tåtorp on Lake Viken (which serves as a storage reservoir for this part of the canal).

At Lyrestad the canal is crossed by the E 3, and at Stora Lanthöjden it reaches its highest point (91.5m/300ft above sea level).

Chain of locks at Berg

The boat continues through Lake Viken (area 46sq.km/18sq. miles, depth 25m/82ft) and the adjoining Lake Botten (13sq.km/5sq. miles) to the south, with the Vaberg (226m/742ft) on the right, to enter Lake Vättern at Karlsborg.

Lake Vättern

The passage across the northern part of Lake Vättern takes 4 hours. The boat reaches the eastern shore at Vadstena (where there is time for a tour of the town and a visit to the castle) and then skirts the shore to Motala, where the Östergötland section of the canal begins.

Vadstena
Motala

On the north bank of the canal can be seen the tomb of Baron von Platen (see above, History), who died in 1829 before the canal was completed. Then a series of six locks leads down to Lake Boren (alt. 74m/243ft), and the boat continues across the lake to reach Borensberg at its east end in the early morning. Over the next 22.2km/14 miles, until the canal enters Lake Roxen at Berg (alt. 32.5m/107ft), it descends another 41.5m/136ft, passing through sixteen locks.

Lake Boren

Passengers travelling in the opposite direction (from Stockholm to Göteborg) have time for a visit to Vreta Abbey (about 20 minutes), south-east of the canal, while the boat is passing through the locks.

Vreta Abbey

Then follows a stretch of 26km/16 miles through Lake Roxen (alt. 32.5m/107ft) and the narrow Lake Asplång (alt. 27m/89ft), 5km/3 miles long, after which the canal descends, through fifteen locks, to the old town of Söderköping, which is reached about 8pm (time for a tour of the town).

Lake Roxen
Lake Asplång
Söderköping

From Söderköping it is another 5km/3 miles to Mem, where the Göta Canal reaches Slätbaken, a 15km/9 mile long inlet on the Baltic. On its south side can be seen the tower of the ruined castle of Stegeborg.

Slätbaken

Baltic

From here the boat turns north through the skerries and the open Baltic, passing the inlet of Bråvik and the steel town of Oxelösund, to enter the long, narrow Himmerfjärd, which leads into the fjord-like Hallsfjärd and the 5km/3 mile long Södertälje Canal (constructed 1806–19), linking Lake Mälar with the Baltic.

Södertälje

At the industrial town of Södertälje the boat passes through its last lock, at about 8am on the fourth day of its voyage, and continues for another 39km/25 miles along the east end of Lake Mälar to Stockholm, which is reached in the evening.

Göteborg   C 6

Country: **Sweden**
Province: Bohuslän. Population: 431,000
Post code: S–40... and S–41...   Telephone code: 031

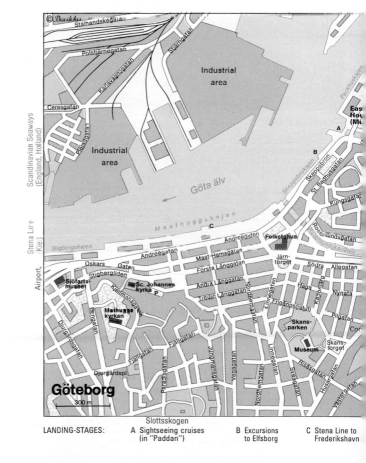

LANDING-STAGES: A Sightseeing cruises   B Excursions   C Stena Line to
                    (in "Paddan")   to Elfsborg   Frederikshavn

Göteborg (in English traditionally Gothenburg), situated in south-western Sweden on the shores of the Kattegat, on both banks of the Götaälv, is Sweden's second largest city and its leading port and commercial centre. The chief town of the county of Göteborg and Bohus, it has a university and a college of technology and is the see of a Lutheran bishop. Its economy is largely dependent on a number of major industries including motor vehicles (Volvo), the manufacture of ball bearings and the chemical industry. There are ferry services to Kiel in Germany and Frederikshavn in Denmark.

★★Situation and characteristics

Göteborg is a relatively young town, having received its municipal charter from Gustavus Adolphus only in 1621. There had been four earlier settlements in the area, but all had been destroyed either by war or by fire. The early development of the town was much influenced by the Dutch settlers who had been brought in: the first town council consisted of ten Dutchmen, seven Swedes and one Scot. The town quickly grew into Sweden's largest port, engaged particularly in the shipment of timber and iron. During Napoleon's continental blockade (1806) it was the focal point for British

History

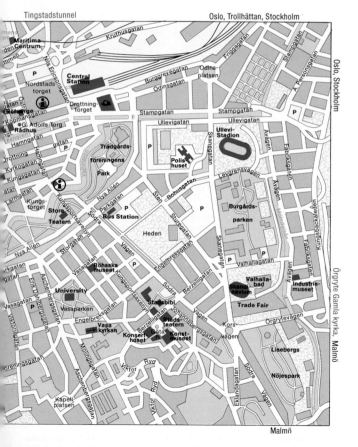

Göteborg

Commercial harbour, Göteberg

trade with northern Europe. This period saw the rise of the commercial aristocracy (East India Company founded 1731) from whose munificence the city frequently benefited. Göteborg's heyday as an international port began in the early 20th century with the development of transatlantic traffic, and it is now the base of about a quarter of the Swedish merchant fleet. With over 20km/12½ miles of quays, the port – which is rarely icebound – is the largest in northern Europe, and can accommodate tankers of up to 225,000 tons. The people of Göteborg are open-minded and liberally disposed, and have always looked towards the West: in their eyes Stockholm is in Siberia. A favourite Swedish joke declares that when it rains in London the people of Göteborg put up their umbrellas.

Old Town

On the Dutch pattern, the main traffic arteries of Göteborg were originally canals, most of which have now been filled in and converted into streets, such as Östra and Västra Hamngatan. Only the central canal, the Stora Hamnkanal, and the old defensive moat which bounds the Old Town on the south have been preserved.

Gustav Adolfs Torg

On the north side of the Stora Hamnkanal is Gustav Adolfs Torg, a large square which was called simply Stora Torget until 1854, when the statue of Gustavus Adolphus (by B. E. Fogelberg) was erected. It is the second version of the statue: the first, cast in Munich, was acquired by Bremen after the ship carrying it ran aground and the citizens of Göteborg refused to pay the salvage money demanded by the men of Heligoland.

Exchange

On the north side of Gustav Adolfs Torg stands the former Exchange, which was built in 1844–49 to plans by Per Johan Ekman; the upper façade terminates in six statues. It now houses the city's Council Chamber.

Town Hall

On the west side of the square is the Town Hall (Rådhus; 1672), designed by Nicodemus Tessin the Elder, with a beautiful inner courtyard. The north wing was built by Erik Gunnar Asplund in 1935–37. The relief of the "Winds" was the work of Erik Grates.

Behind the Town Hall, in Norra Hamngatan, stands the Kristine Kyrka or German Church (rebuilt in 1748–53 after a fire), with the burial vault of Field Marshal Rutger von Ascheberg (1693), governor of Skåne, Halland, Göteborg and Bohuslän.

Farther along Norra Hamngatan (No. 12) is East India House, once the offices of the East India Company (1750). It now houses the Göteborgs Stadsmuseum (municipal museum); on display are archaeological collections (including Sweden's only Viking ship) and cultural history exhibits (development of the town, domestic culture, customs and traditions). The industrial history department is also of interest (tools and machinery from Göteborg's factories; sociology of the industrial age).

Göteborgs Stadsmuseum

A little way to the east the Östra Hamngatan leads to the port area. Building No. 11 houses the Museum of Medical History.

Medicinhistorisk Muset

To the north, in Kronhusgatan, is the Kronhus (1643–53), the city's oldest building. In the great hall (Rikssalen) the five-year-old Charles XI was proclaimed king in 1660.

Kronhus

Across the Stora Hamnkanal from the Municipal Museum, to the right, is the Lilla Torg, with a statue (by Börjesson, 1904) of the textile manufacturer Jonas Alströmer (1685–1761). Farther to the right, at the end of Södra Hamngata, stands the 17th century Governor's Residence. In Skeppsbroplatsen is the town's oldest stone pier (1845), with the Carl Milles Monument.

Lilla Torget

Along Västra Hamngatan, at the intersection with Kungsgatan (on left), is the Cathedral (Domkyrka), built in 1815 on the site of two earlier churches which had been destroyed by fire. It is a three-aisled church with a tower at the west end.

Cathedral

Between Gustav Adolfs Torg and Drottningtorg (to the east along Norra Hamngata) is the Östra Nordstan district, in which the old houses have given place to modern functional buildings. From the shopping centre there is an underground passage to the Central Station in Drottningtorg.

Östra Nordstan

Nils Ericssonsgata runs north to the Götaälv. Moored at the Gullbergskaj are the four-masted barque "Viking" and the lightship "Fladen". To the right is the Götaälv Bridge, leading to the Hisingen peninsula.

Maritima Centrum

The Opera House on Jussi Björlings Plats nearby, was designed by the architect Jan Izikowits and opened in 1994.

★Opera

From the north-east side of Gustav Adolfs Torg Östra Hamngatan runs south to Kungsportsplats, with an equestrian statue of Charles IX (by Börjesson, 1903). Between here and Västra Hamngatan are a number of business and shopping streets. To the south of the square, beyond the old moat, is the Grand Theatre (Stora Teatern, 1859), on the east side of the Kungspark. Opposite the theatre, on the far side of Kungsportsavenyn (called simply Avenyn, "the Avenue", for short), Göteborg's grandest street, can be seen the first version of a well known piece of sculpture by Molin, "The Wrestlers" ("Bältespännare"). Beyond this is the beautiful park of the Horticultural Society (Trädgårdsföreningen), with a large palmhouse and a restaurant (main entrance from Nya Allén). In the Avenue, between Nya Allén and Parkgatan, is a statue (by I. Fallstedt, 1899) of the engineer John Ericsson (1803–89), who after emigrating to the United States perfected the screw propeller and built the warship "Monitor".

Eastern and South-Eastern Districts

Kungsportavenyn

In Liseberg amusement park

Götaplats	At the south-east end of the Avenue lies Götaplats, the city's cultural hub, with the striking Poseidon Fountain by Carl Milles (1931).
★ Museum of Art	A broad flight of steps leads up to the Museum of Art (Konstmuseet; 1921–23), with a comprehensive collection of Scandinavian art as well as works by Italian, French, Dutch and Flemish masters (including Rembrandt's "Falconer", c. 1665, and "Adoration of the Kings", c. 1631, Rubens and Van Gogh) and modern French artists (Cézanne, etc.). Adjoining the museum is the Konsthalle (periodic exhibitions).

On the east side of Götaplats is the Municipal Theatre (Stadsteatern; 1934), on the west side the Concert Hall (Konserthuset; 1935). North-west of the Theatre is the Municipal Library (Stadsbibliotek), with a Doll Museum.

★ Liseberg Scandinavium	South-east of Götaplats (main entrance in Örgrytevägen) is the lively Liseberg amusement park (Nöjespark), one of the largest and finest of its kind in Europe. On the other side of Örgrytevägen are the Trade Fair grounds (Svenska Massan). Adjoining is the Scandinavium (1971), with an arena seating up to 12,000 spectators, and beyond this the Valhalla Baths. Still farther north, in Skånegatan, is the large Ullevi Stadium.
Ethnographic Museum	To the east of the Mölndalsån, which is crossed here by a bridge, lies the Ethnographic Museum; the textiles and ceramics are particularly interesting.
★ Röhsska museet	In Vasagatan (Nos. 37–39), which cuts across the Avenue, is the Museum of Applied Art (Röhsska museet), with modern gold and silver work, textiles, furniture, glass and porcelain. At the entrance are two Chinese marble lions of the Ming dynasty (1386–1644).

Farther along Vasagatan, in the Vasapark, is the University. South of this is the Vasa Church (Vasakyrkan, 1909); at the west end of Vasagatan, is the Commercial College; and to the north of this is the Haga Church (Hagakyrkan, 1859).

On a hill south-west of the Haga Church can be seen a remnant of the old fortifications, Skansen Kronan (Kronen Redoubt), from the top of which there are fine views. The stout tower (1697) now houses a Military Museum, with a collection of weapons and Swedish uniforms from the 17th century to the present day. Around the hill is a working-class housing estate built about 1850.

To the north, at the west end of Södra Allégatan, is Järntorget (Iron Square), with a fountain by Tore Strindberg (1927); on the outside of the basin are various old iron stamps.

    From here Första Långgatan runs west to St John's Church (1866). On a plateau to the south of the church stands the Masthugg Church (Masthuggskyrkan, 1914), from which there is a fine view of the city and the harbour.

Then by way of Stigbergsgatan and Stigbergsplatsen, with the well preserved Gathenhielmska Hus (1710), to the Shipping Museum (Sjöfartsmuseet), which illustrates the development of shipping, fishing and shipbuilding from the Viking period to the present day; there is also an aquarium.

    Adjoining the museum is the Seaman's Tower, 49m/160ft high, topped by Ivar Johnsson's sculpture "Woman by the Sea"; the tower was built to commemorate the seamen who lost their lives in the First World War (good views).

Near the Shipping Museum is the fishing harbour (interesting auctions on weekdays from 7am). It is also well worth visiting the Fish Auction Hall (Feskekörka) on the Rosenlundskanal.

Fish Auction Hall

Farther west is the 933m/1010yd long Älvborg Bridge (1966), which leads to the Hisingen peninsula.

★Slottskogen

South of the Shipping Museum, in Dag Hammarskjöldsleden, lies Göteborg's largest park, Slottskogen (Castle Wood). It is a beautifully wooded area (oaks and conifers), with ponds (seals), animal enclosures, beautiful footpaths and roads, and two restaurants; lookout tower (wide views). At the north-eastern corner of the park is the Natural History Museum (the whales being of particular interest). To the south-east, beyond Dag Hammarskjöldsleden, is the Botanic Garden (Botaniska Trädgården), an open natural park; on its north-east side is the Salgren Hospital, one of the largest in Sweden.

Majorna

Between Slottskogen and the Götaälv lies the Majorna district, originally a working-class housing scheme built about 1875, with the "governor's houses" (*landshövdingehus*) characteristic of Göteborg (so called because they were built in accordance with a decree issued by the governor, the (*landshövding*). Since timber-built houses were not allowed to have more than two storeys the ground floor was built of stone.

Landvetter

Landvetter, Göteborg's airport, is 18km/11 miles east of the city centre on the road to Borås (No. 40).

Southern Surroundings

Nya Elfsborg

From Lilla Bommen it is a half-hour trip by motorboat to the fortress of Elfsborg (1670; renovated 1971), on an island off the mouth of the river. From 1670 onwards it protected the town from attacks from the seashore. Today the building houses a museum which documents the historical beginnings of Göteborg.

There are also attractive trips to the skerries. Particularly popular with bathers is the island of Styrsö.

Långedrag

9km/6 miles south-west of Nya Elfsborg, on the estuary of the Götaälv, is the former fishing village of Långedrag, now a popular seaside resort (summer restaurant) and an attractive residential suburb.

Mölndal

7km/4½ miles south on E 20 is the industrial town of Mölndal (pop. 51,000), now joined up with Göteborg. Aircraft are manufactured here. 2km/1¼ miles east is Gunnebo Castle (1796), in an English-style park. This classical wooden building was constructed for John Hall the Elder; the furnishings are also of interest (guided tours). To the west is Åby racecourse.

Kållered

7km/4½ miles farther south is Kållered, which has a church dating in part from the 13th century with a beautiful painted timber ceiling.

At Lindome the road leaves the province of Bohuslän and enters Halland (see Varberg).

Northern Surroundings

See Bohuslän

Gotland   E 6

Country: **Sweden**
Province: Gotland
Area: 3001sq.km/1159sq. miles. Population: 56,000
Post code: S–621.. Telephone code: 0498

Raukar *on Gotland*

Access

Ferry services: throughout the year by Gotlandslinjen from Oskarshamn (about 4¼ hours) and Nynäshamn, 55km/34 miles south of Stockholm (about 5 hours); booking through Gotslandslinjen.

Air services: flights by the Swedish domestic airline Linjeflyg from 30 airports in mainland Sweden; the flight from Stockholm to Visby takes only 35 minutes.

Situation and characteristics

Gotland, 125km/78 miles long by up to 55km/34 miles across, is the largest island in the Baltic. It lies some 90km/56 miles from the Swedish mainland, and is separated from the island of Öland (see entry) to the south-west by a channel 55km/34 miles wide and up to 200m/650ft deep.

Gotland has a large number of important ancient monuments, including the famous town walls of Visby and 92 churches, none of them built after 1350. For some centuries the island was an important centre of Baltic trade, and as a result frequently came under foreign rule. Tourism is now one of its principal sources of income.

Topography

Gotland is a limestone plateau lying at altitudes of between 20 and 30m (65 and 100ft) with no lakes, rivers or valleys of any size, since water seeps away quickly into the soil. Along the coasts are long sandy beaches alternating with sheer limestone cliffs. Characteristic of the coastal scenery are the bizarrely shaped free-standing crags known as *raukar* (singular *rauk*). The glaciers of the Ice Age have left their mark in the shape of numerous erratic blocks of gneiss, granite and porphyry.

Thanks to its mild climate the island has a varied and abundant plant life; even orchids flourish here. There are large expanses of grazing (sheep-farming) and arable land, but just under half the island's area is covered by forest. Drilling for oil began about 1980.

History

Gotland with its capital Visby was for many centuries an important staging point on the trade route between Asia and Europe. Until the beginning of

175

the 12th century the trade remained firmly in the hands of the Gotlanders, who had established trading posts at Novgorod (northern Russia) and elsewhere; but as the trade grew in importance it came to be increasingly controlled by Germans and Russians. In 1161 the Gotlanders were granted a licence to trade with Germany, and in 1280 Visby and Lübeck entered into a defensive alliance against piracy, which was later joined by Riga. Visby's predominance in Baltic trade was broken in 1293 when the Hanseatic League resolved that Novgorod should trade only with Lübeck. Further difficulty was caused by conflicts between peasants and townspeople.

In 1361 the island was conquered by the Danish king Valdemar Atterdag (betrayed, according to legend, by the lovesick daughter of a Visby goldsmith), and four years later it fell into the hands of pirates. In 1398 the pirates were driven out by the knights of the Teutonic Order, who in 1408 sold the island to Eric of Pomerania, ruler of the united Scandinavian kingdoms. In 1449 it returned to Danish hands. Unsuccessful attempts to conquer the island were made by the Swedes in 1524 and by Lübeck a year later. In 1645, however, it was assigned to Sweden under the treaty of Brömsebro. Thereafter there were two further periods of foreign rule – from 1676 to 1679 by the Danes, in 1808 for 23 days by the Russians. Little remains of the island's former splendour.

Visby

The island's capital, Visby (pop. 20,000), the "city of roses and ruins", on the north-west coast of Gotland, is the seat of the governor of Gotland county and the see of a bishop. Within its enclosing walls it has preserved much of its medieval atmosphere, though of its original seventeen churches ten survive only as ruins and only one (St Mary's) is still used for worship.

★★Town Walls

The most notable feature of Visby is the 3.5km/2 mile long circuit of town walls, built of limestone in the latter part of the 13th century and strengthened about 1300. At regular intervals round the walls are 44 towers standing between 15 and 20m (50 and 60ft) high. At two points there are large breaches in the walls – one on the east side, thought to have been caused by a Swedish attack in 1524, and the other on the west, the result of an attack by the Lübeckers a year later. On the seaward side is the Powder Tower (Kruttornet), probably built in the 11th century and incorporated in the later walls. Near the north end is the Maiden's Tower (Jungfrutornet), in which legend has it that the daughter of a Visby goldsmith was walled up alive for betraying the town to the Danes out of love for the Danish king Valdemar Atterdag. The adjoining corner tower is known as the Silver Cap (Silverhättan). From here the walls run east to the line of cliffs, turn south at the town's main gate, the Norderport, follow the edge of the cliffs to the Söderport (South Gate) and finally turn west to end at the ruins of Visborg Castle. The castle, which at one time dominated the harbour, was blown up in 1679.

Within the Walls

Donnersplatsen

From the harbour Hamngatan leads to Donnersplatsen, with the Burmeisterska Hus, built in 1652 by a Lübeck merchant named Burmeister; in the basement is a tourist information office. The walls and ceilings of the Great Hall on the upper floor, now fitted out as a museum, are decorated with beautiful murals. The furniture is also worthy of note.

South-east of Donnersplatsen are the ruins of the churches of St Per and St Hans, standing side by side. During excavations in 1917 under St Per, the

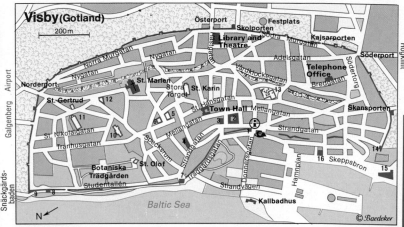

1 Burmeisterska Hus
2 Museum of Antiquities
3 Liljehornska Hus
4 Old Pharmacy
5 St Lars' Church
6 Trinity Church
7 Powder Tower
8 Maiden's Tower
9 Silver Cap
10 St Clement's Church
11 St Nicholas's Church
12 Church of Holy Ghost
13 St Per and St Hans
14 Visborg Castle
15 Harbourmaster's Office
16 Custom House

older and smaller of the two, the foundations of three other churches were found.

From Donnersplatsen Strandgatan leads to the Museum of Antiquities (Golands Fornsal), with a fine collection of Viking and medieval material, including tombstones and runic stones, arms and armour, furniture and religious art. Adjoining the museum is the Liljehornska Hus.

Museum

From here Packhusplan runs north to the Clematishus, near which is the Old Pharmacy (Gamla Apoteket), a 13th century house with a stepped gable (exhibition of arts and crafts).

Old Pharmacy

The Lybska Gränd leads from here to the Market Square (Stora Torget), on the south side of which are the ruins of St Catherine's Church (St Karin) of about 1230, which originally belonged to a Franciscan friary. To the north of the square, in St Hansgatan, are the ruined 13th century churches of the Trinity (Drotten) and St Lars, with massive towers which formed part of the town's defences.

Stora Torget

To the west, higher up, is the Cathedral (St Mary's), the only one of Visby's old churches which is still in use. Built by German merchants and consecrated in 1225, it was much altered in later centuries (restored 1899–1907 and 1945). It has a massive square tower on the west front and two slenderer towers at the east end. The south chapel commemorates Burgomaster Swerting, who was executed in 1350. The church contains a fine carved pulpit of walnut and ebony from Lübeck (1684) and a 13th century font of red Gotland marble.

Cathedral
(St Mary's)

Norra Kyrkogatan runs north from the Cathedral to the ruined Romanesque church of the Holy Ghost (Helgeandskyrkan; 13th c.). This two-storied octagonal structure, of a type unusual in Scandinavia, shows the influence of German architecture. There was probably a bridge linking the upper storey of the church with a hospital which stood close by.

Church of the
Holy Ghost

Visby old town, with the Cathedral

★St Nicholas's Church	From here a side street goes past the remains of the little 15th century chapel of St Gertrude to the ruins of St Nicholas's Church, the largest in Visby. The church, which originally belonged to a Dominican monastery, was begun about 1230 and was destroyed by the Lübeckers in 1525. It has a beautiful rose window in the gable.
St Clement	To the south, among houses, are the remains of the Romanesque church of St Clement, built in the middle of the 13th century. Excavations here brought to light the foundations of three earlier churches, the oldest of which, dating from the 12th century, was probably one of the first stone-built churches in Visby; fine south doorway. To the right of the church can be seen an old weapon-house, in which the men deposited their arms before entering the church.
Botanic Garden	On the north-west side of the town, near Studentallén, lies the Botanic Garden (Botaniska Trädgården), at the south end of which are the ruins of the Romanesque church of St Olof (*c.* 1200). In the Botanic Garden are beds of the roses for which Visby is renowned and which are also found climbing up the walls of its ruins.

Surroundings

★Walk to the Galgenberg	There is a very attractive walk (30 minutes) from the Norderport, past the ruins of the 13th century church of St Göran, which belonged to a leper hospital, to the Galgenberg (Gallows Hill), a medieval place of execution with three 6m/20ft high stone pillars, from which there are fine views of the town and the sea. Below the north side of the hill is the Trojaborg, a stone

Högklint, a sheer cliff on the coast of Gotland ▶

maze which was probably a very ancient cult site; its name recalls the old Roman "game of Troy".

Snäckgärdsbadet 4km/2½ miles north-east of Visby, reached on a road skirting the coast, is the popular bathing beach of Snäckgärdsbadet.

Valdemar's Cross South-east of the town (leaving by the Österport) is the Korsbetning (Cross Meadow), with the ruins of Solberga Abbey (1246). Here is the burial-place of the Gotland peasants killed during the Danish conquest of the island in 1361, and the so-called Valdemar's Cross (Valdemarskors; 2.5m/8ft high, with a Latin inscription). Excavations in 1905 brought to light between 300 and 400 skeletons, together with arms and armour.

★Högklint 4km/2½ miles south-west of the town is the Villa Villekulla, which featured in the films of Astrid Lindgren's "Pippi Longstocking" stories; nearby is a children's playground. 4km/2½ miles beyond this rises the Högklint, a rugged crag (45m/148ft) from the top of which there are wide views of the sea and of Visby. Lower down are a limestone spur, Getsvältan, and a cave. Nearby is the Villa Fridhem, which belonged to Prince Oskar Bernadotte and is now a boarding school, with a large park.

Excursions on Gotland

Remains of the past are to be seen everywhere on Gotland, on a scale found nowhere else in Sweden. The Gotland Tourist Association (Gotlands Turist-förening) operates numerous excursions during the summer to the island's main features of interest. Gotland is also a paradise for the cyclist (with facilities for the rental of bicycles).

Visby to Lickershamn (27km/17 miles)

Leave Visby (Norderport) on Road 149. In 4km/2½ miles a side road goes off to the seaside resort of Snäcksgärdsbadet. 6km/4 miles beyond this is the Herb Garden (Krusmyntgården), on the Brissund road, with some 200 species of medicinal plants.

In another 4km/2½ miles Road 149 comes to Lummelunda, with a stalac-titic cave system discovered only in recent years. In the immediate vicinity are a wildlife park, a mink farm, the remains of an old iron foundry (closed down in 1712) and a large mill-wheel 10m/33ft in diameter.

4km/2½ miles north, still on Road 149, is the late 13th century church of Lummelunda (restored 1960). 9km/6 miles beyond this is the fishing port of Lickershamn. From here a narrow footpath (600m/660yd) runs along the cliffs to a striking *rauk* known as the Jomfru (Maiden; 11.50m/38ft high), from which there are extensive views.

Visby to Fårösund (55km/35 miles)

Leave Visby (Norderport) on Road 148, which passes the airport to Bro (12km/7½ miles). The church, in Romanesque and Gothic style (13th c.), has a Baroque interior; 15th century bell with an inscription in Low German. Built into the façade are stones from an earlier church with animal figures and symbolic devices.

12km/7½ miles farther on is Tingstäde, on the north-western shore of a lake, the Tingstäde Träsk. This was the birthplace of the engineer and inventor Christoffer Polhem (1661–1751). There is a fine 13th century church. Under the waters of the lake are the remains of a pile-built defensive structure of the Iron Age known as the Bulverk.

10km/5½ miles beyond Tingstäde Road 147 goes off on the right to the port of Slite (9km/6 miles south), centre of the Gotland cement industry.

Road 148 continues to Lärbro (3km/2 miles). The church (14th c.) has an unusual octagonal tower and contains numerous sculptures and paintings. Beside the church is a 12th century defensive tower. A few kilometres north-west is the ruined 13th century church of Gann.

From Lärbro the road continues past Rute church (c. 1260) and through a restricted military area to Bunge (13km/8 miles), which has a fortified church (14th c.) richly decorated with sculpture and painting. To the east of the church is an open-air museum with some fifty old buildings.

The village of Fårösund, 2km/1¼ miles beyond this, has a small harbour on the Fårösund (1.5km/1 mile wide), which separates Gotland from the island of Fårö (ferry).

The little island of Fårö ("Sheep Island"), off the northern tip of Gotland, has several beautiful sandy beaches (Sudersandsviken, Ekeviken, Norsta Auren) and large numbers of *raukar*. The island has only recently been opened up to foreign visitors.

Fårö

Visby to Roma and Dalhem (17km/10½ miles, 24km/15 miles)

Leave Visby (Söderport) on Road 143, which runs past the church of Follingbo to Roma, with a fine church built about 1250. 2km/1¼ miles south-east are the ruins of Roma Abbey, a Cistercian house founded in 1164 and destroyed after the Reformation.

7km/4½ miles east of Roma is Dalhem. Above the village is a church of about 1250 (renovated in the early 20th century) which is one of the most interesting on Gotland, notable particularly for its wall paintings and stained glass. 300m/330yd south of the church the old railway station now houses a Railway Museum.

Visby to Burgsvik (81km/50 miles)

Leave Visby (Söderport) on Road 140. In 3km/2 miles a road branches off on the right to Kneippbyn and the Högklint. 13km/8 miles farther on is Tofta church (13th c.); to the right of the road is Tofta bathing beach.

26km/16 miles from Visby is the little seaside resort of Västergarn, with a church which was originally the choir of a larger church. By the beach is Kronholmen golf course. 7km/4½ miles beyond this is the port and seaside resort of Klintehamn.

From Klintehamn motorboats ply to the island of Stora Karlsö (12km/7½ miles south-west), passing Lilla Karlsö, on which there are sheep of the old Gotland breed. Stora Karlsö is famed for its abundance of bird life (250 species recorded, including razorbills, peregrine falcons, eiders and guillemots), and its rare plants (orchids). There are numerous *raukar* and caves, the largest of which, Stora Förvar, was occupied by Stone Age man. Both islands are nature reserves.

Stora Karlsö

From Klintehamn continue either on Road 140, which runs closer to the coast via Fröjel (12th c. church with an old wooden crucifix) to Burgsvik (39km/25 miles), or by the 9km/6 mile longer route on Road 141.

2km/1¼ miles along Road 141, on the right, is Klinte church (13th c.). 20km/12½ miles farther on is Hemse, once an important trading town, with a Romanesque church (c. 1200; 14th and 15th century paintings).

Ship setting at Gannarve (south of Klintehamn)

From here continue south on Road 142, which also comes from Visby. 2km/1¼ miles along this road is Smiss Slott, an old fortified castle. 10km/6 miles beyond this is the fine church of Grötlingbo (1340), with well preserved medieval stained glass; the pulpit (1548) was originally intended for Visby Cathedral.

In another 12km/7½ miles the road comes to Burgsvik, a port and seaside resort on the south side of the inlet of the same name. 2km/1¼ miles east the 13th century church of Öja has a fine 13th century triumphal cross.

From Burgsvik a road leads south, passing the old farm of Bottarvegården (5km/3 miles), now a museum, and Vamlingbo church, to the hill of Hoburgen (37m/121ft; lighthouse), at the southern tip of the island. Here there are curious cliff formations, including the impressive *rauk* known as Hoburgsgubben (4.5m/15ft high), and a number of caves.

An alternative route to Hoburgen is on a narrow road which turns right off the main road 9.5km/6 miles south of Burgsvik, making for Gervalds, and continues close to the coast, through rugged cliff scenery, to Hoburgen.

13km/8 miles south-east of Burgsvik is Holmhällar, with imposing *raukar*. On the beach is an old stone fisherman's cottage. Offshore is the island of Heligholmen, with a "Silver Cave" which is the subject of many legends.

Visby to Ljugarn (48km/30 miles)

On the south-east coast of Gotland, second only to Visby in its attraction to visitors, is Ljugarn, a port and seaside resort with a small Customs Museum. 2.5km/1½ miles north-east are the fields of *raukar*, extending for some 500m/550yd, of Folhammar. 7.5km/4½ miles south west of Ljugarn we come to the 11th century church of Garde, with paintings in Byzantine style. A few kilometres north of Ljugarn, in forest country, is the Torsburg, the oldest fortified settlement on Gotland, probably dating from the 5th century. It occupies a steep-sided limestone crag; on the south side is a wall 1.5km/1 mile long and between 4 and 7m (13 and 23ft) high. There is a lookout tower.

6km/4 miles south at Ljugarn, at Guffride, are seven Bronze Age stone-settings in the form of ships, the largest on Gotland.

★ Stone-settings

Gudbrandsdal

C 5

Country: **Norway**
Region: Southern Norway

The Gudbrandsdal, known as "the valley of valleys", extends north-west of Lillehammer for some 200km/125 miles up the valley of the river Lågen, between the Rondane and Dovrefjell ranges to the east and the mountain region of the Jotunheim to the west. It has a mild climate with long periods of dry weather.

Situation and characteristics

The Gudbrandsdal is one of the most popular tourist and holiday regions in Norway, both in summer and in winter. The people of the valley have preserved much of their old way of life and customs.

★★ Tourist region

From Lillehammer (alt. 180m/590ft: see entry) E 6 follows the river Lågen up the Gudbrandsdal. In 6km/4 miles it comes to Fåberg (alt. 148m/486ft), where the river flows into Lake Mjøsa. To the right is a steep-sided hill, Balbergkamp (660m/2165ft). From here Road 255 goes off on the left and runs north-west into the Gausdal and Espedal (Peer Gynt Trail, Espedal Road: see below).

The Valley

The main road continues north to Hunder and the Hunderfoss power station (conducted tours). The station is supplied with water by a 7km/4½ mile long artificial lake at a higher level formed by a dam 280m/300yd long and 16m/50ft high; fish-ladder and trout hatchery (some 20,000 fish annually). The road running along the top of the dam leads to a camping and chalet site. To the right is Åsletta, from which a private toll road runs 8km/5 miles north-east to the Nermo Fjellstue (mountain inn) and Hornsjö.

★ Hunderfoss power station

6km/4 miles from Hunder, on the hillside to the right, is Øyer church (1725), with an interior in rustic Baroque style. On the other side of the Lågen (bridge) lies the village of Øyer (alt. 181m/594ft). At the Hunderfoss camping site is a children's leisure park, with "trolls' caves", a children's farm, etc. At the Øyer Gjestegård (inn) is a street with shops and workshops for children.

12km/7½ miles farther on we come to Tretten (alt. 191m/627ft; pop. 750), at the south end of the 17km/10 mile long Lake Losna, formed by the widening of the river Lågen. The church (1728) has fine ceiling paintings. Road 254, to the west, leads to the Peer Gynt Trail.

Tretten

E 6 continues along the east side of Lake Losna, coming in 15km/9 miles to the Kirkestuen road junction, with the Fåvang church. This was originally a stave church but was rebuilt in the 17th century as a cruciform church (restored 1951). 4km/2½ miles farther on is the village of Fåvang (alt. 188m/617ft).

Fåvang church

At Elstad, 7km/4½ miles beyond this, a road diverges on the right to the Ringebu stave church (2km/1¼ miles). Built about 1200, the choir, transept

Ringebu stave church

Ringebu stave church

and side aisle were enlarged in 1630 and restoration took place in 1921. It has a carved altarpiece of 1688 and the colourful interior decoration dates from the 17th and 18th c. From here it is another 3km/2 miles to the village of Ringebu (alt. 197m/646ft; pop. 1100).

Enden

Rondane

From Ringebu a side road on the right (No. 27) runs north to Enden (38km/24 miles), continuing to Folldal (50km/31 miles), from which Road 29 leads north-west along the beautiful Rondane range, the third highest in Norway (part of it now a National Park), to rejoin E 6 at Hjerkinn (28km/17 miles).

The Gudbrandsdal near Hundorp

From Ringebu E 6 follows the course of the Lågen, coming in 10km/6 miles   Hundorp
to the village of Hundorp (alt. 193m/633ft), with the Gudbrandsdal Folk
High School. In the school grounds are graves and standing stones of the
Viking period. The church of Sør-Fron (1800), on an octagonal plan, has an
electronic carillon.

8km/5 miles farther on is Harpefoss (alt. 223m/732ft), with an interesting
exhibition of furniture and domestic design. Hydro-electric station (dam
125m/140yd long, 16m/52ft high; the water has a fall of 33m/108ft).

The road continues for 7km/4½ miles to Vinstra (alt. 241m/791ft, pop. 2500),   Vinstra
situated opposite the junction of the rivers Vinstra and Lågen. Features of
interest are the wooden church of Sødorp (1752) and the Peer Gyntgård
(eighteen old houses; privately owned).

Beyond Vinstra the scenery becomes grander. 10km/6 miles farther on is
Kvam, where the decisive battle for the Gudbrandsdal was fought in 1940.
The church (1952) has a 400-year-old Bible; the previous church was destroyed in 1940. 14km/9 miles north (part of the way on a private road, with
toll) are the Rondane Høyfjellshotell (alt. 900m/2950ft) and the Rondablikk
(viewpoint). To the south of Kvam is Teigkamp (1027m/3370ft). On the way
to Sjoa (9km/5½ miles; alt. 285m/935ft) Torgeirkamp (1186m/3891ft) can be
seen on the right.

At Sjoa Road 257 goes off on the left into the Heidal. In 15km/9 miles, after   Heidal
the village of Heidal (many houses and farms protected as national monuments), is the village church, rebuilt in 1938 on the model of the previous
church, which was burned down in 1933. Nearby, on the beautiful farm of
Bølstad, is a chapel of about 1600; parts of doorway from an 11th century
stave church; crucifix of *c.* 1200.

Gudbrandsdal

Kringen	E 6 comes in another 8km/5 miles to Kringen, with a memorial commemo-rating a victory won by the local peasants in 1614 over a band of Scottish mercenaries (said, erroneously, to have been commanded by a certain Captain Sinclair) who were on their way to Sweden. North-west of the village is Pillargurikamp (849m/2786ft), from which according to legend one Pillarguri warned the peasants of the approach of the Scots.
Otta	3km/2 miles farther on is Otta (alt. 288m/945ft, pop. 2500), an important road junction at the confluence of the rivers Otta and Lågen. It is possible to drive up to within a kilometre (1100yd) of the summit of Pillargurikamp, from which there are extensive views.
	From Otta Road 15 runs west via Vågåmo and Lom to the Nordfjord (see entry), and a minor road runs north-east to the Mysuseter Høyfjellspension (13km/8 miles).
Sel church	E 6 continues to follow the course of the Lågen, coming in 3km/2 miles to the church of Sel (1782). An area of some 500 hectares (1250 acres) be-tween the church and the railway station has been transformed within the last thirty years from moorland into fertile arable land. The farms of Romundgård (with the Sinclair Hut, in which the leader of the Scottish mercenaries is said by legend to have spent the night before his death), Laurgård and Jorundgård feature in Sigrid Undset's novel "Kristin Lavransdatter".
	A road on the right (8km/5 miles; toll) leads to Mysuseter. In 3km/2 miles a short path goes off to the Kvitskriuprestinn, a curious group of pyramids of morainic gravel up to 16m/20ft high. From Mysuseter there is a footpath (10km/6 miles) to the Rondvassbu mountain hut on the edge of the Ron-dane National Park (area 570sq.km/220sq. miles: see Rondane).
Høvringen	Over the next 14km/9 miles the valley becomes steadily narrower and the scenery wilder. At Rosten a narrow road (10km/6 miles) branches off on the right to a group of summer grazing stations (*seter*) at Høvringen (alt. 960m/3150ft), which attract many visitors both in summer and in winter.
	E 6 comes in another 8km/5 miles to Brennhaug (alt. 449m/1473ft), with views to the north-east of Storkuven (1452m/4764ft) and to the south of the Jetta range, with Blåhø (1618m/5309ft; road from Vågåmo).
Dovre	The road continues for another 9km/5½ miles to Dovre (alt. 485m/1591ft, pop. 400), chief place in the commune of that name (pop. 3150), with a fine wooden church of 1740. Off the road to the right is the former royal property of Tofte.
Dombås	From Dovre it is 13km/8 miles to Dombås (alt. 659m/2162ft, pop. 1200), at an important road junction. From here Road 9, now following the Lågen valley, runs north-west to Åndalsnes (see Romsdal).

Dovrefjell and Dovrefjell National Park

Dovrefjell	From Dombås E 6 continues north-east through the Hinddal and climbs into the Dovrefjell, the highest peak in which is Snøhetta (2286m/7500ft). Here the coniferous forest gives place to stunted birch-trees, but these in turn soon disappear.
	E 6 is now following the line of the old Kongsvei (Royal Road), along which for several centuries the Norwegian kings travelled to Trondheim for their coronation. In another 10km/6 miles it reaches Fokstua (alt. 982m/3222ft). To the left begins the high moorland region of Fokstumyren, the haunt of many birds (nature reserve). To the right is a view of Fokstuhø (1716m/5630ft), which can be climbed in 2½–3 hours.
	E 6 continues over the moor. To the right can be seen Falketind (1684m/5525ft), to the left, 8km/5 miles farther on, a long lake, the Vålåsjø. At the

end of the lake a side road leads to Dovregubbens Hall (food and accommodation).

Hjerkinn

After passing another lake, the Avsjø, the road comes in 10km/6 miles to Hjerkinn (alt. 956m/3137ft), in a wide high valley in the Dovrefjell. This is the driest place in Norway, with an annual rainfall of only 217mm/8½in. To the west is a military area closed to the public (firing range). The Eystein Church (1969) commemorates King Eystein Magnusson, who built a chain of mountain huts in the 12th century. The Royal Road, travelled by 41 reigning monarchs, is marked by a series of cairns. 1km/¾ mile north is the highest point on the road (1026m/3366ft). On the Tverfjell to the west are the Folldal mines (iron ore, pyrites, copper). To the north is the Hjerkinnhø (1282m/4206ft; 1½ hours' climb), from the summit of which there are magnificent views of Snøhetta, the Rondane range and the Jotunheim.

Road 29 goes off on the right to Folldal (27km/17 miles), from which it is possible either to turn south on Road 27 or to continue via Røros to the Swedish frontier (174km/108 miles).

Dovrefjell National Park

After reaching its highest point to the north of Hjerkinn E 6 descends the valley of the Driva through the Dovrefjell National Park. Here there is a rich variety of mountain flora, and musk-oxen and wild reindeer can also be seen. In 12km/7½ miles the road comes to the Kongsvoll Fjellstue (alt. 887m/2910ft), the newest of the *fjellstuer* (mountain inns) on the Dovrefjell. 750m/820yd farther on, off the road, is a botanic garden.

Kongsvoll is the base from which to climb the Sødre Knutshø (1690m/5545ft; 3–5 hours), to the east, and the starting-point of a walk (4–5 hours) to the Reinheim hut (key in Kongsvoll), from which it is another 4 hours to the summit of Snøhetta (2286m/7500ft).

The Dovrefjell, with Snøhetta

★ Värstig   Farther down the Driva valley some sections of the road have been blasted from the rock. In 9km/5½ miles the Värstig, a section of the old Royal road (now a footpath, offering superb views), runs to the east of the road.

4.5km/3 miles farther on, to the right, is the Drivstua (alt. 680m/2230ft), a former *fjellstue* (accommodation). Beyond this, to the left, is a view into the Åmotsdal. The scanty stands of birches now give place to coniferous forest. 9.5km/6 miles beyond the Drivstua is Magalaupet, a gorge through which the Driva tumbles and foams for a distance of some 100m/110yd.

The road then comes to Rise, with an Iron Age cemetery. Close by are the Smedgården camping site and Driva railway station. A road on the right (toll) ascends into the beautiful mountain scenery of Loseter (alt. 1100m/3600ft). To the north-east is the Sisselhø (1621m/5319ft), which can be climbed in about 5 hours from Oppdal.

Oppdal   The valley now opens up again. To the right rises the steep-sided Ålmenberg (1340m/4397ft; 3 hours' climb from Oppdal). The road then comes to Oppdal, a road junction and tourist centre. E 6 continues north-east to Trondheim (122km/76 miles: see entry). Road 70 diverges to the left and runs through the Sunndal (see entry) to Kristiansund (165km/103 miles).

Peer Gynt Trail (91km/57 miles)

The Peer Gynt Trail offers an attractive alternative (7km/4½ miles longer; tolls) to E 6 between Lillehammer and Vinstra.

From Lillehammer take E 6 as far as Fåberg (6km/4 miles) and then turn left into Road 255. In 3km/2 miles this comes to Fåberg church (1727; runic stone), from which it is another 11km/7 miles to Aulestad, with an old Viking homestead which was acquired by Bjørnstjerne Bjørnson in 1874. The property now belongs to the state and is managed by Bjørnson's grandson (museum; open May–September).

At Segalstad (2km/1¼ miles) Road 255 continues west to Vestre Gausdal, while the Peer Gynt Trail follows Road 254, heading north, and in 5km/3 miles reaches Østre Gausdal, which has a stone-built medieval church. Nearby is the pastor's house (now unoccupied), the largest in the country.

At Svingvoll (alt. 480m/1575ft) Road 254 goes off on the right to Tretten (8km/5 miles). The Peer Gynt Trail leads north-west for 8km/5 miles to the villages of Skeikampen and Gausdal (alt. 800m/2625ft), at the foot of Skeikampen (1123m/3685ft; chair-lift, magnificent views). Then on by way of Frøysehøgda (alt. 970m/3185ft; view of the Gausdal) and Fagerhøy (1018m/3340ft) to Rauhagen, at the highest point on the road (1053m/3455ft). From here there are extensive views – to the north the Rondane range and the Dovrefjell, with Snøhetta, to the north-west the Jotunheim.

In another 8km/5 miles the road comes to Skærvangen, from which a private road (10km/6 miles) branches off to join E 6 at Hundorp. 5km/3 miles farther on is the tourist centre of Golå and Wadahl, 930m/3050ft above the Golåvann (lookout tower). From Vollsdammen a detour (21km/13 miles west) can be made to Dalseter. At Fefor the road runs past Lake Fefor (on left), with Feforkampen (1175m/3855ft; 45 minutes' climb) to the right; from the summit of the hill there are far-ranging views of the Dovrefjell and Jotunheim. From Volldammen it is 10km/6 miles to Vinstra.

Espedal Road (117km/73 miles)

The Espedal Road is another attractive alternative to E 6 between Lillehammer and Vinstra. As far as Segalstad (22km/14 miles) it coincides with the

Peer Gynt Trail. It then runs west to Vestre Gausdal (pop. 400), which has a wooden church on a cruciform plan (1784). From here a winding road (negotiable only in summer) runs south-west to Fagernes (84km/52 miles) through beautiful and varied scenery (many viewpoints), climbing to 1000m/3280ft.

The Espedal Road now follows the Svatsumdal for 22km/14 miles to Svatsum, with an octagonal wooden church (1860). In another 13km/8 miles, at the southern tip of the Espedalsvatn, it passes on the left the remarkable cave system known as Helvete ("Hell"), the largest chamber in which measures 100m/330ft by 40m/130ft. Nearby (2km/1¼ miles) is the abandoned nickel mine of Vassenden.

3km/2 miles farther on is the Strand Fjellstue (alt. 730m/2395ft), with a fine view of the lake, and 5km/3 miles beyond this the Megrund Gård, the oldest farm in the Espedal (c. 1785). From here it is another 4km/2½ miles to the Espedalen Fjellstue (730m/2395ft; good fishing), with a church built in 1974. There was a nickel mine here until 1874.

At Dalseter (4km/2½ miles) the road from Vollsdammen on the Peer Gynt Trail comes in. To the right there is a view of Ruten (1513m/4964ft). 3km/2 miles beyond this is the highest point on the road (972m/3189ft). To the west can be seen the summits of the Sikkildalshø (1783m/5850ft) and Heimdalshø (1848m/6063ft), to the north the Gråhø (1156m/3793ft). To the left of the road is the artificial lake of Olstappen. At Kamfoss is a dam on which, when the water level is high, the overflow forms a beautiful waterfall.

10km/6 miles beyond Dalseter the Espedal Road joins Road 255 at Skåbu, where the Jotunheim Road (a private road; toll) goes off on the left to Bygdin. Road 255 continues, with numerous bends, to Kvikne (church of 1764) and Vinstra (26km/16 miles).

Hallingdal

Country: **Norway**
Region: Southern Norway

The Hallingdal is a broad valley extending north-west from the north end of Lake Krøderen, watered by the Hallingdalselv, here a broad and tranquil stream. The river forms a number of lake-like basins, the largest of which is the Brommavatn. The valley is densely wooded; the hills are bare, with occasional rocky hummocks worn smooth by ice.

Situation and characteristics

At Gulsvik, the "gateway to the Hallingdal", Road 7 runs through a tunnel, with the Hallingdalselv to the right. In 11.5km/7½ miles it passes Flå church (1858) on the right. Farther along the road there are a number of camping sites and a variety of other accommodation – at Stavn, Kolsrud (on an island in the river), Bromma and Roløkken.

The Valley

Gulsvik

In 33km/20 miles the road comes to Nesbyen (alt. 167m/548ft, pop. 2200), situated on a broad detrital cone. To the west is the Hallingdal Folk Museum, with fourteen old buildings. Nesbyen has a church of 1862 and a new chapel in the style of the stave churches. A large market is held here during the first week in July. Among the hidden attractions of the little town is the 30km/19 mile long tunnel through the mountains which brings water to a hydro-electric station. Possible excursions to various beautifully situated summer grazing stations (accommodation charge, road toll) and into the Hardangervidda (see entry).

Nesbyen

From Nesbyen it is 21km/13 miles to Gol (alt. 207m/679ft, pop. 1800), at an important road junction. Chair-lift 1600m/1750yd long climbing 450m/

Gol

1475ft; fine views from top. More than 200km/125 miles of cross-country skiing trails.

1.5km/1 mile beyond Gol Road 51 goes off on the right and runs north-east to Fagernes (52km/32 miles); 25km/15 miles along this road is the Sanderstølen Høyfjellshotell. At Leira Road 51 joins E 16 (Oslo/Hønefoss–Fagernes).

Side trip into Hemsedal

2km/1¼ miles beyond Gol, where the Heslabru spans the Hemsila (waterfall), a tributary of the Hallingdalselv, Road 52 goes off on the right into the Hemsedal. It passes the new church of Gol, and in another 7km/4½ miles crosses the Robru. The valley now begins to open out. At Granheim (alt. 546m/1791ft), 7km/4½ miles farther on, is the 550m/600yd long Eikre dam, from which water is conveyed in a 15km/9 mile long tunnel to the hydro-electric station at Gol. On the way to Ulsåk (alt. 609m/1998ft) the road passes on the left the Helmensbru power station, which is supplied with water by a 14km/8½ mile long tunnel with a fall of 540m/1770ft. View of the Veslehorn (1300m/4265ft), on the east side of which is the Hydnefoss, a waterfall 140m/460ft high, and beyond it the Storehorn (1478m/4849ft).

At Ulsåk a mountain road (toll) diverges on the right to Lykkja, passing the Skogshorn (1728m/5670ft; 2–3 hours' climb). From Lykkja it is possible either to continue to Røn (48km/30 miles) or to turn south to Fjellheim and Gol.

★Hemsedal

3km/2 miles beyond Ulsåk on Road 52 is the holiday and winter sports resort of Hemsedal (alt. 609m/1998ft), with the best alpine skiing facilities in Scandinavia. The road continues to Borlaug, where it joins E 16.

Hallingdal (continuation)

From Gol the road through the Hallingdal continues south-west on Road 7/13, which for most of the way follows the course of the tumultuous Hallingdalselv (many waterfalls).

The winter sports resort of Geilo

In 13km/8 miles Road 7 comes to Torpo (alt. 327m/1073ft), which has a 13th century stave church (fine carving and ceiling paintings).

Torpo

8km/5 miles farther on, at Gullhagen, a road goes off on the right to the alpine skiing centre of Svarteberg (two ski-lifts) and Leveld (chapel), from which there are alternative routes: on the Fanitullvei to Hemsedal, or north-west (27km/17 miles) to the Bergsjø Høyfjellshotell (alt. 1084m/3557ft), or back to the main road via Hovet.

Leveld

3km/2 miles beyond Gullhagen is Ål (alt. 437m/1434ft, pop. 1700), with a large 18th century church. Beyond Ål the Hallingdalselv opens out into the Strandefjord. The road continues along its north side. At Kleivi, at its western end, is the Hol 3 power station, and on the other side of the river the Usta station.

Ål

The road goes on to Hol (church of 1924), where Road 288 (the Aurlandsvei) goes off on the right to the Aurlandsfjord (97km/60 miles). This very attractive tourist road, opened in 1974, runs through numerous tunnels.

Aurlandsfjord

From Hol Road 7/13 runs up the wooded Ustadal, with the Ustaelv flowing in a deep gorge on the left, and comes in 11km/7 miles to Geilo (alt. 795m/2608ft, pop. 2500), a popular holiday resort with excellent alpine skiing facilities, several ski-lifts and a chair-lift up the Geilohøyda (1056m/3465ft; restaurant). The Numedal road from Kongsberg comes in just south of the town.

Geilo

3.5km/2 miles beyond Geilo, at Fekjo, seventeen burial mounds of the 9th and 10th centuries (identified in 1923) can be seen on the left.

Hallingskarv

Over the following 8km/5 miles the road climbs steeply to Ustaoset (alt. 991m/3251ft), on the northern shore of the Ustevann, which is dominated by Hallingskarv (1933m/6342ft; 6–8 hours' climb), to the north. To the south is Ustetind (1376m/4515; 3–4 hours' climb). From here Road 7/13 continues west to the Eidfjord.

Halmstad   D 6

Country: **Sweden**
Province: Halland. Population: 75,000
Post code: S–301..   Telephone code: 034

Halmstad, chief town of the Swedish county and province of Halland, lies near the mouth of the river Nissan in Laholm Bay, on the Kattegat. This situation promoted its rapid development into an important port and trading town, which received its municipal charter in 1307. The town was rebuilt after a fire in 1609, and has preserved much of the appearance of that period.

Situation and characteristics

Tourism is now becoming increasingly important on the coast of southern Halland. The resort of Tylösand (9km/6 miles west of Halmstad), with its long sandy beaches, is one of the most attractive in Sweden.

★Sandy beaches

The Market Square (Stora Torg) is dominated by a fountain, "The Rape of Europa", by Carl Milles (1875–1955). On the south side of the square stands the Town Hall (1938). A notable feature of the interior is the intarsia work by the Halmstad Group, an association (founded 1929) of six painters, most of them from Halmstad, who became known abroad as the Swedish Surrealists. The carillon in the Town Hall plays at 8am, noon, 6pm and 9pm, when the four groups of figures below change places. Beside the Town Hall is a half-timbered building known as the Tre Hjärtan (Three Hearts), once a hospital. Close by is St Nicholas's Church (14th c.), the most notable features of which are the font, the pulpit, the altar and the modern stained glass.

Town

Town Hall

Halmstad

Picasso sculpture

Beyond the Town Hall is the old Castle (early 17th c.), now the governor's residence. On its seaward side is moored "Najaden", a sailing vessel (built 1897) now used as a training ship. On the banks of the Nissan can be seen a 14m/45ft high piece of sculpture in reinforced concrete, "Woman's Head" (1971), created by a Norwegian sculptor on the model of a figure by Picasso.

Norre Katt Park

From the market square Storgatan runs north to the Norre Port (1605), at the south end of the Norre Katt Park. This is the only surviving town gate belonging to the old fortifications, most of which were pulled down in 1734 by order of the town council. North of the park is the Halland Museum, which has an interesting section on ships and the sea (old figureheads, Swedish peasant painting).

Open-air museum

To the north of the town is the wooded Galgenberg, with a lookout tower and an open-air museum, Hallands Gården (old houses, School Museum). The Martin Luther Church in Långgatan (1970) was Scandinavia's first steel church, it has excellent acoustics.

Surroundings

Tylösand

Along the coast to the west is the popular seaside resort of Tylösand (golf course). The road to it runs past the Miniland leisure park, with scale models (1:25) of some 80 of Sweden's tourist sights, in a beautiful setting (open: May to September). The 18th century St Olof's Chapel originally came from Småland; demolished in 1879, it was re-erected at Tylösand in 1949–50.

Haverdalsstrand nature reserve

16km/10 miles north of Halmstad on the coast road lies the Haverdalsstrand nature reserve (about 350 hectares/875 acres), with a 4.5km/3 mile long sandy beach and dunes – a feature rarely found in Sweden.

★Tolarp

To the east of Halmstad on Road 25, at Tolarp (on the road to Simlångsdalen), is the largest passage grave in Halland. Tolarp lies in a beautiful setting amid deciduous forest (marked footpaths), with excellent restaurants. Wild berries and mushrooms are abundant in this area.

Eldsberga

From Halmstad an attractive side trip can be made to Eldsberga (Road 117, then a side road on the left), which has a 12th century Romanesque church with old wall paintings. In this area there are numerous stone tombs of the Bronze Age, often situated on hills with extensive views.

★Tönnersa sand-drifts

South of Halmstad on E 20 are the interesting sand-drifts of Tönnersa, between the river Genevadå to the north and the Laga to the south.

Laholm

30km/19 miles south of Halmstad is Laholm (pop. 22,000), which is probably the oldest town in Halland, the foundation of a settlement on the Laga being recorded in 13th century documents. Nowadays Laholm is an idyllic little town where life still moves at a rather deliberate pace. It is notable for the numerous works of art in its streets and squares, among them a fountain with a sculpture by the Italian Luciano Minguzzi commemorating the work for peace of Count Folke Bernadotte (1895–1948), Dag Hammarskjöld (1905–61) and President J. F. Kennedy (1917–63). In Hästtorg (Horse Square) is the Horse Fountain and in Stora Torg the Laga Fountain (both by John Lundqvist). On the south gable of the Town Hall mechanical figures perform a jousting scene daily at noon and 6pm. In the old part of the town (Gamleby) are picturesque old houses.

At Lagaholm Castle (17th c.; open-air theatre) is a salmon hatchery.

6km/4 miles up the Laga valley is a 15m/50ft high waterfall, the Karsefors (hydro-electric station).

6km/4 miles west lies the seaside resort of Mellbystrand, with a 12km/7½ mile long sandy beach.

Farther south is Skottorp Castle, built about 1660 by Nicodemus Tessin the Elder and remodelled in Neo-Classical style at the beginning of the 19th century.

Skottorp

On the edge of the Hallandsås, near Hassjöv church, can be seen the imposing Bronze Age burial mound of Lugnarohögen. The Hallandsås is a ridge of hills, 40km/25 miles long and between 5km/3 miles and 10km/6 miles across, which was left upstanding when the surrounding land sank. Attractive footpaths through beech and pine forest; skiing in winter.

Lugnarohögen

For the continuation of this route to the south see Ångelholm, Surroundings.

Hämeenlinna (Tavastehus)　　　　　　　　　　　　　　　　　　F 5

Country: **Finland**
Region: Southern Finland
Population: 43,000
Post code: SF–13100　　Telephone code: 917

Hämeenlinna (Swedish name Tavastehus), chief town of Häme province, is attractively situated on a long, narrow lake, the Vanajavesi, with the Hattelmala hills bounding it on the south. The town was founded by the Swedish governor, Per Brahe, in 1639 on a site to the north of the 13th century Tavastehus Castle, which he enlarged and strengthened. The town was moved to its present site in 1777. Its economy depends primarily on timber-processing, with some metalworking.

Situation and characteristics

Hämeenlinna was the birthplace of the Finnish composer Jean Sibelius (1865–1957: see Famous People) and the poet Paavo Cajander (1846–1913). J. K. Paasakivi, President of Finland from 1946 to 1956, went to school here.

In the centre of the town is the Market Square (Kauppatori). On its east side stands the Lutheran church (1798), with a statue of Paavo Cajander in the gardens in front of it. On south side of the square is the Town Hall (1885).

Town

Market Square

At Hallituskatu 11, north of the Market Square, the Sibelius House, in which the composer was born and lived as a child, is now a museum.

★ Sibelius Museum

In the north of the town lies the Sibelius Park, with a statue (by Kain Tapper) of Sibelius as a young man.

Sibelius Park

Nearby, at Lukiokatu 6, is the Historical Museum, with an interesting collection illustrating the history and culture of Häme province, together with much material from the museum of Viipori (Swedish Viborg), now in Russia.

Historical Museum

To the north of the town, on the shores of the Vanajavesi, stands the well preserved castle of Hämeenlinna (Swedish Tavastehus Slott), begun by the Swedish king Birger Jarl in 1260 and completed by Per Brahe in 1639. Still farther north we come to the Municipal Park (fine views).

★ Hämeenlinna

To the east of the river, at Viipurintie 2 (north of the railway station), is the Museum of Art.

Museum of Art

At the Ahvenisto racecourse, on the western outskirts of the town, is the Motor Museum (open in summer), with a collection going back to the early days of motoring and nearby a sports centre.

Motor Museum

Hämeenlinna

Surroundings

Aulanko Park

4.5km/3 miles north of the railway station is Aulanko Park, a nature reserve with extensive recreational facilities (riding, golf, water sports) and a mock ruined castle (performances of fairytale plays in summer). From the tower of the castle there are extensive views. Below, in a cave, is a sculpture of a group of bears by R. C. Stignell. In the Silk House is an exhibition on silk manufacture.

Vanaja

4km/2½ miles south of the station stands the stone-built medieval church of Vanaja, with a finely carved altar and pulpit.

Forssa

54km/34 miles west of Hämeenlinna is the industrial town of Forssa (pop. 20,000). An old spinning-mill (established 1847) now houses the Museum of South-Western Häme. In the Rottismäki district is a museum of workers' housing

A narrow-gauge railway runs in summer between Jokioinen and Minkiö, to the west of Forssa.

Hämeenlinna to Hyvinkää via Riihimäki

Riihimäki

From Hämeenlinna Road 3 (E 12) runs south, coming in 20km/12½ miles to Tervakoski, with the Puuhamaa children's park (over 50 entertainment facilities for both children and grown-ups). 10km/6 miles beyond this is the industrial town of Riihimäki (pop. 25,000), a railway junction where two important lines from Helsinki separate, one going to Tampere and the other to Lahti. In the Riihiraitti open-air museum can be seen exhibits dating from the beginnings of the railway age in Finland. The country's first railway line, between Riihimäki and Hyvinkää, was opened in 1867, and five years later the whole line between Helsinki and Hämeenlinna was in service. Other features of interest are the Glass Museum, housed in an old glassworks adapted for the purpose by the Finnish artist Tapio Wirkkala, and the Finnish Hunting Museum. The town's landmark and emblem is a water-tower of 1952 (viewing platform).

20km/12½ miles from Riihimäki, on the Salpausselkä ridge, is Hyvinkää (pop. 38,000), another old railway town, with an interesting Railway Museum. In the old cemetery are the graves of some 500 railway workers. Near the station is a monument by Wäinö Aaltonen, "The Railway Builders" (1957). A striking feature of the town is the tent-shaped modern church (by Aarno Ruusuvuori, 1961).

Hyvinkää

Hämeenlinna to Tampere by the ★"Silver Line"

The motor vessels of the "Silver Line" sail twice daily from Hämeenlinna, one taking a western and the other an eastern route. The trip allows visitors to experience the harmony between water and woodland in this part of Finland.

From Hämeenlinna the boat sails along the narrow Vanajavesi. To the right can be seen the Rantasipi Aulanko Hotel and soon afterwards the church of Hattula. The boat then continues into the Vanajanselkä, at the west end of which (on right, the old stone church of Sääksmäki) the two routes diverge.

The eastern route continues north, and beyond the industrial town of Valkeakoski passes through locks into the Mallasvesi (ahead, on right, Pälkäne church). In 4½ hours the boat reaches Vehoniemi, on the north side of Lake Roine, from which it is a 35-minute bus ride to Tampere (see entry).

Eastern route

A vessel of the "Silver Line"

Hämeenlinna

Western route

From the west end of the Vanajanselkä the western route goes north-west through the Makkaraselkä to Toijala. At Lempäälä the boat passes under the road and railway from Hämeenlinna to Tampere, enters Lake Pyhäjärvi and continues to Tampere. The trip takes 7 hours.

Hämeenlinna to Tampere via Pälkäne and Kangasala

This route (83km/52 miles) is preferable to the main road (E 12) and is only 3km/2 miles longer. From Hämeenlinna it follows the west side of the Vanajavesi, with Aulanko Park on the opposite shore.

Hattula

In 8km/5 miles the road reaches Hattula, with a brick-built church (14th–15th c.) which before the Reformation was a famous place of pilgrimage. It has many pieces of sculpture, including a figure of St Olav from Lübeck, and fine 15th century wall paintings. Some 2.5km/1½ miles farther on is Hattula's new church. In another 10km/6 miles a country road goes off to the industrial town of Valkeakoski (25km/16 miles); then in another 4km/2½ miles a road on the right leads to Hauho (12km/7½ miles), the oldest parish in Häme province (church of c. 1400; museum).

Pälkäne

11km/7 miles farther on is the junction with Road 12, which skirts Lake Pintele to Pälkäne (10km/6 miles). 1.5km/1 mile north of the town on the road to Ihari is its old church (c. 1400).

★Vehoniemen-harju

In another 11km/7 miles the road comes to the Vehoniemenharju, a beautiful ridge between Lake Roine and the Längelmävesi. It then continues over the Kaivanto Canal, which links the two lakes, and runs along the west side of the Keisarinharju, from which there are extensive views.

Kangasala

Kangasala (pop. 17,500) lies at the south end of the Vesijärvi. The church has a fine carved pulpit (1661) and a portrait of the Swedish queen Karin Månsdotter, who died in 1612 on the old royal estate of Liuksiala (6km/4 miles south).

The road then skirts the long straggling lake of Kaukajärvi. Viatala, to the left of the road, has a modern cemetery chapel, and beyond this is the old church of Messukylä. Then on to Tampere (see entry), 18km/11 miles from Kangasala.

Hämeenlinna to Tampere on E 12

The road runs north-west through wooded country. In 9.5km/6 miles a road goes off on the right to Parola. Before the level crossing, to the left of the road, is an open-air museum of tanks and anti-tank weapons from 1919 onwards. The road then continues to Hattula (6.5km/4 miles).

Iittala
(glassworks)

Beyond the junction with the Parola road E 12 follows the southern shore of the Lehijärvi at some distance from the lake and in 13.5km/8½ miles comes to the well-known glassmaking town of Iittala, off the road to the left on the shores of the narrow Kalvolanjärvi. Attached to the glassworks (conducted tours; showrooms) is a Glass Museum.

11km/7 miles beyond this a road branches off and runs by way of Toijala (railway junction) and along the southern shore of the Makkarselkä; then on E 63, coming from Turku via Lempäälä, to Tampere.

The route continues on E 12, which crosses the 205m/225yd long Sääksmäki suspension bridge at the west end of the Vanajanselkä (restaurant, bathing beach). Soon afterwards the stone-built church of Sääksmäki, one of the oldest in Finland (c. 1550), is seen on the right. Then a road goes off on the right to the industrial town of Valkeakoski (pop. 23,000). In 21km/

13 miles E 12 joins E 63, coming from Lempäälä. From there it is 15km/ 9 miles on the motorway to Tampere (see entry).

Hamina (Fredrikshamn)   G 5

Country: **Finland**
Region: Southern Finland
Population: 11,000
Post code: FIN–49400   Telephone code: 952

Hamina (Swedish Fredrikshamn), situated on a peninsula in the bay of Vehkalahti, in the Gulf of Finland, is one of Finland's leading exporting ports (timber products).

    The town, founded in the 14th century, received its municipal charter in 1653, and was given the name of Fredrikshamn by King Frederick I of Sweden in 1723; the name Hamina (derived from the Swedish *hamn,* "harbour") came later. Here in 1809 was signed the treaty under which Sweden ceded the whole of Finland to Russia – though in 1812 the Tsar returned part of the territory to Finland.

    From Hamina it is 43km/27 miles to the Russian frontier and the crossing point of Vaalimaa, 261km/162 miles to St Petersburg (visa required).

Situation and characteristics

The central feature of the town is an octagonal square, laid out in 1722 to the design of Axel Löwen, with eight streets radiating from it, linked by two outer rings of streets. In the centre of the square stands the Town Hall, originally built in 1796 but altered, with the addition of a tower, by C. L. Engel in 1840. Also in the town centre are the Lutheran church (1843; in the

Town

Bird's-eye view of Hamina

gardens, a monument commemorating the treaty of 1809) and the Orthodox church (1837), a circular building with a dome.

In the market square, to the west, is the octagonal Flag Tower (now housing a small museum), a remnant of the town's defences (1790). The Municipal Museum, at Kadettikoulunkatu 2, occupies the building in which the Empress Catherine of Russia and Gustavus III of Sweden negotiated a treaty in 1783. Another notable building is the School for Officers of the Reserve (1898).

In the old village of Vehkalahti, the original nucleus of Hamina, is a fine medieval church, restored by C. L. Engel in 1823.

Surroundings of Hamina

Karhula

Road 7 runs west to Helsinki (about 150km/95 miles). In 11km/7 miles the road from Kouvola comes in on the right. Ahead can be seen the industrial town of Karhula (pop. 23,000), which is reached in another 7km/4½ miles. The Sunila cellulose factory and the houses round it were built to the design of Alvar Aalto (1936–39 and 1951–54). The Glass Museum is also worth a visit. In the Kymi district is a church of 1850 designed by C. L. Engel.

Kotka

2km/1¼ miles farther on a road (6.5km/4 miles) branches off on the left to the port and industrial town of Kotka (pop. 35,000), on an island in the Gulf of Finland, now linked with the mainland. Situated on the estuary of the largest river in southern Finland, the Kyminjoki, the town rapidly developed into a major exporting port. It also has important industries (particularly woodworking). A naval battle between Sweden and Russia was fought off the coast here in 1790.

In the market square (large market on the first Thursday in the month) stands the handsome Town Hall (by E. Huttunen, 1934). To the south of this is the Municipal Park (Kaupunginpuisto), with the Orthodox church (1795), the only building to survive a British bombardment of the town in 1855. The Lutheran church (1897–98) has an altarpiece by the well known painter Pekka Halonen. Also in Kirkkokatu is the modern Municipal Library (1977).

From the old water-tower (alt. 62m/203ft) and the Norska Berg to the south-east there are fine views of the offshore islands. There are boat trips to the skerries. On some of the islands there are old fortifications. On one of the islands nearer the shore (reached by a side road off the road leading to the E 3) is the "fisherman's hut" of Langinkoski, a timber-built house once presented by the Finnish Senate to Tsar Alexander II. The house, in a beautiful setting, is now a museum; dramatic performances are given here from midsummer to the end of July.

Road 7 continues west via Loviisa and Porvoo (see entry) to Helsinki.

Vyborg

To the east of Hamina is the crossing point of Vaalimaa on the Russian frontier. Some 100km/60 miles from Hamina is Vyborg (Finnish Viipuri, Swedish Viborg), now Russian but formerly the chief town of Finnish Karelia.

Hammerfest   E 2

Country: **Norway**
Region: Northern Norway
Population: 9400. Post code: N–9600

Situation

The busy Norwegian port of Hammerfest lies on the west side of the island of Kvaløy (area 339sq.km/130sq. miles) in latitude 70°39′48″ north and longitude 23°40′ east. The sun never sets here between May 17th and July 28th and never rises between November 21st and January 23rd.

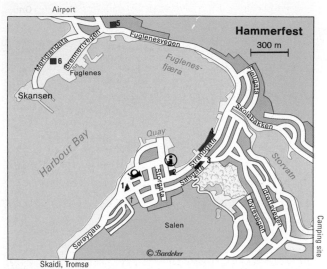

Airport

Hammerfest

300 m

Fuglenes

Skansen

Harbour Bay

Quay

Salen

Skaidi, Tromsø

© *Baedeker*

Camping site

1 Lutheran church
2 Town Hall (Polar Bear Society)
3 Roman Catholic church

4 Fish-processing factory
5 Hospital
6 Meridianstøtten

Long an important commercial and fishing port in virtue of its sheltered and ice-free harbour, Hammerfest received its municipal charter in 1789. The town was bombarded by a British fleet in 1809, almost totally destroyed by fire in 1890 and razed to the ground by German forces in October 1944 after the compulsory evacuation of the population, only the cemetery chapel being left standing. The people of Hammerfest, however, soon rebuilt their town on the narrow strip of land between the hill ridge of Salen and the sea. The rebuilt town is notable for its colourful house-fronts.

History

Hammerfest is the base of Norway's Arctic fishing fleet; it has a large fish-processing industry and a fishery college. It is now also catering for increasing numbers of visitors and in future the town could also profit from the oil boom.

Economy

In the Market Square is the Town Hall (1957). Here, on payment of a single subscription, visitors can become members of the Royal and Ancient Society of Polar Bears. There is also a small museum (open only in summer) displaying relics of the days when Hammerfest was the metropolis of the Arctic and the whalers' capital.

Town

In the square is a bust of the composer Ole Olsen (1850–1927), a native of Hammerfest.

From here Storgata runs north to the quay used by the vessels of the Hurtigrute (see entry) and by local shipping.

To the west of the market square, in Kirkegata, is the Lutheran church (1961), a striking example of modern architecture. In the tent-shaped gable can be seen a large stained glass window (by Jardar Lunde, 1962), 8m/26ft square. Concerts are given in the church every evening in summer. Close by is a little wooden chapel which survived the Second World War.

Lutheran church

From the market square Strandgata runs north-east, passing on the right the little Roman Catholic church (1958), mostly built by German volunteers.

Hammerfest

Hammerfest

The cross was carved by an Austrian who had been a prisoner of war in Narvik. Farther along, also on the right, is the school (1961).

The road continues round the bay to the promontory of Fuglenes, with a prominent granite column topped by a bronze globe. This is the Meridian Column (Meridianstøtten), erected to commemorate the completion of a joint Norwegian-Swedish-Russian survey (1816–52) to determine the size and shape of the earth. Its southern counterpart was set up at Ismail, 2872km/1785 miles away at the mouth of the Danube. The concrete slab beside the column was erected during a further survey in 1929. From here there is a fine view of the town and the hills immediately beyond it.

✶ Skansen

At the end of the Fuglenes peninsula is Skansen, a defensive rampart built during the Napoleonic wars and restored in 1989.

Surroundings

Salen

From the market square a footpath runs up Salen (the "Saddle"; 86m/282ft), the ridge of hills on the south side of the town; the climb to the top takes 20 minutes. It can also be reached on a road running to the east of the town past a small lake, the Storvatn. From the west end of the hill there is a extensive view of the open sea.

On the south side of the town, to the left of the road, is an open-air swimming pool, the Jansvatn. 1km/¾ mile beyond this is the most northerly stretch of woodland in the world. The road continues to Skaidi. To the left is a view of Tyven (the "Thief"; 419m/1375ft), which can be climbed from Hammerfest in 1½ hours. From the summit there are views to the east over the barren island with its many lakes, to the south and west of the mountains with their snowfields and glaciers, and to the north over the infinite expanse of the Arctic Ocean.

Excursion to the North Cape

One of the attractions offered to visitors in Hammerfest is an excursion to the North Cape (see entry), either by sea or by a combination of boat and bus. The fast ships of the Hurtigrute (see entry) leave Hammerfest daily at 8.30am and reach Honningsvåg about 2pm. From there a bus runs to the North Cape and after a short stay returns to Honningsvåg, from which the return to Hammerfest is on the evening bus.

The return boat does not leave Honningsvåg until the following morning, but a night spent there, at the cost of losing one's sleep, is richly rewarded by the fascinating sight of the midnight sun. The morning boat arrives back at Hammerfest about 11.30am.

There are also charter flights from Hammerfest to the North Cape.

Hanko (Hangö)   F 5

Country: **Finland**
Region: South-western Finland
Population: 12,000
Post code: FIN–10900   Telephone code: 911

Hanko (Swedish Hangö), situated on a peninsula in south-western Finland, is the country's most southerly town. The population is about evenly split between Finnish- and Swedish-speakers. It is a popular summer holiday resort with a tradition going back to Tsarist times, offering a wide range of sports and recreational facilities as well as the beautiful beaches round the peninsula. Hanko is also an important port (Finland's only free port) and ferry terminal (services to Lübeck in northern Germany). The harbour is ice-free (or is kept ice-free) throughout the year.

Situation and characteristics

Strategically situated between the Gulfs of Finland and Bothnia, Hanko was settled from a very early period and was a cause of dispute in many wars and the scene of many battles. In the Middle Ages vessels were already anchoring in the sound of Hauensuoli. The peninsula was fortified at the end of the 18th century. Hanko received its municipal charter, however, only in 1874, when the opening of the railway line from Helsinki gave the town's economy a boost.

History

Between 1880 and 1930 hundreds of thousands of Finns emigrating to the United States sailed from Hanko. During the Second World War, in 1940, Finland was obliged to lease the town to the Soviet Union, but in the summer of 1941 the Finns recovered it after a long siege, during which 400 Soviet soldiers were killed. In 1960 Finland and the Soviet Union jointly erected a monument to commemorate these events.

On the Hauensuoli peninsula there are reminders of the sailing ships which once waited off Hanko for favourable winds; these are in the form of names and coats of arms carved from the rock between the 16th and 18th centuries.

Town

In the town centre are a Neo-Gothic church (by Jac Ahrenberg, 1892) on the Vartiovuori (Watch Hill), the modern Town House (1951) and the little Orthodox church (built by Russian merchants in 1895), a wooden structure with an icon mosaic in the towers.

Town House; churches

In the East Harbour (Östra Hamnen), to the south of the town centre, is the Fortress Museum (special exhibitions).

Fortress Museum

The Emigrants Monument (by Mauno Oittinen, 1967) commemorates the emigrants who sailed from Hanko to the United States around the turn of the century.

Emigrants Monument

The picturesque boating harbour is Finland's largest marina. On the peninsula to the east, Lilla Tallholmen, is a charming relic of the early days of tourism, the restaurant known as the "House of the Four Winds" (1910); the house at one time belonged to Marshal Mannerheim.

There are attractive boat trips to the skerries and cruises to Ekenäs and Helsinki.

Surroundings

South-western Finland has been a settled farming region for many centuries and has preserved numerous remains of past times. The coastal region in particular, with its countless islands, is of great scenic beauty.

Hanko to Ekenäs and Lohja

Ekenäs
35km/22 miles from Hanko is Ekenäs (Finnish Tammisaari; pop. 11,000). The name ("Oak Island") refers to the numbers of oak trees – rare in Finland – to be seen here. The whole vegetation of the area, in fact, is of Central European type. The old part of the town, with many wooden buildings of the 19th century, is protected as a national monument. The town church is of stone (rebuilt in 1821 after a fire which destroyed its predecessor of 1672). At Gustav Vasagatan 13 is the Municipal Museum, with a collection illustrating the way of life of this rural area. The Savings Bank was designed by Alvar Aalto (1965–67).

Raasepori Castle
8km/5 miles from Ekenäs on the Helsinki road (No. 53) a country road diverges to the right, signposted to Snappertuna. This leads to the ruined castle of Raasepori (Swedish Raseborg). Although it now lies inland, in the 14th century it was washed by the sea and could be reached by boat. It was abandoned in the 16th century.

Karjaa
From here various country roads lead to the town of Karjaa (Swedish Karis), on Road 53, which has a large church of undressed stone with 15th century wall and ceiling paintings.

Mustio
12km/7½ miles from Karjaa Road 53 intersects with the road to Salo. 3km/2 miles along this road is the ore-mining town of Mustio (Swedish Svartå), where iron ore was being worked as early as the 16th century, in the time of Gustavus Vasa. The town still has metalworking industries. The handsome manor-house of Mustio was built in the 18th and 19th centuries, following Swedish models. There are other ironworks in the neighbouring towns of Pinjainen (Swedish Billnäs) and Fiskari (Swedish Fiskars), both dating from the 17th century and both still working. Fiskari has an interesting museum (industrial history; living conditions of the workers).

Lohja
A side trip can be made to Lohja (19km/12 miles on Road 51), with the headquarters of one of the largest Finnish companies. St Lawrence's Church (15th c.) is built of undressed stone; the interior is almost completely covered with excellently preserved 16th century wall paintings.

Ekenäs to Salo

Tenhola
From Ekenäs Road 52 runs north-west to Salo. 13km/8 miles along the road is Tenhola (Swedish Tenala), situated between two fjords reaching far inland. The town first appears in the records in 1329. The medieval church of St Olof, which still preserves some 14th century work, has a richly furnished interior (crucifix of about 1470, 14th c. triumphal cross, 17th c. wall paintings). Perniö (Swedish Bjärnå) also has a medieval church, much altered in later centuries.

22km/14 miles from Ekenäs is Salo, on Road 1 (Turku–Helsinki). In the
southern district of Uskela is a stone-built church (1813) by C. L. Engel; from
the hill on which the church stands there is a fine view of the town.

Salo

Hardangerfjord

B 5

Country: **Norway**
Region: South-western Norway

The Hardangerfjord, extending for almost 120km/75 miles from Herøysund
to Odda on the Sørfjord, is one of the best known Norwegian fjords, its mild
climate being a particular attraction. Along its shores are large plantations
of fruit-trees (particularly cherries and apples), which are especially beautiful when the trees are in blossom in the second half of May. The people of
the Hardangerfjord are known as Háringers.

Situation and
characteristics

The chief town in the region, Voss (alt. 57m/187ft, pop. 6000), situated at the
east end of the Vangsvatn in the northern part of the fjord system, is an
important junction on the Bergen Railway, a considerable industrial town
and a popular tourist centre, both in summer and for winter sports. The
church (c. 1270) has a fine interior. South-east of the church is St Olav's
Cross, erected in the 11th century to mark the Christianisation of the region.
1km/¾ mile west of the railway station is Finneloftet (c. 1270), a wooden
house which is the oldest secular wooden building in the country
(museum). To the north is the farm of Mølster, with the Voss Folk Museum.

The Fjord

Voss

North-west of Voss lies Bavallen, one of the best equipped alpine skiing
resorts in Norway (cabin cableway 1080m/1180yd long climbing
550m/1800ft; ski-jump, record distance over 100m/330ft).

Bavallen

Fruit-trees in blossom, Hardangerfjord

Hardangerfjord

Flåmdal
From Myrdal station, north of Voss, a branch line runs down the Flåmdal to Flåm and the Sognefjord. The journey in specially designed trains, descending 865m/2838ft in a distance of 20km/12½ miles, takes 45 minutes.

★ Skjervet
E 16 runs south-east to the Hardangerfjord, reaching its highest point (262m/860ft) in 10km/6 miles, at the south end of the Opelandsvatn. 1km/¾ mile beyond this is the beginning of the 3km/2 mile long road (constructed 1863–70) through Skjervet, a valley enclosed by massive rock walls. To the left is the Skjervefoss, a waterfall on the Granvinelv.

Holven
The road then winds its way down for 10km/6 miles to Holven (alt. 30km/100ft), with Granvin church (1720). One of the church's two bells is said to be the oldest in Norway.

Ulvik
Road 572 goes off on the left to the village of Ulvik, one of the most popular holiday resorts in the Hardanger. There is a particularly attractive stretch of road in the descent from a height of 350m/1150ft to the village. Church of 1858. State College of Horticulture, where Kristofer Sjursen Hjeltnes planted the first potatoes in Norway in 1765.
  Ulvik was the home of Norway's best known lyric poet, Olav Hauge.

Granvin
Bruravik
From Holven the road (partly blasted from the rock) runs along the east side of the Granvinvatn and comes in 4km/2½ miles to Granvin (pop. 250), at the north end of the Granvinfjord. From here Road 7/13 runs south through the 10km/6 mile long Vallavik Tunnel to the ferry station of Bruravik, which can also be reached from Ulvik. The ferry (10 minutes) crosses to Brumnes, on the other side of the Hardangerfjord.

Kvanndal
From Granvin the road runs along the west side of the fjord to Kvanndal, from which there are car ferries to Utne, at the mouth of the Sørfjord (15 minutes), and Kinsarvik (35 minutes).

★ Hardangerfjord
Ålvik
The road along the west side of the Hardangerfjord runs through the little industrial town of Ålvik (pop. 1000; precious metal plant), with a hydroelectric station powered by water from the Bjølsegrøvatn, with a fall of 880m/2890ft. Beyond this is Ytre Ålvik, where there used to be a waterfall, the Bjølvefoss, whose water has been diverted to supply the power station.

★ Fyksesund
Bridge
12km/7½ miles farther on the road crosses the narrow, 11km/7 mile long Fyksesund at its junction with the Hardangerfjord on the Fyksesund Bridge (230m/250yd long between the towers, 27.8m/91ft high).

Øystese
9km/5½ miles beyond this is Øystese (pop. 1500), beautifully situated in the bay of the same name. Opposite the church is a museum devoted to the work of the sculptor Ingebrigt Vik (1867–1927). To the north-west rises the Torefjell (1044m/3425ft).

Norheimsund
6km/4 miles on is Norheimsund (pop. 1500), from which there is a fine view across the fjord of the Folgefonn snowfields.

Steinsdal
Beyond Norheimsund the road leaves the fjord and traverses the gentler scenery of the Steinsdal. In 2.5km/1½ miles it comes to the Steinsdalsfoss or Øvsthusfoss, a beautiful waterfall on the Fosselv. It is possible to walk behind the 30m/100ft high wall of water.

★ Tokagjelet
There is now a magnificently engineered stretch of road, 3km/2 miles long, through the wild gorge of Tokagjelet (many bends, four tunnels, steep rock walls).

E 68 then continues to Bergen (85km/53 miles: see entry).

Continuation of
Hardangerfjord
It is not necessary to leave the Hardangerfjord at Norheimsund. Other possibilities are to follow the fjord to Mundheim and from there either

On the Hardangerfjord near Jondal

continue via Eikelandsosen and Tysse to Bergen (an additional 56km/ 35miles), or via Eikelandsosen to Fusa, from there by ferry to Hattvik and then by road to Bergen (an additional 20km/12½ miles).

From Norheimsund the road continues along the west side of the fjord, coming in 4km/2½ miles to the village of Vikøy and in another 4km to the farms of Ystheim and Vangdal (rock carvings of ships and animals).

Vikøy

   3km/2 miles farther on, on the right, is the farm of Berge, with a large stand of oaks (a tree rare in Norway). To the right is a view of Vesoldo (1046m/3432ft).

From here it is another 2km/1¼ miles to the village of Tørvikbygd, from which there is a car ferry to Jondal (15 minutes). From there skiing enthusiasts can continue to the summer skiing centre on the Folgefonn glacier. The road from Jondal to Utne runs past numerous farms, allowing visitors to see something of the agriculture of the Hardangerfjord.

Jondal

   5km/3 miles south of Tørvikbygd is the farm of Ljones. 1km/¾ mile east, at Vikingnes, are a number of large burial mounds.

In another 8km/5 miles the road comes to Fosse, from which there are fine views of Vesoldo to the north-east, the Folgefonn over the fjord to the east and the Hardangerjøkul to the north. 2km/1¼ miles farther on is the village of Strandebarm, on the bay of the same name (beautiful bathing beaches). There was formerly a flourishing boatbuilding industry in this area, but there are now only a few craftsmen making the local type of boat, the "Strandebarmer". The church was built in 1876.

Fosse

Strandebarm

The road then continues by way of Oma (boatyard) to Mundheim, where it joins Road 48 coming from the south (see Stavanger).

Mundheim

The road now bears north-west, away from the shores of the fjord, and comes in 12km/7½ miles to Holdhus (alt. 130m/427ft), with a chapel (fine

Holdhus

interior) which is believed to date from 1726. 6km/4 miles beyond this is Eikelandsosen (pop. 600). Just before the village, on the right, is the Koldedalsfoss. Here Road 48 goes off on the right to Tysse.

Eikelandsfjord
Fusa

Road 552 runs along the south side of the Eikelandsfjord to Fusa, from which there is a ferry to Hattvik (20 minutes). From there a road runs via Osøyra and Syftland to Bergen.

Islands

Off the shores of the Hardangerfjord are numerous islands, some of which can be visited by car or, preferably, by boat.

★Sørfjord

From Kvanndal, at the mouth of the Granvinfjord, a ferry crosses the Utnefjord to Utne and (not all boats) Kinsarvik. Kinsarvik (leisure park) lies at the mouth of the Sørfjord, which is given a particular charm by the contrast between the gentle scenery on the shores of the fjord and the wild and rugged mountain landscape which encloses it. The mild climate favours the growing of fruit, and there are great numbers of cherry and apple trees, particularly in the middle and northern reaches of the fjord.

Lofthus
★Monks' Path

Road 48 runs south along the east side of the fjord for some 40km/25 miles. In 10km/6 miles it comes to Lofthus, one of the most beautiful spots in the Hardanger (folk high school, experimental fruit farm). From here the Monks' Path, constructed by the monks of Lyse Abbey near Bergen, climbs steeply up to the Hardangervidda (900m/2950ft: see entry). From the top there is a breathtaking view of the Hardangerfjord.

South of Lofthus is the parish church of Ullensvang (13th c.; restored 1884 and 1958).

Folgefonn

The road continues along the fjord through attractive country, seen at its best at the end of May when the fruit-trees are in blossom. Above the west side of the fjord rises the great Folgefonn glacier (34km/21 miles long and up to 16km/10 miles across; highest point 1654m/5427ft).

Tyssedal

The road comes in 26km/16 miles to Tyssedal (pop. 1300), at the mouth of the valley of the same name (beautiful waterfalls on the Tysså), with an aluminium plant and a hydro-electric station which supplies power for local industries. Chapel of 1965.

Odda

The road runs through a 1520m/1650yd long tunnel and comes in 6km/4 miles to Odda (pop. 10,000), a considerable industrial town at the south end of the Sørfjord. 16km/10 miles south, on a road which runs past the Sandvinvatn, is the Låtefoss, a mighty waterfall 164m/540ft high.

Agatunet
open-air museum

From Odda a narrower road (No. 550) runs north along the west side of the fjord under the snowfields of the Folgefonn, coming in 29km/18 miles to the village of Aga, with an open-air museum (Agatunet) in the form of a well preserved farming settlement of some 40–50 buildings clustering round an old courthouse.

Utne
(Folk Museum)

16km/10 miles farther north is Utne, which has a cruciform church of 1858, with some furnishings from an earlier medieval church. Here too is the interesting Hardanger Folk Museum.

From Utne there are ferry services to Kvanndal and Kinsarvik.

Eidfjord

From Kinsarvik Road 7/13 runs north-east along the southern shore of the steep-sided Eidfjord, the most easterly branch of the Hardangerfjord, and comes in 18km/11 miles to Brimnes, from which there is a ferry over the Eidfjord to Bruravik.

Eidfjord village

From Brimnes it is 11km/7 miles to the village of Eidfjord, magnificently situated on the south side of the fjord, with a view across it to the north of the snow-capped peak of Onen (1621m/5319ft). At Eidfjord is the Sima power station, a typical example of a Norwegian hydro-electric station.

From Eidfjord a road runs up through a 2.2km/1½ mile long tunnel to the mountain farmstead of Kjeåsen, which has no other communication with the outside world. From the farm there are magnificent views of the Hardanger peaks and down into the fjord.

★Kjeåsen

Hardangervidda   B/C 5

Country: **Norway**
Region: Southern Norway

The Hardangervidda, the largest plateau in Scandinavia, with an area of some 7500sq.km/2900sq. miles, lies at an average altitude of between 1200 and 1600m (3300 and 4600ft), with numerous lakes and a meagre covering of pasture grazed by large herds of wild reindeer. It is a barren landscape, above the tree-line, but immensely impressive in its own way. An area of some 3400sq.km/1300sq. miles is now a National Park, and other parts of the plateau are nature reserves.

This is magnificent walking country, with an extensive system of paths, usually running from one good fishing lake to another and linking the numerous mountain huts (usually overcrowded at the height of the season, between mid July and mid August). In the interior of the Hardangervidda there are no motor roads and no settlements of any size.

The best approach to the Hardangervidda is on Road 7, from Geilo (see Hallingdal) to Eidfjord, which runs between the Hardangervidda proper and the Hardangerjøkul, a snowfield to the north covering an area of 120sq.km/46sq. miles (highest point 1862m/6109ft), the north side of which can be reached from the Bergen Railway. Road 7 climbs from Haugastøl

Hardangerjøkul

The barren landscape of the Hardangervidda

Vøringsfoss

(alt. 990m/3250ft) to its highest point at the Dyranut mountain hut (1246m/4088ft) and then runs down into the valley of the Bjoreia.

★★ Vøringsfoss

20km/12½ miles beyond Dyranut a narrow road (toll) branches off and runs 1km/¾ mile north to the Fosslihotell (alt. 729m/2392ft), commandingly situated above the precipitous Måbødal. From here there is a superb view of the Vøringsfoss, where the Bjoreia plunges vertically 183m/600ft into a narrow rock basin, which is always filled with a dense mass of spray (marvellous play of colour, particularly in the afternoon).

The Fosslihotell is a good base for mountain walks and climbs. Particularly rewarding is the long walk (13–14½ hours) by way of the Demmevass hut (1280m/4200ft), on the western edge of the Hardangerjøkul, to Finse (1222m/4009ft) on the Bergen Railway (the highest station in the country), situated on the Finsevann in a lonely mountain setting. From Finse there are glacier treks on the Hardangerjøkul, with guides.

Måbødal

Beyond the turning for the Fosslihotell the grandest and most interesting section of Road 7 begins. It runs down the wild Måbødal, through tunnels, under almost vertical rock faces, and finally descends in five great hairpin bends to Måbø (alt. 250m/820ft), where it reaches the Eidfjord (see Hardangerfjord).

On the west the Hardangervidda falls steeply down to the Sørfjord (see Hardangerfjord), along the east side of which runs Road 13. The road nearest to it on the south side is the Haukeli Road (see Telemark).

Härjedalen   D 4/5

Country: Sweden

Härjedalen landscape

The province of Härjedalen in central Sweden, with an area of some 12,000sq.km/7455sq. miles and a population of 13,000, is one of the most sparsely settled parts of the country. It lies between two large rivers, the Ljunga to the north and the Ljusna to the south, and is bounded on the west by Norway. It is a region of forests and bare upland plateaux. Härjedalen forms the southern boundary of reindeer herding; bears and wolves are also found here, and there is a varied plant life.

Situation and characteristics

In the past the people of Härjedalen depended for their subsistence almost entirely on the resources of the forest and on farming, but the tourist and holiday trade has now developed into a major source of income, and many old upland grazing stations have provided the basis for the development of modern hotels and other holiday accommodation. The region offers magnificent walking country and excellent facilities for winter sports.

Tourism

Härjedalen is reached by way of Road 81, which runs north from Mora on Lake Siljan. From Sveg Road 84 runs north-west via Glissjöberg and Linsell and in 67km/42 miles comes to Hedeviken, on the northern shore of the Vikarsjö (alt 413m/1335ft). 12km/7½ miles west is Hede.

Access

Some 18km/11 miles south of Hede is the Sånfjäll or Sonfjäll, an isolated peak (1277m/4190ft) rising out of a great expanse of forest. An area of 2700 hectares (6750 acres) is now a National Park, the highest parts of which reach above the tree-line. Sånfjäll is known as Sweden's "Bear Mountain".

Sånfjäll

Road 84 now continues up the wooded valley of the Ljusna. In 46km/29 miles Road 311 goes off on the left and runs south via Tännäs to Särna (104km/65 miles: see Dalarna, Djurås to Särna).

From the junction with the road to Särna Road 84 continues north-west to Funäsdalen (15km/9 miles), chief town of the western Härjedal and a popular tourist centre. From here a road leads 15km/9 miles north-west

Funäsdalen

209

The Rococo church of Vemdalen (near Hede)

up the Ljusna valley to the beautifully situated village of Bruksvallarna (alt. 710m/2330ft).

Helagsfjäll

Another road (No. 41) runs north-east from Funäsdalen to Ljungdalen (alt. 605m/1985ft), from which it is a 19km/12 mile walk to the Helagsfjällets Turiststation (1033m/3389ft), under the north-east side of the Helagsfjäll (1796m/5893ft). From the summit of the Helagsfjäll (2½–3 hours' climb) descends the most southerly glacier in Sweden.

Tänndalen

13km/8 miles west of Funäsdalen, on the Tänndalssjö, is the village of Tänndalen (alt. 725m/2380ft), to the south of which is the Rödfjäll (1245m/4085ft), to the north Skarvana (1254m/4114ft).

Fjällnäs

12km/7½ miles farther north-west is Fjällnäs (alt. 784m/2572ft), an altitude resort which also attracts many skiers in winter, in a magnificent setting on Lake Malmagen, enclosed by hills rising to over 1000m/3280ft (good climbing). 8km/5 miles west is the Norwegian frontier.

Härnösand E 4

Country: **Sweden**
Province: Ångermanland
Population: 27,000
Post code: S–87...   Telephone code: 0611

Situation and characteristics
The Valley

The province of Ångermanland (area 21,071sq.km/8136sq. miles) extends along the Gulf of Bothnia in northern Sweden. The picturesque stretch of coast known as Höga Kusten (the High Coast) offers a variety of scenery: rocks and cliffs, sheltered bays, nature reserves, fishing villages. The principal river is the Ångermanälv, still used for floating down large numbers of logs from the forests but now, unfortunately, one of the Swedish rivers with the greatest number of hydro-electric stations along its course. From Ångermanland comes one of the special delicacies of the Norrland, the pickled herring known as the *surströming*.

Härnösand (pop. 27,000), at the mouth of the Ångermanälv, is the chief town and administrative centre of the county of Västernorrland. It received its municipal charter in 1585.

Nybrogatan runs from the mainland on to the island of Härnö on which lies the old part of the town. The Town Hall with its circular portico (by Olof Tempelmann, 1791) is one of Härnösand's finest buildings. The Neo-Classical Cathedral (1846; restored 1935) has a beautiful Baroque organ-case and 17th century chandeliers. To the west of the Cathedral is the Market Square, with the old Governor's Residence (Länsresidens; 18th c.). A notable feature is the sculpture, "Evolution", by the Norwegian sculptor Hagbart Solløs.

Town

In the Municipal Park can be seen a statue by Carl Milles of Frans Michael Franzén, who was bishop of Härnösand from 1831 to 1847 and was also a notable poet.

To the north of the Nybro (New Bridge), on the Murberg, is an open-air museum, the largest in Sweden after Stockholm's Skansen, with a collection of farmhouses and cottages illustrating the old way of life in the Norrland.

Open-air museum

From the Vårdkasberg (175m/575ft) there are extensive views of the surrounding countryside and the coast. 6km/4 miles south-east of the old town is the bathing beach of Smitingen.

Surroundings

44km/27 miles north-west of Härnösand is the little town of Kramfors (pop. 24,000), which received its municipal charter only in 1947. Here, at the mouth of the Kramforså, Christoffer Kramm established a sawmill in the mid 18th century, and since then woodworking has been the town's principal industry. The main features of interest are the Gudmundrå church (1801) and the local museum, which contains the town's oldest saw.

Kramfors

The old church of Ytterlännäs, a few kilometres north of Kramfors, is one of the finest in Ångermanland. Originally founded in the 13th century, it was rebuilt in the late medieval period with a stellar-vaulted roof.

Ytterlännäs

Road 90 runs north-west to the garrison town of Sollefteå (42km/26 miles; pop. 25,000), which received its municipal charter in 1917. It is attractively situated on both sides of the Ångermanälv, ringed by hills. On the banks of the river are a hydro-electric power station and the Aquarium (open to visitors in summer), and immediately below this lies the Municipal Park, with pleasant walks along the river. Raft and canoe trips on the river; salmon-fishing. In the river stands the Rafters' Monument (by Fredrik Frisendahl, 1940), honouring the work of the raftsmen.

Sollefteå

There is much to see along the "High Coast" between Härnösand and Örnsköldsvik. At Docksta is the Skuleberg (293m/961ft), now a nature reserve, from the top of which there is a fine view of the Gulf of Bothnia and Sweden's highest island, Mjältön (236m/774ft). 5m/16ft below the summit is a cave which seems to have been occupied as a dwelling in the Stone Age.

Höga Kusten

From Köpmansholmen, which has one of the deepest harbours in Sweden, with a 30m/100ft long quay, there are boat trips to the islands of Trysunda and Ulvö.

Köpmansholmen

Örnsköldsvik

106km/66 miles north of Härnösand is Örnsköldsvik (pop. 59,000), the most northerly of Ångermanland's four towns, situated on a bay enclosed by skerries. The town is named after Per Abraham Örnsköld, governor of Västernorrland from 1762 to 1769, who did a great deal to promote the development of the region. The town's economy depends principally on its sawmills and its shipping, which benefits from a deep natural harbour, ice-free for eleven months in the year (services to Vaasa in Finland).

Features of interest are the Town Hall (1909) and the figure of an eagle in the Torgpark, carved in the local granite by Bruno Liljefors, which has become the emblem of the town. On the landward side the town is bounded by wooded crags; farther inland are ranges of hills with good fishing in the lakes and rivers and good skiing in winter. From the Varvsberg there is a fine view of the sea.

Helsingborg   D 7

Country: Sweden
Province: Skåne
Population: 108,000
Post code: S–250..–S–260..   Telephone code: 042

Situation and characteristics

The Swedish town of Helsingborg, strategically situated at the narrowest part of the Öresund (here only 4.5km/3 miles wide) opposite the Danish town of Helsingør (Elsinore), was for centuries hotly disputed between Denmark and Sweden. The town first appears in the records in 1085, and it received its municipal charter in 1649. It is now a busy port, commercial and industrial town, a favoured centre for conferences and trade fairs, and Sweden's main channel of communication by sea with Denmark and mainland Europe. There are plans to build a bridge over the Öresund.

Town

Stortorget
★Kärnan

Visitors arriving in Helsingborg by sea cannot fail to see the town's emblem and landmark, Kärnan (the "Kernel"), a conspicuous brick tower 35m/115ft high which stands at the upper end of the long market square (Stortorget). From the end of the square a broad flight of steps flanked by two towers (lift in left-hand tower) leads up to Konung Oscar II's Terrass (restaurant), at the far corner of which stands the old defensive tower, with foundations up to 4.5m/15ft deep and a circumference of 60m/200ft. In 1400 it was the central feature of a stronghold

built by Valdemar Atterdag on the site of an earlier timber fortress probably dating from the 13th century. Valdemar's castle was destroyed in 1680, leaving only the tower standing. From the top of the tower (190 steps) there are superb views of the town and over the Öresund to Denmark. Beyond Kärnan is Slottshagen, a beautiful park, with a piece of sculpture by Christian Eriksson, "The Hunt", and remains of the old fortress.

Kärnan, Helsingborg's principal landmark

At the lower end of Stortorget is a statue (by J. Börjesson, 1901) of the
Swedish general Count Magnus Stenbock (1664–1717), erected to commemorate his victory over the Danes to the north of Helsingborg in 1710.
Opposite it stands the Neo-Gothic Town Hall (1870), with a 70m/230ft high
tower and stained glass windows depicting events in the history of the
town. In front of the Town Hall are Norwegian and Danish memorial stones,
commemorating the assistance given by Sweden when these countries
were occupied by the Germans during the Second World War.

Town Hall

From the foot of Stortorget Järnvägsgatan runs south-east, passing the
railway station and boat terminal and the Municipal Library (1965).

South-west of Stortorget, flanking the ferry port, is Hamntorget (Harbour
Square), with the Seafarers Monument (by Carl Milles), a column topped
by a figure of Mercury. Nearby can be seen a plaque commemorating the
arrival of the French marshal Jean-Baptiste Bernadotte in 1810. (Bernadotte had been chosen by the Swedish Parliament as heir to the throne and
had been adopted by the childless King Charles XIII; he became king as Carl
XIV Johan in 1818.)

Hamntorget

At the upper end of Stortorget Norra Storgatan goes off on the left. At No.
21 is Jakob Hansens Hus (1641; restored 1931), a handsome old half-
timbered building. In front of it is a fountain topped by a celestial globe
(1927) commemorating the astronomer Tycho Brahe.

Jakob Hansens
Hus

In Södra Storgatan, which runs south-east from the foot of Stortorget, is
the Gothic church of St Mary (13th c.; renovated in 15th c.). Notable
features of the interior are the reredos (c. 1450), the pulpit (1615, with
intarsia decoration), a historical chart (from A.D. 900 to modern times) and
the modern stained glass in the choir.

St Mary's Church

Farther along Södra Storgatan (No. 31) is the Municipal Museum, with
extensive collections, including an art gallery and a natural history section.
Behind it is an open-air museum.

Municipal
Museum

Helsingborg

Concert Hall

From Stortorget Drottninggatan runs north-west to St. Jörgensplats, with a sculpture by A. Wallenberg, "Youth at Play". On the west side of the square is the Concert Hall (Konserthuset; by Sven Markelius, 1932), and beyond this the Municipal Theatre (1976).

Öresund Park

To the north of the town lies Öresund Park, in which is a former spa establishment, Hälsan ("Health"), with the Sophia Spring. On the other side of Hälsovägen, in Vikingberg Park, is the Museum of Art (Konstmuseet), with a collection of both older and modern art (including Frans Hals's portrait of Descartes).

Museum of Art

Fredriksdal open-air museum

In the north-east of the town is Stenbocksgatan, beyond which is the Fredriksdal open-air museum, with a manor-house of 1787, a number of old buildings, a Music Museum, a Botanic Garden and an open-air theatre. In Stenbocksgatan itself is the Sports Stadium (Idrottens Hus), with seating for 5000 spectators.

Southern Surroundings

Ramlösa-Brunn

4km/2½ miles south-east of Helsingborg is the well-known spa of Ramlösa-Brunn (established 1707). In Sweden Ramlösa is not merely a brand name but has practically become a synonym for mineral water. A few kilometres south are Raus church (12th c.) and the picturesque fishing village of Råå, with a fisheries and seafaring museum. In Gantofta is the JIE ceramic manufactory (ornamental ceramics).

Northern Surroundings

Pålsjö Skog

From Helsingborg Strandvägen runs north-west along the coast, passing a number of bathing beaches and the Pålsjö Skog (Wood) nature reserve, in which are a small 17th century castle and the Thalassa guest house.

Sofiero

5km/3 miles farther on stands Sofiero Castle, built in 1865 by Prince Oscar, the future King Oscar II, for Princess Sofie. In 1905 it was given to Gustaf VI Adolf as a wedding present and became his summer residence, where he established a large collection of rhododendrons. After his death in 1973 the castle became the property of the town of Helsingborg. Art exhibitions and open-air concerts are held here in summer.

Hittarp

From the residential suburb of Laröd, on Road 22, a short trip can be made to the seaside resort of Hittarp. Beyond this, some 8km/5 miles from Helsingborg, to the left of the road, is Kulla Gunnarstorp Castle (1865–78), in Dutch Renaissance style. Nearby can be seen an old fortified castle, with ramparts and moats. In the park is the largest beech-tree in Skåne, 6m/20ft in circumference. From Hittarp it is 6km/4 miles to Viken, a fishing village which has developed into a seaside resort.

Höganäs

The road continues along the Öresund, coming in another 6km/4 miles to the town of Höganäs (pop. 22,000), famed for its ceramic industry. The town's largest manufacturer, Höganäs Keramik, produces the well-known "Höganäs jar" (Höganäs kruset). There are many independent potters in the town, whose workshops can be visited.

The road continues past the resorts of Strandbaden and Nyhamnsläge. 10km/6 miles from Höganäs is Krapperup Castle (1790), with extensive plantings of rhododendrons.

★ Kullen

Soon after this there is a first glimpse of the Kullen promontory, at the far end of which, 3km/2 miles away, lies the popular seaside resort of Mölle. Kullen is a 15km/9 mile long gneiss ridge extending into the Kattegat between the Öresund and Skäldervik, formed by the sinking of the sur-

Kullen landscape reserve on the Kattegat

rounding land. The rounded hills, worn smooth by glacial action during the Ice Age, support a varied pattern of vegetation. The flanks of the promontory fall steeply down to the sea, much indented by the waves. Its highest point is Håkull or Högkull (188m/617ft). Many footpaths; golf course; deer park. The north-western part of the promontory is a nature reserve. From Mölle a road (4km/2½ miles) climbs, passing Kullagård farm, to the farthest tip of the promontory, with the highest lighthouse in northern Europe (74m/243ft above sea level). There has been a lighthouse here since 1561; the present light (1900) has a range of 43km/27 miles. From here there is a magnificent view over the Kattegat. Along the coasts of the promontory are numerous caves: on the south side the Silver Cave (Silvergrottan) and the "Stone Huts" (Stenstugorna), on the north side the Josefinelust and Djupadal caves.

Arild

7km/4½ miles from Mölle, on the south side of the Skäldervik, is the idyllic fishing village and seaside resort of Arild. A little way west of this, in an old Skåne farm, is a café and cake-shop, "Flickorna på Skäret" ("The Girls on the Cliff"), which King Gustaf VI Adolf used to frequent.

Brunnby

From Mölle it is a short distance along the north side of Kullen to Ångelholm (see entry). The first 3km/2 miles are on Road 22 to Möllehässle and then on a country road to the left. In another 3km/2 miles this runs past Brunnby church, which dates in part from the 12th century.

Helsinki/Helsingfors with Espoo/Esbo and Vantaa/Vanda   F/G 5

Country: **Finland**. Region: Southern Finland
Population: 498,000 + 177,000 + 152,000
Post code for Helsinki (City): FIN–00...
Telephone code for Helsinki–Espoo–Vantaa: 90

Helsinki/Helsingfors

City tours   Departure from Simonkatu 1 (near Central Station). The 3T tram, starting from the station, runs past some of the principal sights, with commentary in Swedish, English and German.

Cultural events   Helsinki Festival (two weeks at end of August and beginning of September): concerts, exhibitions, opera and ballet of international standard.

Congresses   Numerous congresses are held in Helsinki (Finlandia Hall) and Espoo (Dipoli). Information: Helsinki-Finland Congress Bureau, Helsinki (fax 358–0–65 47 05).

★Capital of Finland: development   Helsinki (Swedish Helsingfors) is capital of Finland and chief town of the province of Uusimaa (Nyland). Around the city itself (which in 1940 had a population of some 300,000) there grew up from 1950 onwards various suburbs, most of them outside the city limits in the province of Uusimaa. This gave rise to administrative problems, which were resolved in the early 1960s by the establishment of the towns of Espoo/Esbo to the west and Vantaa/Vanda to the north-east – independent administrative units without established centres which at once joined the select group of Finland's five largest towns. The only relics of the past in these towns are a few old churches and pastors' houses in grey stone.

Espoo   Under the administrative reform Helsinki's well-known garden suburb of Tapiola became part of the new town of Espoo. The Helsinki University of Technology, now in Espoo, gives the town an excellent congress centre, which in 1972–73 hosted the discussions by 34 European countries, together with Canada and the United States, in preparation for the Conference on Security and Co-operation in Europe.

Vantaa   Within the territory of Vantaa, where Helsinki was originally founded in 1550, are Helsinki's international airport and the Heureka Science Centre (opened in 1989).

Ferries in Helsinki harbour

The Helsinki conurbation, in which a sixth of the population of Finland now lives, has no internal boundaries that matter to the visitor. The following description, therefore, treats it as a single whole.

Most of Helsinki proper lies on a much indented granite peninsula on the north coast of the Gulf of Finland, with numerous offshore islands and rocky islets. Espoo extends along the coast to the west, on which there are many little coves and inlets, and again numbers of offshore islands. In the level parts of the town are parks and gardens, with many deciduous trees as well as spruces and pines. The ground is not entirely flat, however, for it is traversed by outliers of the Salpausselkä ridge. The thin sandy soil is best suited to spruces, while the forests consist mostly of pines.

Situation

With its scientific and cultural institutions Helsinki has been for more than 150 years the centre of Finnish intellectual life. The coexistence – not always without some friction – of Finns and Finland Swedes has been a fertilising influence.

★Importance

Helsinki has a University, a University of Technology (now in Espoo), two business schools and numerous other educational establishments of university standard. In addition it is Finland's largest industrial city (engineering, textiles, chemicals, high technology), with the headquarters of most of the country's major firms. All this, combined with the concentration of population in the conurbation, has made Helsinki Finland's principal importing port. In addition the city's excellent communications and the facilities offered by the Finlandia Hall and Espoo's Dipoli have promoted its development into an important centre for congresses and trade fairs.

The present city centre, in Neo-Classical Empire style, was built in the first half of the 19th century by the German architect Carl Ludwig Engel (1778–1840) in accordance with a plan by Johan Albrecht Ehrenström. With its handsome streets and boulevards, the city has an air of spaciousness, and the white façades of the buildings have earned it the name of the "white city of the North". The new residential areas on the outskirts, including the towns of Espoo and Vantaa, are admirably planned. Finland's first Metro runs from the city centre to Vantaa (underground in the centre, later above ground).

Architecture

Helsinki was founded by Gustavus Vasa in 1550 on a site north-east of the present centre, at the mouth of the Vantaanjoki (Swedish Vanda), as a rival to the trading town of Reval (now Tallinn). In 1639, however, Queen Christina ordered it to be moved to a better site on the Vironniemi peninsula. The construction of a fortress on the offshore island of Suomenlinna was begun in 1748. In 1808 the town, still a place of little consequence, was unable to withstand an attack by Russian forces and was incorporated in the Russian Grand Duchy of Finland, of which Tsar Alexander I made it the capital in 1812. After a great fire which destroyed a third of the town in 1808 C. L. Engel was commissioned in 1816 to rebuild it. In 1828 the University of Turku (Åbo) was moved to Helsinki.

History

After the collapse of the Russian Empire a republic was proclaimed in Helsinki on December 6th 1917. In January 1918 a war began which ended in May of that year with the withdrawal of Russian troops and the expulsion of Finnish socialist forces – for the war was both a war of liberation and a civil war.

During the Second World War Helsinki was one of the few European capitals not occupied by foreign forces. In 1952 the Summer Olympics were held in Helsinki, and in 1975 the Conference on Security and Cooperation in Europe (CSCE) held its final session here.

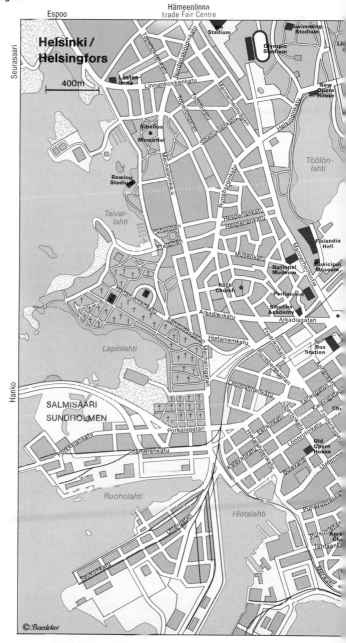

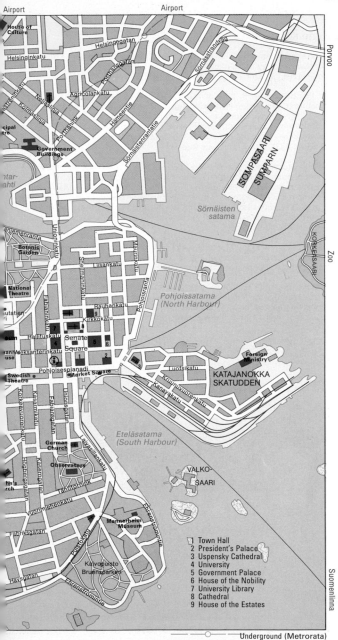

Airport

Airport

Porvoo

House of Culture

Helsingegatan

Helsinginkatu

Porthaniegatan

Agricolankatu

Sörnäistenrantatie

Nelisilinja

Kolmasilinja

Porthankatu

Hämeentie

cipal tre

Government Buildings

Sörnäisten satama

ISOASAARI SUMPARN

ntar- ahti

Unioninkatu

Pohjoisranta

nlejenranta

Botanic Garden

Snellmaninkatu

Liisankatu

Mariankatu

Pohjoissatama (North Harbour)

KOTKESAARI

Zoo

National Theatre

Fabianinkatu

utation- I

Rauhankatu

9

Kirkkokatu

Hallituskatu

4

Senate Square

5

6

ann Aleksanterinkatu use

2

Foreign Ministry

Luotsikatu

KATAJANOKKA SKATUDDEN

Swedish Theatre

Pohjoisesplanadi

Market Square

Kruunuvuorenkatu

Kanavakatu

Korkeavuorenkatu

Kasarmikatu

Unioninkatu

Fabiansgatan

German Church

Unioninkatu

Aleksaterinkatu

Eteläsatama (South Harbour)

hn's rch

Observatory

Tähtitorni

VALKO- SAARI

Högbergsgatan

Kasarmigatan

Vuorimiehenkatu

Ehrenstrómintie

Mannerheim Museum

Fabriksgatan

Puistokatu

Kaivopuisto Brunnsparken

1 Town Hall
2 President's Palace
3 Uspensky Cathedral
4 University
5 Government Palace
6 House of the Nobility
7 University Library
8 Cathedral
9 House of the Estates

Havsgatan

Ehrenstrómintie

Suomenlinna

———○——— Underground (Metrorata)

219

City Centre

Market Square and Katajanokka

Market Square

The heart of Helsinki is the Market Square (Kauppatori), which is the scene of lively activity on market days (Monday to Saturday, 7am to 2pm) and preserves its particular charm even on cold winter mornings.

It lies on the north side of the South Harbour, with an obelisk commemorating a visit to Helsinki by the Russian Empress Alexandra in 1833. From here there are boats to Suomenlinna and to the skerries, and on either side of the harbour are the quays used by the ferries from Sweden. On the north side of the square stands the Town Hall (Kaupungintalo; by C. L. Engel, 1833), with a light blue façade.

At the north-east corner of the square is the President's Palace (Presidentinlinna), and beyond it the Guard-House. At the west end of the square, between the two carriageways of the Esplanade, is the Havis Amanda fountain (by V. Vallgren, 1908). Beyond this is the popular Esplanadikappeli restaurant, with a stage on which concerts are given in summer. A little way south, on the seaward side of the Eteläranta, is the picturesque old Market Hall (Kauppahalli; 1891).

Katajanokka
★ Uspensky
Cathedral

At the east end of the Market Square is a bridge leading on to the island of Katajanokka. Immediately on the left, prominently situated on a hill, stands the Orthodox Uspensky Cathedral (1868), with gilded domes (icons and paintings in interior). The Katajanokka district displays Finnish Art Nouveau architecture at its peak, and it is well worth taking time to look round some of the buildings and into their courtyards. Here too is one of the most impressive of Engel's buildings, the Naval Barracks. After a long period of neglect it has been restored and is now occupied by the Foreign Ministry.

Flower market in the Market Square (Kauppatori)

Havis Amanda Fountain

Between May and November ships of the Finnish icebreaker fleet lie in front of the Naval Barracks. The Finnish fleet of icebreakers is second only to that of Russia (many vessels in which, some of them nuclear-powered, were built in Finnish yards). On the south side of Katajanokka are the old customs warehouses, now converted into hotels, conference halls and various cultural institutions.

Icebreaker fleet

Senate Square and Environs

From the Market Square a street between the President's Palace and the Guard-House leads into Aleksanterinkatu. Along this street to the left are numerous buildings recalling centuries of Finnish history.

Aleksanterinkatu

At the near end of Aleksanterinkatu, on the right, is the House of the Nobility. In Sweden the status of nobility was conferred by being "introduced" in the House of the Nobility, after which the coat of arms of the newly ennobled family was set up in the Knights' Hall. To the rear of the House of the Nobility, running parallel with Aleksanterinkatu, is Hallituskatu. Opposite it are the premises of the Finnish Literary Society (Suomen Kirjallisuuden Seura).

House of the Nobility

Just beyond this, also on the right, is the Government Palace (Valtioneuvostonlinna), formerly the Senate of the Grand Duchy of Finland. In the staircase hall (entrance from Senate Square) the Russian Governor-General, Nikolay Bobrikov, was assassinated by Eugen Schauman in 1904. On the left side of the street stands the bluish-grey Sederholm House, the oldest stone building in Helsinki.

Government Palace

Aleksanterinkatu now leads into the imposing Senate Square (Senaatintori), in the centre of which is a bronze statue of Tsar Alexander II (by W. Runeberg, 1894). As Grand Duke of Finland Alexander encouraged Finnish self-government and in 1864 summoned the Finnish Diet.

★★ Senate Square

On the north side of the square a broad flight of steps leads up to the Lutheran Cathedral (Tuomiokirkko; St Nicholas's), standing 10m/33ft above the square on a granite crag. The Cathedral was begun in 1830 to the design of C. L. Engel and completed in 1852 in a different style. It contains statues of Luther, Melanchthon and the Finnish Reformer Mikael Agricola; fine organ.

Cathedral

On the west side of the square is the University (Yliopisto), built by Engel in 1828–32, with an extension of 1936 on Fabianinkatu. To the north of the University is the University Library (Yliopiston Kirjasto; 1836–45), also designed by Engel, which contains some 1.5 million volumes and 2000 manuscripts, with the largest collection of Slavonic works in the West. The Library is generally regarded as the finest building by Engel in Helsinki.

University

From Senate Square Snellmaninkatu runs north. On the right, just beyond Kirkkokatu, can be seen the former House of the Estates (1891). Over the entrance is a bronze group (by Emil Wikström, 1903) depicting Tsar Alexander I at the Diet of Borgå in 1809. Opposite, in front of the Bank of Finland, is a statue of the Finnish statesman and philosopher J. V. Snellman (1806–81), who secured the recognition of Finnish as an official language on an equal basis with Swedish. Diagonally opposite the Bank, at the corner of Rauhankatu, are the National Archives; here too is an attractive café.

House of the Estates

At the corner of Liisankatu and Marinkatu is a brick-red complex housing the Military Academy and Military Museum. This district of Kruununhaka (originally a small hunting reserve for the nobility) was rebuilt in Art Nouveau style between 1910 and 1925. This part of the town shows more variety of pattern than Katajanokka, with pleasant courtyards, gently curving streets, irregular little lanes and flights of steps. Beyond this we come to an arm of the Baltic, which farther west, near the Finlandia Hall, forms Töölö Bay (Töölönlahti).

Kruununhaka

The arm of the Baltic is crossed by the Pitkäsilta (Long Bridge), beyond which, after the Strand Inter-Continental Hotel (on right), is the district of Hakaniemi. Some 200m/220yd farther on is its market square, with a market hall only slightly inferior to the one in the city centre.

Hakaniemi

From Senate Square Aleksanterinkatu continues west. This section of the street is busier and livelier than the lower part. At its intersection with the broad Mannerheimintie, in the centre of the street, is a sculpture by F. Nyland (1932), "Three Smiths", scarred by Soviet bombing. To the left is Stockmann's department store, established by a Lübeck man, G. F. Stockmann, who began with a small general store at the corner of Aleksanterinkatu and Unioninkatu, on Senate Square. The present store extends to the left along Mannerheimintie to its intersection with the Esplanade.

Stockmann's department store

Esplanade and Boulevard

In the gardens between the two carriageways of the Esplanade is the semicircular Swedish Theatre (Svenska Teatern, Ruotsalainen Teatteri). The present building (by Jarl Eklund and Eero Saarinen, 1936) replaced the original Theatre designed by C. L. Engel (1863–66). To the east of the Theatre are a sculptural group (by G. Finne, 1932) commemorating the Swedish-Finnish poet Zachris Topelius and a bronze statue (by Lauri Leppänen, 1953) of the Finnish poet Eino Leino (1878–1926). Half way along the Esplanade can be seen a bronze statue of the poet J. L. Runeberg by his son W. Runeberg (1885); on the base is the first verse of the Finnish national anthem, "Our Country", which was written by the elder Runeberg.

Swedish Theatre

◀ *Uspensky Cathedral*

Helsinki/Helsingfors

Historic building

On the north side of the Esplanade (Pohjoisesplanadi), at the corner of Kluuvikatu, is a building which was pulled down stone by stone in the early 1960s so that the unstable foundations could be renewed and was then re-erected, leaving the façade unchanged. This building, formerly the Kämp hotel and restaurant (a favourite haunt of Sibelius and Gallén-Kallela), was a centre for the foreign press during the Winter War of 1939–40, and it was here, in March 1940, that a government spokesman announced the signing of an armistice between Finland and the Soviet Union.

Smolna

Diagonally opposite, at the corner of Fabianinkatu on the south side of the Esplanade (Eteläesplanadi), is a small palace designed by C. L. Engel (1824) which from 1832 to 1917 was the residence of the Russian Governor-General. It is now a state guest-house, but it is still popularly known as Smolna, having been the headquarters of the provisional revolutionary government in 1918, as was the Smolny Institute in Petrograd.

At the far end of the Esplanade (corner of Keskuskatu) is Scandinavia's largest bookshop, Akateeminen Kirjakauppa, the Academic Bookshop.

Boulevard

The Esplanade is continued south-westward by the Boulevard (Bulevardi). On the right, beyond Yrjönkatu, are a cemetery which was in use until 1829, the wooden Old Church, built by Engel for use pending the completion of the Cathedral, and two tombs for the Finns and Germans who fell in the battle for Helsinki in 1918. At the corner of Yrjönkatu and Lönnrotinkatu is a mausoleum containing the remains of the planner of Helsinki, J. Sederholm. Many plague victims are buried in the cemetery. Opposite the church can be seen a monument (by Emil Wikström, 1902) to the doctor and philologist Elias Lönnrot (1802–84), who collected, edited and published the various parts of the Finnish national epic "Kalevala". Beside him on the monument is Väinämöinen, the smith in "Kalevala", and at his feet is Suomen Neito ("Maid Finland"). At Yrjönkatu 27 is the Amos Anderson Museum of Art.

Equestrian statue of Marshal Mannerheim

Farther along the Boulevard (to the right, on Albertinkatu) is the Old Opera House. At the far end of the street is the Sinebrychoff Art Collection (pictures of the 17th and 18th c., furniture, etc.).

Old Opera House

Mannerheimintie and around the Station

From the end of the Esplanade Mannerheimintie runs north-west. On the right, beyond Aleksanterinkatu, is the Old Student House (built 1870; rebuilt after destruction by fire in 1978), with two figures from the "Kalevala", Väinämöinen and Ilmarinen. Beyond this is the New Student House (1911); then, beyond Kaivokatu, on right, the Head Post Office (1940), in front of which is an equestrian statue of Marshal Mannerheim (by A. Tukiainen, 1960).

Mannerheimintie

To the right of the Head Post Office is the Central Station (Rautatieasema; 1919), the finest building by Eliel Saarinen in Finland, with a 48m/160ft high clock-tower.

Central Station

On the north side of Station Square (Rautatientoru) is the Finnish National Theatre (Kansallisteatteri; 1901), with a granite façade, and in front of it a monument (by Wäinö Aaltonen, 1934) to the Finnish national writer Aleksis Kivi. Beyond the Theatre lies the Botanic Garden.

National Theatre

On the south side of the square is the National Museum of Art, usually known as the Ateneum after the name of the building it occupies (by C. T. Hoijer, 1884–87), which also houses the Finnish Academy of Art. This is Finland's finest art collection, mostly works of between 1700 and 1960. It is planned to house the collection of contemporary art in a gallery of its own. The Finnish section of the museum includes works by A. Edelfelt (1854–1905), E. Järnefelt (1863–1937), P. Halonen (1865–1933) and A. Gallén-Kallela (1865–1935) among many others. Among works by foreign masters are Rembrandt's "Monk Reading" and examples of contemporary art from many countries. In the sculpture hall are works by the Finnish sculptors V. Vallgren, W. Aaltonen, W. Runeberg and S. Hildén. In front of the entrance is a bronze figure (by V. Vallgren, 1929) of Albert Edelfelt.

★National Museum of Art

Opening times: Tues.–Fri. 9am–5pm, Wed./Thu. to 9pm; Sat.–Sun. 11am–5pm

North-west of the Head Post Office, in Mannerheimintie, rises the Parliament Building (Eduskuntatalo), a monumental pile by J. S. Sirén (1930). In front of it are statues of three ex-Presidents of Finland, P. E. Svinhufvud (1861–1944), K. J. Ståhlberg (1865–1952) and K. Kallio (1873–1940).

Parliament Building

Farther along Mannerheimintie, on the left, is the National Museum (Kansallismuseo, 1912; at present under reconstruction), with a tall spire. It contains a comprehensive collection of material on the culture and ethnography of Finland. Particularly notable stands the Finno-Ugrian collection, with traditional costumes and objects of everyday use. Various displays also document the development of Finland into a modern state.
Opposite the National Museum, in a park, is the Municipal Museum.

★National Museum

North of the Municipal Museum, on the shores of Töölö Bay (Töölönlahti), is the Finlandia Hall, a concert and convention hall (first phase by Alvar Aalto, 1971), with a façade of Carrara marble. The Final Act of the Conference on Security and Cooperation in Europe was signed here in July 1975.

★★Finlandia Hall

To the north of the hall is a park (large chessboards and chessmen), and beyond this again is the new Finnish National Opera House, which was inaugurated at the end of 1993. It is a modern building with two stages. The smaller one, the "Alminsali", is used for experimental operatic performances and workshops.

New Opera House

GROUND FLOOR

Finnish National Museum Helsinki Suomen Kansallismuseo

GROUND FLOOR

Finno-Ugrian Collection
49–51 Sami (Lapps)
53 Ostyaks, Voguls, Hungarians
54 Votyaks, Cheremisses (Mari), Mordvins
55 Estonians, Votians, Livonians
56 Karelians, Veps

FIRST FLOOR

Prehistoric Department
1 Stone Age and Bronze Age
2 Iron Age

Historical Department
5 Medieval sculpture; funerary monuments
6 The medieval church
7 Drinking vessels
8 Lutheran church art (17th/18th c.)
9 Icons
15 Weapons
16 Medieval implements and utensils

Ethnographic Department
41 Woven textiles
43 Ryijy rugs
44 Early 19th c. hut; old furniture
45–46 Furniture (18th and 19th c.)

SECOND FLOOR

Historical Department
18 Renaissance Room
19 Guild paraphernalia; church vessels
20 Burgher Baroque
21 Baroque
22 Church art (18th c.)
23 Chinese porcelain
24 Glass, ceramics
25 Rococo room from Jakkarila manor-house
26 Rococo cabinet from Jakkarila
27 Throne Room
28 Gustavian Room
29 Empire, Biedermeier and neo-Rococo
30 Portraits of Finnish officers
31 Picture, "The Attack" (1899)
32 Dolls' houses, toys

Finland as an independent state (from 1917)
33 History; industry and transport; fashion trends
34 20th century domestic architecture and culture
35 Social conditions, education

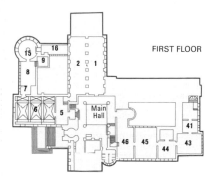

FIRST FLOOR

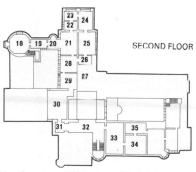

SECOND FLOOR

Northern and Western Districts

Olympic Stadium   To the north of the city, at the junction of Helsinginkatu with Mannerheimintie, is the old Trade Fair Hall, and beyond this the Olympic Stadium (1938), with a 72m/235ft high tower (lift) from which there is a magnificent view of the city. In the Stadium can be found the Finnish Sport Museum,

Finlandia Hall

Rock Church

and in front of the entrance is a statue (by W. Aaltonen, 1952) of the great runner Paavo Nurmi (1897–1973). To the east of the Stadium is the Swimming Stadium and to the north the Ice Stadium. Beyond the lawn in front of the Swimming Stadium lies the Municipal Park, a sea of blossom in summer.

Linnanmäki amusement park

To the east of these sports facilities, beyond the railway line, is the Linnanmäki amusement park, with a water-tower, a switchback and a giant wheel which along with the nearby Television Tower form a striking group on Helsinki's skyline.

House of Culture

Here too is the House of Culture, designed by Alvar Aalto, with acoustics which are among the best in Europe. Behind extends a small park, perhaps the only Lenin Park in Western Europe.

Lastenlinna

At about the level of the Olympic Stadium Linnankoskenkatu branches off Mannerheimintie on the left. At the far end of this street, on the right, is Lastenlinna (the "Children's Castle"), a home and training centre for handicapped children (Mannerheim Children's Hospital).

Sibelius Memorial

From here Merikannontie runs south past the Sibelius Park, in which is the Sibelius Memorial (by Eila Hiltunen, 1967), an eye-catching work of sculpture in steel. This at first aroused criticism for its radical departure from the conventional type of memorial, and by way of compromise the sculptor added a bust of the composer.

Hietaniemi cemetery

Farther down the coast are the Rowing Stadium and the beautiful sandy beach of Hietaniemi. Beyond this lies Hietaniemi cemetery (a military cemetery as well as a civil one), on the highest point of which is a cross commemorating the fallen. Here too Marshal Mannerheim (1867–1951) is buried.

Sibelius Memorial

Near the entrance are the graves of the politicians Risto Ryti, Väinö Tanner, T. M. Kivimäki and E. Linkomies, who – as a condition of the 1944 armistice – were tried by a Finnish court for their political activities during the war and were given prison sentences.

From here Hietaniemenkatu returns towards the city centre. On the left is the Crematorium (by B. Liljeqvist, 1927), with a grove for ash-urns behind it. Hietaniemenkatu then runs into Mechelininkatu: turn left along this street and then right into Arkadiankatu. At the next intersection, on the left, is the Finnish Business School, in front of which can be seen a fountain, "Profit" (by A. Tukiainen, 1954); on the right is the Swedish Business School.

Along Fredrikinkatu, to the left, is the Rock Church (Taivallahdenkirkko; by Timo and Tuomo Suomalainen, 1968–69), an underground church blasted out of the native granite. It has a shallow circular dome (13m/43ft high at its highest point) of copper sheeting and glass borne on concrete ribs. The church is also used as a concert hall.

★★Rock Church

At the junction of Arkadiankatu with Pohjoinen Rautatiekatu is the Sibelius Academy (Conservatoire). Nearby is the Zoological Museum.

Sibelius Academy

Southern Districts

To the south of the Market Square, at the end of Unioninkatu, is the German Church. Beyond it, on Observatory Hill (38m/125ft), is the Observatory (by C. L. Engel, 1833). On a terrace on the east side of the hill is a sculpture by Robert Stigell, "The Shipwrecked Mariners" (1897).

German Church
Observatory

To the west of Observatory Hill is the Neo-Gothic St John's Church (1893), with twin spires 74m/243ft high. Between the hill and the church are Kasarmikatu (Barracks Street) and Kasarmitori (Barracks Square), in which are the headquarters of the Finnish armed forces, in a building designed by Engel in neo-antique style.

St John's Church

South-west of St John's Church stands the brick-built Mikael Agricola Church (1934). From here it is only a few hundred yards to the quay from which there is a ferry to the island of Pihlajasaari (bathing). Near here can be seen a concrete monument with an eternal flame, commemorating seamen lost at sea.

Agricola Church

Off Ehrenströmintie, which runs round the coast to the south, is Kalliolin-nantie, in which (No. 14) is a house once occupied by Marshal Mannerheim, now a Mannerheim Museum. Beyond this is the beautiful Kaivopuisto (Brunnsparken; "Park of the Spring").

Mannerheim
Museum

Vanhakaupunki (Old Town)

To the north-east of the city, some 15 minutes from the centre, on Hämeen-tie (the road to Lahti), is the large Arabia porcelain manufactory (museum). A short distance to the north-east of this, at the mouth of the Vantaanjoki, lies the Vanhakaupunki (Old Town), the site on which Helsinki was founded in 1550.

In Vanhakaupungintie, on the left, can be seen a stone slab marking the position of the first church and the first churchyard. Farther along, on the right, is a granite wall with a portrait of Gustavus Vasa. On the ground is a slab inscribed with a plan of the original town. On the highest point stands a triangular pillar topped by a sphere (by B. Brunila, 1932).

★Suomenlinna

The fortified islands of Suomenlinna (Swedish Sveaborg) are a part of Helsinki which seems remote but is in fact easy to reach by ferry (same ticket as for buses and trams) which takes only 20 minutes.

Sveaborg

The fortress of Sveaborg (Swedish Castle) was built in the mid 18th century to bar Russian access to the Baltic. During the Swedish–Russian war of 1808–09 it fell to the Russians, who thereafter enlarged and strengthened it. In 1918 it passed into Finnish hands and was given the Finnish name of Suomenlinna (Finnish Castle). During the 1950s and 1960s it was handed over by the military to the civilian authorities, and since then has been restored and converted to cultural and recreational uses. It is now included in UNESCO's list of world heritage monuments.

Nordic Art Centre

In Suomenlinna the five members of the Nordic Council (Denmark, Finland, Iceland, Norway and Sweden) have established an Art Centre at which artists are given the opportunity, with the help of an allowance, to pursue their work in peace.

The fortifications themselves are still impressive (Royal Gate, casements). There are also some buildings designed by C. L. Engel. In the old naval dockyard are numbers of wooden ships awaiting restoration. All over the area visitors will find interesting nooks and corners, as well as museums of both traditional and modern art.

Surroundings

Herttoniemi

8km/5 miles east of the city (leaving by way of Itäväylä, the Porvoo road) is the suburb of Herttoniemi, with the Topelius Museum, commemorating the poet Zachris Topelius (1818–98).

Korkeasaari

Also to the east of the city lies the island of Korkeasaari (Swedish Högholmen), with a zoo and a restaurant. It can be reached either by motorboat from the North Harbour or on a footbridge from Mustikkamaa recreation area.

Seurasaari

To the west of the city is the island of Seurasaari (Swedish Fölisö), which is linked with the mainland by a footbridge. It has an interesting open-air museum, with old peasant houses, a church from Kiruna (1686) and other timber buildings.

The island is reached by way of Mannerheimintie, then Linnankoskankatu, right into Paciuksenkatu and left into Seurasaarentie, which leads to the bridge. Nearby, at Meilahti 7, is an old timber house now occupied by the Friends of Finnish Handicrafts, with an exhibition of Rya carpets and other textiles at which visitors can watch the weavers at work.

Tapiola

On the other side of the bay, on the western ring road (Länsiväylä – the Hanko road), 6km/4 miles from the city centre, is the garden city of Tapiola (Swedish Hagalund; pop. 30,000), now part of Espoo. Although built in the 1950s, this is still a fine example of modern town planning. To the northeast, on the Otaniemi peninsula, is the University of Technology, with Dipoli, the unconventionally designed Students' Union (by R. Pietilä and R. Paatelainen, 1966).

Excursions to St Petersburg

In summer there are excursions from Helsinki to St Petersburg by boat or by bus. (Enquire in advance about entry regulations; passport and visa required.) See the AA/Baedeker guide to "Leningrad" (now St Petersburg).

Hønefoss

Country: **Norway**
Region: Southern Norway
Population: 27,000
Post code: N–3500

The Norwegian town of Hønefoss, at the junction of the Begna (Ådalselv) and the Randselv, is the industrial and administrative centre of the district of Ringerike and an important traffic junction. It is divided into a northern and a southern half by the Begna, on which there is a double waterfall, the Hønefoss (hydro-electric station), within the town. The falls are impressive only when the water level is high.

    The falls were the basis of the town's industrial development: in 1668 there were 23 sawmills here. In addition to woodworking the local industries include textiles, skiing equipment and tool manufacture.

Situation and characteristics

Surroundings

An attractive trip from Hønefoss (15km/9 miles on a toll road) is up Ringkollen (701m/2300ft), to the east of the town, from which there are extensive views; meteorological station.

★ Ringkollen

4km/2½ miles south of Hønefoss, on E 16, is Norderhov, with a medieval church containing the tombs of the local pastor, Jonas Ramus and his wife Anna Kolbjørnsdatter. Legend has it that the lady enticed a hostile Swedish force into an ambush in which the the Swedish colonel, Löwen, was taken prisoner (1716). Mementoes of the event are in the Ringerike Museum, in the old pastor's house.

Norderhov

10km/6 miles south of Norderhov is a beautiful stretch of road (3km/2 miles) along the Steinsfjord (on left). The road then crosses the Kroksund, which links the Steinsfjord with the Tyrifjord (alt. 62m/203ft). At the end of the bridge, to the right, is the Sundøya restaurant. Beyond this is Sundvollen (15km/9 miles from Hønefoss; alt. 76m/250ft), a popular resort at the north-east end of the Tyrifjord.

Steinsfjord
Tyrifjord

To the south rises Krokkleiva (443m/1453ft), reached either on a side road (4km/2½ miles; toll) off the main road or by a "barrel lift" (*tønneheis;* 1266m/1385yd long). Below the summit is the Kleivstua (restaurant), with the beautiful "Queen's View" (Dronningens Utsikt). There is an even finer prospect from a projecting spur of rock known as the King's View (Kongens Utsikt; 379m/1243), 25 minutes' walk away.

★ Krokkleiva

3.5km/2 miles farther along E 16, on the right, is the Tyrifjord restaurant. Beyond this point there are a number of fine viewpoints over the fjord. In 9.5km/6 miles the road reaches Skaret (alt. 252m/827ft), with magnificent views of the Tyrifjord and Steinsfjord. Road 285 comes in on the south from Drammen (20.5km/13 miles). E 16 now leaves the shores of the fjord and turns east, climbing in 3km/2 miles, with many bends, to Sollihögda (alt. 341m/1119ft; view of the Tyrifjord below). From here it is 28km/17 miles to Oslo via Sandvika.

From Hønefoss Road 7 runs north-west, passing on the right the large stone bridge carrying the Bergen Railway. It then climbs gradually up the Soknadal and through Sokna (24km/15 miles; alt. 143m/469ft) to Hamremoen (14km/9 miles; alt. 135m/443ft), with an old storehouse raised on posts.

Soknadal

From here it is 5km/3 miles to Noresund, where a road (9.5km/6 miles; toll) branches off to the Norefjell, a popular skiing area, with facilities

Norefjell
(skiing area)

constructed for the 1952 Olympics (2 ski-lifts, chair-lift from 750m/2450ft to 1000m/3289ft).

Lake Krøderen

The road now runs along the east side of the beautiful Lake Krøderen (area 43sq.km/17sq. miles; 1km/¾ mile long, 119m/390ft deep). In 22km/14 miles it comes to Ørgenvika, where, higher up on the right, can be seen the end of the 2312m/2529yd long Haversting Tunnel on the Bergen Railway. From here it is 13km/8 miles to Gulsvik, the gateway to the Hallingdal (see entry).

From Hønefoss E 16 runs north towards the Valdres district (see entry). An alternative route between Hønefoss and Bjørgo is along the east side of the Randsfjord on Road 240 or 34 and then on Road 33 (an additional 37km/23 miles).

★Lake Sperillen

2km/1¼ miles from Hønefoss, at Hov, Road 240 goes off on the right. Road 16 follows the valley of the Begna (Ådalselv), passing through stretches of forest, and comes in 29km/18 miles, at Finsand (alt. 155m/509ft), to Lake Sperillen (118m/486ft; 23km/15 miles long, up to 2km/1¼ miles wide, up to 108m/350ft deep). It then runs for 26km/16 miles along the east side of the lake. Soon after the Buttingsrud camping site the church of Viker can be seen on the opposite side of the lake. Just before Nes there is a fine view of the church with its slender spire (1860).

Hedal
(stave church)

On the right bank of the Begna, above its outflow into Lake Sperillen, is the village of Nes i Ådal (alt. 150m/490ft; pop. 250), where Road 243 goes off on the left to Hedal (25km/15 miles), which has a 13th century stave church (rebuilt on a cruciform plan in 1738; restored 1901) with a fine interior.

From Hedal it is possible either to continue on an unsurfaced road (toll) to Nesbyen (47km/30 miles) or to return to E 16 at Begndal (6.5km/4 miles).

From Nes E 16 continues along the left bank of the Begna through wooded country, crosses the boundary between the counties of Buskerud and Oppland and enters the Valdres district.
For the alternative route to Bjørgo along the Randsfjord, turn right into Road 240 at Hov, 2km/1¼ miles north of Hønefoss. As far as Jevnaker (13km/8 miles) there is an attractive alternative route (beautiful country, large farms), turning left at Klækken (5km/3 miles) into Road 241 (9km/5½ miles).

Randsfjord
Jevnaker

Jevnaker (alt. 141m/463ft; pop. 3000) lies at the south end of the Randsfjord, Norway's fourth largest lake (area 136sq.km/53sq. miles; 73km/45 miles long, up to 108m/350ft deep). The little town has two glass factories – Hadelands Glassverk (founded 1765; conducted tours) and Randsfjords Glassverk (1949) – as well as engineering works.

Road 240 continues along the east side of the fjord. The road on the west side (No. 245; 87km/55 miles to Dokka) is of poorer quality but offers greater variety of scenery.

Halvdanshaugen

From Jevnaker it is 25km/15 miles to Tingelstad, from which a side road runs east to Halvdanshaugen, with a Romanesque church (no longer used for worship) and the Hadeland Folk Museum.

4km/2½ miles farther on is Brandbu (alt. 178m/584ft, pop. 2000), which is also on Road 4 (74km/46 miles to Oslo, 55km/34 miles to Gjøvik).

5.5km/3½ miles south of Brandbu (3.4km/2 miles on Road 4, then turn right) is Gran, with two notable churches of about 1100.

Road 240 continues via Røykenvik (4km/2½ miles; to right Brandbukampen, 522m/1713ft; view) to Hov i Land (37km/23 miles; alt. 134m/440ft;

church of 1781); then on Road 34 to Fluberg (11km/7 miles; alt. 155m/510ft; church with altarpiece of 1752, a copy of one by Rubens) and Singvoll (2km/1¼ miles), where Road 33 goes off on the right to Gjøvik (28km/17 miles).

The road continues through Odnes (ski-jump; record 108m/354ft) to Dokka (14km/8½ miles; alt. 148m/486ft; pop. 2000), chief place of the Nordre Land district; local museum, with fifteen old houses. Here the Dokkaelv flows into the Etna, and Road 245, coming from Jevnaker along the west side of the Randsfjord, joins Road 34 or 33, which now follows the valley of the Etna.

Dokka

5km/3 miles farther on is Nordsinni church (built at Haugnar in 1758, brought to Nordsinni in 1898 and re-erected in 1961), which has an attractive interior.

At Møllerstugufossen, 8km/5 miles farther on, is a group of twelve rock carvings some 4000 years old.

Rock carvings

At Tonsåsen (16km/10 miles; alt. 624m/2047ft) the road from Bagn comes in on the left. Road 33 soon reaches its highest point (726m/2382ft) and then descends to 510m/1675ft at Bjørgo (12km/7½ miles). Here, in the wooded Valdres region, it joins E 16, coming from Hønefoss.

Hudiksvall   E 5

Country: Sweden
Province: Hälsingland
Population: 38,000
Post code: S–824..   Telephone code: 0650

Hudiksvall harbour

Hudiksvall

Situation and characteristics

Hälsingland is a farming region with great expanses of pasture where old folk dances are danced in summer. The high spot of the year is the Hälsingehambon, a popular festival celebrated on the Hårga Meadow to the south of Bollnäs, with dances in colourful traditional costumes. The district has many attractions for visitors: in addition to the beauty of the country areas there are the beaches and fishing villages on the "Maidens' Coast". The chief town of Hälsingland is the port and woodworking town of Hudiksvall (pop. 38,000), on the Hudiksvallfjärd, the oldest town in the Norrland after Gävle (municipal charter 1582) and the oldest of the towns founded by the Vasa kings. In the past the town was frequently ravaged by fire.

Town

The old part of the town, with many wooden houses, is Fiskarstaden, on the harbour. Rebuilt after a fire in 1792, it is the best preserved part of the town. The church dates from the 17th and 18th centuries. Another notable building is the Hantverksgådens Hus (19th c.), with a richly decorated façade on Storgatan – an early example of a specially built shop front.

Nearby is the Hälsingemuseum, with exhibits illustrating local history and life and a picture gallery with works by Swedish artists. The Theatre (1881; restored 1972) is beautifully situated in a park by the Lillfjärd. To the east of the town is the Köpmanberg, with a park and a restaurant.

Surroundings

Hälsingtuna

3.5km/2 miles north-west of Hudiksvall is the medieval church of Hälsingtuna, with an old burial vault.

Maidens' Coast

Off the E 4, both north and south of Hudiksvall, are attractive little fishing villages and seaside resorts on the "Maidens' Coast", notably Stocka and Mellanfjärden (north of the town), Skärså, Stenö (particularly suitable for families with children) and Ljusne (to the south).

Söderhamn

56km/35 miles south of Hudiksvall on E 4 lies Söderhamn. In the days when Sweden was a great power this was an important arms manufacturing town: it is now an industrial and commercial town noted for its parks and gardens. From the Oscarsborg lookout tower there are extensive views. Kvarnen, an old mill, is now a cultural centre (exhibitions). A pleasant excursion is to the Losemyra Fäbod, an upland grazing station a few kilometres north of Söderhamn.

A trip into the interior: Bollnäs

From Söderhamn Road 301 leads inland to Bergvik, where the first sulphite factory in the world was established in 1874; industrial museum. The road to Bollnäs runs past Rengsjö Hambygsgård, an open-air museum with old farmhouses and cottages, some of them dating from the 15th century; one notable feature is the "sun door" on one of the houses.

Bollnäs lies in a long settled farming area at the confluence of the rivers Voxna and Ljusna (fishing, canoeing). From the top of the Bolleberg (262m/860ft) there are fine views of the surrounding country.

Doll Museum

A few kilometres west of Bollnäs is Alfta, with the Linnea Avenberg doll factory and a Doll Museum (700 dolls ranging in date from 1730 to the present day).

Hamra National Park

North-west of Edsbyn, in northern Dalarna, is the Hamra National Park, with elks, bears, roe-deer and many species of woodland birds.

Bollnäs to Ljusdal

From Bollnäs Road 83 goes north towards Ljusdal. At Växbo, on the east side of the road, is a 19th century mill which has been brought back into use (conducted tours). On the western shores of the Orsjö are good bathing beaches. To the west of Road 83 is the farm of Harsagården, a good base for walkers and anglers. Near here is the Svedbovallen upland grazing station (cows and goats; farm-made cheese). A few kilometres north, beautifully situated on the river Ljusna, lies the village of Järvsö, with Sweden's largest parish church (1838) on an island in the river. The farm of Stene Gård (19th c.), on the east bank of the river, is now a craft and cultural centre. From the top of the Järvsjöklack (389m/1276ft) there are fine views of the surrounding countryside.

Around the town of Ljusdal is an area of hills and lakes. On Lakes Södra and Norra Dellen there are beautiful beaches and ideal canoeing waters.

Hurtigrute ("Coastal Express")

Country: **Norway**

The Hurtigrute ("Coastal Express") is an essential element in the life of Norway's western coastal regions. Every day at 10pm one of the eleven black steamers of the Hurtigrute service sails from Bergen for Kirkenes, on the Russian frontier, calling at 44 intermediate ports. Formerly a vital transport link for places otherwise difficult of access on the west coast, it has within the last thirty years developed into a major tourist attraction. The Hurtigrute operates on 365 days in the year, and although the violent winter storms may sometimes lead to delays the small but very seaworthy vessels have always got through.

A regular service between southern and northern Norway was first established in 1893. An all-year-round service between Trondheim and Hammerfest transported goods and passengers (including, even in those days, some tourists) as well as mail: hence the name of mailship which the vessels have borne since then.

The ships of the Hurtigrute provide passengers with cabins, traditional Norwegian food, entertainment and talks on the history of Norway and of the mailships. The voyage can be interrupted by shore excursions or overnight stops at intermediate ports. For tourists the journey is a memorable one, with the experience of crossing the Arctic Circle, the scenery of some of the most impressive fjords in western and northern Norway, the midnight sun between May and August and, on clear autumn and winter nights, the aurora borealis or "northern lights". In addition they see something of the way of life, the fisheries, architecture and traditions of the coastal settlements. Over the eleven days that the trip takes, however, no guarantees can be given about the weather.

Lake Inari/Inarijärvi   F 2

Country: **Finland**
Region: Northern Finland

Lake Inari, in the far north of Finland, is the country's third largest lake, with an area of 1300sq.km/500sq. miles (80km/50 miles long by 41km/25 miles wide) – though the area of the lake, with its numerous indentations and ramifications, cannot be exactly determined. The number of islands in the lake is usually given as 3000. This bizarre world on the 69th parallel is one of the most fascinating regions in Finland.

Situation and characteristics

The shores of the Inarijärvi are rocky, lined with forests of spruce, pine and birch, all in dwarf arctic forms. On the north-western shore of the lake, north-east of Partakki (on the Kaamanen–Sevettijärvi road), the line above which the spruce will not grow reaches down to the lake. Until well into spring the climate is of arctic severity, since the Scandinavian mountains block the moderating influence of the Gulf Stream which washes the Norwegian coast. The ice on the lake frequently does not break up until

Topography

235

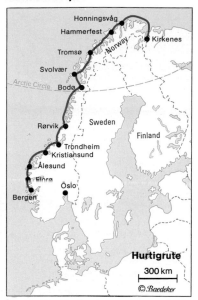

Route of the Hurtigrute

Flag of the Norwegian postal service

A Hurtigrute ship in Vardø harbour

Fishing on Lake Inari

June. Here late winter merges almost imperceptibly into early summer, with at most one or two weeks which can be called spring.

The country around Lake Inari is thinly populated. The commune of Inari is the largest in Finland, with an area of 17,000sq.km/6560sq. miles. Of the 7000 inhabitants a fifth are Sami (Lapps: see Lapland). In the little town of Inari there are separate schools for Sami and Finns.

Population

The great attraction of this region is its unspoiled natural scenery, with large expanses which show no trace of the hand of man. Visitors travelling on Road 4 (E 75) in the direction of Norway will get some impression of the particular world of Lake Inari on the stretch of road between Ivalo and Inari. Those spending at least one night in the region should include a boat trip on the lake – perhaps to the island of Ukkokivi, which in pagan times was regarded by the Sami as the most sacred of the many islands on the lake (one to three departures daily in summer from Inari; the trip takes 2 hours).

★Lake Inari and Surrounding Area

There is good fishing on the shores of the lake and the islands and on the open lake. Information about fishing permits can be obtained in the villages and hotels.

Fishing

Lake Inari, which extends from south-west to north-east, is served by only three roads. Road 4 (E 75), coming from the south (Sodankylä), runs along the south-western shore. Beyond Inari E 75 turns north. At Kaamanen Road 4 branches off and runs west to Karigasniemi and the Norwegian frontier, while Road 970 (E 75) continues north to Utsjoki, from which a road descends the Tenojoki valley to Nuorgam. From Kaamanan a country road leads north-east via Partakko and the Skolt (Sami) village of Sevettijärvi to reach the Norwegian frontier in 130km/80 miles, 10km/6 miles before the Norwegian village of Neiden. From Ivalo another road (No. 9681) runs north-east to Nellimö and the Russian frontier (no crossing). The actual

Roads

237

Landscape near Ivalo

frontier cannot be reached either by car or on foot, for a strip of territory on the Finnish side 1km/¾ mile wide is closed except to permit-holders and patrolled by frontier guards. (Under a frontier agreement between Finland and Russia both countries are required to protect the frontier.)

There are no motor roads on the much indented north-eastern shores of the lake, and even walkers find it hard going here, since much of the area is boggy and impassable. This is country for fit and experienced walkers only. There are no villages here, only isolated cottages and huts.

Ivalo

Ivalo lies on the Ivalojoki, here spanned by a large bridge, and has the most northerly airport in Finland. There is a monument commemorating the Arctic port of Petsamo, now in Russia, which formerly belonged to Finland. Half way between Ivalo and Inari is the Karhunpesäkivi ("Bear's Den Rock"), with a café, picnic area and telephone; good fishing. The hill of Akku (327m/1073ft) offers a rewarding climb.

Inari

Inari, at the mouth of the Joenjoki (good fishing), has a folk high school for Sami. Next to the forestry office is an open-air museum on the culture of the Sami, with a Lapp settlement. Inari has a modern town hall (1983) and a church built in 1952 to replace the earlier church, destroyed by bombing in 1940.

Pielppajärvi church

A walk of 7.5km/4½ miles to the north-east leads to the old Sami church of Pielppajärvi (originally 17th c.; rebuilt 1762). In earlier times the Sami had to bury their dead on islands in the lake, since the bears which were still numerous in the 19th century used to dig up the graves.

★ Lemmenjoki National Park

Ivalojoki Lemmenjoki

A boat trip on the rivers Ivalojoki and Lemmenjoki offers the experience of unspoiled natural scenery. The Lemmenjoki National Park extends to the

Norwegian frontier. There are still a few gold-panners living in huts around the little port of Kultahamina. Some welcome visitors, others do not; but all benefit from the tourist trade, since washing for gold does not provide a living. The base for a tour of this area is the Lemmenjoki hotel (46km/29 miles south-west of Inari).

Jämtland   D 4

Country: Sweden

Jämtland, a mountainous region in central Sweden bordering on Norway, is one of the last unspoiled areas of natural landscape in Europe. Only 1.4% of this forest-covered territory is under cultivation. With its great expanses of lush green pasture, its crystal-clear waters and its snow-capped peaks, Jämtland offers attractions to visitors in both summer and winter.

Situation and characteristics

Here animals threatened with extinction, including bears, gluttons and martens, live undisturbed, and Jämtland's 3000 lakes and streams contain many species of fish to attract the angler. The best months for fishing the mountain streams are July and August; in the forest regions June is preferable.

Western Jämtland

The chief town of Jämtland is Östersund (see entry), on the Storsjö, from which E 14 runs west to the Norwegian frontier.

68km/42 miles from Östersund on E 14 is Järpen (alt. 324m/1063ft), a busy industrial town on the Indalsälv (power station), which drains the Kallsjö. The area is well wooded. To the west, beyond the Indalsälv, the 14m/45ft high Rista Falls tumble into the Åresjö. The calcareous soil favours the growth of rare mosses and other plants.

Järpen

Åre (alt. 378m/1240ft; pop. 10,000) is a popular climbing and winter sports centre. It has a stone-built church (probably 13th c.) with an image of St Olof. A large cabin cableway runs up to 1300m/4265ft, and there are also several chair-lifts and ski-tows as well as a funicular. From the summit of Åreskutan (1420m/4659ft), to the north of the town, there are magnificent views.

Åre

8km/5 miles west of Åre is Duved (alt. 384m/1260ft), also a winter sports centre, with lifts to the Mullfjäll (1031m/3383ft).

Duved

West of Duved Road 322 branches off and runs north-west to the Tännfors, one of the finest waterfalls in the north, in a nature reserve. Here the Indalsälv plunges down into the Nornsjö from a height of 32m/105ft, with a width of 60m/200ft.

★★Tännfors

At Handöl is a small Lapp chapel (1804). There is another impressive waterfall here, the Handölsfall, with a drop of 120m/395ft (suspension bridge).

Handöl

Storlien (alt. 592m/1942ft), with Sweden's highest railway station, lies in a winter sports area (numerous lifts). In summer there is pleasant canoeing. The Norwegian frontier runs 4km/2½ miles west of the town. The mountainous region to the south extends as far as Härjedalen. The tourist resort of Storulvån is a good base for winter sports and for mountain walks in summer.

Storlien

The Tännfors falls

Northern and Eastern Jämtland

Strömsund

The handsome little town of Strömsund (alt. 288m/945ft, pop. 16,000) is reached on Road 45, which runs north-east from Östersund. South of the town is the Russfjärd. 2.5km/1½ miles north-east is Grelsgården, with a lookout tower from which the view reaches to the mountains on the Norwegian frontier.

North-west of the town is the string of lakes known as Ströms Vattudal, extending to the Norwegian frontier. This lake system, through which flows the Faxälv, is an anglers' paradise. Near the frontier, in a nature reserve, is the Hällingsåfall (55m/180ft high).

North of this, reached on a minor road from Gäddede, is the village of Ankarede, a traditional Sami meeting-place (chapel of 1896). The annual Lapp fair held here at midsummer attracts many visitors.

Hammarstrand

East of Östersund (Road 87) is Hammarstrand, situated in the Ragunda valley at the foot of the Kullstaberg. From the lookout terrace on this hill there is a fine view of the Indalsälv, which was a lake, 15m/50ft deep, until a channel for rafts was opened in 1796, when the lake disappeared within four hours.

Joensuu   G 4

Country: **Finland**
Region: Eastern Finland
Population: 47,000
Post code: FIN–80100   Telephone code: 973

Joensuu at night

Joensuu, situated at the outflow of the Pielisjoki into the Pyhäselkä, on the north-eastern fringe of the Finnish Lakeland, was founded in 1848. It is now the administrative, commercial and educational centre of northern Karelia and a university town.

Situation and characteristics

The Town Hall (by Eliel Saarinen, 1914) is a red brick building with a massive tower which also houses the Municipal Theatre.

Between the Town Hall and the market square lies the Freedom Park. Near the Town Hall, on the river, is the quay used by the boats to Savonlinna (see entry) and Koli and by cruise ships.

Town

Town Hall

Saarikatu leads over a bridge on to the islands of Niskasaari and Ilosaari. On the latter island are a bathing beach and the Karelian House, founded in 1954 to promote Karelian culture, with the interesting Museum of Northern Karelia. A festival of Karelian song is held annually in Joensuu.

The Museum of Art has a collection of Finnish art of the 19th and 20th centuries, Russian icons and an exhibition of holography. Also in this area is the Orthodox church of St Nicholas, a wooden church on a cruciform plan. At the mouth of the river is the Hasanniemi open-air theatre, with a revolving stage; nearby are a camping site and a hostel for hikers.

★Museum of Northern Karelia

Surroundings

17km/10½ miles west of Joensuu, near Liperi, is the holiday village of Harila, on the shores of the Orivesi.

Harila

71km/44 miles east of Joensuu on Road 74 is Ilomantsi, with an Orthodox church. At Möhkö (20km/12½ miles east of Ilomantsi, on the Russian frontier) is an industrial museum in which old methods of smelting iron ore are demonstrated. To the south-east lies the Petkeljärvi National Park (visitor centre, waymarked trail).

Ilomantsi

241

Uusi Valamo	See Finnish Lakeland
Lintula Abbey	See Finnish Lakeland
Koli Hills	See entry

Jönköping D 6

Country: Sweden
Province: Småland
Population: 110,000
Post code: S–55...　Telephone code: 036

Situation and characteristics

The Swedish town of Jönköping in north-western Småland, picturesquely situated at the southern tip of Lake Vättern (see entry), was granted its municipal charter by Magnus Ladulås in 1284. After being several times destroyed by fire it was largely rebuilt from 1836 onwards. It is now a centre of agriculture and forestry, enlarged by the incorporation of the neighbouring communes of Huskvarna and Gränna. It is the chief town of Jönköping county.

Town

In the original heart of the town, between Lake Vättern and the little lakes of Munksjö and Rocksjö, a number of older buildings have been preserved. In Hovrättstorget are the Provincial Court (Göta Hovrätt; 1639–55) and the former Town Hall, built in the late 17th century. To the north-west stands the Kristina Church (17th/18th c.), to the south-east the County Museum (Länsmuseet), with a collection which includes Småland pottery and ironware and naïve art.

★Match Museum

To the west of the station is the old Match Factory (Tändstickfabriken), founded in 1844 by J. E. Lundström, which began to produce safety matches in 1852 and soon gained an international reputation. It is now occupied by the Match Museum (Tändstickmuseet), with a collection of matchbox labels, designed both for the domestic market and for the various countries to which the matches were exported.

Municipal Park

Farther west is the Municipal Park, in which is an Ornithological Museum (some 700 species of birds, collection of eggs). Also in the park is an open-air museum, with old wooden houses from Småland (15th–18th c.). At the west end of the park are a church from Bäckaby and a belfry from Solberga (18th c.).

Huskvarna

From Jönköping E 4 runs north up the west side of Lake Vättern to the little town of Huskvarna, one of the attractions of which is Dr Skoda's Waxworks. The road then continues to Gränna (see Lake Vättern).

Surroundings

Habo church

15km/9 miles north-west of Jönköping is Habo church, a large red-painted wooden building of the late 16th century, with vividly coloured wall paintings on Biblical themes in rustic Baroque style.

Taberg

14km/8½ miles south of Jönköping is the Taberg (343m/1125ft), a hill of iron ore (no longer worked). This area is now a nature reserve. From the top of the hill there is a view extending in clear weather for 80km/50 miles.

Eksjö

Roads 31 then 33 run south-east from Jönköping by way of the railway junction of Nässjö to the town of Eksjö (pop. 18,000), which received its municipal charter about 1400. There are a number of well preserved old wooden houses in the town. The Municipal Museum displays the picture collection of the artist Albert Engström (1869–1940), who lived in Eksjö. The

Courtyard of a house in Eksjö

countryside round the town is very attractive. To the north-east are Skuru-gata, a deep gorge, and Skuruhatt (337m/1106ft), highest hill in Småland.

From Jönköping E 4 runs south to Värnamo (pop. 31,000), on the banks of the Lagå, the chief town in southern Småland. Although known in 1236 as a meeting-place of the *ting* (assembly) and in 1620 as a trading post, the town failed to develop, and in 1859 it still had no more than 300 inhabitants. Since then the growth of industry and the incorporation of neighbouring communes has brought its population to over 30,000. Some 60% of the population are engaged in industry and craft trades, with furniture manufacture playing a leading role. The Swed-Expo trade fair is held here annually. In the centre of the town is Apladalen, a nature park with a local museum.

Värnamo

An old-time steam train runs on Sundays in summer on a 15km/9 mile long line between Bor and Osbruk, to the east of Värnamo.

Old-time railway

In a nature reserve 25km/15 miles north-east of Värnamo is Nydala Abbey (12th c.), of which only a chapel now remains. Part of the abbey church is incorporated in a modern church.

Nydala

Jostedalsbre

B 5

Country: **Norway**
Region: Western Norway
Altitude: up to 2038m/6687ft

The Jostedalsbre, between the Sognefjord to the south and the Nordfjord to the north, is the largest inland ice-sheet in continental Europe (almost 100km/62 miles long), of similar type to the great icefields of Greenland.
   Together with the adjoining icefields the Jostedalsbre covers an area of over 1000sq.km/380sq. miles. Only a few low rocky hummocks emerge

The Brikdalsbre, a branch of the Jostedalsbre

from the mass of ice, which is estimated to be some 500m/1650ft thick. Twenty-six major glaciers reach down into the surrounding valleys, including the Tundbergdalsbre, the largest glacier in Europe after the Aletsch glacier in Switzerland. Since the ice of these glaciers, like the ice almost everywhere in Norway, has been retreating for many years the ascent to the ice-sheet has become steadily steeper and more strenuous.

★Lusterfjord
Into the Jostedal

At Røneid on the Lusterfjord (on the south side of which is the Urnes stave church) Road 604 branches off Road 55 (which follows the north side of the fjord) and ascends the Jostedal, a rift running north–south through the massive mountain plateau, bounded on the west by the Jostedalsbre. The road follows the tumultuous course of the Jostedalselv.

Jostedal

The village of Jostedal (alt. 201m/660ft), 25km/15 miles from Røneid, has a wooden church of 1660. The road continues over the Høghbru (bridge); then at Gjerde a narrow road goes off on the loft into the Krundal. This road is followed as far as Berset, above which to the south towers Høgenipa (1535m/5036ft).

★Jostedalsbre

From Bergset there is a magnificent but strenuous climb (3 hours, with guide) past the Bjørnestegbre to the Jostedalsbre, continuing over the icefield to the Høgste Breakullen (1953m/6408ft); from there an hour's walk north-west, when an impressive view opens up of the mountains along the Nordfjord; and then a descent (sometimes difficult) through the Kvanndal to Nesdal, near the south end of the Loenvatn.

★Nigardsbre

From the turn-off at Gjerde Road 604 continues north. At Elvekrok (alt. 340m/1115ft) a private road branches off on the left to the Nigardsbre.

Innvikfjord

North-west of the Jostedalsbre Road 60 skirts the Innvikfjord. Near its east end is Olden, with a church built in 1746–49 (restored 1971).

From Olden a road runs south into the beautiful Olderdal. Running along-side the 11km/7 mile long Oldenvatn and passing many waterfalls, it comes to Briksdal (alt. 150m/490ft). From here there is a footpath (1 hour) to the Briksdalsbre, an arm of the Jostedalsbre rearing its blue masses of ice above the scrub forest.

★ Oldenvatn
★★ Briksdalsbre

Jotunheim   B/C 5

Country: Norway
Region: Western Norway

The Jotunheim, the largest of the few regions of Alpine type on the Nor-wegian high plateau, extends from the Sognefjord in the west to the Gudbrandsdal in the north-east. The name Jotunheim ("Home of Giants") was coined by Norwegian students in allusion to the frost and ice giants of the Edda. Most of the mountains in the Jotunheim rise to heights of no more than 1800–2000m (6000–6500ft), but it also includes the two highest peaks in Scandinavia, Galdhøpiggen (2468m/8098ft) and Glittertind (2452m/8045ft). Since the valleys are mostly above the tree-line, they pre-sent a notably barren aspect; but the extensive views over rocky crags and fields of ice add up to a memorable experience of natural beauty. The Jotunheim was designated a National Park in 1980.

Situation and characteristics

Visitors who set out to explore this grand landscape of mountains, glaciers and valleys should be properly equipped; for the weather here can change with surprising suddenness.

The Jotunheim is best reached from E 4 (Lillehammer to Trondheim), taking Road 15, which branches off E 4 at Otta and heads west towards the Nordfjord. It runs up the Ottadal, passing Vågåmo, with the church of Vågå (first mentioned in 1270; font of 1050), and then along the south side of the

Access
(Ottadal, Bøverdal)

Autumn in the Jotunheim

Pass on the Sognefjell road

Vågåvatn by way of Randen to Lom (stave church). From here Road 55 (the road to the Sognedal) ascends the Bøverdal, with the Jotunheim rearing above the road to the left (south-east). It can be explored from numerous points in the valley.

Jyvashytta

At Galdesand a road branches off on the left and climbs steeply, with 21 hairpin bends, to the Jyvashytta (14km/9 miles). This mountain hut, in a rugged and treeless region, is the highest point in Norway reachable by car (1817m/5962ft).

★ Galdhøpiggen
★ Glittertind

From the Jyvashytta Galdhøpiggen, the highest peak in Scandinavia (2468m/8098ft) can be climbed in about 4 hours (guide required). From the summit there are superb views. To the east, beyond the Visdal, is Glittertind (2452m/8045ft), with its massive crown of snow.

Leirdal
Sognefjell

Beyond Galdesand Road 55 continues up the Leirdal, passing the magnificently situated Jotunheimen Fjellstue (mountain inn). The road then climbs up the Breiseterdal, through grand mountain scenery, to the Sognefjell, a passage through the mountains used from time immemorial. To the left is an imposing glacier, the Smørstabbe.

★ Hurrungane

Beyond the pass (1400m/4593ft) the road descends, passing a number of mountain lakes and the Oscarshaug, to the Turtagrø hotel, a good base for walks and climbs in the Hurrungane (Horunger), the finest mountain group in the Jotunheim.

★★ Skagastøls-botn

A particularly rewarding climb in the Hurrungane group is to the Skagastølsbotn, with the Skagastølsbre glacier (1350m/4429ft) and the Skagastølstinder behind it. About 4 hours should be allowed for the climb; for the ascent of the Store Skagastølstind (2404m/7888ft; strenuous) an additional four hours are required.

From Turtagrø Fanaråk (2075m/6808ft), to the east, can be climbed in 4 5 ★Fanaråk
hours; Klypenåsi (1145m/3757ft), to the north-west, in 2½ hours. A guide is ★Klypenåsi
required for all climbs.

From Turtagrø the road winds its way down to Hauge on the Lusterfjord
(see Sognefjord).

In the southern part of the Jotunheim there are several beautiful lakes. Lakes
From Randen, on the south side of the Vågåvatn, Road 51 runs past the
Lemonsjø and below Rindehøvda (155m/509ft; views), and then up the
Sjodal to Maurvangen. A little to the west is Lake Gjende. ★Lake Gjende

Beyond the Valdresflya plateau, much of which is covered by bog, is Valdresflya
Bygdin, with Lake Bygdin to the right and the Vinstervatn to the left. This
section of road is regarded by many Norwegians as the finest pass road in
the country.

On Lake Bygdin motorboats ply between Bygdin and the Eidsbugaren Lake Bygdin
Høyfjellshotell (Høyfjellsmuseum). From there a road (3.5km/2 miles;
views) leads to the Tyinholmen hotel on the north side of the Tyinsjø (area ★Tyinsjø
35sq.km/13½sq. miles; motorboat trips). On the south side of the lake is
the Tyin Høyfjellshotell.

Jyväskylä F 4

Country: **Finland**
Region: Southern Finland
Population: 67,000
Post code: FIN–40100   Telephone code: 941

Jyväskylä, founded by Tsar Nicholas I in 1837, is attractively situated on the Situation and
north side of a small lake, Jyväsjärvi, which is linked by a narrow strait, the characteristics
Aijälänsalmi, with Lake Päijänne, Finland's second largest lake and its
deepest (95.3m/313ft), to the south.
   Jyväskylä is an important traffic junction, the administrative and cultural
centre of central Finland and an industrial town (woodworking, metalworking) which is also noted for its trade fairs. The first Finnish-language
secondary school was established here in 1858. The University was
founded in 1934.

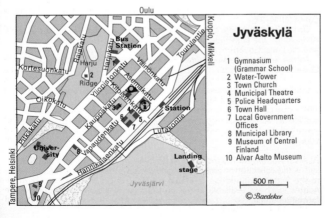

Jyväskylä

1 Gymnasium
  (Grammar School)
2 Water-Tower
3 Town Church
4 Municipal Theatre
5 Police Headquarters
6 Town Hall
7 Local Government
  Offices
8 Municipal Library
9 Museum of Central
  Finland
10 Alvar Aalto Museum

500 m

© Baedeker

Municipal Theatre, Jyväskylä   *Old church, Keuruu*

Buildings by Alvar Aalto	The town is given its particular character by a mingling of old wooden houses and modern stone buildings. It also has many buildings designed by the famous Finnish architect Alvar Aalto, who spent his early years in Jyväskylä.
Cultural events	Jyväskylä Winter Festival (January or February) and Jyväskylä Summer Festival (end of June to beginning of July): programmes of cultural and artistic events; debates and discussions, extending also to social and political questions.
Town	In the centrally situated Church Gardens (Kirkkopuisto) is the Neo-Gothic Town Church (1880). Nearby is a monument to the Finnish writer Minna Canth (1844–97).
	On the way from here to the harbour and the lake are three buildings by Alvar Aalto: the Municipal Theatre (1982), the Police Headquarters (1970) and the Local Government Offices (1978).
	To the north, in Rajakatu, are the Orthodox church (1954) and a Neo-Classical church of 1929.
Museum of Central Finland	An the near end of Keskussairaalantie, south-west of the Town Church, is the Museum of Central Finland (Keski-Suomen Museo; by Alvar Aalto, 1961), with collections of material on the history of the town, ethnology and applied art. A short distance north is the University (new buildings by Alvar Aalto), with the University Museum (Yliopiston Museo; history of education).
★Alvar Aalto Museum	At Alvar Aaltonkatu 7 is the Alvar Aalto Museum, designed by Aalto himself, with a collection on architecture and design and works of art belonging to the Sihtola Foundation (periodic special exhibitions). Brochures on Aalto's work are available in the museum as well as in the tourist information office.

The Water-Tower (Vesilinna) in the Harju Park (Harjupuisto), in the centre of the town, is a landmark which it is difficult to ignore. It is approached by 143 stone steps ("Nero's Steps"), laid in 1925. From the viewing terrace there is an extensive prospect over the forests and lakes of the surrounding area. Other fine viewpoints are the Syrjänharju to the north-east of the town (with park) and the ski-jump on the Laajavuori (café), 4km/2½ miles north-west of the town centre.

To the east of the town, on the road to Vaajakoski, is the Viherlandia garden centre (period displays).

Surroundings

32km/20 miles west of Jyväskylä on the road to Virrat can be found the historic wooden church of Petäjävesi (1763–64). 60km/37 miles west, at the north end of the Keuruunselkä (lake), is the village of Keuruu, which also has an old wooden church (1756–58), as well as a museum of art.

10km/6 miles south of Jyväskylä on E 75 is Rannankylä, with a ceramic manufactory housed in the former school.

4km/2½ miles farther south Muurame has an interesting "sauna village", a collection of 24 saunas from different parts of the country (café; sale of handicrafts).

See Finnish Lakeland

Kajaani

Country: Finland
Region: Central Finland
Population: 36,000
Post code: FIN–87100   Telephone code: 986

Kajaani, chief town of the Kainuu district (roughly half way between the Gulf of Bothnia and the Russian frontier), was founded by the Swedish governor-general, Per Brahe, in 1651 beside the castle of Kajaaninlinna (built by Charles IX of Sweden in 1605). It lies on the banks of the Kajaaninjoki, which flows into the Oulujärvi, a large lake with an area of 1002sq.km/387sq. miles, just north-west of the town. At the mouth of the river is a hydro-electric station.

Around the turn of the century the Kainuu district around Kajaani was the largest producer of wood tar in Europe. The tar was bought by merchants in the barren country of eastern Kainuu and conveyed by water in special tar boats to the ports on the Gulf of Bothnia, from which it was shipped, as "Stockholm tar", to Sweden and later to Britain and used for the caulking of boats. The area now has a considerable woodworking industry.

The doctor and writer Elias Lönnrot (1802–84) lived in Kajaani from 1833 as district medical officer. From this base he travelled round the country collecting fragments of the Finnish national epic "Kalevala", which he then brought together and supplemented by work of his own. Urho Kekkonen (1900–86), President of Finland, went to school in Kajaani.

In the centre of the town is the Market Square, with the new Town Hall (1906). The old Town Hall, a wooden building designed by C. L. Engel (1831), is in Vanhatori and is now a cultural and congress centre (concerts, etc.).

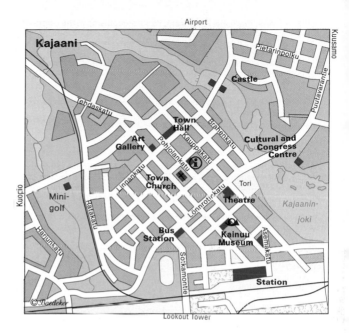

Castle	North-east of the Town Hall, on the little island of Linnasaari, are the ruins of the fortress of Kajaaninlinna, built in 1607–66, captured and destroyed by the Russians in 1716, and restored in 1937. The Swedish historian and poet Johannes Messenius (1579–1636) was confined in the castle as a state prisoner from 1620 to 1635 and wrote a rhyming chronicle of Finland.
Town Church	The Town Church, a wooden building in Neo-Gothic style (by Jacob Ahrenberg, 1896) has an altarpiece by Toivo Tuhkanen (1925). Nearby is the Orthodox church. Other interesting wooden buildings are the railway station and Urho Kekkonen's family home. The President is commemorated by an unusual monument (by Pekko Kauhanen, 1991), "Great Times".
Kainuu Museum	In Asemakatu (Station Street) is the Kainuu Museum, with collections on the history and economy of northern Finland (tar), the history of the town and the national epic "Kalevala".

Surroundings

Paltaniemi	12km/7½ miles north-west of Kajaani lies Paltaniemi, on the south side of the Paltaselkä, a wide inlet on the Oulujärvi, with a large wooden church (1726), originally Paltamo parish church. Notable features of the interior are the altarpiece (by Margareta Capsia, c. 1725) and the 18th century ceiling paintings by Emanuel Granberg. Nearby is the so-called Emperor's Stable, recalling Tsar Alexander I's visit to Finland. Paltaniemi was the birthplace of the great Finnish lyric poet Eino Leino (1878–1926).
Vuokatti Sports Centre	At Sotkamo, 30km/19 miles east of Kajaani om Road 18, is the Vuokatti Sports Centre. The hill (326m/1070ft) is one of the leading skiing areas in southern and central Finland, and in addition there are 250km/155 miles of

cross-country trails in varying degrees of difficulty (distances between 5km/3 miles and 16km/8 miles; several hotels). Vuokatti is the starting-point of the popular ski run on the UKK trail to Lieska, a distance of 220km/137 miles (February/March).

From Vuokatti it is another 66km/41 miles to Kuhmo, a small town in the barren territory of eastern Finland which has become world-famed for the Chamber Music Festival held annually in July. The town's most notable building is the New Library (by Nurmela, Raimoranta and Tasa, 1989) on the banks of the Pajakka rapids, an outstanding example of contemporary Finnish architecture. Outside the town on the road to Suomussalmi can be found the "Kalevala Village", with reconstructions of old houses and crafts-men's workshops.

Kuhmo

Kalmar   E 6

Country: **Sweden**
Province: Småland
Population: 55,000
Post code: S–39...   Telephone code: 0480

Kalmar, chief town of the county of Kalmar in south-eastern Sweden, lies on the Kalmarsund, which separates the island of Öland from the main-land. Thanks to this favourable location, there was already a trading post here in Viking times.

Situation and characteristics

Fortified in the 11th century as a coastal stronghold against Denmark, Kalmar became a member of the Hanseatic League. In 1397 the Union of Kalmar, under which Denmark, Sweden and Norway were united in a single kingdom under Eric of Pomerania, was signed here. The Union remained in force until 1523.

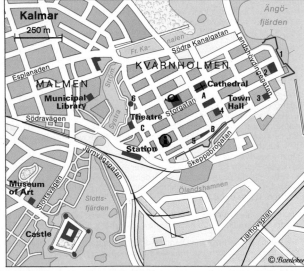

A Stortorget	1 Town walls	4 17th c. stone house
B Lilla Torget	2 Seafaring Museum	5 Bishop's Palace
C Larmtorget	3 County Museum	6 Water-Tower

Kalmar

During the 16th century Kalmar, with its strong fortifications, was one of the most important towns in Sweden.

From the 18th century the population of Kalmar became mainly occupied in craft production, trade and seafaring. The town's modern industries include engineering and motor vehicles (Volvo branch factory).

Kvarnholmen

The town originally lay below the castle, but after it had been largely destroyed during the wars with Denmark and by a great fire it was rebuilt on the island of Kvarnholmen from 1647 onwards.

Stortorget
Cathedral

The central feature of the old town on Kvarnholmen is the Market Square (Stortorget), in which are the Cathedral and the Town Hall, both built in the second half of the 17th century to the design of Nicodemus Tessin the Elder. The Cathedral is in Italian Baroque style; notable features of the interior are the pulpit, of North German workmanship, the reredos and some fine sculpture.

Town walls

Some sections of the old town walls have been preserved. To the south of Stortorget, at the entrance to the harbour, is one of the old town gates, Kavaljeren (1697).

Södra Långgatan

Between Stortorget and Kavaljeren runs Södra Långgatan, at No. 40 of which is the house of Burgomaster Rosenlund, the oldest stone-built house on Kvarnholmen.

Museums

Södra Långgatan leads east to two museums, the Seafaring Museum and the County Museum (Kalmar Länsmuseet). An exhibition of underwater archaeology in the County Museum includes remains of the royal ship "Kronan", which sank in 1679.

Lilla Torget

South-west of the town gate is Lilla Torget, around which are the old Bishop's Palace (Domprostgården), the Burgomaster's House (Borgmestaregården) and the Governor's Residence (Länsresidenset; 1676).

Larmtorget

Storgatan runs south from Stortorget to Larmtorget, with a fountain (1928) in honour of Gustavus Vasa, who landed at Stensö, south-west of Kalmar, in May 1520. On the west side of the square is the Theatre (1863), with a Neo-Renaissance façade.

A little way north is the 65m/215ft high Water-Tower, in Art Nouveau style, now converted into flats. Near the Theatre is one of the bridges linking Kvarnholmen with the mainland, and immediately beyond this is the Municipal Park.

★ Kalmar Castle

To the south of the Municipal Park, on a small island, is Kalmar's medieval Castle, surrounded by walls and bastions. It is a massive five-towered structure, the earliest parts of which were built at the beginning of the 11th century. It was enlarged in the 16th century and restored at the end of the 19th century. Between 1307 and the beginning of the war with Denmark in 1611 it withstood no fewer than 24 sieges.

In the courtyard is a Renaissance fountain. The chapel, in the south wing, was completed in 1592. In the North Tower are the royal apartments of Eric IV, with intarsia panelling and 16th century hunting scenes. Other fine rooms are the Lozenge Room and the Golden Room (Gyllene Salen), which date from the reign of John III.

Near the Castle, in Slottsvägen, is the Museum of Art. Near here too stands Krusenstjernska Gården, an 18th century burgher's house.

★ Öland Bridge

To the north of the town the Öland Bridge (Ölandsbron), links the island of Öland (see entry) with the mainland. Opened in 1972, it is the longest bridge in Europe (6072m/6641yd).

Also to the north of Kalmar is the new Water-Tower (Nya Vattentornet), from the top of which there are extensive views.

Kalmar Castle

Surroundings

E 22 runs south from Kalmar, with fine views of the Kalmarsund, into the province of Blekinge. The little town of Bergkvara, which is famed for its traditional crafts (woodwork, pottery), has a Shipping Museum.

Bergkvara

North of Kalmar is the 12th century fortified church of Kläckeberga.
   On E 22 to the north of Kalmar are many little seaside resorts and fishing villages. The next town is Oskarshamn (see Västervik, Surroundings).

Kläckeberga

Karasjok

F 2

Country: Norway
Region: Northern Norway
Population: 1400
Post code: N–9730

Karasjok lies on the river Karasjohka, 145km/90 miles east of Alta (see entry) on E 6 and 14km/8½ miles from the Finnish frontier. The bus to Rotaniemi (Finland) stops in Karasjok, and the "Nord-Norge" buses also stop here several times a day. This little town is regarded as the Sami capital, and the Sami parliament, the Same-Ting, has recently been established here.

Situation and characteristics

The town has a markedly continental climate, with extreme cold in winter (down to −50°C/−58°F) and very hot summers (up to +30°C/86°F).

The economy of the town is of characteristically Lapp type. There are some 3000 reindeer within the commune of Karasjok, and farming, hunting,

Economy

In the Karasjok . . .   *. . . open-air museum*

fishing and tourism all make their contributions to the subsistence of the population.

Sights

The church (1807) is the oldest Lutheran church in Finnmark. This was the only building left intact when German troops withdrew from the region during the Second World War: the rest of the town had to be completely rebuilt.

The Sami Centre (tourist information) was opened in 1991. There is a restaurant serving typical Sami dishes.

Sami culture

The Sami Museum (Samiid Vuorka Davvirat) has a large collection of material on the culture of the original inhabitants of Scandinavia, and the Karasjok Library has the largest collection of Sami literature. Sami crafts are represented by a cutler's and a silversmith's workshop.

Surroundings

Excursions

Excursions available from Karasjok are boat trips on the Karasjohka, visits to Sami settlements, either in summer or in winter, and trips on dog sleighs (in winter). At the confluence of the Karasjohka and the Anarjokka are world-famed salmon-fishing waters.

Øvre Anarjåkka National Park
★Views

The Øvre Anarjåkka National Park, south-east of Karasjok along the Finnish frontier, is the largest nature reserve in northern Norway (1290sq.km/ 498sq. miles). With its extensive areas of bog, this is not good walking country, but from any of the hills within the park (none of them rising above 600m/2000ft) visitors will get a fantastic view of the endless expanses of the Finnmarksvidda, the northern Norwegian plateau.

Karlskrona

Country: **Sweden**
Province: Blekinge
Population: 59,000
Post code: S–37...   Telephone code: 0455

The smallest Swedish province (area 2941sq.km/1136sq. miles), Blekinge lies in the south of the country on the Baltic, at the entrance to the Kalmarsund. Blekinge was frequently devastated during the wars between Sweden and Denmark, until in 1658, under the treaty of Roskilde, it finally became Swedish. Known as the "garden of Sweden", it has the country's largest forests of beech and oak, planted up to 1830 by the royal forestry administration (nature reserves, with marked footpaths). Blekinge was the seafaring province of Sweden, with the ports of Karlskrona and Karlshamn. Karlskrona was a Swedish naval base and later had large shipyards, while Karlshamn was the port from which many farming people from the district of Småland to the north emigrated to America in the 19th century.

Karlskrona is built on some thirty islands linked with one another by bridges. The town was founded by Charles XI on the island of Trossö in 1680, when the headquarters of the Swedish fleet were also established there. In the 18th century Karlskrona was Sweden's second largest town, but thereafter it declined in importance. It is now an industrial town (principally foodstuffs and fish-processing), with Sweden's largest cold-storage depots. The Swedish economic situation has led in Karlskrona, as in other ports, to the closing down of many shipyards.

Situation and characteristics

In the town's central square, Stortorget, stands a statue of Charles XI (by Börjesson, 1897). Around the square are the Neo-Classical Town Hall, the Baroque Frederikskyrka (1774) and the round Trinity Church (1709). Both churches were designed by Nicodemus Tessin the Younger. A colourful flower market is held in the square four days before Midsummer's Eve, when garlands and bouquets of flowers from the hillsides and meadows of Blekinge are sold.

Town

Stortorget

To the west, on Fisktorget (Fishmarket Square), is the Blekinge Museum (regional history and culture), with a Baroque-style garden on the terrace. Farther west lies the Björkholmen district, with picturesque little wooden seamen's houses. This is the old dockyard area (conducted tours in summer). To the north of Fisktorget, moored at the Borgmästarekaj, is the former training ship "Jarramas", now a restaurant. In Amiralitetstorget is a bell-tower.

Fisktorget

Farther south the Maritime Museum houses a collection which includes carved figureheads from 17th century vessels and original ship models.

★Maritime Museum

On the edge of the dockyard area is the Admiralty Church (1685), the largest wooden church in Sweden. In front of it can be seen an appealing wooden figure of "Old Rosenbom", a character in Selma Lagerlöf's book "The Wonderful Adventures of Nils".

Admiralty Church

Surroundings – East

South-east of Karlskrona we come to Ramdala, with a 13th century church. At Möckleryd is the site known as Hästhallen ("Horse's Hall"), with rock carvings. The promontory of Torhamns Udde is the haunt of large numbers of birds, particularly in autumn when the migrants pause here.

A side road off E 66, north of Karlskrona, leads to the little coastal town of Kristianopel, founded in 1600 by the Danish king Christian IV, which pre-

Kristianopel

"Old Rosenbom", Karlskrona

serves parts of its old town walls. Church of 1624, with stepped gables; picturesque old houses.

From Kristianopel a long-distance trail (Blekingeleden) goes to Olofström in western Blekinge. At Brömsebro, on the boundary between Blekinge and Småland, is a stone commemorating the peace of 1645 between Denmark and Sweden. There are ruins of the Danish fortress of Brömsehus.

Surroundings – West and South-West

West of the town is the Hjortahammar cemetery area. There are also numerous prehistoric remains around Johannishus, the largest manor-house in Blekinge, built in 1772 in French Renaissance style.

Ronneby

28km/17 miles west of Karlskrona lies the little town of Ronneby (pop. 29,000). In the 19th century this was a much-frequented spa, with a chalybeate spring first discovered in 1705. The old spa hotel has now given place to the Ronneby Brunn hotel and conference complex.

Holy Cross Church (Heliga Korskyrka), which dates from the 11th century, has frescos of the 15th/16th century, brought to light during restoration work. In the church is a door bearing the marks of burning and axe-strokes, believed to date from 1564, when Eric XIV's forces took Ronneby and massacred the inhabitants. Near the church, in the Bergslagen district, can be found a local museum, Möllebackagården.

On the Ronnebyå, 3km/2 miles downstream at Djupadal, is a gorge 16m/52ft deep but only 1.5m/5ft wide. Here, in a typical old Blekinge farmhouse, is a restaurant. From the picturesque skerry-fringed coast there are boat trips to the island of Karö.

30km/19 miles north of Ronneby is the Flower Garden (Blomstergården) of Göljahult (Eringsboda). In the garden, originally private but now open to the public, are a variety of pieces of sculpture, some of them on fairytale themes.

Karlshamn (pop. 31,000), which received its municipal charter in 1664, is now a modern port and industrial town, with the largest vegetable oil and margarine plants in Scandinavia. On the way there from Karlskrona (E 22) a detour should be made to the coast with its fringe of skerries (bathing).

Karlshamn

In the old part of the town are wooden buildings of the 17th and 18th centuries, including the Asschierska Hus, built in 1682 as the town hall, and the Skottsberska Gård, a well preserved merchant's house of about 1760. The Smithska Gård now houses a museum. In the Hamnpark can be seen a monument by Axel Olsson, "The Emigrants Kristina and Karl Oskar", recalling Karlshamn's role as the port from which many Swedes emigrated to America in the 18th century. On the island of Kastelholm, off the mouth of the harbour, are fortifications dating from 1675. On the east side of the town extends the Väggapark. To the west, on the river Mörrumså (salmon fishing), is the village of Mörrum, with a salmon aquarium.

The smallest, but also the oldest, town in Blekinge is Sölvesborg (pop. 16,000), on the borders of Skåne. With its narrow streets and low houses, it has preserved its small-town charm. Features of interest are the parish church of St Nicholas (14th c.), with 15th century wall paintings, and a runic stone, Stentoftestenen. Gammelgården, originally a poorhouse, is now a museum, displaying objects recovered by excavation.

Sölvesborg

South-east of Sölvesborg is the seaside resort of Hällevik. From Nogersund there are boat services to the island of Hanö, with a British cemetery – a reminder of the days during the Napoleonic wars (1810–12) when a British squadron was based on Hanö.

Hällevik

Karlstad

D 6

Country: Sweden
Province: Värmland. Population: 75,000
Post code: S–65...   Telephone code: 054

Karlstad, the cultural and commercial centre of Värmland (see entry), chief town of the county and the see of a bishop, lies in the delta of the Klarälv, at the point where the river flows into Lake Vänern after a course of 500km/310 miles. The town is named after Charles IX, who in 1584 granted a municipal charter to the settlement on the island of Tingvalla which had existed since the early medieval period as a trading station and place of assembly (the meeting-place of the *ting*). In 1905 negotiations took place here on the dissolution of the union between Sweden and Norway. Karlstad is now a considerable industrial town (mainly woodworking).

Situation and
characteristics

Älvgatan, with its old burghers' houses, gives some impression of what the town was like before a great fire in 1865. The Cathedral (1723–30) and Bishop's Palace (1780) also survived the fire.

Town

In the market square, Stora Torget, stands a Peace Monument by Ivar Johnsson commemorating the dissolution of the union of Sweden and Norway. On the west side of the square is the Town Hall (1869). To the east, in Kungsgatan, is the Old Grammar School, in its day one of the handsomest school buildings in Sweden, which now houses a School Museum.

Stora Torget

To the west of Stora Torget is Residenstorget, with the Governor's Residence. In front of it can be seen a bronze statue of King Charles IX (1926). To the south-west is the Town House (1963).

Residenstorget

Monument to Selma Lagerlöf, Karlstad

Also on the south-west side of the town is Marienbergsskogen, a wooded area within which are a zoo, an open-air museum, a theatre and an amusement park.

Värmland Museum

In the north of the town extends the Sandgrund Park, with the Värmland Museum (art and history; textile collection; exhibitions on topical subjects). To the north-east is the twelve-arched Östra Bro (East Bridge) spanning the Klarälv, the longest stone bridge in Sweden (1761–70).

Surroundings

Skoghall Hammarö

8km/5 miles south-west of Karlstad, on a peninsula in Lake Vänern, is the little town of Skoghall, with sawmills and cellulose plants. 5km/3 miles east of the town the old wooden church of Hammarö has a medieval reredos and wall paintings.

Alster

At Alster, 6km/4 miles north of Karlstad, is the manor-house of Alster Herrgård, in which the lyric poet Gustav Fröding (1860–1911) lived as a child. In a grove on the estate can be found the Fröding Stone (Frödingsstenen).

Kristinehamn

See Lake Vänern

Kemi   F 3

Country: **Finland**
Region: Northern Finland
Population: 26,500
Post code: FIN–94100   Telephone code: 698

The ice-breaker "Sampo"

The Finnish town of Kemi lies at the north end of the Gulf of Bothnia, at the mouth of the Kemijoki. Well placed for water transport, it was already a busy settlement trading in skins and fish in the Middle Ages. It received its municipal charter in 1869, and with the development of industry became an important port. Woodworking plays a major role in its economy.

Situation and characteristics

The Kemijoki was once well stocked with fish, particularly salmon, which came here in large numbers at spawning time: hence the salmon which features in the town's coat of arms. The growth of industry and the construction of hydro-electric stations, however, have restricted their habitat.

The town is well laid out, with wide streets. In the Town Hall (Kaupungintalo; 1939) is a "panoramic café", with fine views. Another notable modern building is the Municipal Theatre (by Jan Söderlund, 1980).

Town

The Neo-Gothic brick church in the Church Gardens was built in 1902. In the Cultural Centre at Pohjoisrantakatu 9–11 is the Art Gallery, with works by Finnish artists. The Museum occupies a typical old Nordland farmhouse, complete with a fish-smoking hut.

The Gemstone Gallery has a collection of 3000 gemstones, with copies of crown jewels from many European countries, including a crown made in 1918 for the king of Finland – a king who never was.

Gemstone Gallery

Surroundings

12km/7½ miles south of Kemi is Ajos, base of the icebreaker "Sampo" (built 1961). In winter visitors can take a trip in the "Sampo", which can accommodate 150 passengers; in summer they can look round it in harbour (cafeteria).

Ajos

Kemi

Kemi
parish church

9km/5½ miles north of the town centre is the 16th century parish church of Kemi, built of undressed stone, the oldest stone church in northern Finland. The vaulted timber ceiling has paintings of Christ's Passion. Under the choir is the mummified body of a 17th century pastor, Nikolaus Rungius (d. 1628).

Hydro-electric
station

To the north of the town, on the Kemijoki, is the large Isohaara hydroelectric power station. A picturesque road runs up the Kemijoki to Rovaniemi (see entry).

Kirkenes   F 2

Country: Norway
Region: Northern Norway
Population: 5000
Post code: N–9900

Situation

The Norwegian port and industrial town of Kirkenes lies on the south side of the Varangerfjord, on a promontory between the Langfjord and the broad estuary of the Pasvikelv. The Russian frontier runs only a few kilometres east of the town centre.

Midnight sun

The midnight sun provides a memorable experience here; it is visible for two months, beginning May 20th.

In the town centre are a number of modern office buildings. The town's economy is centred on the mining and processing of iron ore.

Stone mazes

To the north of the town, on the Holmengrå peninsula and the island of Kyøøy, are two stone mazes, probably medieval but possibly dating back to the Iron Age.

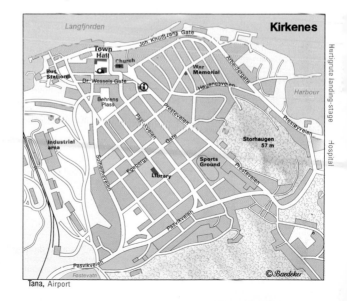

Surroundings

To the north of the town the Varangerfjord cuts deep inland from the east and combines with the Tanafjord to cut off the Varanger peninsula from the mainland. From Kirkenes there is a ferry service to Vadsø, on the north side of the Varangerfjord, and also daily sailings to the Russian port of Murmansk.

Varanger peninsula

Vadsø (pop. 6000), on the south side of the Varanger peninsula, is the chief town of Finnmark county and a busy port, shipping fish and fish products. There are boat services to Hammerfest several times a week on the Hurtigrute (see entry).

Vadsø

Espengården, an old patrician house (1840), is now part of the Vadsø Museum. The Immigrants Monument in the town centre commemorates the many Swedes and Finns who came to live in Vadsø.

On the offshore island of Vadsøy is an airship anchoring mast which was used by Amundsen in 1926 and Nobile in 1928.

From Kirkenes and Vadsø there are boat services to Vardø (pop. 3000), the most easterly town in Norway, which received its municipal charter in 1788. The North Harbour, sheltered by two breakwaters, is the base of a considerable fishing fleet which brings in most of the town's income. Note the large racks for drying stockfish.

Vardø

Fridtjof Nansen sailed from Vardø in the "Fram" on July 21st 1893 on a voyage which took him to latitude 86°4' north, returning to Norwegian soil here in 1896.

To the west of the town is Vardøhus, an old fortress which was strengthened in 1737. From the Vardefjell, a rocky hill 59m/195ft high, there are far-ranging views of the town, the island and the rugged hills of the Varanger peninsula.

Vardø is connected with the mainland by a road tunnel running under the sea.

Kirkenes, in the far north of Norway

Kiruna   E 3

Country: **Sweden**
Province: Lapland
Altitude: 506m/1660ft
Population: 27,000
Post code: S–981..
Telephone code: 0980

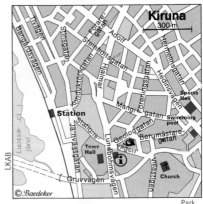

Kiruna, the most north-
erly town in Sweden,
lies in the same latitude
as central Greenland.
It is the chief town
of the largest com-
mune in the country
(area   20,000sq.km/
7700sq.miles), which
borders on both Norway
and Finland. The mid-
night sun is visible here
from mid May to mid
July. Originally a Lapp

Park

settlement, the town began to develop when mining of the local iron ore
started about 1900. Kiruna received its municipal charter in 1948, by which
time the population had risen to 11,000.

Sights

South-east of the railway station is the Town Hall (1963), with a carillon in
the tower; art collection. The wooden church, built by Gustav Wickman in
1912 on the model of a Lapp hut, has an altarpiece painted by Gustaf V's
brother, Prince Eugen of Sweden, depicting a summer landscape in central
Sweden and an altar group of carved wood by Christian Eriksson and
Ossian Elgström.

★Kirunavaara

The town is dominated by the ore mountain of Kirunavaara, terraced by
opencast workings. The existence of the iron ore in the hill had been known
since 1730, but it was only after the construction of the railway lines to
Luleå and Narvik that it became possible to work the ore. Working is now by
opencast methods. There are conducted tours of the old underground
workings, the largest in the world.

Surroundings of Kiruna

★Kebnekaise

Within the commune of Kiruna, though some 90km/56 miles west of the
town itself, is Sweden's highest mountain, Kebnekaise (2117m/6946ft). The
ascent of the south peak takes about 8–9 hours and should be undertaken
only by experienced and properly equipped climbers. In a high valley on
the slopes of Kelpack (789m/2589ft) can be found the Kebnekaise climbing
hut.

**Research
stations**

45km/28 miles north of Kiruna the Esrange rocket station was established
in 1965 by the European Space Research Organisation (ESRO) for the
launching of research rockets. In the Tarfala valley is the Glaciological
Research Station, at Abisko the Scientific Research Station.

National Park

Also at Abisko (see entry), 95km/60 miles north-west of Kiruna, is the
Abisko National Park, a large nature reserve extending along the shores of
Lake Torneträsk.

From Abisko the Lapland (Ofot) Railway runs west to Narvik (see entry) on
the Norwegian coast.

Kiruna, against the backdrop of Kirunavaara

Kebnekaise, Sweden's highest mountain

Kokkola (Gamlakarleby) F 4

Country: **Finland**
Region: Western Finland. Population: 35,000
Post code: FIN–67100   Telephone code: 968

Situation and characteristics

Kokkola, one of the oldest towns in Finland (founded 1620), was almost entirely Swedish-speaking, and was known only under the name of Gamlakarleby, until the 20th century. With the development of industry, however, the language boundary was obliterated and Finnish came increasingly into use. Nowadays only about a fifth of the population are Swedish-speaking. Originally situated on the sea, the town is now 5km/3 miles inland as a result of the rise in the level of the coast. The harbour is the deepest on the west coast of Finland.

History

The town was founded by Per Brahe in 1620 at the behest of King Gustavus Adolphus. Its excellent situation from the point of view of communications led to the rapid growth of its commerce and shipping around 1800. Kokkola lost much of its merchant shipping fleet during the Crimean War (1854–56).

Town

In Mannerheim Square (Mannerheiminaukio) stands the Town Hall (by C. L. Engel, 1845). The church in the centre of the town is modern (1960). The old part of the town with its wooden houses has preserved much of its original character. The Kaarlela district has an old church (1460). The Renlund Historical Museum (history of the town, ship models) occupies an old wooden house dating from 1696. The Renlund Art Gallery displays works by Finnish artists.

On the banks of the Kaupunginsalmi is the English Park (Englantilainen Puisto) – a name which recalls a British attack on the town in 1854, during the Crimean War. A captured British longboat is displayed in the park.

Kokkola Museum

Southern Surroundings

The area south of Kokkola abounds in historical associations, not only for Finland but for the kingdom of Finland and Sweden as a whole, which was torn apart by Tsar Alexander I's victorious campaign in 1808–09.

The best route south is the road via Öja and Risöhäll, which runs over islands and round inlets of the sea, with fine views of the Gulf of Bothnia.

Jakobstad (pop. 20,000), 40km/25 miles from Kokkola, was founded in 1652 by Ebba Brahe, widow of the Swedish general Count Jacob de la Gardie. In the 17th century the area around the commune of Pedersöre on which the town now stands was a fief of the de la Gardie family. Queen Christina of Sweden revoked the fief, but granted Count Jacob the right to found a town. After his death Ebba Brahe – whose youngest brother Per Brahe had founded Gamlakarleby and Nykarleby – founded the town and named it after her late husband. Jacobstad is predominantly Swedish-speaking; its name in Swedish is Pietarsaari, which is derived from the original name of the commune of Pedersöre.

Jakobstad

In Jakobstad can be found the Strengberg tobacco factory, the oldest in Scandinavia, with a Tobacco Museum.

Jakobstad was the birthplace of J. L. Runeberg (1804–74), one of the greatest 19th century poets writing in Swedish. His best known work is the "Songs of Ensign Ståhl", a glorification of the Swedish-Finnish resistance to the Russian invasion of 1808–09. Since the war was waged under Swedish command – Finland providing the soldiers and NCOs, Sweden the officers – the work is also a reflection of Swedish attitudes. Runeberg's school, in the Westmansmors Stuga, is now a museum. In the gardens adjoining the Town Hall is a monument to the poet by his son Walter Runeberg (1905).

The church in Pedersöre probably dates from the 14th century. Originally it was a square building in grey stone, providing a model for the wooden churches with pointed spires built in northern and eastern Finland in the 17th century, but was rebuilt on a cruciform plan by Jacob Rijf in 1787–95.

The old part of Jakobstad, with its harbour, is picturesque. The School Park occupies the area where, 200 years ago, the Strengberg family tried to grow tobacco in glasshouses. The park itself contains more than a thousand different species of plants. At Alholmsgatan 8 is a Motorcycle Museum.

10km/6 miles from the town centre is the sandy beach of Fäboda, with the Nanog Arctic Museum.

Fäboda beach

20km/12½ miles south of Jakobstad lies the town of Nykarleby (Finnish name Uusikaarlepyy), founded in 1620, where Per Brahe established the first secondary school in Österbotten (1640). The little town is still mainly Swedish-speaking. Nykarleby was the birthplace in 1818 of Zachris Topelius, the most important Finland-Swedish poet of the 19th century after Runeberg; the house in which he was born is now a museum.

Nykarleby

The wooden church of St Brigitta (1708) has fine wall paintings; the bell-frame dates from 1702.

Near Nykarleby General von Döbeln defeated a Russian army during the Swedish-Russian war of 1808–09.

Surroundings of Kokkola – North

From Kokkola Road 8 leads north along the coast and comes in 30km/19 miles to Lohtaja, lying a little off the main road. In the hamlet of Perttulan Puhto are three timber-built 18th century manor-houses.

At Kalajoki, 65km/40 miles from Kokkola, are the most frequented sandy beaches in Finland, sheltered by a fringe of dunes. As a result of the steady

Kalajoki
★Sandy beaches

Sandy beach, Kalajoki

rise in the level of the land the coastline is continually moving farther seaward. On the beach is the Jukujukumaa amusement park.

Maakalla	The island of Maakalla, a relatively recent product of the rise in the land, emerged from the sea in the 16th century. On the island is a fishing village in 18th century style. The fishermen brought over their huts from the mainland to provide an advanced base for their activities. There is even a little church on the island. Boat services from Kalajoki in summer.

Koli Hills   G 4

Country: **Finland**
Region: Eastern Finland

Situation	The Koli Hills, one of the most attractive areas in Finland, lie on the south western shores of Lake Pielinen, on the north eastern fringe of the Finnish Lakeland (see entry). The hills are due to be designated a National Park.
Ukko-Koli	At Ahmovaara a side road branches off Road 18 (Joensuu–Kajaani) and runs east through rugged country, with expanses of forest, to end at a parking place at the Koli Hotel. From there a stepped path climbs up the rocky hill of Ukko-Koli (347m/1139ft), from where there is a magnificent view of Lake Pielinen, 253m/830ft below, with its many wooded islands. To the south are two other peaks in the Koli range, Akka-Koli (339m/1112ft) and Paha-Koli (334m/1096ft). To the north is Ipatti (316m/1037ft).
Walking and winter sports	Around the hotel there are more than 20km/12½ miles of marked footpaths, as well as facilities for winter sports.
Holiday centre	10km/6 miles north is the Loma-Koli holiday centre, with a hotel, chalets and a camping site. Within easy reach is Lieksa (see Finnish Lakeland).

Kongsberg   C 5

Country: **Norway**
Region: Southern Norway
Altitude: 170m/560ft. Population: 20,000
Post code: N–3600

Kongsberg owed its foundation and early prosperity to the nearby silver-mines, which began to be worked in 1624, during the reign of Christian IV, and were closed down only in 1957. The town – one of the oldest in Norway – lies in the southern Numedal on both sides of the river Lågen, on which there are a series of rapids in this area.

Situation and characteristics

In the market square, on the right bank of the river, stands a large wooden church (1741–61), with a fine organ and church plate. Opposite the church, to the north, is a statue of Christian IV and in Hyttegate, to the east of the church, a small Silver-Mine Museum. On the other bank of the river, spanned here by the Nybro (New Bridge), is the Lågdal Museum, with a collection of antiquities from the surrounding area.

Town

7km/4½ miles south of the town are the old silver-mines (conducted tours). The Kongensgruve (Royal Mine) at Saggrenda extends 2300m/2500yd into the hill (mine railway).

Silver-mines

Surroundings

The Heddal is reached by taking the road which runs past the old silver-mines and then turning west on E 11. This passes through Notodden (pop. 9000) and comes in 38km/24 miles to Heddal stave church (see Telemark).

Heddal

There is a very attractive road up the Numedal to Geilo. The valley, with particularly fine scenery in its upper reaches, is traversed by the river Lågen, which rises in the central Hardangervidda (see entry). Leave Kongsberg on Road 40, going north. Beyond Flesberg (31km/20 miles) the valley narrows. At Djupdal station (46km/29 miles) the road crosses the river, here flowing through a deep gorge, and runs past the old church of Rollag and beyond this the Mykstufoss hydro-electric station.

Numedal

At Rødberg is another hydro-electric station (Nore I and II), powered by water from two lakes in a side valley to the north, Pålsbufjord and Tunnhovdfjord.

Rødberg

Shortly before coming to Vasstulen the road reaches its highest point (1100m/3610ft). To the left can be seen the Sigridfjell (1231m/4039ft). After going over two other hills the road comes to Geilo in the Ustadal, a popular holiday and winter sports resort (several ski-lifts). There is a chair-lift up Geilohøgda (1056m/3465ft); restaurant at the upper station. To the north-west is the Prestholtskarv (1857m/6093ft), with a road ascending to 1350m/4430ft.

Kristiansand   B 6

Country: **Norway**
Region: Southern Norway. Population: 61,000
Post code: N–4600

The port of Kristiansand lies on a level and almost square peninsula in the Skagerrak at the mouth of the Torridalselv (the lower course of the Otra).

Situation and characteristics

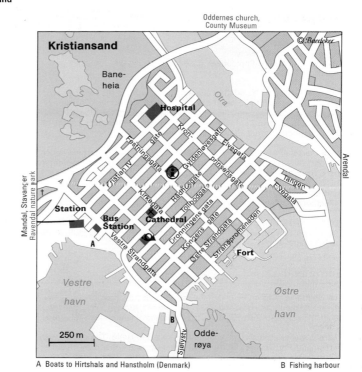

Oddernes church,
County Museum

Kristiansand

© Baedeker

Bane-
heia

Hospital

Otra

Station

Bus
Station

Cathedral

Fort

Mandal, Stavanger
Ravendal nature park

Arendal

Vestre
havn

Østre
havn

250 m

Odde-
røya

A Boats to Hirtshals and Hanstholm (Denmark)   B Fishing harbour

The town, founded by Christian IV in 1641, was destroyed by fire on several occasions in subsequent centuries (most recently in 1892), and was rebuilt on a regular grid plan.

Kristiansand is the chief town of Vest-Agder county and the see of a bishop. Its main sources of employment are industry and shipping. Its harbour makes it one of Norway's major ports.

Town

Cathedral

In the Market Square (Torget), in the centre of the town, is the Cathedral, rebuilt in Neo-Gothic style in 1882–85 after a fire; open only from 9am to 2pm. It has a fine altar with a painting of Christ at Emmaus and wood figures of the Evangelists from the old church.

In the adjoining gardens can be seen a monument (by Gustav Vigeland) to the poet Henrik Wergeland (1808–45), a native of the town. On the east side of the square is a bronze statue of King Håkon VII (1872–1957).

West Harbour
Fishing harbour

On the south-west side of the town is the West Harbour (Vestre Havn) bounded on the south by the little peninsula of Langmannsholm, and to the east, between Langmannsholm and Odderøy, the fishing harbour (harbour cruises). There are remains of old fortifications on Odderøy.

Fort
Christiansholm

On the south-east side of the peninsula is the East Harbour (Østre Havn), with the 17th century Fort Christiansholm (art exhibitions in summer).

Vest-Agder
County Museum

Outside the town, to the north-east, the Vest-Agder County Museum (Fylkesmuseum) is one of the largest open-air museums in Norway, with old

The port of Kristiansand, on the Skagerrak

cottages and farmhouses from Vest-Agder and the Setesdal, a street of old houses (Bygaden) from Kristiansand. Several rooms in the houses display furniture, textiles, glass, stoneware and old liturgical utensils.

Near the museum stands the early medieval church of Oddernes, with a runic stone in the churchyard.

North-west of the town, beyond the park-like Baneheia (several lakes with facilities for bathing), is the Ravnedal Nature Park.

Ravnedal Nature Park

From the crags which rear above the park there are fine views of the town, the sea and the islands.

Surroundings

Mandal (pop. 12,000) 45km/28 miles west of Kristiansand on E 18, lying on both banks of the Mandalselv, is the most southerly town in Norway, with handsome old burghers' houses and a large wooden church (1821). From the rocky hill of Uranienborg, to the north of the town, there are wide views.

Mandal

28km/17 miles south-west of Mandal is Lindesnes (alt. 38m/125ft), the most southerly point on the mainland of Norway (lat. 57°58′43″ north), on which Norway's first lighthouse was built in 1655.

Lindesnes

From Kristiansand a road runs north by way of Vennesla to Grovane, from which a train drawn by an old steam locomotive (1894) operates on Sundays along a 5km/3 mile stretch of the old Setesdal railway.

Grovane old-time railway

See entry

Setesdal

Kristiansand to Arendal via Grimstad (72km/45 miles)

From Kristiansand E 18 runs north-east to the coastal towns of Grimstad and Arendal.

Lindesnes lighthouse

Wildlife Park	E 18 crosses the much indented Topdalsfjord on a suspension bridge 608m/660yd long and in 11km/7 miles passes the Dyrepark (Wildlife Park), in which almost all the species found in Scandinavia are represented. It is also well known for its breeding of camels.
Grimstad	The road runs by way of Lillesand (pop. 1500) and the manor-house of Norholmen, once the home of the Norwegian writer Knut Hamsun (museum), to Grimstad (pop. 14,500). In Østregate, near the harbour, is the former pharmacy in which Henrik Ibsen was an apprentice from 1847 to 1850. While in Grimstad he wrote his first drama, "Catiline", which was published in 1850 under a pseudonym. The interior of the pharmacy has been preserved in its original state and is now a museum; it contains a number of Ibsen manuscripts and pictures which he painted in Grimstad.
Arendal	Arendal (pop. 12,000), chief town of Aust-Agder county, is picturesquely situated on the slopes of a hill, with an important harbour and shipyards. In the south of the town stands the Town Hall, the largest wooden building in Norway after the Stiftsgård in Trondheim.
Hisøy, Tromøy	Offshore are the islands of Hisøy and Tromøy (bridge). Tromøy has a 13th century church and a good viewpoint on the hill of Vardåsen.

Kristianstad D 7

Country: **Sweden**. Province: Skåne. Population: 70,000
Post code: S–291.. Telephone code: 044

Situation and characteristics	Kristianstad, situated on the Helgeå in south-eastern Sweden, was founded by King Christian IV of Denmark in 1614, when Skåne still belonged to

Denmark. The town was surrounded by ramparts and bastions, for it was designed as a stronghold to ward off Swedish attacks on Skåne. The layout of the town was the earliest example of Renaissance town-planning in northern Europe, with a rectangular street grid adjusted to the line of the fortifications.

In the main square, the Stora Torg, is the Town Hall (1891), on the central gable of which is a statue of Christian IV, with his greeting to the towns-people of Kristianstad, "Frid med Eder" ("Peace be with you"). Also in the square are the Freemasons' Lodge; the Burgomaster's House (1640), which was given its present form about 1800; the 19th century Stora Kronohus, a white building in Empire style which was originally occupied by a court and a regiment of artillery and is still in military hands; and the Municipal Museum, housed in the old Armoury (local history, art).

Town

Stora Torg

Trinity Church (1617–28), the largest and finest Renaissance church in northern Europe, has a magnificent organ and carved choir-stalls, for the most part excellently preserved.

★Trinity Church

Outside the Norreport, a town gate of 1760, are barracks, once occupied by a regiment which took part in the campaigns against Napoleon. A memorial stone commemorates the battles of Grossbeeren, Dennewitz and Leipzig in 1813. From the Water-Tower, 50m/165ft high, there are superb views.

Water-Tower

In Östra Storgatan is a Film Museum, housed in the studios in which the first Swedish films were shot. At Västra Storgatan 40 is Cardell House (1760), with a beautifully carved doorway. This was the home of General Cardell, who is said to have had the street closed to traffic so that his afternoon nap should not be disturbed. At Västra Storgatan 39 can be seen a house which was occupied by Charles XII about 1700 and by Stanislaus Leszczynski, the exiled king of Poland, from 1711 to 1714.

Film Museum

In Tivoligatan are a tannery of 1660 and a number of 17th century houses. At the end of the street, on the banks of the river, extends the large Tivoli Park, laid out by a Danish landscape gardener, with a theatre in Art Nouveau style (by Axel Anderberg, 1906).

Tivoli Park

Surroundings

In the area around Kristianstad there are many old castles and churches. 3km/2 miles south are the ruins of Lillhöhusborg, birthplace of Herluf Trolle, a well-known Danish nobleman. 6km/4 miles south is Norra Åsum church, built in 1200 by Bishop Absalon of Roskilde in Denmark. There are interesting medieval churches at Färlöv, Kiaby, Vittskövle and Fjälkinge. To the south of the town can be found the castles of Malteshol, on Linderödsåsen, and Vittskövle, and the Forsaker falls (10m/35ft high), in a beautiful wooded setting. On the coast is Åhus, a fishing village and seaside resort with an eel-smoking factory.

Road 21 runs north-west from Kristianstad to Hässleholm. Just before it reaches the town it comes to Ignaberga, near which is the Tykarpsgrotta, a limestone cave. Hässleholm (pop. 48,000), which received its municipal charter in 1914, grew up around a railway junction. In the park is a piece of sculpture by Axel Ebbe, "The Brigand". At Osby, north of Hässleholm, is the interesting Brio Toy Museum. In the forests in the surrounding area there are good canoeing waters.

Hässleholm

17km/10 miles north-east of Kristianstad stands Kongsgård Castle, originally (in medieval times) a monastery and now a hotel and restaurant. There are other castles at Ovesholm (with a beautiful English-style park) and Trolle Ljungby, which was rebuilt about 1660; from the same period

Kongsgård

Vittskövle Castle, near Kristianstad

dates Råbelöv Castle, on the lake of that name. In the Ivösjö is the island of Ivö (deposits of china clay; porcelain manufactory).

Kuopio   G 4

Country: Finland
Region: Central Finland. Population: 80,000
Post code: FIN–70100   Telephone code: 971

Situation and characteristics

Kuopio is beautifully situated on a peninsula projecting into the Kallavesi, with Puijo Hill rising above the town to the north. It is the economic and cultural centre of the province of Kuopio, the see of a Lutheran bishop and of the Orthodox Archbishop of Finland, and has a university, founded in 1972. Kuopio is the focal point of both boat and land traffic in the flat but richly diversified region of Savo with its intermingling of woodland and water. It is linked with the Gulf of Finland by Lake Saimaa and the Saimaa Canal.

History

Kuopio received its municipal charter from Per Brahe in 1654. After losing its municipal rights for a period it was granted a new charter by Gustavus III in 1782. During the 1808–09 war the town surrendered to the Russians without a fight, but was later recaptured in a surprise attack by a Finnish force led by Colonel Sandels.

J. V. Snellman

One of the outstanding Finnish figures of the 19th century, the philosopher, politician and statesman Johan Vilhelm Snellman, was rector of the grammar school in Kuopio from 1843 to 1849. Later, in 1863, he persuaded Tsar Alexander II to agree that Finnish should be one of the official languages, together with Swedish and Russian (in practice little used), of the Grand Duchy of Finland.

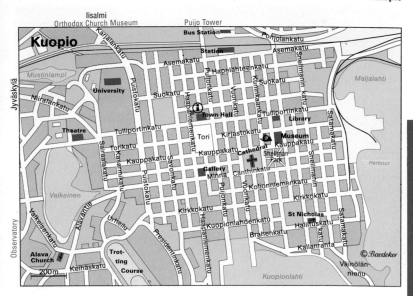

The central feature of the town is the Market Square (Kauppatori), where visitors can buy the local delicacy, *kalakukko* (a fish and pork pie). In the square are the Town Hall (by F. A. Sjöström, 1884) and, opposite it, the Art Nouveau Market Hall. On the far side of Kauppakatu stands the Grammar School (1825).

Town

Market Square

Kauppakatu leads to the Cathedral (designed by Jacob Rijf; completed in 1815 by Pehr Granstedt) which stands on a low hill to the east. Beyond it is Snellman Park (Snellmaninpuisto), with a bronze statue of Snellman (whose house at Snellmaninkatu 19 is now a museum).

Cathedral
Snellman Park

To the north of the park, in Kauppakatu, the Municipal Museum has frescos by Juho Rissanen (1909). The displays illustrate the history and culture of the region, and there is also an aquarium. Immediately adjoining is the Municipal Library.

Municipal
Museum

Maaherrankatu extends along the east side of Snellman Park. At its north end, in a small garden on the left, is a monument to the great Finnish writer Minna Canth (1844–97).

Monument to
Minna Canth

In the south-east of the town can be found the Orthodox church of St Nicholas (1903), seat of the Archbishop (Metropolitan) of the Finnish Orthodox church. The church has two dioceses, each with some 30,000 members – Karelia, with fourteen parishes, and Helsinki, with eleven.

St Nicholas's
Church

To the south of the Orthodox church is the narrow peninsula of Väinölänniemi, with a park, sports grounds, a bathing beach and (at the southern tip) a summer restaurant, the Peränniemen Kasino. At the landward end of the peninsula is a statue of Hannes Kolehmainen, who won the marathon in the 1920 Olympic Games.

Väinölänniemi
peninsula

On the west side of the town, to the north of the Lake Valkeinen sports complex (fishing), is the modern Municipal Theatre (by Risto-Veikko Luukkonen and Helmer Stenros, 1962). Farther north, on Lake Mustinlampi, are an indoor swimming pool and a bowling alley.

Theatre

View of Kuopio and the Kallavesi from Puijo Hill

Kuopio Town Hall and Market Square

Karjalankatu, to the east, runs north to the Orthodox Church Museum (1969), part of a complex which also includes the Archbishop's residence, a seminary for priests and the offices of the Finnish Orthodox Church, Finland's second largest religious community. The museum displays objects from the Valamo, Petsamo and Konevitsa monasteries, which had to be evacuated during the Second World War.

★Orthodox Church Museum

Farther north, in Vuorikatu, Kirkkokatu and Savonkatu, are wooden houses in the Finnish style developed in the 18th century.

Surroundings of Kuopio

Immediately north of the town, on the wooded Puijo Hill (Puijomäki), stands a 75m/245ft high lookout tower, rising to a height of 225m/740ft above the Kallavesi. The tower has two viewing platforms and a revolving restaurant (turning through 360 degrees every hour) at a height of 65m/213ft.

★Viewpoint (Puijo Hill)

There are "water-buses" to the Ritoniemi holiday village on the island of Soisalo.

Kuusamo   G 3

Country: **Finland**
Region: North-eastern Finland
Altitude: 250m/820ft. Population: 18,000
Post code: FIN–93600   Telephone code: 989

Kuusamo lies on a plateau at the north-west end of the Kuusamojärvi, a lake from which a number of rivers flow in different directions – eastward into the Gulf of Dvina on the White Sea, westward into the Gulf of Bothnia. The extensive area included within the commune of Kuusamo, with its lakes and rivers, attracts many visitors in both summer and winter – in summer it draws anglers and walkers, and in winter it offers excellent skiing (ski-jump, a ski-lift and good pistes and cross-country trails on Rukatunturi).

Situation and characteristics

As early as the 15th century Kuusamo was an important meeting-place of the two cultures of Sweden from the west and Russia from the east.

A quarter of the population live by agriculture and forestry, including reindeer-herding and the breeding of animals for their fur. The local industries are mostly small-scale (manufacture of timber products and angling equipment, fish-processing). Only about half the population of the commune live in the town of Kuusamo, which is fairly loosely built-up.

Population and economy

In the centre of the town is the small market square (market on weekdays).

Town

Near the centre stands the church (1951), with two bells which have an interesting history. In 1944 they were removed from the church by German troops and buried in the churchyard to save them from the advancing Soviet forces. Thereafter they were lost from sight until 1959, when the one-time commander of the regiment visited Kuusamo and produced a plan showing where the bells were hidden.

The larger of the two bells was presented to the church by King Charles XI in 1698. The smaller one was a thanksgiving gift in 1721 from Protestant clergymen who had found a refuge in Kuusamo during the wars of 1700–21.

Surroundings

Kuusamo is a good base from which to explore the natural beauties of the surrounding area, either by car or on foot. The scenery of this region is given its particular stamp by the contrast between the extensive areas of water and bogland and the tracts of rocky country. The lakes are frequently edged by sheer granite cliffs, and in many places the rivers are hemmed in by rocks, flowing through deep gorges and over rapids.

Rukatunturi

For an attractive excursion in the country around Kuusamo, leave on Road 5 (E 63), which runs 25km/15 miles north to the hill of Rukatunturi (462m/1516ft), which has 25 pistes and 18 lifts for skiers. The chair-lift also operates in summer, offering visitors panoramic views. The longest bob-sleigh run in Finland returns to the starting-point of the lift.

Juurna

From here take Road 5 for 10km/6 miles and then turn right into Road 950, which in 5km/3 miles after passing a side road to Säkkilänvaara, reaches Juurna, with the Jyrävä rapids (good fishing).

Oulanka
National Park
Rapids

From here return to Road 950, which comes in 9km/5½ miles to the village of Käylä; then turn right into the road to Liikasenvaara. 15km/9 miles along this road are the Oulanka National Park information centre and the Kiuta-köngäs rapids on the Oulanjoki, which here flows between sheer rock walls with a fall of 14m/45ft over a distance of 600m/660yd.

Bear Trail

Here the road cuts across the Bear Trail (Karhunkierros), a waymarked footpath some 70km/45 miles long, with shelter huts, which ends at Ruka-tunturi. Experienced walkers can begin the walk there: others should start from the Suorajärvi bus stop on Road 950, from which the going is easier. Since the trail is never too far from human settlement it is possible to take a break at any time.

Evening on the Alakitka, near Juurna

Kiutaköngäs rapids, in Oulanka National Park

Lahti   G 5

Country: **Finland**
Region: Southern Finland. Population: 95,000
Post code: FIN–15100   Telephone code: 918

Lahti lies 100km/60 miles north-east of Helsinki on the north-western edge of the Salpausselkä ridge, at the south end of the Vesijärvi (alt. 82m/269ft; area 113sq.km/44sq. miles), which is surrounded by wooded hills. One of Finland's largest towns, Lahti owed its rapid rise to prosperity to its excellent situation, with good communications. It received its municipal charter, however, only in 1905. It now has a varied range of industries (large furniture factories; glass, textiles, metalworking, electrical goods). It also has a powerful radio transmitter and an Academy of Music. | Situation and characteristics

International Organ Festival (August): Writers' Seminar (August); Poster Biennale (alternate years in summer). | Cultural events

Lahti is a popular winter sports resort. Every February the Finlandia Run, a cross-country skiing race, is held here; and this is followed in March by the Salpausselkä Winter Games. The Nordic skiing championships were held in Lahti in 1978 and 1989. | ★Winter sports

The central feature of the town is the Market Square (Kauppatori), surrounded by shops and office, on the north side of which stands a wooden church. In Kirkkokatu is the brick-built Holy Cross Church (Ristin Kirkko), designed by Alvar Aalto (1978). | **Town** / Market Square

To the west, at the end of Kirkkokatu, can be found the Historical Museum, which has been housed since 1968 in a mansion built by a local industrialist | Historical Museum

277

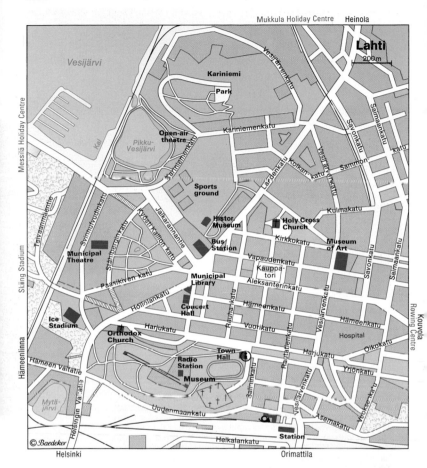

at the end of the 19th century. The collection includes pictures and prehistoric material from Viipuri, formerly a Finnish town but now in Russia. In the adjoining park is the Kariranta Open-Air Theatre.

Town Hall

South of the Market Square stands the Town Hall (by Eliel Saarinen, 1912), a monumental Art Nouveau building in rough brick. Also in the town centre is the Concert Hall (by Kaija and Heikki Sirén, 1954). To the west is the modern Municipal Theatre (1983).

Monuments

Standing in the park adjoining the Town Hall the Freedom Monument commemorates the liberation of the town from Communist forces. In front of the railway station, to the south-east, is an equestrian statue of Marshal Mannerheim (by Veikko Leppänen, 1959).

Radio Museum

In the centre of the park is the old radio station, with the Radio Museum (over 1000 exhibits).

The Museum of Art at Vesijärvenkatu 11 houses works by Akseli Gallén-Kallela. Two specialised museums are the Poster Museum and the Skiing Museum.

Museum of Art

At Harjukatu 5 is the Orthodox church (1954), a copy of the church of the Prophet Elijah in Viipuri.

Orthodox church

Surroundings

In the district of Kiveriö rises the 50m/165ft high Water-Tower (Mustankallionmäki), a modern structure with a café at 40m/130ft.

Water-Tower

To the west of the town is the Skiing Stadium, with a ski-jump 90m/295ft high (viewing platform) and three other jumps, cross-countrytrails and a floodlit sawdust run 1000m/1100yd long. There are also an ice rink and a swimming pool.

Skiing Stadium

11km/7 miles north-west of Lahti lies Tiirismaa (223m/732ft; radio transmitter), a skiing resort with two ski-lifts and a slalom run. The hill is an outlier of the Salpausselkä ridge, a massive terminal moraine which bounds the Finnish Lakeland (see entry) on the south and extends north-east for 550km/340 miles into Karelia.

Tiirismaa

5km/3 miles north of Lahti, on the east side of the Vesijärvi, is the Mukkula recreation and holiday centre, and a few kilometres north-east, on the road to Heinola, the Takkula recreation area. 8km/5 miles north-west of the town can be found the Messilä holiday centre, with facilities for water sports, adventure playgrounds and restaurants (open in summer).

Recreation centres

8.5km/5 miles farther north-west is Hollola, with a stone-built 14th century church (fine woodcarving).

Hollola

Sports facilities on the Selpausselkä ridge in summer

Boat trips

There is a hydrofoil service from Lahti to Jyväskylä (3½ hours each way). In summer there are also steamer trips to Jyväskylä (10½ hours) and Heinola (4½ hours).

Landskrona

D 7

Country: **Sweden**
Province: Skåne. Population: 36,000
Post code: S–261.. Telephone code: 0418

Situation and characteristics

The port and industrial town of Landskrona, on the Öresund, received its municipal charter from Eric of Pomerania in 1413, but suffered severely from the wars between Sweden and Denmark in the three following centuries. There are many market gardens and nurseries in the fertile surrounding area (e.g. at Weibulls).

Town

Landskrona has many 18th century buildings, and its little houses have been carefully restored. In the centre of the town is Town Hall Square, on the north side of which, housed in the 18th century Adolf Fredrik Barracks, is the Municipal Museum.

Citadel

Behind the barracks is the Citadel, within the area of which are a beautiful park and a Museum of Art. The Citadel, built by the Danish king Christian III in the 16th century, is surrounded by a triple ring of ramparts and moats, reinforced by bastions. From 1825 it was used as a prison, and from 1940 it provided accommodation for refugees.

Selma Lagerlöf's house

Behind the Sofia Albertina Church (18th c.; fine stained glass), at Kungsgatan 13A, stands the house in which the Swedish writer Selma Lagerlöf (Nobel Prize, 1909) lived from 1885 to 1891. While here she wrote her novel "Gösta Berling's Saga" (published 1891).

Citadel, Landskrona

From the harbour there are boat services to the Tuborg Harbour in Copenhagen and to the island of Ven. From the new water-tower there is a fine view over the Öresund.

Surroundings

3km/2 miles north of the town centre lies the fishing village of Borstahusen (good bathing). A few kilometres farther north is the hilly region of Glumslövs Backar, a landscape shaped by Ice Age glaciers.

East of the town, on the Malmö road, are the Weibullsholm gardens.

The Island of ★Ven

5km/3 miles off the Swedish coast, in the Öresund, is the island of Ven (area 7.5sq.km/3sq. miles; pop. 300), probably a relic of a former land link between Skåne and Zealand in Denmark. The island, a plateau with steeply sloping eroded sides, was already occupied in the Stone Age.

Ven owes its fame to the Danish astronomer Tycho Brahe (1546–1601), who lived from 1578 to 1598 in Uranienborg, a castle in the centre of the island. King Frederick II of Denmark (to which Ven belonged until 1658) granted the estate to Tycho Brahe so that he could carry on his astronomical observations in its dust-free air. From his observatory of Stjärneborg Brahe discovered the first super-nova star, recording his observations in his book "De nova stella" ("Of the New Star")

Visitors can see the remains of Uranienborg and Stjärneborg and the Brahe Museum. There is also a statue of the great astronomer.

The best way to explore the island is by bicycle (which can be hired at Bäckviken, where the boat comes in) or on foot. There is also a bus service from Bäckviken to Kyrkbacken, on the north-west coast of the island, near which is the 12th century church of St Ibb (St James). It is advisable to take a picnic with you, for there are considerable distances between the kiosks selling snacks. Good bathing.

Lapland

Countries: **Norway** (Lapland), **Sweden** (Lappland), **Finland** (Lappi), **Russia** (Laplandiya)

The name of Lapland is applied to the northern part of Scandinavia, extending over parts of Norway, Sweden, Finland and Russia. It has a total area of around 260,000sq.km/100,000sq. miles, sloping down towards the east from the mountains of Norway and northern Sweden. In the south it is mostly forest-covered; in the north it consists of treeless tundra and bog. It has a population of some 380,000, of whom 30,000–32,000 are Sami (Lapps).

The climate, except in the coastal regions, is continental, with short summers (many mosquitoes) and long, cold winters. Since most of Lapland lies north of the Arctic Circle, the midnight sun shines in summer, while in winter the Arctic night prevails.

In the fauna of Lapland the reindeer occupies a special place. Brown bears are now rare, and with the advance of modern civilisation the lynx has almost disappeared. During the winter wolves venture near human settlements.

Those who want to do any walking in Lapland should be equipped with sturdy footwear, good maps, a compass and sufficient food. Lapland is beautiful, but it has a character of its own which finds expression in sudden and violent changes in the weather. Walkers should never go on their own.

Ecology and Tourism

The ecological balance of Lapland is extremely delicate, and visitors should be very careful not to disturb it. It may take many years, for example, for a tin to rust away, since it is subject to corrosion only during the few frost-free months in the year.

In the dry summer months great caution is required with open fires. During this period there are different stages of alert restricting the lighting of fires, and visitors must be sure to check up on the current alert situation: ignorance is no defence against failure to comply with the restrictions, which may result in a heavy fine. They should ensure, before leaving a camping site, that any fire they have lit is completely extinguished. If they are travelling by mountain bicycle they should remember that the layer of topsoil in Lapland is extremely thin and slow to build up, and should, therefore, ride only on made-up roads.

One possible hazard for motorists in Lapland is a collision with an elk or reindeer. Animals tend to like main roads, where there is likely to be a breeze to keep the mosquitoes away. If an animal is critically injured in an accident it should be put out of its misery. If you are unable or reluctant to do so, a local inhabitant should be informed and driven to the spot in order to do what is necessary. The nearest police station or frontier post should then be informed. Elks belong to no one; but a motorist who kills one has no right to it, since under the veterinary regulations only the holder of an elk-shooting permit is entitled to dispose of a dead elk. Reindeer always belong to someone, and any visitor who takes the meat of a reindeer is guilty of theft.

In accidents of this kind the facts are recorded by the authorities, and that ends the matter. The question of responsibility for the accident is not pursued. The motorist is not liable for compensation, which the owner of the animal can claim from the state. Since he is not exposed to any legal action, either criminal or civil, the driver need have no hesitation in reporting the matter and giving all the information required. Failure to do so will usually have unpleasant consequences, since the local people will realise what caused the bump on your car and the bush telegraph will associate it with an accident which may have occurred hours or days before and many miles away.

Population

Sami

In the whole of Lapland there are 30,000–32,000 Sami (Lapps), some 20,000 of them in Norway and 8500 in Sweden. They call themselves Sabmek (singular Sameh), the "bog people". Their origins are obscure; they are short in stature, round-headed and broad-faced, with yellowish skin and dark hair. Their language is related to Finnish. Although Christian missions to the Sami began in the 17th century they have preserved certain pagan practices.

Three broad groups of Sami are distinguished: the nomadic Mountain Sami, now steadily declining in numbers, who move between the forest and mountain regions with their herds of reindeer in regular migrations; the Forest Sami, who live a settled life with their herds in particular areas; and the Lake or Fishing Sami, who live by fishing.

Costume

The characteristic Sami costume, which differs little between men and women, consists of a knee-length skirt of blue or brown material, with red and yellow trimming, and close-fitting trousers, with a cap of the same material (which in Norway has four stiffened points and in Sweden is tall and topped with a red ball of wool). The shoes are of soft reindeer-skin, with turned-up toes (*gabmagak; skalkomager,* skin boots). The winter garment is of reindeer skin. The local costumes and articles of carved reindeer horn are now also made for the tourist trade.

Houses, transport

The normal Sami dwelling is a small timber or earth hut (*gammen;* Sami *darfe goattek*). The nomadic Sami have canvas tents (Finnish *kota,* with an

A herd of reindeer

opening at the top to let the smoke out. The *pulka* or *akja,* a boat-shaped sleigh hauled by a reindeer on a single trace, is now rarely used; in recent years the motor sleigh (snowmobile) has become the principal means of transport.

The main property of the Sami is their reindeer (Norwegian and Swedish *ren,* Finnish *poro),* a species of deer accustomed to cold conditions in which both sexes have antlers. There are estimated to be something like 750,000 reindeer in Lapland. A Sami requires at least 100–200 head for subsistence, but rarely possesses more than 500. With 800 he is a rich man. Herds of several thousand are sometimes found, but these belong to nomadic families travelling together. The hooves of a herd of reindeer make a characteristic clicking sound as they move about on the hard ground. Since the vegetation takes many years to recover after being cropped by reindeer, the herds require very large areas for grazing. The Chernobyl disaster of 1986 did grave damage to the grazing grounds. In addition to their reindeer many Sami have other livestock and may grow certain crops.

Reindeer

During the 1980s the Sami in the Scandinavian countries gained extensive political rights as a minority community. In Norway and Sweden they have their own autonomous parliament, the Sameting; there are radio and television programmes in the Sami language, and many schools offer tuition in Sami as well as in the national language. On the other hand it is the case that many Sami are unable to live by the traditional economy and to follow their traditional way of life.

Political and cultural autonomy

Norwegian Lapland

Norwegian Lapland includes the counties of Troms and Finnmark, the coasts of which are much indented by fjords and inlets. In Troms arable

Sami in traditional costume

Lapp tent near Kautokeino

farming is still possible and there is rich pastureland, but the country to the north-east becomes increasingly bare and inhospitable. From the high ranges of mountains in the west the land falls to low-lying plateaux in the east, with occasional bare rounded hills. The chief towns of the two counties are Tromsø (see entry) and Vadsø (see Kirkenes, Surroundings).

Alta

On the Altafjord in western Finnmark is the important commercial town of Alta (see entry), formerly known as Bossekop in Alta ("Whale Bay", from the Sami word *bosso*, "whale"). The population live mainly by salmon-fishing and working the local slate. The country round the fjord, which can be surprisingly warm in summer, has a remarkably varied growth of vegetation.

Kautokeino

130km/80 miles south of Alta on Road 93, on the Finnmarksvidda, is Kautokeino, with a mainly Sami population of 1600. Features of interest are the church (1958; replacing an earlier church of 1703 which was destroyed in 1944) and a silversmith's workshop. The Sami Institute of Kautokeino is a scientific and cultural centre for the Sami of Scandinavian Lapland.

Karasjok

145km/90 miles east of Alta is Karasjok (see entry), which ranks as the capital of the Norwegian Sami. Here is the Sami Centre (Samelandssenter), which accommodates both tourist facilities and cultural and political activities; it is the seat of the Sami parliament, the Sameting. It occupies a handsome modern building (1991) in the form of a traditional Sami tent, constructed of timber, metal and glass.

Porsangerfjord

From Alta Road 6 (Skarzeberg Tunnel and Sortvik Tunnel) runs north-east to the little settlement of Kistrand, on the Porsangerfjord, which extends south for some 120km/75 miles from Honningsvåg on the island of Magerøy (see North Cape). The road follows the head of the fjord and continues to Kirkenes (see entry).

The midnight sun on the Porsangerfjord (Norwegian Lapland)

Swedish Lapland

This is the most northerly province in Sweden, the largest in area (120,000sq.km/46,000sq. miles) and the most sparsely populated. It extends from north to south for some 600km/370 miles, with an average width of 250km/150 miles. The land rises from east to west in a series of plateau-like steps. Towards the Norwegian frontier is a wild mountain region, largely untouched by man, which reaches its highest point in Kebnekaise (2117m/6946ft: see Kiruna, Surroundings). A number of rivers (Umeälv, Skellefteälv, Piteälv, Luleälv, Kalixälv, Torneälv, etc.), well stocked with fish, rise in this area and flow south-east towards the Gulf of Bothnia. Most of the area is covered with bog and forest; towards the east and north the forests become increasingly sparse and finally end in a scrub of stunted birch-trees.

The inhabitants live mainly by timber-working, with some arable and stock farming. In addition there are the iron-mines of Gällivare and Kiruna. There are numerous hydro-electric stations on the rivers; among those best worth seeing are Akkats, Porjus and Vietas. The area is traversed by a number of roads and by the mineral railway from Luleå to Narvik.

Jokkmokk, originally a Sami village, is now the chief town of the commune of the same name, the second largest in Sweden with an area of 19,500sq.km/7530sq. miles (half of it above the tree-line) and a population of 3400. The village, on Lake Talvatis, was established by Charles IX as a winter meeting-place for the Lapps, where a Lapp assembly, a church festival and a fair were held every February. Some of the old traditions, including the fair, have been preserved. The old church (1753) was burned down in 1972 and replaced by a new one in 1974–75. The modern Ajtte Museum has an interesting collection of material on the culture of the Sami and of the Swedish settlers; displays of Sami handicrafts for sale. There is a Sami secondary school, established in 1942, as well as a school for nomad children.

Jokkmokk

Lapp church at Saltoluokta (northern Sweden)

From Jokkmokk a motor road and a footpath run up Storknabben, the "Hill of the Midnight Sun" (café). To the north are the Kaitum Falls. The Arctic Circle (see entry) passes 7km/4½ miles south of the town; on Road 45 is the Arctic Circle Fishing Camp, with services and holiday chalets. To the east of Jokkmokk are Muddus National Park and the Siemi nature reserve. 12km/7½ miles south is Kåivovallen, an old summer settlement of the Sami and their reindeer.

Vuollerim

43km/27 miles south of Jokkmokk on Road 97 at Vuollerim archaeological finds have revealed the existence of a settlement dating back 6000 years (interesting modern museum).

Riksgränsen

Riksgränsen (alt. 552m/1811ft) is a tourist centre and the last Swedish station on the Lapland Railway (see Abisko, Surroundings). It is Sweden's leading summer skiing resort (chair-lift), which has frequently temperatures of 15–20°C (60–70°F) when the temperature of the snow is at freezing point. The midnight sun is visible here from May 26th to July 17th.

Nearby is the tourist resort of Björkliden, on Lake Torneträsk, with good skiing country and a chair-lift up Njula (1199m/3934ft) from a height of 750m/2460ft. Lake Torneträsk, at the head of the Torneälv, is surrounded by high crags. Along its north side are various Sami settlements.

★Kungsleden

Kungsleden, the 500km/310 mile long Royal Trail (22–25 days; experienced walkers only; proper equipment, including maps, compass, rubber boots, etc., essential), crosses the mountain world of Lapland, with huts providing overnight accommodation at regular intervals. It extends from Abisko (see entry) in the north by way of the Kebnekaise massif (see Kiruna, Surroundings) and the Padjelanta National Park to Hemavan in southern Lapland. Features not to be missed are the Abisko National Park, with its unusual vegetation, and the Njula gorge (reached by a chair-lift).

Stora Sjöfallet National Park

The Stora Sjöfallet National Park, with a waterfall on the Stora Luleälv, is Sweden's third largest nature reserve. This is the source area of the Stora

Stora Sjöfallet National Park

Luleälv, a hilly region slashed by valleys with the highest peak in the area, Akka (2015m/6611ft). The National Park, established in 1909, extends from the coniferous forests in the east over a mountain region of varying height and with varied flora and fauna. The nature reserve originally covered an area of 1500sq.km/580sq. miles, but after ten years the central area round the lakes (120sq.km/45sq. miles) was excluded from the National Park to permit the construction of a dam pounding water for the Porjus hydroelectric station. The waterfall from which the park takes its name was formed by water plunging down from the mountain lake of Kårtjejaure into Lake Langas; the falls have now been reduced to a trickle.

The Royal Trail (Kungsleden: see above) runs through the National Park. Shooting and fishing are prohibited.

Sarek, between the Stora and the Lilla Luleälv, is another typical mountain region, with a National Park (area 1950sq.km/750sq. miles). Within this area are something like a hundred glaciers, 87 peaks over 1800m/5900ft and eight others over 2000m/6500ft, with plateaux and valleys between the hills. ★Sarek

The best known valley is Rapadal, on Lake Laidaure. Shooting and fishing are prohibited; sleigh dogs may be used from January to April, but otherwise dogs are banned. Through the Rapadal flows the Rapaälv, which receives melt-water from some thirty glaciers and deposits sediment in its delta on Lake Laidaure. There is a remarkable contrast between the barren world of the mountains and the rich plant and animal life of the valley.

To the west is Alkavare, where silver was still being worked in the late 17th century. Remains of silver-mines; chapel of 1788.

The Sarek nature reserve was established in 1909 in order to preserve this characteristic mountain region in its unspoiled state. A mountain walk through the National Park takes more than a week, and should be undertaken only by experienced hill walkers, with proper equipment, a tent and adequate supplies of food. This is regarded as one of the most difficult walking areas in Scandinavia, and prospective visitors should beware of over-estimating their capabilities.

Lapland

Tärnaby

Tärnaby lies in a magnificent mountain setting, 38km/24 miles from the Norwegian frontier, on the southern slopes of the Luxfjäll (824m/2704ft). In the little town, which is equipped to cater for skiers, there are a Lapp Museum and a school for nomad children.

12km/7½ miles west on a waymarked footpath or a motor road are the Västensjö and the hill of Gieravardo (views). The neighbouring village of Hemavan also offers good skiing and has developed into a tourist centre. From Hemavan there are good views extending to the hills of Jofjäll and Okstinder on the Norwegian frontier. In summer canoes and gliders can be hired. Fishing is permitted in the lakes below the village.

Ammarnäs

60km/38 miles north-east of Tärnaby (road only from Sorsele) is the village of Ammarnäs, with an old Lapp church. Fishing, cross-country and downhill skiing.

Vilhelmina

Vilhelmina, in southern Lapland, is the headquarters of the body officially representing the Lapp community and has an interesting Lapp Museum 95km/60 miles north-west by way of Laxbäcken (school of agriculture) is the village of Saxnäs, in a grand mountain setting on the southern shore of the Kultsjö (alt. 540m/1770ft), with good walking, fishing and skiing.

Finnish Lapland

Finnish Lapland, a forest-covered region of hills and bog with an area of some 94,000sq.km./36,000sq. miles, is similar in many respects to Swedish Lapland, but the hills are lower. Only in the extreme north-west, where a finger of territory reaches into the Scandinavian mountains, is there a peak of greater height – Haltiatunturi (1328m/4357ft), the highest peak in Finland. Almost the whole of Finnish Lapland is covered with forests; in the south spruce predominates, but beyond Lake Inari (see entry) there are only pines and birches. At higher altitudes there are expanses of lichen-covered tundra. The area has been made more easily accessible to visitors by the construction of roads and the provision of hotels and other accommodation. The administrative centre of Finnish Lapland is Rovaniemi (see entry), a few kilometres south of the Arctic Circle.

★Arctic Highway
Sodankylä

Rovaniemi is the starting-point of the main traffic artery of Finnish Lapland, the Arctic Highway (Road 4; E 75 for part of the way). This runs north in long straight stretches, passing the beautiful Portikoski waterfall, to Sodankylä, the commercial and cultural centre of its extensive commune which is very popular with tourists. Features of interest are the old church (1689, now a museum) and the new church (1859), the modern Town Hall and a gallery displaying the works of the Lapp painter Andreas Alariesto. A Film Festival is held here in June.

Urho Kekkonen
National Park

Road 4 (E 75) continues north, passing the two large reservoirs of Porttipahta and Lokka, and comes in just under 100km/62 miles to Vuotso, where the first road signs in the Sami language appear. At Tankavaara visitors can see something of the old gold-digging tradition (museum village, Gold Museum) and can try their hand at washing for gold. Here too is the information centre of the Urho Kekkonen National Park, an area of 2550sq.km/985sq. miles extending to the Russian frontier. On the borders of the National Park (30km/19 miles farther on) is the skiing and holiday area of Saariselkä. From the summit of Kaunispää (438m/1437ft) there are extensive views of the surrounding country – particularly impressive in the light of the midnight sun.

The Arctic Highway continues to Ivalo (see Lake Inari), where it branches off Road 4 and heads north-east, ending in 54km/34 miles at the Russian frontier. Formerly it went on to the Finnish port of Petsamo on the Arctic Ocean, now in Russia and renamed Pechenga.

Road 4 continues to Kaamanen and then bears north-west to reach the
Norwegian frontier at Karigasniemi. From Kaamanen Road 970 (E 75)
continues north to the Norwegian frontier by way of Utsjoki and then along
the frontier river of Tenojoki (good salmon-fishing), beyond the frontier, to
the Norwegian port of Berlevåg on the Arctic Ocean.

Berlevåg

Lappeenranta (Villmanstrand)   G 5

Country: **Finland**
Region: South-eastern Finland. Population: 55,000
Post code: FIN–53100   Telephone code: 953

The Finnish town of Lappeenranta (Villmanstrand), on the south side of the
Lappvesi, was founded by Queen Christina in 1649. It is the most southerly
port of call of the boats on Lake Saimaa (see entry). In view of its exposed
situation on the frontier with the Russian Empire it was garrisoned by a
cavalry regiment in the 17th century. Near the town are two frontier cross-
ings into Russia, Nuijamaa (road) and Vainikkala (rail). Lappeenranta is one
of the Finnish towns most popular with visitors.

Situation and
characteristics

The town grew up in the medieval period as a trading station. In 1741 it was
the scene of a decisive battle in which a Swedish and Finnish army was
defeated by the Russians. Under the treaty of Åbo (Turku) Lappeenranta
passed to Russia in 1743, remaining Russian until 1811. There are remains
of fortifications dating from the 17th and 18th centuries and from the
Russian period.
   After the discovery of a radioactive mineral spring in 1824 the town
developed as a spa, much favoured by the Russian nobility. Since 1974 the
spa has operated throughout the year; it specialises in the treatment of
cardiac and circulatory disorders and rheumatism.

History

Lappeenranta lies at the north end of the Saimaa Canal, the construction of
which was planned by several Swedish kings but was carried out only in
the reign of Tsar Alexander II and completed in 1856. Until 1944 it was
wholly within Finnish territory, but in 1944 almost its whole length fell
wihin the territory which Finland was compelled to cede to Russia and it
was closed. In the 1960s, however, the Soviet Union leased the canal zone
back to Finland, and the Finns then built a new canal on the old line, with
modern locks. The canal is now open to pleasure boats.

Saimaa Canal

The town's main street is Kauppakatu, running from north to south. To the
east of its intersection with Valtakatu, in the Central Park (Keskuspuisto),
near the market square, stands the old parish church of Lappee (1794), with
a separate belfry (1856). Nearby is a military cemetery with the graves of
Karelians who fell in the war with the Soviet Union (1941–44); monument
by Wäinö Aaltonen (1951). Near the church, at the corner of Kauppakatu
and Raastuvankatu, is the timber-built Town Hall (by C. L. Engel, 1829).

Town

Lappee church

Along Kauppakatu to the north, on a hill to the left (alt. 130m/427ft;
60m/200ft above Lake Saimaa), is the Town Church (1924). Farther north, at
the head of a peninsula projecting into Lake Saimaa to the left of the road,
extends the Old Park, with a monument commemorating a battle in 1741 in
which the Swedish and Finnish army which had launched an attack on
Russia was defeated by the Russians.

Town Church

To the north-west, beyond the monument, are remains of old fortifications.
In the fort (Linnoitus) are the Museum of South Karelia (cultural history of
southern Karelia, including material from the Viipuri museum) and the
Museum of Art. In the old guard-house of the fort is the Cavalry Museum,
which documents the history of the Finnish cavalry.

Museums

North-east of the monument stands the oldest Orthodox church in Finland
(1785).

Orthodox church

The oldest building in Lappeenranta (Cavalry Museum)

Harbour

To the east of the town, in an inlet on the lake, is Lappeenranta harbour, Finland's largest inland port. On the south side of the inlet can be found the spa establishment. At the north end of Ainonkatu is an old boat which used to sail on Lake Saimaa, the "Prinsessa Armaada", now housing a restaurant. On the east side of the inlet at Kimpinen Park there is a bathing beach.

To the east of the town, on the right of the Imatra road, there are extensive views from the Water-Tower (café). In the Lauritsala district (also on the Imatra road) are an old (1785) and a new church (1969).

Surroundings

Boat trips

Lappeenranta is the base for boat trips on Lake Saimaa. There are regular services to Mikkeli and to Savonlinna (see entries), as well as cruises on the lake lasting a few hours or several days. In summer there are excursions to the Saimaa Canal and the Russian frontier, through the Saimaa Canal to the Russian town of Vyborg (formerly the Finnish port of Viipuri) and to St Petersburg (to which there are also coach trips; visa required).

Imatra (waterfalls)

40km/25 miles north-east of Lappeenranta is Imatra (pop. 40,000), famous since the 19th century for its waterfalls. At Imatra the river Vuoksen, which flows from Lake Saimaa into the Gulf of Finland, falls 18m/60ft within a very short distance, and the force of the water has gouged a channel 20m/65ft wide out of the granite. The river has now been diverted to power a hydro-electric station, and it flows in its old bed only when the sluices are opened on Sunday afternoons in summer. The construction of the Valtionhotelli at the rapids during the Russian period established Imatra's position as a holiday resort. On the west bank of the river is a tourist complex, with a camping site, chalets, hostels for walkers, a riding school, a marina and bathing beaches.

Boats in Lappeenranta harbour

In the Vuoksennista district the fine new Community Centre, designed by Alvar Aalto (1957–59), includes a church, a pastor's house, a cemetery chapel and parish houses.

★Community Centre by Alvar Aalto

Larvik

C 6

Country: **Norway**
Region: Southern Norway. Population: 9000
Post code: N–3251

The former county town of Larvik is finely situated on the south coast of Norway. To the south of the town is the Larvikfjord; to the north is a 20km/12½ mile long lake, the Farrisvatn. The town has gained importance through its wood processing industry.

Situation

Larvik has two mineral springs – Kong Håkons Kilde (King Håkon's Well), a spring of sulphurous saline water which is marketed under the brand name Farris, and a chalybeate spring. It does not, however, operate as a spa.

Mineral springs

Larvik was the birthplace of the anthropologist Thor Heyerdahl (b. 1914), famed for his voyages on the balsa-wood raft "Kon-Tiki" from Peru to Polynesia and in the papyrus boat "Ra" (1969–70) and the reed boat "Tigris" (1978).

Birthplace of Thor Heyerdahl

The central feature of the town is the Market Square (Torget). On the outskirts of the town to the north-west extends a magnificent beech forest (Bøkeskogen), with a hill offering extensive views and a 1500-year-old cemetery area. North-east of this is the Farris Bad district of the town, with a beautiful park.

Town

To the south-east of the town, on Herregårdsbacken, is the Herregård, a large wooden manor-house (1670–80), formerly the residence of the Counts of Larvik, which now houses the Municipal Museum.

Herregård (Museum)

A giant raft of logs on the Larvikfjord

Church	To the south, beyond the railway, a 17th century church contains a portrait of Martin Luther by Lucas Cranach the Elder (to left of altar). From the church there is a fine view over the fjord.
Museums	North-west of the church, on the harbour, is the old Custom House, now occupied by a small Seafaring Museum. Storgata runs west, parallel to the railway, to the Bødkerfjell. On this hill is a privately owned museum with material on the ironworking industry which flourished in Larvik from 1640 to 1868 (stove plates, casting moulds).

Surroundings

Stavern	7.5km/5 miles south of Larvik we come to the seaside resort of Stavern, with a church of 1756. In the churchyard is the grave of the writer Jonas Lie (1833–1908) and his wife.
Tjølling	7km/4½ miles east of Larvik is Tjølling, with another interesting church (Romanesque, with a Renaissance pulpit and a Rococo baptistery containing a font of about 1700).

Lillehammer   C 5

Country: **Norway**
Region: South-eastern Norway
Altitude: 180m/590ft. Population: 20,000
Post code: N–2600

Situation and characteristics	Lillehammer, chief town of Uppland county, is attractively situated above Lake Mjøsa at the south end of the Gudbrandsdal. The town is divided into

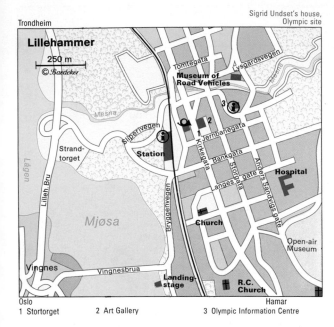

Trondheim

Sigrid Undset's house,
Olympic site

Lillehammer

250 m

© Baedeker

Tomtegata

Lysgårdsvegen

Museum of
Road Vehicles

Mesna

3

Sliperivegen

Strand-
torget

Station

Jernbanegata

Kirkegata

Bankgata

Storgata

Langes gate

Anders Sandvigs gate

Hospital

Church

Open-air
Museum

Vingnes

Vingnesbrua

Landing-
stage

R.C.
Church

Oslo

Hamar

1 Stortorget   2 Art Gallery   3 Olympic Information Centre

two by the river Mesna. It is one of the best known tourist centres in
Norway, visited both in summer as a holiday resort and in winter for the
excellent skiing in the surrounding area (lifts, floodlit pistes). A skier figures
in the town's coat of arms.

In 1994 the Winter Olympic Games were held in Lillehammer, and new
sports facilities were constructed in and around the town for the event. The
Olympic Village lies above the town.

Ice rink, curling rink, sleigh rides, excellent cross-country skiing (over
500km/300 miles of trails). Hafjell Alpine Centre, with two chair-lifts, four
chair-lifts and a children's lift (greatest height difference 850m/2790ft);
20km/12½ miles of alpine cross-country trails; ski school. At Nordseter
(850m/2790ft) there are 350km/220 miles of cross-country trails, two ski-
lifts, a ski-tow and a ski school. At Sjusjøen (850m) there are some
300km/185 miles of cross-country trails, a ski-lift, a ski school and a large
group of ski huts. Kvitfjell, near Ringebu, is one of the most difficult downhill slopes.

Winter sports

Lillehammer's principal tourist attraction is the open-air museum in Maihaugen Park, on the south-eastern outskirts of the town. Founded by a local
dentist, Anders Sandvig (1862–1950), in 1887, it consists of more than a
hundred old buildings, all re-erected here in their original form and furnished with old domestic equipment and implements. Among them are
18th century farmhouses from the heyday of peasant culture and various
craftsmen's workshops. The museum is constantly being extended and
altered; near the car park is a Municipal Museum. The oldest building in the
collection is a stave church from Garmo. Another notable items is Peer
Gynt's Cottage (Peer Gynts Stue), dating from about 1700, which is said to
have been the home of the prototype of Ibsen's hero.

**Maihaugen
Open-Air Museum**

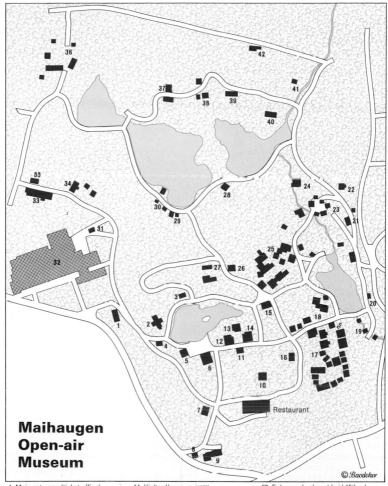

Maihaugen
Open-air
Museum

© *Baedeker*

1 Main entrance (ticket office)
2 Church (*c.* 1200) from Garmo (Gudbrandsdal)
3 Smoke house (*c.* 1700) from Hesta (Romsdal)
4 Tolstad House (15th c.) from Tolstadløkken, Vågå
5 Headman's house or widow's house (mid 17th c.) from Mytting, Ringebu
6 Presbytery (mid 17th c.) from Vågå
7 "Guest-house"
8 Workshop
9 Constable's house
10 Armoury (mid 18th c.) from Toftemnen, Dovre
11 Store-house from Dagsgård
12 Lykre House (mid 18th c.), the first house in the Museum
13 Vigenstad House (early 18th c.)

14 Hjeltar House (*c.* 1600)
15 Schoolhouse (mid 19th c.), Skjåk
16 Village office with prison cells
17 Bjørnstad Farm (*c.* 1700) from Bjørnstad, Vågå
18 Chapel and presbytery from Isum, Sør-Fron
19 Mills
20 Smithy
21 Brassfounder's workshop (manufacture of belts)
22 Hut from Skrefsrud
23 Knutslykkja Farm (*c.* 1800)
24 Dyer's workshop
25 Øygård Farm (18th c.), Skjåk
26 Peer Gynt Hut
27 Meviken
28 Hut from Knuvel, Fåberg
29 Fisherman's huts

30 Fisherman's chapel (mid 15th c.) from Fåberg
31 Toilets
32 Old workshops and concert hall
33 Church houses (summer restaurant)
34 Changing House
35 Potter's workshop
36 Valbjør shieling (summer grazing station) from Vågå
37 Barhus shieling (*c.* 1800) from Gausdal
38 Øygård shieling (*c.* 1700) from Skjåk
39 Korpberg shieling (*c.* 1700) from Nord-Fron
40 Kleiv shieling (*c.* 1600) from Vågå
41 Sheiling huts from Lesja and Ringebu
42 Lunde shieling (mid 19th c.) from Ringebu

Lillehammer

Skjåk farmhouse in the Maihaugen open-air museum

Town	In the market square (Stortorget) the Municipal Art Gallery (Malerisamling) contains works by Norwegian painters. North-east of this is the Museum of Road Vehicles. In Nordseterveg can be seen the house once occupied by the writer Sigrid Undset (1882–1949; Nobel Prize 1928).

Lillehammer also has a number of interesting monuments commemorating local personalities: Anders Sandvig, in the market square; Sigrid Undset, in front of the Merchants' Hall in Storgata; Ludvig Wiese, "father" of Lillehammer, in Lilla Torget; and at the corner of Kirkegata and Langesgate "Peter the Tower-Man", a local character who specialised in the repair of church towers. |
| Kanten | From the north bank of the Mesna there is a chair-lift up Kanten (restaurant). |

Surroundings

	From Maihaugen Park a road runs up to the south-east, passing the Langseth Hotel (alt. 350m/1150ft) and the little lake of Bådshaugtjern (585m/1919ft), and soon afterwards crosses the Bustokelv, which flows out of Lake Sødre Mesna (512m/1680ft), on the right, into Lake Nordre Mesna (511m/1677ft). Beyond Mesnalien (520m/1706ft) the road turns north and continues climbing.
Sjusjøen	The road then runs past the Sjusjø (795m/2608ft) and comes to the village of Sjusjøen (830m/2723ft), with hotels and numerous huts and summer chalets. Beyond this point the road is narrow but still negotiable. Then in another 6km/4 miles turn into a road on the left which follows the south side of the Mellsjø (893m/2930ft).
Nordseter	This road runs into another coming from Lillehammer. Along this, to the left, is Nordseter (786m/2580ft), from which it is a rewarding 1¼ hours' climb to the summit of Neverfjell (1086m/3563ft; wide views). The road then runs down to Lillehammer through forest country.
Along the Gausdal	Leave Lillehammer on a road which leads south-west and crosses the narrow north end of Lake Mjøsa on a long bridge; then turn right into Road 253, which runs along the west side of the lake, passing Jørstadmoen and the airport on the right. At the church of Faberg (1724) turn left into Road 255, which goes along the Gausdal (the valley of the Gausa), with another
Follebu	road parallel to it on the hillside to the east. At Follebu (alt. 310m/1015ft) a road goes off on the right and comes in 2km/1¼ miles to the stone built medieval parish church, higher up on the hillside. 1km/¾ mile beyond Follebu, in Østre Gausdal (to the right of the road), is the large farmhouse of
Aulestad	Aulestad, in which the writer Bjørnstjerne Bjørnson (1832–1910) lived from 1875 onwards. The house is now a museum.

At Segalstadbru the continuation of Road 255, to the left, runs up the valley, which grows steadily narrower, to Vestre Gausdal (church of 1784), while to the right Road 254 continues to climb up the Østre Gausdal to Stingvoll (alt. 480m/1575ft), where it is possible either to bear left for the Peer Gynt Trail (see Gudbrandsdal) or right via Tretten into the beautiful Gudbrandsdal (see entry). |

Linköping   D 6

	Country: **Sweden**
Province: Östergötland. Population: 119,000
Post code: S–58... Telephone code: 013
Situation and characteristics	Linköping, chief town of the province of Östergötland, the see of a bishop and a university town, lies on the west bank of the Stångå, which flows into

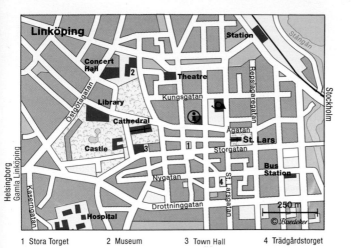

1 Stora Torget   2 Museum   3 Town Hall   4 Trädgårdstorget

Lake Roxen just to the north of the town, on the road from Stockholm to Göteborg. The name of the town first appears in the records in 1120 in connection with the foundation of Vreta Abbey (see Surroundings, below). At a church council held in Linköping in 1152 it was decided that Sweden should become a province of the Church of Rome. Here in 1598, on the banks of the Stångå, Duke Charles of Södermanland (later King Charles IX), a supporter of the Reformation, defeated the Roman Catholic King Sigismund of Poland. Sigismund's followers were executed in the market square of Linköping in 1600, in what became known as the "Linköping massacre".

The main square of Linköping is Stora Torget, with the Folkung Fountain (Folkungabrunn, 1927), one of Carl Milles's best known works. It depicts Folke Filbyter, the legendary ancestor of the royal dynasty of the Folkungs, riding out in search of his grandson.

Town

Stora Torget

To the east of Stora Torget is St Lars' Church (1802), with a 12th century tower. It contains a number of pictures by Pehr Hörberg (1746–1816), one of the leading Swedish painters of his time, noted for his fine use of colour and naïve Romantic manner.

St Lars' Church

North-west of Stora Torget is the Cathedral, begun about 1150 in Romanesque style (north doorway) and later altered and enlarged in Gothic style. The south doorway has rich figural decoration. The 105m/345ft high tower dates only from 1886. The Late Gothic choir was the work of Master Gerlach of Cologne. To the right of the altar is the marble sarcophagus of the Lutheran bishop Terserus (d. 1679). In the south transept is a winged altar with paintings by the Dutch master Marten van Heemskerk (1543), which was presented to the Cathedral by King John III. To the north of the Cathedral are the Bishop's Palace (1773) and the Diocesan Library, which possesses numerous old manuscripts and rare printed books.

★Cathedral

South-west of the Cathedral, in the King's Garden (Kungsträdgården), is the Castle, originally a stronghold of the bishop's. It is now, much altered and restored, the Governor's Residence.

Castle

In the north of the town, in Vasatorget (reached from the Cathedral by way of Gråbrödragatan), are the Municipal Museum and the Östergötland

Museums

County Museum. The County Museum has collections of archaeological, local and folk interest and an art gallery containing works both by foreign masters (Cranach) and by Swedish painters (including Pehr Hörberg).

Stångebro
The town is bounded on the east by the Stångå, on the banks of which stands the Stångebro Monument, commemorating the battle in 1598. The bridge itself, linking the two halves of the town, was built in 1655.

Gamla Linköping
To the west of the town the Gamla Linköping open-air museum consists of an assemblage of 18th and 19th century buildings, mostly wooden, which were transferred here from the town centre during slum clearance and redevelopment operations. A number of historic old buildings from the province of Östergötland were also re-erected here. Here too is the Valla recreation area.

Air Force Museum
Also on the western outskirts of the town can be found the Air Force Museum, with a collection of Swedish military aircraft and air force equipment.

Surroundings

Kinda Canal
An attractive excursion from Linköping is a trip on the Kinda Canal, which links Lake Roxen with a number of other lakes to the south, through which the Stångå flows. 80km/50 miles in length, the canal has a total of fifteen locks. The boat passes a number of old manor-houses (including the handsome Sturefors manor-house of 1704 on Lake Erlang), and the trip ends at Horn, at the south end of Lake Åsund.

Vårdsberg
8km/5 miles east of Linköping is the round church of Vårdsberg (12th c.; restored 1940), with fine paintings in the vaulting (16th c.). 6km/4 miles east is Askeby church, with the remains of a 12th century nunnery.

Kaga church
7km/4½ miles north-west of Linköping the Kaga church was built by King Sverker (d. 1156) on the old pagan cult site of Allguvi (the "shrine of all the gods"). The church is richly decorated with paintings; those in the nave are by Master Amund, those in the choir by his teacher the Master of Risinge.

Vreta Abbey
11km/7 miles north-west, on the road to Motala, stands Vreta Abbey, a 13th century church (restored c. 1920) which belonged to a house of Cistercian nuns. On the north side of the church, which contains numerous monuments, are the foundations of the conventual buildings and the cloister.

Lofoten Islands   C/D 2/3

Country: **Norway**
Region: Northern Norway. Area: 1308sq.km/505sq. miles
Population: 27,000

Access
Boats to Svolvær from Bodø (6 hours), Skutvik (2 hours) and Narvik (9 hours). The coastal steamers also call in at the Lofotens. Air services from Bodø, Evenes and Narvik to Svolvær and other places. There are also plans to link the islands with the mainland by car-ferry in the years to come.

Recreation and sport
Fishing from the pier or from small boats, deep-sea angling; climbing; shooting.

Situation and characteristics
The Lofotens – the Norwegian name Lofoten is singular (Lofot + the definite article -en) – are a chain of hilly islands strung out from north-east to south-west and separated from the mainland by the Vestfjord. The four

main islands of Austvågøy, Vestvågøy, Moskenesøy and Flakstadøy, together with a number of medium-sized islands, lie so close together that they appear from a distance to be a single long jagged range of mountains. The main islands are surrounded by a swarm of stacks and skerries, and are indented by numerous inlets and fjords with rock walls up to 1000m/3300ft high. The mountains are of Alpine type with characteristic steep-sided summits (highest point 1266m/4154ft), bare and often snow-capped.

At numerous points on the islands there are cliffs and crags on which large numbers of seabirds nest. There are few trees. Near the coasts of the islands are bogs, lakes, pastureland and some areas of arable land. The climate is wet, but mild in winter.

Fauna and flora; climate

The main sources of income are fishing and its associated industries (see below). There is also a certain amount of sheep-farming, and mink-farming has been introduced in recent years. Tourism also makes a significant contribution to the economy at all times of year; holiday accommodation can be rented in fishermen's huts (*rorbuer*), either old-style (with very limited amenities) or modernised.

Economy

The fishing season in the Lofotens, for which thousands of fishermen gather with their boats, is from the beginning of February to the middle of April. The main catch is cod (Norwegian *torsk*). From the beginning of January the cod – predatory fish which normally live deep in the Atlantic – head for coastal waters in long shoals many feet deep to spawn. The depth at which they swim depends on the temperature of the water, ranging between 100m/330ft and 300m/990ft.

Fishing and fish-processing

Once landed, the cod are cut into sections (*rundfisk*) or split lengthwise (*klippet*), and the head and guts are removed. They are then hung up on timber racks (*hjeller*) to dry, remaining on the racks until June (*tørrfisk*, stockfish), or they are salted and laid out on the rocks (*klippfisk*), and then piled up in heaps, which are covered to protect them from rain. Some of the fish are not dried but are salted in barrels (*laberdan*). The heads are used to make fertilisers, the roes are canned and the livers are used to make cod liver oil.

Austvågøy

The chief town and administrative centre of the Lofotens is Svolvær, on the south coast of the island of Austvågøy. The town has a normal population of 4000, which swells during the fishing season (February–April) to almost 10,000. It is the main fishing port (fish-processing industries), the hub of communications and the principal commercial centre of the islands.

Svolvær

In the "Artists' House" (Kunstnernes Hus) on the island of Svinøy is an exhibition of works by the many painters who have found inspiration in the Lofotens. On the little island of Gunnarholm (road bridge from Svolvær), opposite the landing-stage, can be found the grave of the Nordland painter Gunnar Berg (b. Svolvær 1864, d. Berlin 1894).

Painters of the Lofotens

North of Svolvær is the steep-sided hill of Blåtind (597m/1959ft; 5 hours there and back for fit walkers), from which there are superb views; midnight sun visible from the end of May to mid July.

Blåtind

An attractive trip is by motorboat (2 hours) from Svolvær to the south end of the island of Hinnøy, in the Vesterålen group (see entry), where Digermulkollen offers a rewarding climb (1¼ hours). The boat sails through the southern part of the 8km/5 mile long Raftsund between the Lofotens and the Vesterålen group.

Hinnøy

From the Raftsund a narrow rocky opening gives access to the Trollfjord, beyond which can be seen the snow-capped Higravtinder (1161m/3908ft)

★★Trollfjord

Svolvær, on the island of Austvågøy

and the jagged Trolltinder (1045m/3429ft), rising above the Trollfjordvatn, a 3km/2 mile long mountain lake which is usually frozen over.

The most popular day trip to the Trollfjord is by bus from Svolvær by way of Fiskebøl to Stokmarkness and back by the express boat, which sails via the Trollfjord.

Kabelvåg

10km/6 miles south-west of Svolvær (bus service) is Kabelvåg, where there are many of the holiday houses known as *rorbuer* or *sjøhus*. Here too there are a Fisheries Museum and the Lofoten Aquarium (fish and other marine fauna of the Vestfjord). The church of Vågan is the largest wooden church north of Trondheim.

Festvåg

At the south-western tip of Austvågøy, under Vågekalle (942m/3091ft; 3½ hours' climb), is Festvåg, from which there is a ferry (12 minutes) to the typical little fishing settlement of Henningsvær, in the middle of a group of little islands where a large fishing fleet gathers in winter.

Vestvågøy

Stamsund

On the south-east coast of the large island of Vestvågøy is Stamsund (Lofoten Hotel, with *rorbuer,* and other holiday accommodation), one of the largest fishing ports in the archipelago and the transport centre of the western Lofotens.

Ballstad

At the south-west end of Vestvågøy lies the fishing village of Ballstad, at the foot of Ballstadaksla (466m/1529ft).

Flakstadøy

Ramberg

On the north-west coast of the island of Flakstadøy is the little settlement of Ramberg (holiday houses in Nusfjord), administrative centre of the island.

To the east is Flakstad church (1780), which was originally built of driftwood.

Moskenesøy

The chief place on the island of Moskenesøy is the fishing village of Reine (Reine Kro; holiday houses), on the Kirkefjord, a favourite haunt of painters and climbers. 10km/6 miles south-west is the little settlement of Å, at the end of the Lofoten road. From the higher ground above the village there is a view of the Moskenstraumen, between the cape of Lofotodden and the island of Mosken – the Maelstrom described by Jules Verne and Edgar Allan Poe.

Reine

From Reine there are boat trips to the little island of Værøy to the south-west. At the south end of this island is the Mostadfjell, rising steeply above the abandoned village of Mostad. These hills are a paradise for birds, where more than a million birds – mainly puffins, but also guillemots, cormorants and white-tailed eagles – breed between May and August. The nesting sites can be reached by hiring a boat from the village of Værøy (20 minutes).

Værøy

On Værøy are the last specimens of a curious breed of six-toed dogs, known as puffin hounds, which are used in catching puffins.

There are also boat trips from Reine (5 hours), as well as from Bodø (5 hours) and Værøy (2¼ hours), to the remarkable Røst Islands, almost 100km/62 miles from the mainland, with a series of high crags (Vedøy, Storfjell, Stavøy, the Nykan rocks) inhabited by a large colony of seabirds, including some 3 million puffins as well as rare species like the greater and lesser storm petrel and the fulmar. The crags can be reached by boat from Røstland, and during the season by helicopter from Bodø.

Røst Islands
★ Bird crags

Rainbow on the Tind (Moskenesøy)

Luleå   E 3

Country: **Sweden**
Province: Norrbotten
Population: 70,000
Post code: S–95...   Telephone code: 0920

Situation and characteristics

The Swedish port of Luleå, at the north end of the Gulf of Bothnia, is the largest town in Norrbotten and the see of a bishop. It is the gateway to the mountain world of Lapland and the northern tundras. The offshore islets and skerries, more than 300 in number, are notable for their fauna and flora. Although Luleå is only 110km/70 miles from the Arctic Circle, it has a mild climate, with an average temperature only about 2°C/3.5°F lower than at Malmö in southern Sweden. In July Luleå has the highest number of hours of sunshine in Sweden (300–310). During the summer it ranks with Narvik as one of the two principal ports for the shipment of iron ore from northern Sweden, which is conveyed from Gällivare and Kiruna on the Lapland Railway. The harbour of Luleå is usually ice-bound until May.

History

Luleå was founded by Gustavus Adolphus in 1621 and moved in 1649 to its present site on a promontory in the Luleälv. Most of its old houses have been destroyed by fire. Until 1940 the town had a population of no more than 14,000, but it was given a great boost when a state-owned ironworks (Norrbottens Järnverk AB, now SSAB Luleå) was established on the island of Svartö: within ten years the population had doubled, and thereafter it continued to grow.

Town

In the centre of the old town stand the Cathedral (1887–93) and the ten-storey Town Hall (1957). To the east, in Storgatan, the town's main business street, is a modern shopping centre. At the west end of Storgatan extends Hermelinspark. On the south side of the town in the Norrbotten Museum can be seen an interesting collection of material on Lapp customs and traditions. To the west of the Museum the Länsresidens, a handsome wooden building, houses local government offices. To the north-west is the promontory of Gültzauudden, with a bathing beach, tennis courts and other sports facilities. Open-air theatre in summer.

House of Technology

The House of Technology on the campus of the University of Technology (outside the town on the Haparanda road) illustrates modern technological developments in an understandable way.

Surroundings

Gammelstad

10km/6 miles west, on the original site of Luleå, is the "church town" of Gammelstad – a settlement of little wooden houses providing overnight accommodation for churchgoers coming from a distance and for their horses and carts. With almost 500 "church houses" (kyrkstugor), this is the largest church town in Sweden. The church itself, which dates from the 14th century, has a richly decorated interior, with an altar of 1520 from Antwerp. Here too is the Hägnan open-air museum.

Characteristic features of the Norrland coast are the little chapels on the skerries, all dating from the 18th century. In the Luleå skerries alone there are three (Uddskär, Måsskär, Rödkallen).

Boden

40km/25 miles north-east of Luleå up the valley of the Luleälv is Boden (pop. 29,000), a garrison town and railway junction where the mineral railway from Gällivare to Luleå cuts across the main north–south line. The rather military stamp of the town has a long tradition. The fortress built here in 1901 was almost entirely blasted from the rock. There is an Army Museum.

Park in Luleå

Farther inland is the little town of Älvsbyn (pop. 9000). Beside the church (1808–13) are forty wooden "church houses". 40km/25 miles west of Älvsbyn is Europe's largest unregulated waterfall, Storforsen, 82m/270ft high. Here too can be found an interesting Forestry Museum illustrating the work of the raftsmen and forestry workers.

Älvsbyn
★Storforsen

80km/50 miles north-east of Luleå, at the mouth of the Kalixälv, is the town of Kalix (pop. 19,000), which shows a combination of old peasant traditions with the early development of industry. The church (1472) has a late medieval reredos, a fine font and a modern window over the altar (by Pär Andersson). In the local government offices is the Kalix Museum. North of the town, on the Lappträsk road, is Englundsgården, with furniture and furnishings illustrating the way of life of a 19th century farming family. The manor-houses of Björknäs, Filipsborg and Grytnäs, at the mouth of the Kalixälv, similarly give a view of the life of the wealthier classes at the end of the 19th century. Some 10km/6 miles beyond Kalix is an area extending to the Arctic Circle within which there are restrictions on traffic.

Kalix

Piteå (pop. 39,000), 58km/36 miles south-west of Luleå on the Gulf of Bothnia, is a port and industrial town at the mouth of the Piteälv. It was originally founded by Gustavus Adolphus in 1621 on the site now occupied by Öjebyn, but in 1666 was moved 6km/4 miles south-east to its present position. The church at Öjebyn (15th c.) is surrounded by "church houses". Piteå has a wooden church built in 1648 and restored about 1950. The town's old wooden houses are concentrated round the market square, in which stands the Town Hall.

Piteå

6km/4 miles south-east of Piteå, on Pitholmen, extends a 10km/6 mile long bathing beach. The coast from Piteå to Haparanda is known as the Norrland Riviera. At Jävre, south of Piteå, is an archaeological trail (Bronze Age remains).

Lund   D 7

Country: **Sweden**
Province: Skåne
Population: 86,000
Post code: S–22...   Telephone code: 046

Situation and characteristics

Lund, 20km/12½ miles north-east of Malmö (see entry) in the province of Skåne, is thought to have been founded in 990 by the Danish king Swein Forkbeard as the secular and spiritual centre of the eastern part of his kingdom. It has a university founded in 1666 and a college of technology and is the see of a bishop. From the 12th to the 15th century it was the seat of a Danish archbishop and the largest town in Scandinavia, known as the "Metropolis Daniae".

★**Cathedral**

The Cathedral, founded about 1080 by the Danish king Knut IV (St Knut or Canute), is the oldest and finest Romanesque church in Sweden. The present building dates from the 12th century. The twin towers, popularly known as the "Lads of Lund" (Lunna Påga), were formerly a prominent landmark. The Cathedral now stands in the heart of the town – a reminder of the fact that Lund was the oldest archiepiscopal see in Scandinavia, with authority over 27 churches and eight religious houses.

Interior

Over the altar is a magnificent 14th century carved reredos, the work of a North German master. The 15th century carved choir-stalls were originally made for a monastery attached to the Cathedral. In the apse is a mosaic of Christ by Joakim Skovgaard (1925).

★Crypt

In the crypt – the oldest part of the church – are the tombs of Archbishop Birger (d. 1519) and Archbishop Herman. The well, with inscriptions in Low

Doorway of the Romanesque Cathedral

German, was the work of a Westphalian master named van Düren who lived in Lund from 1512 to 1527. The roof of the crypt is borne on stone piers. The figures on the piers are traditionally believed to represent a giant named Finn, who is said to have built the cathedral for St Lawrence, and his wife.

In the aisle can be seen the famous 14th century astronomical clock ("horologium mirabile lundense"), with figures of the Three Kings which emerge twice daily (at noon and 3pm on weekdays, 1 and 3pm on Sundays).

Astronomical clock

North of the Cathedral lies the Lundagård, a park which features prominently in the life of the University. In the park is the Kungshus (King's House) or Lundagårdshus, built in the 16th century as a residence for the Danish king Frederick II. King Charles XII of Sweden is said to have ridden up the spiral staircase in the palace when he took up his quarters in Lund after his campaigns in Europe. The Kungshus was occupied by the University until 1882, when the present University buildings nearby were built.

Town

Lundagård

At the north end of Sandgatan are the Bishop's Palace and beyond it the University Library, which possesses old 12th century manuscripts and some 2½ million volumes in all fields of knowledge. Near the Library are various other University buildings and the campus of the College of Technology. In this area too is the Zoological Museum.

University Library

South-east of this along Sölvegatan is the Archive of Decorative Art, where visitors can follow the creation of a work of art from its first conception to its completion. Farther south-east is the Botanic Garden, with 7000 plants from all over the world.

In Tegnérsplats, at the south-east corner of Lundagården, is a monument to the Swedish poet Esaias Tegnér (1782–1846), author of "Frithiof's Saga", a

Tegnérsplats

Astronomical clock

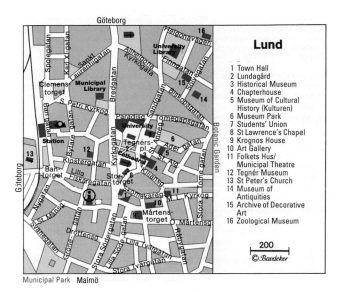

Göteborg

Lund

1 Town Hall
2 Lundagård
3 Historical Museum
4 Chapterhouse
5 Museum of Cultural History (Kulturen)
6 Museum Park
7 Students' Union
8 St Lawrence's Chapel
9 Krognos House
10 Art Gallery
11 Folkets Hus/ Municipal Theatre
12 Tegnér Museum
13 St Peter's Church
14 Museum of Antiquities
15 Archive of Decorative Art
16 Zoological Museum

200

© Baedeker

Municipal Park **Malmö**

romantic cycle on an Old Norse theme. His house in Gråbrödergatan is now a museum.

★ Museum of Cultural History

Also in Tegnérsplats is the Museum of Cultural History (Kulturhistoriska Museet; popularly known simply as Kulturen), an open-air museum with farmhouses, pastors' houses and town houses from all over southern Sweden; particularly notable is an old church from Bosebo in Småland. There are also collections of pottery, porcelain, textiles and folk art. To the south, in Kraftstorget, are the Historical Museum and the Cathedral Museum.

Mårtenstorget

In the south of the town is Mårtenstorget (fruit, vegetable and flower market). In the square are the Market Hall and the medieval Krognos House. To the rear stands the Art Gallery (1957), with a collection of modern Swedish art and periodic special exhibitions of work by leading international artists.

Drotten church

On the Kattesund, south-west of Stortorget (tourist information office), are the remains of the Drotten church, excavated in 1984 and 1985. The site is open to the public.

Surroundings

Dalby

South-east of Lund on Road 12 is Dalby, with one of the oldest stone-built churches in northern Europe (12th c. crypt). Nearby is Dalby Söderskog National Park (mixed deciduous forest). Farther east is the farm of Östarp, an outstation of the Museum of Cultural History in Lund.

Bosjökloster

30km/19 miles north of Lund on Road 23 are the Castle and recreation area of Bosjökloster, picturesquely situated on the shores of the Ringsjö. At Höör is the Skåne Wildlife Park (Skånes Djurpark), with some 400 animals from the Nordic countries.

Lyngenfjord   E 2

Country: **Norway**
Region: Northern Norway

The Lyngenfjord, perhaps the most magnificent fjord in the Nordland,   Situation
extends south for some 80km/50 miles from the Lyngstuen promontory
(395m/1296ft) at the northern tip of the Lyngen peninsula, a snow- and
glacier-covered granite ridge which rises directly out of the sea between
the Lyngenfjord and the Ullsfjord to the west.

The Fjord

The Lyngenfjord is reached by leaving Tromsø on E 78, which runs south-   Access
east to Nordkjosbotn, and then turning east up the valley of the Nordkjoselv, through birch forests and between hills, to Øvergård. The road
then descends, with a view of the fjord ahead, to Oteren, at the south end of   Storfjord
the Storfjord, the southern arm of the Lyngenfjord, with the jagged ridge of
the Mannfjell (1533m/5030ft) to the south-east. E 78, here coinciding with
E 8, then continues close to the east side of the Storfjord.

After passing a side road on the right into the beautiful Signaldal (the valley   ★★ Lyngenfjord
of the Storfjordelv) the main road crosses the Skibotnelv and comes to a
road junction at Olderbakken. E 6 continues north, hugging the eastern
shore of the Lyngenfjord. From Skibotn there is a fine view of the west side
of the fjord, with the glaciated peak of Jeggevarre beyond the Pollfjell.

At Odden, from which there is a good view of the glaciers at the northern   Kåfjord
end of the west side of the Lyngenfjord, the road turns south-east and runs

Fishermen's cabins on the Lyngenfjord

along the west side of the 20km/12½ mile long Kåfjord, hemmed in between steep-sided hills, to Kåfjordbotn at the head of the fjord.

Olderdal

E 6 now turns north-west again and runs along the east side of the fjord to Olderdal. From here it is possible either to follow the beautiful road along the east side of the Lyngenfjord towards Rotsund, with magnificent views, or to take the ferry to Lyngseidet on the west side of the fjord.

West side of
Lyngenfjord

There are two good climbs from Lyngseidet, each taking 4 hours – Goalsevarre (1289m/4229ft) and Rørnestind (1250m/4101ft). A road runs south along the west side of the fjord to Furuflaten, with the Pollfjell (1280m/4200ft) rising above it on the north. From there it is a 4–5 hours' climb up Njallasvarre (1530m/5020ft), from which there is a magnificent view to the west of the glaciers on Jiekkevarre (1833m/6014ft), one of the highest mountains in northern Norway, first climbed by Geoffrey Hastings in 1898. From here the road continues to Oteren, on the main road to Tromsø.

Excursion into Finland (Kilpisjärvi and Saanatunturi)

From the road junction at Olderbakken E 8 leads south-east to the lake of Kilpisjärvi in Finland. The first section of the road follows the broad and well wooded valley of the Skibotnelv (good fishing), passing on the right the little lake of Øvrevann. It then passes the winter customs post at Helligskogen, followed by the summer customs post, and crosses the Finnish frontier. Beyond this point the road becomes the Finnish Road 21 (still E 8). Ahead there is a view (to right) of Kilpisjärvi. In another 5km/3 miles the Finnish frontier post (customs) is reached.

Kilpisjärvi

The road continues close to Kilpisjärvi (alt. 476m/1560ft; area 39sq.km/15sq. miles), a lake well stocked with fish lying along the Swedish frontier. At the north-western tip of the lake (reached by motorboat from the hotel) is a round boundary stone marking the point where the frontiers of Sweden, Norway and Finland meet. To the left can be seen the characteristic silhouette of Saanatunturi.

★★Saanatunturi

Some 3km/2 miles beyond the frontier post, on the left of the road, is a climbers' hostel. From here there is a rewarding climb (2 hours; stout footwear essential) to the summit of the distinctively shaped Saanatunturi (1024m/3360ft), the sacred mountain of the Lapps, from which there are panoramic views: to the west the Norwegian mountains, partly snow-covered; to the south Kilpisjärvi, to the east the undulating forest country of Finland and to the north Finland's highest mountain, Haltiatunturi (1324m/4344ft), a remote and inaccessible peak (from the village of Kilpisjärvi a walk of some 120km/75 miles; organised parties, with guides).

5km/3 miles beyond the climbers' hostel, off the road to the right, is Kilpisjärvi tourist hotel, with a number of chalets in addition to the main building.

Road 21 continues south-east along the Swedish frontier to Muonio; then on to Tornio or Rovaniemi (see entries).

Lake Mälar/Mälaren   D/E 5/6

Country: **Sweden**
Provinces: Södermanland, Uppland, Västmanland

Situation and
characteristics

Lake Mälar, Sweden's third largest lake (after Lakes Vänern and Vättern), lies immediately west of Stockholm. 117km/73 miles long, it extends through the provinces of Västmanland, Södermanland, Uppsala and Stockholm to the Baltic, with a total area of 1140sq.km/440sq. miles. It is irregularly shaped, its shores indented by numerous arms and inlets. Its principal tributary rivers are the Eskilstunaå, Arbogaå, Hedström, Kolbäckså, Svartå, Örsundaå and Fyriså.

At one time Lake Mälar was an arm of the Baltic, but since the 12th century, because of a fall in the water level, it has been an inland lake. Since 1943 the lake has been regulated to prevent flooding and to avoid unduly low water levels which would hinder the movement of shipping. Vessels with a draught of up to 5.5m/18ft can now sail from the Baltic to Stockholm on the Södertälje Canal and Hammarbyleden.

Around the shores of the lake – which are partly fertile and partly rocky – there are many castles, manor-houses and estates. There are over a thousand islands in the lake, with boat services to many of them (including Björkö) in summer. The principal towns on the lake are Stockholm, Västerås and, farther north, Uppsala (see entries).

Malmö

D 7

Country: **Sweden**
Province: Skåne
Population: 232,000
Post code: S–21... Telephone code: 040

Malmö lies on the west coast of Skåne, facing the Danish capital of Copenhagen across the Öresund. A major port and Sweden's third largest city, it is an important economic and cultural centre.

Situation and characteristics

A settlement was established on this site in the second half of the 13th century and thanks to its sheltered anchorages in the shallow Lomma Bay, where the vessels of the Hanseatic towns came to fish for herring, rapidly developed. The town's first fortifications were built during the reign of the Danish king Eric of Pomerania, who also granted Malmö its coat of arms in 1473. The town passed to Sweden under the treaty of Roskilde (1658).

History

The construction of the harbour and the energy and enterprise of a merchant named Frans Suell (statue in Norra Vallgatan) brought the town great prosperity in the 18th century, and it developed still further after the construction of the railway between Stockholm and Malmö in the following century.

During the summer there are daily sightseeing tours of the city, starting from Gustav Adolfs Torg at 11am and 1pm, as well as harbour and canal cruises.

City tours

In the centre of the city, to the south of the harbour, is the Old Town (Gamla Staden), enclosed on all sides by canals. It has preserved much of its original layout, particularly around Stortorget, the main square. In the centre of the square stands an equestrian statue (1896) of King Charles X, who conquered Skåne in 1658 and united it with Sweden.

Old Town

Stortorget

On the east side of the square is the Town Hall, built in 1546 in Dutch Renaissance style (altered in 19th c.). On the first floor are St Knut's (Canute's) Hall, once the meeting-place of the influential Guild of St Knut, and the Council Chamber (Landstingssalen), with portraits of Danish and Swedish kings. At the north-east corner of the square is the Governor's Residence (Residens).

Town Hall

The street between the Governor's Residence and the Town Hall leads to St Peter's Church (St Petri), an imposing 14th century brick building modelled on St Mary's Church in Lübeck. Notable features of the interior are the pulpit (1599) and the Baroque altarpiece (1611). To the left of the entrance is the baptismal chapel, with Late Gothic wall paintings of flowers and animals and a font of 1601.

St Peter's Church

Immediately south-west of Stortorget lies Lilla Torget, with houses of the 16th–18th centuries and, on its west side, the new Market Hall (Saluhallen).

Lilla Torget
Burghers' houses

309

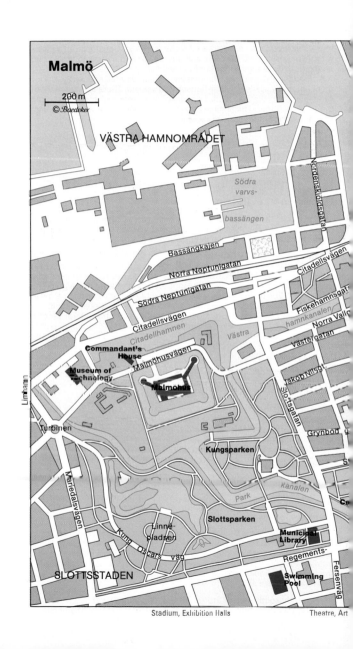

Malmö

200 m

© *Baedeker*

VÄSTRA HAMNOMRÅDET

Södra varvs-bassängen

Nordenskiöldsgatan

Bassängkajen

Norra Neptunigatan

Citadellsvägen

Södra Neptunigatan

Fiskehamnsgat

Citadellsvägen

hamnkanalen

Citadellhamnen

Västra

Norra Vall

Västergatan

Commandant's House

Malmöhusvägen

Museum of Technology

Jakob Nilsg.

Malmöhus

Slottsgatan

Limhamn

Turbinen

Grynbod

Kungsparken

S

Mariedalsvägen

Kanalen

Park

Ce

Slottsparken

Linné-pladsen

Municipal Library

Kung Oscars väg

Regements-

Fersenväg

SLOTTSSTADEN

Swimming Pool

Stadium, Exhibition Halls   Theatre, Art

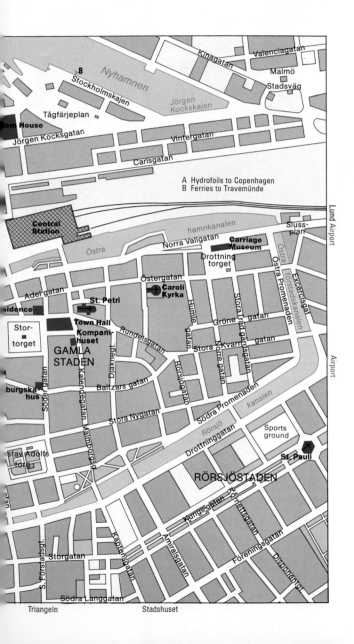

A Hydrofoils to Copenhagen
B Ferries to Travemünde

Malmö

Town Hall, Malmö

Of the many old burghers' houses in Malmö the following are particularly notable: the Flensburgska Hus (1595) at Södergatan 9; Jörgen Kocks Hus (1525; now a guest house) at Västergatan 5; the Rosenvingeska Hus (1542) at Västergatan 5; Tunnelns Hus or Ulfeldtska Hus (1519) at Adelgatan 4; the Diedenska Hus (1620) at Östergatan 6; and the Thottska Hus (1558) at Östergatan 8. The Kompanihus in Stortorget, built in the 16th century for a commercial firm, is now used for meetings and other functions.

Form Design Center
Doll House

In Hedmanska Gården, on Lilla Torget, is the Form Design Center, with examples of modern Swedish design (furniture, textiles, glass, ceramics, decorative art). To the north of this is Charlotte Weibull's Doll House (Dockhus), which sells dolls in traditional costumes from all over Sweden.

Gustav Adolfs Torg

Södergatan, a busy shopping and business street, runs south to Gustav Adolfs Torg. Beyond this, over the canal, is Södra Förstadsgatan, which leads to the elegant Triangeln shopping centre, with a modern hotel.

Carriage Museum

East of the city centre, in Drottningtorget, is the Carriage Museum, housed in the old Town Hall (old carriages; history of the motor car). Nearby in the St Gertrud district are a number of carefully restored old houses (16th–19th c.), now a leisure centre.

Malmö Castle (Municipal Museum)

West of the Old Town lies the Kungspark (King's Park), with a summer restaurant. From the Kungspark a bridge leads into the Slottspark (Castle Park), in which, surrounded by a moat, is Malmö Castle (Malmöhus), built 1537–42 and restored in 1870 after a fire. It now houses the Municipal Museum (archaeology, art and culture, natural history). From the Castle it is only a few yards to the Museum of Technology, associated with which is a Seafaring Museum.

Municipal Theatre

In the south-west corner of the Slottspark is Linnépladsen (Linnaeus Square), with a sculpture, "Pegasus", by Carl Milles. At the south-east

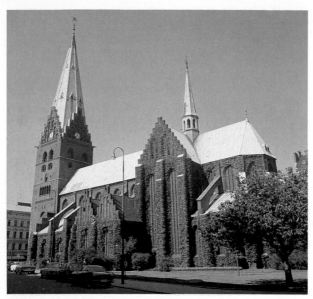

St Peter's Church, Malmö's oldest building

Baptistery, with old frescos

corner of the park is the Municipal Library. To the south of this is the Municipal Theatre (1942–44), the largest theatre in Scandinavia, with seating for 1700 (visitors admitted).

Still farther south is Pildammspark, with an open-air theatre and the Margareta Pavilion. In this area too are the Stadium and the Exhibition Halls. The Hyllie Water-Tower (77m/253ft high) is open to visitors.

Recreation; transport

In the south-east of the city, in Amiralsgatan, lies the Folkets Park, an amusement park with numerous restaurants. Farther to the south-east is Sturup Airport.

To the south-west, on the Öresund, are the Ribersborg bathing beach and Limhamn, from which there is a ferry service to the Danish fishing village of Dragør. There are plans for a bridge over the Öresund to Denmark.

From Malmö harbour there is a hydrofoil service to Copenhagen (45 minutes).

Surroundings

Torup Castle

14km/9 miles east of Malmö, set in a beautiful park, is the well preserved Torup Castle (16th c.), which is now owned by the city of Malmö (conducted tours in summer). Another attractive country house is Svaneholm, which also dates from the 16th century; it now houses a restaurant which serves typical local dishes.

Skanör-Falsterbo

To the south of Malmö on E 22 are extensive residential suburbs. The idyllic seaside resort of Skanör-Falsterbo, at the south-western tip of Skåne, is remarkable for its unusual beach flora and for the numbers of birds to be seen here.

Mikkeli (St Michel)   G 4

Country: **Finland**
Region: Southern Finland
Population: 32,000
Post code: FIN–50100   Telephone code: 955

Situation and characteristics

The Finnish town of Mikkeli (Swedish St Michel), chief town of the province of the same name, lies on one of the western arms of Lake Saimaa. There were human settlements in this area more than a thousand years ago, and the first Christian community in the Savo region was established here, as the little stone sacristy of Savilahti's wooden medieval church still bears witness.

History

The village of St Michel was granted the right to hold a market in 1745 and received its municipal charter in 1838. In 1843 it became the chief town of the province and in 1945 the see of a bishop. A garrison town from the 17th century, it played a military role in the 20th century as the headquarters of Marshal Mannerheim in three campaigns during the Second World War (the Winter War of 1939–40, the renewed war of 1941–44 against Soviet forces and the Lapland War of 1944–45 against the German occupying forces) – events commemorated by the Cross of Freedom and the marshal's batons in the town's coat of arms.

A secondary school was established in Mikkeli in 1872. In the second half of the 19th century, with the development of industry, the town's economy made great strides. Its principal industries are woodworking, textiles and metalworking.

Town

Cathedral

The brick-built Cathedral (1897) has an altarpiece (c. 1900) by Pekka Halonen (Christ crucified, with the Virgin and St John); stained glass over the altar.

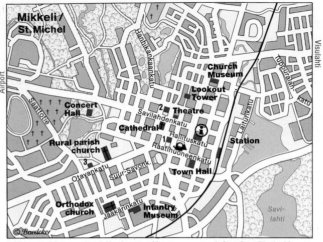

1 Museum of Art   2 Headquarters Museum   3 Suur-Savo District Museum

In the town centre are the Museum of Art (20th c. painting, sculpture), the provincial government offices (by C. L. Engel, 1843) and the Town Hall (1912).

Museum of Art

On the west side of the town stands the rural parish church (1816), a large wooden building in a style characteristic of eastern Finland, on a double cruciform plan, which can accommodate a congregation of 2000.

Parish church

Near the church, in a converted granary at Otavankatu 11, is the Suur-Savo District Museum (history and ethnology of the Suur-Savo district).

Suur-Savo Museum

Farther south is the Orthodox church, a modern building by Ilmari Ahonen (1957).

Orthodox church

In the centre of the town, on the hill of Naisvuori (open-air theatre in summer), stands a lookout tower (café) from which there are fine panoramic views. Indoor swimming pool hewn from the rock. Nearby is the interesting Headquarters Museum (see History, above).

Lookout tower

To the north-east, at the end of Porrasalmenkatu, is the stone-built sacristy (*kivisakasti*) of Savulahti church, a wooden building (1320) which was pulled down in the 18th century. The sacristy now houses a Church Museum.

Church Museum

Outside the town, to the north, is the Visulahti tourist centre, with a wax museum, a motor museum and Miniland (scaled-down models of Finnish buildings).
   3km/2 miles south on Road 18, at Tuukkola, can be found a cemetery with graves dating from the 12th century.

Visulahti

Surroundings

From Mikkeli there are boat services to the nearby holiday centre of Pistohiekka (chalet village) and to Lappeenranta and Savonlinna (see entries).
   To the north is the esker (a gravel ridge deposited by a glacier) of Pikku-Punkaharju.

Miniland, Visulahti (Mikkeli)

Brahelinna	6km/4 miles south of Mikkeli on Road 13 is the narrow sound of Porrassalmi, and 18km/11 miles beyond this, at Ristiina, are the ruins of Brahelinna, a castle begun by Per Brahe but never completed. The church at Ristiina, built by Eskil Collenius, a Karelian architect, in 1775, contains portraits of Per Brahe and his wife.

Lake Mjøsa   C 5

Country: **Norway**
Region: South-eastern Norway
Altitude: 124m/407ft

Situation and characteristics	Lake Mjøsa, Norway's largest lake, extends for 100km/60 miles through a fertile region from Eidsvoll in the south to Lillehammer (see entry) in the north. With a width of up to 15km/9 miles, it has an area of 362sq.km/140sq. miles – slightly less than Lake Garda in northern Italy – and is up to 443m/1450ft deep. The lake is well stocked with trout.

Around ★Lake Mjøsa

Eidsvoll	Lake Mjøsa is reached from Oslo on E 6. From the little town of Eidsvoll, on the right bank of the wide, clear river Vorma, there is a boat service up the lake to Lillehammer from mid June to mid August. The trip, in the oldest paddle-steamer in the world still in service (1856), takes about six hours, with calls at the main places on the lake.
Minnesund	Beyond Minnesund E 6 crosses the river Vorma at its outflow from the lake and continues along the east side of Lake Mjøsa through attractive scenery, climbing slightly.

Lake Mjøsa (south-eastern Norway)

Soon after Espa, a little place on the picturesque Korsødegårdsbugt, E 6 leaves the lake, to return to it only at Hamar. Those who want to keep close to the lake should take Road 222, which runs parallel to E 6 on the west, passing through Stange. West of Stange is the village church, one of the two most beautiful churches in Hedmark (the other being Ringsaker), built about 1250 and remodelled in the 17th century. Between the road and the lake, sometimes directly on the lakeside, are numbers of prosperous farmhouses *(storgårder),* many dating from the 18th century, which bear witness to the wealth of this fertile region.

Espa

Stange church

The next place of any size is Hamar (pop. 16,000), chief town of Hedmark county, which lies on the north side of the Akersvik, at the mouth of the Furnesfjord, which runs north for some 15km/9 miles. The symbol of the town is the Olympia Hall, with its unusual roof construction reminiscent of an upturned Viking ship. West of the town, on the Storhamarodde (Domkirkeodde) peninsula, are the ruins of the 12th century Cathedral of Hamar and the Hedmark Museum, with numbers of old wooden buildings (the oldest dating from 1583), an open-air theatre and a restaurant.

Hamar

North of the Hedmark Museum lies Norway's only Railway Museum (Jernbanemuseet). In the museum, which dates from 1896, visitors can see locomotives, carriages and signals. In the grounds are the buildings of Norway's first railway (1854) and a 300m/330yd long stretch of track.

Railway Museum

28km/17 miles east of Hamar, on the Glåma, is Elverum (alt. 188m/615ft, pop. 17,000), once a fortified town. Features of interest are the Glomsdal Museum, an open-air museum (80 old peasants' houses from the prosperous Østerdal, with period furnishings), and the Norwegian Forest Museum (forestry, shooting, fishing).

Side trip to Elverum

Beyond Brumunddal E 6 comes to the north end of the Furnesfjord and turns west. The motorway passes Moelv, crosses to the west side of Lake Mjøsa on a bridge and continues towards Lillehammer.

Brumunddal

Ringsaker   A side trip can be made to Ringsaker, on the shores of the lake. The beautiful village church has a carved and painted altar. From here a road follows the east side of the lake by way of Moelv to Lillehammer.

Gjøvik   On the west side of the lake (reached by a ferry from Mengstol) is Gjøvik (pop. 28,000; fish-hook factory), chief place in the Toten district, known as "the white town on Lake Mjøsa". From here Road 4 goes north to Lillehammer.

Toten Museum   From Gjøvik Road 33 runs south along the west side of Lake Mjøsa. To the west of Kapp (pop. 1100) is the Toten Museum, an open-air museum established in the 1930s round a farmhouse of 1790 (period furnishings).

Balke church   On a peninsula to the north of Skreia (pop. 900) is Balke church (c. 1200; restored 1967). The road now keeps close to the shore of the lake, with the Skreia ridge of hills to the west (Skreikamp, 708m/2323ft).

Feiring ironworks   From the farm of Bjørnstad a road leads north to the Feiring ironworks (Feiring Jernverk), established in 1797, with 24 buildings (stamping mill, blast furnace, etc.) which illustrate the technology of this early stage of the industry.

At Minnesund we return to the starting-point of the tour.

Mo i Rana   D 3

Country: **Norway**
Region: Northern Norway
Population: 6500
Post code: N–8600

Situation and characteristics   Mo i Rana is a busy industrial and commercial town at the east end of the Nordranafjord, dominated by the extensive steelworks and rolling mill of the Norsk Jernverk corporation. The Norwegian National Library is based in Mo.

There are conducted tours of the steelworks, to the north-east of the town, during the holiday season.

Sights   In the town centre is the 19th century church, with an altarpiece (1780) from an earlier church. Near the railway station is the Municipal Museum (history of the town, local arts and crafts, mining, natural history, geology). 10km/6 miles outside the town is the Stenneset open-air museum with buildings dating from the 18th c. to the early 20th c.

Mofjell   Above the town to the south rises the Mofjell (410m/1345ft; cabin cableway), from which there are fine views (particularly towards sunset) of the town and the Svartisen glacier.

Surroundings

Reinforshei   E 6 runs north-east from the town, through beautiful scenery, and in 2.5km/1½ miles crosses the Rana. There is a salmon ladder in the river at Reinforshei.

Røssvoll   At Røssvoll (13km/8 miles) is a small round wooden church. Here a road goes off on the left, passes Mo airport and comes in 10km/6 miles to the village of Grønli, from which there is a footpath (800m/½ mile) to the farm of Grønli, near the Grønli Cave.

Grønli Cave, Mo i Rana

The Grønli Cave (1200m/1300yd long) is the best known of the 120 caves which have been discovered in this area. There are conducted tours of the cave (care required: the path is not good).

★Grønli Cave

The road ends in 32km/20 miles at the Svartisvatn, above which rear the great Svartisen snowfield and glacier. A motorboat takes visitors to the other side of the lake, from which it is a 45 minutes' walk to the foot of the massive Svartisen glacier (see Saltfjell).

Svartisvatn

91km/57 miles south-west of Mo i Rana on E 6, at the outflow of the Vefsnelv into the Vefsnfjord, is the attractive little town of Mosjøen (pop. 10,000), with weaving mills and an aluminium plant. The church in the Dolstad district (1734) is the oldest octagonal church in the country. Nearby is an open-air museum with ten old houses. From the hill of Haravoll there are fine views of the town and the fjord.

Mosjøen

From Mosjøen Road 78 leads to Leirosen, from which Road 17 runs south to Sandnessjøen; then ferry to the island of Dønna, which has a 12th century stone church with underground passages and a burial vault. From the Dønnesfjell (127m/417ft) there is one of the finest prospects of the varied landscape of the Norwegian west coast – the bird island of Lovund, the Seven Sisters waterfall and the snow-capped peaks on the mainland. The road to the summit of the hill was built by German troops during the Second World War.

Side trip to
Sandnessjøen
and Dønna

Molde

B 4

Country: **Norway**
Region: Western Norway. Population: 21,000
Post code: N–6400

Molde, chief town of the county of Møre og Romsdal, lies on the north side of the Moldefjord, sheltered on the north and west by a range of hills. In its

Situation and
characteristics

Church, Molde

mild climate roses flourish which normally do not grow so far north and as a result it is known as the "city of roses".

During the summer the town is a busy tourist centre. An international Jazz Festival is held here in August. There is good fishing in the surrounding area.

Founded in the 15th century, Molde received its municipal charter in 1742. During the Second World War it was largely destroyed but after the war was rebuilt in modern style. The main industries are textiles and ship fittings. Molde is also an educational centre.

Sights

Church

In the centre of the town is the Town Hall (1966). East of this is the church (by Finn Bryn, 1957), with a separate belfry. On the wall of the aisle is a painting of the Resurrection by the 19th century artist Axel Ender, an altarpiece from the earlier church which was destroyed in 1940; fine stained glass by O. Kristiansen.

★Rekneshaug

To the west of the town is the hilly, wooded park of Rekneshaug, with a monument to the Norwegian writer Alexander Kielland (1849–1906), who was a local government official in Molde for some years. At the far end of the park is the Romsdal Museum, with many old houses from the Romsdal. North-east of the park is the Stadium, with an indoor swimming pool.

Surroundings

Hjertøy

In the fjord to the south of the town is the little island of Hjertøy (motorboats from harbour), with a small Fisheries Museum.

★Fannestrand

There are pleasant walks on the shores of the fjord, particularly to the east along the Fannestrand beach.

Two fine viewpoints near Molde are Tusten (696m/2284ft; 3 hours' climb) and Varden ("Heap of Stones"; 407m/1335ft), up which there is a road (4km/2½ miles).

Tusten
Varden

28km/17 miles north of Molde on Road 64 is the Trollkirka (Trolls' Church), a limestone cave in the Tverfjelle (see Atlantic Highway).

Trollkirka

Narvik

D 2

Country: **Norway**
Region: Northern Norway
Population: 19,000
Post code: N–8500

The northern Norwegian port of Narvik lies at the western end of a peninsula between the Rombaksfjord to the north and the Beisfjord to the south. Both of these fjords are branches of the Ofotfjord, which gives Narvik its access to the Atlantic. Silhouetted to the south can be seen the famous mountain known as "den sovende Dronning" (The Sleeping Queen).

Situation and characteristics

The town, which received its municipal charter in 1902, is of great economic importance as the terminus of the Ofot Railway (Lapland Railway) from the Kiruna iron-mines in Sweden and an ice-free port. During the Second World War the German occupation of Norway facilitated the export of Swedish iron ore to Germany. British efforts to prevent this led to fierce fighting, during which Narvik suffered heavy damage. In the postwar reconstruction of the town the old wooden houses were replaced by new stone buildings.

The town is divided in two by the extensive installations, modernised and extended in 1977, of the ore terminal. The ore brought from Sweden by rail

★Ore Terminal

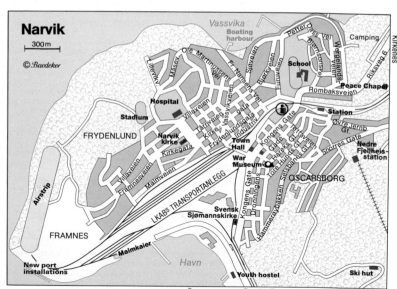

Passenger quay Fauske, Trondheim

Narvik

is carried by long conveyors to various stores and to the Malmkaier (Malm Quays). The port can now handle ore-carriers of up to 350,000 tons, and has a total handling capacity of some 30 million tons a year. To the south of the port, adjoining the loading installations, is a small park with an attractive sculpture of a group of children.

Town

To the east of the railway line to the ore terminal lies Kongensgate, the town's main street. In the Torg (Market Square) stands the Town Hall (1961), in front of which is a large signpost with 23 signs giving the distances to the North Pole and to cities throughout the world. Nearby is a War Museum. At the south end of Kongensgate is the Swedish Seamen's Church (Svensk Sjømannskirke), with a library. Diagonally opposite is a monument commemorating the Norwegian warships "Norge" and "Eidsvold", which were sunk during the fighting in 1940. To the north, beyond the railway, is the Gulbransonspark, and to the west of this are some 4000-year-old rock carvings.

To the east of the town is the cemetery, with the graves of both Allied and German soldiers.

Frammeåsen

20 minutes west of the town is a good viewpoint, Frammeåsen (102m/335ft), from which there is a prospect of the Ofotfjord and Kongsbaktind.

Surroundings

Fagernesfjell

South-east of Narvik is the Fagernesfjell (1250m/4100ft), with a cableway running up to 700m/2300ft (restaurant at upper station). From the top of the hill there are extensive views; the midnight sun is visible from the end of May to the middle of July. There are excellent skiing facilities on the slopes of the hills round Narvik.

See entry   Lofoten Islands

See entry   Vesterålen

Narvik to Abisko by Rail (also new road)

The section of the line within Norwegian territory is known as the Ofot Railway, the Swedish section as the Lapland Railway. The line, completed in 1903, serves primarily for the transport of iron ore from the Swedish iron-mining area of Kiruna and Gällivare to Narvik. In good weather a rail trip into Swedish Lapland is a fascinating experience, taking passengers in just under two hours from the western fjords to the desolate Arctic mountains. The best views are on the left-hand side. In addition to the numerous ore trains using the line there are regular passenger trains.

From Narvik the line runs along the south side of the Rombaksfjord, already beginning to climb. Beyond Rombak there is a further ascent, with impressive views to the rear of the Rombaksbotn and the end of the fjord. The line traverses numerous tunnels and over viaducts, through country in which trees and shrubs are increasingly rare.

Beyond Bjørnfjell, the last Norwegian station, the train crosses the   Riksgränsen
watershed between the Arctic and the Baltic (525m/1720ft) and soon afterwards crosses the frontier into Sweden. 2km/1¼ miles beyond this, in a magnificent mountain setting, is the Swedish town of Riksgränsen, in the centre of a popular skiing area. Then on to Abisko (see entry).

Nordfjord   B 5

Country: **Norway**
Region: Western Norway

The Nordfjord, lying almost exactly on the 62nd degree of northern lati-   Situation and
tude, extends, parallel with the Sognefjord to the south, for a distance of   characteristics
more than 90km/55 miles from Måløy to Olden, with a depth of up to
565m/1850ft. The various parts of the fjord have different names, though in
the past the name of Nordfjord was applied to the whole area. The juxtaposition of wide expanses of water, mighty mountains and glaciers gives the
inner branches of the fjord their particular charm.

There are mini-cruises from Bergen, usually lasting two or three days,   Mini-cruises
which call in at various places in the Nordfjord.

The Fjord

The Nordfjord is reached from the south on E 6, which runs via Lillehammer   Access
to Otta, from which Road 15 leads west by way of Lom to Stryn on the north   Innvikfjord
side of the Innvikfjord, the most easterly ramification of the Nordfjord.

After crossing the Strynselv the route continues on Road 60 along the steep   Loen
north side of the fjord to Loen, at the mouth of the beautiful Loendal, with a
small octagonal wooden church (1937). From here Skåla (1937m/6355ft)
can be climbed (6 hours; guide required).

From Loen a narrow road (14km/9 miles) runs along the east side of the   ★Loenvatn
beautiful Loenvatn (alt. 43m/140ft; area 10.2sq.km/4sq. miles; greatest
depth 193m/635ft) by way of the Bødal tourist centre to Kjenndal, below the
north side of the Nonsnibba (1823m/5981ft). Above the western shore of
the Loenvatn rises the snow-capped peak of the Ramnefjell or Ravnefjell

323

Fruit-blossom on the Nordfjord

(2003m/6570ft), a northern outlier of the extensive snowfields of the Jostedalsbre (see entry). To the east of Kjenndal rises the Lodalskappa.

Olden

From Loen Road 60 continues along the shores of the Innvikfjord to Olden, at the south end of the fjord, with a church of 1746–49 (restored 1971).

★Oldenvann

From Olden a road runs 4.5km/3 miles south through the beautiful Olden valley to Eide, on the northern shore of the Oldenvann (alt. 37m/120ft; area 8.4sq.km/3sq. miles; length 11km/7 miles; up to 90m/295ft deep), and continues along the lake (motorboat services), passing several waterfalls, with snow-covered hills to right and left, to Rustøy (13km/8 miles), at the south end of the lake.

Briksdal

From Rustøy it is 5.5km/3½ miles (narrow road, with passing places) to Briksdal (alt. 150m/490ft), from which it is an hour's walk to the Briksdalsbre, an offshoot of the Jostedalsbre rearing its blue masses of ice above the scrub forest.

Innvik

Road 60 continues along the south side of the fjord from Olden to Innvik (17km/10 miles), with a view to the south of the snow-covered Storlaugpik (1556m/5105ft) and Ceciliekruna (1775m/5824ft).

Utvik
Utvikfjell

Beyond the attractive little settlement of Utvik the road leaves the shore of the fjord and climbs in hairpin bends, with extensive views over the fjord, on to the Utvikfjell (640m/2100ft), from which there is a splendid panorama, with the Jostedalsbre to the south.

Gloppenfjord
Sandane

The road now descends to Byrkjelo, on Road 1. To the left is the road to the Sognefjord (see entry); to the right is Sandane (pop. 2000), beautifully situated at the east end of the Gloppenfjord, another branch of the Nordfjord. At Sandane is the Nordfjord Folk Museum (16 old buildings). On the west side of the fjord are the church of Gjemmestad and a number of Iron Age burial mounds; on the east side one of the largest burial mounds in Vestland, Tinghogjen (50m/165ft across, 7m/23ft high), which catches the last rays of the setting sun on Midsummer Day.

The road now follows the east side of the Gloppenfjord to its junction with the Utfjord, another section of the Nordfjord. To the right is Sandane's little airstrip. From Anda, on the point between the two fjords, there is a car ferry to Lote (10 minutes), on the north side of the fjord.

Utfjord

From Lote Road 1 runs north-west to Nordfjordeid (pop. 1700), crossing the tongue of land between the Hundvikfjord and the Eidsfjord, and then continues west along the north side of the Eidsfjord.

Nordfjordeid
Eidsfjord

Beyond Stårheim, birthplace of the folk poet Mathias Orheim (1884–1958; hut with relics and mementoes), the road comes to the main arm of the fjord system, the Nordfjord proper. The route continues along the north side of the fjord on Road 15.

Nordfjord

From Maurstad a rewarding side trip can be made (north on Road 620) to the Stadlandet promontory, at the end of which is the West Cape, with the crag known as the Old Woman (Kjerringa) and a superb view of the open North Sea. With its shifting currents the West Cape is a notorious hazard for shipping.

Stadlandet
★★View

Road 15 continues west to Almenningen, with a view of Hornelen, Europe's highest cliff, rising vertically from the sea to a height of 860m/2820ft. In popular legend this was the place where witches and trolls held their revels.

Almenningen

Soon after this a 1224m/1339yd long bridge crosses the Ulvesund to the port of Måløy on the island of Vagsøy. Features of interest here are the

Måløy

Måløy, on the island of Vågsøy

Kannesten, a rock eroded into hourglass shape on the beach 11km/7 miles from Måløy, and the old trading station on the Vagsberg, with seven historic buildings.

★Rock carvings

A boat can be taken from Hagens Hotell to Vingen (opposite Hornelen), with the largest group of rock carvings in the north, the Helleristningsfelt (2000 figures, mostly of deer).

Norrköping   D 6

Country: **Sweden**
Province: Östergötland
Population: 119,000
Post code: S–60... Telephone code: 011

Situation and characteristics

The town of Norrköping lies at the outflow of the Motalaström into the Bråvik, an inlet on the Baltic which extends inland for some 50km/30 miles. The Bråvik forms a natural boundary between the wooded region of Kolmård to the north and the fertile arable country of Vikboland to the south. Norrköping is an industrial town.

Town

Johannisborg

To the east of the railway station are the remains of the Johannisborg. Although nothing is left standing but the gateway and adjoining walls, there is enough to give some impression of what this 17th century castle was like in its heyday. The gate tower was restored in 1934.

Karl Johan Park

To the south of the station lies the Karl Johan Park, with a fine collection of cacti. In the park is a monument (by Schwanthaler, 1846) to King Carl XIV Johan (Bernadotte). Facing the park stands the Town House. Near the station is the Neo-Gothic St Matthew's Church (1892).

Norrköping town centre

On the south bank of the Motalaström is the Tyska Torg (German Market), with St Hedvig's Church, built in the 17th century for the town's German community (altered in the 18th century), with an altarpiece by Pehr Hörberg. On the south side of the square is the Town Hall (1907–10); the carillon in the 68m/225ft high tower plays daily at noon and 5pm.

Tyska Torg
Town Hall

In Drottninggatan, the town's main street, rises the City Tower (1750), the great symbol and landmark of Norrköping, from which the fire-watchers used to call the hours.

City Tower

Östra Eneby church (12th c.), one of the town's oldest churches, has medieval ceiling paintings, valuable tapestries and a beautiful font with a basin of Kolmård marble.

The Gamla Torg (Old Square), where the Town Hall and the Burghers' Guildhall once stood, is now surrounded by handsome early 19th century houses. In the square can be seen a monument (by Carl Milles) to Louis de Geer, a Dutchman who brought industry to the town in the 17th century; it faces the Holmen works founded by de Geer (tower painted in the colour known as Norrköping yellow).

Gamla Torg

The Municipal Museum (Stadsmuseet), on the site of an old factory in Västergatan (beyond the Gamlebro), displays implements and machinery used in over fifty different trades (textile industry). In Kristinaplats is the Museum of Art (Konstmuseet), with departments of older and modern art (Swedish painting and sculpture). In St Persgatan is a Dyeing Museum (Färgargården).

Museums

To the west of the town are the People's Park and Himmelstalund Park, in which are the old spa establishment and a theatre, as well as 3000-year-old rock carvings (including representations of ships).

★Rock carvings

Northern Surroundings

5km/3 miles north-west of the road to Svärtinge is the manor-house of Ringstad. Near here are cemetery areas and the remains of a 7th century Viking stronghold, believed to be one mentioned in the Helgi lays of the Edda.

Ringstad

29km/18 miles north-west of Norrköping is Finspång, in an old mining area, now an industrial town, with a castle of 1668. 10km/6 miles north-east of Finspång is Rejmyra, with a glassworks (showroom for sale of glassware produced here).

Finspång

Kolmård Forest lies on the boundary between Södermanland and Östergötland, to the north of the long inlet of Bråvik. This well wooded upland region extends for some 100km/60 miles from west to east. The rocks are mainly reddish gneiss, together with some red and black granite. Stone from here was used in the construction of the Parliament Building in Stockholm in the 19th century. There is also a certain amount of iron and copper in the area. The famous green marble found in the eastern part of the region was worked at intervals over a period of almost 300 years, from 1673 to 1960.

Kolmård Forest

To the east is the Kolmård Wildlife Park (Djurpark) or Zoo, with an elephant house, a tiger house, a dolphinarium, a tropical section, a cableway and a safari park. Nearby, at Fagervik, is a Stone Age occupation site.

Wildlife Park

Eriksgatan, the old main road between Götaland and Svealand, ran through the Kolmård area from the Krokek inn to Unnerberg Castle. A forerunner of our present-day inns was the Monastery of Our Lady (Vårfruklostret) in Kolmård, which provided accommodation for travellers.

Eriksgatan

Giraffes in Kolmårdens Djurpark

Stones from the ruins of the monastery were used in the construction of a chapel and later of the old church of Krokek (1747), now also in ruins.

Southern Surroundings

Lövstad

10km/6 miles south-west of Norrköping, in an English-style park, is Lövstad Castle, now a museum with a collection of pictures. Concerts are given in the castle during the summer months.

Söderköping

15km/9 miles south-east of Norrköping we come to Söderköping (pop. 13,000), founded in the 13th century as a trading station for Lübeck merchants, who built a large church here (as they did at Skänninge). The church (St Lawrence's) was completed 200 years later, at the end of the 15th century. Excavations in Storgatan, Vintervadsgatan and elsewhere in the town have brought to light merchants' and craftsmen's houses and equipment which show that for a time during the Middle Ages Söderköping was one of Sweden's principal trading towns. In 1567 the town was partly destroyed by Danish troops, but was rebuilt in stone. King John III made Norrköping the administrative centre of the region and promoted the development of mining; and thereafter Söderköping's trade declined, and the German merchants left the town. Its inhabitants then turned to fishing in the skerries for their subsistence. A trading settlement which was now established on the islands of Björkeskär and Viskär held a monopoly of the fisheries off the coasts of Östergötland until 1731. Later the mineral water of St Ragnhild's Spring acquired some reputation and was marketed commercially.

Among features of interest in the town are the Drothem quarter with its church and a number of old buildings around St Lawrence's Church, including the belfry (1582) and the schoolhouse. On Gilleskullen is an open-air museum with old houses from the surrounding area. There are fine views from the Ramunderberg with its castle.

North Cape

Country: **Norway**
Region: Northern Norway

By car: leaving Tromsø, Road 6 at first keeps close to the coast for most of the way, passes through Alta and comes to Olderfjord. From there E 69 runs along the Porsanger peninsula to Kåfjord, from which there is a car ferry (several times daily; 45 minutes) to Honningsvåg. There is also a bus from Lakselv (airstrip), the administrative centre of the Porsanger district, to Kåfjord.

Access

By sea: the best way is on one of the fast ships of the Hurtigrute (see entry) from Hammerfest (about 6 hours; limited accommodation).

By air: there are flights from Hammerfest to Honningsvåg.

From Honningsvåg there are buses and taxis to the North Cape.

The North Cape (alt. 307m/975ft; lat. 71°10′21″ N, longitude 25°47′40″ E), in Norwegian Nordkapp, is a crag of greyish-black slate, furrowed by deep clefts, which rises abruptly from the sea on the north side of the island of Magerøy. It is regarded as the northernmost point in Europe, though in fact the cape of Knivskjelodden reaches slightly farther north (71°11′8″ N). The most northerly point on the mainland is the promontory of Nordkinn (or Nordkyn or Kinnarodden), between the Laksefjord and the Tanafjord, 68km/42 miles east of the North Cape in latitude 71°8′1″ north and longitude 27°40′9″ east.

Situation

The island of Magerøy is the most northerly outpost of Scandinavia. Between fjords cutting deep into the land, its promontories jut out into the Arctic Ocean – massive and much fissured ridges of rock between 300 and 400m (1000 and 1300ft) high, flat-topped and for the most part falling steeply down to the sea. Only an occasional patch of vegetation can be seen in this desolate landscape.

Magerøy

The little port of Honningsvåg lies on the south-east coast of Magerøy. It has an interesting North Cape Museum. From here there are boat trips to Norway's biggest bird cliff and to various abandoned fishing villages.

Honningsvåg

Hewn from the rock of the North Cape is the North Cape Hall (admission charge). A tunnel lined with tableaux on the history of the North Cape leads to the main hall (bar; North Cape certificates, special stamps and postmarks) with a panoramic window on the Arctic Ocean. An arrow indicates the direction of true north. In good weather the view extends west, north and east over the open sea. To the south-east are the islands of Hjelmsøy and Rolvsøy; to the east, in the distance, the Nordkinn promontory; to the south the plateau of Magerøy with its snowfields, its lakes and its scanty

★★North Cape

329

On the North Cape (island of Magerøy)

Midnight sun over the North Cape

vegetation. A granite column on the North Cape commemorates a visit by King Oscar II in 1873.

Since 1929 the North Cape has been under statutory protection as a nature reserve, and the removal of plants is prohibited.

The midnight sun is visible here from May 14th to July 30th, reaching its lowest point at 10.35pm (GMT).

Nyköping   E 6

Country: **Sweden**
Province: Södermanland
Population: 65,000
Post code: S–61100   Telephone code: 0155

Nyköping, chief town of the county of Södermanland, lies on the Baltic coast just above the mouth of the Nyköpingså. In the Middle Ages it was one of the most important towns in Sweden, and between the 13th and the 16th centuries it was the meeting-place of the Riksdag (Parliament) on fifteen occasions. It is now a busy industrial town (motor vehicles, furniture, etc.).

Situation and characteristics

Flanking the main square, the Stora Torg, are the Town Hall (1720), the Governor's Residence (1803) and the old church of St Nicholas (rebuilt in the 18th century).

Town

From the Stora Torg Slottsgatan runs south to the massive castle of Nyköpingshus, on the right bank of the Nyköpingså. The original castle probably dated from the time of the Folkung kings. In 1318 King Birger Jarl imprisoned his two brothers, who had disputed his claim to the throne, in the castle and left them to starve to death. The castle was burned down in 1665 and later partly rebuilt. There survive the main gateway (Vasaporten) and Duke Charles's Tower or Kungstornet on the west side. In the tower is Södermanland County Museum, which documents the history of Nyköpingshus (model of the castle) and the province of Södermanland (material recovered by excavation, portraits of Swedish rulers). North-west of the castle is the Museum of Art, with works by Swedish painters of the 18th–20th centuries.

Nyköpingshus (Museum)

In the south-east of the town stands All Saints Church (Allhelgonakyrkan), built in the 13th century and rebuilt in the 17th. Notable features of the interior are a 15th century triumphal cross and a 17th century reredos.

All Saints Church

Surroundings

For nature-lovers there are pleasant excursions to the lakes north of the town (Yngaren, Långhalsen, Båven).

Lakes

13km/8 miles south-east of Nyköping (motorway) is the port of Oxelösund (pop. 13,000), with a large steelworks and an interesting modern church (1975).

Oxelösund

7km/4½ miles from Nyköping on the Stockholm motorway is an exit (Road 223) leading to the large (10m/33ft high) burial mound of Uppsa-Kulle, 15km/9 miles north.

Uppsa-Kulle

11km/7 miles farther north Ludgo church has an altar by Burchard Precht and two 15th century sculptures from western Europe (French or Flemish).

Ludgo

20km/12½ miles farther north on the motorway and 1.5km/1 mile on the ordinary road Road 218 goes off on the right to the seaside resort of Trosa, 6km/4 miles south on the Baltic coast (large fish-smoking plant).

Trosa

Tullgarn

3.5km/2 miles farther along the main road a side road on the right (2km/ 1¼ miles; signpost) leads to the Neo-Classical manor-house of Tullgarn (1719–28), in a beautiful park, for many years a royal summer residence (open to the public in summer).

Öland   E 6/7

Country: **Sweden**
Province: Öland
Area: 1346sq.km/525sq. miles
Population: 25,000
Post code: S–38...   Telephone code 0485

Situation and characteristics

Öland, lying off the south-east coast of Sweden, is the country's second largest island, now linked with the mainland by Europe's longest bridge, which spans the Kalmarsund in a bold arch. The chief place on the island is the little town of Borgholm, and there are two rural communes. The landscape and vegetation are very different from those of the adjoining mainland. Since the island is no more than 16km/10 miles across at its widest point, there is usually a light sea-breeze blowing. The most unusual part of Öland is the Alvar steppe country, where the limestone rock is exposed or covered only by a thin layer of soil.

Topography

The Stora Alvar, an area some 40km/25 miles long by 10km/6 miles across, extends from Vickleby on the west coast to Ottenby, near the southern tip of the island: an expanse of treeless steppe made up of bare rock, karstic formations, grassy heathland and flat moorland. This southern part of Öland, however, also has some of the most fertile land on the island (e.g. around Mörbylånga).

The landscape of central Öland, between Borgholm and Färjestaden, is very different, with deciduous and coniferous forest predominating along the Kalmarsund and a broad swathe of hazel scrub and wooded meadowland in the interior.

Northern Öland has a rocky west coast and a series of alternating promontories and shallow inlets on the east coast. In between are expanses of meadowland and some steppe country, with junipers. At Böda a belt of coniferous forest extends from coast to coast.

Öland has a long history of human habitation. Among the most striking remains of the past are the cemetery areas, mostly dating from the Iron Age, and the refuge forts constructed for the protection of the settled population during the period of the Great Migrations. In the 12th and 13th centuries the churches were fortified by the construction of defensive towers – sometimes one at each end of the church. Although most of the island's churches date only from the 19th century there are still some surviving medieval churches. Other relics of earlier days are the stone walls, the fishermen's huts, the long straggling villages and the windmills.

★Windmills

The windmills of Öland, some 400 in number, have become the very symbol of the island. They are mainly post-mills, built to serve the needs of individual farms. All of them are now statutorily protected ancient monuments.

Northern Öland

In the north of the island, 2km/1¼ miles from the little fishing village of Byxelkrok, is an area to which Linnaeus gave the name of Neptuni Åkrar ("Neptune's Fields"): a curious beach formation of loose stones which in summer is covered with blue flowers. From the beach there is a view of the crag known as the "Blue Maiden" (Blå Jungfrun). Above the beach is a cemetery area with 35 graves and a ship tomb of the Viking period.

Windmills on the island of Öland

To the north, east and south extends a large park (some 6000 hectares/15,000 acres) with over fifty different species of trees. Within the park is Trollskogen, a wood of pine-trees twisted into bizarre shapes by the wind. At the north-western tip of the island stands a lighthouse popularly known as Långe Erik (Long Eric). South of this, on the east coast, is the Böda inlet, with a sandy beach and a wood, Kronoskogen (wild orchids). On the west side are Byerums Raukar, the only *raukar* (see Gotland) on Öland. To the south is the Hornsjö, Öland's only lake.

Trollskogen

Near Löttorp is Källa Ödekyrka, a 13th century fortified church which has preserved its defensive aspect. The church, dedicated to St Olof, provided lodging for travellers and others coming from the nearby port of Källahamn. In the interior of the island to the west, south of the new church of Källa, lies the Vi Alvar cemetery area, with Iron Age sacrificial stones.

Källa Ödekyrka

At Jordhamn, on the west coast, can be seen a *skurverk,* a wind-operated mill for grinding limestone. Limestone is also worked at Sandvik, farther south, which has the largest Dutch windmill in Sweden (8 storeys; restaurant). To the south is the Knisa Mosse nature reserve (birds).

Jordhamn
limestone mill

At a road junction (south-west to Borgholm, south-east to Egby) is Föra church, with a fine 12th century defensive tower; outside the church is the 15th century St Martin's Cross. The road continues by way of the seaside resorts of Bruddestad and Äleklinta (cliffs) to Köpingsvik, on the west coast, with the overhanging limestone cliffs of Köpings Klint, on which are burials and "judgment rings". Some 300m/330yd from the church is a 3m/10ft high runic stone. 4km/2½ miles west is Borgholm.

Föra church
Köpingsvik

From Borgholm to Färjestaden

Borgholm (pop. 11,000), the only town on the island (municipal charter 1516), is a popular holiday resort. At Tullgatan 22 is Ölands Forngård, a

Borgholm

Öland

museum of local history. In Strandgatan, on the harbour, is the Kronoma-gasin, an archaeological museum housed in a building of 1819. Here too is an interesting Motor Museum.

★Borgholm Castle 1km/³⁄₄ mile south-west of the town are the imposing ruins of Borg-holm Castle, begun in 1572 on the site of an earlier castle, subsequently rebuilt, and destroyed by fire in 1806; it is now the setting of a musical festival. From the ramparts there are fine views of the island and Kalmar-sund.

Solliden Here too is the visitors' entrance to Solliden, a country house built in 1903–06 for Queen Victoria, now a royal summer residence. In the beautiful park much of the original vegetation has been preserved, but there is also a Dutch rose garden, as well as many deciduous trees not normally found in this region. The park is open daily in summer from noon to 2pm.

Egby church 12km/7½ miles east of Borgholm is Egby church, the smallest on the island. In spite of alterations carried out in 1818, when the tower was built, the church has preserved its original Romanesque character. It has a fine font and a stone altar of the 12th century. The Baroque pulpit and reredos date from about 1750.

Gärdslösa church 15km/9 miles south-east of Borgholm stands the Romanesque church of Gärdslösa (12th c.), Öland's best preserved medieval church. The Gothic choir, with wall paintings on Old Testament themes, dates from the end of the 13th century. There are also fragments of 14th century frescos. The pulpit (1666) is richly painted, and there is a beautiful Rococo altar (1764).

Karums Alvar 17km/10 miles south of Borgholm is Karums Alvar, a large Iron Age ceme-tery area, with a stone-setting in the shape of a ship, 30m/100ft long, known as Noah's Ark. Nearby are two limestone hills to which Odin is said to have tethered his horse Sleipnir.

Himmelsberga open-air museum 23km/14 miles south-east of Borgholm is Himmelsberga open-air museum: typical local farms, with old furniture and furnishings; hand-some old half-timbering, mostly of oak. Norrgården (1842) has more the air of a manor-house, while Karls-Olsgården (late 18th c.) is a modest turf-roofed cottage (wall paintings in parlour).

Lerkaka 25km/15½ miles south-east of Borgholm is Lerkaka, with five well pre-served windmills. Nearby can be seen a large runic stone.

Ismantorpsborg 27km/17 miles south of Borgholm is Ismantorpsborg, the most striking of the refuge forts on Öland, probably dating from the period of the Great Migrations. It has a diameter of some 125m/400ft, and within its well preserved ramparts are 88 hut bases. Unusually, it has no fewer than nine entrances, suggesting that it was primarily a cult site.

Färjestaden ★Öland Bridge On the west coast of Öland, opposite Kalmar, lies the little port of Fär-jestaden. From Möllstorp, to the north of the town, the Öland Bridge (6070m/6600yd long, with 153 piers), built in 1972, spans the sound to Kalmar (see entry). 500m/550yd from the end of the bridge can be found Ölands Djurpark (Zoo).

Gråborg 8km/5 miles north-east of Färjestaden is the Gråborg, the largest refuge fort on the island, which was probably constructed during the Great Migrations and remained in use into the Middle Ages. Its ramparts, up to 6m/20ft high, enclose an elliptical area 220m/240yd long by 165m/180yd across. There are remains of an impressive vaulted gateway. Near the Gråborg are the ruins of St Knut's Chapel (13th c.).

Ruins of St Knut's Chapel (near the Gråborg)

Southern Öland

4km/2½ miles south of Färjestaden (signposted "Runsten") is the oldest runic stone on Öland, the Karlevisten, with a long inscription recording that it was set up at the end of the year 1000 by Sibbe the Wise, a Danish sea-king (who probably owned no land).

★Karlevisten

6km/4 miles north-east of the little port of Mörbylånga stands the Romanesque church of Resmo (c. 1150), with 12th century frescos in the choir. The upper part of the east tower was pulled down in 1826, but the south wall has been preserved.

Mörbylånga
Resmo church

5km/3 miles east of Mörbylånga is Mysinge Hög, a Bronze Age burial mound from which there is a magnificent view of the Stora Alvar. In this area are a number of Neolithic tombs, the only ones of their kind in eastern Sweden. The remains of some 30 people were found in these 4000-year-old tombs, each constructed of nine large blocks of granite.

Mysinge Hög

At the south end of the island, on the west coast, is the little port of Degerhamn, 3km/2 miles north of which is the Gettlinge Gravfält, a large Iron Age cemetery area with two limestone mounds marking the graves of chieftains. Nearby are a ship-setting, a judgment ring and a number of burials of different types.

Degerhamn
Gettlinge
cemetery

9km/5½ miles east of Degerhamn is the Seby Gravfält, another Iron Age cemetery area, with the remains of limestone mounds which are still prominent features of the landscape. 1km/¾ mile away, by the roadside, is a large runic stone with the inscription "Ingjald and Näf and Sven set up this stone in honour of their father Rodmar".

Seby cemetery

The Stora Alvar, the steppe country of southern Öland

View of the coast from the Långe Jan lighthouse

16km/10 miles south-east of Degerhamn we come to another refuge fort, Eketorps Borg, with ramparts enclosing an almost exactly circular area. Originally built in the 4th century, it was enlarged during the period of the Great Migrations and developed into a fortified settlement which was occupied for several hundred years. The inhabitants lived by farming and stock-rearing. In the western part of the site excavations have brought to light the foundations of huts. At the end of the Viking age wooden houses were built which remained in occupation well into the medieval period. Finds of material dating from this period have shown that the inhabitants of the fort had by then taken to trading and seafaring. Some of the Iron Age houses have been reconstructed, and there is a museum.

Eketorps Borg

The south end of the island is occupied by the Stora Alvar, a great expanse of steppe country which is aglow with colour when the thyme and heather are in bloom; in certain favoured spots, too, thousands of orchids flower in spring. A very common flower is the trailing tormentil, but there are also such rare species as the large sand-lily and the little blue globularia. Many plants are protected by law, including the yellow pheasant's-eye which grows on coastal grassland.

★Stora Alvar

Near the southernmost tip of the island is Ottenby, which in the 13th century belonged to a monastery. In the 16th century it was taken over by Gustavus Vasa, and thereafter remained Crown property. The manor-house of Kungsgård dates from 1804. To the north, visible from the road, is an Iron Age cemetery area. 2km/1¼ miles farther west are two tall limestone mounds known as the King's Stones. The Kungsgård estate is bounded by a wall ("Charles X's Wall") running right across the island, built in 1653 to protect the cultivated land to the north from the deer on the royal estate.

Ottenby

On the promontory at the southern tip of Öland stands the lighthouse known as Långe Jan, the tallest in Sweden (42m/140ft), built in 1785. Nearby are a bird-watching station and an ornithological museum.

Lighthouse
Bird-watching
station

Örebro

D 6

Country: Sweden
Province: Närke
Population: 119,000
Post code: S–70...   Telephone code: 019

Örebro is the chief town in the province of Närke, the small region between the upland province of Västmanland and the wooded country of Värmland. The town lies in the plain on both sides of the Svartå, near the west end of Lake Hjälmar. It has a long tradition as a commercial town, having for centuries served as a link between the mining region and the farming country of central Sweden. It grew up around a ford on the Svartå, which from the end of the 13th century was protected by a 25m/80ft high tower built by Birger Jarl to watch over and defend the river crossing. Later the watch-tower gave place to a fortified castle, rebuilt in the 16th century, in which the Riksdag (the Swedish Parliament) frequently met.

Situation and
characteristics

In the centre of the town is the main square (Stortorget). At the west end of the square stands St Nicholas's Church (Nikolaikyrka; 18th c.), in which the French Marshal Bernadotte was chosen as heir to the throne in 1810. The church also contains the tomb of the legendary national hero Engelbrekt Engelbrektsson, a bronze statue of whom (by Carl Gustav Qvamström, 1865) can be seen opposite the church in front of the Neo-Gothic Town Hall (1856–62).

Town

St Nicholas's
Church

337

Örebro

To the west of the church, on the banks of the Svartå, is the Concert Hall, with the Municipal Library in the same building.

Medborgarhus (Theatre)

From the Stortorg Drottninggatan runs south to Olof Palmes Torg, in which is the Medborgarhus (Community House; 1964), now occupied by a youth club. The same building houses the Hjalmar Bergman Theatre, named after the well-known Swedish novelist of that name (1883–1931), who was born in Örebro.

★Castle

From the Stortorg Kungsgatan runs north to the Castle, an imposing four-towered Renaissance structure on an island in the river. It dates in its present form from the 16th century (restored 1897–1900):

note particularly the richly decorated doorways in the inner courtyard. The Castle is now occupied by provincial government offices.

Museums

To the south-east of the Castle lies the Castle Park, with a summer restaurant. On the east side of the park are the Örebro County Museum (local history and culture; special exhibitions, including shows of modern art) and the Museum of Technology.

Wadköping open-air museum

From the Castle Kanalvägen leads along the south bank of the Svartå to the Municipal Park, on the east side of which, on the banks of the river, is the Wadköping open-air museum, with a number of old Swedish wooden houses, including the King's House (Kungsstugan; 15th or 16th c.) and the Burgher's House (Borgarstugan; 17th c.).

Svampen Water-Tower

In the north of the town, in Storgatan, is the Olaus Petri Church (1812). In front of it can be seen a bronze monument (by Nils Sjörgren) to the brothers Laurentius and Olaus Petri, leading figures of the Reformation in Sweden during the reign of Gustavus Vasa.

North-east of the church is Svampen (the "Mushroom"), a 60m/200ft high water-tower (restaurant) from which there are extensive views of the surrounding countryside.

Karlslunds Herrgård

On the western outskirts of the town is the historic old manor-house of Karlslunds Herrgård (16th c.), with an interesting Farming Museum.

Gustavsvik Motor Museum

South-west of the town centre, on the road to Karlstad, is an open-air swimming pool, Gustavsviksbadet. The Gustavsvik Motor Museum (open in summer) has a collection of veteran and vintage cars and motorcycles.

Örebro Castle (photograph by Landmäteriet, 1989)

2km/1¼ miles east of Örebro town centre can be found the Oset bird sanctuary: 45 hectares/110 acres of land and 85 hectares/210 acres of water, frequented by many species of birds.

Bird sanctuary

Surroundings

10km/6 miles north-east of Örebro, on the old Fellingsbroväg, is the Nastasten, a runic stone with the inscription "Tored had this stone set up for Lydbjörn, his good son".

Nastasten

15km/9 miles north-east of Örebro is Ekebergs Herregård, home of Gustavus Vasa's second wife Margareta Leijonhufvud. The famous Ekberg marble (used, for example, in the Town Hall and the Dramatic Theatre in Stockholm) came from the nearby village of Glanshammar.

Glanshammar

The village church, which dates from the middle of the 12th century, is one of the richest churches in the province, with Renaissance paintings and a fine processional cross. 200m/220yd west of the church are the old silver-mines which gave the place its name. (Silver-mining ceased about 1530).

North-east of the church is a ship burial, part of a cemetery area which extends along the road to Fellingsbro.

40km/25 miles east of Örebro on E 20, on the Arbogaå, is Arboga (pop. 14,000), in the province of Västmanland. It was founded in the 12th century, when the river was made navigable, and rapidly developed into a busy trading town. Until the early 17th century Arboga was one of the best known towns in Sweden, but its trade declined when the mining towns of Nora and Lindesberg were established (1643) and the Hjälmar Canal was built.

Arboga

The town centre has largely preserved its old-world atmosphere, with many old merchants' and craftsmen's houses. The medieval church of St Nicholas, in which provincial assemblies were held, was restored in 1921; it has a beautiful reredos (German work, 16th c.) and old wall paintings. In front of the church is a statue (1935) of the national hero Engelbrekt Engelbrektsson, who was elected Rikshövitsman (Governor of the Realm or Regent) at the first meeting of the Swedish Riksdag in 1435. To the west of the church stands the Town Hall (18th c.).

Lake Hjälmar

Lake Hjälmar (area 483sq.km/190sq. miles, greatest depth 28m/90ft) extends eastward into Södermanland, and is linked with Lake Mälar (see entry) by the Hjälmar Canal and the Arbogaå. Between 1877 and 1888 the water level was lowered by 1.80m/6ft, thus making an additional 27,000 hectares/67,500 acres of land available for cultivation. The lake is well stocked with fish and is frequented by many species of birds. At Segersjöviken is a bird-watching tower.

Mosjö church

17km/10½ miles south of Örebro is Mosjo church, a medieval church which has survived practically unchanged. It contains a reproduction of the 12th century Mosjö Madonna (75cm/30in. high), the original of which is in the National Historical Museum in Stockholm. This wood figure in the costume of a Nordic goddess is believed to be one of the oldest representations of the Virgin in Scandinavia. To the east of the church are a number of tombs and a "judgment ring".

Hallsberg

South of Örebro lies the town of Hallsberg (pop. 16,000), a railway junction. In Västra Storgatan is an Art Nouveau house built for a businessmman named Adolf Bergöö in 1889, with wall paintings by his son-in-law Carl Larsson in the banqueting hall.

South-east of Hallsberg, on Lake Avern, is the Neo-Gothic manor-house of Boo (1876–82). The chapel has a bell-tower built by Field Marshal H. J. Hamilton (1728–33) in thanksgiving for his safe return from imprisonment in Russia.

Kopparberg

Between Nora and Kopparberg (Road 60; both in the province of Västmanland) are many old mining and ironworking settlements such as Pershyttan. At Klacka-Lerberg, in the mining area, are stalactitic formations.

Kopparborg (10km/6 miles from Örebro) has a number of unusual museums – Sweden's only Photographic Studio Museum, a Postal Museum, a Goldsmiths' Museum, a Shoemakers' Museum and a Mine Museum.

Oslo   C 5

Country: **Norway**
Region: Southern Norway
Population: 461,000
Post code: N–.... Oslo (various)

City tours,
harbour cruises

City sightseeing tours: departures from Town Hall Quay and Trafikanten (at Central Station). Harbour cruises: departures from Town Hall Quay.

Winter sports

The Oslo region (Oslomarka), with Nordmarka, Krogskogen, Vestmarka, Østmarka, etc., offers excellent skiing, with a reasonable assurance of good snow conditions from January to March. The Nordmarka is most easily reached on the Holmenkollen railway.

There are 2200km/1400 miles of prepared cross-country trails, 200km/125 miles with floodlighting. There are downhill pistes, with lifts, at Tryvannskleiva, Rødkleiva, Wyllerløypa, Kirkerudbakken, Ingierkollen, Grefsenkleiva, Fjellstadbakken, Trollvannskleiva, Vardåsen and Varingskollen.

The most easily accessible Alpine skiing area is on the Norefjell (north-west of the city, via Hønefoss and Noresund; 2½ hours by car), with four lifts up to 1800m/5700ft.

In the surrounding area there is a ski school and ski-hiring station (Voksenkollen Stasjon). Within the city itself there are three ice rinks.

Oslo lies at the north end of the Oslofjord (see entry), which here cuts deep inland and is joined by the Akerselv. The city is surrounded by forest-covered hills from which there are far-ranging views.

Situation

Oslo, known from 1624 to 1877 as Christiania and from 1877 to 1924 as Kristiania, is the capital of Norway and, in terms of area, one of the largest capitals in the world. Of the city's total area of 450sq.km/175sq. miles only around 20% is built-up. Oslo has an underground railway and a suburban railway system.

★Capital of Norway

Oslo is the seat of government and the chief town of the two counties of Oslo and Akershus, the see of a Lutheran and (since 1953) a Roman Catholic bishop, and a university town, with two universities and several other higher educational institutions. The modern university at Blindern in the north offers tuition in most subjects. It has numerous cultural institutions, including museums, libraries, theatres and Norway's only opera house.

Importance

Oslo is Norway's most important port, the base of many shipping lines, with a large merchant fleet and shipyards. Its principal industries, in addition to shipbuilding, are electrical engineering, printing and publishing, foodstuffs and clothing manufacture.

★Port; industry

Oslo, the oldest Scandinavian capital, is thought to have been founded in 1050 by King Harald Hårdråde, but it is likely that there was already a landing-place for ships and a small settlement on the site. Harald's son,

History

View of Oslo from Holmenkollen

Holmenkollen Blindern (University)

Sørkedalsveien

Parkveien

Kirkeveien

Suhms gate

Pilestredet

MAJORSTUEN

Middelthuns gate

Sørgenfrigata

Fagerborg
Church

Sten
Park

Vigeland
Sculpture
Park

Frogner
Park

Kirkeveien

Neuberggata

Bogstadveien

Rosenborg

Amaldus
Nielsens
plass

Professor Dahls gate

THOMAS
BYEN

Municipal Museum

Halvdan Svartes gate

Vigeland-
Museum

Niels Juels gate

Nobels gate

Gimle

Frognerveien

Eckersbergs gate

Oscars gate

FROGNER

Uranienborg
Church

Riddervolds
plass

Parkveien

Slottparken

Nord

Palace

Carl Johan

Elisenbergveien

Bygdøy allé

Frognerveien

Bygdøy allé

Colbjørnsens gate

Nobel
Institute

Drammensveien

Thomas Heftyes gate

SKILLEBEKK

Drammensveien

Niels Juels gate

Drammensveien

Solli
plass

Observatoriet terrasse

University
Library

Observatory

Olaf
Bulls
plass

Munkedamsveien

Vestb.-
plassen

Dokkveien

Aker
Brygge

Frognerstranda

Frognerkilen

Filipstadveien

Piperv.

BYGDØY

Shipping
Museum

Oslofjord

© *Baedeker*

Henie-Onstad Art Centre
Airport, Trade Fair, Bygdøy, Drammen

Museum of Technology

Lilleborg-Kirche

Oslo

400m

St. Hans-

Haugen

Sannergata

Thorvald Meyers gate

St Paul Church

Seilduksgata

Falck Ytters plass

Old Aker Church

Helgesens gate

Gruners gate

Helgesens gate

Sofienberggata

Sofienberggata

Riks-Hospitalet

Vår Frelsers Gravlund

Nordre gate

Thorvald Meyers gate

Rathkes gate

Sverdrups gate

Museum of Applied Art

St. Olav

St James

Trondheimsveien

Munch Museum
Botanic Garden

Histor. Museum

Trinity Church

Deichman Library

Torggata

Rudolf Nilsens plass

National Gallery

Henrik Ibsens gate

Government Buildings

Youngs torget

Ting hus

Opera House

Brugata

Storting (Parlament)

Stortorget

Cathedral

Steners gate

Grenland

Grenlands

Bus Station

Greenland Church

Central Station

Custom House

Exchange

Akershus Festning

Bjørvika

Bispegata

Lade-gård

Bispegata

Trondheim

Festnings-plassen

Military Museum

Bispe-vika

Moss

Olav Kyrre, made the town the see of a bishop and built a cathedral, and thereafter Oslo remained for centuries Norway's religious centre, while the kings resided in Bergen. Around 1300, however, Håkon V moved his capital from Bergen to Oslo and began to build the stronghold of Akershus. About the same time the Hanseatic League established a trading station in Oslo. This period of prosperity came to an end when plague wiped out a third of Norway's population in 1349. Then in 1397 Norway came under Danish rule, and Oslo declined steadily in importance. After a great fire in 1624 Christian IV rebuilt the town on the north side of Akershus Castle and renamed it Christiania. It was only after the separation of Norway from Denmark in 1814 that Christiania again became the capital of Norway and the residence of the king; and during the reign of King Carl XIV Johan it enjoyed a new rise to prosperity. In 1925 the town reverted to its old name of Oslo.

Central Area

Karl Johansgate and district

Central Station

Oslo's main shopping and business street is Karl Johansgate (partly pedestrianised), which runs north-west from the Central Station (Sentralbanestasjonen) to the Royal Palace. South-east of the station, at Oslogate 13, is the Ladegård, a Baroque building (1725) which was restored between 1957 and 1968.

Stortorget

Half way between the station and Eidsvollplass, to the right, is the old market square, Stortorget, originally laid out in the late 17th century. In the centre of the square can be seen a statue of Christian IV (by C. L. Jacobsen, 1874).

Cathedral

On the south-east side of Stortorget is the Cathedral (consecrated 1697). The tower was rebuilt in 1849–50 by Alexis de Châteauneuf, a Hamburg architect, and the interior was renovated in 1948–50 under the direction of Arnstein Arneberg. The main doorway has bronze doors decorated with reliefs (1938). Notable features of the interior are the ceiling paintings (by H. L. Mohr, 1936–50; "God the Father, the Son and the Holy Ghost"), the Baroque pulpit and altar (c. 1699), the organ-case (1727) and the stained glass by Emanuel Vigeland (1910–16). In the octagonal Chapel of the Redeemer (built on to the Cathedral in 1949–50) is a sculpture in silver by Arrigo Minerbi, "The Last Supper".

Bazaar Halls

Behind the Cathedral, along the old church walls, are the Bazaar Halls (1841–42, enlarged 1858), now occupied by craftsmen, antique-dealers and greengrocers.

Egertorget

The busiest part of Karl Johansgate begins to the south of Stortorget. To the west is Egertorget, an important junction point on the city's underground system (T-Banen).

Storting

Beyond the intersection of Karl Johansgate with Akersgate, on the left, is the Parliament Building (Storting; 1861–66). In the Chamber is a large picture by O. Wergeland of the constitutional assembly at Eidsvoll in 1814.

To the south of the Parliament Building, in Akersgate, can be seen a monument to the poet J. H. Wessel (1742–85). Opposite it is the Freemasons' Lodge.

In Eidsvollplass, adjoining the Parliament Building, is a statue (by Bergslien) of the poet Henrik Wergland (1808–45). A short distance away lies the Studenterlund, originally a park with a bandstand, now the haunt of street musicians, with stalls selling a variety of wares and beer-gardens.

Oslo Town Hall

In Rosenkrantzgate (No. 10), which crosses Karl Johansgate at this point, is the Nye Teater (New Theatre: modern plays, revues, etc.), which opened in 1929 with a performance of Knut Hamsun's play "At the Gates of the Kingdom".

Nye Teater

North-west of Eidsvollplass is the National Theatre, a Neo-Classical building designed by H. Bull (1895–99). The interior is partly in Art Nouveau style, with fine ceiling paintings in the auditorium. In front of the building are bronze statues (by S. Sinding) of Ibsen and Bjørnson; to the rear is a statue of the actor J. Brun.

National Theatre

North-east of the National Theatre, in the gardens on Karl Johansgate, is a statue of the playwright Ludvig Holberg, a native of Bergen, who created the Danish-Norwegian comedy.

A little way south of the National Theatre, in Fridtjof Nansensplass, stands the monumental Town Hall (Rådhus; 1931–50), one of the city's great landmarks. This massive four-square building, built of concrete faced with brick, was designed by Arnstein Arneberg and Magnus Poulson. It has two towers; in the one to the east is a carillon of 38 bells. The façade is decorated with sculpture and reliefs. The interior has rich fresco decoration by Henrik Sørensen, Per Krohg, Edvard Munch and other artists.

★Town Hall

Behind the Town Hall is the landing-stage from which boats leave for Bygdøy and various islands in the fjord and also for cruises.

South-west of the landing-stage, on the west side of the Pipervika dock, is the Aker Brygge, a shopping and cultural centre in the former Aker shipyard (restored), with numerous restaurants.

★Aker Brygge

Near here is the old West Station, in which the Norwegian Information Centre was established in 1991. Art and other exhibitions are also held here.

North-east of the National Theatre, on the other side of Karl Johansgate, is the University, founded by Frederick VI of Denmark in 1811 and built

Old University

between 1839 and 1854. The new University buildings are in the north-western district of Blindern, and the old building is now mainly occupied by the Faculty of Law. In front of the central block are statues of the legal scholar A. M. Schweigaard (1808–70; on left) and the historian P. A. Munch (1810–63).

The Great Hall (1911) has paintings by Edvard Munch (1926).

Norske Teater

To the east of the University, in Kristian IVs Gate, is the Norske Teater, Oslo's largest theatre, famed for its musicals and productions of modern works by Norwegian and foreign playwrights.

Museums

★National Gallery

Opening times:
Mon. and Wed.–
Sat. 10am–4pm,
Sun. 11am–3pm

In Universitetsgate (No. 13), which flanks the east side of the University, is the National Gallery (Nasjonalgalleriet; built 1879–81, with extensions in 1907 and 1924), which displays mainly works by Norwegian painters from the 19th century to the present day. Among the artists represented are J. C. Dahl (1788–1857), T. Fearnley (1802–42), H. F. Gude (1825–1903), H. O. Heyerdahl (1857–1913), C. Krohg (1852–1925), G. P. Munthe (1849–1929), E. Peterssen (1852–1928) and A. Tidemand (1814–76). A special room is devoted to Edvard Munch. There are also works by Danish and Swedish artists, pictures by El Greco, Rubens and Rembrandt and a collection of paintings by modern French artists (Cézanne, Degas, Gauguin, Manet and Matisse), as well as a room containing casts of antique sculpture.

★Historical
Museum

Opening times:
Tues.–Sun. 11am
or noon to 3pm

Beyond the National Gallery (entrance at Frederiksgate 2) is the Historical Museum (1903), which contains the University's historical and ethnographic collections. Among the Nordic antiquities the rich collection of material on the Viking age (c. 800–1050) is particularly noteworthy. There are also a collection of material on the Eskimo and Siberian peoples and a coin cabinet.

Royal Palace

Royal Palace

At the north-west end of Karl Johansgate, on higher ground, stands the Royal Palace (Det Kongelige Slott), a long building erected between 1825 and 1848 (not open to the public). In front of the palace is an equestrian statue (by B. Bergslien, 1875) of King Carl XIV Johan. In the park surrounding the palace, near Karl Johansgate, can be seen a monument (by G. Vigeland) to the mathematician N. H. Abel (1802–29), and behind the palace, to the right, is a statue, also by Vigeland, of the woman writer Camilla Collett (1813–95).

Nobel Institute

Along the south side of the park runs Drammensveien, and at its intersection with Parkveien, to the right, is the Norwegian Nobel Institute. The Nobel Peace Prize is presented annually on December 10th in the Great Hall of the University to a person selected by the Norwegian Nobel Committee from among names put forward by parliamentarians from all over the world.

City Centre – North

Trinity Church

From the Storting Akersgate leads north-east past the modern Government Buildings (1957–59; Nos. 42–44) to the Trinity Church (Trefoldighetskirke; 1853–58), a Neo-Gothic brick building. Notable features of the interior are the stained glass (by F. Haavardsholm) in the choir, the altar, with a painting of the Baptism of Christ, and the fine organ-case.

Beyond the church, to the east, are the Deichman Library (the Municipal Library, with some 850,000 volumes) and the Swedish Margaretakirke (1926). To the south-east, in Youngstorg, is the Norske Opera (1958).

At the north end of Akersgate is St Olav's Church (1853; R.C.). Opposite the church, at St. Olavsgate 1, is the Museum of Applied Art (Kunstindustrimuseet), which gives an excellent survey of the development of the applied and decorative arts in Norway (tapestries, including the fine Baldishol Tapestry of about 1180 from Baldishol church in Hedmark county; metalwork, glass, furniture, etc.). Associated with the Museum is a School of Arts and Crafts.

Museum of Applied Art

Opening times: Tues.–Fri. 11am–3pm, Sat. and Sun. noon to 4pm

Farther north, between Ullevålsveien and Akersveien, is the Cemetery of Our Saviour (Vor Frelsers Gravlund), with the graves of Bjørnson and Ibsen, the painter H. F. Gude and the poet Henrik Wergeland.

Cemetery of Our Saviour

At the north end of Akersveien is Old Aker Church (Gamle Akerskirke), a basilican church in Anglo-Norman style which first appears in the records before 1150 and may have been founded by Olav Kyrre (restored 1861).

Old Aker Church

To the north of the cemetery, between Ullevålsveien and Geitmyrsveien, lies the beautiful park of St. Hanshaugen (concerts in summer).

City Centre – South

In the old part of the town to the south of the Storting and Karl Johansgate are the head offices of large banks and business houses. South-west of the Central Station is the Exchange (1827; enlarged 1910).

Farther west, in Bankplass, a large granite building in Norwegian Art Nouveau style (by I. O. Hjort, 1902), originally the head office of the Norwegian National Bank, now houses the National Museum of Contemporary Art (Museet for Samtidskunst), opened in 1990. The museum displays works by modern Norwegian and international artists from the end of the Second World War to the present day (periodic special exhibitions, covering particular fields or particular periods; travelling exhibitions). The museum has a total exhibition area of 4000sq.m/43,000sq.ft, on three floors; cafeteria.

★National Museum of Contemporary Art

Opening times: Tues.–Fri. 11am–7pm, Sat. and Sun. 11am–4pm

To the west of this part of the town, rising above the Oslofjord on the promontory of Akersnes, is Akershus Castle, begun by Håkon V at the end of the 13th century. In the reign of Christian IV the medieval stronghold was converted into a Renaissance castle and the fortifications were extended. The entrance, in Festningsplass, leads up to the Castle proper, now used for government receptions and other functions. Visitors are shown various rooms, including Christian IV's Hall and the chapel, with the tomb of Håkon VII (1872–1957) in the crypt.

★Akershus Castle

Within the castle is the Museum of the Norwegian Resistance (Norges Hjemmefrontmuseum), illustrating the activities of the Norwegian resistance during the Second World War. There is a monument commemorating the resistance fighters who were executed in Akershus.

Museum of the Resistance

In the old Arsenal in Nedre Akershus is the Military Museum, with displays of weapons and other exhibits illustrating the history of the Norwegian forces and the defence of Norway down the centuries.

Military Museum

Frognerpark (Vigelandpark)

To the north-west of the city, reached by way of Drammensveien and Frognerveien, lies the beautiful Frognerpark, also known as the Vigelandpark. The main entrance, with a wrought-iron gate, is in Kirkeveien. Within the park are several restaurants and a very popular open-air swimming pool.

The Monolith and other sculpture by Vigeland in the Frognerpark

Norwegian Folk Museum: a house from Setesdal . . .

The principal attraction in the Frognerpark is the Vigeland Sculpture Park, an extraordinary assemblage of sculpture by Gustav Vigeland (see Vigeland Museum, below). Extending for some 600m/660yd are a total of no fewer than 650 individual sculptures, on which Vigeland worked for forty years. The Vigeland Bridge alone is flanked by 58 bronze groups, and under the bridge are sculptures of children. The oldest item is the fountain group, depicting the cycle of human life. Beyond this can be seen the 17m/55ft high Monolith, with 121 intertwined human bodies. At the far end is the Wheel of Life (1933–34; erected after Vigeland's death), consisting of seven linked human bodies. To the north stands a monument erected in 1987, Slekten ("The Family").

★Vigeland
Sculpture Park

The Municipal Museum (Oslo Bymuseum; open in summer), housed in an old mansion, the Frogner Hovedgård, offers a survey of the history of Oslo from the 13th century to the present day, including transport and housing conditions.

Municipal
Museum

South-west of the Municipal Museum, beyond Halvdan Svartesgate, is the studio of the Norwegian sculptor Gustav Vigeland (1869–1943), now a museum. In the tower is an urn containing Vigeland's ashes.

Vigeland Museum

Near the Frognerpark, in front of the Colosseum cinema (Fridtjof Nansensveien 6), can be seen a bronze statue of Charlie Chaplin (by Nils Aas, 1976).

Eastern and Northern Districts

On the eastern outskirts of the city is the Botanic Garden (Botanisk Have; entrance in Trondheimsveien), with a great variety of trees and shrubs, flowers and useful plants. It includes a museum containing large herbaria.
 On the hill above the Botanic Garden are the Zoological Museum, the Museum of Mineralogy and Geology and the Palaeontological Museum.

Botanic Garden
Museums

. . . and the stave church from Gol in the Hallingdal (detail)

349

Oslo

★★Munch Museum

Opening times:
Mon. or Tues.
to Sat.
10am to 4 or 6pm,
Sun. noon to 6pm

On the south side of the Botanic Garden, at Tøyengate 53, the Munch Museum has a collection of paintings, graphic art, drawings, watercolours and sculpture by Edvard Munch (1863–1944), Norway's greatest painter, representing almost all the different phases of his art. Characteristic features of Munch's work are fantasies of life and death, Nordic melancholy and a mystical feeling for nature. The museum puts on special exhibitions devoted to particular aspects of the artist's work, and also participates in exhibitions of Munch's work in Norway and abroad. Attached to the museum are rooms for study and research and a restoration department. Other events (concerts, etc.) are organised from time to time. In the inner courtyard of the museum is a sculpture by Naum Gabo.

Museum of Technology

In the north of the city, at Kjelsåsveien 143, is the Norwegian Museum of Technology and Industry (telecommunications, transport, etc.). There are numerous press-button working models and apparatus which visitors can try out for themselves.

★★ Bygdøy

To the west of Oslo (6km/4 miles by road; motorboats from Rådhusplass) lies the Bygdøy peninsula, with the Folk Museum, the Viking ships and other attractions. Bathing beaches.

★Norwegian Folk Museum

The Norwegian Folk Museum (Norsk Folkemuseum) consists of a number of different buildings. The main building contains collections of everyday objects, silver, carpets, furniture, etc., together with a Lapp Exhibition (costumes, tents and equipment for reindeer herding, hunting and fishing). In the same building is Ibsen's study from his house in Oslo. Visitors can take an interesting walk through the Old Town (Gamle Byen) with its medieval houses; Pharmacy Museum (mortars and herbaria of 1857).

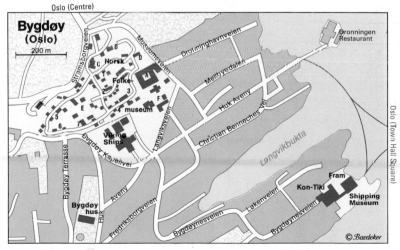

Norsk Folkemuseum

A	Main building (furniture, etc.)
B	Gol stave church
C	Restaurant
D	Theatre
E	Square
F	Gamle Byen (old town houses)

Norwegian Folk Museum

PEASANT HOUSES	
1 Østerdal	4 Hallingdal
2 Numedal	5 Vestland
3 Telemark	6 Jæren
	7 Østland

There is also a large open-air museum, with old wooden buildings, arranged according to the part of Norway from which they come. Of particular interest are the stave church (*c.* 1200) from Gol in the Hallingdal, brought here in 1885, and the Raulandstue (*c.* 1300) from the Numedal.

To the south of the Folk Museum is the Vikingskiphus, a large hall specially built to house three Viking ships, seaworthy vessels of the 9th century. Boats of this kind were used by the Vikings on their long sea voyages and also for the burial of their chieftains.

★Viking Ships Museum

The Oseberg Ship (21.50m/70ft long and just over 5m/16ft wide), discovered north of Tønsberg in 1904, is the largest and finest pre-Christian object found in the northern countries. Built about 800, it was the state barge of the chieftain's wife, Åsa, and was used for her burial about 850. Of particular interest are the rich grave goods found in the ship.

Oseberg Ship

The Gokstad Ship (23.30m/76ft long by 5.24m/17ft wide), found at Gokstad in 1880, was also used for a burial; unlike the Oseberg Ship, it was a seagoing vessel, and accordingly was less richly decorated. It was designed for use either under sail or with oars; the warriors' shields would be hung along the thwarts. An exact replica of this ship sailed to America in six weeks in 1893.

Gokstad Ship

The Tune Ship, found in 1867 some 10km/6 miles above Fredrikstad, is the most poorly preserved of the three, only part of the ship's bottom having survived.

Tune Ship

On the south-east side of Bygdøy (at the landing-stage used by the motor-boats) can be found the Fram Museum, containing the famous vessel in which Nansen sailed to the Arctic in 1893–96. Here too is the Shipping Museum. In front of it is the "Gjøa", in which Amundsen sailed through the North-West Passage in 1903–06.

★Fram Museum

Shipping Museum

In the Viking Ships Museum

Oslo

★ Kon-Tiki Museum

In an adjoining building is the balsa-wood raft "Kon-Tiki" in which the Norwegian anthropologist Thor Heyerdahl and five companions sailed from the Peruvian port of Callao to Eastern Polynesia (April 28th to August 7th 1947). Here too are a 9.50m/30ft high figure from Easter Island, prehistoric boats, an underwater exhibition and an Easter Island family cave, as well as the 14m/46ft long papyrus boat "Ra II" in which Heyerdahl and a crew of men from eight nations crossed the Atlantic in 1970.

Surroundings

Ekeberg

3km/2 miles south-east of the city centre rises the Ekeberg, with Ekeberg Park (riding school, camping site, restaurant) and the former Nautical College, in the entrance hall of which are frescos (signs of the Zodiac) by Per Krohg. From the terrace of the College there are fine views of Oslo harbour and the fjord. Between the College and Kongsveien is an area containing a number of 5000-year-old rock carvings (*helleristninger*), with thirteen figures, mostly of elks. From a viewpoint below the camping site can be seen the remains of the old settlement of Oslo, including part of the royal stronghold (Kongsgården) and St Hallvard's Church.

★ Holmenkollen

A pleasant excursion from Oslo is to Holmenkollen (371m/1217ft), the wooded range of hills north-west of the city, which attracts large numbers of visitors for the sake of the views it offers. Holmenkollen is part of the Nordmarka, in winter Oslo's favourite skiing area. There is a good road to Frognerseteren (13km/8 miles) and Tryvannstårn (lookout tower); also reached by the city's T-Bane from the National Theatre and the Storting (35 minutes).

By car, Holmenkollen is best reached by leaving Oslo on Drammensveien, turning right into Frognerveien, continuing alongside Frognerpark on Kirkeveien and then turning left at the junction with Valkyriegate. After running parallel with the Holmenkollen railway for some time the road bears right and winds its way up through the forest, passing many villas.

Ski-jump

11km/7 miles from the city centre the towering Holmenkollen ski-jump is seen on the left (access road). There is a lift up the tower; on the platform are a restaurant and a Skiing Museum (skiers and skiing equipment, including some of the equipment used by Nansen and Amundsen in the Arctic). In front of the museum can be seen a statue of Nansen.

★ View

The road continues uphill, passing a small chapel, 1km/¾ mile from the ski-jump Voksenkollvelen goes off on the left, and another kilometre along this road is a viewpoint (479m/1572ft) with an orientation table and a bronze statue of Hans Krag, the engineer in charge of the construction of the road. From Voksenkollen it is 10 minutes to the Tryvannshögda.

Tryvannstårn

1km/¾ mile beyond the turn-off for Voksenkollen the main road comes to the popular Frognerseteren restaurant (alt. 437m/1434ft), from which there is a magnificent view of Oslo. Opposite the restaurant are a number of old wooden buildings from Telemark and the Hallingdal. From here it is a 20–25 minutes' walk north-west to the Tryvannshögda (529m/1736ft), with a lookout tower 118.50m/389ft high, the Tryvannstårn (1962; lift), from which there are panoramic views.

Grefsenkollen

Another possible excursion from Oslo (9km/5½ miles) is to Grefsenkollen (364m/1194ft), north-east of the city. From the summit of the hill there are superb views of Oslo and the Oslofjord (viewpoint restaurant).

★ Henie-Onstad Art Centre

12km/7½ miles south-west of the city centre on E 18, on Høvikodden, is the Henie-Onstad Art Centre (1966–68), founded by Sonja Henie and Niels Onstad, with Norway's largest collection of international art, including works by Matisse, Miró and Picasso. The cups won by the champion skater Sonja Henie (1912–69) are displayed in one of the rooms. There are rooms used for various cultural events (theatrical performances, concerts, etc.).

Holmenkollen ski-jump

Oslofjord   C 5/6

Country: **Norway**
Region: Southern Norway

The Oslofjord, extending more than 100km/60 miles northward from the
Skagerrak to the Norwegian capital, is made up of a series of narrow straits
and wider basins. Along its rocky shores, of moderate height, are many
little towns and settlements. The western shore of the fjord was one of the
earliest areas of settlement, but the trim towns on the west side can also
look back on a long tradition. The first settlers here, coming by boat,
established themselves around 10,000 years ago, at the end of the last ice
age, and thereafter followed the retreating ice ever farther inland. In addition to farming and forestry there has been a lively development of industry, and the coastal towns are the home ports of a large merchant fleet.

Situation and
characteristics

West Side of the Fjord

From Oslo the motorway runs south-west by way of Sandvika, at the mouth
of the Sandvikelv, and after passing the old church of Tanum and Skaugum,
traditionally the residence of the Crown Prince, reaches Drammen (pop.
52,000), chief town of Buskerud county, situated at the mouth of the Drammenselv, a river with an abundance of water which here flows into the
Drammensfjord. The town has considerable industry and is an important
port, shipping timber, cellulose and paper; it is also the country's principal
port for the import of motor vehicles.

Drammen

In the market square (Bragernes Torg) is the attractive modern St Hallvard's Fountain. In the Bragernes district are a church of 1877 – a prominent
landmark – and the Town Hall (1872), which in 1986 was awarded the

Europa Nostra Prize for a particularly successful restoration. From here a toll road runs up in a spiral tunnel 1700m/1850yd long (six turns with a radius of 35m/115ft and a gradient of 10%) to the summit of Bragernesåsen (293m/960ft; fine views; Åspaviljongen summer restaurant). To the north-east lies the lonely forest lake of Klopptjern (alt. 218m/715ft).

In the Stromsø district on the south bank of the Drammenselv is the Drammen Museum (history of the town and of Buskerud county). Attached to the museum is the 18th century farmhouse of Marienlyst. There is a church of 1667, rebuilt in Empire style in 1840.

Sande
Holmestrand

Beyond Drammen there are two routes – either on a road hugging the coast of the Drammensfjord or on the main road running inland – to Sande, on the Sandebukt. From here the road continues down the west side of the Sandebukt to Holmestrand (pop. 9000), which has an aluminium plant. The church (1674), on a Y-shaped plan, has stained glass by Per Vigeland (1957). Also of interest is the Holmestrand Museum (history of the town; ships and the sea, etc.).

Horten

The first place on the Oslofjord proper is the port of Horten (pop. 22,000), with Karl Johansvern (Naval Museum), the main base of the Norwegian navy from 1940 until the end of the Second World War. In front of the museum is the "Rapp" (1872), the oldest torpedo boat in the world. The Preus Museum of Photography at Langgate 82 is the only one of its kind in Norway. From Horten there is a car ferry (45 minutes) to Moss, on the east side of the fjord.

Borre church
Royal tombs

Near here are the medieval church of Borre, with a fine Baroque interior, and a cemetery area with the largest group of royal tombs in northern Europe, Ynglingeætten: six large burial mounds up to 6.50m/21ft high and twenty-one smaller ones.

Åsgårdstrand

South-east of Horten, on the shores of the fjord, is the well-known seaside resort of Åsgårdstrand, where the painter Edvard Munch lived for several years (memorial museum in "Munchs Lille Hus", Munch's Little House) and where among other things he painted the famous "Girl on the Bridge".

Tønsberg

Farther south, at the north end of the narrow Tønsbergfjord, is Tønsberg (pop. 31,000). Norway's oldest town, founded by Harald Fairhair in 871, Tønsberg is now chief town of Vestfold county, with a considerable merchant fleet and a Nautical College. The whaling ships sailed from here until 1951, when whaling ceased for reasons of conservation. At the near end of the town, on left, stands a monument to the Polar explorer Roald Amundsen (1872–1928), who reached the South Pole in 1911, flew over the North Pole in a semi-rigid airship in 1926 and was lost on a flight to Spitzbergen in 1928. To the west of the town is the rocky Slottsfjell (Castle Hill; 63m/206ft), with a lookout tower and the foundations of the old Tønsberghus, a castle built in 1150 by Håkon Håkonsson and enlarged by Magnus Lagabøter, who wrote Norway's first code of laws here between 1263 and 1280. From the top of the hill there is a fine view of the harbour. Other features of interest are the Vestfold County Museum, on the road to Larvik, with an Arctic section (whaling); the Cathedral (1858), with the Minnepark (mosaics by Per Vigeland and sculpture by Gustav Vigeland); and St Olav's Church, the largest round church in the Nordic countries.

A minor road runs south to the long straggling islands of Nøtterøy and Tjørne, which lie between the Tønsbergfjord and the Oslofjord, linked by a large bridge; beautiful bathing beaches. Offshore is the Lille Ferder lighthouse (1923).

Sandefjord

To the south-east, off the main road, is Sandefjord (pop. 35,000), on the fjord of that name. A former whaling port, it is now a seaside resort, with a

Skerries in the Oslofjord ▶

Whaling Museum and a Seafaring Museum. On the harbour, which is the base of a modern merchant fleet, can be seen a monument to the whalers by Knut Steen. Good bathing and sailing. At the south end of the island of Østerøy is a beacon, the Tønsberg Tønne. To the east of Sandefjord is the Gokstad mound, under which the Gokstad Ship (now in the Viking Ships Museum in Oslo) was found in 1880.

Larvik

South-west of Sandefjord, at the north end of the Larviksfjord, lies the town of Larvik (see entry). South of this is the seaside resort of Stavern (see Larvik, Surroundings), with the old coastal stronghold of Frederiksvern, built by King Frederick V in 1760 as a naval base (Citadel on the island of Citadelløy). Nearby are the smaller resorts of Helgeroa and Nevlunghamn.

East Side of the Fjord

Drøbak

The road from Oslo leads down the east side of the fjord to the attractive seaside resort of Drøbak in Østfold county, lying off the main road, with a handsome wooden church (1736), the Treegaarden Julehus ("Christmas House") and the castle of Oscarsborg in the Oslofjord, where the German heavy cruiser "Blücher" was sunk in April 1940.

Moss

Farther south is the town of Moss (pop. 25,000), on the Mossesund, which separates the island of Jeløy (Alby manor-house, with the F 15 Gallery) from the mainland (bridge). The treaty of union between Norway and Sweden was signed at Moss in 1814. Car ferry (45 minutes) to Horten, on the west side of the Oslofjord. To the south, on the shores of the fjord, is the seaside resort of Larkollen.

Sarpsborg

The main road continues to Sarpsborg (pop. 12,000), originally founded by St Olav in the 11th century. It is now a busy industrial town (papermaking, cellulose, electrical engineering). Borgarsyssel Open-Air Museum (old houses, pastor's house of 1660, ruined church of St Nicholas, built by King Øystein in the 12th century); beautiful Kulås Park (Iron Age burial mound).

Fredrikstad

A secondary road (No. 109) runs south-west to the commercial and industrial town of Fredrikstad (see entry), at the mouth of the Glåma.

To the west of Vikene there is a ferry to the island of Hankø (beautiful coniferous forest), now a popular holiday resort, with a sailing school.

Oldtidsveien
★ Rock carvings

Between Fredrikstad and Skjeberg (pop. 13,500) runs the "Prehistoric Trail" (Oldtidsveien), along which are a series of prehistoric remains: rock carvings at Solberg (human figures, solar symbols, ships) and Hornnes (ships with animals' heads on the prow), 200 burial mounds at Store Dal Felt and rock carvings at Begby, including solar symbols, human figures, animals, and men with swords and phalluses (Bronze Age).

Halden

2km/1¼ miles before the Swedish frontier a road branches off on the left to Halden (pop. 26,000). The town, known from 1665 to 1927 as Frederikshald, withstood several attacks by the Swedes and after suffering severe damage in a fire was rebuilt on a regular plan in 1826. It has a variety of industries, including particularly woodworking, and is an important centre of the timber trade in eastern Norway.

Fredriksten

On the high ground to the east of Halden stands the fortress of Fredriksten (alt. 113m/370ft; fine views), built in 1661–71. An iron pyramid (erected 1860) commemorates King Charles XII of Sweden, who was killed during the siege of the town in 1718. Here too is the Municipal Museum (Haldens Minner).

Halden has a theatre in the manor-house of Rø (1830), with a Baroque stage. On the east side of the town is the Atomic Energy Institute, with a reactor which came into service in 1959.

Rock carvings, Solberg

Östersund

D 4

Country: **Sweden**
Province: Jämtland
Altitude: 292m/960ft
Population: 57,000
Post code: S–831.. Telephone code: 063

Östersund, the only town of some size in Jämtland (see entry), is the economic and cultural centre of the province. The town, rising in terraces above the eastern shore of the Storsjö, was founded by Gustavus III in 1786, and still preserves its original rectangular street plan. In the lake, opposite the town, lies the hilly island of Frösö. — Situation and characteristics

In Rådhusgatan, the town's main street, stands the Town Hall (by F. B. Wallberg, 1912). Diagonally opposite it are the Municipal Museum and the Old Church (1846). The New Church (by L. I. Wahlman, 1940) has fine frescos by H. Linnqvist in the choir. Parallel with Rådhusgatan to the west is Storgatan, lined by 19th century houses. — Town

In the north of the town is the Jämtland County Museum (by F. B. Wallberg, 1928–30), with a collection of material on the history and culture of the province (tapestry from Överhögdal). To the north-west is an open-air museum, Fornbyn Jämtli, with old wooden houses from Jämtland and Härjedalen. — Museums

Surroundings

In the Storsjö (area 448sq.km/175sq. miles; greatest depth 74m/240ft) is the fertile island of Frösö. At the old Frösö bridge can be seen an 11th century — ★Storsjö Frösö

357

Church on the Storsjö

runic stone. From the Östberg (468m/1536ft) there are fine views of the lake and the extensive forests on the island. 7km/4½ miles west of the bridge is a church, rebuilt in 1898, the earliest parts of which date from the 12th century, with a separate belfry. In the churchyard is the grave of the composer W. Petersen-Berger, whose country house, Sommarhagen, is nearby. 1km/¾ mile west of the church is the farm of Stocke, with the Stocketitt, a lookout tower with a view reaching to the mountains on the Norwegian frontier. An old steamer, the "Thomée", plies on the Storsjö. Legend has it that a monster, the Storsjöodjur, lives in the lake.

Andersö

There is a car ferry from Frösö to the island of Andersö, which – like Skansholmen and Isö – is a nature reserve. There are remains of 17th century fortifications on the island.

On the shores of the lake opposite the island can be seen the church of Sunne, with remains of a fortress built by King Sverre in 1178 after defeating the men of Jämtland in a battle on the frozen Storsjö.

Brunflo church

To the south of Östersund is the 18th century church of Brunflo, with a belfry which was originally a defensive tower.

Hackås church

The church of Hackås, 40km/25 miles south-east of Östersund, has 13th century paintings.

Oulu (Uleåborg)   F 3

Country: **Finland**
Region: Northern Finland
Population: 100,000
Post code: FIN–90100.   Telephone code: 981

Oulu (Swedish Uleåborg), chief town of Oulu province and the see of a bishop, lies near the north end of the Gulf of Bothnia at the mouth of the Oulujoki. It has a University, founded in 1959. In spring there are numerous sporting events (skiing competitions, etc.) in the Oulu area.

Situation and characteristics

Towards the end of the 16th century King John III of Sweden built a castle (Finnish *linna*) on the island of Linnansaari at the mouth of the river, and the town grew up on this island, receiving its municipal charter in 1610. In 1822 it was almost completely destroyed by fire, and thereafter was rebuilt in accordance with a plan prepared by Johan Albrecht Ehrenström. During the 19th century the trade in tar flourished, and the town prospered accordingly.

History

At the north end of the busy Kirkkokatu stands the Cathedral, built in 1770–72 and, after being destroyed by fire in 1822, rebuilt in 1828–32; the interior was renovated and redecorated with paintings in 1932. To the left of the entrance a monument (by Wäinö Aaltonen) commemorates those who fell in the fight for liberation in 1918. In the gardens in front of the church is a bronze bust of the Finnish-Swedish bishop and poet F. M. Franzén (1772–1849), who was born in Oulu.

Town

Cathedral

On the north side of the gardens, at Linnankatu 3, are the Provincial Government Offices (Lääninhallitus; 1888).

From the north end of Kirkkokatu a small bridge leads into the beautiful Ainola Park, on an island. At the west end of the island is a handsome building (1930) which houses the Municipal Library (Kirjasto) and the Provincial Museum (historical and ethnographic collections; exhibition on Lapland). In front of the building a stone commemorates the woman writer Saara Wacklin (1790–1846), a native of Oulu. Farther north is the Botanic Garden and on the island of Hupisaari a summer theatre.

Ainola Park

To the east of the Botanic Garden, beyond a small stream, is the Tietomaa Science Centre, an introduction to science for the whole family, with an

★Tietomaa Science Centre

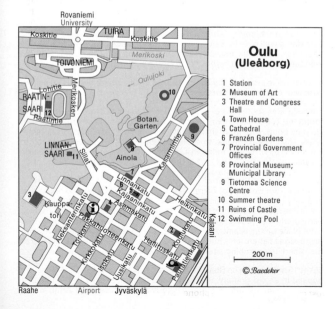

Oulu
(Uleåborg)

1 Station
2 Museum of Art
3 Theatre and Congress Hall
4 Town House
5 Cathedral
6 Franzén Gardens
7 Provincial Government Offices
8 Provincial Museum; Municipal Library
9 Tietomaa Science Centre
10 Summer theatre
11 Ruins of Castle
12 Swimming Pool

200 m

© Baedeker

observatory, a computer exhibition and a cinema showing films on science and natural history.

Town House	South-west of the Cathedral, in Hallituskatu, is the Town House (Kaupungintalo; 1894), and beyond this, in Torikatu, the old Town House, now the police headquarters. At the far end of Asemakatu is the Museum of Art.
Market Square	To the west, on the banks of the Oulujoki, lies the spacious Market Square (Kauppatori), with the Theatre and Congress Hall. There is a library nearby.
Linnansaari	To the east of the Market Square are two bridges leading on to Linnansaari (Castle Island), on which there are the scanty remains of the Castle (built 1590), which was destroyed by an explosion in 1793 (summer café). The road goes over another arm of the river to the island of Raatinsaari, with a park, stadium, indoor swimming pool and a number of high-rise blocks.
Modern residential district	Another bridge leads north on to the island of Toivoniemi, on which is a modern residential district built in the 1940s to the design of Alvar Aalto. To the east of this is a hydro-electric station powered by the Merikoski, the last of the rapids on the Oulujoki. The power station (by Aarne Ervi, 1949–57) is one of the finest examples of Finnish industrial architecture of the postwar period.
Tuira	A fourth bridge leads to the suburb of Tuira, on the north bank of the river, in which are a number of schools.
	To the north of the town, in the Puolivälinkangas district, is the Water-Tower (viewing platform).
University	Farther north, in the Linnanmaa district, is the University with a Geological and a Zoological Museum on the campus.

Surroundings

Haukipudas	20km/12½ miles north of Oulu is Haukipudas, with a wooden church of 1762 containing wall paintings by the well-known Finnish church painter Mikael Toppelius. 17km/10½ miles beyond this is the fishing village of Ii, with old wooden houses in the harbour quarter (Iin Hamina).
Ranua	A worthwhile visit is to Ranua, north-east of Olu where there is an animal park with elk, deer and reindeer.
Turkansaari open-air museum	13km/8 miles south-east of Oulu, on the left bank of the Oulujoki, can be found the Turkansaari open-air museum (which can also be reached from Oulu by boat), with more than twenty old buildings, including a church of 1694. The road continues to Muhos, with the oldest wooden church in Finland (1634). 6km/4 miles upstream is the Pyhäkoski hydro-electric power station.
Hailuoto	Off the coast, in the Gulf of Bothnia, is the island of Hailuoto (ferry in summer from Oulunsalo, 27km/17 miles south-west of Oulu). This is a flat and very young island which came into being in the medieval period as a result of a rise in the level of the land. Thanks to its beautiful sandy beaches, particularly on the west coast, it is now a very popular holiday area. The chief place on the island, Hailuoto, is a little town in traditional style, with picturesque fishermen's huts along the shore. At Marjaniemi, at the end of the island, is a camping site with holiday cabins.
Liminka	25km/15 miles south on Road 4 is Liminka, which has a Historical Museum, housed in an old granary, illustrating the traditional activities of the area (dairy farming, fishing, hunting). There is also a Museum of Art in an old school (1868).

52km/32 miles south of Liminka on Road 8 is Raahe (Swedish Brahestad;   Raahe
pop. 14,000), founded by Per Brahe in 1649. In the Pekkatori, a square
surrounded by burghers' houses, can be seen a statue of Per Brahe (a copy
of the original, which is in Turku). The town, which was rebuilt in 1810 after
a fire and preserves some houses of that period, is attractively laid out. The
Museum (opened in 1862) has a collection of material on ships and seafaring. The church has an altarpiece by the painter E. Järnefelt (1863–1937).

Pallastunturi Hills   E/F 2

Country: Finland
Region: Northern Finland

The Pallastunturi Hills – with their treeless slopes one of Finland's most   Situation and
popular skiing areas – lie in the north-west of the country, near the Swedish   characteristics
frontier, in the middle of a chain of hills extending from Yllästunturi
(740m/2428ft) in the south to Ounastunturi (738m/2421ft) in the north. The
highest point is Taivaskero (821m/2694ft); to the north-west is Laukukero
(777m/2549ft), to the east Pallaskero (646m/2120ft).

From Muonio, a trim village at the junction of the Jerisjoki with the
Muonionjoki, Road 79 runs east to Rovaniemi. 7km/4½ miles along this
road, on the right, is Olostunturi (509m/1670ft; skiing pistes), with a footpath running up to the top. 5km/3 miles beyond this, at Särkijärvi, take a
road on the left which climbs through beautiful hill scenery; then at a
junction 15km/9 miles farther on, where a road goes off on the right to
Pallasjärvi, turn left into a road which climbs in 7km/4½ miles to the
Pallastunturi Turisthotel, at the foot of Taivaskero (good skiing area; lift).
Adjoining the hotel is the National Park information centre. Here the midnight sun is visible from May 27th to July 16th.

Pallastunturi (northern Finland)

Pori

Pallastunturi-
Ounastunturi
National Park

From here a waymarked trail runs 60km/40 miles north-west (five mountain huts providing overnight accommodation) to Enontekiö, with a modern church and a silversmith's workshop. The trail passes through the Pallastunturi-Ounastunturi National Park (area 500sq.km/200sq. miles), an area typical of the barren upland regions of Lapland.

Pori (Björneborg)   F 5

Country: **Finland**
Region: South-western Finland
Population: 77,000
Post code: FIN–28100   Telephone code: 939

Situation and
characteristics

The commercial and industrial town of Pori (Swedish Björneborg) lies for the most part on the south bank of the Kokemäenjoki some 20km/12½ miles above the mouth of the river, on the Gulf of Bothnia. The town was originally farther upstream, but was moved in 1365 and again in 1558, since the mouth of the river was reaching steadily farther west due to the rise in the level of the land.

The town was granted its municipal charter in 1558 by Duke John, son of the Swedish king Gustavus Vasa. The last of a series of fires, in 1852, made it necessary to replan the town, which was now laid out around two wide avenues intersecting at right angles.

Pori's economy is centred on its fishing harbour and two commercial harbours, with some industry (woodworking, metalworking).

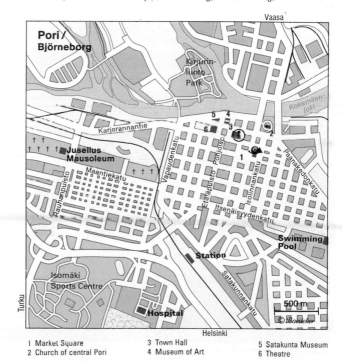

I Market Square	3 Town Hall	5 Satakunta Museum
2 Church of central Pori	4 Museum of Art	6 Theatre

The main features of interest in Pori lie at the north end of the north–south avenue, Pohjoispuisto, on the banks of the Kokemäenjoki. This part of the town has preserved its late 19th century aspect. On the east side of the avenue stands the Town Hall, in the style of a Venetian palazzo (by August Krook, 1895), originally built as the mansion of the Junnelius family.

To the west of Pohjoispuisto, at Hallituskatu 11, is the Satakunta District Museum (founded in 1888) with a large and varied collection (some 50,000 items), including material on the history of the town, objects from the surrounding area and period furniture of several centuries. The present building dates from the 1970s. Nearby are the Municipal Theatre (1884; restored in 20th c.) and the Law Courts (by C. L. Engel, 1841).

On the south bank of the river (Eteläranta) is the Museum of Art (renovated by Kristian Gullichsen, 1977–81). In addition to its permanent collection (modern painting and sculpture; Maire Gullichsen Collection) the museum puts on special exhibitions of work by Finnish and foreign artists.

To the east of Pohjoispuisto, set in gardens, stands the Neo-Gothic church of central Pori (by G. T. Chiewitz, 1863), with a 72m/246ft high tower. Altarpiece (the Resurrection) by R. W. Ekman; stained glass in choir by Magnus Enckell.
In Paanakedonkatu, which runs south-east from the church to the Tampere road, is an indoor swimming pool with a sports hall nearby.

To the west of the town centre are the Old Cemetery and beyond this the New Cemetery, with the Juselius Mausoleum (by Josef Stenbäck, 1902), built by a local industrialist, F. A. Juselius, for his daughter, who died at the age of eleven. The mausoleum was originally decorated with frescos by the well-known painter of the Finnish "National Romantic" school, Akseli Gallén-Kallela, but when these deteriorated they were replaced by

Town

Town Hall

Satakunta Museum

Museum of Art

Church

Juselius Mausoleum

Juselius Mausoleum, Pori

paintings executed by Gallén-Kallela's son Jorma, following his father's original designs.

Kirjurinluoto Park

On the north bank of the Kokemäenjoki, in the angle formed by its tributary the Luotsimäenhaara, lies Kirjurinluoto Park, with a summer theatre. The Pori Jazz Festival is held in the park annually in July – part of the Finland Festival, a programme of events (music, drama and opera), often lasting several days, which take place in various Finnish towns during the summer months.

Surroundings

★Yyteri beach

A very attractive excursion from Pori is on Road 265 to Yyteri, with its fine sandy beach, continuing to Mäntyluoto and over a causeway to the island of Reposaari. The road passes the water-tower at Kaana (café, with view). At Yyteri are a hotel, a camping site and holiday chalets. On Reposaari is a fine church in Norwegian style; on the harbour (which played an important part in the 19th century) can be seen a monument commemorating the gunboat S 2, which sank in a storm in 1927.

Ulvila

7km/4½ miles from Pori on the Helsinki road (No. 2) a road diverges to the left to Ulvila, the site of Pori from 1365 to 1558, with a church of 1429.

Harjavalta

29km/18 miles beyond the turn-off for Ulvila Road 2 comes to Harjavalta. Here, in the house and studio of the Finnish sculptor Emil Cederkreutz, is displayed a collection of his works and of early 20th century Finnish art.

Rauma

South of Pori on Road 8 is Rauma (pop. 30,000), a town with distinctive traditions of its own. Many of the inhabitants speak a special dialect which is not understood in the rest of Finland.

The town was founded in the 13th century and received its municipal charter from King Kristoffer in 1442. Around 1550 Rauma was temporarily depopulated when its inhabitants were ordered to move to the newly founded town of Helsinki, but after a few years they were allowed to return. In the 17th century Rauma developed into a busy seafaring town, and its seamen learned in foreign countries the art of making pillow lace which is still practised in the town. Every year in July there is a Lace Week in Rauma.

The layout of the old town with its wooden houses (included in the UNESCO list of world heritage monuments) dates from the 16th century, though the present buildings are mainly 18th and 19th century. In this area are the church of the Holy Cross (with 16th century wall paintings), which originally belonged to a 15th century Franciscan friary, and the ruined Trinity Church (14th c.). The old Town Hall (by C. H. R. Schröder, 1776) now houses the Municipal Museum. A 19th century burgher's house, Marela, is also a museum. There are many specialised shops in the old town.

To the south of the old town are an indoor swimming pool and a water-tower. By the tower can be seen a sculpture by Aila Salo, "Through Difficulties to Victory" (1976). To the north-west beyond the railway, is the Otanlahti recreation area, with sports facilities, a swimming pool, baths and saunas. Here too are the Poroholma camping site and the landing-stage used by the motorboats which in summer run regular cruises among the offshore islands.

Porvoo/Borgå   G 5

Country: Finland
Region: Southern Finland
Population: 20,000
Post code: FIN–06100   Telephone code: 915

Porvoo (Swedish Borgå), 50km/30 miles north-east of Helsinki, is attractively situated on the left bank of the Porvoonjoki (Borgåå), near the mouth of the river, which flows into an inlet on the Gulf of Finland. The town was founded in 1346 by the Swedish king Magnus Eriksson, and some 45% of the population are still Swedish-speaking. The town was burned down by the Danes in 1508 and by the Russians in 1708. In 1732 Porvoo became the see of a bishop. In 1809 Tsar Alexander I, who under the treaty of Frederikshamn had become Grand Duke of Finland, received the homage of the Estates here. Porvoo was the birthplace of the sculptors Walter Runeberg and Ville Vallgren and the home of a number of other artists.

Since the 1960s an important element in the town's economy has been the oil port of Sköldvik, around which many industrial plants have been established.

The old town, with its narrow winding streets and many wooden houses, is built on a hill which rises above the river at the north end of Porvoo. Here too stands the Gothic Cathedral (1414–18; renovated 1978), its white gable with red brick ornament facing the river. In the beautiful Rococo interior is a bronze statue of Tsar Alexander I by Walter Runeberg (1909), commemorating the Diet of Porvoo in 1809 at which Alexander received the homage of the Estates and guaranteed the inviolability of the Finnish constitution and religion.

South-east of the Cathedral are the belfry and a small wooden church (1740).

In a square below the Cathedral is the Municipal Museum, housed in the old Town Hall (1764). Of particular interest is the material relating to the Iris factory, which produced Art Nouveau furniture and ceramics around the turn of the century. The corner house opposite the Museum, to the east, contains a collection of sculpture by Ville Vallgren (1855–1940) and pictures by Albert Edelfelt (1854–1905).

Situation and characteristics

Town

Cathedral

Municipal Museum

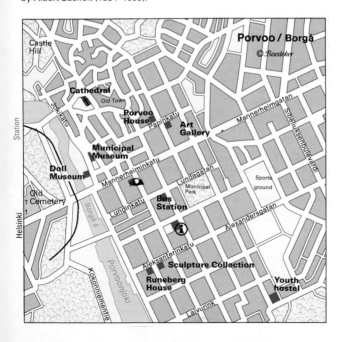

Old town, Porvoo

On the banks of the river are a series of picturesque red-painted 18th century boat-houses. Here too, at Jokikatu 14, is the Doll Museum.

Runeberg House

Some 500m/550yd south, in Runeberginkatu, can be seen a bronze statue of J. L. Runeberg, a smaller copy of the statue in Helsinki. Farther south, at the corner of Runeberginkatu and Aleksanterinkatu, is the Runeberg House, home of the poet Johan Ludvig Runeberg (1804–77), who taught in the grammar school from 1837 to 1857. In the adjoining house is the sculpture collection of Walter Runeberg, the poet's son.

Old Cemetery

In the Old Cemetery on the west bank of the Porvoonjoki, on the Helsinki road, are the graves of J. L. Runeberg and of Eugen Schauman, who shot the Russian General Bobrikov in Helsinki in 1904 and then took his own life.

Museums

To the east of the Cathedral, in Kaivokatu, is a building which houses the Natural History Museum, the Hunting and Wildlife Museum and an Art Gallery (periodic special exhibitions, particularly of contemporary art).

Yrjö A. Jäntti Art Gallery

A short distance away, in Papinkatu, is the Yrjö A. Jäntti Art Gallery, with Yrjö A. Jäntti's collection of Finnish painting, together with graphic art, drawings and woodcarving.

Surroundings

Skerries; manor-houses

To the south of the town is a charming scatter of skerries. Some 6km/4 miles south-east of Porvoo is the old manor-house of Haikko (main building converted into a hotel), with the studio of the 19th century painter Albert Edelfelt, now a museum. 10km/6 miles north-east is another old manor-house, Sannäs (1836–37; national monument), now a conference centre.

30km/19 miles east of Porvoo, just off Road 7, is Pernaja (Swedish Pernå), birthplace of the Finnish Reformer Mikael Agricola (1509–57). St Michael's Church (14th c.) has a 16th century altar from Lübeck.

5km/3 miles beyond this stands the imposing manor-house of Sarvilahti (17th and 18th c.), in a beautiful park.

5km/3 miles farther east is the little town of Loviisa (Swedish Lovisa; pop. 9000), picturesquely situated at the north end of the Lovisavik, a long inlet opening off the Gulf of Finland. The town, still mainly Swedish-speaking, was founded in 1745. It was originally called Degerby, but was renamed in 1752 in honour of Queen Luise Ulrike of Sweden, sister of Frederick the Great. In the centre of the town, now a well-known health resort, are a large Neo-Gothic church (1865) and the Town Hall (1856).

North of the town centre is a trotting course, near which is the Municipal Museum. On the outskirts of the town are the remains of old fortifications.

At Korttia, 26km/16 miles from Porvoo on the Lahti road (No. 55), can be found a group of some twenty potholes up to 10m/33ft deep, scoured out of the granite by the grinding action of pebbles swirled round by melt-water during the retreat of the glaciers in the last ice age, some 10,000 years ago.

At Mäntsälä Road 55 joins the Helsinki–Lahti motorway (E 75). 2km/ 1¼ miles south-west, at Hirvivaara, is the Sepänmäki Craft Museum, an old craftsmen's quarter with buildings and workshops preserved in their original state.

Rago National Park   D 3

Country: Norway
Region: Northern Norway

The Rago National Park, north of Bodø between E 6 and the Swedish frontier, has an area of only 171sq.km/66sq. miles. Beyond the frontier are the Swedish National Parks of Padjelanta and Sarek. The park is reached by turning off E 6 at Nordfjord, north of Fauske; cars must be left in the village of Lakshola.

This is good walking country, but there is little in the way of overnight accommodation, and walkers need to be properly equipped for the damp climate. The variety and beauty of the scenery, however, make Rago well worth a visit: nowhere else in Norway can such variety be found within such a small area.

The main artery of the National Park is the Storskog valley, through which flows the Trolldalselv. Waterfalls tumble down through the fresh green pine forests which climb up the slopes of the hills to a height of 400m/1400ft above the valley bottom. At 1000m/3300ft begins the glacier zone with its fields of snow and ice. The wooded valley is the haunt of elks, beavers and gluttons.

From Lakshola a trail runs east up the valley and then climbs gradually into the hills with their sparse growth of vegetation. Passing the only mountain hut in the National Park (overnight accommodation), the trail follows the old route into Sweden which was used by the Sami driving their reindeer from their summer to their winter grazing grounds. To the right rises the bare Ragoberg (1300m/4265ft), in which silver and lead were discovered before the First World War, but in such small quantities and in such difficult conditions that they were not worth working.

Romsdal   B/C 4/5

Country: Norway
Region: Western Norway

Situation

The Romsdal (the valley of the Rauma), one of Norway's most beautiful valleys, extends south-west from Åndalsnes, on the magnificent Romsdalsfjord, for a distance of some 60km/40 miles.

Access

The Romsdal is reached either from Åndalsnes or from the south-east through the Gudbrandsdal (see entry), from the head of which E 9 runs over the watershed between the Atlantic and the Skagerrak into the upper Romsdal. Beyond the inn at Stugaflåten, the last place in the Gudbrandsdal, the road passes from the county of Oppland into Møre og Romsdal.

Along the ★Romsdal

The road now winds its way down the Romsdal, which becomes steadily narrower, with views of the river Rauma flowing tumultuously below. At the Slettafoss it has cut a wild gorge through the rock.

Vermå

At Vermo (alt. 273m/895ft) can be seen a stone commemorating the opening of the railway in 1924. Here the line crosses the river on the Kyllingbru (76m/80yd long, 59m/195ft high). Nearby is the Vermafoss hydro-electric station.

Flatmark

A few kilometres farther on the road reaches the valley bottom, with steep hills on either side. At Flatmark (alt. 127m/417ft) the peak of Døntind (1676m/6000ft) is seen on the left.

Kors church

The church at Kors was built in 1919, incorporating masonry from the old church at Flatmark. Notable features are the reredos by Jacob Klustad, the "Master of the Acanthus", and the Renaissance pulpit.

Marstein
★Romsdalshorn

In a wider part of the valley, below the massive bulk of the Kalskråtind (1799m/5903ft), is Marstein. To the north, dominating the scene, is the

Romsdal, near Åndalsnes

View of the Trollstigvei

Romsdalshorn (1550m/5086ft); to the west are the Trolltinder (1794m/5866ft), with almost vertical rock faces which were first climbed only in 1966. The height of the mountains means that the sun does not reach down into the valley for almost five months in the year.

At the Sogge bridge the Trollstigvei ("Trolls' Road") goes off on the left and traverses the Isterdal to Valldal. It crosses the Stigfoss, continues up to the Trollstigheimen Fjellstue, on the pass, and then descends to Valldal, on the magnificent Tåfjord.

★Trollstigvei (side trip)

At the Grøtør bridge a side road branches off to Grytten church. The E 9 continues to Åndalsnes (pop. 3000), a lively tourist centre picturesquely situated on the Romsdalsfjord. The town has an important harbour and shipyards (which among other things build oil-rigs).

Åndalsnes

Rondane

C 5

Country: **Norway**
Region: Eastern Norway

The Rondane is the range of mountains lying between the Gudbrandsdal (see entry) to the west and the Atnedal to the east, 572sq.km/221sq. miles of which were declared a National Park in 1962. Although the Rondane has ten peaks over 2000m/6600ft, it is a very popular and relatively easy walking area. It is a region of dry Alpine climate and sparse vegetation, with greyish-yellow lichens covering the calcareous limestone which predominates in the Rondane.

Situation

In the Middle Ages the Rondane formed a natural barrier for peasants and merchants travelling to the important markets in the copper town of Røros

In Rondane National Park

(see entry). Numbers of ruined stone cottages bear witness to the traffic on this route and to the popularity of this area with British sportsmen in the 19th century – successors to the men of prehistoric times who hunted reindeer in this area.

Walkers will come across numbers of pits dug in Viking times to trap game.

★Rondane National Park

The natural centre of the National Park is the Rondvassbu mountain hut, where all the trails in the mountains meet. The hut – a good base for walks, either short or long, in the surrounding area – is just under an hour's walk from the western border of the park above Otta. From here the long Rondesjö runs north through the mountains. To left and right are the highest peaks in the range. The ascent of the Rondeslott ("Ronde Castle"; 2178m/7146ft) takes less than five hours for a climber of average fitness.

Around the Rondane National Park is a network of mountain huts run by the Norske Turistforening, making it possible to explore the area in convenient day trips on well marked trails.

With E 6 on the west side and Road 27 to the east, the Rondane can be easily reached from Oslo. A very popular walk with Norwegians is through the Rondane and into the Dovrefjell (see Gudbrandsdal), which lies immediately north.

Røros   C 4

Country: **Norway**
Region: Eastern Norway
Altitude: 628m/2060ft
Population: 3300. Post code: N–7460

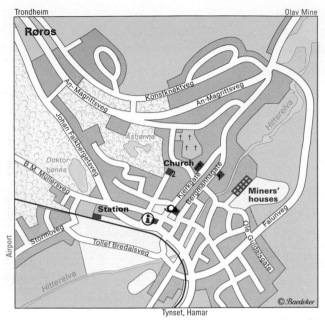

1 Copperworks Collections   2 Aasengård

The mining town of Røros, situated on both banks of the Hitterelv, was founded in 1644 after the discovery of large deposits of copper ore in the surrounding area, and during the 17th century many German miners were brought in to work here and the mines were worked until well into the 20th century. The town, now on UNESCO's World Heritage List, attracts many visitors in summer.

Situation and characteristics

The old houses of Røros, excellently restored, preserve something of the aspect of this old mining town in past centuries. In Slaggveg can be seen a row of miners' houses up to 250 years old. The more prosperous inhabitants of the town lived in the main street, Bergmannsgate. The size and furnishings of the houses give clear evidence of sharp class distinctions.

★Town

At the north end of Bergmannsgate are the Kobberverks Samlingern (Copperworks Collections), a museum illustrating the mining and processing of copper (mining equipment and implements, miners' lamps, etc.), together with the banners and weapons of the Miners' Corps. The mining company failed in the late 1970s as a result of economic difficulties.

Museum

Parallel to Bergmannsgate to the north-west is Kjerkgate, in which is the church (1784), once the only stone building in the town, with a square tower; Baroque interior. It contains a portrait of Hans Olsen Aasen (see below).

Church

In the centre of the town is its oldest surviving building, the Aasengård. The site of the house was cleared in the 17th century by Hans Olsen Aasen, who discovered the first copper ore in this area. The house can be seen by arrangement with the tourist office.

Aasengård

Røros

Surroundings

Christianus Sextus mine

8km/5 miles east of Røros is the Christianus Sextus mine, an old copper-mine which is open to the public in summer. The tourist office in Røros arranges bus trips to the mine, with conducted tours of the workings.

Rovaniemi   F 3

Country: **Finland**
Region: Northern Finland
Population: 33,000
Post code: FIN–96200   Telephone code: 960

Events

Reindeer-sleigh races (February); Ice Marathon, an international skating competition (March); Ounasvaara Winter Games (end March); Santa Claus Artic Golf Tournament (also in March); Midnight Sun Festival on Mt Ounasvaara (June 23rd); Ars Arctica exhibition (end of June to end of July); All Saints Ice Regatta on the Vikajärvi (November).

Situation and characteristics

Rovaniemi, situated at the junction of the Kemijoki, Finland's longest river (510km/320 miles), with the Ounasjoki (320km/200 miles), is the chief town and economic and cultural centre of the Finnish province of Lapland, by far the largest of the country's provinces, with an area of over 90,000sq.km/35,000sq. miles.

There was a settlement here in the 16th century, when Swedish and Russian tax-collectors first began to appear in these northern regions. With the increase in the demand for timber following the development of industry Rovaniemi grew considerably in importance, lying as it did at the

Reindeer-driving race, Rovaniemi

junction of two of the principal rivers down which logs could be floated from the interior of Lapland to the Baltic. The town was detached from the surrounding rural district in 1929, and in 1938 became the chief place in the Finnish province of Lapland. It received its municipal charter in 1960.

Until quite recent times Rovaniemi, like other places in the northern territories, consisted almost entirely of wooden houses. During the winter of 1944–45 over four-fifths of the town was burned down during the fighting between Finnish and German forces. After the war Alvar Aalto was given the task of rebuilding the town, and based the layout of the main streets on the pattern of a reindeer's antlers. The buildings erected since the war are almost all of stone, and some of the public buildings have provided a model for the whole of Lapland with their functional design and adaptation to the landscape.

Rovaniemi now attracts some 400,000 visitors a year, and accordingly the service trades are of major importance to the town's economy.

★Tourism

Although the main part of the town lies on the left bank of the Ounasjoki (or the Ounaskoski rapids), there are a number of public buildings and sports facilities on the right bank. Within the area of the town there are numerous peninsulas and inlets. The river is spanned by two bridges.

Town

In the south-east of the town, near the large two-level road and rail bridge, are the Provincial Government Offices.

To the south, beyond the railway, stands the Lutheran church (by Bertel Liljequist, 1950), with an altar fresco by Lennart Segerstråhle, "The Source of Life". To the left of the entrance a stone marks the site of the earlier church (1817–1944). Adjoining the church is the churchyard, with a large memorial to the Finnish soldiers who fell in the Second World War. Opposite the church is a monument to the Finnish freedom fighters of 1918.

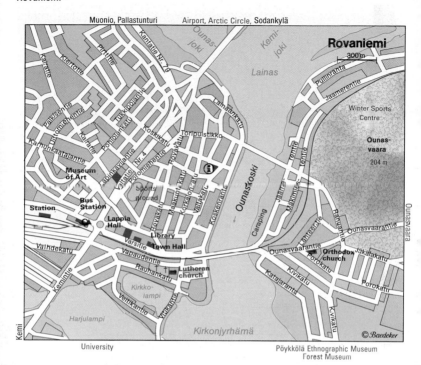

Muonio, Pallastunturi   Airport, Arctic Circle, Sodankylä

Rovaniemi

University   Pöykkölä Ethnographic Museum / Forest Museum

Lappia Hall	At Hallituskatu 11 is the Lappia Hall (by Alvar Aalto, 1975), which serves as a theatre, concert hall and conference centre. Housed in the same building is the Lapland Provincial Museum (culture of the Sami and the gipsies). Next door (No. 9) the Municipal Library, also by Alvar Aalto (1965), has a room for exhibitions.
Orthodox church	On the east side of the Ounaskoski rapids is the Orthodox church (by Toivo Paatela and Ilmari Ahonen, 1957), with valuable icons from Valamo monastery (now in Russia).
★ New Bridge	In the north-west of the town, in the gardens on the banks of the Kemijoki, can be seen a bronze statue of a bark-stripper (by Kalervo Kallio, 1939–52). The river is spanned by the 320m/350yd long New Bridge (1989), with a striking central pier to which the suspension cables are fixed. After dark the bridge is attractively illuminated.
Ethnographic Museum Forest Museum	4km/2½ miles south of the town centre, on the Kemijoki, are the Pöykkölä Ethnographic Museum (peasant houses, furnishings and equipment) and the Lapland Forest Museum, which illustrates the life of the timber-workers immortalised in the sculpture of Kallervo Kallio.

Surroundings

Ounasvaara	South-east of Rovaniemi, on the left bank of the Kemijoki, rises the hill of Ounasvaara (204m/670ft), with a café, a hotel, a winter sports centre (large

Ski-jump on Ounasvaara

ski-jump) and a skiing hut. From the top of the hill the midnight sun is visible from June 18th to 28th.

8km/5 miles north of Rovaniemi the road to Kemijärvi crosses the Arctic Circle (Finnish Napapiiri: see entry). Here there are a regular shopping centre (souvenirs), a "Children's Land" and a post office (special postmark). Here too visitors can obtain a certificate to prove that they have crossed the Arctic Circle. Nearby is the SOS Children's Village, "Lapland", opened in 1979.

Arctic Circle

30km/19 miles south-west of Rovaniemi on the Aavasaksa road lies the tourist and sports centre of Pohtimolampi, with a ski-lift and a reindeer-driving school for tourists.

Pohtimolampi
sports centre

Lake Saimaa

G 4/5

Country: **Finland**
Region: South-eastern Finland

Lake Saimaa, the "lake of a thousand islands", is the most southerly element in an intricate and widely ramified system of lakes, linked by numerous rivers and channels, which occupies the whole of the eastern part of the Finnish Lakeland. The lake is abundantly stocked with fish.

Situation and
characteristics

Lake Saimaa itself, lying at an altitude of 76m/250ft, has an area – excluding its numerous islands – of some 1300sq.km/500sq. miles, with a greatest depth of 90m/295ft. (The area of the Finnish Lakeland as a whole is about 7000sq.km/2700sq. miles.) The Salpausselkä ridge, a terminal moraine, forms the low southern rim of Lake Saimaa and prevents any outflow from the lake to the south.

The ★Lake

Lake Saimaa from the air

The whole lake system – the dark colouring of which, taking on a yellowish hue in the shallower parts, comes from the numerous expanses of bog in the region – is drained by the river Vuoksi, which leaves Lake Saimaa to the north of the town of Imatra and after a course of 150km/95 miles through Russian territory flows into Lake Ladoga. The hilly shores of the lake and most of the islands are almost entirely covered with coniferous forest, with some birch forest farther north.

Cruises on lake

A number of agencies, most of them in Lappeenranta (see entry), run day trips and longer cruises on Lake Saimaa.

Saimaa Canal

Lake Saimaa is linked with the Baltic, to the south, by the 50km/30 mile long Saimaa Canal, which ends at Vyborg in Russia. There are cruises on the canal (visa required) from Lappeenranta and Helsinki.

Exhibitions

There are interesting exhibitions on the Saimaa region in the Provincial Museum in Savonlinna (see entry).

Saltfjell   D 3

Country: **Norway**
Region: Northern Norway

Situation and characteristics

The Saltfjell National Park (area 2250sq.km/870sq. miles), established in 1989, is the largest and most varied National Park in northern Norway. Bounded on the west by the North Sea and the Svartisen glacier and in the east by the Swedish frontier, it is bisected by the Arctic Circle. The E 6 and the railway running parallel to it between Mo i Rana in the south and Bodø in the north are the only inroads by man and the only means of communication on a plateau which becomes impassable in winter under great masses of snow. The Saltfjell is still used by the Sami for grazing their herds of reindeer.

The great tourist attraction of this area is the Svartisen ("Black Ice") glacier, the largest icefield in northern Scandinavia, extending westwards to the coastal fjords. For the most part the plateau lies between 1200m/3900ft and 1400m/4600ft, with individual peaks rising above this, including Snetind (1599m/5246ft), Sniptind (1591m/5220ft) and Istind (1577m/5174ft). The best access from the south is by way of Mo i Rana (see entry) and from there north-west to Svartishytta or Melfjorden. Both roads end at the foot of an offshoot of the Svartisen glacier.

★Svartisen glacier

Road 17, running south from Bodø to Glomfjord, offers the possibility of a visit to a glacier as well as perhaps the most beautiful stretch of road in northern Norway. The narrow Nordfjord to the west, with its precipitous sides and innumerable waterfalls, is Norway's most dramatic fjord.

Glomfjord

E 6 crosses the Arctic Circle at an altitude of 650m/2130ft. 100m/110yd south is a stone commemorating the Yugoslav prisoners of war who died during the construction of the railway to the north in 1942–45, during the German occupation of Norway.

Arctic Circle

The best approach to the Saltfjell for a walking holiday is by way of E 6 to Rognan and Roads 812 and 813, running west to Storfjord. The striking feature of the Saltfjell is the juxtaposition of glaciers to the west with wide valleys and ridges of hills to the east. The differences in topography are reflected also in differences of climate: in the west it is damp, with relatively mild winters, while the eastern part of the area has a typical inland climate, with low rainfall and cold winters.

The ★ Saltfjell

Some 70% of all the natural caves in Norway are in the Saltfjell, and the Grønli Cave to the north of Mo i Rana is a celebrated tourist sight. The

Caves

Svartisen glacier

limestone and marble which are the predominant rocks in the Saltfjell have been dissolved by the numerous watercourses in the mountains, thus forming the caves. The famous Saltfjell marble is still worked on the fringe of the National Park.

National Park

Like other National Parks, the Saltfjell has a network of paths and "self-service" huts at a day's march from one another; information about them can be obtained from local tourist offices. Old sacrificial sites, pits for trapping game and stone boundary lines show that many centuries ago the Sami used the Saltfjell as hunting and grazing grounds. There were a number of trade routes between Rana in the south and Saltdal in the north, and the Arctic climate with its heavy falls of snow made it necessary to have shelter for the night available all over the area. The last farms in the Saltfjell were abandoned in the mid 20th century, and after the establishment of the National Park no further hydro-electric stations were built in the Saltfjell.

Surroundings

Junkerdal

From Storfjord, on E 6, Road 77 runs through the dramatic and fertile Junkerdal to the Swedish frontier. The vegetation in this densely wooded country includes both Arctic species of orchids and plants normally found only much farther south.

Sulitjelma

From Fauske (pop. 5400), on E 6, Road 830 runs east to Sulitjelma. Deposits of iron ore were discovered here by chance in the 1880s, and mining continued until 1990. The Mining Museum in the town tells the story of the mine. From Sulitjelma there are organised climbing parties to the Blåmannisen glacier (1571m/5154ft) and Suliskongen (1913m/6277ft).

Jakobsbakken

In the old mining village of Jakobsbakken, 11km/7 miles beyond Sulitjelma, accommodation for visitors is provided in the former miners' houses.

Savonlinna   G 4

Country: **Finland**
Region: South-eastern Finland
Population: 29,000
Post code: FIN–57100   Telephone code: 957

Events

★Savonlinna Opera Festival (part of the Finland Festival), with concerts and music seminar (June–July); exhibitions in the Retretti Art Centre during the summer.

Situation and characteristics

Savonlinna, a popular spa and holiday resort, lies in the middle of the Saimaa lake system in south-eastern Finland, between the Haapavesi to the north and the Pihlajavesi to the south. The town grew up around the castle of Olavinlinna and received its municipal charter in 1639. The oldest part of the town is picturesquely situated on an island between two waterways, with the newer districts on the mainland to the west. Savonlinna is one of the main centres of the boat services on Lake Saimaa.

Town

The town's main traffic artery is Olavinkatu, a long street running from east to west. At the west end of the old town, on the strait of Haapasalmi, is the Market Square, with the landing-stage used by the Lake Saimaa boats. From here a bridge leads north over the inlet of Koulolahti to the Vääräsaari peninsula, with the Spa Establishment (modern treatment facilities) and the Casino Hotel, an attractive park and an open-air theatre.

Little Church

Olavinkatu runs east from the Market Square to another spacious square, Olavintori, in which is the Little Church (by L. T. K. Visconti, 1845), originally

Harbour-front promenade, Savonlinna

Orthodox (for the Russian garrison) but Lutheran since 1940. Over the west gable is a dome topped by a lantern.

On the south side of the island, reaching out into the Pihlajavesi, is the Riihisaari peninsula, on which is the Provincial Museum (periodic special exhibitions), housed in a former granary (1851). South of this is the Saimaa Museum, with a number of old ships, including the "Salama", a steam-powered schooner launched at Viipuri in 1874 which carried passengers and cargo between Savonlinna, St Petersburg and Lübeck. It sank in Lake

Provincial Museum

Museum ships

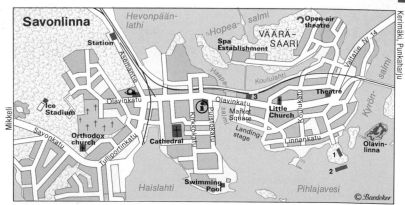

1 Provincial Museum   2 Museum ships   3 Opera Festival Office

Saimaa in 1898 and lay in more than 30m/100ft of water until 1971, when it was raised, restored and opened to the public as a museum ship in 1978 (displays on shipping on Lake Saimaa).

Cathedral

On the Savonniemi peninsula, between the Haapasalmi and the Kirkkolahti, stands the Lutheran Cathedral, a Neo-Gothic brick church (by A. H. Dahlström, 1879) which was damaged by bombing during the Winter War of 1939–40 and reconsecrated in 1949. In the adjoining gardens is a war memorial by Wäinö Aaltonen (c. 1920).

★★ Olavinlinna
Castle

The principal sight of Savonlinna is Olavinlinna Castle (Swedish Olofsborg), which lies south-east of the old town on an islet in the Kyrönsalmi (reached by a bridge). The castle, founded in 1475 by Erik Axelsson Tott, governor of Viipuri (Viborg) Castle, was ceded to Russia in 1743, after the Northern War, and thereafter was several times enlarged and strengthened. It is entered through a vaulted gateway on the west side which leads into the small inner courtyard, the oldest part of the castle. The castle, which has been excellently restored, contains a number of handsome rooms which are used for receptions and conferences, among them the King's or Knights' Hall, the Congress Hall and the Great Hall. Three massive round towers have survived, and in one of them (the Church Tower) is a small chapel, still used for worship and for weddings. In the Great Bastion there is a summer café. From the loopholes and small windows in the towers there are fine views of the surrounding country. Housed in the castle are a Historical and an Orthodox Museum.

Opera Festival

The Savonlinna International Opera Festival, Finland's best-known cultural event, is held in the courtyard of Olavinlinna Castle in June and July. In addition to opera, including works by Finnish composers and productions by visiting foreign companies, the programme of the festival also includes a variety of concerts.

Olavinlinna

Surroundings

From Savonlinna there are boat trips to the other towns on Lake Saimaa, to Punkaharju (see Finnish Lakeland), with the Retretti Art Centre, the largest in the Nordic countries, to the monasteries of Uusi Valamo and Lintula and, nearer Savonlinna, the Rauhalinna Hotel, a handsome timber building which was originally a hunting lodge of the Tsars.

Boat trips

15km/9 miles east of Savonlinna on Road 71, on the Puruvesi, lies Kerimäki (see Finnish Lakeland), with the largest wooden church in the world.

Setesdal   B 5/6

Country: **Norway**
Region: Southern Norway

The Setesdal or Sæterdal, the valley of the Otterå (Otra), extends almost due north for a distance of some 230km/140 miles from Kristiansand, on the south coast of Norway, forming an important traffic route to Bergen and the Hardangerfjord (see entries). It has much to offer visitors, with its beautiful scenery and a population which still observes old customs and traditions.

Situation and characteristics

Along the ★Setesdal

Road 39 runs north-west from Kristiansand (see entry), turning away from the west bank of the river Otra and passing the cemetery and the road to Ravnedal Park. At Mosby a road goes off on the right to Vennesla and Grovane (old-time railway: see Kristiansand, Surroundings).

Access

Road 39 then continues past the Langevann and Eigelandsvann, passes through Hægeland (octagonal church, 1830), crosses an expanse of wooded heathland and crosses the Otra on the Birkeland bridge.

Evje (alt. 185m/607ft, pop. 1400) has boatyards, woodworking industry and felspar quarries. In Evjemoen, to the south, was a nickel plant (closed down in 1946) using ore from Flåt. The minerals of this region (amazonite, beryl, aquamarine) will be of interest to geologists. Hornnes, 5km/3 miles south of Evje, has an interesting octagonal wooden church (1826–29).

Evje

Byglandsfjord (alt. 207m/680ft), on the south side of the lake of that name, through which the river Otra flows, was formerly the terminus of the Setesdal railway, which closed in 1962; it is now a winter sports resort (chair-lift, pistes).

Byglandsfjord

Road 39 (blasted from the rock at certain points) now runs along the east side of the Byglandsfjord, with the Årdalsfjell (760m/2495ft) rearing above it on the right.

The village of Årdal has a fine wooden church (1827), with a runic stone (c. 1100) in the churchyard. 300m/330yd south of the church can be seen a 900-year-old oak tree. On a hill to the north-east is Landeskogen, a home for the mentally handicapped.

Årdal

Farther north, at the foot of Lysheia (845m/2772ft), is Bygland, with a 19th century church. In the churchyard are prehistoric cult stones, and there are several old burial mounds in the surrounding area. Good fishing in the fjord.

Bygland

The road crosses the fjord on the Storestraum bridge and continues along its western shore. To the left is the Reiårsfoss waterfall. At the north end

Storestraum bridge

The Otterå (Otra), Setesdal

Rustfjell	of the fjord are a number of old store-rooms built on piles (*stabbur*). Following the course of the Otra, the road now skirts the Rustfjell (1070m/ 3511ft), to the left.
Helle	The road continues through magnificent scenery to Helle, which has a long tradition of silversmithing.
Collection of silversmiths' work	At Nomeland a road branches off on the left to the Brokke power station, from which there is a beautiful view of the valley. Nearby is Sylvartun, an old wooden house with a collection of silversmiths' work.
★Hallandsfoss Valle	Soon afterwards the Hallandsfoss, a 15m/50ft high waterfall, is seen on the left, with a number of deep potholes (gouged out by swirling melt-water). Beyond this, in a wider part of the valley, is Valle (alt. 307m/1007ft), chief place in the Setesdal, with old houses and a church of 1844.
Setesdal Museum	9km/5½ miles beyond Valle is the farm of Flateland, where a side road (2km/1¼ miles) goes off to the Setesdal Museum (old wooden houses).
Bykle	Road 39 continues high above the Otra, which here flows through a gorge, and comes to Bykle (alt. 549m/1801ft), an old village steeped in the peasant traditions of the valley lying a little to the east of the Bossvatn. The church (13th c.) has a fine 16th century interior which was decorated in the 19th century with acanthus patterns. To the north of the church is the Huldrehein Museum, with 16th century wooden houses.

A short distance east of the village is the Sarvsfoss, the finest waterfall on the Otra, 30m/100ft high. From Bykle there are marked footpaths into the surrounding hills. North of Bykle the valley becomes flatter and the landscape more mountainous in character.

The road now crosses the Otra again on the Berdal bridge and continues east along the shores of the Hartevatn.

Hovden (alt. 740m/2428ft), beautifully situated above the outflow of the Otra into the Hartevatn, is the main winter sports and climbing centre in the Setesdal (lifts).

North of Hovden the road runs past the Lislevatn, the Breivatn and the Sessvatn, reaching the highest point between Kristiansand and Haukeligrend (917m/3009ft). From Haukeligrend the Haukeli Road descends to Haugesund (see Telemark).

Lake Siljan
D 5

Country: **Sweden**
Province: Dalarna

Lake Siljan lies in the heart of the province of Dalarna (see entry), surrounded by gently rising hills with expanses of forest. 36km/22 miles long by 25km/15 miles wide, the lake has an area of 290sq.km/110sq. miles. The Österdalälv flows into the lake at one end and out at the other. Near the north-western end of the lake is the island of Sollerö. The average depth of Lake Siljan is about 60m/200ft, but there is a curious channel between Mora and Leksand where it reaches a depth of 120m/390ft.

Situation and characteristics

Lake Siljan, which has been artificially regulated since 1926, is a very popular holiday area. The beauty of the lake and the surrounding area is best seen by taking a boat trip from one of the towns on the lake.

★Boat trip

The little market town of Mora (pop. 20,000), at the north-west end of the lake, where the Österdalälv flows into it, attracts visitors in both summer and winter. The 13th century church (with stellar vaulting) has a separate belfry of 1672 which is the great landmark of Mora.

Mora

Mora has associations with two very different characters, Gustavus Vasa and the artist Anders Zorn. It was here that the founder of the Swedish state, Gustavus Vasa, called on the men of Dalarna in 1520 to rise against Danish rule. He is commemorated by the Vasa Run (Vasaloppet), the longest cross-country ski race in the world, held every year at the beginning of March. The Vasaloppsmuseum in the Sports Club tells the story of the race. On Klocksgropsbacken can be seen the Vasa Monument, a statue of Gustavus Vasa by Anders Zorn.

Vasa Monument

Anders Zorn (1860–1920) – painter, etcher and sculptor – was Mora's most famous son. The Zorn Collections, presented to the town by Anders and Emma Zorn, comprise the Zorn Museum, the Zorngård, Zorns Gammelgård and Gopsmor, the artist's "painting room" (open only in summer). The Zorn Museum shows a selection of Zorn's work, including watercolours, oil paintings, sculpture and graphic art. In the grounds of the museum is the Zorngård, the artist's house and studio, with turn-of-the-century furniture and furnishings.
    Zorns Gammelgård, on the outskirts of the town, gives a comprehensive view of the old popular culture of Mora and the surrounding area. It is an open-air museum of some forty houses and farmsteads, with old furniture and equipment, illustrating the development of the local style of timber architecture.

Zorn Collections

A bridge leads on to the island of Sollerö (good fishing and bathing; golf course). On the island is Bengtsarvet, a large cemetery area of the Viking period, with 123 burials.

Surroundings

Sollerö

South-east of Mora, on the shores of the lake, is Nusnäs, where visitors can watch the making of the little wooden horses of Dalarna (see entry).

Nusnäs

383

Cabin on Lake Siljan

Gesundaberg

An attractive trip, within easy reach of Mora, is to the Gesundaberg (501m/1644ft; cableway), from the top of which there are extensive views. Nearby is the interesting Siljanfors Forest Museum, an open-air museum illustrating the development of forestry in the region.

Orsasjö

North of Mora is the Orsasjö (alt. 161m/528ft; area 56sq.km/22sq. miles; greatest depth 97m/320ft), on the northern shore of which are Våmhus (basketwork demonstrations in Lissolbakken) and Orsa (see Dalarna).

Rättvik

Rättvik (pop. 11,000), between Leksand and Mora on the north-eastern shore of Lake Siljan, is the chief place in a commune which also takes in Vikarbyn, Boda, Furudal and Bingsjö. As a tourist resort it offers year-round attractions. The church, on a promontory reaching out into the lake, dates from the 13th century but was rebuilt in the 18th century. Beside the church are some ninety "church houses", some of them dating from the 17th century, which provided overnight accommodation for worshippers and their horses. To the south of the church is the Vasa Stone (1893), commemorating Gustavus Vasa's first address to the men of Dalarna in 1520 on the precinct wall of the church.

In a park (which also includes a holiday village and a swimming pool) is Rättviks Gammelgård, an open-air museum with a display of old tools and implements, household goods and local costumes. In Gudmunds Slöjd visitors can see the little wooden horses of Dalarna being made, particularly the grey horses which are a speciality of Rättvik. In the church school is a Natural History Museum (geology, flora and fauna of the region). From the Tolvåsberg and the Vidablick lookout tower (325m/1066ft) there are fine views of Lake Siljan.

Leksand

Leksand (pop. 14,000), on the Österdalälv at the south-east end of Lake Siljan, is the chief place in the commune of Leksand, which includes more than ninety small villages. Leksand church, originally built in the 13th

Folk-dancing display

century, has an onion-domed tower added in the 18th century and a Baroque interior; 14th century crucifix. The Hembygsgård houses a local museum, with a varied collection of material (including a school museum). The Tinghus contains a collection of pictures by local artists.

Every year, in the first week in July, groups of fiddlers in traditional costume perform not only in Leksand but all over the commune, during the Lake Siljan musical festival, "Musik vid Siljan". (There is a local saying, "When two Rättvikers meet three of them play the fiddle".)

Musik vid Siljan

The focal point of the midsummer celebrations in Leksand is the Sammilsdal open-air museum, where in the second half of July every year a mystery play similar to "Everyman", the "Himlaspel", is performed. Also of interest to visitors are the church boats, in which, from midsummer to August, the local people, often still wearing traditional costumes, row to church and on occasions race against each other.

Midsummer celebrations

In winter large numbers of winter sports enthusiasts come to Leksand, which has an ice rink and a cableway up the Åsledsberg (437m/1390ft).

Surroundings
Winter sports

The well preserved old wooden farmhouses of Matsgården in Östbjörka and Skräddargården in Stumsnäs have collections of the famous folk paintings (*dalmålningar*) of Dalarna.

Folk paintings

South-east of Lake Siljan is the hilly region of Bergslagen, with an old-established mining and smelting industry. The local mines still yield iron and some copper (Falun). Near the Bergslagen mines are numbers of ironworks – at Borlänge, Fagersta, Domnarvet, Avesta, Uddeholm, Degerfors, etc.

Bergslagen

Skåne

Country: **Sweden**

Situation and characteristics

Skåne (Scania), Sweden's most southerly province, lies between the Kattegat, the Öresund and the Baltic. It has a coastline of some 500km/300 miles, fringed by sandy beaches and wooded dunes, with some stretches of rocky coast in the north-west. The fertile plain of Skåne is Sweden's granary. The northern part of the province is a region of granite and gneiss, forests and gently rolling country.

The white farmhouses of Skåne are built on an elongated ground-plan which provides protection from the strong winds blowing over the plain. The grass-covered field walls which were formerly characteristic of the province have frequently had to give way to the requirements of modern traffic; and few of the Hollander windmills and post-mills which were still common at the end of the 19th century now survive.

History

The large Iron Age chambered tombs to be seen in Skåne are a reminder that this area was settled at a very early period. In the Bronze Age roads were constructed across the mud-flats to Denmark; and this, combined with the mild climate, led to a steady increase in the number of settlements. Many Vikings sailed from Skåne on their long voyages to Britain and France.

Until the middle of the 17th century Skåne belonged to Denmark, and many towns and buildings were given their particular stamp by Danish bishops, kings, nobles and merchants. Examples of this are the town of Kristianstad and Glimmingehus, a well preserved early 16th century castle near Simrishamn. Many fine old castles and manor-houses have survived and are open to the public.

Under the treaty of Roskilde in 1658 Skåne finally became part of Sweden.

Mixed woodland and heath on the Baltic coast near Boorby

Glimmingehus Castle, Skåne

Towards the end of the medieval period Skåne had established a prosperous economy based on agriculture, fishing (herring), coal-mining, its resources of clay and the brickworks which they supplied.

Economy

The traditional costumes of Skåne, with their rich adornment of silver, recall the prosperity of the region in the 16th century, when the inhabitants began to wear finer clothing and jewellery. The styles of that period have largely survived in the various local costumes and in the decoration of furniture.

Traditions

Among the most interesting towns in Skåne are Helsingborg, Landskrona, Malmö, Lund, Trelleborg, Ystad and Kristianstad (see entries).

Towns

Skellefteå

E 4

Country: **Sweden**
Province: Västerbotten
Population: 74,000
Post code: S–93... Telephone code: 0910

Skellefteå, lying between the Skellefteälv and the Gulf of Bothnia, is mentioned in the records as a trading town in 1621, but received its municipal charter only in 1845. In 1912 the railway reached the town, and this, combined with the expansion of the Boliden mines, led to rapid development in the 1920s. The incorporation of neighbouring settlements, some of them as much as 20km/12½ miles away, has contributed to giving the town its present population of 74,000.

Situation and characteristics

The central area, still showing its original rectangular plan, is well preserved, with wooden houses in typical Norrland style. In the Nordanåparken and Bonnstan districts are numbers of 17th century "church

Town

houses" (providing overnight accommodation for churchgoers travelling from a distance). Close by are the Regional Museum (bronze ornaments of A.D. 300–400) and the 18th century Church of the Provincial Assembly, which incorporates some medieval work and contains a collection of medieval sculpture in wood and a beautiful reredos. Below the church is the Lejonströmsbro (1737; 312m/341yd long), the longest wooden bridge in Sweden still carrying motor traffic.

Adjoining the Municipal Park is the Town House (1955), which contains a fine mosaic by Evert Lundquist. The Town Church, in Neo-Baroque style (1927), has a striking doorway of black granite; the interior was designed by Carl Fagerberg and Gunnar Torhamn.
Skellefteå also has the most northerly terrarium and tropical house in the world.

Surroundings

Skelleftehamn

16km/10 miles south-east of the town centre is the port of Skelleftehamn. St Örjan's Church (1935), has a roof and bells of Boliden copper and contains an altarpiece of the Spanish school, perhaps by Velázquez.
From Skelleftehamn there are boat services to Jakobstad and Kokkola in Finland.

3km/2 miles farther on is Rönnskärsviken, which is noted for its output of gold and other metals.

To the south of Skellefteå lies the Bjuröklubb nature reserve (archaeological trail, fishermen's chapel, lighthouse).

In the "church town" of Lövånger, 50km/30 miles south of Skellefteå, are 100 wooden houses for the overnight accommodation of worshippers,

"Church town" at Lövånger (south of Skellefteå)

some dating from the 14th century. They have been carefully restored and are now rented to holiday visitors.

35km/22 miles north-west of Skellefteå is the mining town of Boliden. Large deposits of copper ore were discovered here in 1925–26, and gold, silver, lead and arsenic are now mined in the area; there are also deposits of selenium and sulphur. There is a small museum on the history of the mines. From Boliden there is a 96km/60 mile long industrial cable railway via Rakkejaur to Kristineberg, where deposits of copper, sulphur and zinc are worked.

Boliden

Farther west, near the Lapland border, is a very beautiful corner of Västerbotten whose principal attractions are the Malåns waterfall, the primeval forest of Kryddgrovan and, near Jörn, Storeklinta (515m/1690ft), the highest hill in Västerbotten. There is a 13km/8 mile long cableway between Örträsk and Mensträsk.

Skövde

D 6

Country: **Sweden**
Province: Västergötland
Population: 46,000
Post code: S–54...   Telephone code: 0500

The town of Skövde lies between Lakes Vänern and Vättern (see entries), on the eastern edge of the Billingen Hills. This is an area of great historical importance, since it is believed that Sweden had its origins in Skaraborg (now a county within the province of Västergötland). Skövde is thus one of the oldest settlements in the country. Material recovered by excavations, including a hoard of gold which is now in the Historical Museum in Stockholm, is dated to between A.D. 400 and 500. The church at Forsby, to the east of Skövde, is thought to be Sweden's oldest church (consecrated 1135).

Situation and characteristics

Skövde, a garrison town since the 19th century and the base of armoured forces, is now an expanding industrial town, using minerals from the Billingen Hills, it is also the cultural and educational centre of the area. Its largest firm, Volvo Komponenter, manufactures car engines and other components. There are also cement factories.

With a single exception (Peter Helen's little house in Kyrkogatan, now used for exhibitions) the buildings of Skövde all date from after a great fire which wrought havoc in 1759. The Art Gallery and Theatre in the Oden House of Culture (a building of architectural interest) offer a varied cultural programme. The old 18th century Town Hall is now occupied by the Municipal Museum. St Helen's Church (13th c.; altered 1888), in the main square, was formerly a popular place of pilgrimage where a local St Helen was venerated.

Town

Surroundings

The Billingen Hills, to the west of the town, are a plateau 23km/14 miles long by 11km/7 miles across – the largest in Västergötland – reaching 299m/981ft at its highest point. This is an area of varied landscape, with expanses of bog, lakes, coniferous forests and pastureland (rare flowers, including orchids and lilies), traversed by an attractive waymarked trail 29km/18 miles long. There are excellent facilities for both summer and winter sports. The mineral resources of the hills have long provided raw materials for the industries of the surrounding area.

Billingen Hills

Småland

Falköping

Road 46 runs south from Skövde through a region rich in prehistoric sites. Half way between Skövde and Falköping is the oldest Cistercian nunnery in Sweden, probably founded in 1161 by King Karl Sverkersson. Falköping (pop. 32,000) is one of the highest towns in Sweden (alt. 220m/722ft). Its 18th and 19th century streets, with a sprinkling of modern architecture, have preserved their charm. An unusual feature of the town's layout is that the streets curve round to avoid a passage grave. St Olof's Church (12th c.) is one of the many churches in the area, which is reckoned to have one of the largest numbers of churches in any Swedish commune. In the Municipal Park are an impressive passage grave and a museum.

A few kilometres farther south, near Åsarp, is the Stone Age village known as Ekehagens Fornby. To the east of Falköping, at Skörstorp, is a picturesque little church, the only round church in the area.

Tidaholm

Also to the east of Falköping, on the river Tida, is Tidaholm, with the large Vulcan match factory. On Vulcan Island is a museum concerned not only with matches but with veteran and vintage cars. On Turbine House Island is a turbine-house built in 1898 to drive a metal-turning lathe, now an art gallery. On the island there are also three old forges (18th c.).

Småland   D 6

Country: **Sweden**
Region: Southern Sweden

Situation and characteristics

Småland, the region round Växjö, is notable among the provinces of Sweden for its numerous lakes. The uplands in the northern part of the region slope down towards the south and south-west and give way to a plain. Here begins the "endless forest" celebrated in so many Swedish songs. The landscape of Småland is patterned by the innumerable rocky hills,

After the harvest, Småland

smoothed and rounded by Ice Age glaciers, interspersed with shallow lakes and peat-bogs. The barren soil is covered with mosses and lichens.

Until the 18th century the population of Småland depended almost exclusively on agriculture for their subsistence, but the stony morainic soil yielded poor returns. Many peasants, therefore, sought employment in factories to eke out a meagre living. A rapid increase in population, poverty, high taxes and compulsory military service led many young Småland families to emigrate to America between 1750 and 1850.

Economic problems

The working of iron ore began in Småland in the 15th century, the main mining centre being Taberg. There was a great surge of activity in ironworking when foreign smiths came to Sweden and imparted their skills to the local people. In the 16th century Gustavus Vasa brought in skilled glassblowers from Venice, and thereafter glass manufacture played a major part in the Swedish economy. In the mid 19th century woodworking and glass were the leading Swedish industries. In time over 200 glassworks were established in Sweden.

Development of glass industry

More than half the country's glassworks are in the south-eastern corner of the wooded region of Småland, and as a result the belt of forest between Nybro and Växjö has become known as the "Glass Kingdom" (Glasriket). Most of the glassworks started out as iron foundries, in the days when bog-ore (impure iron ore) was still being used. The history of the Glass Kingdom really began, however, in 1742, when the glassworks at Kosta, west of Orrefors, were established. After difficulties in the seventies the small family firms combined to form larger concerns, and the two great rival firms of Kosta and Orrefors now belong to the same corporation. A few small glassworks, however, still remain independent, perpetuating the pattern of the old days.

The ★"Glass Kingdom"

A relic of these early days can be seen in the old hammer-mill at Orrefors, 17km/10 miles north-west of Nybro. In this village of some 900 inhabitants

Orrefors

Swedish glass

an old iron foundry using bog-ore was still operating in the latter part of the 19th century. The glassworks established here in 1898 is now part of the Orrefors Glasbruk company founded in 1937. Originally producing window glass and glass for industrial use, the company now makes lamps and decorative glassware; and in association with the Sandvik glassworks in Hovmantorp it also produces good-quality glassware for everyday use at moderate prices.

The Orresfors works can claim to have pioneered the manufacture of the glassware for which Sweden is now famed, having been the first firm to employ designers in this field in 1915. This marked the beginning of what is known as the Gate-Hald period, which made Swedish glass famous throughout the world. Simon Gate and Edvard Hald were the two designers who, together with Lindstrand, Landberg, Palmqvist, Öhrström and Lundin, gave Orrefors glass its artistic form and developed a distinctive style.

At the Orrefors works is a Glass Museum, with an interesting display of glass of the Gate-Hald period. The largest glass museum in northern Europe is at Växjö (see entry). All the glassworks in the Glass Country have showrooms in which their products are on sale, and visitors can usually also watch the glass-blowers at work. In many of the glass-making towns there are annual fairs and festivals, frequently accompanied by musical events.

Sognefjord   B 5

Country: Norway
Region: Western Norway

Situation and
characteristics

The Sognefjord is the largest of the Norwegian fjords, surpassing the gentler scenery of the Hardangerfjord with the sombre grandeur of its mountain setting. It extends inland for some 180km/110 miles from Sygnefest in the west to Skjolden at the eastern end of the Lusterfjord, with an average width of no more than 5km/3 miles. Its greatest depth is 1245m/4085ft.

At its eastern end the fjord is split into a number of narrow arms, enclosed by steep rock walls rising to over 1700m/5500ft. Here and there along the shores are cornfields, orchards and trim houses. The east end of the fjord already has a continental climate, with warm summers and long, cold winters.

Boat travel

Since there are no roads along the whole length of the Sognefjord the best way to explore it is by boat. From Bergen (see entry) a number of ships run cruises along the fjord.

During the summer the ships of the Hurtigrute (see entry) sail twice daily from Bergen to Årdalstangen at the east end of the Sognefjord, calling at Lavik, Balestrand, Leikanger, Midfjord (transfers to Gudvangen and to Revsnes and Årdalstangen) and Flåm.

Within the Sognefjord there are numerous local boat services (sometimes carrying cars) which offer the prospect of rewarding side trips.

There are also car ferries on the following routes: Balestrand–Hella–Fjærland, Hella–Vangsnes, Flåm–Aurland–Gudvangen, Kaupanger–Revsnes and Gudvangen–Kaupanger–Årdalstangen.

Information:
Fylkesbaatane i Sogn og Fjordane
Strandgate 197, N–5024 Bergen

Along the Sognefjord

Rysjedalsvika

At the extreme western end of the Sognefjord, which at this point is bordered by low hills worn smooth by glacier action, with only a sparse covering of vegetation, is Rysjedalsvika.

Lavik is the chief place in the western Sognefjord and an important junction of land and water-borne traffic (ferry to Oppedal on the south side of the fjord). The church dates from 1865.

Vadheim (pop. 600), at the head of the Vadheimsfjord, has an electro-chemical factory.

Nordeide, a little holiday resort at the mouth of the Høyangsfjord, is connected by ferry with Måren on the north side of the Sognefjord and with Svortemyr on the south side.

Høyanger (pop. 2200), at the head of its fjord, has a hydro-electric station and an aluminium works. Good hill walking in the surrounding area; fishing.

Balestrand (pop. 700), with high hills rearing above it, is the main tourist centre on the Sognefjord. To the north-west is the little Esefjord.

To the north of Balestrand, extending to near the foot of the Jostedalsbre (see entry), is the Fjærlandsfjord. From Balestrand there is a boat service up the 26km/16 mile long fjord to Fjærland, a popular base for walks and climbs in the glacier area. From Fjærland an 11km/7 mile long tunnel runs under the glacier area to Skei (Road 1), in the heart of the Sogn og Fjordane region.

There is a ferry from Balestrand to Hella, on the east side of the Fjærlandsfjord.

Opposite Balestrand, on the south side of the Sognefjord (ferry), is Vik, with a hydro-electric station and aluminium and woodworking plants. Nearby are the stave church of Hopperstad (12th c.) and a stone-built Romanesque church. From here it is possible to drive back to Bergen by way of Voss.

Balestrand on the Sognefjord

Sognefjord

Vangsnes

At Vangsnes, situated on a promontory on the south side of the Sognefjord, opposite Hella, can be seen a 12m/40ft high statue of Fridtjof (hero of a 13th century Icelandic saga) presented by Kaiser Wilhelm II. Nearby are three burial mounds.

Leikanger
Hermansverk

Leikanger and Hermansverk, lying close together in a fertile area on the north side of the Sognefjord (fruit orchards), combine to form the chief place in the county of Sogn og Fjordane. Leikanger has a stone church of the 13th century. To the south is a fine view of the Aurlandsfjord.

★Aurlandsfjord

The Aurlandsfjord is a southern arm of the Sognefjord, a cleft in the mountains 1.5km/1 mile wide flanked by rock walls rising to 900–1200m (2900–3900ft). In Aurlandsvangen, chief place in the commune of Aurland, is the oldest stone-built church in the region (c. 1200). Nearby is the church of Undredal (only 3.7m/12ft wide, with seating for 40), a stave church which was altered about 1700.

Flåm

At the southern tip of the Aurlandsfjord, surrounded by mountains, is the tourist resort of Flåm, at the mouth of the Flåmdal. This is the terminus of the railway line, a branch of the Bergen Railway, which runs down the Flåmdal from Myrdal (see Hardangerfjord).

★★Nærøyfjord

The western branch of the Aurlandsfjord is the Nærøyfjord, which is hemmed in by almost vertical rock faces, so that for months during the winter the sun never reaches the bottom of the fjord. At the head of the fjord is Gudvangen. Nearby is the Kjelsfoss (waterfall).

From Gudvangen E 16, which is joined at Vinje by Road 13, coming from Vik, runs back by way of Voss to Bergen.

Kaupanger

Kaupanger, at the head of the Amlabugt, an inlet on the north side of the Sognefjord, is connected by ferry with Revsnes, Gudvangen and Årdal-

On the Nærøyfjord

stangen. It has a 13th century stave church (restored 1862) and an open-air museum, the Heibergske Samlinger, with a number of old houses.

To the east of Kaupanger the Sognefjord splits into the Lusterfjord, which leads north towards the Jotunheim (see entry), the Årdalsfjord to the east and the Lærdalsfjord to the south-east.

The Lusterfjord, 45km/30 miles long, owes the milky colouring of its water to the numerous glacier-fed streams which flow into it. At Urnes, on the east side of the fjord, is one of the oldest stave churches in the country, originally dating from before 1100. From Skjolden, at the northern tip of the fjord, there is a road to the Jotunheim.

★Lusterfjord
Urnes stave
church

The Årdalsfjord is the most easterly arm of the Sognefjord. At its head, on an old raised beach, is the little town of Årdalstangen or Årdal (pop. 2300), with a large aluminium plant. To the south is the highest peak in the Slettefjell, Sauenosi (1352m/4436ft).

Årdalsfjord
Årdalstangen

To the north, on the Årdalsvatn, is the industrial township of Øvre Årdal. From here a road runs north to Hjelle, from which it is a 3–4 hours' walk up the Vettisgjel gorge to the Vettisfoss, a waterfall 260m/850ft high, which has been protected since 1924 as a natural monument.

Øvre Årdal

The Lærdalsfjord extends south-east from Kaupanger. At the head of the fjord, at the mouth of the Lærdal, is Lærdalsøyri, with a number of old houses, including the Hanseatic House.

Lærdalsfjord
Lærdalsøyri

From the Lærdal to Florø by Road

The only roads of any consequence in the Sognefjord are E 16, coming from Valdres (see entry), and its continuation, Road 5.

From the road junction beyond Øye take E 16, which runs along the Otrovatn, through the Smeddal and via Borlaug to the Lærdal.

Borgund (alt. 345m/1130ft), at the mouth of the Lærdal, has a small stave church, black with pitch, the best preserved in the country. It is thought to have been built about 1150. Apart from a window inserted at a later period it has been carefully restored to its original form, preserving its original layout. The two doorways are richly decorated, and the west doorway has a runic inscription which helped to date the church. The belfry, between the old and the new church, was restored about 1660 in its old form.

★Borgund
state church

From Borgund the road runs through the picturesque Svartegjel gorge, carved by the Lærdalselv (a good salmon river) through the rock barrier of the Vindhella. Beyond Husum (alt. 316m/1037ft) it passes through another magnificent gorge and comes to Lærdalsøyri (see above).

The road now runs along the south side of the Lærdalsfjord. From Revsnes there is a ferry across the Sognefjord to Kaupanger.

At Sognedal, on the Sognedalsfjord, are a runic stone (c. 1100) and several burial mounds.
    The road continues along the north side of the Sognefjord, passes through Hermansverk and Leikanger and comes to Hella, from which there is a ferry to Balestrand (see above).

Sognedal

From Balestrand the road turns north, following the west side of the Vetlefjord, and continues by way of Førde, at the head of the Førdefjord, chief place in the Sunnfjord district, to Florø (pop. 5000), a port and industrial town attractively situated on the island of Brandsøy (bridge).

Førde
Florø

Spitzbergen/Svalbard

Country: **Norway**
Area of archipelago: 62,700sq.km/24,200sq. miles

Situation and characteristics

The Norwegian archipelago of Svalbard, centred on the main island of Spitzbergen (Spitsbergen), lies between the 74th and 81st parallels, some 700km/435 miles north of the North Cape (see entry) and 1300km/810 miles from the North Pole. With a total area of 62,700sq.km/24,200sq. miles, it has a population of only 3700, who live in five settlements on the main island.

The main island, Spitzbergen (area 39,000sq.km/15,000sq. miles), is broken up by fjords cutting deep inland. To the north-east, separated from the main island by the Hinlopen Strait (usually ice-bound), is Nordaustland (North-East Land; 15,000sq.km/5800sq. miles), which is almost completely covered by glaciers. To the south-east are Edgeøy (Edge Island; 5000sq.km/1930sq. miles) and Barentsøy (Barents Island; 1300sq.km/500sq. miles).

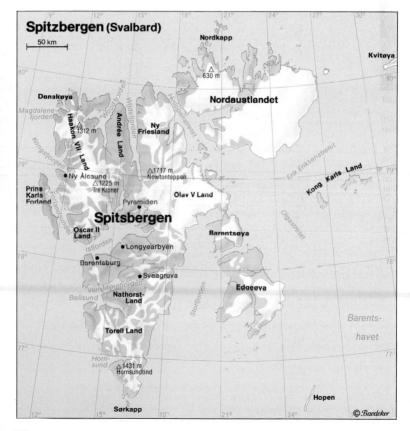

Spitzbergen: view from the Grønfjord towards the Isfjord

Farther south are the long, narrow island of Hopen and Bjørnøy (Bear Island), with meteorological stations.

Access

The opening of the Svalbard Airport at Longyearbyen, the chief place on Spitzbergen, in 1975 ended the islanders' isolation during the winter. There are now three or four flights weekly from Tromsø, as well as direct flights from Oslo and increasing numbers of charter flights. Twice monthly, too, there are scheduled flights from Moscow via Murmansk.

During the summer cruise ships sail along the ice-free west coast of Spitzbergen with its magnificent backdrop of fjord scenery. The regular service formerly provided by ships of the Hurtigrute in summer came to an end when the airport was opened. There are no local boat services, though there may sometimes be spare places on boats chartered by tour operators, and motorboat cruises are run in the Isfjord if there is sufficient demand.

Accommodation

Spitzbergen has no tourist infrastructure in the ordinary sense, such as hotels or roads between the settlements on the island. The only facilities offered to visitors are the camping site at the airport and the modest (and expensive) accommodation provided by SNSK (the local coal-mining company) in the Nybyen district of Longyearbyen.

Visitors must therefore be equipped to look after themselves (tent, sleeping bag, etc.). They should also bring sufficient food with them, particularly if they want to do some walking. The few shops in Longyearbyen cater for the needs of the local population – whose main requirements, however, are supplied by the mining company. Guns and ammunition may be brought in by visitors who have a gun licence.

Live animals may not be brought in because of the danger of rabies.

Visitors who intend to undertake walks of any length on the island are strongly recommended to carry a gun (for protection against polar bears), and they must inform the Governor's office before setting out and on their return. Under a new law which came into force at the beginning of 1992 any walking tour outside the settlements requires an authorisation from the Governor (Sysselmann) of Spitzbergen, who (depending on the applicant's experience, equipment and proposed route) may impose restrictions, refuse permission or ask for an assurance of reimbursement of the cost of a possible search and rescue operation – a regulation made necessary by experience with thoughtless or inadequately equipped visitors in the past.

History

Vikings found their way to the archipelago in 1194, reporting that they had found the "cold coast" ("Svalbardi fundinn"). Then 400 years later, in 1596, it was rediscovered by the Dutch navigator Willem Barents, who named it Spitzbergen after its prominent peak. Searching for the North-West Passage to China, he found only an abundance of seals and whales on the edge of the permanent ice cap. Soon afterwards the whaling settlement of Smeerenburg ("Blubber Town") was established on a flat peninsula on Amsterdamøy (Amsterdam Island), in the far north-west of Spitzbergen; but the whaling era lasted only a few decades, the whales and seals having been exterminated.

Thereafter, for many years, Spitzbergen was left to itself. During the 18th and 19th centuries a few Russian monks lived a hermit's life as fur-trappers. Towards the end of the 19th century Nansen's polar expeditions stimulated interest in the islands, and in 1899 a Norwegian seafarer named Søren Zachariassen discovered rich deposits of coal. In 1906 the first coal-mine on Spitzbergen was established by an American millionaire named Longyear, and the settlement which he founded was called Longyear City. In 1916 the mines were taken over by the Norwegian mining company SNSK, and Longyear City became Longyearbyen.

Subsequently other mining settlements were established by the Russians (Grumant on the Isfjord), the Dutch (Barentsburg on the Grønfjord) and the Swedes (Svea on the Van-Mijenfjord). The rich deposits of high-grade coal which Spitzbergen was now found to possess brought to the fore the question of sovereignty over the islands, which had not hitherto been settled; and in 1925, under the treaty of Sèvres, they were assigned to Norway, on condition that it would permit all the signatory states to carry on economic activities on an equal basis and would keep the islands permanently demilitarised.

During the Second World War Svalbard, lying on the route of the Allied convoys to Murmansk, acquired great strategic importance, and as a result Longyearbyen was destroyed in 1943 by the German battleships "Tirpitz" and "Scharnhorst".

Most of the mines were closed down during the great depression, and there now remain on Spitzbergen only the three Norwegian settlements of Longyearbyen (pop. 1100), Ny Ålesund (pop. 70) – the world's most northerly settlement – and Sveagruva (pop. 30) and the two Russian settlements of Barentsburg (pop. 1400) and Pyramiden (pop. 1200). The Norwegians and the Russians each produce around 250,000 tons of coal a year. High transport costs mean that the mines can be worked only with considerable subsidies; but in spite of the political thaw between East and West neither country seems willing to leave the other in sole possession.

Geology

Svalbard displays a very varied geological pattern, ranging from the Pre-Cambrian granite peaks in the north-west by way of the Carboniferous coal measures to the younger rocks of the Tertiary era in the centre of the main island. Fossils dating back some 120 million years show that at an early stage in the history of the earth this was a region of subtropical climate which moved steadily farther north as a result of continental drift.

Although Svalbard lies in the Arctic region its average temperatures, particularly on the west coast and in winter, are much higher than at other places in the same latitude. But even so average winter temperatures lie between −8° and −16°C (+18° and +3°F), rather lower in the north and east. The lowest-ever temperature, recorded in 1917, was −49°C (−56°F).

Temperatures in July and August rise to an average of 5°C (41°F), the highest recorded being 22°C (72°F); but there may be frost and snow at any time of year. Offshoots of the Gulf Stream bring higher temperatures along the west coast and ice-free waters between June and December.

Almost the whole of the east coast – like two-thirds of Spitzbergen – is covered with glaciers. Only in the central areas with their arid Arctic climate (annual precipitation only about 300mm/12in.) are there glacier-free zones of any size.

The proximity of the sea leads to frequent fog; the sky is usually overcast but the weather dry. At Longyearbyen the midnight sun is visible from April 19th to August 24th, while the Arctic night lasts from October 27th to February 15th.

The Arctic flora comprises some 140 different species, including low-growing flowering plants, ferns, mosses and lichens. The fauna includes some thirty species of seabirds, seals, polar bears, reindeer and Arctic foxes. Since 1973 the polar bear has been fully protected, and there are now estimated to be a few thousand of them, living mainly on the ice-covered east coast. There is always the possibility, even in summer, of encountering a polar bear on the west coast, and since they are extremely aggressive when hungry and may attack without warning visitors are advised to carry a rifle when outside the settlements.

Flora and fauna

In recent years some 27,000sq.km/10,400sq. miles (44% of Svalbard's total area) have been declared nature reserves. There are now three National Parks (South Spitzbergen, Forlandet and North-Western Spitzbergen), two nature reserves, three plant reserves and fifteen bird reserves. The extreme climatic conditions mean that rubbish thrown away may not decompose for many years. In order to avoid upsetting the delicate ecological balance, therefore, visitors should be sure to take their litter away with them.

Nature reserves

Cruise ship in the Magdalenefjord

★Sailing along the West Coast

Hornsund

Cruise ships usually sail only along the west side of the archipelago. After rounding the South Cape (Sørkapp) of Spitzbergen the ship passes the 15km/9 mile wide Hornsund, which even in summer is often covered with thick drift ice. Above its coasts rise Alpine peaks (Hornsundtind, 1431m/4695ft) and mighty pinnacles (Sofiekammen, 925m/3035ft).

★Isfjord

Some 50km/30 miles north of the wide Bellsund is the Isfjord (100km/60 miles long including its branches), which cuts more than half way across the island of Spitzbergen. While the north side is partly covered by glaciers, the south side falls down to the fjord in steep-sided tabular hills. In this fjord are the two principal settlements on the island, Longyearbyen on Advent Bay and Barentsburg on the Grønfjord.

Kongsfjord

Farther up the west coast, in the Forlandsund, is the long island of Prins Karls Forland with its jagged glacier-covered peaks (Monacofjell, 1084m/3557ft). Beyond the northern tip of the island the Kongsfjord is seen on the right, with the pyramidal peaks known as the Tre Kroner (Three Crowns, 1225m/4020ft) rising above a 14km/9 mile wide glacier.

On the south side of the fjord lies the former mining settlement of Ny Ålesund (mines closed down in 1962 after a number of accidents). Features of interest in the little town are the Ny Ålesund Railway (steam engine of 1909), a monument to the mining history of Spitzbergen; the world's most northerly post office (special postmark); and the airship mooring mast from which Roald Amundsen set out in the airship "Norge" in 1926 to fly over the North Pole (monument commemorating the flight). Two years later Umberto Nobile also set out from here in an airship but it was wrecked on the return flight, and Amundsen was lost in the course of a rescue mission.

Krossfjord

To the north of the Kongsfjord are the Krossfjord and the Møllerfjord, with Møllerhavn. Some 30km/19 miles north are the Sju Fjella – seven rivers of ice reaching down to the sea between steep and jagged rocks. Still farther north is the Magdalenefjord, at the head of which is the Waggonway glacier, 2km/1¼ miles wide, with a cliff-like front up to 100m/330ft high.

To the north lies the island of Danskøy (Danes' Island), at the north-western corner of Spitzbergen. In 1897 a Swede named Andrée set out from here to fly to the Pole in a balloon, but after three days was compelled to make an emergency landing and on the way back on foot through the pack-ice perished on Kvitøy, the most easterly island in the Svalbard archipelago. Both on Danskøy and on the neighbouring Amsterdamøy there were whaling bases in the 17th and 18th centuries.

Woodfjord
Wijdefjord

On the north coast of Spitzbergen, which has few glaciers, are two long fjords, the Woodfjord and the Wijdefjord (100km/60 miles long), at the head of which are the two highest peaks in Svalbard, Newtontoppen and Perriertoppen, each 1717m/5633ft high.

Stavanger B 6

Country: **Norway**
Region: South-western Norway
Population: 98,000   Post code: N–4000

Situation and
characteristics

Stavanger, chief town of Rogaland county, lies on the south-western coast of Norway on the Byfjord or Boknafjord, an arm of the Stavangerfjord. It has an excellent harbour sheltered by offshore islands and is the commercial centre of the surrounding area. Major elements in the town's

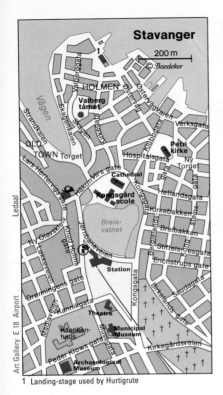

Stavanger

200 m

© *Baedeker*

1 Landing-stage used by Hurtigrute

economy are an oil refinery, fish-canning factories and, most importantly, its shipyards (which construct oil-rigs as well as ships). Some 320km/200 miles south of Stavanger, in the North Sea, are a number of Norwegian offshore oilfields (Tor, Ekofisk and Eldfisk).

Stavanger is one of the oldest towns in Norway. It was the see of a bishop from the 12th to the 17th century, when it lost this status to Kristiansand (1682). Towards the end of the 18th century the town had its own merchant shipping fleet, and a great economic upswing began in the second half of the 19th century with the growth of the herring and sprat fisheries and the fish-canning industry. In recent years Stavanger has gained increased importance with the development of the North Sea oil industry.

History

In the centre of Stavanger, at the north end of Kongsgata, stands the Cathedral, the most important in Norway after Trondheim Cathedral. It was built at the end of the 11th century by Bishop Reinald, an Englishman also known as Reginald of Worcester (d. 1135), as a three-aisled Romanesque basilica. The choir was rebuilt in Gothic style after a fire in 1272, and the whole church was renovated in the 19th century. Notable features of the interior are the richly carved Baroque pulpit (1658), a stone font of the Gothic period and the stained glass in the east window (by Victor Sparre, 1957) depicting New Testament scenes.

Town

★Cathedral

To the south of the Cathedral, on the northern shore of the Breiavatn, is the Kongsgård, originally the Bishop's Palace. Later a grammar school, the Kongsgård Skole, was built on the foundations of the palace. The bishop's private chapel (Bispekapellet) has been restored.

Kongsgård

North-west of the Cathedral, extending to the harbour inlet (Vågen), is the Market Square (Torget), the scene of lively activity on weekdays. In the square can be seen a bronze statue (by Magnus Vigrestad) of the Stavanger-born novelist and playwright Alexander Kielland (1849–1906).

Market Square

To the north of the Market Square, between Vågen and the East Harbour (Østre Havn), is the Holmen peninsula, the oldest part of the town. In this area, near Kirkegata, which runs north from the Cathedral, stands the Valbergtårn, an old watch-tower on the highest point in the town (views; exhibition of arts and crafts).

Valbergtårn

401

Stavanger Cathedral

Stavanger harbour

North-west of the Market Square, on the far side of Vågen, lies Gamle Stavanger (Old Stavanger), with many old houses. In Nedre Strandgate, occupying an old merchant's house, is the Maritime Museum (history of seafaring, etc.).

Old Town

Immediately south of the Breivatn is the railway station, and beyond this are the Theatre and, in Muségata, the Municipal Museum (antiquities, natural history, ethnography, ships and the sea). An item of particular interest in the museum is the earliest skeleton found in Norway (at Viste, 10km/6 miles north-west of Stavanger, where there are caves which were inhabited in Stone Age times).

Municipal Museum

To the south-west, in Storgate, are the Archaeological Museum (with a special exhibition, "Kaleidoscope") and the Vestland School Museum (old furnishings, equipment and teaching material).

Archaeological Museum

Farther west, at Madlaveien 33, the Art Gallery houses works by the painter Lars Hertervig.

Art Gallery

To the west of Stavanger is Ledaal House, a mansion built about 1800 for the Kielland family. It features in Alexander Kielland's novels under the name of Sandsgård. The house is now used for receptions and other functions.

Ledaal House

Outskirts of the Town

The best views of the town, the fjord and the surrounding hills are to be had from the Vålandshaug (85m/280ft), in a park to the south of the town. It is reached by way of Hornklovesgate.

★ Vålandshaugen

To the north-west of the town, reached by way of Løkkeveien, is Bjergsted Park, with a restaurant and several viewpoints.

Bjergsted Park

Surroundings

To the west of the town is Byhaugen (76m/250ft), from which there is a fine view of the Ryfylkefjell to the north-east.

Byhaugen

3.5km/2 miles south-west of Stavanger is Ullandhaugen (131m/417ft), with a telecommunications tower (viewing platform) and a plaque commemorating Harald Fairhair's naval victory in 872, which gave him control of the whole country.

Ullandhaugen

In the fjord to the north of the town are numerous islands and islets. On the little Klosterøy, which is linked with the larger island of Mosterøy by a bridge, is the Augustinian abbey of Utstein (first mentioned in the records in the 13th century), the best preserved monastic house in Norway. Klosterøy can be reached from Stavanger by motor launch.

Klosterøy

To the east of Stavanger, beyond the Høgsfjord (pleasant trip by motor launch from the Strandkai), lies the Lysefjord, a cleft in the mountains 37km/23 miles long, up to 2km/1¼ miles wide and up to 457m/1500ft deep, with bright green water. The fjord is enclosed by sheer walls of rock rising to above 1000m/3300ft.

★ Lysefjord

The most striking feature in the fjord is the Prekestol ("Pulpit"), a flat-topped crag 597m/1960ft high. It can be reached from Stavanger on Road 13, which comes in 24km/15 miles to Lauvvik, on the Høgsfjord, from which there is a ferry across the fjord to Oanes. From there Road 13 continues north to Jøssang, where a side road goes off on the right to the Prekestol-hytta, from which it is a 2 hours' walk to the Prekestol.

★ Prekestolen

Stockholm E 5/6

Country: **Sweden**
Provinces: Södermanland and Uppland
Population: 651,000 (with suburbs 1.6 million)
Post code: S–10... Telephone code: 08

City tours
: City Sightseeing (bus), departure from Gustav Adolfs Torg (Opera); Stockholm Sightseeing (bus and boat), departure from Town Hall. Also attractive, in good weather, are boat trips to the skerries.

Events
: Detailed information about events in Stockholm is given in the booklet "Stockholm This Week", obtainable from tourist information offices.

Situation
: Stockholm lies on a number of islands and peninsulas at the outflow of Lake Mälar into the Baltic, which here forms a deep inlet. The charm of its setting lies in the intermingling of land and water   the skerries fringing the coast, the crags rearing up from the sea, the intricate pattern of waterways encompassing the city. The surrounding area, with its woodlands and lakes, its old castles and coastal towns, is also very beautiful.

★Capital of Sweden
: Stockholm is the capital of Sweden, linked by lakes and canals with the interior of the country. The city is surrounded by suburbs, many of them developed from old residential districts, and since the end of the Second World War new commuter areas equipped with shopping centres and satellite towns have grown up around the capital.

Importance
: Stockholm is the seat of government, Parliament (the Riksdag) and the Supreme Court and the see of a Roman Catholic archbishop, with a University and several other higher educational establishments and scientific institutes, an Academy of Music, many libraries, a great variety of cultural

In the old town of Stockholm

institutions and the Nobel Institute. It is also an important industrial city (particularly metalworking, engineering and textiles), and in addition it is a great tourist centre and congress city.

An underground railway system (Tunnelbana, or T-Bana for short), begun in 1930 but actively developed only after 1945, links the city centre with its various suburbs. The T-Bana stations are a kind of city-wide art exhibition: the tunnels blasted out of the rock were left in their natural state, painted in bright colours and skilfully lit.

★Underground (T-Bana)

Stockholm's Arlanda Airport (for long-distance flights) is 45km/28 miles north of the city centre (fast airport buses from City Terminal). Arlanda and Stockholm's other airport at Bromma handle more than half of all Swedish air traffic.

Airports

Stockholm originally grew up on the islands of Stadsholm, Helgeandsholm and Riddarholm, which were fortified by Birger Jarl in 1252 in order to protect the townspeople against the attacks to which they were continually exposed, particularly from the sea. These islands now form the Old Town (Gamla Stan) of Stockholm. Thereafter the town gradually spread on to the mainland to the north and south. The great days of Stockholm came in the 17th century, when it was the capital of Sweden's Baltic empire. During the 18th and 19th centuries the town's old wooden houses were repeatedly destroyed by fire, and now the buildings are mostly of stone, effectively combining Nordic traditions with modern styles. The new city centre round the Hötorg and Sergels Torg, developed since 1950, is a showpiece of contemporary Swedish architecture.

History

Central Area

Old Town (Gamla Stan)

Helgeandsholm, the nearest to the mainland of the three islands on which the first settlement developed, is reached by way of the Norrbro (North Bridge). The east end of the island is occupied by a small park, Strömparterren, with a summer café, while the western half is dominated by the Riksdag (Parliament), a Neo-Baroque building erected between 1898 and 1904, with the Riksbank (Swedish National Bank) beyond it to the west. The interior of the Riksdag was altered when Sweden adopted a single-chamber system in 1971.

Riksdag

At the south end of the Norrbro, on the island of Stadsholm, is the Royal Palace (Kungliga Slottet), a building in Renaissance style designed by Nicodemus Tessin the Younger (d. 1728) and completed by his son K. G. Tessin. It occupies the site of a medieval Vasa castle destroyed by fire in 1697. The palace contains some 500 rooms decorated in Baroque and Rococo style. On the first floor are the apartments occupied by King Oscar II (d. 1907), the Bernadotte Våning, on the second floor the state apartments (Festvåning) and guest rooms (Gästvåning). In the south wing are the chapel and the Hall of the Estates (Rikssal).

★Royal Palace

In the Treasury are the royal regalia, including the crown of Eric XIV. In the Armoury are displayed magnificent suits of armour and coronation and ceremonial robes. Also in the palace are Gustavus III's Museum of Antique Sculpture and a museum containing models of the medieval castle (open only in summer).

Beyond the palace, to the south-west, stands the Cathedral (Storkyrka). After its consecration in 1306 building work continued for another 200 years, and between 1736 and 1743 it was remodelled in Baroque style. Here the kings and queens of Sweden are married and crowned. The church has a richly furnished interior. Near the altar, which has a beautiful reredos of silver and ebony (c. 1640), is a Gothic sculpture in polychrome wood of St George and the dragon by the Lübeck master Bernt Notke (d. 1509),

★Cathedral

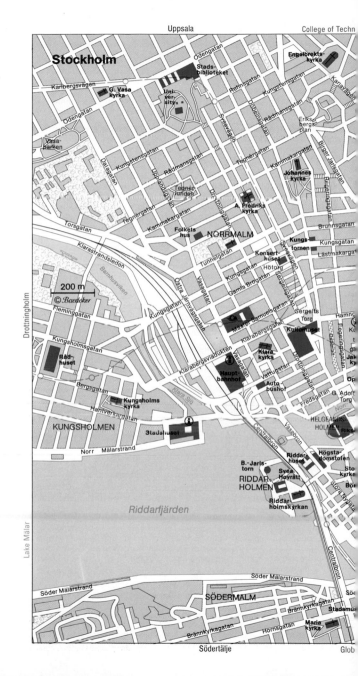

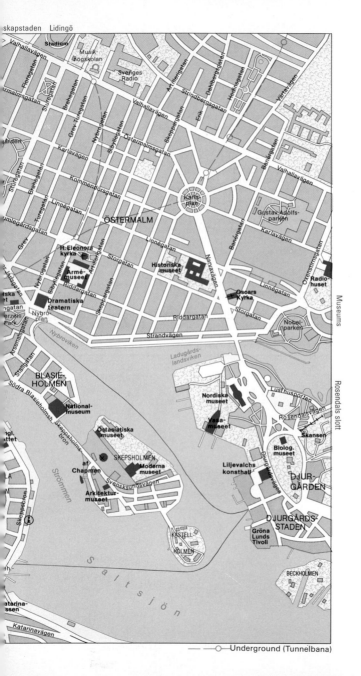

skapstaden Lidingö

Stadion
Musik-Högskolan
Sveriges Radio
Valhallavägen
ÖSTERMALM
Karla-plan
Gustav-Adolfs-parken
Karlavägen
Linnégatan
H. Eleonora kyrka
Armé-museet
Historiska museet
Oscars Kyrka
Dramatiska teatern
Nybro-plan
Riddargatan
Nobel-parken
Strandvägen
Nybroviken
Ladugårds-landsviken
BLASIE-HOLMEN
National-museum
Nordiska museet
Lusthusporten
Rosendalsvägen
Östasiatiska museet
Vasa-museet
Skansen
SKEPPSHOLMEN
af Chapman
Moderna museet
Biolog. museet
Liljevalchs konsthall
Arkitektur-museet
DJUR-GÅRDEN
KASTELL-HOLMEN
DJURGÅRDS-STADEN
Gröna Lunds Tivoli
BECKHOLMEN
Strömmen
Skeppsbron
Katarina-ssen
Katarinavägen
S a l t s j ö n

Museums
Rosendals slott
Radio-huset

— —O— Underground (Tunnelbana)

presented to the Cathedral by Sten Sture, Regent of Sweden, to commemorate the Swedish victory over the Danes in the battle of Brunkeberg (1471). The organ is 18th century.

Stortorg

To the south of the Cathedral, in the centre of the island, is the Stortorg, a square surrounded by 17th and 18th century buildings. One of the finest of these is the Exchange (Börse), built by Erik Palmstedt in 1778, which now houses the Swedish Academy and the Nobel Library. In 1520 the Stortorg was the scene of the Stockholm Massacre, in which Christian II of Denmark executed 82 leading Swedes in order to strengthen his hold on the country.

German Church

South-east of the Stortorg is the German Church (Tyska Kyrka; St Gertrude's), which, more than any other church in the city, preserves the character and style of the 17th century. It has a richly gilded altar by Markus Hebel of Neumünster, a magnificent pulpit in ebony and alabaster designed by Nicodemus Tessin the Elder, a royal pew and an organ (by the firm of Peter in Cologne) presented to the church in 1971 on the 400th anniversary of the German community in Stockholm.

To the east of the church, in Österlånggatan, is the Gyldene Freden ("Golden Peace") restaurant, which has associations with the 18th century Stockholm poet Carl Michael Bellman, among whose best known songs are "Fredmans Epistlar".

To the west of Gamla Stan, Västerlånggatan runs south, lined by small shops, to the Järntorg. In this square is the old Riksbank (c. 1670), one of the oldest bank buildings in the world.

Riddarhustorg

At the north-west corner of Gamla Stan is Riddarhustorg, with a monument to Gustavus Vasa, who re-established the independent Swedish kingdom in 1523. On the north side of the square can be seen the Old Town Hall (17th c.), now occupied by the Supreme Court (Högsta Domstolen).

Roof of the Riddarhus (detail)

The Riddarhus (Knights' House; by Justus Vingboons and Simon de la Vallée, 1641–74), in Baroque style with Neo-Classical features showing Dutch influence, is one of Stockholm's finest buildings. The façade, articulated by columns, is flanked by two wings facing Lake Mälar. The green copper roof is topped by gilded figures. The Knights' Hall, with the coats of arms of Swedish noble families, was until 1866 the meeting-place of the Estate of the Nobility.

★ Riddarhus

From the west side of Riddarhustorg a bridge leads on to the little island of Riddarholm. In Birger Jarlstorg are a column bearing a statue of Birger Jarl, the founder of Stockholm, and Birger Jarl's Tower (15th c.), from which there are fine views of Lake Mälar and the Town Hall.

Riddarholmen

Birger Jarlstorg

Also in the square is the High Court (Svea Hovrätt), housed in the old Wrangel Palace (*c.* 1650), whose round tower is a relic of the old fortifications of Stockholm.

On the south side of the square is the Riddarholm Church (Riddarholmskyrka), which originally belonged to a Franciscan friary but was much altered in later centuries. The cast-iron steeple (1841), 90m/295ft high, is a prominent Stockholm landmark. The church, the burial-place of the Swedish monarchs, has been used since 1807 only for burials and memorial services.

★★ Riddarholm Church

The interior of the Riddarholm Church is particularly fine. The walls are covered with the coats of arms of knights of the Order of the Seraphim, founded in 1336, and the floor is paved with gravestones.

Interior

In the choir, in front of the high altar (1679), are the tombs of King Magnus Ladulås (d. 1290) and King Karl Knutsson (d. 1470). To the right is the burial chapel of Gustavus Adolphus (killed in the battle of Lützen in 1632), with a green marble sarcophagus. Opposite it is the Caroline Chapel (Karolinska Gravkoret), with the tombs of Charles XII (d. 1718) and Frederick I (d. 1751).

Adjoining the Gustavus Adolphus Chapel is the burial chapel of the

Riddarholmen

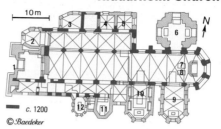

Riddarholm Church

© Baedeker

c. 1200

1	West Doorway	8	Tomb of Karl
2	Torstensson Chapel (1651)		Knutsson (d. 1470)
3	Wachtmeister Chapel (1654)	9	Gustavus Adolphus Chapel (1633–34)
4, 5	Lewenhaupt Chapels (1654)	10	Bernadotte Chapel (1858–60)
6	Caroline Chapel (1671–1743)	11	Vasaborg Chapel (1647)
7	Tomb of Magnus Ladulås (d. 1290)	12	Banér Chapel (1636)

House of Bernadotte (Bernadotteska Gravkoret; 19th c.). In the centre of this, to the rear, can be seen the massive red porphyry sarcophagus of Carl XIV Johan (d. 1844), with the sarcophagus of his wife Desideria (d. 1860) in front of it. Here too is the tomb of Gustaf V (1858–1950).

In the south aisle are the burial chapels of the Counts of Vasaborg and Field Marshal Johan Banér (d. 1641).

In the north aisle, to the left of the entrance, is the chapel of the Counts of Torstensson, and beyond this are the chapel of General Wachtmeister (d. 1652) and the two chapels of the Counts Lewenhaupt.

Norrmalm

From Gamla Stan the Norrbro leads into the Norrmalm district of Stockholm. At the end of the bridge is Gustav Adolfs Torg, with an equestrian statue of Gustavus Adolphus (1796). In the square, to the left, stands the Crown Prince's Palace (1783), which has been occupied since 1906 by the Foreign Ministry. To the right, with a view of the inlet of Strömmen, is the Opera House, and north of this is St James's Church (Jakobskyrka, 1643; tower 1735). From here a series of public gardens extend northward, with the Kungsträdgård (King's Garden), a favourite meeting-place, and statues of Charles XII and XIII. In the Kungsträdgård is Sverigehus (Sweden House), with a tourist information office.

Museums

★National Museum

Opening times:
Tues.–Sun.
11am–5pm,
Tues. and Thur.
to 9pm;
closed Mon.

South-east of Gustav Adolfs Torg, at the southern tip of the Blasieholm peninsula, is the National Museum, with Sweden's finest art collection, including painting and sculpture, decorative art and a department of modern applied art.

The gallery has important works by Dutch and Flemish artists, including Rembrandt ("Conspiracy of Claudius Civilis" and "The Painter's Cook"), Rubens ("Bacchanale" and "Sacrifice to Venus") and Frans Hals the Elder ("Fiddler") and many pictures by 18th century French painters (Boucher, Watteau, etc.). Modern Swedish painting is represented by D. K. Ehrenstrahl, Al Roslin, Carl Fredrik Hill, Prince Eugen, Ernst Josephson, Carl Larsson, Bruno Liljefors, Karl Norström and Anders Zorn. There is also a department of graphic art, with interesting architectural drawings.

In the gardens on the north-west side of the museum is a bronze group, "The Wrestlers" ("Bältespännare", 1867), depicting an old Nordic form of wrestling in which the contestants were tied together at the waist.

To the south of the National Museum is a bridge leading on to the island of Skeppsholm, formerly occupied by the Swedish navy, on which are the Skeppsholm Church (1842), the Museum of Architecture, the Museum of East Asian Art and the Modern Museum, with a large collection of contemporary art (periodic special exhibitions) and a Museum of Photography.

Museums on Skeppsholmen

Moored off the west side of Riddarholm the former training ship "af Chapman" is used in summer as a youth hostel.

"af Chapman"

Along the north end of the Kungsträdgård is Hamngatan, now regarded as Stockholm's main street. There are magnificent views of the city from the rooftop restaurant of the NK (Nordiska Kompaniet) department store. At Hamngatan 4 is the Hallwyl Palace, with a façade showing Spanish inspiration. Formerly the home of the Counts Hallwyl, this is now a museum (interior in turn-of-the-century style, collection of Countess Hallwyl), and is also used for theatrical performances. In Berzelius Park (named after the famous chemist J. Berzelius) is a very popular restaurant, Berns Salonger.

City Centre

Hamngatan

Near Berzelius Park, in Nybroplan, stands the world-famed Royal Dramatic Theatre (Kungliga Dramatiska Teatret), an imposing building in Art Nouveau style popularly known as "Dramaten", which was inaugurated in 1908 with a performance of Strindberg's "Master Olof". The theatre, which has several houses, puts on both classical and modern plays and comedies. Ingmar Bergman has been responsible for a number of productions here.

"Dramaten"

At the west end of Hamngatan, in the centre of the district known as the City, is Sergels Torg, with a modern fountain and a glass column almost 40m/130ft high (by E. Öhrenström, 1974). On the south side of the square is the House of Culture (Kulturhuset; by Peter Celsing, 1974), with a glass frontage which gives it a cheerful and attractive aspect. It contains exhibition rooms, restaurants (with view of Sergels Torg), a library and reading rooms and the Municipal Theatre (Stadsteatern).

Sergels Torg

House of Culture

Sergelsgatan, a pedestrian zone with many shops and an underground market hall, runs north, past five high-rise blocks, to the Hötorg, in which markets are held in spring, summer and autumn. In Hötorg is the Concert Hall (Konserthuset, 1962), home of the Stockholm Philharmonic Orchestra, in which the annual presentation of the Nobel Prizes takes place. In front of it can be seen the Orpheus Fountain (by Carl Milles, 1936).

Concert Hall

From Hötorg Kungsgatan, one of Stockholm's principal shopping streets, runs east, with Sturegallerian, an exclusive shopping centre, the PUB department store and two 17-storey tower blocks, the Kungstornen ("King's Towers").

Kungsgatan

From the Concert Hall a broad avenue, Sveavägen, runs north-west, passing on the left the Adolf Frederikskyrka (1774), which contains sculpture by the Swedish sculptor J. T. Sergel (d. 1814) and a monument to the French philosopher Descartes, who died in Stockholm in 1650 (his remains were taken to Paris in 1666). Towards the far end of Sveavägen are the Commercial College and the Municipal Library (Stadsbiblioteket), and at the end the Wenner-Gren Research Centre (1961). From the Municipal Library Karlbergsvägen runs west to Karlberg Castle (17th c.), now a military academy, on the lake of the same name.

Adolf Frederikskyrka

Parallel to Sveavägen is Drottninggatan, another busy shopping street. At No. 85, once the home of the dramatist August Strindberg (1849–1912), can be found the Strindberg Museum.

Strindberg Museum

At the north end of Drottninggatan are the main buildings of Stockholm University (founded 1878). Near its south end stands the Klarakyrka, with a spire 104m/340ft high; in the churchyard is the grave of the 18th century poet C. M. Bellman. To the west is the Central Station.

University

Kungsholm (King's Island) is separated from the rest of the city by a narrow inlet. Here, on the shores of the Riddarfjärd, is the Town Hall (Stadshuset), a red brick building with green copper roofs which is the great landmark and emblem of Stockholm (by Ragnar Östberg, 1911–23). At the south-east corner of the building is a square tower crowned by an open lantern, on the tip of which (106m/350ft) are the three golden crowns of the Swedish coat of arms. From the platform below the bellcote (lift) there are fine views. On the north front is the "Spectacle of St George", with mechanical figures which perform twice daily, at noon and 6pm, when the bells in the tower play "St George's Tune". At the foot of the east side of the tower, under a pillared canopy, can be seen a recumbent figure (by G. Sandberg) of Birger Jarl, founder of Stockholm.

Kungsholmen

★Town Hall

There are conducted tours of the interior of the Town Hall, taking in both offices and reception rooms, including the Blue Hall, an enclosed inner courtyard surrounded by arcading, the Council Chamber and the Golden Chamber, richly decorated with mosaics and wall paintings. In the gardens fronting the Town Hall are sculptures by Carl Eldh (1873–1953).

To the west of the Town Hall, in Hantverkargatan, stands the Baroque Kungsholm Church (17th c.) and north-west of this, in Scheelegatan, the Council House (Rådhuset; by C. Westmann, 1911–15), occupied by the Law Courts.

Council House

To the east of Norrmalm is the Östermalm district, which is bounded on the west by Birger Jarlsgatan and on the south by the inlet of Nybrovik. Along the waterfront, between Nybroplan and the Djurgård, runs one of Stockholm's finest streets, Strandvägen, along which are a series of palatial buildings, most of them occupied by foreign embassies.

Östermalm

Strandvägen

To the north, in Riddargatan, is the Royal Army Museum (Armémuseet), with a collection of uniforms and weapons illustrating Sweden's military history.

Army Museum

Farther north, in the Humlegård Park, is the Royal Library, Sweden's National Library (built 1870–77, with later extensions). Among its treasures is the Codex Aureus, an 8th century Latin translation of the four Gospels.

Royal Library

To the east of the park, at Sturegatan 14, is the Nobel Foundation, established in 1900 by the Swedish chemist Alfred Nobel. The Foundation annually awards six prizes for outstanding achievements in physics, chemistry, medicine, economics, literature and the cause of peace. (The Peace Prize is presented in Oslo.)

Nobel Foundation

In Karlavägen is the Engelbrektskyrka (by Lars Israel Wahlman, 1914), built of granite and red brick. East of this, in Valhallavägen, can be seen the Stadium built for the 1912 Olympic Games. To the north is the College of Technology.

Engelbrektskyrka

In the southern part of the Östermalm district is the National Historical Museum (Historiska Museet), which offers an excellent survey of the early historical period, the Viking age and the Middle Ages in Sweden; of particular interest are the inscribed stones from Gotland. In the same building is the Royal Coin Cabinet. Nearby are the headquarters of Swedish Radio and Television and, in Borgvägen, the Swedish Film Institute.

National Historical Museum

In Djurgårdsbrunnsvägen, the continuation of Strandvägen to the east, are the National Maritime Museum (Sjöhistoriska Museet), the Museum of Science and Technology (Tekniska Museet) and the Museum of Ethnography (Etnografiska Museet; peoples and cultures of the Third World, with material brought back by travellers of the 18th–20th centuries).

Museums in Djurgårdsbrunnsvägen

◄ *Stockholm Town Hall*

Water Festival in Stockholm

★ Kaknäs Tower

To the north-east of these museums, outside the city centre, rises the Kaknäs Tower, built in the 1960s as a radio and television tower. 155m/510ft high, it is the tallest structure in Scandinavia. At a height of 128m/420ft is an open viewing platform, and there is also a glazed viewing platform, with restaurants, offering panoramic views.

Södermalm

The southern district of Södermalm was incorporated in Stockholm only about 1570. It is a very characteristic part of the city with its picturesque situation and street layout adapted to the rocky terrain. It is reached from the old town (Gamla Stan) by way of a double bridge over the Söderström. At this point there is a sluice (Slussen), separating the fresh water of Lake Mälar from the salt water of the Baltic.

★ Viewpoint

In Södermalms Torg (to the left) is the Katarinahiss, a lift giving access to a platform and restaurant at a height of 36m/120ft, from which there are fine views of the old town and the northern districts of the city. From the viewing platform an iron gangway leads to Mosebacketorg.

On the south side of Södermalms Torg is the former Town Hall (17th c.), now occupied by the Municipal Museum (Stadsmuseet). To the south, in Medborgarplats, is the Medborgarhus (Community House; 1939), which serves a variety of purposes. In Hornsgatan stands St Mary's Church (Mariakyrka; 16th–17th c.), with a steeple added in 1825. Opposite the church is the Hornsgatspuckel, a hill on which there are numerous art galleries and craft shops. In Mariatorg, to the west, can be seen a fountain with a sculpture of Thor and the Midgard snake.

Globe Arena

On the south side of Södermalm are bridges leading to Södra Hammarby-hamnen and Johanneshov, in which is the Globe Arena, a domed building 85m/280ft high erected in the late eighties, with seating for 16,000. It is used for a variety of events (sporting contests, opera, etc.).

★Djurgården

On an island reached from Strandvägen on the Djurgårdsbro lies Djurgården, a park laid out on the site of an earlier deer park which was a royal hunting preserve between the 16th and 18th centuries. In the park are a number of interesting museums.

Immediately beyond the bridge, to the right, is the Nordic Museum (Nordiska Museet), a massive building in Renaissance style which gives a survey of life and work in Sweden over the past 500 years. On the ground floor is the Royal Armoury, with material illustrating the life of the privileged classes, and there are other sections devoted to peasant life in the various provinces of Sweden and to the culture of the Sami (Lapps).

★ Nordic Museum

To the south of the Nordic Museum can be found the Biological Museum, a wooden building in the style of the Norwegian stave churches, with a comprehensive collection of the birds and mammals of Scandinavia. Nearby is Liljevalchs Konsthall, a gallery which puts on exhibitions of Swedish and international art and handicrafts.

Biological Museum

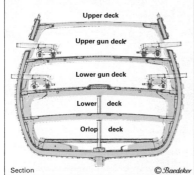

The "Wasa" (1628)

Upper deck

Upper gun deck

Lower gun deck

Lower deck

Orlop deck

Section   © *Baedeker*

On the west side of the island (also accessible from the city by boat) is the Wasa Museum, housing the warship "Wasa", which sank in Stockholm harbour on its maiden voyage in 1628 and was brought to the surface again in 1961.

The "Wasa" was located on the seabed in 1956 at a depth of 32m/105ft, and work began three years later on recovering and preserving it. This was a large-scale operation for which entirely new techniques had to be devised. The vessel, 62m/200ft long, is the only completely preserved 17th century ship in the world. It is now displayed in its own museum, together with numerous items of equipment (everyday objects, carved ornaments, etc.) recovered from the vessel.

★★ Wasa Museum

Opening times: daily 9.30am–7pm, in winter 10am–5pm

Between the Wasa Museum and the Gröna Lund fairground in the south lies an interesting Aquarium (Akvaria Vatten Museum).

Aquarium

The Skansen open-air museum, a branch of the Nordic Museum, extends over a large area to the east of the Biological Museum. The initiator and founder of the museum, which was opened in 1891, was Artur Hazelius, who was concerned to save something of the older Sweden before the development of industry had gone too far in changing the country. The old buildings brought together here include a church and a manor-house, Lapp dwellings and an upland shieling (summer grazing station), smallholders' cottages and peasant farmhouses, and a whole quarter of a town, with craftsmen's workshops. Over the years some 150 old buildings of historical interest have been assembled at Skansen, which is now ten times its original size. In the various houses and workshops visitors can see something of many traditional crafts – butter and cheese making, baking, weaving, basketwork, wood-turning, glass-blowing, etc.

★Skansen open-air museum

Opening times: daily 9am–5pm, in summer to 10pm

Skansen Open-air Museum

Scandinavian animals

Högloftet-Restaurant

Exit

Little Skansen

Tingvallen

Bollnäs-torget

Post office

WC

Rose Garden

Hazelius entrance

Exit

Solliden

Solliden entrance

Restaurant

WC

Main entrance

100 m

1 Town buildings (17th–19th c.)
2 Non-Scandinavian animals
3 Älvrosgården (farmhouse from Mora, 16th–17th c.)
4 Skogaholms Herrgård (manor-house from Närke, c. 1680, reconstructed 1793–94)
5 Agricultural worker's house (1920)
6 Belfry from Östergötland (1732)
7 Belfry from eastern Jämtland (1778–79)
8 Seglora church, from Västergötland (1729–30, tower 1780)
9 Oktorsgården (farmhouse from Halland, 18th c.)

10 Skånegården (farmhouse from Skåne)
11 Delsbogården (farmhouse from Hälsingland, 18th/19th c.)
12 Moragården (farmhouse from Dalarna, 16th/17th c.)
13 Miner's house from Västmanland (17th c.)
14 Peasants' houses from upland Dalarna (17th–18th c.)
15 Lapp encampment
16 Finngården (peasants' houses from Lekvattnet in Värmland, 16th/17th c.)

© Baedeker

Skansen Zoo   But Skansen is a Zoo as well as a museum of cultural history. In its spacious grounds are examples of the various species of animals found in Sweden. Goats, hill cattle, etc., live in their appropriate setting, and there are separate enclosures for brown bears, polar bears, bison, elks and reindeer. There are also specimens of animals not found in Scandinavia, including monkeys, elephants, sealions and penguins; and many small animals and birds live wild. The zoo is open throughout the year.

At the north end of the park rises the Bredablick lookout tower, and to the east of this is the 19th century Rosendal Castle, a wooden building once occupied by King Carl XIV Johan and later converted into a Carl Johan Museum. To the south of the park is the Solliden restaurant, where concerts, displays of folk dancing and theatrical performances are given daily in summer. In this area too is Grönalund, a modern amusement park.

At the south end of the island extends the promontory of Waldemarsudde, on which Prince Eugen (1865–1947), son of Oscar II, built himself a house. Himself a painter, he gathered round him a large circle of artists and writers. Visitors can see his studio and a collection of pictures, including both his own work and works by other Swedish artists of his day.

Waldemarsudde

In the Villa Thiel, at the east end of Djurgården, is another collection of pictures, mostly by 19th and 20th century Swedish artists.

To the east of Djurgården are four small islands, the Fjäderholmarna, with restaurants, craft shops and the Baltic Aquarium. In summer the islands can be reached by boat (about 30 minutes) from Slussen and Ropsten.

Islands off Djurgården

Vetenskapsstaden and Lidingö

On the north side of Stockholm is the district of Vetenskapstaden ("City of Learning"), in which are the Royal Academy of Sciences and the Natural History Museum (Naturhistoriska Riksmuseet). The latter's most recent attraction is the "Cosmonova", a planetarium with a circular cinema in which visitors can see the wonders of the heavens.

Natural History Museum

On an island to the north-east of the city can be found the residential suburb of Lidingö, in which is Millesgården, the former home and studio of the Swedish sculptor Carl Milles (1875–1955), now a museum, which in addition to major works by Milles himself displays his collection of Greek and Roman art. In the grounds of the house, from which there is a fine view of Stockholm, are replicas of various sculptures by Milles.

Millesgården

Surroundings

11km/7 miles west of the city centre (45 minutes by boat), on the island of Lovö, is Drottningholm Palace, now the residence of the royal family. The palace, based on French and Dutch models, was built for Queen Eleonora in 1662 by Nicodemus Tessin the Elder. It contains pictures by David Klöker Ehrenstrahl and Johan Philip Lempke and sculpture by Nicolaes Millich and Burchard Precht. In the beautiful park with its terraces and avenues of lime-trees are various bronze sculptures brought back from Denmark and Bohemia as trophies of war. In 1744 Drottningholm was given to Queen Luise Ulrike (sister of Frederick the Great) as a wedding present, and new wings were added to the palace by Carl Hårleman and Carl Fredrik Adelcrantz, with rooms in French Rococo style, notably the Library. Adelcrantz was also the architect of the theatre (1766), which is still frequently used for performances and still preserves the stage machinery of Gustavus III's reign; 18th century scenery and costumes are displayed in the theatre museum.

Drottningholm Palace

The Chinese Pavilion (1766) in the park was also built for Queen Luise Ulrike as a summer residence; the interior shows a mingling of French Rococo and Chinoiserie. Nearby is the little settlement of "Canton" (1750–60), built to house the craftsmen making furniture and wallpaper for the Chinese Pavilion.

28km/18 miles west of Stockholm, in Lake Mälar, lies the little island of Björkö (Birch Island). During the Viking period Björkö was a trading station, with a population in the 10th century of some 1000 people – craftsmen,

★Björkö

Drottningholm Palace from the park

merchants, peasants and slaves. Here too, about 830, St Ansgar preached the Gospel.

Cemetery area

Outside the area of the settlement is a cemetery with some 2500 burials, the largest in Sweden. Excavations brought to light silver coins from Arabia, silk from China, pottery from Friesland and glass from France, an indication of Björkö's extensive trading connections. The area around the old settlement is now protected as an ancient monument. Nearby is St Ansgar's Chapel (consecrated 930).

In summer there are boat services from Stockholm and Södertälje to Björkö.

Södertälje

South-west of Stockholm is the industrial town of Södertälje (pop. 60,000), which grew out of a Viking trading post situated between Lake Mälar and the Baltic. Originally called simply Tälje, it took the name of Södertälje when the town of Norrtalje was founded. Its industrial development was fostered by the construction of the Södertälje Canal (1807–19) and the railway line from Stockholm to Göteborg, which passed through Södertälje. In Stortorg are St Ragnhild's Church (which preserves some 13th century work), the new Town Hall (1965) and other modern buildings. The old Town Hall was moved to the banks of the canal. In an open-air museum (Östra Sörmlands Museet) on the Torrekällberg old houses and workshops have been re-erected. There is also a working bakery which makes a local speciality, Södertälje *kringlor*. 2km/1¼ miles south of the town is a bathing station, Södertälje Havsbad.

Mariefred

An attractive excursion from Stockholm is a boat trip on Lake Mälar (about 3 hours) to Mariefred (pop. 2600), an idyllic little town in a beautiful setting. Mariefred owes its origin and its name to the Carthusian monastery of Pax Mariae which was founded here in 1493 and continued in existence until the Reformation. It is dominated by its 17th century church, situated on a hill. Below this is the oldest part of the town, with wooden houses lining narrow lanes, most of them running down to the lake. In the market square, to the north of the church, stands the Town Hall (1784), also timber-built. On the south side of the hill, below the church, is a local museum. On the west side of the town, beyond Stallarholmsvägen, can be found the ruined church of Kärnbo.

The most notable building in Mariefred is Gripsholm Castle, on an island close to the shores of Lake Mälar. It takes its name from an earlier stronghold built in 1380 by Seneschal Bo Johnsson which was burned down during the peasant rising led by Engelbrekt Engelbrektsson. The present castle was built by Henrik von Göllen between 1537 and 1544 for Gustavus Vasa. Its last occupant, in 1864, was King Carl XV. Gripsholm featured in Swedish history on several occasions, and was also used as a prison. In 1809 Gustavus IV Adolphus was compelled to abdicate here.

★ Gripsholm Castle

With its thick walls, massive towers and fortifications Gripsholm has preserved its medieval character in spite of extensive alteration and new building. The two bronze cannon in the cobbled courtyard were trophies of the Russian wars in the reign of John III. One of the runic stones beside the drawbridge has an inscription recording a journey to Russia by Ingvar Vitfarnes.

In the interior of the castle, which is now state property, visitors can see 60 of its 102 rooms, including the Round Saloon and the pretty little theatre in the Knights' Wing, built for Gustavus III in the 18th century. The collection of 2800 portraits of royal personages and other notabilities is one of the largest in Europe. Portraits of private citizens from 1809 onwards are housed in the folk high school in Mariefred.

There are regular boat services between Stockholm and Mariefred.

Vaxholm lies on the island of Vaxö, north-east of Stockholm on the channel used by seagoing vessels making for the capital. On a rocky island between Vaxö and Rindö Gustavus Vasa built a defensive tower to protect this channel. During the 17th century it was developed into a powerful fortress,

Vaxholm

Gripsholm Castle on Lake Mälar

419

Runic stone in the park of Gripsholm Castle

and in the following century Rindö was also fortified. The fortress of Vaxholm was given its present form in 1838, but immediately after this rebuilding lost any military significance, since its walls could not withstand modern artillery. It now houses a museum, with a collection of material from its days as a fortress. Until 1912 there was a ban on the construction of stone houses in Vaxholm. During the 19th century this was a favourite summer resort of the people of Stockholm, and the little summer houses with carved decoration and enclosed verandas, in which the inhabitants drank their evening punch, are relics of that period.

Saltsjöbaden   20km/12½ miles south-east of Stockholm (25 minutes on suburban railway), on an inlet in the Baggensfjärd, is the little residential town of Saltsjöbaden, a fashionable seaside resort (yacht marina, golf course, tennis courts, etc.). Here too is the Stockholm Observatory.

Nynäshamn   60km/40 miles south of Stockholm, on the Södertörn peninsula, is Nynäshamn, an industrial town with a modern church. There is a boat service to Visby, on the island of Gotland (see entry).

Lake Mälar   See entry

Sundsvall   E 4

Country: **Sweden**
Province: Medelpad
Population: 93,000
Post code: S–85...   Telephone code: 060

Situation and characteristics   Sundsvall is the only town in the little province of Medelpad (area 7086sq.km/2736sq. miles), half way up the eastern coast of Sweden, which is watered by two rivers, the Indalsälv and the Ljunga. The valleys of the rivers have a luxuriant flora, and the Indalsälv forms Sweden's largest delta, which has many features of geological interest.

Sundsvall is one of the most important ports and commercial towns in the northern countries. It lies at the mouth of the Selångerå between two hills, the Norra and Södra Stadsberg. The layout of the old town was the work of Nicodemus Tessin the Elder, but much of the town was destroyed by a devastating fire in 1888, only the district of Norrmalm remaining unscathed. Thereafter the town was rebuilt in stone, with wide streets, and became known as Stenstaden, the "Stone Town".

Thanks to its excellent situation and to the trade routes to the west which ran through this area Sundsvall was an important trading settlement as early as the 6th century. The town received its municipal charter from Gustavus Adolphus in 1624. A period of some prosperity began in the 19th century, when numerous sawmills were established here: at times there were no fewer than forty operating on the offshore island of Alnö alone. Sundsvall now has an oil terminal and is an important woodworking and papermaking centre.

Economy

Around the main square, the Stora Torg, a great variety of architectural styles are represented. In the centre of the square is a bronze statue (1911) of Gustavus Adolphus, and on its south side stands the Town Hall. At Storgatan 29 is the Municipal Museum. Along this street to the west is the Neo-Gothic Gustav Adolfs Kyrka (1894), with wood sculpture by Ivar Lindenkrantz.

Town

West of the church, in a small park, lies the Bünsowska Tjärn (lake). On the Esplanade, which cuts across Storgatan in the centre of the town, is the Hirschska Hus (1890), a handsome mansion built by a wholesale merchant named Isaak Hirsch.

From Sundsvall's two hills, the Norra and Södra Stadsberg, there are extensive views of the town and the island of Alnö. On the Norra Stadsberg is the Norra Bergets Hantverks- och Friluftmuseum (Craft and Open-Air Museum), with many old wooden houses from the province of Medelpad and comprehensive collections of other material illustrating the way of life of the pre-industrial period.

Open-air museum

Surroundings

To the north of the town a road bridge (1024m/1100yd long, 40m/130ft high) crosses the Alnönsund to the island of Alnö. 2km/1¼ miles north of Alvik is a 13th century stone church with stellar vaulting which has vividly coloured wall paintings, fine sculpture and a triumphal cross of about 1500. The new church (1896) has a richly carved wooden font of the 12th/13th century. At the south-eastern tip of the island is the attractive little fishing village of Spikarna, with the popular Vindheim summer restaurant.

Alnö

To the west of the island of Alnö, reached by way of E 14 and the village of Matfors, is Lake Marmen, on the shores of which are numerous prehistoric remains. In front of the beautiful 18th century church of Attmar can be seen the largest runic stone in Medelpad. Other features of interest are the church of Tuna (1776–77; 13th c. font) and the Tunabacken cemetery area.

Lake Marmen

South of Sundsvall on E 4, around Njurunda, is an attractive region of lakes (waterfowl) and moorland (orchids), fishing villages and islands with good beaches.

Njurunda

50km/30 miles north-west of Sundsvall is Liden. From the Vettaberg (381m/1250ft) there is a fine view into the valley of the Indalsälv. On the lower slopes of the hill can be found a late medieval church.

Liden

Sunndal   C 4

Country: **Norway**
Region: Central Norway

Situation The Sunndal is traversed by the lower course of the river Driva, which is
joined at Oppdal by the Ålma. The valley extends west from Oppdal, half
way between Dombås and Trondheim, to reach the Sunndalsfjord at
Sunndalsøra.

★Along the Sunndal

Oppdal Oppdal (alt. 545m/1790ft, pop. 3500) lies in a wider part of the valley at an
important junction where Road 16 branches off E 6 (Dombås–Trondheim)
and leads west. Here the Ålma, coming from the east, flows into the Driva.
Oppdal is a considerable tourist resort and winter sports centre, with a
chair-lift and several ski-tows, as well as more than 70km/45 miles of
cross-country ski trails. There is an interesting district museum, with old
houses, store-houses (*stabbur*) and other exhibits.

Oppdal church Road 70 runs west down the valley of the Driva, passing a Viking cemetery
area, and comes in 2.5km/1½ miles to Oppdal church, at the foot of Ørsni-
pen (1378m/4520ft). This 17th century wooden church, with a conspicuous
steeple, has 17th and 18th century furnishings (pulpit, altar).

Side trip At Vognill a road branches off and runs north-west (22km/14 miles) to the
to Trollheim Gjevilvass hut (700m/2300ft), on the northern shore of the Gjevilvatn
(663m/2175ft). From here it is an 8–9 hours' walk north-west to the Trollheim hut (531m/1740ft), from which several peaks in the Trollheim range
can be climbed, including Trollhetta (1614m/5295ft; there and back 7–8
hours, with guide) and Snota, the highest peak in the area (1668m/5473ft;
there and back 8–9 hours, with guide).

Farther down the valley is the old manor-house of Gravaune, with an
interesting collection of everyday objects and old weapons. The road then
continues past the Ålbu power station to Lønset (alt. 521m/1710ft). From
here a road goes up the Storlidal, passing the Storfall, to the Storli hut
(652m/2140ft), another good base for climbs in the Trollheim range.

Gjøra After crossing the county boundary the road winds its way down (fine
views) to Gjøra. A side road on the left traverses the Jenstadjuv, a gorge
with a waterfall, into the Gruvedal (good walking country). The main road
continues down the Sunndal following the river, now called the
Sunndalselv.

Romfo Romfo (alt. 138m/453ft) has a church of 1824; to the west of the village is the
Grøa Driva power station (140MW). The village of Fale is a good salmon fishing
centre. Beyond this is Grøa (alt. 100m/330ft); ahead, to the right, can be
seen Hovsnebba (1609m/5280ft).

Sunndal A little farther on the river is crossed on the Elverhøy bridge. On the far side
Bygdemuseum of the bridge are the Sunndal Bygdemuseum and an Iron Age cemetery
area.

Sunndalsøra Sunndalsøra (pop. 5000) lies at the head of the Sunndalsfjord, which is
★ Sunndalsfjord enclosed by snow-covered hills. The town has a large power station
(290MW) and an aluminium plant. Visitors can visit the fishery research
station. At Sunndalsøra a road branches off and follows the south-west
side of the fjord to Eidsvåg (40km/25 miles) and Molde (95km/60 miles: see
entry).

Aursjø 39km/25 miles south of Sunndalsøra (2km/1¼ miles along the Molde road,
then turn left) is the Aursjø (mountain hut at 860m/2920ft), with one of the

Kristiansund

largest dams in Norway, from which water is channelled under pressure to the Sunndalsøra power station.

Sunndalsøra to Kristiansund

The road to Kristiansund runs for 8.5km/5 miles along the steep eastern shore of the Sunndalsfjord (several tunnels) and then through the wooded Øpdalseid area. In another 11.5km/7 miles the octagonal church of Ålvundeid is seen on the left. At the Ålvundfoss, a waterfall 85m/280ft high, the road divides. Road 70, to the left, now runs along the south-west side of the Ålvundfjord.

Tingvoll (pop. 1000), on the Tingvollfjord, has an interesting 13th century stone church containing a runic stone and remains of frescos.

Tingvoll

The road now skirts the north-east side of the fjord. From Kvisvik there is a ferry to Kvalvåg on the island of Frei, from which Road 70 continues to Kristiansund.

Kristiansund (pop. 18,000), chief town of the county of Møre og Romsdal, was founded in 1742. Built on three islands which enclose the harbour, it is the base of a fishing fleet and does a large trade in the shipment of fish products.

Kristiansund

Previously accessible only by ferry, it has been linked with the mainland since 1992 by a suspension bridge over the Gjemnessund and an underwater tunnel. It has a fine modern church. From the Vardek lookout tower to the north-west of the town there is a good view of the islands of Nordland, Gomaland, Kirkeland (on which the main part of the town lies) and Innland, connected with each other by bridges.

15km/9 miles north-west of Kristiansund (boat service), in the open sea, is the island of Grip, the largest of a group of 82 little islands and islets. On Grip are a lighthouse and a 15th century wooden church.

Grip

Tampere (Tammerfors) F 5

Country: **Finland**
Region: Southern Finland (Pirkanmaa). Population: 176,000
Post code: FIN–33210   Telephone code: 931

Events

Tampere Theatre Summer (mid August), part of the Finland Festival; also, in summer, performances in Pyynikki open-air theatre.

Situation and characteristics

Tampere (Swedish Tammerfors) was founded in 1779 as an industrial settlement and is now Finland's third largest town (the largest inland town in Scandinavia) and the country's leading industrial city. It lies between two lakes, Näsijärvi to the north and Pyhäjärvi to the south, which are linked by the Tammerkoski, a stretch of rapids 945m/1000yd long with a fall of 18m/59ft. After Finland came under Russian control in 1809 the development of the town was promoted by the Tsars: thus between 1821 and 1906 its exports to Russia were exempted from customs duties.

Tampere's main industries are now metalworking, textiles and footwear. In addition to its theatres, which have an international reputation, it offers a wide range of cultural and recreational facilities, including the modern Municipal Library, the Lenin Museum, numerous parks and lakes and the Särkänniemi amusement park. Within the city limits are almost 200 lakes, and several inland shipping lines are based in Tampere, including the

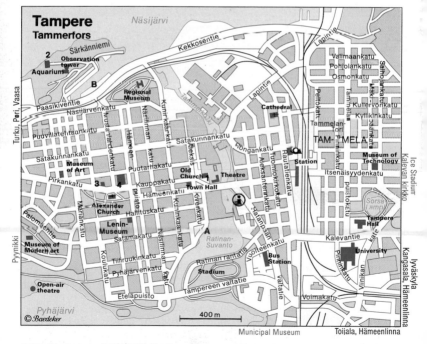

A Silver Line boats   B "Poets' Way" boats

1 Central Square   2 Sara Hildén Museum of Art   3 Hiekka Museum of Art   4 Municipal Library

motor vessels of the Silver Line and the appealing old steamers which ply on the "Poets' Way".

Tampere's principal street is Hämeenkatu, which runs from the railway station by way of Keskustori (Central Square) to the wide avenue Hämeenpuisto. In the square is the Hämeensilta (bridge), with four figures by Wäinö Aaltonen (1929): the Tax-Collector, the Hunter, the Tradesman and the Finnish Maiden. Nearby is the former municipal library, in Neo-Classical style, in front of which is another work by Aaltonen, a monument (1928) to Aleksis Kivi ("The Muse blessing the Poet").

Town

Central Square (Keskustori)

The most notable buildings in Keskustori are the Neo-Classical Old Church (by Carlo Bassi, 1824), on a cruciform plan, with an Empire-style belfry (by C. L. Engel, 1828); the Town Hall, in Neo-Renaissance style (by Georg Schreck, 1890) and the neo-Classical Tampere Theatre (by Kauno S. Kallio, 1913). By the rapids (*koski*) is the Koskikeskus shopping centre.

Tampere's imposing Cathedral is reached from Hämeenkatu by way of the Koskipuisto (park) along the Tammerkoski to Satakunnankatu, then to the right along this street to Rautatienkatu. The Cathedral (by Lars Sonck, 1902–07) is a very typical example of Finnish Art Nouveau architecture, with wall and ceiling paintings by Hugo Simberg, an altar fresco of the Resurrection by Magnus Enckell and liturgical utensils by Eric O. V. Ehrström.

★Cathedral

Notable buildings to the east of the station are the University (by Toivo Korhonen, 1961) and the Tampere Hall, an ultra-modern concert and congress hall (by Sakari Aartelo and Esa Piironen, 1990). A few minutes' walk north-east of the Tampere Hall is the Kaleva Church (by Reima and Raili Pietilä, 1966), an austere concrete structure which is still the subject of controversy a quarter of a century after its completion. In the Liisanpuisto (park) is the Kalevala Monument, a massive bronze sculpture by Terho Sakki (1973). At the east end of the park is Kauppakatu.

University
Tampere Hall

Näsinneula observation tower

Municipal Library, Tampere

425

Tampere

Kauppi Park

Along Kauppakatu to the north lies Kauppi Park, with an extensive range of recreational facilities, including a marina, a riding school, an archery range, a greyhound racing track, a sports institute and an observatory.

Hämeenpuisto

From the Central Square Hämeenkatu runs west into Hämeenpuisto, on or near which are a number of notable buildings – the Alexander Church (by Theodore Decker, 1881), Tampere's second oldest Lutheran church; the Natural History Museum; the Hiekka Museum of Art (with works by Wäinö Aaltonen and many examples of goldsmiths' work), and close by is Moomin Valley (Muumilaakso), with drawings and sketches by Tove Jansson, the internationally popular children's author. Farther west, in Pirkankatu, the Museum of Art (Taidemuseo); the Tampere Workers' Theatre, a brick building designed by Marjatta and Martti Jaatinen (1985); the new Municipal Library (by Raili and Raima Pietilä, 1986); and the Lenin Museum (Hallituskatu 19).

★Pyynikki Park

South-west of the city centre, on the slopes of a hill (152m/499ft), lies the large Pyynikki Park, in which is an open-air theatre with a revolving auditorium; in summer performances are given here by the Workers' Theatre. To the west of the park is the old district of Piispala, a hilly part of the town with old wooden houses.

Särkänniemi Amusement Park

North-east of Pyynikki and east-north-east of Piispala, on the shores of the Näsijärvi, we come to the Särkänniemi Amusement Park, in which is the Sara Hildén Museum of Art (1979; modern Finnish and international art). A conspicuous landmark in the park is the Näsinneula observation tower (173m/568ft), with a revolving restaurant at 120–125m/390–410ft. In addition to merry-go-rounds and other diversions there are an aquarium, a dolphinarium and a planetarium.

Surroundings

★Vehoniemenharju

An attractive trip from Tampere (14km/8½ miles east) is by way of the prettily situated village of Kangasala to the Vehoniemenharju, the narrow strip of land between Lake Roine to the west and the Längelmävesi to the east.

Tampere to Virrat by Boat

The trip from Tampere to Virrat by boat takes about 8 hours. The distance by road, via Teisko, is 120km/75 miles. This route, renowned for its scenic beauty, is known in Finland as the "Poets' Way" and will introduce visitors to a stretch of very typical Finnish scenery.

From Tampere (Mustalahti, to the north of the town) the ship sails north up the Näsijärvi with its many bays and inlets. On the east side of the lake is the village of Teisko, with the Maisansalo leisure centre (tennis courts, saunas, boating harbour, etc.). In about 2½ hours the ship reaches the Murole Canal (lock). While it is passing through the lock there is time to see the Murole Falls, a short distance away to the right. The canal leads into the next lake, Palovesi, and the ship then continues through narrow channels and the open Jäminselkä to the Kautu Canal (swing bridge) and along this into the Ruovesi. On a crag to the left can be seen a house once occupied by the well-known Finnish painter Akseli Gallén-Kallela (1865–1931).

Ruovesi

Farther along the west side of the lake (about 4¾ hours from Tampere) is the beautifully situated village of Ruovesi, now a popular summer resort, where the poet J. L. Runeberg was tutor in a private household (commemorative plaque).

Virrat

The ship then continues north into the Tarjannevesi, a lake dotted with islands, and through the Visuvesi Canal into the Vaskivesi, at the north end of which is the village of Virrat.

Särkänniemi Amusement Park

Tampere to Hämeenlinna by the "Silver Line"

Another very attractive trip through beautiful scenery is on a motor-launch of the Silver Line to Hämeenlinna (see entry), south-east of Tampere.

Telemark   B/C 5/6

Country: **Norway**
Region: Southern Norway

The Norwegian county of Telemark extends north from the Skagerrak to the southern Norwegian uplands and the outliers of the Hardangervidda (see entry). Along its rocky coast are numerous seaside resorts; the hinterland is mostly hilly and well wooded, while the Hardangervidda is a desolate plateau.

Telemark played an important part in the development of skiing techniques. The telemark turn was much practised between the two world wars, and has recently returned to favour, particularly among young people.

Situation and characteristics

Skien (pop. 46,000), situated on the north bank of the Skienselv near the Skagerrak, is a busy industrial town and the administrative centre of Telemark county. The church (1894), with two tall spires, stands on higher ground. South of the church is a monument to the great Norwegian dramatist Henrik Ibsen (1828–1906), who was born in Skien.

Skien

To the east of the town, on the low hill of Brekke (55m/180ft), is Brekke Park (restaurant, summer theatre), with the Telemark County Museum (Fylkesmuseum), which has a small Ibsen collection as well as a number of old peasant houses from the Telemark region.

★County Museum

427

Telemark

2km/1¼ miles north-east of the town is Gjerpen church (13th c.; restored 1921). 6km/4 miles beyond this a narrow side road on the left (signposted) leads up to the Kikuthytta (325m/1065ft), from which there is a superb view.

Telemark Canal

From Skien the Telemark Canal runs north-west through the Norsø and the Bandaksvatn, a picturesque lake shut in by high hills, to Dalen (105km/65 miles from Skien). From the beginning of June to the middle of August motor-ships sail from Skien to Dalen daily (about 10 hours).

Notodden

50km/30 miles north of Skien as the crow flies, at the outflow of the Tinnelv into the Heddalsvatn, is the town of Notodden (alt. 31m/100ft, pop. 12,000), which lies on E 76. To the east along E 76 is Kongsberg (see entry); to the west is the stave church of Heddal.

★★Heddal stave church

The stave church of Heddal (Hitterdal), which dates from the middle of the 13th century (restored in 1849–51 and again in 1952–54), is the largest of Norway's old wooden churches. It has fine 14th century wall paintings and a carved bishop's throne. The windows were inserted during the 19th century restoration work. The belfry stands opposite the church on the other side of the road.

Near here is the Heddal District Museum.

Sauland

E 76 continues to Sauland (alt. 90m/295ft), prettily situated at the junction of the Tuddalsdal and the Heddal. The village has a church built in 1857 on the site of an earlier stave church and a store-house (*stabbur*) of 1718.

Gausta (side trip)

From Saudal a narrow road on the right runs 22km/14 miles up the Tuddalsdal to the 18th century church of Tuddal (alt. 468m/1535ft). 6km/4 miles beyond this is the Tuddal Høyfjellshotell, the starting-point of the ascent of Gausta (1883m/6178ft), the highest peak south of the Bergen Railway (skiing; views).

Heddal stave church

E 76 continues to Seljord (alt. 120m/395ft), to the east of which is the Lifjell, the highest peak in which is Gyrannaten (1550m/5085ft). In November 1870 two Frenchmen who had escaped from the besieged city of Paris by balloon landed on the south-western slopes of the Lifjell.

Seljord
Lifjell

At Høydalsmo Road 45 branches off E 76 on the left to Dalen, at the end of the Telemark Canal from Skien. Just before Dalen is the village of Eidsborg, with a stave church (first mentioned in the records in 1354 but later much altered) and an open-air museum. Dalen is beautifully situated at the west end of the 26km/16 mile long Bandaksvatn.

Dalen
★Bandaksvatn

From Dalen Road 38 runs north, passing the steep rock face of the Ravnejuv (gorge), and returns to E 76 at Åmot.

Ravnejuv

E 76 continues north-west to Haukeligrend, situated at an important junction where Road 39 goes off on the left and runs south to Kristiansand (see entry). Straight ahead is the continuation of E 76, which from here to Haugesund, on the coast (197km/123 miles), is known as the Haukeli Road. Only the first 30km/20 miles of this road is in Telemark; at Haukeliseter it enters the county of Hordaland.

Haukeligrend

The Haukeli Road (toll), opened in 1886 and later partly re-aligned, is one of the most rewarding routes to the southern part of the Norwegian west coast, with superb views of mountain scenery. There are many unlighted tunnels, particularly in the eastern section of the road.

  From Haukeligrend the road climbs up the Haukelifjell, passing an old *stabbur* at Botn (915m/3000ft). Soon it rises above the tree-line, and the view to the west opens up.

★Haukeli Road

Haukeliseter lies on a passage through the mountains, in a lonely setting at the east end of the Ståvann. It is now a popular climbing and skiing centre, with numerous cross-country ski trails. The road now passes from Telemark into Hordaland. Ahead, to the right, can be seen the steep rock faces of the Store Nupsfonn.

Haukeliseter

The old road reaches its highest point on Dyrskar (1145m/3757ft), a pass barely exceeded in magnificence by the great Alpine passes, on the watershed between the Atlantic and the Skagerrak. The modern road runs under the pass in a tunnel 5682m/6214yd long.

★Dyrskar

The road continues over a wasteland of rocks and snow and through a number of tunnels to Røldal (alt. 390m/1289ft), at the north end of the lake of that name, with a stave church (13th century, with later alterations) and an Iron Age cemetery area.

Røldal

The road now climbs the slopes of the Røldalsfjell, with a view ahead of the great Folgefonn glacier, which rises to a height of 1654m/5427ft. It then runs through several tunnels, passes the impressive Seljestad Gorge and comes to a junction where Road 47 goes off on the right and continues north to Odda, on the Sørfjord (see Hardangerfjord). Here E 76 turns south-west along the south side of the Åkrafjord.

★Seljestad Gorge

The village of Etne, on the Etnefjord, has a wooden church of 1675, with a tower added in 1930. There is good fishing in the Etneelv.

Etne

Finally E 76 comes to Haugesund (pop. 27,000), in Rogaland county, a busy port (services to Stavanger and Bergen) and industrial town, with an airport. The Town Hall also houses the Municipal Museum. A large International Film Festival is held in Haugesund every September. The town is linked with the little island of Risøy (fishing port; extensive quays) by an arched concrete bridge.

Haugesund

2km/1¼ miles north of the town centre is the Haraldshaug, said to be the burial mound of Harald Fairhair, whose naval victory at Stavanger in 872

Landscape near Haukeligrend

is commemorated by a 17m/55ft high granite obelisk erected in 1872, the 29 blocks of stone in the monument representing the tribes which he united into a single nation.

Karmøy

To the south of Haugesund town centre is the Karmsund Bridge, which leads to the island of Karmøy. At the east end of the bridge are five standing stones known as the "Fem Dårlige Jomfruer" ("Five Poor Maldens"). In Avaldsnes (2.5km/1½ miles south of Haugesund) is St Olav's Church (c. 1250). 6km/4 miles south of Avaldsnes is a large aluminium plant. At the south end of the island (35km/22 miles from Haugesund) lies the port of Skudeneshavn (pop. 1500), from which there is a ferry to Stavanger.

Tornio (Torneå)   F 3

Country: Finland
Region: Northern Finland
Population: 23,000
Post code: FIN–95400   Telephone code: 698

Situation and characteristics

The Finnish frontier town of Tornio (Swedish Torneå) lies on the Gulf of Bothnia, at the mouth of the Tornionjoki (Torneälv). It consists of three parts, the most westerly of which is on the former island of Suensaari, now joined to the mainland on the Swedish west bank of the river.

The town first appears in the records in the 14th century, when Archbishop Hemming baptised Finns and Sami (Lapps) here. Tornio received its municipal charter in 1621, and thanks to its strategic situation soon developed into a considerable trading town.

Tornio's wooden church (1684–88) is one of the best preserved 17th century wooden churches in Finland. Its high saddle roof is covered with shingles arranged in a pattern; the separate belfry has a steeple surrounded by five turrets. The interior is attractive, with a painted timber ceiling, a carved wooden pulpit and a brass chandelier. To the north of the church is a water-tower with a viewing platform and a café.

Town

Church

A modern building in Torikatu houses the Aine Museum of Art (19th and 20th century Finnish art). In Keskikatu is the Regional Museum (folk material from the Tornio valley and Lapland).

Museums

3km/2 miles south of the town centre we come to the district of Alatornio, which was incorporated in Tornio in 1973. It has a fine church (by Jacob Rijf, 1794–97) in Swedish Neo-Classical style.

Alatornio

Surroundings

9km/5½ miles south of the town is the island of Röyttä, Tornio's port for ocean-going vessels. Boat trips to the skerries.

Röyttä

An attractive excursion from Tornio is a drive up the Tornio valley to the north.

Tornio valley

17km/11 miles from Tornio a side road goes off to the Kukkolankoski rapids, which have a fall of 13.8m/45ft over a distance of 3.5km/2½ miles. There is a restaurant with good fish dishes.

Kukkolankoski

On the last Sunday in July a Whitefish Festival takes place at the rapids, with rafting races.

26km/16 miles beyond the turning for Kukkolankoski another side road branches off to the rapids of Matkakoski.

Matkakoski

At Karunki, half way between the two rapids, can be seen a handsome old wooden church (1817).

Beyond this is Ylitornio, with a modern stone church, beside which is an old wooden belfry. 10km/6 miles north of the church we reach a road junction where Road 930 goes off on the right to Rovaniemi (see entry). A short distance along this road is a narrow side road leading to a car park on the slopes of Aavasaksa (242m/794ft), round which flows the Tengeliönjoki. From the car park a footpath (350m/380yd) leads to the top of the hill, from which the midnight sun can be seen on Midsummer Day, although the hill is actually south of the Arctic Circle.

Ylitornio

Aavasaksa

Accommodation in this area is available in both summer and winter in comfortable holiday cabins. There is a ski-lift (605m/660yd long; height difference 114m/374ft).

Haparanda (Finnish Haaparanta) is Tornio's Swedish neighbour and counterpart, on the west bank of the Torneälv (Tornionjoki). The town was founded in 1809, after Tornio, together with the rest of Finland, had passed to Russia. The boundary wall in the sports ground to the north of the town is a relic of these earlier frontier confrontations: the present frontier between Sweden and Finland is now regarded by both sides as the most peaceful frontier in the world. Haparanda is Sweden's most easterly town.

Haparanda

During the First World War Russia and the Central Powers exchanged prisoners of war unfit for further service through Haparanda. In the churchyard of Nedertorneå, on the west side of the town, are the graves of Austrian, German and Turkish prisoners who died on the journey.

Trelleborg   D 7

Country: **Sweden**
Province: Skåne. Population: 35,000
Post code: S–231.. Telephone code: 0410

Situation and characteristics	Trelleborg, on the coast of Skåne, is the most southerly town in Sweden. Founded in the 12th century, it owed its prosperity in the Middle Ages mainly to the abundant supplies of herring in the Baltic. In 1619 it lost its municipal charter to Malmö, but recovered it in 1867. A period of rapid development began with the construction of the harbour and the coming of the railway in 1875, when Trelleborg was linked to the Swedish network by a branch line from Lund.

The town now plays an important part in communications with the mainland of Europe. A ferry service to Sassnitz on the German island of Rügen was opened in 1897, and this was later followed by a link with Travemünde.

Town

Central area

In the oldest part of the town the medieval street layout has been partly preserved. The church, originally dating from about 1250, was almost completely rebuilt at the end of the 19th century. Around the church and the old market square, the Gamla Torg, some of the little single-family houses characteristic of Skåne have been preserved.

Foundations of a 13th century church belonging to the Franciscan friary which once stood in the square were brought to light in 1932.

Art Gallery

On the east side of the Municipal Park is the Art Gallery (1935), with a collection of sculpture by Axel Ebbe (1868–1941). In the Stortorg is the Sea Serpent Fountain, also by Ebbe.

Nearby is the Water-Tower (by Ivar Tengbom, 1912; 58m/190ft high).

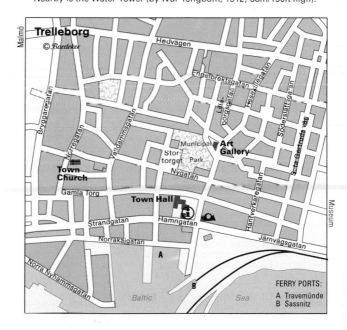

On the harbour, near the railway, can be seen a monument presented by
Germany in 1926 in gratitude for the help of the Swedish Red Cross in
returning wounded prisoners of war from Russia during the First World
War. A few hundred metres east of the harbour, in Skyttsgården, is the
Municipal Museum.

Harbour

Surroundings

Road 9 runs east from the town to the Smygdehuk lighthouse, marking the
most southerly point in Sweden. From here it is 1581km/982 miles to
Treriksröset on the Norwegian–Swedish frontier near the Lyngenfjord.

The village of Västra Vammenhög, north-east of Trelleborg, achieved
world fame after featuring in Selma Lagerlöf's book "The Wonderful
Adventures of Nils".

Tromsø   E 2

Country: **Norway**
Region: Northern Norway
Population: 47,500. Post code: N–9000

The Norwegian port of Tromsø lies between Narvik and Hammerfest, in
latitude 69°39' north, on a small island connected to the mainland by a
bridge 1036m/1100yd long and 43m/140ft high. The town grew up around a
church founded in the 13th century and received its municipal charter in
1794. Tromsø is now the largest town in northern Norway, chief town of
Troms county and an important fishing port, with a university, an observatory for the study of the aurora borealis and the meteorological station
for northern Norway. The midnight sun is visible here, in good weather,
from May 21st to July 23rd. In 1944 the German battleship "Tirpitz" was
sunk by British aircraft off the island of Kvaløy.

Situation and
characteristics

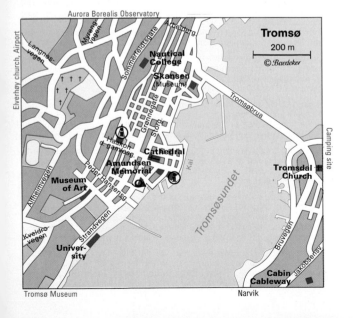

Tromsø

Bird's-eye view of Tromsø

Economy and transport	Tromsø has been, and still is, a base for expeditions to the Arctic (monument to Amundsen). Ships are fitted out here for fishing in the Arctic Ocean, and many fishing boats use the harbour of Tromsø as a base. The fast ships of the Hurtigrute (see entry) from Bergen to Kirkenes and vice versa call in at Tromsø every day, and in summer this is the starting-point for cruises to Spitzbergen. There are regular air services between Tromsø and Oslo and other major Norwegian cities.
Town Tromsdal Church	On the mainland, just before the bridge, is the Tromsdal Church, a striking example of modern architecture (by Jan Inge Hovig, 1965), known as the "Cathedral of the Arctic". The whole of the east end is occupied by a stained glass window (140sq.m/1500sq.ft), "The Return of Christ".
Skansen Museum	Near the west end of the bridge, on the site of an old fort, is the Skansen Museum (local history and traditions). On the fjord, in a separate building, is the Polar section of the museum, which displays, among much else, fishing and other equipment from Amundsen's South Pole expedition.
Cathedral	South-west of the landing quay, in the centre of Tromsø, stands the large wooden Cathedral (1861). The altarpiece, a copy of one in the Bragernes Church in Drammen, depicts the Resurrection. The church has stained glass by Per Vigeland.
★Tromsø Museum	In a park 2km/1¼ miles south-west of the town centre, reached from the Cathedral by way of Storgate and Strandveien, passing the University, is Tromsø Museum, with natural history and ethnographic collections (including a section on the culture of the Sami) and a number of old 18th and 19th century buildings. Near the museum is its aquarium.
Elverhøy Church	To the west of the town centre stands the Elverhøy Church (1802), a wooden church on a cruciform plan which from 1803 to 1861 was the cathedral of Tromsø. It was moved to its present site in 1975. Notable features of the interior are the altar and a medieval Madonna in wood.

Fjord landscape near Tromsø

Surroundings

A cabin cableway runs up from a station to the south of the Tromsdal Church to a height of 420m/1380ft (restaurant; extensive views).

Viewpoint

Some 30km/20 miles south of Tromsø, on the east side of the island of Kvaløy, lies the village of Hella, with an open-air museum containing a number of houses from old Tromsø.

Open-air museum

Trondheim

C 4

Country: **Norway**
Region: Central Norway
Population: 137,000. Post code: N–7000

Trondheim, Norway's third largest city, lies in latitude 63°25′ north and longitude 10°33′ east in an inlet on the south side of the Trondheimfjord, surrounded by a ring of hills. The town is built on a peninsula formed by the Nidelv which is linked with the mainland only at its west end. Trondheim is the chief town of the county of Sør-Trøndelag and the see of both a Lutheran and a Roman Catholic bishop, with a number of scientific and educational institutions. SINTEF, Scandinavia's largest technological research centre, also has its headquarters here.

Situation and characteristics

The favourable temperature conditions (average in January rarely below −3°C/+27°F) ensure that the fjord is always ice-free and foster a rich growth of vegetation.

The principal industries are foodstuffs, metalworking and engineering. The main exports are fish products and canned fish.

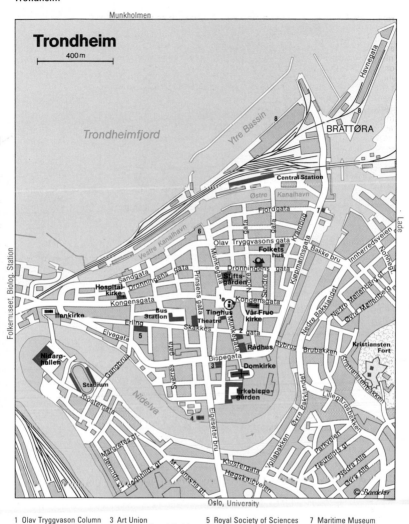

Trondheim

400 m

1 Olav Tryggvason Column 3 Art Union 5 Royal Society of Sciences 7 Maritime Museum
2 Museum of Applied Art 4 St Olav's Church (ruin) 6 Fishmarket 8 Hurtigrute landing-stage

History   Trondheim (formerly spelt Trondhjem) was originally the name given to the whole of the Trondheimfjord area, the original nucleus of the kingdom of Norway, where the Norwegian kings were elected by the Øreting. Here in 997 Olav Tryggvason (or Tryggvessøn) built the royal stronghold of Nidarnes and a church dedicated to St Clement.

King Olav the Saint is regarded as the real founder of the town (1016), which was known until the 16th century as Nidaros ("mouth of the river Nid"). The town developed rapidly after Olav's death in 1030, when hosts of pilgrims travelled to the shrine of the sainted king. The cult of St Olav made

Trondheim the largest and wealthiest town in Norway, with nine churches and five religious houses in addition to the Cathedral.

The Reformation put an end to the pilgrimages; the saint's shrine was carried off to Denmark and destroyed, and his remains were buried at an unknown spot within the Cathedral. All but a few of the churches and convents disappeared. Thereafter the town was destroyed by fire, either wholly or partially, no fewer than fifteen times. In spite of all this, however, at the beginning of the 19th century it was still as large as Oslo, with a population of some 9500.

After the coming of the railway, connecting the town with the rest of the Norwegian system in 1877 and with the Swedish system in 1881, Trondheim enjoyed a period of rapid growth.

A decision by the Norwegian Parliament (Storting) that the town should revert to its old name of Nidaros as from January 1st 1930 was reversed in February of the following year in recognition of the townspeople's preference for Trondheim (the spelling now adopted instead of the previous Trondhjem).

The central feature of the town and the hub of its traffic is the Market Square (Torget), at the intersection of its two main traffic arteries, Kongensgata and Munkegata. In the centre of the square rises a tall octagonal column bearing a statue of Olav Tryggvason (1923). At the foot of the monument, set into the paving, are letters marking the four cardinal points (N–V–S–Ø).

Central Area

Torget

From the Market Square Munkegata runs south to the Cathedral. On the right (No. 20) is the imposing Tinghus (1951), with two bronze doors and coloured ceramic reliefs depicting episodes in the history of the town. Beyond this, also on the right (No. 8), is the Cathedral School, in an 18th century brick building. On the opposite side of the street is the Nordenfjeld Museum of Applied Art (Kunstindustrimuseum), with examples of modern Scandinavian design. To the south stands the Town Hall (Rådhus).

Munkegata

Trondheim Cathedral was built by King Olav Kyrre (1066–93) over the tomb of St Olav and considerably enlarged after the establishment in 1151 of the archbishopric of Nidaros, with authority over the whole of Norway. In conception and execution it is the most magnificent church in the Scandinavian countries. The transept and chapterhouse are in a Late Romanesque transitional style influenced by the Norman architecture of England, and the fine Early Gothic domed octagon dates essentially from the same period. The long choir, with the beautiful south doorway, was built in the early 13th century, the massive nave and the tower, also in Gothic style, between 1230 and 1280. After being ravaged by fire in 1531, 1708 and 1719 the whole western half of the church, from the transept to the west front, was reduced to ruin. The reawakening of national consciousness in the 19th century, however, saved the Cathedral from total destruction. Restoration work began in 1869, and on July 28th 1930, the 900th anniversary of St Olav's death, the church was re-consecrated. The organ (1930), in its Baroque organ-case, was moved in 1936 to a new position under the rose window, and the west front was restored between 1914 and 1968.

★★Cathedral (Domkirke)

Origins and architecture

The Cathedral is built of bluish-grey soapstone (*klebersten*) quarried to the south and east of Trondheim. In the 11th and 12th centuries the Cathedral was the burial-place of the Norwegian kings. In the 15th century a number of kings were crowned here, and since 1814 it has been a requirement of the constitution that the monarch should be crowned in Trondheim Cathedral.

Over the high choir is the domed octagon, in richly decorated Gothic. From the ambulatory there is a view of St Olav's Spring, which was probably a factor in determining the site of the earliest church here. Adjoining the high choir is the aisled long choir (26m/85ft long), with a beautiful font based on fragments of an earlier one. The south chapel in the Romanesque transept

Interior

437

Trondheim Cathedral

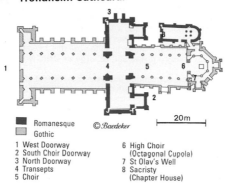

Romanesque   © *Baedeker*
Gothic

1 West Doorway	6 High Choir
2 South Choir Doorway	(Octagonal Cupola)
3 North Doorway	7 St Olav's Well
4 Transepts	8 Sacristy
5 Choir	(Chapter House)

was consecrated in 1161. The aisled nave, almost completely rebuilt, is 42.50m/140ft long by 20m/65ft wide, with fourteen piers supporting the vaulted roof. The large organ, under the rose window, was made by Steinmeyer, of Øttingen in South Germany (1930). Fine stained glass (1913–34) by Gabriel Kielland.

Archbishop's Palace (Museum)

To the east and south-east of the Cathedral lies the old churchyard. To the south-west the Archbishop's Palace (Erkebispegården), a medieval stone building, now houses a collection of weapons and the Museum of the Resistance (1940–45).

Façade of Trondheim Cathedral (detail)

Stiftsgård

North-west of the Cathedral, in Bispegata, is the art gallery of the Art Union (Kunstforening), which puts on periodic special exhibitions.

From the Bybru (Town Bridge), which crosses the Nidelv to the north-east of the Cathedral, there is a fine view of the old warehouses along the river.

North of the Market Square, in Munkegata, can be seen the Stiftsgård, a substantial yellow wooden mansion (*c.* 1770) in which the king stays when visiting Trondheim.

In Kongensgata, to the east of the Market Square, is Vår Frue Kirke, the Church of Our Lady (13th and 16th–17th c.). In the adjoining gardens is a small bronze statue of the Norwegian naval hero Peter Tordenskjold, born in Trondheim in 1691; it is a replica of the original statue by H. W. Bissen in Copenhagen.

South-west of the Market Square, in Erling Skakkesgata, is the headquarters of the Royal Society of Sciences (Kongelige Norske Videnskabers Selskab), founded in 1760, with a fine library (old manuscripts) and large collections of material in a variety of fields (bird diorama; botany, mineralogy, zoology; church art; antiquities).

Farther west, at the end of Kongensgata, can be found the Ilen Church, built of bluish quartz sandstone. To the south of this, reached by a bridge over the Nidelv, are the Nidarø Trade Fair Grounds, with halls for sporting events, etc.

The oldest port installations are those at the mouth of the Nidelv. On the Øvre Elvehavn, which extends north from the Bybru, are a series of old wooden warehouses built on piles. The Kanalhavn lies between the railway station, at the north end of the town, and the mainland. To the north of the station, on the Ytre Basseng, is the quay used by the Hurtigrute ships.

Around the Market Square and Cathedral

Art Union

Stiftsgård

Vår Frue Kirke

Royal Society of Sciences

Nidarø Trade Fair Grounds

Harbour

Trondheim

Maritime Museum

At Fjordgata 6 the Maritime Museum has ship models and pictures illustrating many centuries of ships and seafaring.

Kristiansten Fort

On a low hill (72m/236ft) to the east of the town, reached by way of the Bybru and the Bakklandet district, is the little 17th century fort of Kristiansten (open in summer 4–6pm), from which there is a fine view of the town (best by morning light).

★View

There is a magnificent view of Trondheim and its fjord from the revolving restaurant in the Television Tower to the east of the city (120m/395ft; restaurant at 80m/260ft).

Western Outskirts

Folk Museum

On a low hill to the south-west of the city, once occupied by the Sverresborg, a stronghold built by King Sverre (1177–1202), is the Folk Museum (Folkemuseet), an open-air museum with old buildings from the Trondheim area.

Biological
Research Station

North-west of Trondheim, on the shores of the fjord, stands the Biological Research Station, with an aquarium and a large marine laboratory.

Surroundings

Munkholmen

2km/1¼ miles north of the city, in the Trondheimfjord, is the fortified island of Munkholm (motorboats from Ravenkloa fish market, at the north end of Munkegata; hourly service, 10-minute trip). On the island stands a round tower belonging to the former Benedictine abbey of Nidarholm (founded in the 12th century), the site of which is now occupied by a fort built in 1658, the Gammel Festning.

Ringve Gård
Museum

3.5km/2 miles north of the city centre, in the Lade district, can be found the manor-house of Ringve Gård, childhood home of the naval hero Peter Nordenskjold. It now houses the Ringve Museum, with a fine collection of musical instruments, which visitors can play (concert hall).

Fjellseter
Gråkallen

A pleasant excursion from Trondheim is on the Fjellsetervei to the Fjellseter (367m/1204ft; skiing area, ski-jump), 8km/5 miles west of the city. From here there is a path (15 minutes) to the summit of Gråkallen (556m/1824ft), from which there are views of much of the Trondheimfjord, extending east to the mountains along the Swedish frontier and south to Snøhetta and the Trollheim hills. The hill can also be reached on the Gråkallen electric railway from St Olavsgata, or by bus from Dronningensgata to Lian (30 minutes; alt. 272m/892ft), continuing on foot by way of the Fjellseter and Skistua to Gråkallen (a pleasant walk, 2–2½ hours there and back).

Trondheim to Namsos

Værnes

E 6 (the Narvik road) runs east from Trondheim along the shores of the fjord. There is also a motorway (No. 706; toll). In 35km/22 miles, at Værnes (shortly before the tunnel under the airport), is a 13th century church.

Steinkjer

125km/78 miles from Trondheim is Steinkjer (pop. 20,000), on the Steinkjerfjord, an agricultural market centre in the county of Nord-Trøndelag. On the north bank of the Steinkjerelv is an open-air museum, with old peasant houses. 10km/6 miles west of the town, at Bardal, are Stone Age and Bronze Age rock carvings.

Stiklestad

Near Steinkjer is the little town of Stiklestad, where King Olav II (St Olav) was killed in 1030. Documents relating to him and the battle can be seen in the Stiklestad Nasjonale Kulturhus and in the St Olav Museum.

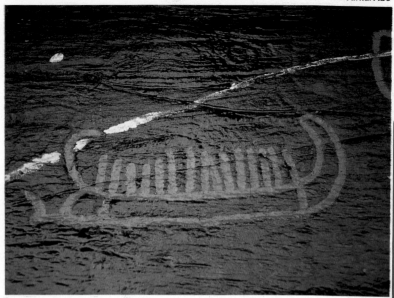

Rock carving, Bardal

The road to Namsos (No. 17) branches off at Asphaugen. Namsos (pop. 11,000) lies at the mouth of the Namsenelv, which here flows into the Namsenfjord, 205km/128 miles from Trondheim. To the east of the town is the Namsdal Museum, with old boats, tools and everyday objects. From Bjørumsklompen (115m/377ft) there is a fine view of the town.

Namsos

Turku/Åbo

F 5

Country: **Finland**
Region: South-western Finland
Population: 174,000
Post code: FIN–20100
Telephone code: 921

City sightseeing tours are run in summer; departure from tourist information office.

City tours

The Turku Music Festival, part of the Finland Festival, is held in the first half of August.

Music Festival

The southern Finnish town of Turku (Swedish Åbo), the country's oldest town and once its capital, lies on the Gulf of Bothnia, at the mouth of the Aurajoki, sheltered by a number of larger islands and a swarm of skerries. Some 5% of the population is Swedish-speaking, and the town attracts many visitors from neighbouring Sweden. Turku is the chief town of the province of Turku-Pori, with the Provincial Court of Appeal (established here in 1623), and the seat of the Lutheran Archbishop of Finland. It has a Finnish and a Swedish university and a commercial college. Together with neighbouring Naantali the port of Turku handles a busy import and export

Situation and characteristics

441

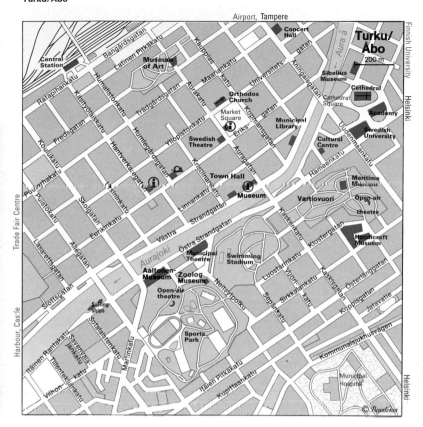

trade. Turku is also an important industrial town (shipbuilding, engineering, foodstuffs, textiles, etc.); most of the industrial plants are on the outskirts of the town.

History

Turku lies in the area where the successors to the Swedish Vikings landed in the 12th century and set out to conquer what is now Finland. The Swedish name means "settlement by the river", the Finnish name "market place". In 1525 the town received its municipal charter from Gustavus Vasa; then in 1630 Gustavus Adolphus established a grammar school in the town which was raised to university status in 1640. In 1743 the treaty ending the two years' war between Russia and Sweden was signed in Turku. In 1809 the town, together with the rest of Finland, came under Russian control. In 1810 the seat of government was transferred to Helsinki, and in 1827, after a devastating fire, the university also moved there.

After Finland became independent a new Swedish-language university was established as a private foundation in 1918, followed two years later by a state Finnish-language university. Thereafter Turku took on a new lease of life, and from the late 1950s onwards the town developed even more rapidly. For many years it was an important centre for the building of

Bird's-eye view of Turku

icebreakers and other specialised types of vessel. During the seventies it developed into a considerable tourist centre.

The hub of the city's traffic is the Market Square (Kauppatori; market on weekdays until 2pm), on the north bank of the Aurajoki. Flanking the square are the Swedish Theatre (1838), the glass-roofed Hansa shopping centre, offering an endless variety of wares, and the Orthodox church (by C. L. Engel, *c.* 1840).

Town

Market Square

From the Market Square the busy Aurakatu runs north-west to the Museum of Art (Taidemuseo), an imposing granite building (by G. Nyström, 1904) standing on high ground surrounded by gardens. It contains a varied collection of pictures and sculpture, mainly by Finnish artists. On the steps leading up to the entrance are figures by Wäinö Aaltonen of the Finnish painters R. W. Ekman (1809–73) and V. A. Westerholm (1860–1919). To the west of the Museum is the Central Station.

Museum of Art

Aurakatu ends at the bridge over the river Aura (Aurasilta). On the banks of the river, to the right, stands the Town Hall (Kaupungintalo; 1885). Nearby is the town's oldest surviving timber building (restored 1957), Quensel House (named after its first known owner, Wilhelm Quensel, appointed an assessor to the Court of Appeal in 1694), which now houses the Pharmacy Museum. Part of the furnishings of the museum came from an old pharmacy in Oulu. Here too are a tourist information office and the departure point of the water-buses which sail to the skerries.

Town Hall
Pharmacy
Museum

Farther upstream, also on the near bank of the river, is the Municipal Library (by C. Wrede, 1903), modelled on the Ritterhaus in Stockholm, with an attractive fountain.

443

Turku/Åbo

Old Town Hall

Upstream from the Library a bridge crosses the river to Cathedral Square, on the west side of which are a bronze statue of the Finnish historian H. G. Porthan (1739–1804), the Swedish Lyceum (founded 1630; present building 1724) and the Old Town Hall, from the balcony of which the peace of Christmas is proclaimed in December every year.

★Cathedral

Standing on the east side of the square, on Unikankari Hill, the Cathedral (Tuomikirkko; formerly St Henrik's) was founded about 1230 and consecrated in 1290. It is a massive brick church in Late Romanesque style with Gothic and Renaissance additions and a 98m/320ft high tower.

Interior

The interior of the Cathedral (restored after a fire in 1827) contains the monuments of many notable figures. To the right of the main entrance is the burial chapel of Torsten Stålhandske (d. 1644), the Swedish commander of the Finnish cavalry during the Thirty Years' War, and to the left is the Tavast Chapel, with the tombs of Bishops Magnus Tavast (d. 1452), Olaus Tavast (d. 1460) and Magnus Stjernkors (d. 1500). To the left of the choir is the Kankas Chapel, the finest in the church, built for the Horn and Kurck families, in the centre of which is the granite sarcophagus of the much-tried Queen Katharina Månsdotter (d. 1612), daughter of a poor common soldier, whom Eric XIV raised to the throne. To the right of the choir is the Tott Chapel, built by Per Brahe in 1678, with the tombs of the Swedish general Åke Tott (d. 1640) and his wife Sigrid Bjelke.

Museums

To the north of the Cathedral, in Piispankatu, is the Sibelius Museum, in a low modern building, with a collection of musical instruments; periodic concerts. In the same street is the "Ett Hem" museum, a reconstruction of a 19th century middle-class house with furnishings of the period.

Finnish University

500m/550yd north-east of the Cathedral is the Finnish University (Turun Yliopisto), opened in 1922; the present buildings were erected between 1954 and 1960.

Facing the Cathedral to the south-east, in Hämeenkatu, can be found the former Academy (1802–15), occupied by the University until its transfer to Helsinki in 1827. It now houses the offices of the provincial government, the Court of Appeal and the Cathedral chapter.

Swedish University

Immediately south-west of the Academy, at the corner of Uudenmaankatu, is the Swedish University (Åbo Akademi), opened in 1919. In the gardens in front of the building can be seen a bronze statue (by W. Runeberg, 1888) of Per Brahe, Swedish governor of Finland 1637–40 and 1648–54; on the base is the inscription "Jagh war med landett, och landett med mig wääl tillfreds" ("I was well satisfied with the country, and the country with me").

From Cathedral Square Uudenmaankatu runs south-east to Kupittaa Park. In the southern half of the park are a swimming pool and St Henry's Spring, with whose water the first Christians in Finland are said to have been baptised.

Vartiovuori

South-west of the Old Town Hall, at the foot of Vartiovuori, are the headquarters of the Economic Society, founded in 1797 to promote the development of agriculture, the arts and industry. Diagonally opposite this, in the little Runeberg Park on the banks of the Aurajoki, is a sculpture by Wäinö Aaltonen, "Lilja". On Vartiovuori itself are attractive public gardens, a Second World War anti-aircraft position and the very interesting Maritime Museum, housed in the former Observatory (by C. L. Engel, 1819) and an old water-tower of 1903 (astronomical collection; art collection).

Handicraft Museum

On the south side of the hill (which escaped the great fire in 1827) is a group of old wooden houses, now forming a very interesting Handicraft Museum (Käsityölaismuseo). The craftsmen working here produce a variety of everyday objects which make very attractive souvenirs.

On Sampanlinna Hill are an open-air theatre, an old windmill and (on the west side) the Swimming Stadium. Beyond Neitsytpolku is the Zoological Museum, which offers an excellent survey of the fauna of Finland (including birds which nest there). To the south-west extends a sports park.

North-west of the Swimming Stadium, in Itäinen Rantakatu, which runs along the south bank of the Aurajoki, stands the Municipal Theatre (1962). In front of it is a statue of the writer Aleksis Kivi (by Wäinö Aaltonen, 1949).

Farther west, at Itäinen Rantakatu 11, is the Wäinö Aaltonen Museum (1967), with a collection of sculpture and other works of art.

Moored at St Martin's Bridge (Martinsilta) are two old sailing ships – the "Suomen Joutsen", now a training school for seamen, and the barque "Sigyn" (built 1887, restored 1971–78) – which are open to the public in summer. On the banks of the river are a number of old vessels which have been converted into restaurants and the landing-stage used by the steamer "Ukko-Pekka", which sails to the skerries.
   South-west of the "Sigyn", in Vilhonkatu, is St Martin's Church (1933).

The New Cemetery, on the eastern outskirts of the city, has a notable chapel by the Turku-born architect E. Bryggman (1941), a showpiece of the romantic variant of functionalism.

On the west side of the town (reached from Aurakatu by way of Linnankatu), on the right bank of the Aurajoki near the harbour, stands Turku Castle (Turunlinna). It was probably built about 1300 on what was then an island at the mouth of the river and was enlarged in the 16th/17th century (renovated 1959–61). It now houses the Turku Historical Museum, which offers an excellent survey of the development of Finnish culture (portraits, furniture, tapestries, costumes, arms and armour, etc.).

Turku Castle

Surroundings

St Karin's Church	2km/1¼ miles north-east of Cathedral Square (along Hämeenkatu, then beyond the railway turn left into Kirkkotie) is the little 14th century church of St Karin (Kaarinankirkko). In the churchyard can be seen the grave of the legal scholar Mathias Calonius (1738–1817), first governor of Finland after its annexation by Russia, who insisted that the country's old laws should be maintained.
St Mary's Church	3km/2 miles north-east of Turku station on the Tampere road (Tampereentie) is St Mary's Church (Maariankirkko), a well preserved 14th century church of undressed stone. Nearby, at the village of Räntämäki, are the remains of the first Christian church in Finland, believed to have been built in 1161.
Ruissalo	South-west of Turku, off the mouth of the Aurajoki lies the island of Ruissalo, which is linked with the mainland by a bridge. Here there is a large recreation area, with a camping site, a golf course, minigolf and facilities for riding and water-skiing. In August every year a rock festival, Ruisrock, is held here. On the island is a spring with an inscription commemorating the Swedish writer M. Choräus (1774–1806), who lived on Ruissalo for some time. On the south coast is a bathing station. The shores of the island are lined with handsome villas (mostly timber-built) dating from the turn of the century. In the centre of the island is the Villa Roma (art exhibitions; artists' studios). South of Ruissalo (reached by motorboat) the little island of Pikku-Pukki, in the Ruissalo Sound (the main shipping channel to Turku), is a popular excursion from Turku (Airisto Yacht Club; summer restaurant).
Naantali	On the coast 17km/10 miles west of Turku is the charming little town of Naantali (Swedish Nådendal; pop. 11,000), a popular seaside resort. The town grew up around a Brigittine convent founded in 1443. The old church, situated on the coast north of the town, has a number of monuments and a 15th century altar from Danzig. Near the church can be seen a stone commemorating Jöns Budde (d. 1491), the earliest identifiable Finnish writer, who was a monk in Naantali. Naantali is now Finland's principal oil-importing port.
Kultaranta Castle	On the island of Luonnonmaa to the west of Naantali, which is linked with the mainland by the Ukko-Pekka Bridge, stands Kultaranta Castle, the summer residence of the President of Finland.

Turku to Parainen

Kuusisto	Leave Turku on Road 1 and in 9km/5½ miles, at Kaarina, turn right into Road 180, which runs south over the Pohjoissalmi (North Sound) on to the island of Kuusisto (Swedish Kustö). Just beyond the bridge a road branches off on the left to the ruins of Kuusisto Castle, at the east end of the island. Founded in 1317, it belonged to the Bishops of Finland and was demolished in 1528, after the Reformation.
Rävsund ★Kirjala	From Kuusisto a 300m/330yd long suspension bridge (1963) crosses the Rävsund to the island of Kirjala, where a road goes off on the left to the well preserved 15th century castle of Kvidja, 7km/4½ miles south-east on the north side of the island of Lemlahti, which once belonged to Bishop Magnus Tavast.
Parainen	2km/1¼ miles beyond the turning for Kvidja the road crosses the Hässund and comes in another 4km/2½ miles to Parainen (Swedish Pargas), a town noted for its limestone quarries (cement factories). It has an old stone church with a beautiful interior.

13km/8 miles south-west of the town, amid a great scatter of skerries, is the island of Stormälö, with the Airisto Hotel, run by the Finnish Tourist Board (open in summer).

16km/10 miles south-west of Parainen (leaving on the road to the Airisto Hotel) is the little port of Lillmälö, from which the route continues on a ferry (free) and then a country road running south-west by way of the Nagu Islands to the island of Korpo, lying far out to sea (35km/22 miles to Korpo church, which contains some old wood sculptures).

Korpo

Turku to Uusikaupunki

Leave on Road 8, which leads via Raisio and Mynämäki to Laitila, from which Road 198 continues 19km/12 miles south-west to the port and commercial town (granite industry) of Uusikaupunki (Swedish Nystad; pop. 15,000) on the Gulf of Bothnia. The town was founded in 1616, during the reign of Gustavus Adolphus. Here in August 1721 the treaty of Nystad was signed which ended the Northern War, giving Russia possession of Ingermanland, Estonia, Livonia and part of Karelia; monument (1961) in the Market Square. In Town Hall Square stands the new church (1863). The old church (1629) now houses a museum of cultural history.

Uusikaupunki

From Uusikaupunki there are attractive boat trips to the offshore islands. To the south of the town is the old manor-house of Sundholm. A country road runs north to Pyhäranta, from which Road 8 continues to Rauma.

Sundholm
manor-house

Seven Churches Route

An attractive round trip which takes in seven old churches.

Raisio

Windmills in the Windmill Park, Uusikaupunki

447

Umeå

Masku Nousiainen	Leave Turku on Road 8. 7km/4½ miles from the city centre, before the turning for Naantali, the stone church of Raisio (14th c.) is seen on the left. 10km/6 miles farther on is the little stone church of Masku. To the southwest is Kankainen Castle. 4.5km/3 miles beyond Masku is Nousiainen. In its 13th century stone church (3.5km/2 miles north-east, off the main road) can be seen the tomb of St Henry (Henrik), an English missionary who spread the Christian faith in Finland and is venerated as the country's patron saint.
Lemu Askainen	The route continues on a country road which branches off Road 8 on the left, heading for Askainen. In 7.5km/4½ miles it comes to Nyynäinen, 1.5km/1 mile south-west of which is the church of Lemu. Askainen, 8km/ 5 miles beyond Nyynäinen, has an old stone church. 2km/1¼ miles west, on the coast, is the manor-house of Luohisaari (1655), birthplace of Marshal Mannerheim.
Merimasku Rymättylä	From Askainen the route continues south, crossing by ferry on to a much indented island at the north end of which is Merimasku (11km/7 miles from Askainen), with a wooden church of 1726. 4km/2½ miles beyond Meri masku we reach a road junction, from which it is 15km/9 miles straight ahead to the 15th century church of Rymättylä (wall paintings). The road to the left is the return route to Turku: 1.5km/1 mile beyond the junction a bridge leads to the island of Luonnonmaa, on which the road runs along the east coast, passing close to Kultaranta Castle; then over the Ukko-Pekka bridge, on to Naantali (6km/4 miles) and from there via Raisio to Turku (17.5km/11 miles).

Umeå   E 4

Country: **Sweden**
Province: Västerbotten
Population: 89,000
Post code: S–90...   Telephone code: 090

Situation and characteristics	Umeå, chief town of the county and province of Västerbotten, lies on the left bank of the Umeälv 5km/3 miles above its outflow into the Gulf of Bothnia. A port and commercial town, it is also the cultural centre of northern Norrland, with a library, an opera house, a university (founded 1963) and a college of forestry. It has a variety of industry, in particular woodworking. Umeå received its municipal charter in 1622, but its development really began only with the rise of the woodworking industry in the second half of the 19th century. In 1888 three-quarters of the town and its three shipyards were destroyed in a great fire, and thereafter it was rebuilt with broad streets lined by birch trees. The town is particularly attractive in May, when the trees burst into leaf.
Town	In the centre of the town is Rådhustorget (Town Hall Square), in which is a large bust of Gustavus Adolphus, founder of the town. To the south of the square, in Storgatan, is the town's principal church (1892), brick-built in Neo-Gothic style. Beside the church stands an obelisk marking the common grave of a Swedish colonel, J. Z. Duncker, and a Cossack colonel, Aerekoff, who were killed in the fighting at Hörnefors in 1809. In Döbeln Park, adjoining the church, can be seen a monument commemorating General von Döbeln, commander of the last Swedish-Finnish army, which was disbanded here after the war with Russia in 1808–09, when Sweden was compelled to cede Finland to Russia.
Gammlia open-air museum	On a hill north-east of Umeå is the Gammlia open-air museum, with the Västerbotten Museum (folk museum). Among the buildings in the open-air museum is an 18th century house, Sävargården, which was the head-

quarters of the Russian General Kamensky during the Swedish-Russian war. The Helena Elisabeth Church, originally a fishermen's chapel on the island of Holmö (off Umeå in the Gulf of Bothnia), is in part built of timber from wrecked ships. An example of an old craftsman's house is Lars Fägrares Gård, now a Skiing Museum.

Surroundings

17km/10½ miles south-east of Umeå is its outer harbour, Holmsund (large sawmill). From here there are ferries to Vääsä in Finland and to the island of Holmö (swimming pool; Stora Fjäderägg nature reserve). Holmsund lies on the "Blue Highway", which cuts across E 4 and E 79 to the west of Umeå and runs through the magnificent scenery of southern Lapland into Norway, following the Umeälv, on which there are numerous rapids.

Holmsund

9km/5½ miles west of Umeå on E 12, which runs alongside the Umeälv, we reach Klabböle, with the Energy Centre (informative displays on the technology of power production).

Klabböle
(Energy Centre)

At Sörfors, 15km/9 miles north-west of Umeå, the large underground hydro-electric power station of Stornorrfors has a fall of 75m/250ft and a turbine hall 24m/80ft high hewn from the rock (conducted visits in summer). Here too is the Stornorrfors salmon hatchery, which releases 100,000 salmon annually into the Umeälv. The salmon can be seen leaping up the small waterfall below the huge dam.

Sörfors
(power station)

The country around the village of Bjurholm, to the west of E 12, is of great scenic beauty and has many features of geological interest. Here there is a bridge over the Öreälv. From the Balberg (487m/1598ft) there are extensive views; on the south side of the hill is a very varied flora.

Bjurholm

North-west of Umeå, on the Vindelälv, one of the Norrland rivers which has not been artificially regulated, visitors can enjoy a "waterfall trip" down the river. Farther upstream is the Mårdseleforsarna nature reserve, with tumultuous waterfalls crossed by suspension bridges. From Åmsele there are canoe trips on the Vindelälv.

Vindelälv

Uppsala

E 5

Country: **Sweden**
Province: Uppland
Population: 161,000
Post code: S–75...
Telephone code: 018

The famous Swedish university town of Uppsala lies 70km/45 miles northwest of Stockholm in a fertile plain on the banks of the Fyriså. It is the chief town of the county of Uppsala and the province of Uppland and the seat of the Lutheran Archbishop of Sweden. There is a variety of industry around the town (engineering, pharmaceuticals, printing).

Situation and characteristics

    The county of Uppsala occupies the central part of the province of Uppland, which played a prominent part in the early history of Sweden. The people of Uppland, the Svea, enjoyed the right of electing and deposing their kings. The name of Sweden (Sverige) is derived from Svea, and the term Svea Rike, the kingdom of the Swedes, is still found in this form in the traditional painting of Dalarna (*dalmålningar*).

Uppsala can claim to be the historic centre of Sweden. At the time when the Swedish kings resided in Gamla Uppsala (Old Uppsala) the present town, then known as Östra Aros, was merely the port and trading station of the

History

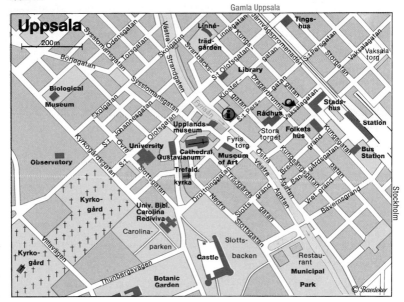

capital. In 1273 the see of the archbishop of Gamla Uppsala was transferred to Östra Aros, while the royal residence was moved to Stockholm.

The University, which plays a central role in the life of Uppsala, was founded in 1477 by Archbishop Jakob Ulvsson and, thanks to the patronage of Gustavus Adolphus, developed into a major centre of learning.

Town

Uppsala is made up of two very different parts – the ecclesiastical and academic town to the west of the Fyriså and the central area, with the Town Hall and the shopping and business streets – much altered by new building in the 1960s and 1970s – to the east of the river. Most of the features of interest are in the older part of the town.

★ Cathedral

The original Cathedral was based on English models, but later received its High Gothic stamp from a French builder, Etienne de Bonneuil. The Gothic cathedral was finally consecrated in 1435. Its total length is 118.70m/390ft and its internal width 45m/150ft; the towers are 118.70m/390ft high. The towers were partly rebuilt in 1702 after a fire, and were given new spires in 1745. Restoration work carried out about 1880 gave rise to much criticism, and in recent years extensive alterations have been made to restore the church so far as possible to its medieval form.

Interior

The interior of the Cathedral is of impressive effect. The sumptuous Baroque pulpit (1707) was carved by Burchard Precht to the design of Nicodemus Tessin the Younger. At the east end of the choir is the burial chapel of Gustavus Vasa, with the king's tomb (Netherlandish work of about 1576). On the north side of the church are the tomb of Katarina Jagellonica (1583) and the marble monument of her husband, John III. On the north side is the Oxenstierna Chapel. Also buried in the Cathedral are Carl von Linné (Linnaeus), Archbishop Nathan Söderblom and the philosopher Emanuel Swedenborg.

Uppsala Cathedral

Interior of the Cathedral, with the Baroque pulpit

In the Silver Chamber, among other treasures, can be seen the gilded reliquary (1574–79) of King Eric IX (St Eric), who was killed by the Danes in 1160. In the north tower is a museum with, among much else, a gold brocade robe (c. 1400) which belonged to Queen Margaret, ruler of the united kingdoms of Denmark, Norway and Sweden.

Museums

Below the Cathedral, on the banks of the Fyriså, is the Uppland Museum (regional history and culture), with interesting models of the Cathedral and the Castle. To the south, in Fyristorg, is the Museum of Art.

Gustavianum

Facing the west end of the Cathedral is the Gustavianum (c. 1620), which was presented to the University by Gustavus Adolphus. It contains the University's cultural history collections, the Museum of Nordic Antiquities and the Victoria Museum (Egyptian antiquities).

To the south of the Gustavianum is the Trinity Church (Trefaldighetskyrka), the oldest parts of which date from the 12th century (medieval wall paintings).

University

The New University buildings in Slottsgatan were erected in 1879–86, in sumptuous style (staircases of green Swedish marble). In the Chancellor's Room is a magnificent carved cabinet from Augsburg. In the University gardens behind the Gustavianum are runic stones and a bronze statue of the historian and poet E. G. Geijer.

University Library
★★Codex
Argenteus

The University Library (Carolina Rediviva) is the largest library in Sweden, with over 2 million volumes and some 30,000 manuscripts. Its greatest treasure (in its display collection) is the famous Codex Argenteus, probably written at Ravenna in the reign of Theodoric the Great (6th c.). It contains the translation of the Gospels by the Gothic bishop Wulfila or Ulfilas (d. 383), written in silver and gold letters on 187 pages of purple parchment, in a 17th century silver binding. Other valuable items are the Codex Upsaliensis (the oldest manuscript of Snorri Sturluson's Younger Edda, c. 1300), the Decretum Concilii Upsaliensis of 1593, with many signatures, and Olaus Magnus's Carta Marina (a map of northern Europe printed in Venice in 1539). The oldest Swedish printed book is dated 1483.

Castle

To the south of the University Library is the Botanic Garden, and to the south-east, on higher ground, the Castle, begun by Gustavus Vasa in 1548 but only half completed; it now houses the governor's residence, various offices and the provincial archives. Here Eric IV had Count Sture murdered, and here too, in the Great Hall (Rikssalen), Queen Christina abdicated. From the bastions there are fine views of Uppsala and the surrounding countryside. On the north-west bastion is a bell made for Queen Gunilla Bielke which rings daily at 6am and 7pm. Behind the Castle is a bust of Gustavus Vasa (by Fogelberg) surrounded by cannon.

South-east of the Castle lies the Municipal Park (summer restaurant).

Cemetery

In the cemetery (Kyrkogård) to the west of the town can be found the grave of Dag Hammarskjöld (1905–61), a former Secretary General of the United Nations.

Stora Torg

From the University Library Drottninggatan runs north-east to the Stora Torg, with the Town Hall (1883). To the east of the square are the Folkets Hus ("People's House") and the Municipal Theatre. North of this is the Town House (Stadshus), to the east the railway station. From the nearby East Station (Uppsala Östra) Sweden's longest old-time railway runs to Länna.

Linnaean Museum

From the Stora Torg Svartbäcksgatan runs north-west to the Linnaean Garden (Linnéträdgården), of which the great botanist Linnaeus (Carl von Linné, 1707–78) was curator, with the Linnaean Museum. Linnaeus devised the technical language of botany and the Linnaean system of botanical nomenclature, the binomial system which is still in use.

Surroundings

5km/3 miles north of the town lies Gamla Uppsala (Old Uppsala), once capital of the old Svea kingdom. The little church of undressed stone is a remnant of the cathedral which was built about 1125. The old offertory box has been preserved, and the bishop's throne is one of the oldest pieces of furniture in Sweden. Three large burial

Uppsala

mounds dating from around the 6th century contain the remains of kings Adil, Egil and Aun. To the east is the Tingshög, an eminence from which the kings addressed their people. In the Odinsborg Inn visitors can drink mead from silver-mounted drinking horns. To the north is the open-air museum of Disagården, with old houses from the surrounding area.

In northern Uppland are a number of little industrial towns with old-established ironworks (Strömbergsbruk, Lövstabruk, etc.). In this area there are also numerous prehistoric remains and medieval churches. Öregrund and Östhammer are typical little skerry towns with old wooden houses, some of them dating from the 18th century.

Northern Uppland

11km/7 miles south-east of Uppsala, in a house built in 1779, are the Mora Stones, on which kings took the oath after being elected; the name of the king was then inscribed on the stone. 3km/2 miles from here is Hammarby, Linnaeus's country house, now a museum. Also near the Mora Stones stands the church of Lagga, which has 15th century wall paintings.

Mora Stones
Hammarby

Sigtuna

30km/20 miles south of Uppsala, on Lake Skarven, is Sigtuna (pop. 30,000), one of the oldest towns in Sweden, founded by Olof Skötkonung in the 11th century. The first Swedish coins, with the inscription "Situne Dei", were struck here by coiners brought from England by Olof. The first episcopal see in the land of the Svea and in its early days a busy trading town, Sigtuna declined in importance when the bishop moved his residence to Uppsala in 1130. The town suffered a further setback in 1187 when it was attacked and set on fire by the Estonians. It took another fifty years for Sigtuna to recover and, after the foundation of a Dominican monastery in 1237, regain a measure of prosperity.

Sigtuna's main street, Stora Gatan, follows the same line as it did about the year 1000, as was shown by the discovery of the old road surface 3m/10ft below the present ground level. Material recovered in the excavations, including remains of the earliest buildings on the site, can be seen in the museum in Lilla Torget. Evidence of Uppsala's one-time importance is provided by the remains of the churches of St Lars, St Per and St Olof. St Olof's Church (mid 12th c.) was probably built on the site of an old sacred spring. Nearby is St Mary's Church, an old monastic church built in the 13th century, with wall paintings of that period, the tomb of Archbishop Jarler (d. 1255), who had been a monk in the monastery, and a 15th century reredos in the choir.

The Lundströmska Gård is an old burgher's house with its original furniture and furnishings. To the west of the town is the Sigtuna Foundation (1915), with a Lutheran folk high school and a guest house.

★Skokloster Castle

10km/6 miles north-west of Sigtuna as the crow flies, but accessible only from the Stockholm–Enköping road (E 18), stands Skokloster Castle, on the Skofjärd. As its name indicates, the castle was originally a monastery, founded by Cistercians in 1244. In 1574, however, the monastery was pulled down, with the exception of the church, and in 1611 the estate passed into the hands of Field Marshal Herman Wrangel, whose son Karl Gustav, Count of Salamis, was born in Skokloster in 1613.

Karl Gustav Wrangel, later Grand Admiral and Grand Marshal of Sweden, built the present castle in 1654–57. The architect was first de la Vallée and later Nicodemus Tessin the Elder. The castle, in Baroque style, is brick-built, laid out on a square ground-plan around a central courtyard, with octagonal towers at the corners. The richly decorated interior, with stucco ornament and wall and ceiling paintings, is well preserved. It contains a collection of pictures and of arms and armour; among items of special interest are the ceremonial shield of the Emperor Charles V (probably made in Augsburg), a sword which belonged to the Hussite leader Jan Žiška and the executioner's sword used in the "Linköping massacre".

The church to the north of the castle contains a 13th century triumphal cross, the Wrangel burial vault and a pulpit which was brought from Oliva, near Danzig, during the Thirty Years' War. Near the church can be seen a runic stone with carved figures of two horsemen, probably older than the runic inscription. Adjoining the car park is a Motor Museum.

Härkeberga

South of Uppsala on Road 55 is Härkeberga, with a church containing well preserved wall paintings by Albertus Pictor (15th c.).

Skokloster Castle

Enköping

50km/30 miles south-west of Uppsala and 34km/21 miles east of Västerås (see entry), on the Enköpingså, is Enköping (pop. 34,000), whose economy depended until the middle of the 19th century on craft production and the growing of herbs and spices (earning it the name of the "horse-radish town"). From the 1880s onwards some of the craft workshops developed into small industrial firms and new firms were established, mainly in the engineering field. As a result a large proportion of the population is now employed in industry. After a great fire in 1799 the town was rebuilt on a rectangular plan, which is still preserved in the town centre. Most of the buildings are relatively low. The Church of Our Lady (Vårfrukyrkan), built of grey stone, was a bishop's church in the 12th century, but has been much altered and restored since then. On the Minksund are the ruins of a Franciscan friary (restored), the ground-plan of which can still be recognised.

Around Enköping there are large numbers of rock carvings, particularly at Boglösa, to the south of the town.

Vaasa (Vasa)   E 4

Country: **Finland**
Region: Western Finland
Population: 54,000
Post code: FIN–65100
Telephone code: 961

Vaasa (Swedish Vasa), on the Gulf of Bothnia, is the chief town of Vaasa province and the seat of the Provincial Court of Appeal. About a third of the inhabitants are Swedish-speaking. The town lies at the narrowest part of the Gulf of Bothnia, sheltered by a girdle of skerries, the archipelago of the Valsöarna and the islands of Vallgrund and Björkö. The shortest route between Finland and Sweden is the Vaasa–Umeå ferry.
Situation and characteristics

The town, named after the Swedish royal house of Vasa, was founded in 1606 at Mustasaari, now 6km/4 miles inland but then on the coast. Vaasa was twice destroyed by war (1714, 1800) and again by a great fire in 1852. Thereafter, from 1862 onwards, it was rebuilt on the new coastline, which had moved west as a result of a rise in the level of the land. The rebuilding was directed by the provincial architect, Carl Axel Setterberg; and, as at Pori, the new town was laid out with broad avenues (*puistikko*) to reduce the fire hazard. Setterberg favoured the Neo-Gothic style; other architects built in a variety of styles.
History

In December 1917, after the proclamation of Finnish independence, Vaasa became the temporary capital of the country when the socialist militia seized control of Helsinki and the Senate took refuge in Vaasa. From here General Mannerheim directed operations against the Red Brigades and the Russian forces supporting them. Hence the cross of freedom which figures in the town's coat of arms, as it does in that of Mikkeli.

Between the two wide avenues, Hovioikeudenpuistikko and Vaasanpuistikko, which run south-west from the railway station through the centre of the town is the Market Square, with an imposing monument to Liberty (by Yrjö Liipola, 1938), commemorating the 1918 civil war and war of liberation.
Town
Market Square

South-west of the square is the Neo-Gothic Trinity Church (by C. A. Setterberg, 1868), which has altarpieces by A. Edelfelt, L. Sparre and R. W. Ekman. Opposite the church, to the north, is a bronze statue of the writer Zachris Topelius (19th c.).
Trinity Church

455

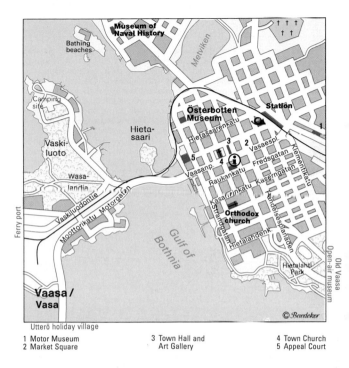

Utterö holiday village

1 Motor Museum	3 Town Hall and	4 Town Church
2 Market Square	Art Gallery	5 Appeal Court

Appeal Court

At the west end of Hovioikeudenpuistikko (Appeal Court Avenue), in a square by the sea, is the Provincial Court of Appeal, a 19th century Neo Gothic brick building with corner turrets. To the south is a monument commemorating the landing here in February 1918 of a German rifle battalion of young Finns trained in Germany.

Österbotten Museum

To the north of the Appeal Court lies the Mariepark, in which is the Österbotten Provincial Museum (Pohjanmaa-Museum), with collections illustrating the culture of the province and the history of the town, together with works of art of various periods, including 19th and 20th century Finnish painting.

Open-air museum
Motor Museum

To the south of the town is Hietalahti Park, with the Braga open-air theatre (peasant culture of the Finland Swedes) and a summer restaurant.
To the east, beyond the station, is a Motor Museum.

Wasalandia

Vaasanpuistikko crosses a narrow channel on a causeway, which also carries the railway, to the island of Vaskiluoto, on which is the Wasalandia amusement park (with Zoo). From the causeway a short side road gives access to the island of Hietasaari (Swedish Sandö; park, with bathing beaches).

Surroundings

Old Vaasa

Old Vaasa lies 6km/4 miles south-east of the town centre, on the site occupied by the town before the 1852 fire. Here are the ruins of St Mary's

Old Vaasa

Church, originally (14th c.) on a basilican plan but converted by successive alterations into a cruciform church. The old Appeal Court, in Gustavian style, built during the reign of Gustavus III, is now Mustasaari church (1786). The ruined 14th century church of Korsholm/Mustasaari is the setting of a musical festival which forms part of the Finland Festival. There is an interesting museum in the late 18th century house of the Wasastjerna family.

On the south side of E 12, at Sulva, is the craftsmen's village of Stundars, with over forty old buildings, several workshops and a summer theatre.

Stundars

The ring of skerries in the Gulf of Bothnia offers great variety of beauty and recreation. Boats can be hired for fishing trips, or visitors can accompany the local fishermen. There are large numbers of holiday cabins on the islands which can be rented through the tourist information office in Vaasa. In particularly cold winters it is possible to drive to Björköby and continue across the ice on the Gulf of Bothnia to Umeå on the Swedish side.

Skerries

Just under 100km/62 miles south of Vaasa, off Road 8, is the little town of Kristiinankaupunki (Swedish Kristinestad), whose 9000 inhabitants are mainly Swedish-speaking. The town was founded by Per Brahe in 1649 and named after Queen Christina of Sweden, a daughter of Gustavus Adolphus. During the 18th and 19th centuries, as a busy port for the shipment of tar, Kristiinankaupunki prospered, but thereafter it declined. The town centre still preserves the grid pattern of its original layout.

Kristiinankaupunki

Kristiinankaupunki was spared the devastating fires which afflicted so many towns, and there are large numbers of 18th and 19th century wooden houses in the old part of the town. A picturesque feature is the red-painted Old Church (1698–1700), which has a handsome organ, a Rococo pulpit and a separate belfry (1703). Other notable buildings are the centrally situated Town Hall, in Empire style (1858), and the house of the Lebell family in

Rantakatu, which is now a museum, with rooms furnished in various different styles.

Visitors who are not pressed for time should take the coast road rather than the main road. Between Malax and Närpes there are many little fishing villages, and windmills add variety to the landscape. There is a particularly fine example at Harrström in the commune of Korsnäs.

Valdres   C 5

Country: **Norway**
Region: Southern Norway

Situation

The fertile region of Valdres in southern Norway lies on both banks of the river Begna, which rises in the southern Jotunheim and flows into the Tyrifjord at Hønefoss. It is a region of many farms and lush pastureland. There are a number of stave churches in the area.

Into Valdres

The starting-point for a trip into the Valdres area is the town of Hønefoss (see entry) on the river Begna, here also known as the Ådalselv. From there E 16 runs north up the Begna valley, along the east side of Lake Sperillen (23km/14 miles long). On the opposite side of the lake can be seen the Høgfjell (1010m/3314ft). At the north end of the lake, where the Begna flows into it, is the village of Nes. Here Road 243 diverges on the left to Hedal, which has a 13th century stave church.

Bagn

E 16 now follows the right bank of the Begna to Begndal and continues to Bagn, a pretty village straggling up the valley (radio transmitter), with a wooden 18th century church on a cruciform plan. At Bagn a side road branches off to the stave church of Reinli (12th c.).

Winter in Valdres

Fagernes, situated amid hills covered with spruce forests at the mouth of the Neselv, which here forms beautiful waterfalls as it flows into the Strandefjord, is a popular holiday resort, much frequented by anglers. The Valdres Folk Museum, one of the largest open-air museums in Norway, has numerous old buildings, as well as collections of domestic equipment, textiles, musical instruments and hunting weapons.

Fagernes

At Fagernes the road divides. E 16 bears west, while Road 51 continues north-west towards the Jotunheim (see entry).

E 16 now runs along a number of small fjords, passing through Lomen (13th century stave church with fine interior) and Ryfoss, to the southern shore of Lake Vangsmjøsa (19km/12 miles long), which it follows to Grindaheim (alt. 471m/1545ft). The stave church which once stood at Vang, just before Grindaheim, was dismantled in 1841 and taken to Brückenberg in Silesia (now in Poland), and the site is now occupied by Vang's white wooden church. Beside the church is a runic stone with the inscription "Gose's sons set up this stone for Gunnar, their brother's son".

★Vangsmjøsa

Øye, at the west end of Lake Vangsmjøsa, has a stave church (12th c.) which was rebuilt from parts found under the floor of a later church.

Øye

11km/7 miles beyond Øye is a road junction where Road 53 diverges on the right to the Tyinsjø, while E 16 continues towards the Sognefjord (see entry).

Lake Vänern   C/D 6

Country: Sweden
Provinces: Värmland, Dalsland, Västergötland

Lake Vänern, Sweden's largest lake (area 5546sq.km/2170sq. miles), lies in a tectonic basin in the south of the country, north-west of the road from Göteborg to Örebro. The lake is divided into two parts, Stora Vänern to the north-east and the Dalbosjö to the south-west, by two peninsulas, Värmlandsnäs and Kållandshalvö, the island of Kållandsö, off the Kållandshalvö, and a number of smaller islands. Since the country around the lake is considerably lower the water level is falling at the rate of about 8cm/5in. in a century.

Situation and characteristics

There were plans for regulating the lake and the associated waterways from the 16th century onwards, but it was only in 1938 that regulatory measures were carried out. There is now heavy shipping traffic on the lake, largely because of the link it provides between the Kattegat and the Baltic by way of Trollhättan and the Göta Canal.

Around ★Lake Vänern

For motorists coming from Göteborg the starting-point of the tour is Trollhättan. Those coming from Stockholm via Örebro can join the route described below at Kristinehamn, at the north-eastern corner of the lake.

The industrial town of Trollhättan (pop. 50,000), on the Götaälv, received its municipal charter only in 1916 – though the prehistoric remains found in this area provide evidence of human occupation dating back 7000 years. The name of the town first appears in 1413 in the tax records of King Eric of Pomerania, which state that corn was ground for the castle by the Trollhättan mill. The mills and sawmills of earlier times have now given place to such well-known industrial enterprises as SAAB and NOHAB and various engineering and electrical engineering plants.

Trollhättan

The once-renowned Trollhättan Falls, at the point where the Götaälv had cut its way through a ridge of gneiss, formerly plunged down from a height

Trollhättan Falls

459

of 38.50m/126ft to 5.7m/19ft over a distance of 1500m/1640yd, but are now almost dry. They can be seen in their former magnificence only in the month of July, when the water level of Lake Vänern usually makes it possible to release water over the falls; and "Waterfall Day" is celebrated in mid July.

The huge masses of water which once poured over the falls are now conveyed in underground tunnels to a power station. As early as the middle of the 17th century the Trollhättan Falls were seen as an obstacle to the creation of a navigable waterway from Sweden to Norway and thus to the North Sea, for which the Götaälv provided a basis, and Christoffer Polhem was commissioned by Charles XII to construct a waterway bypassing the falls. Work was suspended in 1755, and the project, involving the provision of eight locks, was completed only in 1800.

Since this canal did not meet the increased demand created by the development of industry it was enlarged in 1844 by Nils Ericsson. The final stage came in 1916, when a new canal with four locks, overcoming a height difference of 32m/105ft, was opened to traffic. Some 20,000 vessels now pass through the locks every year.

Visitors can see the locks in operation and have a conducted tour of the Oliden power station. Other features of interest in Trollhättan are the open-air museum in a nature park, the Saab Automobile Museum and the "King's Cave" (Kungsgrottan) at the east end of Kong Oscars Bro (King Oscar's Bridge). There is a fine view of the town from Kopparklinten, a hill on the west bank of the river.

Vänersborg

Vänersborg (pop. 36,000), chief town of Älvsborg county, lies at the northern tip of a promontory reaching out into Lake Vänern. It has an attractive lakeside promenade, Birger Sjöbergsväg. with Sträcklan Park. Here too can be seen a statue by Axel Wallenberg of "Frida", a figure much celebrated in song.

Nearby is the Municipal Museum, with material on the history of the town and a collection of exotic birds presented by the explorer Axel Ericson. In the town centre are a number of handsome 18th century buildings, among them the Governor's Residence (by Carl Hårleman, 1754). Nearby is the church (1780).

Lidköping

Lidköping (pop. 35,000), a port town at the mouth of the Lidaå, in the Kinnevik, an inlet on the southern shore of Lake Vänern, has a number of small industrial undertakings, the best known of which is the Rörstrand porcelain manufactory, established here in 1935.

Lidköping received its municipal charter in 1446, when the town lay on the east bank of the Lidaå. Then in 1670, when Magnus Gabriel de la Gardie was granted the right to build a town in the county of Läckö he laid it out on the west bank, reaching right down to the river, and the street pattern of the new quarter he built largely survives in the present town. A hunting lodge was built in the Stora Torg, and this later became the Town Hall, a prominent landmark of the town; destroyed by fire in 1960, it was rebuilt on the basis of the original plans. In the market square can be seen a statue of Gabriel de la Gardie. Gamla Staden, the "Old Town" round the Limtorg, has preserved its old-world character, with the original buildings.

★Läckö Castle

To the north of the town the peninsula of Kållandshalvö reaches out into Lake Vänern. Off its northern tip is the island of Kållandsö, on the shores of which is Läckö Castle, built in 1298 by Bishop Brynolt Algotsson. Excavations have shown that the original fortified castle, much altered in later centuries, had broadly the same ground-plan as the present castle. After the Reformation, in 1557, the castle became Crown property, but soon afterwards passed into the hands of Sven Sture and in 1571 to the Hogenskild Bielke family, who carried out a thorough restoration. In 1615 General Jacob de la Gardie, husband of Ebba Brahe, was granted possession of Läckö Castle, together with the title of count. His son considerably altered and enlarged the castle, bringing in two German architects, Elias Holl and

Town Hall, Lidköping

Läckö Castle, on an island in Lake Vänern

461

Franz Stiemer, who added a fourth floor, new kitchen premises and outer works. In 1746 Frederick I had the portrait of Jacob de la Gardie in the Knights' Hall (which was richly decorated with murals depicting scenes from the Thirty Years' War) removed to Stockholm, where it can now be seen in the Military Academy on the Karlsberg. In 1810 Läckö Castle was granted to General Carl Johan Adlercreutz, victor in the battle of Siikajoki, and renamed Siikajoki. In 1920 it was thoroughly restored, and since 1965 it has belonged to the Västergötland Tourist Association, which puts on exhibitions in the castle in summer.

Skara

South-east of Lidköping, 24km/15 miles from the shores of the lake, lies the little town of Skara (pop. 18,000), which grew up round an ancient place of assembly (*ting*) and cult site and during the Middle Ages became a centre of Christian missionary activity and the see of a bishop. A seminary for priests established in the 13th century was the forerunner of the grammar school founded in 1641. The Cathedral, originally Gothic (1312–50), was much altered in later centuries but preserves its High Gothic choir (13th c.) and nave (14th century). The towers were added during an early 19th century rebuilding. After a clumsy restoration in the late 19th century the church was largely restored to its original character after a fire in 1947. In the aisle is the marble sarcophagus of Erik Soop, a cavalry colonel who saved Gustavus Adolphus's life in 1629, during the Thirty Years' War. In the Romanesque crypt under the choir can be seen the tomb of one of the first bishops, Adalvard.

Opposite the Cathedral is the Diocesan Library (1857), and farther north can be found the Municipal Park (Stadsträdgården), with Skaraborg County Museum and the Fornbyn open-air museum, which together give a picture of life in this part of Sweden in earlier times. The open-air museum contains a number of old peasants' houses and a church.

In the Stortorg is an attractive bronze fountain by Nils Sjögren (1894). To the west of the square the picturesque Rådhusgata (Town Hall Street) is an old market street still paved with cobbles. To the east of the town centre is a leisure park, Skara Sommarland.

Varnhem

14km/9 miles east of Skara is Varnhem, with a 13th century church which belonged to a Cistercian abbey, the burial-place of King Eric's dynasty. Birger Jarl, who died in Västergötland in 1266, is also buried here. After the Reformation and a series of fires the abbey and its church fell into disrepair. It was restored by Magnus Gabriel de la Gardie in 1654–73, when the buttresses which give the church its characteristic aspect were added. De la Gardie and his wife are buried in the church. Conservation work has been carried out on the ruins of the abbey, and some of the finds made during excavations in 1923–27 are displayed in the museum.

From Varnhem it is a short trip south-east to the Hornborgasjö, the haunt of large numbers of birds, including cranes.

★Kinnekulle

Kinnekulle (306m/1004ft) is a tabular hill (14km/8½ miles long by 6km/4 miles wide) covered with fir forests, of a type very characteristic of Västergötland. From the top of the hill there are extensive views of Lake Vänern. The hills in this area came into being some 500 million years ago, when the ancient rocks (gneiss) sank under the sea. For millions of years sand, soil and remains of algae, insects, crustaceans and fish were deposited on the sea floor and in course of time turned into stone. Streams of lava later thrust up through clefts in the rock, enclosing certain areas; then, when the land gradually re-emerged from the sea, the more exposed strata were eroded away, while those protected by the lava remained. The result of this development can be seen on Kinnekulle, with its series of "steps" showing the succession of strata from the ancient rocks upward and throwing important light on the geological history of the region.

Wall paintings in Södra Råda church, Gullspång

Mariestad (pop. 24,000), at the mouth of the Tida, is a busy industrial town. **Mariestad**
It was almost completely rebuilt after a fire in 1895. To the north of the town
is the Cathedral (1593–1619; restored 1958–59). On an island in the river
stands Marieholm Castle, residence of the governor of Skaraborg county,
with a local museum.

From Mariestad the road continues by way of Gullspånd, on the boundary **Kristinehamn**
between Västergötland and Värmland, to Kristinehamn (pop. 26,000), a
town whose character has been shaped by its situation on Lake Vänern. A
market centre and port in the Middle Ages, it grew in importance with the
development of iron-mining in Bergslagen, when the ore was shipped from
Kristinehamn.

The town received its municipal charter in 1642, during the minority of
Queen Christina, after whom it was named. The importance of Kristinehamn as a port for the shipment of iron ore and timber was further increased in the mid 19th century, when the railway came to the town; and it
is still a considerable port.

On a promontory reaching out into the lake stands a 15m/50ft high
concrete sculpture by Picasso which he presented to the town in 1965.
Some 4km/2½ miles south of the town centre can be seen a runic stone
dating from the year 500. 5km/3 miles west of the town is the Östervik
Chapel, built by Georg Adlersparre in 1869.

At Kristinehamn E 18, coming from Stockholm, joins the road round Lake
Vänern.

25km/15 miles from Kristinehamn, at the north end of Lake Möckeln, is **Karlskoga**
Karlskoga (pop. 34,000), which received its municipal charter only in 1940.
This has been a mining area for many centuries. On the east side of the
town are the large Bofors steelworks and rolling mill, founded in 1646,
which were acquired in the late 19th century by Alfred Nobel, the inventor
of dynamite and founder of the Nobel Prizes; Nobel Museum.

Nobel Museum, Karlskoga

To the north of the town is a wooden church with 16th century wall paintings.

From Kristinehamn the road continues along the shores of Lake Vänern to Karlstad (see entry).

Säffle

25km/15 miles beyond Karlstad the road turns south and comes to Säffle (pop. 18,000), on the west side of the Värmlandsnäs peninsula. The town lies on the Byälv, a short distance from Lake Vänern and the Harefjord. In addition to the Billerud woodworking and papermaking plant it has a number of metalworking, engineering and furniture-making factories. It is traversed by the Säffle Canal, which links the Glavsfjord to the north-west with Lake Vänern. In Kungsgården, by the water-tower, is Olof Trätäljas Hög, said to be the burial mound of the legendary King Olof Trätälja.

Åmål

Åmål (pop. 13,000) is the only town in Dalsland, the area to the west of Lake Vänern, founded in the reign of Queen Christina (1643). After numerous fires which destroyed many of the town's old wooden houses it was largely rebuilt in stone. The old quarter by the Municipal Park – the area, including the old market square, which is known as Plantaget – is therefore a tourist attraction. Vågmästaregården, an early 18th century house, was for many years the residence of the local railway manager, and frequently also of the burgomaster. Nearby is another 18th century house, Dalgrensgården, with a slate roof. In the beautiful Örnäspark are Hembygdsgården, with a collection of furniture and domestic equipment from the surrounding area, and a wildlife park. Nearby is a beach restaurant from which there is a fine view of Lake Vänern.

Dalsland Canal

At the Köpmannebro (bridge) begins the magnificent Dalsland Canal constructed by Nils Ericsson, 254km/160 miles long, with 29 locks. It links a whole string of lakes, with only about 10km/6 miles of its total length that can be described as a canal in the normal sense. This navigable lake system extends from Dalsland into Värmland and Norway. It was originally constructed in order to provide a means of transport for the products of the ironworks and sawmills of Dalsland and Värmland, and also as a convenient link with Norway and the North Sea. Nowadays the canal is no longer used for the transport of freight, but it has become a popular tourist route, running as it does through beautiful and varied scenery which alternates between fertile farming country, dark forests, rugged hills and barren wastelands. Visitors planning to sail their own boat (or a rented one) through the canal should consult the appropriate tourist information office, since the locks are not in operation every day in the week or every week in the year.

The road now turns away from the shores of Lake Vänern and returns to Vänersborg, at the south-western tip of the lake. In the neighbourhood of the town elk can sometimes be seen on the Hunneberg and the Halleberg.

Varberg   C 6

Country: **Sweden**
Province: Halland
Population: 47,000
Post code: S–432..   Telephone code: 0340

Varberg is an attractive seaside resort and spa on the west coast of Sweden. From here E 20 runs north to Göteborg and south to Halmstad (see entries). Around the town are miles of cliff-fringed and sandy beaches, including a naturist beach. The town is also a sea-angling centre (several trips daily).

Situation and characteristics

The most prominent feature of Varberg is the fortress on a rocky promontory to the west of the town, which came into Swedish hands in 1645. Originally built in the 13th century, it was much altered in later centuries. It now houses a local museum, notable in particular for the clothes of the "Bocksten man", a body dating from medieval times which was found in 1938 in a bog at Bocksten, to the east of the town. Within the precincts of the fortress is a café with a superb view out to sea.

Town

★Fortress (Museum)

In an old warehouse on the harbour is a glassworks (conducted tours). To the north of the town, close to E 6, are the interesting excavations of Nyby (as Varberg was originally called), including the remains of a Carmelite convent.

Glassworks
Excavations

North-west of the town lies Getterö, a beautiful island which is connected with the mainland by a causeway. A striking feature of the landscape is the large number of stone cairns. The island has a great variety of birds and a good bathing beach. There is a ferry from here to Grenå in Denmark.

Getterö

Surroundings

7km/4½ miles south of Varberg is Träslövsläge, the largest fishing village in Halland, which has a wooden church with interesting paintings. On E 6 is Varbergs Sommarland, a leisure park. Farther south is Falkenberg (see entry).

Träslövsläge

To the east, at Torstorp (golf course), are modern rock carvings – some 130 proverbs cut from the rock in the early 19th century by a local landowner named Bexell. The road to Ullared (No. 153), the headquarters of a mail order company, runs through beautiful country, passing numbers of prehistoric tombs, in particular the cemetery of Broåsen (at Gödestad), with the longest burial mound on the west coast.

Rock carvings; cemetery

Village church, Torpa (southern Sweden)

Torpa

A rewarding side trip is to Torpa, to the north, which has a medieval church with a 14th century font and 18th century ceiling paintings. The wooden tower points to the east.

Beaches and features of interest on the coast

There are many attractive beaches on the coast to the north of Varberg. E 20 runs via Åskloster, where the river Viska flows into the Kattegat. At the tip of a promontory reaching out into the Kattegat is the Ringhals nuclear power station. To the east of E 20 are Värö church and the Åkraberg nature reserve. At Landa a road goes off to the little seaside resort of Åsa, which has a long sandy beach. 6km/4 miles north, on a peninsula, stands the imposing Tjolöholm Castle (1898–1904), in English Renaissance style, built by a Göteborg businessman named James Fredrik Dickson (conducted visits; interesting Carriage Museum). On the east side of E 20 is Fjärås Bräcka, a long bank of shingle at the west end of Lake Lygnern, an elongated lake extending north-east. Here too are an Iron Age cemetery area and more than a hundred standing stones, the largest of them 4.75m/16ft high.

Kungsbacka

8km/5 miles farther north is the town of Kungsbacka (pop. 52,000), with handsome old 19th century houses and an open-air museum in the beautiful Kungsbackaskog nature park. North of Kungsbacka the road enters the province of Bohuslän. Until 1645 this was the frontier between Sweden and Denmark. 11km/7 miles north-west of Kungsbacka lies the former island of Särö, now linked with the mainland.

A road runs south-west from Kungsbacka, along the shores of the Kungsbackafjord, to Onsala, which has a richly decorated church (17th–18th c.; restored 1918–19). In the octagonal burial vault are the massive marble sarcophagi of the Swedish naval hero and privateer Lars Gathenhielm (1689–1718) and his wife Ingela. Nearby is a Carriage Museum. At the tip of the peninsula is the seaside resort of Gottskär.

Värmland

Country: **Sweden**

Värmland lies in central Sweden to the north and north-west of Lake Vänern, extending to the Norwegian frontier. The beauty of the province lies in its scenic variety, its alternation between uplands, expanses of plain and its many lakes. Although archaeological finds have shown that the region was inhabited in the Stone Age, it was only thinly populated in the medieval period. In those days there was an active border trade with Norway, and this was also a route by which Christianity made its way from Norway into Sweden.

Situation and characteristics

Given the nature of the soil, agriculture yielded only meagre returns. The main crop grown by the peasants of Värmland on their smallholdings was oats, both for their own subsistence and as fodder for the horses which were used on other farms or, more commonly, on the landowners' estates.

Economy

During the 16th and 17th centuries many Finns settled in Värmland, attracted by the exemption from taxes which was offered as an inducement to settlers. These peasants, known as *svedjebönder,* obtained land for cultivation by burning down the standing trees. In course of time this created difficulties for the mining industry, which needed the timber. The normal practice in those days was to light fires in the mine shafts so as to heat the rock, which cracked as it cooled and could be extracted with a pick. This meant that the mines required great quantities of timber, and since the transport of timber was difficult the mines were located close to areas of forest. The burning of the forests by the *svedjebönder,* therefore, led the mine-owners to complain to the Crown.

The development of industry in the 19th century brought a period of prosperity to the mining industry. The ore, originally carried by pack-horses and small boats, now began to be transported on the canals and by rail.

Värmland is now a popular holiday and recreation area, with good fishing, canoeing and walking, as well as rafting on the Klarälv.

An attractive holiday area in Värmland lies around the three Fryken Lakes (Lower, Middle and Upper), which in addition to their scenic beauty have many associations with Selma Lagerlöf.

★**Fryken Lakes**

From Karlstad (see entry) Road 61 follows the right bank of the Klarälv, through wooded country for most of the way. 13km/8 miles from Karlstad, on the left, is a small lake. Then comes a road junction where Road 62 branches off on the right, following the Klarälv valley. Road 61 bears left, coming in 7.5km/4½ miles to another road junction where a road goes off to Kil (3km/2 miles south-west), an important railway junction from which a line runs north to Torsby (pop. 15,000), at the north end of Upper Lake Fryken.

Access

Road 61 continues to the south end of the three Fryken Lakes (alt. 62m/203ft; total length 71km/44 miles; boat trips), an area familiar to readers of Selma Lagerlöf's novel "Gösta Berling's Saga". It passes the church of St Kil (on right); then, 6.5km/4 miles beyond the turning for Kil, crosses the Norsälv, which drains the Fryken Lakes, and reaches a junction. Here we turn right into Road 45, which runs up the Fryksdal, passing numbers of farms and small lakes. Off the road to the west is Frykerud church (1799), with modern stained glass.

Fryksdal

In 25km/15 miles the road comes to the village of Västra Ämtervik, charmingly situated above the 27km/17 mile long Middle Lake Fryken (Mellan-Fryken). Opposite it, on the east side of the lake, is the church of Östra Ämtervik.

Middle Lake Fryken

On Middle Lake Fryken

Room in Mårbacka, Selma Lagerlöf's family home

1km/¾ mile beyond Västra Åmtervik church a country road (signposted to Arvika) goes off on the left and climbs to Kringerås (272m/892ft), a hill from which there are superb views of the beautiful Fryksdal (an attractive side trip of 5km/3 miles).

The road continues at some distance from the shores of the lake and in 6.5km/4 miles crosses the Rotnaälv, which links Mellan-Fryken with the beautiful Lake Rotnen (Finnfall skiing area).

Soon after this the road comes to Rottneros and beyond this, on the right, the manor-house of that name, the Ekoby of "Gösta Berling's Saga", set in a beautiful park, with a large collection of sculpture.

Rottneros

4.5km/3 miles farther on is Sunna, a pleasant little town on the channel between the Middle and Upper Lakes which attracts many summer visitors; it features in "Gösta Berling's Saga" as Broby. Above the village can be found the church (19th c.).

Sunne

9km/5½ miles south-east, off the main road, is the manor-house of Mårbacka, where Selma Lagerlöf (1858–1940) was born and lived until her death. The house now belongs to a foundation and is open to visitors in summer. Her grave is in the churchyard at Östra Åmtervik (6km/4 miles south-west of the house).

★Mårbacka

From Sunne there are two possible routes: either on Road 45, which runs along the east side of Upper Lake Fryken (Övre Fryken) by way of Lysvik to Torsby (41km/25 miles), or (preferably) on a country road which follows the west side of the lake, passing the manor-house of Stöpfors (14km/8½ miles) and Tossebergsklätten (342m/1122ft; views), to Torsby.

Upper Lake Fryken

To the south of Arvika (pop. 26,000) – the farthest inland of Sweden's inland ports, with a connection to the Skagerrak – is the Glaskogen nature reserve (area 28,000 hectares/70,000 acres), with marked footpaths and canoeing routes and overnight accommodation in mountain huts.

Glaskogen nature reserve

Västerås   E 5

Country: **Sweden**
Province: Västmanland
Population: 118,000
Post code: S–72...
Telephone code: 021

Västerås, chief town of the county and province of Västmanland, lies in an inlet on Lake Mälar, at the mouth of the Svartå. The town takes its name from its original site on the west side of the river mouth, Västra Aros (aros = river mouth"), which in course of time became Västerås. In the medieval period the town was the see of a bishop. Eleven meetings of the Swedish Diet were held here, the most important being the Diet of Västerås in 1527, during the reign of Gustavus Vasa, at which it was decided to adopt the Reformed faith.

Situation and characteristics

The town grew rapidly during the 20th century with the development of industry. In 1900 it had barely 12,000 inhabitants – a figure which since then has multiplied almost tenfold. Among the town's principal industries is the manufacture of electrical appliances (ASEA Brown Boveri, ABB). Västerås is also an important inland port, used by many pleasure craft.

The central feature of the town is the Stora Torg, to the south and east of which are Stora Gatan and Vasagatan (both pedestrian zones). Round the central area there is a ring road (Ringvägen).

Town

Stora Torg

469

Västerås

★Cathedral

To the north of the Stora Torg stands the Cathedral, a Gothic brick church built on the foundations of a Romanesque predecessor and consecrated in 1271 (much later alteration; restored 1959–61). The 103m/338ft high tower was added by Nicodemus Tessin the Younger in 1694.

Interior

Between the nave and the choir, on the site of an earlier choir screen, is a 14th century triumphal cross. The three carved reredoses in the choir came from Antwerp and Brussels. Other notable features are the marble sarcophagus of King Eric XIV, the altar of St Veronica and the marble monument of Marshal Magnus Brahe (1633). In the panelled baptistery is a carving of the Baptism of Christ by a North German master. The church contains numerous other monuments and epitaphs.

In the square in front of the Cathedral can be seen a bronze statue by Carl Milles of Bishop Johannes Rudbeckius (d. 1646), who founded the Grammar School and the Diocesan Library (east of the Cathedral), which is now combined with the Provincial Library. Opposite the Cathedral is the old Bishop's Palace.

Kyrkbacken

To the north of the Cathedral lies Kyrkbacken, the oldest part of the town, which has preserved its original character, with old workers' houses. To the west is Djäkneberg Park, with a monument commemorating famous Swedes.

Castle (Museum)

The Castle, on the banks of the Svartå, was originally built in the 13th century. It now houses the Västermanland Provincial Museum (prehistoric remains, local history and culture) and provincial government offices.

Town House
Museum of Art

In the Fiskartorg (Fishmarket) is the Town House (by Sven Ahlborn, 1959), with a 65m/215ft high tower containing a carillon. In the former Town Hall (restored 1972) is the Museum of Art (art from the 17th century to the present day).

Vasa Park

On the south side of Vasa Park is the railway station. To the east of the park are the imposing offices of ASEA Brown Boveri (electrical appliances). Farther east along Stora Gatan is the Folkets Park (People's Park) or Arosparken, with amusements and sports facilities.

Surroundings

2km/1¼ miles south-west of the town centre, on E 18, is Vallby open-air museum, with old wooden buildings (a pharmacy, a silversmith's work-shop, a potter's workshop, etc.) in which various craftsmen ply their trades.

Vallby
open-air museum

6km/4 miles north-east of the town is the Anundshög, on which there is a Viking cemetery (burial mounds, stone-settings).

★Anundshög

2km/1¼ miles west of the town, in Lake Mälar, lies the little island of Elba, with a summer restaurant. There are regular boat services from Västerås harbour to Elba and also to the island of Östra Holmen (good bathing).

Elba

15km/9 miles south-west, on the shores of Lake Mälar, is Tidö Castle (17th c.; Toy Museum, etc.).

Tidö Castle

Sala (pop. 40,000), 40km/25 miles north of Västerås, enjoyed a period of prosperity in the 16th century, when the local silver-mines made a major contribution to the country's revenue. The silver ore worked here was said to have one of the highest silver contents in the world. The town received its municipal charter in 1625, but the mines were already being worked at the end of the 15th century. The mines were controlled by a bailiff residing in Väsby Kungsgård, now a museum. There are conducted tours of the town, the mines and the museum. The deepest shaft is the Charles XI Shaft (318.80m/1046ft). The Queen Christina Shaft, at the entrance to the mine, is 257m/843ft deep. The power supply of the mines was provided by water-mills. By the time the mines closed down in 1908 they had yielded a total of 500 tons of pure silver and 30,000 tons of lead. Although mining continued on a very small scale until about 1950, the annual yield declined into insignificance.

Sala

In the Stora Torg, in the centre of the town, are the Town Hall and the Town House. Suckarnas Allé ("Avenue of Sighs"), which extends along the Övre Damm, commemorates Gustavus Adolphus's love affair with Ebba Brahe.

1km/¾ mile north of the town stands the 14th century Provincial Assembly Church, with wall paintings of 1465, the earliest known work by Albertus Pictor. The reredos (c. 1520) came from Brussels.

Road 66 runs north from Västerås, passing the Strömsholm Canal, con-structed in the 18th century for the transport of ore and iron to the ports on Lake Mälar. On the north-eastern shore of Lake Åmänningen, in a beautiful setting, is the little town of Ängelsberg, notable for its handsome turn-of-the-century houses. Some 15km/9 miles west is the "steel town" of Fager-sta (pop. 14,000), with mines which have been worked since the 14th century.

Ängelsberg

40km/25 miles south-west of Västerås is Köping, a trading town since the 15th century. Here in the 18th century Carl Wilhelm Scheele, a native of Stralsund, worked as a pharmacist; one of the founders of modern chem-istry, he discovered the elements oxygen and nitrogen. The Köping Museum has an interesting pharmacy section commemorating Scheele.

Köping

Västervik   E 6

Country: **Sweden**
Province: Småland
Population: 39,000
Post code: S–593.. Telephone code: 0490

Situation   The Baltic port of Västervik, on the coast of Småland, is one of the most
               attractive examples of Sweden's old timber-built towns of the 18th century.

Town   St Gertrude's Church (15th c.) has fine wall paintings and an altar by the
               Swedish Baroque master Burchard Precht (1651–1738).
               The Cederflycht Poorhouse (Cederflychtska Fattighuset; by Carl Hårle-
               man, c. 1750) led a contemporary historian to remark, "In Västervik the
               poor live better than the rich." Aspagården, the oldest house in the town, is
               now occupied by craftsmen's workshops.
               In the Fiskaretorg (Fishmarket) visitors can sample the local fish speciali-
               ties, and in nearby Batmansgränd can be seen a row of little red-painted
               seamen's houses recalling the days when Västervik was an important port.
               Nearby are the ruins of Stegeholm Castle (14th c.), which in recent years
               has been the scene of an annual song festival. Here too is the Slottsholmen
               summer restaurant. On Kulbacken, a hill from which there is a good view of
               the town, is the Provincial Museum (Tjustbygden Museum; local history
               and crafts, with a section on ships and seafaring).

Skerries   3km/2 miles east of the town centre lies the Lysingsbad recreation area.
               One of the great attractions of Västervik is its girdle of skerries: the so-
               called "skerry garden" consists of some 5000 islands and islets.

Surroundings

               10km/6 miles south of Västervik is Lundsby (17th c.), an interesting market
               village (torgby) laid out round a central square.

Oskarshamn   65km/40 miles south of Västervik is Oskarshamn (pop. 27,000), a port and
               industrial town on Döderhultsvik, an inlet on the Baltic between Kalmar and
               Västervik, which received its municipal charter in 1856. Oskarshamn was
               the birthplace of the Swedish doctor and author Axel Munthe (1857–1949),
               whose "Story of San Michele" (1931) was a bestseller in many languages.
               Munthe, who lived in Paris and Rome and on Capri, died in Stockholm.
               Oskarshamn is a town of many ups and downs, reflecting its hilly topo-
               graphy. At Hantverksgatan 18–20 can be found the House of Culture,
               containing the Maritime Museum, a library and an art gallery displaying
               Småland woodcarving and works by the sculptor Axel Petersson (1868–
               1925), who was born at Döderhult, near Oskarshamn. The church, on a hill
               in the Municipal Park, is Neo-Gothic (19th c.). Opposite the harbour is the
               Fyknet quarter, a district of little wooden houses.

               On the way to Döderhult is Fredriksberg Herrgård, an 18th century manor-
               house with a handsome great hall, now housing an interesting local
               museum.

               From Långa Softan (the "Long Bench"), in the old seamen's quarter around
               the harbour, there is a fine view of the coast. 20km/12½ miles out to sea,
               half way between the mainland and the island of Öland (see entry), lies the
               rocky island of Blå Jungfrun, the "Blue Maiden" (alt. 85m/280ft; National
               Park).
               In summer there are daily ferry services from Oskarshamn to Byxelkrok
               on Öland and Visby on Gotland (see entry).

Vimmerby   Inland from Västervik, to the west, is the former market town of Vimmerby
               (pop. 16,000), with old houses and a medieval street layout. Open-air
               museum. The Grankvistgård (18th c.) has finely executed wall and ceiling
               paintings.

               To the west of Vimmerby is one of the oldest wooden churches in Sweden.
               The writer Astrid Lindgren (see Introduction, Famous People) was born in

Market Square, Vimmerby

this area, and this was the setting of some of her books, the fairytale village of Sagobyn.

North of Vimmerby, near the border between Småland and Östergötland, extends the Norra Kvill National Park – 27 hectares/ 67 acres of unspoiled natural woodland. In the park is Sweden's largest oak-tree, the "thousand-year-old oak", which has a girth of 14m/46ft.

Norra Kvill
National Park

Lake Vättern   D 6

Country: **Sweden**
Provinces: Västergötland, Östergötland, Närke, Småland

Lake Vättern, Sweden's second largest lake (area 1912sq.km/738sq. miles; 130km/80 miles long, greatest width 30km/19 miles) extends through the four provinces of Västergötland, Östergötland, Närke and Småland. Its water is so clear that the bottom can be seen at depths of up to 10m/33ft, and at these depths the surface appears green as a result of the reflection of light from the sandy bottom. The clarity of the water is due to the fact that the lake is fed partly by springs and partly by water from mountain streams, purified by passing over gravel.

Situation and
characteristics

The lake has an average depth of 40m/130ft, but reaches as much as 128m/420ft at the deepest spots around Visingsö. This great mass of water stores so much heat that the lake does not freeze until late in the year – rarely before New Year, and in many years not at all. On the other hand it is slow to warm up in summer. The colder water on the bottom supports a large fish population, including the Vättern salmon, a species of trout.

473

Regatta on Lake Vättern

Around ★Lake Vättern

Gränna

40km/25 miles north-east of Jönköping (see entry) is Gränna (pop. 2200), one of the few towns with old wooden houses which have not been devastated by fire. With its charming old-world architecture and its beautiful situation on Lake Vättern, at the foot of the Grännaberg, this idyllic little town has become a popular holiday resort.

The town was founded in 1652 by Count Per Brahe, who laid out the main street (Brahegatan), which then consisted of only ten houses, in such a way that he could see it from his castle of Brahehus (now a ruin). He also built the Town Hall, with its belfry, and enlarged the medieval church. The church, now a handsome Baroque edifice, stands above the village at the foot of the hill. In the cobbled market square is the Medborgargård (Community House). In Museigården can be found the Andrée Museum, commemorating the engineer and Arctic explorer Salomon Andrée, a native of the town (b. 1854) who was lost in 1897 during an attempt to fly to the North Pole from Spitzbergen in a balloon.

Gränna is noted also for its *polkagrisar* ("polka-dotted piglets") – sticks of red-and-white striped peppermint rock.

★Visingö

From Gränna there are boats (20 minutes) to the largest island in Lake Vättern, Visingö (pop. 750; area 25sq.km/10sq. miles; 14km/8½ miles long, up to 3km/2 miles wide). The prehistoric cemetery areas on the island point to early human settlement here. Visingsborg Castle, built by the Brahe family, was once the most splendid castle in Sweden, but was destroyed by fire in 1718 and is now a ruin. At the southern tip of the island is the "Castle on the Näs", Sweden's oldest secular building. Pleasant walks in the forest (on the south side of which are a number of mulberry-trees); rides in horse-drawn carriages.

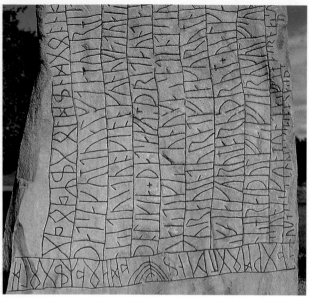

Detail of runic stone at Rök, near Alvastra

27km/17 miles north of Gränna, at Ödeshög in Östergötland, Road 50 goes off on the left, running at some distance from the shores of the lake, and comes in 8km/5 miles to Alvastra, with the ruins of a Cistercian abbey (founded 1143), at the foot of the Omberg (Hjässan, 263m/863ft; viewing platform), a range of hills 10km/6 miles long which is wooded on the east side and falls steeply down to Lake Vättern on the west.

Alvastra

6km/4 miles beyond this, off the road to the right, is Väversunda, which has a 12th century Romanesque church with a triumphal cross (replica: the original is in the National Museum in Stockholm). To the east lies Lake Tåkern, the haunt of large numbers of birds, which features in Selma Lagerlöf's "Wonderful Adventures of Nils" and in Bengt Berg's animal stories.

Väversunda

17km/10 miles farther north is Vadstena (pop. 7500), a town noted for its lace, which owes its origin to St Birgitta. Birgitta was principal lady-in-waiting at the court of King Magnus Eriksson and Queen Blanka, but withdrew from the court after receiving a divine revelation and in 1346 was granted the property of Kungsgården for the foundation of an abbey, which was completed only six years after her death, in 1379. She was canonised in 1394.

Vadstena

Thereafter the little settlement of Vadstena rose to importance as a place of pilgrimage and market town, and was granted a municipal charter in 1400.

After the Reformation Vadstena declined, but it has recently recovered some importance with the growth of the tourist trade.

By the harbour stands Vadstena Castle, in Renaissance style, built by Gustavus Vasa in the 16th century and later altered and enlarged by his son, John III, and grandson, Duke John. The high curtain walls along the lake front were pulled down to supply stone for the construction of the harbour pier.

★Vadstena Castle

Lake Vättern

Vadstena Castle

Blåkyrkan

North of the Castle is the Blue Church (Blåkyrkan), so called from the colour of the limestone of which it is built (restored 1898). The most notable feature of the interior is the 15th century St Birgitta's Altar, by a Lübeck master. To the left of the altar is the reliquary of St Birgitta, with the figure of the saint in the central part. On a pillar in the nave is a sculpture of St Birgitta in ecstasy which was much venerated in the Middle Ages. The nuns' quarters are still largely preserved, as are the more modest buildings to the south which were built for the monks in the 18th century. Gustavus Adolphus converted the abbey into a home for old soldiers.

Immediately outside the abbey is Mårten Skinners Hus (16th c.). The situation of the Town Hall (15th c.) shows how the centre of the town had moved away from the abbey towards the castle. In Rådhustorget (Town Hall Square) are a number of well preserved burghers' houses, notably Udd Jönssons Hus. In Storgatan is the Finspång Hotel.

Motala

16km/10 miles north of Vadstena lies Motala (pop. 41,000), which was the meeting-place of the local *ting* (assembly) as early as the 14th century. The church dates from that period. Motala became a place of some consequence, however, only after the construction of the Göta Canal (see entry). The engineer responsible for the canal, Count Baltzar von Platen, also planned the layout of the district around the Motalavik. There is a statue of Platen in the Stortorg (Market Square), and his mausoleum stands on the banks of the canal. Other features of interest in the town are the nine-arched Storbro and Borenhuits Slusstrappa, a "staircase" of five locks leading into Lake Boren.

Medevi

From Motala Road 50 runs north to Medevi, Sweden's oldest spa.

Askersund

Askersund (pop. 12,000) is the most northerly of the towns on Lake Vättern. Around the market square are a number of old wooden houses and a

476

beautiful little Baroque building. In the Municipal Park is an interesting local museum.

Road 49, running along the west side of Lake Vättern, is one of the most beautiful roads in Sweden. Tiveden National Park (28km/17 miles) is a hilly and well wooded area with a number of lakes (good walking).

Tiveden National Park

At Karlsborg (pop. 4000) the Göta Canal runs into Lake Vättern. Karlsborg Fort, built in the 19th century, is still of military importance. Within the ring of walls and moats are a number of separate buildings; the Museum and the park are open to the public.

Karlsborg

From Road 195, which leads south from Mölltorp, there are fine views of the long island of Visingsö, the town of Jönköping at the south end of Lake Vättern and the attractively situated suburb of Bankeryd.

★Views

Växjö   D 6

Country: **Sweden**
Province: Småland
Altitude: 160m/525ft
Population: 70,000
Post code: S–35...
Telephone code: 0470

Växjö lies at the north end of the lake of that name. It received its municipal charter in 1342 and is now chief town of Kronoberg county. There was a trading settlement here in the Iron Age and in Viking times, and the town's name comes from its situation at the meeting-place of trading routes (*väg*) on the lake (*sjö*). It became a religious centre in the 12th century, when its first church was built by St Sigfrid, a missionary from England. Within recent years Växjö has developed into an industrial town, with modern buildings and a wide range of recreational facilities.

Situation and characteristics

The 12th century Cathedral, after undergoing much alteration in later centuries, was given its present appearance in a restoration carried out in 1959. It has modern stained glass by Jan Brazda, Bo Beskow, Elis Lindquist and Erik Höglund and a mosaic by Bo Beskow. The organ-case dates from 1779. Under the tower is an exhibition of the church's treasures.

Town

Cathedral

Near the Cathedral is the Karolinska Gymnasium, a grammar school at which Linnaeus, Per Henrik Ling and Peter Wieselgren were pupils. The Bishop's Palace, Östrabo, was the residence of the poet Bishop Elias Tegnér until his death in 1846. There is a statue of Tegnér in the gardens outside the Cathedral.

There is a twice-weekly market in Växjö's main square, the Stortorg, immediately in front of the Bishop's Palace.

Market

On a low hill to the south of the railway station can be found the Småland Museum, with an art collection, a coin cabinet and a section on forestry. Of particular interest is the museum's collection of Swedish and foreign glassware, illustrating the history of glass-making.

Småland Museum (★glass collection)

The Emigrants' House (Utvandrarnas Hus; 1968) contains an exhibition on the theme "The Dream of America", archives and a library documenting the emigration movement in the second half of the 19th century, when more than 200,000 people left the country. This provided the source material for Vilhelm Moberg's novels about the life of the emigrants ("The Emigrants", 1949, etc.).

Emigrants' House

Vesterålen

Teleborg   On the south side of the town is Teleborg Castle (19th c.), now the administrative offices of the nearby college.

Kronoberg Castle   5km/3 miles from the town centre, on the Helgasjö, are the ruins of Kronoberg Castle; originally an episcopal residence, it later became Crown property (Kungsgård). Near the castle is the old Ryttmästaregård ("Captain's House"), re-erected on this site and now occupied by a café.
From Kronoberg there are steamer trips on the lake.

Surroundings

Dädesjö   To the north of Växjö are great expanses of forest and lakes. There are medieval churches at Drev, Dädesjö (wooden ceiling, with paintings) and Sjösås. On Lake Örken is Braås Hembygdsparken (open-air museum). From the lookout tower at Tolg there are extensive views of the surrounding countryside.

Ljungby   West of Växjö on Road 25 (possible side trip to Hjärtenholm Agricultural Museum, north of Alvesta) is Ljungby (pop. 27,000). Gamla Ljungby Torg (Old Ljungby Square) was created in 1972, with a number of surviving 19th century houses. Ljungby lies in a wooded part of Småland, with many lakes and numerous prehistoric remains and old churches. To the west of the town is Lake Bolmen, with many islands, the largest of which is Bolmsö.

Bergkvara   Road 23 runs south-west from Växjö, passing the ruins of Bergkvara Castle
Råshult   on the Bergkvarasjö. 20km/12½ miles from Växjö, to the east of the road, is the manor-house of Huseby, which was left to the state by Florence Stephensen in 1979 (open to the public). A side road on the right leads to Liatorp, from which it is a short distance to Diö, on the shores of Lake Möckeln. In the lake lies the beautiful island of Höö (nature reserve). At Råshult, near Stenbrohult, can be found the small cottage in which Linnaeus was born in 1707 (open to the public in summer).

Älmhult   10km/6 miles farther south is Älmhult, where the IKEA furniture-making
Lake Åsnen   firm was established over 40 years ago. From Älmhult Road 120 runs east to Lake Åsnen (canoeing; cycle trails). To the east of the lake lies a part of Småland from which many emigrants left in the 19th century (villages of Ljuder, I ångasjö and Moshult, birthplace of Vilhelm Moberg); "Emigrants' Trail" (Utvandrarleden), starting from the Korrö youth hostel. Farther east on Road 25 are the glass-making area of Småland and the town of Kalmar (see entries).

Narrow-gauge   A narrow-gauge railway (operated only during the summer months) runs
railway to   through the forests of Småland from Växjö to Västervik on the east coast.
Västervik   The line (opened in 1879) is privately owned.

Vesterålen   D 2/3

Country: **Norway**
Region: North-western Norway

Situation and   The island group of Vesterålen, lying off the Vestfjord on the north-west
characteristics   Norwegian coast, is the north-eastern continuation of the Lofoten group. The landscape of these islands is less rugged than that of the Lofotens; the hills are less precipitous, usually grass-covered to a considerable height and frequently wooded.
    The islands can be reached by way of a suspension bridge over the Tjeldsund or by ferry; the best starting-point is Narvik (see entry). The midnight sun is visible here from the end of May to the end of July.

On the Vågsfjord

The much ramified island of Hinnøy is Norway's largest island after Spitzbergen (see entry). Half of the island (the western and southern parts) is in
Nordland county, the other half (the north-eastern part) in Troms county.

Hinnøy

Harstad, the chief place on the island (pop. 22,000), reached on Road 83 by
way of the Tjeldsund bridge, lies in a sheltered situation on the Vågsfjord, in
the north-east of the island. It is an important fish-processing centre. A
festival (concerts, theatre, exhibitions, jazz) is held here at the end of June.
In summer there is an angling competition.

Harstad

On a peninsula 3km/2 miles north-east of Harstad stands the stone church
of Trondenes (built about 1250), which in the Middle Ages was the most
northerly church in Christendom.

Trondenes church

Offshore, north-east of the town, is the little island of Kjeøy, with rock
paintings (*hellemalerier*) dating from the Stone Age.

Kjeøy

From the Tjeldsund bridge Road 19 runs south along the coast. At the south
end of the island a side road goes off on the left to Lødingen (church,
pastor's house), from which there is a ferry to Bognes, to the south.

Lødingen

After the turning for Lødingen Road 19 runs north, follows the shores of the
Gullesfjord and then turns inland, continuing west to the Sortlandsund.
Here Road 82 branches off and runs up to the north end of Hinnøy, then
crosses the Andøy bridge on to Andøy, the most northerly island in the
group, with extensive areas of moorland from which hills rise to heights of
up to 600m/2000ft. To the east is a coal seam (not worked) extending into
the sea.

Andøy

At the northern tip of the island lies the little fishing port of Andenes, with a
breakwater 2500m/2735yd long. With its population of 4200 it has the air of
a small town. In an old burgher's house is a Polar Museum. On the harbour
is a whaling centre, and in summer visitors can take part in a "whale safari".

Andenes

Langøy

Sortland

Beyond the turning for Andøy Road 19 crosses the Sortlandsbru over the Sortlandsund, which separates Hinnøy and Langøy. Langøy, with its numerous peninsulas and fjords, occupies most of the western part of the Vesterålen group. Sortland (pop. 3000), an old-established settlement at the most easterly point on the island, is a port of call for the ships of the Hurtigrute (see entry).

Hadseløy

Stokmarknes

Road 19 crosses from Langøy to Hadseløy on the Hadselbru (toll) and comes to the little town of Stokmarknes (pop. 3000), another port of call on the Hurtigrute. From here there are boat trips to the Eidsfjord, to the north.

Melbu

At the south end of Hadseløy is the little port of Melbu, the base of a large trawling fleet. There are magnificent views of the islands from Husbykollen (513m/1683ft). Ferry service to the Lofoten Islands (see entry). From the road running along the west coast to Stokmarknes there are fine views of the sea and the islands.

Ystad   D 7

Country: **Sweden**
Province: Skåne
Population: 24,000
Post code: S–271..
Telephone code: 0411

Situation and
characteristics

Ystad is a port on the south coast of Skåne from which there are ferry services to the Danish island of Bornholm and to Swinoujście in Poland. In the Middle Ages it was one of the principal herring-fishing towns in the Baltic. The town enjoyed a period of prosperity in the early 19th century, when Napoleon imposed his continental blockade and many of the town's inhabitants carried on a very profitable smuggling trade.

Half-timbered houses, Ystad; to the rear St Mary's Church

Ystad has the finest and best preserved medieval half-timbered houses in Sweden. The Old Town Hall in the Stortorg is a building in Empire style (1838–40) erected over 14th century cellars with groined vaulting, relics of the original Town Hall destroyed by the Swedes in 1659. The cellars are now a bar.

Also in the Stortorg is the 13th century St Mary's Church, a familiar landmark with its copper-sheathed steeple (16th c.). From the tower a watchman still looks out over the town, sounding his horn four times every hour during the night. A tower added in the 14th century collapsed during a storm, destroying part of the nave. With assistance from the Danish king Frederick III the church was rebuilt and enlarged to twice its previous size. The interior is richly decorated, with fine wood-carving and crucifixes.

Farther north can be found another 13th century church, St Peter's, near which is the Gråbrödrakloster (Monastery of the Grey Friars), a Franciscan friary which is the best preserved religious house in Sweden after Vadstena Abbey (see Lake Vättern). It was founded in 1267 and after the Reformation, about 1530, was used at various times as a hospital, a brandy distillery and a warehouse.

South-east of the Stortorg, at Dammgatan 23, is the Charlotte Berlin Museum, a burgher's house with 19th century furniture and furnishings. In the same building are the Museum of Art and the Dragoon Museum.

At the corner of Stora Östergatan and Pilgränd stands the Pilgränsgård, a handsome half-timbered house of about 1500 (restored 1947). The Aspelinska Gård, at the corner of Östergatan and Gåsegränd, consists of three half-timbered buildings grouped round a courtyard, erected in 1778 for a goldsmith named Jonas Aspelin.

At the corner of Stora Norregatan and Sladdergatan is the Brahehus, a 16th century mansion built by the Brahe family, who had large estates in this area and enjoyed great political influence. Also in Sladdergatan is a very decorative half-timbered house, the Änglahus (17th c.), built for a town councillor named Hans Raffn; on the façade are the carved angels from which it takes its name.

On the east side of the town, in the Österportstorg, stands the New Town Hall, a building in Empire style (1812) which was originally the mansion of a local dignitary named C. M. Lundgren.

Farther east is Sandskogen, the "Sand Forest", a belt of trees planted in the early 19th century as a protection from drifting sand. This area is now the "Riviera" of Sweden's south coast.

Surroundings

5km/3 miles north-west of the town is the 12th century church of Bjäresjö, with interesting wall paintings.

15km/9 miles north of Ystad on Road 19 is Örups Stenhus, one of the oldest castles in Skåne (c. 1490). It shows some similarity to Glimmingehus (see below).

17km/10½ miles east of Ystad on Road 9 is the Vallaberga Kyrka (12th c.), Sweden's only surviving round church. It has the same ground-plan as the round churches on the Danish island of Bornholm, which at one time belonged to the same diocese. The font was the work of the 12th century Gotland stonemason known as the Magister Majestatis. The church's

Standing Stones "Ales Stenar" near Kåseberga

separate fortified tower, dating from the late medieval period, is now a museum.

Kåseberga

On the coast to the east of Ystad is the little fishing village of Kåseberga, famed for the Ales Stenar, a Viking stone-setting in the shape of a ship, 67m/220ft long by 19m/62ft across, consisting of 59 standing stones. From the low hill there is a view extending in clear weather to the Danish island of Bornholm.

Backåkra

At Backåkra, between Lödderup and Sandhammaren, can be seen a house once occupied by Dag Hammarskjöld, Secretary General of the United Nations, now the Dag Hammarskjöld Museum.

★Glimmimgehus
(ill., p. 387)

Glimmingehus, south-west of Simrishamn, is one of the best preserved castles in Sweden, giving some impression of the life of a large landowner in the Middle Ages. It was built in 1499 by Rikcamiral Jens Holgersen Ulfstad; the architect was Adam van Düren, who also worked on the cathedrals of Cologne and Lund. The castle has remained unchanged since it was built. It was a residence as well as a defensive structure, and was equipped with a heating system. The castle, which is mentioned in Selma Lagerlöf's "Wonderful Adventures of Nils", has belonged to the state since 1924 and is open to the public.

Simrishamn

There are good beaches along the whole coastal strip between Ystad and Simrishamn, particularly at Sandhammaren, at the south-eastern tip of Skåne. Simrishamn is a fishing town (pop. 20,000) founded in the 14th century, with St Nicholas's Church and picturesque little houses gay with climbing roses.

20km/12½ miles north on Road 9 is Kivik, where Sweden's best known summer market is held. Here too is the "King's Grave" (Kungsgraven), a Bronze Age royal tomb.

Kivik

In summer a steam train runs between Brösarp and St. Olof, to north and south of Kivik.

South of Kivik, on the coast, lies the Stenshuvud National Park, a hill (98m/322ft) with a varied pattern of vegetation from which there is a good view of the Danish island of Bornholm.

Stenshuvud
National Park

Practical Information from A to Z

N.B. In **Norway**, telephone area codes ceased to exist from 1993, having been incorporated into the customer number. As a result, all telephone and fax numbers now have eight digits instead of six as before.

Accommodation

See Camping and Caravanning; Hotels; Youth Hostels, Holiday Houses and Cabins

Airlines

Airline Offices in Britain

Air UK Ltd
Stansted House
Stansted Airport
Essex CM24 1AE
tel. (01279) 660400;
reservations (0345) 666777; fax (01279) 660330
Services from Aberdeen, Edinburgh, Humberside, Teesside and Norwich to Stavanger and Bergen (change at Aberdeen from last 4 points of departure)

Brymon European Airways
Brymon House, Coventry Road
Birmingham B26 39G
Reservations: (0345) 222111
Services from Birmingham to Oslo, Göteborg and Stockholm (via Copenhagen or Amsterdam)

Braathens
Newcastle International Airport
Woolsington
Newcastle upon Tyne NE13 8BZ
Reservations: (0191) 214 0991
Services to Oslo and Stavanger/Bergen

British Airways
156 Regent Street
London W1
tel. (0181) 897 4000
(reservations)
Services from London Heathrow to Stavanger, Oslo, Stockholm and Helsinki

Finnair
14 Clifford Street
London W1X 1RD
tel. (0171) 408 1222
fax (0171) 629 7289

◄ *A ferry ship of the Silja Line off Mariehamn (Åland Islands)*

Air Travel

SAS Scandinavian Airlines
52–53 Conduit Street
London W1E 5Y2
tel. (0171) 734 6777
fax (0171) 465 1025

Services from London Heathrow to Bergen, Oslo and Stavanger; from Aberdeen and Glasgow to Stavanger; and from Manchester via Copenhagen to Norway; from Manchester to Oslo

Widerøe Norsk Air
c/o Air UK (see above)
Services from London Stansted via Kristiansand to Sandefjord

Airline Offices in Scandinavia

Norway

SAS Norway Hot Line (information and reservations)
tel. 81 00 33 00

British Airways
Karl Johansgate 16B (3rd floor), P.O. Box 487
010 05 Oslo 1
tel. (02) 33 16 00
and Fornebu Airport
tel. (02) 59 70 19

Sweden

SAS
Sveavägen 22
S–10396 Stockholm
tel. (08) 24 00 40

British Airways
Norrmalmstorg 1
LS–111 46 Stockholm
tel. (08) 6 11 02 34

Finland

Finnair
Mannerheimintie 102
FIN–00250 Helsinki
tel. (90) 8 18 81;
Air Terminal
Töölönkatu 21
tel. (90) 8 18 77 70

British Airways
Keskuskatu 7 (7th floor)
00100 Helsinki 10
tel. (90) 65 06 77

Air Travel

Air services within Scandinavia are provided mainly by SAS (Scandinavian Airlines System) and Finnair. In Norway there are Braathens SAFE and Widerøe, in Sweden Linjeflyg.

Norway

Braathens SAFE

The Norwegian airline Braathens SAFE, flying Boeing 737s, serves 15 airports from Kristiansand in the south to Tromsø and Spitzbergen in the north.

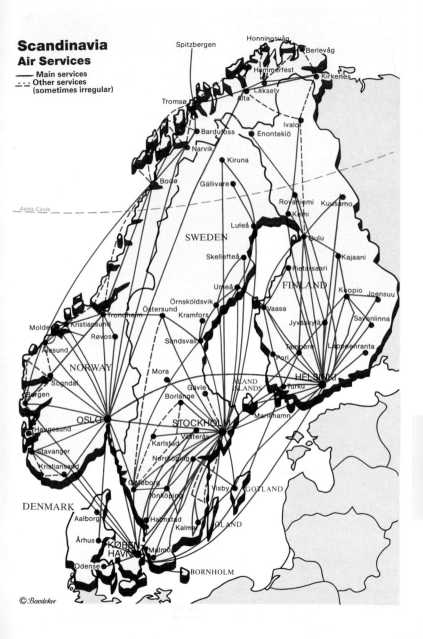

Scandinavia
Air Services
— Main services
--- Other services
(sometimes irregular)

Spitzbergen

Honningsvåg
Berlevåg
Hammerfest
Kirkenes
Tromsø
Alta
Lakselv
Bardufoss
Enontekiö
Ivalo
Narvik
Kiruna
Bodø
Gällivare
Rovaniemi
Kemi
Kuusamo
Luleå
Oulu
SWEDEN
Skellefteå
Kajaani
Pietarsaari
Umeå
FINLAND
Kuopio
Joensuu
Örnsköldsvik
Östersund
Vaasa
Trondheim
Kramfors
Savonlinna
Molde
Kristiansund
Jyväskylä
Røros
Sundsvall
Tampere
Lappeenranta
Ålesund
Pori
Sogndal
NORWAY
Mora
ÅLAND
ISLANDS
HELSINKI
Bergen
Gävle
Turku
Haugesund
OSLO
Borlänge
STOCKHOLM
Mariehamn
Stavanger
Karlstad
Västerås
Kristiansand
Norrköping
Göteborg
Visby
GOTLAND
DENMARK
Jönköping
Aalborg
Halmstad
ÖLAND
Århus
Kalmar
KØBEN-
HAVN
Malmö
Odense
BORNHOLM

Arctic Circle

© Baedeker

SAS aircraft

Visit Norway Pass	Braathens's Visit Norway Pass (for visitors from outside the Scandinavian countries only) gives discount-rate flight coupons valid for a month.
Information	Braathens SAFE Markedsavdeling Postboks 55 N–1330 Oslo Lufthavn tel. 67 59 70 00
Widerøe	Widerøe and its subsidiary Norsk Air serve 40 airports within Norway. Their aircraft in their green and white livery connect with SAS and Braathens services to convey passengers to tourist centres in western and northern Norway. Through fares are available at very reasonable rates. It is also possible to fly one way and return by rail or bus.
Information	For further information and reservations apply to SAS agencies or direct to: Widerøe Postboks 82 Lilleaker N–0216 Oslo 2 tel. 22 73 66 00, fax 22 73 65 90

Sweden

SAS Inrikes	SAS Inrikes, a subsidiary of SAS, serves 38 airports in Sweden. The most important of these, from south to north, are Malmö, Visby, Göteborg, Jönköping, Norrköping, Karlstad, Stockholm, Västerås, Falun, Mora, Östersund, Umeå, Luleå, Gällivare and Kiruna.
Information	Information about special fares for "red departures" (see Railways, Sweden) and other reductions can be obtained from:

SAS
Box 550
S–19045 Stockholm-Arlanda
tel. (08) 7 97 50 00, fax (08) 7 97 86 20

Smaller airports are served by a variety of small local airlines. Information about flights can be obtained from the airports.

Finland

Turku, in south-western Finland, has daily connections with Copenhagen and Stockholm. Within Finland Finnair and its subsidiaries serve 22 airports: from south to north Helsinki, Mariehamn (Åland Islands), Turku, Lappeenranta, Tampere, Pori, Mikkeli, Savonlinna. Jyväskylä, Varkaus, Joensuu, Kuopio, Vaasa, Kokkola/Jakobstad, Kajaani, Oulu, Kemi, Kuusamo, Rovaniemi, Kittilä, Enontekiö and Ivalo.

Finnair

The fares for domestic flights in Finland are very reasonable, particularly with the Finnair Holiday Ticket and Youth Holiday Ticket, which give unlimited use of domestic services for 15 days. The adult ticket costs about £230, the youth ticket (for young people under 24) about £190.
For other reductions and further information apply to Finnair offices or to a travel agent.

Holiday Tickets

Information about "Fly and Drive" holidays in Finland can be obtained from travel agencies, Finnair offices and the Finnair Tour Desk in Helsinki, tel. (90) 8 18 79 00. A brochure produced by Finnair Tours, "Finland Fly and Drive", contains information about other possibilities.

"Fly and Drive"

Business Hours

There are no general statutory provisions on shop opening hours. Most shops are open Monday to Wednesday from 9am to 4 or 5pm, Thursday and Friday 9am to 7 or 8pm, Saturday 9am to 1 or 3pm.
The Narvesen kiosks are frequently also open on Sundays and in the evening until 10pm. Some foodshops stay open until midnight.
Vinmonopolet: see Food and Drink, Alcohol.

Norway

Shops are usually open from 9.30am to 6pm, on Saturdays until 1pm, often until 4pm; some central supermarkets are open until 8pm and on Sundays from noon to 4 or 5pm. Foodstuffs can be bought at many petrol stations and in Näröppe shops from early in the morning until late in the evening.
Systembolaget: see Food and Drink, Alcohol.

Sweden

Shops are normally open Monday to Friday 9am–6pm, Saturday 9am–3pm; large shops and department stores are open until 8pm Monday to Friday, until 4pm on Saturday. Some of the shops in the underpass at Helsinki station stay open until 10pm.
Alko: see Food and Drink, Alcohol.

Finland

For opening times of banks see Currency; for post offices see Postal Services.

Bus Services

Railway services in northern Scandinavia are much more limited than in the south, and the gaps are filled by buses, which run many services connecting with the railway. There are a variety of reduced fares on particular routes and for certain age groups. Detailed information about services can be obtained from local tourist information offices or from the following addresses:

Norway

Nor-Way Bussekspress AS
Karl Johans gt. 2
N–0154 Oslo
tel. 22 17 52 90, fax 22 17 59 22

Sweden

Swe-Bus
Gullbergs Strandgatan 34
S–41104 Göteborg
tel. (031) 38 20/50/56, fax (031) 15 53 56

P.O. Box 8936
Katrinerovägern IC
40273–Göteborg
tel. (031) 103 840

Linjebuss
Torsgatan 8
S–11423 Stockholm
tel. (8) 729 13 00, fax (08) 6 26 94 73

Finland

Matkahuolto
Lauttasaarentie 8
FIN–002001 Helsinki
tel. (90) 682 701, fax (90) 692 2864

Camping and Caravanning

Scandinavia is ideal for a camping holiday. In all the Scandinavian countries there are numerous official camping sites (Norwegian *campingplass,* Swedish *campingplads,* Finnish *leirintäalue*). Most sites are open to all campers, but at some sites an international camping carnet (or a membership card from a national camping club) is required.

The various national tourist boards, motoring organisations and camping clubs publish annually lists of camping sites, showing their situation, size, facilities and general quality.

In addition to the usual sanitary installations and cooking facilities the larger sites usually have showers and shops selling foodstuffs. Many also have wooden camping cabins offering simple sleeping accommodation. In areas of particular natural beauty there are often holiday villages of chalets and log cabins.

"Wild" campers should ask locally for permission before setting up their camp. Camping is prohibited in nature reserves and military areas.

On the coast or on the shores of fjords tents should be sited with their entrances away from the wind. In Lapland a mosquito net is essential.

Norway

Norway has around 1400 camping sites, which are classified in three categories (with one, two or three stars).

Information:
Norges Automobil Forbund (NAF)
Storgaten 2
N–0155 Oslo 1
tel. 22 34 16 00

Sweden

Around 750 camping sites in three categories; some are open throughout the year.

Camping site in the forest (Finland)

Information:
Sveriges Campingvärdars Riksförbund (SCR)
Box 255
S–45117 Uddevalla
tel. (0522) 3 93 45, fax (0522) 3 38 49

Some 360 camping sites in three categories.   Finland

Information:
Finnish Travel Association, Camping Department
Mikonkatu 25, FIN–00100 Helsinki 10
tel. (90) 17 08 68, fax (90) 65 43 58

Car and Passenger Ferries

There are ferry services from British ports to Norway and Sweden, and also
to Denmark, from which there are ferries to Norway and Sweden. There are
no direct car ferries from Britain to Finland, but numerous ferries from
Swedish ports.

Ferries to Denmark

Harwich–Esbjerg (19 hours): Scandinavian Seaways
Newcastle–Esbjerg (20 hours): Scandinavian Seaways

Ferries to Norway

Newcastle–Stavanger (20 hours) and Bergen (27 hours): Color Line

Car and Passenger Ferries

Via Denmark   Copenhagen Helsingborg–Oslo (16 hours): Scandinavian Seaways
Hirtshals–Oslo (8 hours): Color Line
Hirtshals–Kristiansand (4½ hours): Color Line
Frederikshavn–Larvik (6–11 hours): Larvik Line
Frederikshavn–Oslo (12 hours): Stena Line, DA–NO Linjen
Frederikshavn–Moss (7 hours): Stena Line

Ferries to Sweden

Harwich–Göteborg (24 hours): Scandinavian Seaways
Newcastle–Göteborg (22 hours): Scandinavian Seaways

Via Denmark   Helsingør–Helsingborg (25 minutes): Scandlines
Dragør (Copenhagen)–Limhamn (Malmö) (55 minutes): Scandlines
Frederikshavn–Göteborg (3 hours): Stena Line
Grenå–Varberg (4 hours): Lion Ferry
Grenå–Halmstad (4 hours): Lion Ferry

Ferries to Finland

From Sweden

Stockholm–Helsinki (15 hours): Silja Line, Viking Line
Stockholm–(Mariehamn)–Turku (6 hours): Viking Line
Stockholm–Turku (11 hours): Silja Line, Viking Line
Stockholm–Naantali (23 hours): Viking Line
Kapellskär–(Mariehamn)–Naantali (2–8 hours): Viking Line
Sundsvall–Vaasa (7 hours): Wasa Line
Örnsköldsvik–Vaasa (5 hours): Wasa Line
Grisslehamn–Eckerö (2 hours): Eckerö-Linjen
Skellefteå–Jakobstad (6 hours): Jakob Lines
Skellefteå–Karleby (4 hours): Jakob Lines
Umeå–Vaasa and Uneå–Jakobstad (6 hours): Silja Line, Jakob Line

Addresses of Shipping Lines

Color Line   The International Ferry Terminal
Royal Quays
North Shields NE29 6EE
tel. (0191) 296 1313

Scandinavian   15 Hanover Street
Seaways   London W1R 3HG
(No telephone bookings)

The International Ferry Terminal
Royal Quays
North Shields NE29 6EE
tel. (0191) 296 0101

Silja Line   Scandinavian Seaways
Scandinavia House
Parkeston Quay
Harwich
Essex CO12 4QG
tel. (01255) 241234, 240240 (reservations)

Stena Line
Charter House, Park Street
Ashford, Kent TN24 8EX
tel. (01233) 647047 (reservations)

4th Floor
21–24 Cockspur Street
Trafalgar Square, London SW1Y 5BN
tel. (0171) 839 2927

Car Rental

Facilities for car rental are widely available in the Scandinavian countries. All the main international hire firms are represented, and cars can be booked before leaving home through their local offices. There are also numerous local firms (easily found in the Yellow Pages of the telephone directory) from whom cars can be hired on the spot; their rates are usually lower, the cars perhaps not quite so well equipped.

Car rental firms have desks in international airports and railway stations. The age of the hirer varies from 18 to 25 years, so please check first. They must produce an international driving licence. Rates vary according to type of car, duration of rental and time of year.

Chemists

See Medical Aid and Chemists

Currency

The unit of currency is the Norwegian krone (abbreviated kr or NOK), which consists of 100 øre. There are banknotes for 50, 100, 500 and 1000 crowns and coins in denominations of 50 øre and 1, 5 and 10 crowns.

Norway

Exchange rates are subject to fluctuation. Current rates can be obtained from banks, travel agencies and tourist information offices; they can also be found in the principal national newspapers.

Exchange rates

There are no restrictions on the import or export of either Norwegian or foreign currency, but the export of more than 25,000 kr must be declared on a customs form.

Opening times of banks: Mon.–Wed. and Fri. 8.15am–3.30pm, Thur. 8.15am–5pm.

The unit of currency is the Swedish krona, plural kronor (abbreviated kr or SEK), which consists of 100 öre. There are banknotes for 20, 50, 100, 500 and 1000 kronor and coins in denominations of 50 öre and 1 and 5 kronor.

Sweden

See under Norway above

Exchange rates

There are no restrictions on the import or export of either Swedish or foreign currency.

Opening times of banks: Mon.–Fri. 9.30am–3pm, also between 4 and 5.30pm on Thursday. In large towns until 5.30pm. In smaller places the opening hours are frequently shorter, and banks close at 1pm on the day before a public holiday.

The national unit of currency is the markka or Finnmark, for which the abbreviation FIM is commonly used; which consists of 100 penniär (singular penni). There are banknotes for 10, 50, 100, 500 and 1000 mk and coins in denominations of 10 and 50 p and 1 and 5 mk.

Finland

Customs Regulations

See under Norway above

There are no restrictions on the import of either Finnish or foreign currency, but foreigners bringing in more than 10,000 mk must declare it on entry. They cannot take out a larger sum than 10,000 mk unless they can show that they have brought it into the country on arrival.

Opening times of banks: Mon.–Fri. 9.15am–4.15pm.

Customs Regulations

Customs regulations are broadly similar in Norway, Sweden and Finland, which are members of the Nordic Passport and Customs Union. Personal effects and travelling equipment may be taken in without payment of duty. The bringing in of hunting weapons, the import and use of walkie-talkies and the export of works of art are subject to special regulations, information about which can be obtained from the tourist office of the country concerned.

Duty-free allowances

	Alcohol	Tobacco goods	Gifts, etc. max. value
Norway	1 litre wine, 1 litre spirits and 2 litres beer, or 2 litres wine and 2 litres beer (min. age 20)	200 cigarettes or 250gr of other tobacco goods (min. age 16)	1200 kr
Sweden	1 litre spirits, or 3 litres fortified or sparkling wine, 5 litres wine and 15 litres strong beer (min. age 20)	300 cigarettes or 150 cigarillos or 75 cigars or 400gr tobacco (min. age 15)	1000 kr
Finland	Persons aged 20 years: 1 litre strong alcohol; plus if 18 years: 3 litres sparkling wine and 5 litres other wine and 15 litres beer. (All refer to travellers entering from another EU country.)	300 cigarettes or 150 cigarillos or 75 cigars or 400gr tobacco (min. age 17)	1500 mk

Electricity

Generally 220 volts AC (plugs have 2 round-edged prongs – you will need an adaptor).

Embassies and Consulates

Norwegian Embassies

25 Belgrave Square
London SW1X 8QD; tel. (0171) 235 7151

2720 34th Street NW
Washington DC 20008, 2714 USA
tel. (0101) 333 6000

United States

Royal Banks Centre
90 Sparks Street, Suite 532
Ottawa, Ontario K1IP 5B4
Tel. (613) 238 6571

Canada

Swedish Embassies

11 Montagu Place
London W1H 2AL
tel. (0171) 724 2101

United Kingdom

1501 M Street
Washington DC 20005
tel. (202) 467 2600

United States

Mercury Court, 377 Dalhousie Street
Ottawa, Ontario K1N 9N8
tel. (613) 241 8553

Canada

Finnish Embassies

38 Chesham Place
London SW1X 8HW
tel. (0171) 235 9531

United Kingdom

3301 Massachusetts Avenue NW
Washington DC, 20008 USA
tel. (202) 298 5800

United States

55 Metcalfe Street, Suite 850
Ottawa, Ontario
tel. (613) 236 2389

Canada

British Embassies and Consulates

Thomas Heftyesgate 8
0244 Oslo
tel. (02) 22 55 24 00

Norway

Consulates in Ålesund, Bergen, Harstad, Haugesund, Kristiansand, Kristiansund, Stavanger, Trømsø and Trondheim

Skarpögatan 6–8
S–11593 Stockholm
tel. (08) 671 9000

Sweden

Consulates in Göteborg, Luleå, Malmö and Sundsvall

Itäinen Puistotie 17
FIN–00140 Helsinki
tel. (90) 66 12 93

Finland

Consulates in Jyväskylä, Kotka, Kuopio, Mariehamn, Pori, Tampere, Turku and Vaasa

United States Embassies and Consulate

Drammensteien 18
Oslo 2
tel. (02) 22 44 85 50

Norway

Sweden	Strandvägen 101

Sweden   Strandvägen 101
S–11589 Stockholm
tel. (08) 7 83 53 00

Consulate General in Göteborg

Finland   Itäinen Puistotie 14A
FIN–00140 Helsinki
tel. (90) 17 19 31

Canadian Embassies

Norway   Oscarsgate 20
0244 Oslo
tel. (02) 22 46 69 55

Sweden   Tegelbacken 4 (7th floor)
S–10323 Stockholm
tel. (08) 453 3000

Finland   Pohjoisesplanadi 25B
FIN–00100 Helsinki
tel. (90) 17 11 41

Emergencies

Norway   There is no uniform emergency call for police, fire and ambulance throughout Norway, and each town and country area has its own numbers. These
can be found inside the front cover of the local telephone directory, under a
large SOS in red letters. For Oslo the emergency number for police is 002,
for fire and ambulance 003.

Sweden   The emergency number throughout Sweden is 9 00 00 or 112.

Finland   Throughout Finland dial 112 for fire and ambulance, 1 00 22 for police.

Events

January   Norway
Tromsø: Northern Lights Festival

Sweden
Kiruna: Snow Festival
Örebro: Fur Market
Stockholm: International Antiques Fair

Finland
Jyväskylä: Winter Festival
Tampere: Winter Games

February   Norway
Kristiansund: Opera Festival

Sweden
Jokkmokk: Lapp Winter Fair
Stockholm: International Fashion Fair (trade)
Karlstad: Swedish Rally (car rally)
Mora: Tjejvasan Ski Race (Vasa Run for women)
Växjö: Siegfried Fair

The Vasa Run (Vasaloppet) in Sweden

Finland
Country-wide: Shrove Tuesday celebrations, skating races, tobogganing
Ähtäri-Ikaalinen: Sata-Häme Ski Trek (30–40km daily)
Helsinki: Snow Rally
Helsinki: International Boat Show
Jyväskylä: Winter Festival
Lammi-Lahti: Pikku Reppu (Finlandia Ski Race)
Oulu: Musical Festival
Rovaniemi: Kultakelloajot (reindeer-sleigh race)
Savonlinna: International Snow Sculpture Competition
Vuokatti-Lieksa: Ski Race on the UKK trail

Norway   March
Lillehammer: Birkebeiner Cross-Country Ski Race (50km)
Oslo: Holmenkollen Nordic Skiing Festival
Voss: Voss Jazz Festival

Sweden
Ammarnäs: Vindelälvsdraget (dog-sleigh races from Ammarnäs to
    Vännäsby in Lapland)
Falun: Swedish Ski Games
Gällivare: Winter Fair
Göteborg: "Viking" Exhibition
Göteborg: TUR (Swedish International Travel and Tourist Fair)
Mora: Vasaloppet (the Vasa Run, a 90km cross-country ski race from Sälen
    to Mora)
Stamsjön: Åsele Nappet (fishing under the ice)
Stockholm: International Boat Show

Events

Finland
Espoo: International Squash
Hetta: Church Music Days
Inari: Reindeer-Driving Competition
Ilomantsi: Pogosta Ski Race (70 and 50km)
Jyväskylä: International Bridge Competition
Kuopio: Finnish Skating Marathon
Kuopio: Puijo International Winter Games
Kuusamo: Ruka Winter Games
Lahti: Salpausselkä Games
Niinisalo-Tampere: Pirkka Ski Race (90km)
Oulu: Tar Ski Race
Pyhäjärvi: Ice-Fishing Competition
Rovaniemi: Arctic Snow Week
Rovaniemi: Arctic Circle Ski Race
Rovaniemi: Ounasvaara Winter Games
Tampere: Short Film Festival
Turku: Boat Fair
Vantaa: International Fur Auction

April

Norway
Karmøy: International Sea-Fishing

Sweden
Göteborg: Horse Show
Helsingborg: International Stamp and Coin Fair
Mörrum: Beginning of the salmon-fishing season
Country-wide (April 30th): Walpurgis Night celebrations (with student processions in the university towns)

Finland
Espoo: April Jazz
Muonio: Lapponia Cross-Country Ski Race (40, 50, 60 and 80km)
Oulu: Ice-Fishing Marathon
Country-wide (April 30th): Walpurgis Night celebrations

May

Norway
Bergen (until June): Festival (classical music, theatre, folklore)
Bergen: Natt jazz
Bømlo: Mostraspelet (traditional open-air theatre)
Country-wide (May 17th): National Day (parades, fireworks)
Frederikstad: Old Time March
Kristiansand: International Folklore Festival

Sweden
Emmaboda: Carnival
Rättvik: Street Market
Salsta (until September): Music in the Baroque castle
Stockholm (until September): Performances in the Drottningholm Theatre
Stockholm: Tjejtrampet (cycle race, 42km)
Strömsholm: Horse Show
Varberg: Sea-Angling Competition

Finland
Country-wide (May 1st): Spring Festival (with parades)
Helsinki: 10,000 Metre Street Race (for women)
Kajaani: Jazz Spring
Punkaharju (until September): Retretti Arts Centre (applied arts exhibition)
Rautalampi: Pradznik Festival (orthodox church and folk festivals)
Tankavaara-Saariselkä: Night Ski Race (55km)
Valkeakoski, Ritvala: Ritvala Helka Festival (a traditional Easter festival)

All over Scandinavia there are Midsummer celebrations on the second-last Friday and Saturday in June.

Norway
Äl: International Folk Festival
Countrywide bonfires and dancing to celebrate Midsummer D Day (23rd)
Førde: International Folklore Festival
Harstad: North Norway Musical Festival
Kalvøya near Oslo: Rock Festival
Kvindesdal: Emigrants Festival
Loftus (June 15th): Edvard Grieg's Birthday Festival
Oslo: Færder-Seilas (sailing regatta in Oslofjord)
Oslo: Summer Concert (classical concert, with other events)
Røros: Festival of Culture
Røros (until August): Summer Exhibition of Arts and Crafts
Seljord: Seljordspelet (games)

Sweden
Country-wide (June 6th): National Day (Flag Day) also June 21st–23rd
    Midsummer Celebrations
Alingsås: Potato Festival
Askersund: Jazz Festival
Göteborg: Musical Festival
Göteborg: PostGirot Open (cycle race)
Gränna: Gränna-polkan (the Gränna Polka)
Hällefors: Festival of Folk Music
Karlshamn: Golf Week
Kopparberg: Mineral Fair
Laholm: Aurora Days (hot-air balloon festival)
Lidköping: Summer Exhibition in Läckö Castle
Motala: Vättern Runt (cycle race round Lake Vättern)
Motala: Tjej-Vättern (cycle race for women)
Örebro: City Marathon
Östersund: Expo Norr (Food Fair)
Rättvik: Festival on Lake Siljan
Rättvik (until July): Church Boat Races
Sala: Festival in the Silver-Mine
Stockholm: City Marathon
Uppsala: Carnival
Vadstena: St Birgitta Pageant Play

Finland
Åland Islands: Organ Festival
Eckerö: Mail Rowing Races
Enontekiö: Midsummer Ski Race
Hämeenlinna (also in July): Children's Theatre (by children for children)
Hämeenlinna (until August): Music in Sibelius's Home Town
Hämeenlinna: Cycle Races
Praasniekka at various locations in June, July and August; in June at
    Nurmes and Ilomantsi (Prazdnik; Orthodox church festival and folk
    festival)
Helsinki: Sea Jazz
Helsinki: International Light Athletics
Ikaalinen: Sata-Häme Soi (Accordion Festival)
Ilmajoki: Musical Festival
Iisalmi: Finlandia Canoeing Relay Race (6 days, 545km)
Imatra (until July): Big Band Festival
Joensuu: Song Festival
Joensuu: Karelian Folk Festival
Jyväskylä: Summer Festival
Jyväskylä: International Art Festival
Jyväskylä: Finlandia Marathon

Kemijärvi: International Wood Sculpture Week
Kilpisjärvi: Midsummer Skiing Contests
Kokkola: Midnight Jazz
Korsholm (until July): Musical Festival
Kuopio: Festival of Music and Dance
Lahti: Suur-Hollola Ajot (trotting races)
Lappajärvi: International Relay Orienteering Competition
Lappeenranta: South Karelian Folk Festival
Naantali: Musical Festival
Nilsiä: Bach Week
Nurmes: Bomba Festival (Karelian folk songs and dances)
Nurmijärvi (until July): Aleksis Kivi Festival
Orivesi: Klemetti Summer Festival
Oulu: Midnight Golf
Oulu: Tar-Burning Week
Porvoo: Summer Sounds
Savonlinna (until July): Opera Festival
Seinäjoki: Provincial Rock
Sodankylä: Midnight Sun Film Festival
Sodankylä: Lapland Festival
Tampere: Pirkka Cycle Trek (43 and 128km)
Tornio: Jazz Blues
Turku (until August): Craft Weeks
Turku: Ruis Rock
Vaasa: International Puppet Theatre Festival
Valtimo: Praasniekka (Prazdnik; Orthodox church festival and folk festival)
Vammala: Old Literature Days
Ypäjä: Finn Derby (international jumping display)

July

Norway
Bodø (until August): Northern Music Festival
Kongsberg: International Jazz Days
Koppang: Kaukangermart'n (Historical Market)
Molde: International Jazz Festival
Oslo: Bislett (international light athletics festival)
Risør: Nordic Dragon Festival
Rodenda (Hardanger): Baronspelet (Historical Play)
Seljie: Vestkappfestival (culture, sport and fishing)
Stiklestad (until August): Play about St Olav
Trondheim (until August): St Olav Days (concerts and operas in Cathedral)
Vesterålen, Melbu (until August): Summer Music Days
Many places (July 29th): Olsok Eve (St Olav's Day)

Sweden
Arboga: O Ringen (5-day international orienteering competition)
Åsele: Folk Festival
Båstad: Swedish Open (tennis)
Borgholm: Victoria Day
Brunskog: Värmlänningarna Festival
Falun: Festival of Folk Music
Göteborg: Gothia Cup (international youth football tournament)
Gotland: Round Gotland Race (sailing regatta)
Gränna: Andrée Day (anniversary of Andrée's attempt to reach the North Pole by balloon)
Helsingborg: International Antiques Fair
Järvso: Hälsinge-Hambo (folk dancing festival)
Karlstad: Wermland Open Golf Tournament
Kivik: Biggest Country Fair in Scandinavia
Kukkolaforsen: Herring Festival
Lake Siljan: Music Festival
Leksand: Himlaspelet (play in open-air theatre)

Girl dressed for the Midsummer celebrations

Östersund: Storsjö Festival
Pajala: Fair
Sandhamn: Round Gotland Race (sailing regatta)
Trollhättan: Waterfall Days

Finland
Åland Islands: Craftsmen's Days
Åland Islands: International Tennis Tournament
Ekenäs: Nordic Guitar Festival
Hailuoto: Sand Castle Building Championships
Hanko and Naantali: Sleepy-Head Carnival
Hanko: International Regatta
Hanko: International Tennis Tournament
Ilomantsi: Praasniekka (Prazdnik; Orthodox church festival and folk
   festival)
Joroinen: Finnish Triathlon
Kajaani: Language and Melody (recitations)
Kaustinen: Festival of Folk Music
Kilpisjärvi-Tornio (until August): Arctic Canoe Race (535km)
Kuhmo: Chamber Music Festival
Lappeenranta: Karelian International Games
Lahti (until August): International Organ Week
Lahti: Finn Cykling (international cycle trek, 170km)
Lieksa: Brass Band Week
Lieksa: Rafting Competition
Lohtaja: Festival of Church Music
Mikkeli: International Trotting Races
Oulu: Kuusrock (International Rock Festival)
Outokumpu: Stone and Mineral Fair
Pielavesi: Orthodox church festival and folk festival
Pori: Jazz

Events

Ruovesi: Witches Festival (concerts, exhibitions, drama)
Rovaniemi: Ars Arctica (art exhibition)
Seinäjoki: Tango Festival
Sodankylä: Minerals Market
Sotkarno: International Orienteering Competition
Sulkava: Rowing Marathon
Sysmä: Summer Sounds
Tankavaara (until August): Gold-Panning Championships
Tornio: Nordic Harmonica Festival
Turku: Musical Festival
Turku: Airisto International Regatta
Utsjoki-Helsinki: "Finland Runs"
Uusikaupunki (until August): Crusell Week (Woodwind Festival)
Valkeakoski: Workers' Musical Festival
Viitasaari: Music of Today

August

Norway
Elverum: Festivals
Haugesund: Herring Jazz Festival (jazz and seafood)
Måløy: Kaplein Linge Cup (sailing regatta)
Oslo: Festival of Chamber Music
Risør: International Wooden Boat Festival
Vadsø Varanger: Jazz Festival
Vinstra: Peer Gynt Festival

Sweden
Ängelholm: Festival of Light
Göteborg: The Göteborg Party
Jokkmokk: Autumn Market
Malmö: Skåne International Fair
Malmö: Crayfish Festival
Stenungssund: Round Tjörn Race (sailing regatta)
Stockholm: Water Festival
Stockholm: Scandinavian Masters (golf)
Stockholm: Tjejmilen (10km race for women)
Storuman: Nordic Musical Festival
Sunne: Culture Week
Växjö: Karl Oscar Days (village life in the 19th century)
Visby: Medieval Week
Country-wide (August 14th): opening of the crayfish season

Finland
Åland Islands: Åland Cultural Festival
Hämeenlinna: Children's Festival in the Castle
Helsinki: City Marathon
Helsinki: Finnish Amateur Open (golf)
Helsinki: International Trotting Races
Helsinki: Nordic Fashion Show
Helsinki (until September): Festival Weeks
Jyväskylä: Finnish Horse Championships
Jyväskylä: Rally of the Thousand Lakes
Kilpisjärvi: Frontier River Cycling Fitness Run
Kotka: Maritime and Shanty Festival
Sevettijärvi: Praasniekka (Prazdnik; Orthodox church festival and folk festival)
Tampere: Festival of Drama
Tankavaara: Gold-Panning Competition
Turku: Musical Festival

September

Norway
Notodden: Blues Festival
Oslo: Marathon

Sweden
Filipstad: Market (with a tradition going back 330 years)
Göteborg: International Book Fair
Kopparberg: Market
Stockholm: International Fashion Show

Finland
Helsinki: Baltic Herring Market
Kouvola: International Volleyball Tournament
Mutalahti: Praasniekka (Prazdnik; Orthodox church festival and folk
  festival)
Oulu: Nordic Rally (international car rally)
Rautalampi: Hiring Market
Tampere: Finlandia March (10, 20 and 40km)
Tampere: Antiques Fair

Norway   October
Oslo: Ultima (festival of contemporary music)

Sweden
Lidingö: Lidingöloppet (30km race)
Stockholm: Stockholm Open (tennis)
Rättvik: Market
Uppsala: Film Festival

Finland
Helsinki: International Horse Show
Ruokolahti: Autumn Festival and Market
Tampere: Pirkka Jogging (33km run, starting from Valkeakoski)
All over Lapland: Separation of the reindeer

Sweden   November
Vadstena: Christmas Bazaar

Finland
Helsinki: Skiexpo
Inari: Jazz in the Polar Night
Oulu: International Festival of Children's Films
Rovaniemi: All Saints Ice Regatta
Tampere: Jazz Happening

Norway   December
Oslo (December 10th): Presentation of the Nobel Peace Prize

Sweden
Lund: Christmas Bazaar in Kulturen
Stockholm: Christmas Market
Stockholm (December 10th): Presentation of Nobel Prizes
Country-wide (December 13th): St Lucia's Day celebrations

Finland
Helsinki: Christmas Charity Market
Vantaa: International Fur Auction
Country-wide (December 6th): Independence Day celebrations
Country-wide (December 13th): St Lucia's Day celebrations
Turku and Naantali (December 24th): Proclamation of the Christmas peace
  at noon from Town Hall balcony
Country-wide (December 31st): Welcome to the New Year in town squares

"Everyman's Right"

"Everyman's Right" – the right of free access to land even when it is private property – is a characteristically Scandinavian idea. It is a right based on customary law, never written down but generally respected. The right should, of course, be exercised with discretion: before camping on privately owned ground the owner's permission should be sought; tents must not be pitched or caravans parked within 150 metres of a house or other dwelling.

Information

A booklet about "Everyman's Right" can be obtained from:
Naturvårdsverket
Smidesvägen 5
S–17185 Solna
tel. (08) 7 99 10 00, fax (08) 29 23 82

Ferries within Scandinavia

Ferry services play an important part in maintaining communications within Scandinavia. In Norway in particular the car ferries crossing the fjords are essential elements in the road network.

The following list of ferry services gives the places connected by the ferry, the frequency of the service and the name of the shipping line concerned.

Norway

Horten–Moss: daily: Alpha A/S (Moss)
Stavanger–Bergen: daily: Askøy-Bergen Rutelag (Bergen)
Bergen–Kirkenes: daily: OVDS (Narvik) and DNDS (Trondheim)
Bruravik–Brimnes (Hardangerfjord): daily: Hardanger Sunnhordlandske Dampskipsselskap (Bergen)
Kvanndal–Utne–Kinsarvik (Hardangerfjord): daily: Hardanger Sunnhordlandske Dampskipsselskap (Bergen)
Løfallstrand–Fjermundshavn (Hardangerfjord): daily: Hardanger Sunnhordlandske Dampskipsselskap (Bergen)
Steinestø–Knarvik (Osterfjord): daily: Bergen Nordhordland Rutelag
Ytre Oppedal–Lavik (Sognefjord): daily: Fylkesbaatane i Sogn og Fjordane (Bergen)
Vangsnes–Dragsvik (Sognefjord): daily: Fylkesbaatane i Sogn og Fjordane (Bergen)
Vangsnes–Hella (Sognefjord): daily: Fylkesbaatane i Sogn og Fjordane (Bergen)
Balestrand–Hella–Fjærland (Sognefjord): daily: Fylkesbaatane i Sogn og Fjordane (Bergen)
Kaupanger–Revsnes (Sognefjord): daily: Fylkesbaatane i Sogn og Fjordane (Bergen)
Gudvangen–Kaupanger–Årdalstangen (Sognefjord): daily: Fylkesbaatane i Sogn og Fjordane (Bergen)
Lote–Anda (Nordfjord): daily: aatane i sogn og Fjordane (Bergen)
Geiranger–Hellesylt (Geirangerfjord): daily: Møre og Romsdal Fylkesbåt (Molde)
Eidsdal–Linge (Norddalsfjord): daily: Møre og Romsdal Fylkesbåt (Molde)
Folkestad–Volda (Voldafjord): daily: Møre og Romsdal Fylkesbåt (Molde)
Festøy–Solevåg (Vartdalsfjord): daily: Møre og Romsdal Fylkesbåt (Molde)
Aursnes–Magerholm (Storfjord): daily: Møre og Romsdal Fylkesbåt (Molde)
Vestnes–Molde (Moldefjord): daily: Møre og Romsdal Fylkesbåt (Molde)
Bremsnes–Kristiansund–Leirvåg: daily: Møre og Romsdal Fylkesbåt (Molde)

Valset–Brekstad (Trondheimsfjord): daily: Fosen Trafikkselskap (Trondheim)

Forvik–Tjøtta: daily: Helgeland Trafikkselskap (Sandnessjøen)

Bodø–Værøy–Røst–(Lofoten): daily: Ofoten og Vesteraalens Dampskips-selskap (Narvik)

Skutvik–Svolvær (Lofoten): daily: Ofoten og Vesteraalens Dampskips-selskap (Narvik)

Fiskebøl–Melbu (Lofoten-Vesterålen): daily: Nordtrufikk A/S

Kåfjord–Honningsvåg: daily: Finnmark Fylkesrederi og Ruteselskap (Hammerfest)

Sweden to Üland: Sweden
Oskarshamn–Byxelkrok: daily: Ö-Linjen

Sweden to Gotland:
Nynäshamn–Visby: daily: Gotlandslinjen
Oskarshamn–Visby: daily: Gotlandslinjen

Finland to Åland Islands: Finland
Naantali–Mariehamn: daily: Viking Line
Turku–Mariehamn: daily: Silja Line, Viking Line

Food and Drink

Restaurants

In addition to the restaurants in hotels there are many other restaurants in Scandinavian towns, offering a wide range of choice from good home cooking to *haute cuisine*. The Norwegian and Swedish terms (restaurant, restaurang) are familiar enough; the Finnish ravintola is less obvious. The restaurants are often full of character, and the cuisine is almost always of a high standard.

Restaurant prices in Norway, Sweden and Finland are high compared with   Prices
other European countries. A glass of beer may cost at least £4, and a bottle of decent wine may be £25 or even more. *Husets vin* (Finnish *kaarahvivini*), served in carafes, is somewhat cheaper.

Prices tend to be slightly lower in Sweden and lower still in Finland. For visitors on a normal budget, therefore, a gourmet evening out will be a very special occasion indeed.

Prices are more reasonable in snack bars and cafeterias (*gatekjøkken* in Norway, *bar, matbar, kafeteria* or *gatuköken* in Sweden, *ruokobaari* in Finland). The meal may not be a gastronomic experience, but it will at least be filling. The prices of the various dishes offered are usually posted up above the counter or bar.

Drinks

The sale of alcohol is closely regulated in the Scandinavian countries,   Alcohol
though some of the severer restrictions imposed in the past have now been relaxed. Visitors frequenting the larger hotels and restaurants are unlikely to be affected by the regulations. The usual drink is beer of lager type (Norwegian *øl*, Swedish *öl*, Finnish *olut*), usually bottled.

Norway: Opening times
Vinmonopolet: Mon.–Wed. 10am–4pm, Thur. 10am–5pm, Fri. 9am–4pm,   of off-licence
Saturday 9am–1pm (from May 15th to Sept. 1st 8.15am–3pm).   shops

Sweden:
Systembolaget: Mon.–Wed. and Fri. 9.30am–6pm, Thur. 9.30am–7pm; closed Sat. and the day before public holidays.

Finland:
Alko: Mon.–Thur. 10am–5pm, Fri. 10am–6pm; Sept. to May also Sat. 10am–2pm.

Milk

Milk (*melk*) is a very popular drink in Norway, often served at breakfast or dinner without extra charge. Also popular are cream (*fløte*) and sour cream (*rømme*).

Coffee

In Sweden coffee is a kind of national drink, and Swedish coffee is the best in Scandinavia.

Specialities

Like other countries, Norway, Sweden and Finland have a variety of specialities, only a few of which can be mentioned here.

Sweden

In Sweden the meal usually begins with cold hors-d'oeuvre (*smörgås),* either served at the table on a small plate or set out on a side table (*smörgåsbord*). The selection usually includes cold meat, fish, vegetable salads, egg dishes and cheese, and is known, according to the quantity and variety of food offered, as *assiett* or *delikatessassiett.* A special delicacy is smoked salmon or reindeer meat. The largest smörgåsbord is the *gående bord,* a long table with both cold and hot dishes to which guests help themselves.

Visitors to Sweden at the beginning of August should try one of the "crayfish meals" offered at that time of year.

Captain's Buffet on the ferry ship "Peter Pan"

A popular snack, sold at street kiosks, is *korv med mos* (sausage and mash). *Knäckebröd* and *hårtbröd* are types of crispbread, the popularity of which has now spread to many other countries. A meal is often accompanied by a glass of *snaps*.

In Norway the cold buffet (*kolbord*) is also a national tradition, and the large side table set out with a great variety of appetising dishes is a regular feature of breakfast or dinner in a Norwegian restaurant. The special menu listing various kinds of open sandwiches is less commonly found than in Finland. There are only a few kinds of sausage of European type, and most visitors are likely to prefer ham or cold meat. Particularly popular in Norway are goat's-milk cheese (*geitost*) and *mysost*, a sweetish whey-cheese, brownish in colour, sliced thin and eaten on bread. A meal often ends with preserved fruit, served with cream.

Norway has excellent fish dishes (salmon, trout, cod). Norway

One Finnish speciality which every visitor should try is reindeer meat, either roasted or smoked. A particular delicacy is crayfish, which are served between July 20th and September 20th, boiled in salt water with dill seasoning and eaten ice-cold. A speciality of the province of Savo (Kuopio) is *kalakukko* ("fish-chicken"), a pie made of small whitefish and pork baked in a rye dough. The Finnish cold buffet, the equivalent of the Swedish smörgåsbord, is *voileipäpöytä*. Finland

The Nordic Menu

English	Norwegian	Swedish	Finnish
restaurant	restaurant	restaurang	ravintola
snack bar	kafeteria	kafeteria, barservering	ruokabaari, baari
breakfast	frokost	frukost	aamiainen
lunch	middagsmat	lunch, middag	päivällinen
dinner	kveldsmat	kvällsmat	illallinen
eat	spise	ata	syödä
drink	drikke	dricka	juoda
a lot, many	mye, mange	mycket, måga	paljon, moni
a little	lite	lite	vähän
the bill	regningen	notan	lasku
pay	betale	betala	maksaa
at once	med en gang, straks	gemast, bums	heti
menu	menu	matsedel	ruokalista
soup	suppe	soppa	keitto
meat	kjøtt	kött	liha
grilled	grillet, grilleret	grillat	pariloitu
roast	stek	stekt	paisti
beef	oksekjøtt	oxkött	naudanliha
ham	skinke	skinka	kinkku
lamb	lam	lamm	lammas
mutton	gjeldvær	gällgumse	lammas
roast mutton	fåresteik	fårstek	lampaanreisi
pork	svin	svinkött	sika
roast pork	svinestek	grisstek	sianpiasti
reindeer	rein	ren	poro
sausage	pølse	korv	makkara
veal	kalv	kalv	vasikka

Food and Drink

English	Norwegian	Swedish	Finnish
fish	fisk	fisk	kala
fried	stekt	stekt	paistettu
boiled	kokt	kokt	keitetty
fish balls	fiskekaker	fiskbullar	
cod	torsk	torsk	turska
crayfish	kreps	kräfta	rapu
herring	sild	sill	silli
lobster	hummer	hummer	hummeri
salmon	laks	lax	lohi
smoked salmon	røkelaks	rökt lax	savustettu lohi
shrimp	reke	räka	katkarapu
trout	ørret	forell, laxöring	taimen
vegetables	grønnsaker	grönsaker	vihanneksia
bean	bønne	böna	papu
cabbage	käl	kål	kaali
cauliflower	blomkål	blomkål	kukkakaali
cucumber	agurk	gurka	kurkku
green salad	hodesalat	huvudsallat	salaatti
peas	erte	ärta	herne
potatoes	potet	potatis	peruna
red cabbage	rødkål	rödkål	punakaali
spinach	spinat	spenat	pinaatti
tomato	tomat	tomat	tomaatti
ice	is	glass	jäätelö
stewed fruit	kompott	kompott, sylt	hillo, jälkiruoka
custard, flan	pudding	pudding	vanukas
whipped cream	krem	vispgrädde	vispikerma, vaahtokerma
fruit	frukt	frukt	hedelmät
apple	eple	äpple	omena
bilberry	blåbær	blåbär	mustikka
cherry	kirsebær	körsbär	kirsikka
cranberry	tyttebær	lingon	puola
lemon	sitron	citron	sitruuna
orange	appelsin	apelsin	appelsiini
pear	pære	päron	päärynä
plum	plomme	plommon	luumu
raspberry	bringebær	hallon	vadelma
strawberry	jordbær	jordgubbe	mansikka
drinks	drikk	dryck	juoma
beer	øl	öl	olut
coffee	kaffe	kaffe	kahvi
cream	fløte	grädde	kerma
milk	melk	mjölk	maito
mineral water	mineralvann	mineralvatten	kivennäisvesi
tea	te	te	tee
water	vann	vatten	vesi
wine	vin	vin	viini
red wine	rødvin	rödvin	puunaviini
white wine	hvitvin	vitt vin	valkoviini
bread	brød	bröd	leipä
white bread	hvetebrød	vetebrod	ranskanleipä
roll	rundstykke	franskt bröd	sämpylä
cake	kake	kaka	kaaku

Frontier Crossings

There are many roads linking Norway, Sweden and Finland. Only the most important and scenically most attractive are listed here.

The list gives the last town of some size in the first country, the number of the road to the frontier, the name of the frontier crossing point, the number of the road beyond the frontier and the first town of some size in the other country. Where the crossing point has no name the name of the last place before the frontier is given.

Direct connections:
Oslo–Göteborg: E 6 – Svinesund (E 6) – Uddevalla
Oslo–Stockholm: E 18 – Hån (E 18) – Karlstad

Norway–Sweden

Kongsvinger (R 2) – Edabruk (R 61) – Arvika
Trondheim (R 26) – Långflon (R 62) – Karlstad
Røros (R 26/218) – Flötningen (R 70) – Mora
Røros (R 31) – Fjällnäs (R 84) – Sveg
Trondheim (E 14) – Storlien (E 14) – Östersund and Sundsvall
Eidet (R 765) – Valsjöbyn (R 340) – Östersund
Mo i Rana (E 12) – Umbukta (E 12) – Storuman and Umeå
Storfjord (E 6/R 77) – Graddis (R 375) – Arjeplog and Luleå
Narvik (E 6/Bjørnfjellveien) – Riksgränsen (E 10) – Kiruna

Tromsø (E 8) – Galgojavare (E 8) – Kilpisjärvi
Hammerfest and Alta (R 93) – Aiddejavre – Kivilompolo
North Cape (R 93) – Karasjok – Karigasniemi (R 4)
Varanger peninsula (E 6) – Polmak – Nuorgam
Kirkenes and Neiden (E 6/R 893) – Näätämö
Tana (E 75) – Utsjoki (E 75) – Inari

Norway–Finland

Luleå (E 4) – Haparanda (E 4) – Tornio and Kemi
Gällivare (E 10 and R 400) – Övertorneå – Aavasaksa (E 8)
Pajala (R 400) – Pello (E 8) – Rovaniemi
Kiruna (R 45) – Karesuando (E 8) – Kilpisjärvi
Gällivare (R 939) – Kolari – Kittilä

Sweden–Finland

Kotka and Vaalimaa (E 18) – Vyborg and St Petersburg (E 18)
Lappeenranta and Nuijamaa (R 13) – Vyborg
Ivalo and Raja-Jooseppi – Murmansk

Finland–Russia

The frontier crossing to the east of Kirkenes is closed for private cars, but day and weekend excursions for groups or individuals can be arranged through the Kirkenes tourist information office (see Information).

Norway–Russia

During 1992 there were many changes in the numbering of European highways (identified by the letter E plus a number), and numerous other roads in Norway and Sweden were also renumbered. Account has been taken of the changes in this Guide on the basis of the information available.

N.B.

Getting to Scandinavia

The easiest means of access to the Scandinavian countries from Britain and North America is by air. There are flights to Norway, Sweden and Finland from cities throughout the world. From London and some other British airports there are frequent direct flights to Oslo, Stockholm, Helsinki and other towns, flown by British Airways and other British airlines, SAS Scandinavian Airlines and Finnair (see Airlines).

By air

See Car and Passenger Ferries

By sea

Help for the Disabled

By car

Taking a car to Scandinavia gives greater freedom of movement but involves a fairly long (and expensive) crossing on a car ferry from a British port (see Car and Passenger Ferries).

Help for the Disabled

Information

In Britain the main sources of information and advice on travel by the disabled are the Royal Association for Disability and Rehabilitation (RADAR), Unit 12, City Forum, 250 City Road, London EC1V 8AF, tel. (0171) 250 3222; the Spinal Injuries Association, 76 St James's Lane, London N10 3DF, tel. (0181) 444 2121; and Holiday Care Services, 2nd Floor, Imperial Buildings, Victoria Road, Horley, Surrey, RH6 7PZ; tel. (01293) 774535.

Useful
publications

"European Holidays and Travel Abroad – A Guide for Disabled People", published by RADAR (small charge plus postage and packaging).

The AA also publishes a "Guide for the Disabled Traveller" (free to members).

Major sources of information in the United States are Louise Weiss's "Access to the World: A Travel Guide for the Handicapped" (available from Facts on File, 460 Park Avenue South, New York NY 10016) and the Society for the Advancement of Travel by the Handicapped, 26 Court Street, Penthouse Suite, Brooklyn NY 11242.

Facilities in
Scandinavia

Scandinavia is well equipped with facilities for disabled visitors. Many hotels have specially adapted rooms; all public institutions have lavatories for disabled people; the pavements at street corners often have lower kerbs for the convenience of wheel-chair users, and there are lifts for wheel-chairs; traffic lights have audible signals; and camping sites have sanitary installations adapted for use by the disabled.

Information about facilities for disabled people:

Norway

Norges Handikapforbund
(Norwegian Association for the Disabled)
Postboks 9217 Vaterland
N–01234 Oslo 1; tel. 22 17 02 55

Sweden

A new "Holiday Guide for the Disabled", listing suitable accommodation, sightseeing and activities throughout Sweden, is available from the Swedish Tourism and Travel Council. For general information contact: De Handikappades Riksforbund, Katrinebergstägen 6, S–117 43 Stockholm, Sweden (tel. 818 910).

The annual guide "Hotels in Sweden", also available from the Swedish Tourism and Travel Council, indicates hotels with rooms adapted for disabled visitors.

Finland

Invalidilitto ry
(Association for the Disabled)
Kumpulantie 1A
FIN–00520 Helsinki; tel. (90) 71 84 66 and 1 85 51

Holidays can be booked through the following agencies:

Rullaten ry
Pekka Jarvansalo
Vartiokyläntie 9
FIN–00950 Helsinki; tel. (90) 32 20 69

Area Travel Agency
Pohjoisesplanadi 2
FIN–00130 Helsinki
tel. (90) 1 85 51, fax (90) 1 85 52 45

Holiday Houses

See Youth Hostels, Holiday Houses and Cabins

Hotels

The hotels in the Nordic countries, which are noted for their cleanliness, are fully up to international standards of comfort and service in the different price categories. The large towns have luxury establishments, but many smaller places have hotels of a very high standard. Even in the far north there are good hotels and comfortable inns. Many hotels have "family rooms" with three to five beds which provide accommodation at very reasonable rates. Some mountain hotels are open only during the summer or winter season, and there are also special summer hotels.

Many hotels have special facilities for the disabled (a ramp for wheelchairs at the entrance, etc.) and guests suffering from allergies.

Norway

There are luxury hotels in Oslo and other large towns. A *turisthotell* or *høyfjellshotell* offers comfortable accommodation in isolated areas in the mountain regions. A *pensjonat* is a smaller hotel with a good standard of comfort; a *gjestgiveri* is an inn.

Sweden

There are excellent hotels – often called Stadshotell or Stora Hotell – even in the smaller towns. There may be a Järnvägshotell near the station. A *gästgivaregård* is a country inn. The *turiststationer* run by the Swedish Tourism and Travel Council are usually excellent.

Finland

There are luxury hotels in Helsinki and other large towns. The Finnish Tourist Board also runs comfortable and well equipped tourist hotels in the main tourist areas. In the remoter parts of the country there are roadside inns (*matkustajakoti*) – more modest establishments, but invariably clean. A *majatalo* is a country inn.

Details of value-for-money guest houses can be obtained from:
Finlandia Hotels
Teollisuuskatu 27
FIN–00511 Helsinki
tel. (90) 7 01 65 00, fax (90) 7 01 65 10

Tariffs

Hotel tariffs in Norway, Sweden and Finland are fairly high, but many first-class hotels offer reduced rates during the summer season or at weekends throughout the year. In Finnish hotels in particular it is always worth enquiring about reductions. Many national and international hotel chains offer reduced rates in the form of a hotel pass or hotel cheque system, usually covering accommodation and breakfast. In Finland there is the Finncheque, valid in hotels belonging to several Finnish chains; in Norway the Fjord Pass; in Sweden the Sweden Hotels Pass and the CountrySide Sweden hotel cheque. Some concessions of this kind apply to both Norway and Sweden and usually also Finland: e.g. the Scandinavian Bonus Pass, the Best Western hotel cheque, the Pro-Scandinavia cheque and the Scandic Hotel cheque. Hotel cheques must be bought in advance, either before leaving home or in one of the Scandinavian countries.

There are additional reductions for children (for example a child's bed may be provided free of charge in its parents' room).

In the following list of hotels – which is merely a selection – b. = beds and r. = rooms.

Hotels

Göta Hotel, on the Göta Canal

Abisko
(Sweden)

Gästgården, tel. (0980) 4 01 00, 102 b.; STF Abisko, tel. 4 00 00, 338 b.

Åland Islands
(Finland)

In Mariehamn: Adlon, Hamngatan 7, tel. (928) 1 53 00, 124 b.; Arkipelag, Strandgatan 31, tel. 2 40 20, 215 b.; Park Alandia, Norra Esplanadgatan 3, tel. 1 41 30, 180 b.; Pommern, Norragatan 8–10, tel. 1 55 55, 140 b.; Savoy, Nygatan 12, tel. 1 54 00, 85 b.

Ålesund
(Norway)

Atlantica/Havly, Rasmus Rønnebergsgate 4, tel. 70 12 91 00, 90 b.; Baronen, Vikasenteret, tel. 70 14 70 00, 62 b.; InterNor Hotel Scandinavie, Løvenvoldgate 8, tel. 70 12 31 31, 120 b.; Rica Parken, Storgate 16, tel. 70 12 50 50, 276 b.; Rica Skansen, Kongensgate 27, tel. 70 12 29 38, 179 b.

Alingsås
(Sweden)

Parkaden (no rest.), Magasinsgatan 3, tel. (0322) 1 70 20, 38 b.; Scandic Hotel Alingsås, Bankgatan 1, tel. 1 40 00, 135 b.

Alta
(Norway)

★SAS Alta, Løkkeveien, tel. 78 43 50 00, 184 b.; Alta Fjordhotell, Strandveien, tel. 78 43 70 11, 147 b.; Alta Gjestestue, Bekkefaret 3, tel. 78 43 55 66, 49 h.; Alta Motell, Bossekop, tel. 78 43 47 11, 44 b.

Ängelholm
(Sweden)

Dahlman (no rest.), Östergatan 27–29, tel. (0431) 1 10 02, 16 b.; Paletten, Östergatan 57, tel. 8 22 80, 68 b.

Balestrand
(Norway)

See Sognefjord

Bergen
(Norway)

★Reso Hotel Norge, Ole Bullsplass 4, tel. 55 21 01 00, 680 b.; SAS Royal Hotel Bryggen, tel. 55 54 30 00, 500 b.; Grand Hotel Terminus, Zander Kaaesgade 6, tel. 55 31 16 55, 220 b.; Hordaheimen, C. Sundtsgate 18, tel. 55 23 23 20, 117 b.; InterNor Hotel Neptun, Valkendorfsgate 8, tel. 55 90 10 00, 198 b.; Rosenkrantz, Rosenkrantzgate 7, tel. 55 31 50 00, 205 b.; Strand, Strandkaien 2B, tel. 55 31 08 15, 80 b.
In Kokstad: Bergen Airport Hotel, Kokstadveien 3, tel. 55 22 92 00, 500 b.; Scandic Hotel Bergen, Kokstadsflaten 2, tel. 56 22 71 50, 406 b.

Summer hotel: Fantoft (May 20th–August 20th), Fantoftveien 14, tel. 55 27 60 10, 300 b.

★Radisson SAS Hotel Bode, Storgate 2, tel. 75 52 41 00, 384 b.; Central, Prof. Schyttesgate 7, tel. 75 52 40 00, 76 b.; Grand, Storgate 3, tel. 75 52 00 00, 90 b.; Skagen Hotel, Nyholmsgate 11, tel. 75 52 24 00, 80 b.

Bode
(Norway)

★Plaza, Allégatan 3, tel. (033) 11 01 00, 268 b.; Borås, Sandgärdsgatan 25, tel. 11 70 20, 117 b.; Gustav Adolf, Andra Villagatan 5, tel. 10 81 80, 78 b.; Mark (no rest.), Yxhammargatan 1, tel. 10 81 90, 92 b.; SARA Hotel Grand, Hallbergsgatan 14, tel. 10 82 00, 134 b.; Scandic Hotel Borås, Hultasjögatan 7, tel. 15 70 00, 200 b.
In Borås-Brämhult: Nya Motel Lage, Kornellgatan 2, tel. 4 87 20, 70 b.

Borås
(Sweden)

See Öland

Borgholm
(Sweden)

City Hotell i Eskilstuna (no rest.), 100m from station, Drottninggatan 15, tel. (016) 13 74 25, 100 b.; Country, Strängnäsvägen, tel. 11 04 10, 118 b.; SARA Hotel Eskilstuna, Hamngatan 9–11, tel. 13 72 25, 485 b.; Smeden, Drottninggatan 9, tel. 13 76 90, 142 b.; Sundbyholms Slott & Konferenshotell, tel. 9 65 00, 190 b.

Eskilstuna
(Sweden)

Dipoli, Otaranta, tel. (90) 43 58 11, 456 b.; Espoo, Nihtisillantie 1, tel. 53 35 33, 320 b.; Hanasaari, Hanasaari, tel. 45 15 66, 120 b.; Korpilampi, tel. 8 67 21, 330 b.; Kuninkaantie Espoo, Lakelankatu 1, tel. 85 91 91, 182 b.; Tapiola Garden, Tapiontori, tel. 46 17 11, 164 b.

Espoo
(Finland)

Grand, Ågatan 1, tel. (0346) 1 44 50, 102 b.; Värdshuset Hvitan, Storgatan 24, tel. 8 20 90, 65 b.; Vita Hästen, Elvägen, tel. 8 00 20, 115 b.

Falkenberg
(Sweden)

Bergmästaren, Bergskolegränd 7, tel. (023) 6 36 00, 160 b.; Birgittagården (no rest.), Uddnäs Josjö, tel. 3 21 47, 47 b.; SARA Hotel Grand, Trotzgatan 9–11, tel. 1 87 00, 322 b.; Scandic Hotel Falun, Kopparvägen/Norslund, tel. 2 21 60, 215 b.

Falun
(Sweden)

See Öland

Färjestaden
(Sweden)

Hennickehammars Herrgård, tel. (0590) 1 25 65, 93 b.; Kalhyttans Herrgård, Kalhyttevägen 8, tel. 1 41 00, 44 b.; Scandic Hotel Filipstad, John Ericssonsgatan 8, tel. 1 25 30, 105 b.

Filipstad
(Sweden)

City, Nygårdsgate 44–46, tel. 69 31 77 50, 216 b.; Victoria, Turngate 3, tel. 69 31 11 65, 100 b.

Fredrikstad
(Norway)

Nex (no rest.), Lasarettsgatan 1, tel. (0970) 11 02 0, 220 b.; Polar, Per Hogströmsgatan 9, tel. 1 11 90, 90 b.

Gällivare
(Sweden)

Aveny, Södra Kungsgatan 31, tel. (026) 61 55 90, 60 b.; Gävle, Staketgatan 44, tel. 11 54 70, 93 b.; RESO Grand Central, Nygatan 45, tel. 12 90 60, 317 b.; SARA Hotel i Gävle, Norra Slottsgatan 9, tel. 17 70 00, 403 b.; Scandic Hotel Gävle, Johanneslötsvägen 6, tel. 18 80 60, 392 b.

Gävle
(Sweden)

In Geiranger: Geiranger, tel. 70 26 30 05, 125 b.; Grande Fjord Hotell, tel. 70 26 30 90, 57 b.; Union Hotel, tel. 70 26 30 00, 285 b.; Hotel Utsikten Bellevue, tel. 70 26 30 03, 57 b.

Geirangerfjord
(Norway)

★ RESO Hotel Rubinen, Kungsportsavenyn 24, tel. (031) 81 08 00, 270 b.; ★ SARA Hotel Europa, Köpmansgatan 38, tel. 80 12 80, 1000 b.; ★ SARA Hotel Gothia, Mässansgata 24, tel. 40 93 00, 600 b.; ★ SARA Hotel Scandinavia, Kustgatan 10, tel. 42 70 00, 600 b.; ★ SAS Park Avenue Hotel, Kungsportsavenyn 36–38, tel. 17 65 20, 530 b.; ★ Scandic Crown Hotel,

Göteborg
(Sweden)

Hotels

Polhemsplatsen 3, tel. 80 09 00, 320 b.; ★ Sheraton Göteborg Hotel and Towers, Södra Hamngatan 59–65, tel. 80 60 00, 680 b.; Eggers, Drottningtorget, tel. 80 60 70, 150 b.; Ekoxen Göteborg (no rest.), Norra Hamngatan 38, tel. 80 50 80, 118 b.; Excelsior (no rest.), Karl Gustavsgatan 7, tel. 17 54 30, 120 b.; Kung Karl (no rest.), Nils Ericsonsgatan 23, tel. 80 58 35, 130 b.; Liseberg Heden, Sten Sturegatan, tel. 20 02 80, 159 b.; Lorensberg (no rest.), Berzeliigatan 15, tel. 81 06 00, 200 b.; Novotel Göteborg, 4km/2½ miles from station and 30km/19 miles from airport, tel. 14 90 00, 450 b.; Onyxen (no rest.), Sten Sturegatan 23, tel. 16 01 36, 82 b.; Örgryte, Danska Vägen 68–70, tel. 2 75 65, 140 b.; Panorama, Eklandagatan 51–53, tel. 81 08 80, 340 b.; Ramada, Gamla Tingstadsgatan 1, tel. 22 24 20, 242 b.; RESO Hotel Opalen, Engelbrektsgatan 73, tel. 81 03 00, 459 b.; Ritz (no rest.), Burggrevegatan 25, tel. 80 00 80, 140 b.; Riverton, Stora Badhusgatan 26, tel. 10 12 00, 347 b.; Royal (no rest.), Drottninggatan 67, tel. 80 61 00, 120 b.; Vasa (no rest.), Victoriagatan 6, tel. 17 36 30, 75 b.; Windsor, Kungsportsavenyn 6, tel. 17 65 40, 91 b.

Gotland
(Sweden)

In Visby: ★ Snäck, 1km/¾ mile from airport, tel. (0498) 6 00 00, 426 b.; Donnersplats (no rest.), Donnersplats 6, tel. 1 49 45, 52 b.; Solhem/ Palissard, Solhemsgatan 3, tel. 7 90 70, 215 b.; St Clemens, Smedjegatan 3, tel. 7 95 75, 80 b.; Strand, Strandgatan 34, tel. 1 26 00, 200 b.; Värdshuset Lindgården, Strandgatan 26, tel. 1 87 00, 16 b.; Villa Borgen, Adelsgatan 11, tel. 7 11 70, 36 b.

Gudbrandsdal
(Norway)

In Otta: Grand Gjestegård, tel. 61 23 12 00; Otta, tel. 61 23 00 33, 170 b.; Rapham Høyfjellshotell, tel. 61 23 02 66, 112 b.; Rondane Høyfjellshotell, Kro og Hyttegrend, tel. 61 23 39 33, 140 b.

Halmstad
(Sweden)

★ Grand Hotell, Stationsgatan 44, tel. (035) 11 91 40, 187 b.; Amadeus, Hvitfeldtsgatan 20, tel. 10 97 70, 100 b.; Continental, Kungsgatan 5, tel. 11 85 75, 65 b.; Mårtenson, Storgatan 52, tel. 11 80 70, 163 b.; Norre Park, Norra Vägen 7, tel. 11 85 55, 93 b.; Scandic Hotel Hallandia, Rådhusgatan 4, tel. 11 88 00, 254 b.; Scandic Hotel Halmstad, Strandvallen 3, tel. 10 43 00, 250 b.
In Symlångsdalen: Tallhöjdens Värdshus, tel. 7 02 45, 66 b.
In Tylösand: ★ RESO Nya Hotel Tylösand, tel. 3 05 00, 400 b.

Hämeenlinna
(Finland)

Cumulus, Raatihuoneenkatu 16–18, tel. (917) 5 28 81, 191 b., Vaakuna, Possentie 7, tel. 58 31, 281 b.
Outside town: ★ Rantasipi Aulanko, tel. 5 88 01, 500 b.

Hamina
(Finland)

Seurahuone, Pikkuympyränkatu 5, tel. (952) 4 48 20, 30 b.

Hammerfest
(Norway)

Hammerfest, Strandgate 2–4, tel. 78 41 16 22, 89 b.; Turistsenter, Storsvingen, tel. 78 41 11 26, 230 b.; Rica, Sørøygate 15, tel. 78 41 13 33, 160 b.; Hammerfest Bed & breakfast, Skytterveien 24, tel. 78 41 15 11, 140 b.

Hanko
(Finland)

Hangon Motelli, Lähteentie, tel. (911) 8 28 81, 40 b.

Härnösand
(Sweden)

Royal (no rest.), Strandgatan 12, tel. (0611) 2 04 55, 50 b.; Scandic Vägkrog (with Motel), Ådalsvägen, tel. 1 95 60, 49 b.

Harstad
(Norway)

See Vesterålen

Helsingborg
(Sweden)

★ Grand Hotel, Stortorget 8–12, tel. (042) 12 01 70, 210 b.; Anglais (no rest.), Gustav Adolfs Gata 14–16, tel. 12 61 20, 90 b.; Högvakten, Stortorget 14, tel. 12 03 90, 81 b.; Kärnan i Helsingborg, Järnvägsgatan 17, tel. 12 08 20, 98 b.; Mollberg, Stortorget 18, tel. 12 02 70, 190 b.; RESO Hotel Horisont, Gustav Adolfs Gata 47, tel. 14 92 60, 350 b.; Scandic Hotel Helsingborg, Florettgatan 41, tel. 15 15 60, 530 b.; Stadsmotellet i Helsingborg, Hantverkaregatan, tel. 12 79 55, 70 b.; Stena Hotel Nouveau, Konsul Perssons Plats, tel. 18 53 90, 175 b.; Viking, Fågelsångsgatan 1, tel. 14 44 20, 60 b.

★ Grand Marina (Art Nouveau building), Katajanokanlaituri 7, tel. (90) 1 66 61, 1000 b. (restaurants); ★ Hesperia, Mannerheimintie 50, tel. 4 31 01, 596 b.; ★ Inter-Continental Helsinki, Mannerheimintie 46–48, tel. 4 05 51, 1100 b.; ★ Kalastajatorppa, Kalastajatorpanti 1 (2.8km/1¾ miles from city centre, on lake, with own beach), tel. 4 58 11, 467 b.; ★ Marski, Mannerheimintie 10, tel. 6 80 61, 290 b.; ★ Palace, Eteläranta 10, tel. 13 45 61, 96 b.; ★ Ramada Presidentti, Eteläinen Rautatiekatu 4, tel. 69 11, 1000 b.; ★ SAS Royal, Runeberginkatu 2, tel. 60 30 00, 260 r.; ★ Strand Inter-Continental, John Stenberginranta 4, tel. 3 93 51, 358 b.; Anna, Annankatu 1, tel. 64 80 11, 100 b.; Aurora, Helsinginkatu 50, tel. 71 74 00, 140 b.; Haaga, Nuijamiestentie 10, tel. 57 83 11, 250 b.; Helka (open Jan. 2nd–December 22nd), Pohjoinen Rautatiekatu 23, tel. 44 05 81, 255 b.; Helsinki, Hallituskatu 12, tel. 17 14 01, 230 b.; Hospice, Vuorikatu 17B, tel. 17 04 81, 341 b.; Marttahotelli, Uudenmaankatu 24, tel. 64 62 11, 70 b.; Merihotelli, John Stenberginranta 6, tel. 70 87 11, 154 b.; Metrocity, Kaisaniemenkatu 7, tel. 17 11 46, 200 b.; Olympia, Läntinen Brahenkatu 2, tel. 75 08 01, 185 b.; Park Hotel Käpylä, Pohjolankatu 38, tel. 79 97 55, 80 b.; Pasila, Maistraatinportti 3, tel. 14 22 11, 506 b.; Seurahuone Socis, Kaivokatu 12 (at station), tel. 17 04 41, 224 b.; Torni, Yrjönkatu 26, tel. 13 11 31, 275 b.; Ursula, Paasivuorenkatu 1, tel. 75 03 11, 70 b.; Vaakuna, Asema-aukio 2 (at station), tel. 13 11 81, 510 b.
Summer hotels: Academia (June 1st–Sept. 1st), Hietaniemenkatu 14, tel. 13 11 42 65 and 4 02 02 06, 404 b.; Satakuntatalo (May 20th–Sept. 7th), Lapinrinne 1A, tel. 6 94 03 11, 120 b.

Espoo and Vantaa: see entries

Helsinki
(Finland)

Grand Hotel, Stabellsgate 8, tel. 32 12 27 22, 70 b.; Klækken, tel. 32 13 22 00, 200 b.; Inter Nor Hotel Ringerike, Kongensgate 3, tel. 32 12 72 00, 158 b. In Sokna: Bergland Hotell, tel. 32 14 51 44, 94 b.

Hønefoss
(Norway)

Hammering, on E 4 in Hudiksvall Norr, tel. (0650) 2 44 20, 180 b.; Hudik, N. Kyrkogatan 11, tel. 1 50 40, 100 b.; Stadshotellet, Storgatan 36, tel. 1 50 60, 276 b.

Hudiksvall
(Sweden)

Atrium, Siltakatu 4, tel. (973) 1 26 91 11, 88 b.; Karelia, Kauppakatu 25, tel. 2 43 91, 62 b.; Kimmel, Itäranta 1, tel. 17 71, 500 b.; Joensuun Vaakuna, Torikatu 20, tel. 2 73 11, 160 b.; Viehka, Kauppakatu 32, tel. 2 95 31, 67 b.

Joensuu
(Finland)

Grand Hotel, Hovrättstorget, tel. (036) 11 96 00, 80 b.; Klosterkungen, Klostergatan 28, tel. 10 08 00, 155 b.; RESO Hotel Portalen, Västra Storgatan 9, tel. 11 82 00, 303 b.; Scandic Hotel Jönköping, Rosenlund, tel. 11 91 60, 368 b.; Stora, Hotellplan, tel. 11 93 00, 185 b.
In Huskvarna: Ramada, Strandvägen 1, tel. 14 24 00, 224 b.

Jönköping
(Sweden)

Alexandra, Hannikaisenkatu 35, tel. (941) 65 12 11, 266 b.; Arenaa, Asema-katu 2, tel. 61 17 00, 180 b.; Cumulus, Väinönkatu 3, tel. 65 32 11, 369 b.; Jyväshovi, Kauppakatu 35, tel. 63 02 11, 215 b.; Milton, Asema-aukio, tel. 21 34 11, 72 b.

Jyväskylä
(Finland)

Summer hotels: Amis (June 1st–Aug. 10th), Sepänkatu 3, tel. 61 29 20, 200 b.; Rantasipi Laajavuori, Laajavuori recreation area, tel. 62 82 11, 500 b.

Kajanus, Koskikatu 3, tel. (986) 16 41, 450 b.; Seurahuone, Kauppakatu 11, tel. 2 30 76, 135 b.; Valjus, Kauppakatu 20, tel. 15 02 00, 160 b.; Vanha Välskäri (reception in Valjus Hotel), tel. 15 02 00, 55 b.

Kajaani
(Finland)

Continental (no rest.), Larmgatan 10, tel. (0480) 1 51 40, 64 b.; Kalmar Stadshotellet, Storgatan 14, tel. 1 51 80, 240 b.; Kalmarsund, Fiskaregatan 5, tel. 1 81 00, 168 b.; Packhuset (no rest.), Skeppsbrogatan 26, tel. 5 70 00,

Kalmar
(Sweden)

Hotels

100 b.; Ritz (no rest.), Larmgatan 6, tel. 1 55 40, 56 b.; Romantik Hotel Slottshotellet (no rest.), Slottsvägen 7, tel. 8 82 60, 60 b.; Scandic Hotel Kalmar, Dragonvägen 7, tel. 2 23 60, 321 b.; Witt, Södra Långgatan 42, tel. 1 52 50, 177 b.

Karasjok
(Norway)

Annes Overnatting og Motel, tel. 78 46 64 32, 11 b.; SAS Karasjok Turisthotell, tel. 78 46 74 00, 112 b.

Karlskrona
(Sweden)

Ja Hotels, Borgmästaregatan 13, tel. (0455) 2 70 00, 120 b.; Siesta (no rest.), Borgmästaregatan 5, tel. 8 01 80, 29 b.; Statt Hotel, Ronnebygatan 37–39, tel. 1 92 50, 149 b.

Karlstad
(Sweden)

Drott, Järnvägsgatan 1, tel. (054) 11 56 35, 120 b.; Grand Hotel, Västra Torggatan 8, tel. 11 52 40, 111 b.; Gösta Berling, Drottninggatan 1, tel. 15 01 90, 100 b.; Plaza, Torggatan 2, tel. 10 02 00, 180 b.; RESO Hotel Gustaf Fröding, Höjdgatan 3, tel. 83 10 00, 315 b.; Ritz (no rest.), Västra Torggatan 20, tel. 11 51 40, 87 b.; SARA Hotel Winn, Norra Strandgatan 9–11, tel. 10 22 20, 358 b.; Scandic Hotel Karlstad, Sandbäcksgatan 6, tel. 18 71 20, 345 b.; Stadshotellet, Kungsgatan 22, tel. 11 52 20, 215 b.; Wåxnäs, Ventilgatan 1, tel. 16 00 80, 81 b.

Kemi
(Finland)

Cumulus, Hahtisaarenkatu 3, tel. (9698) 2 28 31, 220 b.; Kemi, Meripuistokatu 9, tel. 2 39 51, 38 b.; Merihovi, Keskuspuistokatu 6–8, tel. 2 34 31, 157 b.; Palomestari, Valtakatu 12, tel. 1 71 17, 94 b.; Yöppu (guest house), Eteläntie 4, tel. 3 20 34, 49 b.

Kirkenes
(Norway)

Rica Arctic Hotel Kirkenes, Kongensgate 1–3, tel. 78 99 29 29, 160 b.; Rica Hotel Kirkenes, Pasvikveien 63, tel. 78 99 14 91, 88 b.

Kiruna
(Sweden)

Kebne, Konduktörsgatan 7, tel. (0980) 1 23 80, 120 b.; RESO Hotel Ferrum, Lars Janssonsgatan 15, tel. 1 86 00, 315 b.; Vinterpalatset, Järnvägsgatan 18, tel. 8 31 70, 35 b.

Kokkola
(Finland)

Chydenius, Rautatienkatu 6, tel. (968) 31 40 44, 90 b.; Kantarellis, Kauppatori 4, tel. 2 50 00, 280 b.; Seurahuone, Torikatu 24, tel. 1 28 11, 130 b.; Vaakuna, Rantakatu 16, tel. 2 87 11, 412 b.

Kongsberg
(Norway)

Gyldenløve, Herm. Fossgate 1, tel. 32 73 17 44, 84 b.; InterNor Grand Hotel Kongsberg, Christian Augustsgate 2, tel. 32 73 20 29, 178 b.

Kristiansand
(Norway)

Bondeheimen, Kirkegate 15, tel. 38 02 44 40, 64 b.; Christian Quart, Markensgate 39, tel. 38 02 22 10, 250 b.; Ernst Park, Rådhusgate 2, tel. 38 02 14 00, 250 b.; Norge, Dronningensgate 5, tel. 38 02 00 00, 250 b.; RESO Hotel Caledonien, V. Strandgate 7, tel. 38 02 91 00, 400 b.; Rica Fregatten, Dronningensgate 66–68, tel. 38 02 15 00, 69 b.; Savoy, Kristian IVs Gate 1, tel. 38 02 75 00, 50 b.

Kristianstad
(Sweden)

Christian IV (no rest.), Västra Boulevarden 15, tel. (044) 12 63 00, 145 b.; Grand Hotel, Västra Storgatan 15, tel. 10 36 00, 225 b.; Turisten (no rest.), Västra Storgatan, tel. 12 61 50, 65 b.

Kuopio
(Finland)

Atlas, Haapaniemenkatu 22, tel. (971) 15 26 11, 88 b.; Captain's Inn, Snellmaninkatu 23, tel. 11 31 12, 56 b.; Cumulus, Puijonkatu 32, tel. 15 41 11, 228 b.; Iso-Valkeinen, Päiväranta, tel. 34 14 44, 325 b.; Martina, Tulliportinkatu 23, tel. 12 35 22, 69 b.; Sokos Hotel Puijonsarvi, Minna Canthinkatu 16, tel. 17 01 11, 459 b.; Rauhalahti, Katiskaniementie 8, tel. 31 17 00, 300 b.; Rivoli Kuopio, Satamakatu 1, tel. 19 51 11, 250 b.; Savonia, Sammakkolammentie 2, tel. 22 53 33, 190 b.

Kuusamo
(Finland)

Iivaaran Lomakeskus, 682 Hiltunen, tel. (989) 8 21 91, 90 b.; Kuusamo, Kirkkotie 23A, tel. 20 20, 227 b.; Kuusamon Tropiikki, Kylpylätie, tel. 20 60, 190 b.
On Rukatunturi: Rantasipi Rukahovi, tel. 20 10, 440 b.

Ascot, Rauhankatu 14, tel. (918) 8 97 11, 420 b.; Grand, Vapaudenkatu 23, tel. 52 51 46, 153 b.; Lahti, Hämeenkatu 4, tel. 8 97 21, 178 b.; Musta Kissa, Rautatienkatu 21, tel. 5 77 22, 128 b.; Scandic Hotel Lahti, Vesijärvenkatu 1, tel. 81 34 11, 308 b.; Seurahuone, Aleksanterinkatu 14, tel. 5 77 11, 210 b. Out of town: Mukkulan Kartanohotelli, tel. 30 65 54, 30 b.; Mukkula Summer Hotel (May 2nd–August 31st), Ritaniemenkatu 10, tel. 6 86 11, 86 r.; Tallukka, Tallukantie 1, Vääksy, tel. 6 86 11, 300 b.

Lahti
(Finland)

Kronan (no rest.), Lilla Strandgatan 11, tel. (0418) 1 62 25, 26 b.; Öresund, Kungsgatan 17, tel. 2 90 00, 250 b. In Glumslöv: Örenäs Slott, tel. 7 02 50, 236 b.

Landskrona
(Sweden)

Carelia Congress Hotel, Marssitie 3, tel. (953) 5 22 10, 100 b.; Cumulus, Valtakatu 31, tel. 57 81, 170 b.; Grand Hotel Patria, Kauppakatu 21, tel. 57 51, 300 b.; Lappee, Brahenkatu 1, tel. 58 61, 413 b.; Lappeenranta Spa, Ainonkatu 17, tel. 1 74 00, 63 b.; Matkahovi, Kauppakatu 52, tel. 1 84 35, 37 b. Summer hotel: Karelia Park (June 1st–Aug. 31st), Korpraalinkuja 1, tel. 1 04 05, in summer 55 21), 200 b.

Lappeenranta
(Finland)

Helgeroa, Krabbegate, tel. 33 18 93 00, 60 b.; InterNor Grand Hotel, Storgate 38–40, tel. 33 18 78 00, 190 b.

Larvik
(Norway)

Birkebeineren Hotel, Olympiaparken, tel. 61 26 47 00, 414 b.; Bjørns Kro og Motell, Vignes, tel. 61 25 83 00, 120 b.; Dølaheimen Breiseth Hotell, Jernbanegate 3, tel. 61 26 95 00, 205 b.; Hammer Home Hotel, Storgate 108, tel. 61 26 35 00, 144 b.; Inter Nor Lillehammer, Turisthotelveien 278, tel. 61 26 60 00, 500 b.; Langseth, Bakkøkka, tel. 61 25 78 88, 92 b.; Oppoland Hotel Lillehammer, Hamarveien 2, tel. 61 25 85 00, 140 b.; Rica Victoria, Storgate 84B, tel. 61 25 00 49, 195 b.

Lillehammer
(Norway)

In Nordsæter (14km/8½ miles NE): Nordsæter Fjellstue og Hytter, tel. 61 26 40 08, 350 b.

In Sjusjøen (22km/14 miles E): Rustad Hotell og Fjellstue, tel. 62 36 34 08, 89 b.; Sjusjøen Fjellstue, tel. 62 36 34 13, 105 b.; Sjusjøen Høyfjellshotell, tel. 62 36 34 01, 160 b.; Panorama Hotel, tel. 62 36 34 51, 110 b.

★Ekoxen, Klostergatan 68, tel. (013) 14 60 70, 317 b.; Baltic, Hantverkaregatan 1, tel. 12 90 00, 107 b.; Park Hotell (no rest.), Järnvägsgatan 6, tel. 12 90 05, 48 b.; RESO Frimurarehotellet, St. Larsgatan 14, tel. 12 91 80, 349 b.; Scandic Hotel Linköping, Rydvägen, tel. 17 10 60, 297 b.; Stora Hotellet, Stora Torget 9, tel. 12 96 30, 150 b.

Linköping
(Sweden)

In Svolvær: Havly Sjøgate, tel. 76 07 03 44, 86 b.; Knutmarka Feriesenter, Leirskoleveien 16, tel. 78 07 21 64, 92 b.; Royal, Siv Nilsensgate 21, tel. 76 07 12 00, 96 b.; Svolvær, Austnesfjordgate 12, tel. 76 07 19 99, 34 b.; Vestfjord, Havna, tel. 76 07 08 70, 130 b.

Lofoten
(Norway)

See Spitzbergen

Longyearbyen
(Norway)

Arctic, Sandviksgatan 80, tel. (0920) 1 09 80, 156 b.; Luleå Stads Hotell, Storgatan 15, tel. 1 04 10, 175 b.; Max (no rest.), Storgatan 59, tel. 2 02 20, 189 b.; Nordkalotten, Lulviksvägen 1, tel. 8 93 50, 520 b.; Scandic Hotel Luleå, Mjölkudden, tel. 2 83 60, 406 b.

Luleå
(Sweden)

Good Morning Hotels (no rest.), Förhandlingsvägen 4, tel. (020) 73 11 22 and (046) 30 31 20, 207 b.; Grand Hotel, Bantorget 1, tel. (046) 11 70 10, 130 b.; Lundia, Knut den Stores Gata 2, tel. 12 41 40, 158 b.; Sparta, Tunavägen 39, tel. 12 40 80, 110 b.

Lund
(Sweden)

★SAS Royal Hotel, Östergatan 10, tel. (040) 7 02 30, 442 b.; ★Sheraton Malmö Hotel & Towers, Triangeln 2, tel. 7 40 00, 430 b.; Anglais, Stortorget

Malmö
(Sweden)

Hotels

15, tel. 7 14 50, 135 b.; Garden, Baltzarsgatan 20, tel. 10 40 00, 260 b.; Noble House, Gustav Adolfstorg 47, tel. 10 15 00, 228 b.; RESO Hotel St. Jörgen, Stora Nygatan 35, tel. 7 73 00, 460 b.; SARA Hotel Winn (no rest.), Jörgen Kocksgatan 3, tel. 10 18 00, 202 b.; Savoy, Norra Vallgatan 62, tel. 7 02 30, 150 b.; Scandic Crown Hotel, Amiralsgatan 10, tel. 10 07 30, 244 b.; Scandic Hotel Segevåg, Segesvängen, tel. 43 36 20, 348 b.; Skyline, Bisittaregatan 2, tel. 8 03 00, 535 b.

Mariehamn
(Finland)

See Åland Islands

Mikkeli
(Finland)

Alexandra Mikkeli, Porrassalmenkatu 9, tel. (955) 2 02 01, 127 b.; Cumulus, Mikonkatu 9, tel. 2 05 11, 250 b.; Kaleva, Hallituskatu 5, tel. 20 61 500, 64 b.; Nuijamies, Porrassalmenkatu 21, tel. 36 31 11, 65 b.; Varsavuori, Kirkonvarkaus, tel. 36 71 11, 260 b.
Summer hotel: Tekuila (June 1st–Aug. 15th), Raviradantie 1, tel. 36 65 42 and 36 02 11, 232 b.

Mo i Rana
(Norway)

Bech's Motor Hotell, Hammerveien 10, tel. 75 13 02 11, 92 b.; Holmen, Th. von Westensgate 2, tel. 75 15 14 44, 80 b.; Meyergården, O. T. Olsensgate 24, tel. 75 15 05 55, 300 b.

Molde
(Norway)

Alexandra , Storgaten 1–7, tel. 71 25 11 33, 250 b.; Knausen, Bermo, tel. 71 25 15 77, 156 b.; Molde, Storgate 19, tel. 71 21 58 88, 72 b.

Mora
(Sweden)

See Lake Siljan

Narvik
(Norway)

InterNor Grand Royal, Kongensgate 64, tel. 76 94 15 00, 220 h.; Narvik Sportell, Skistuaveien 8, tel. 76 94 75 00, 110 b.; Nordstjernen, Kongensgate 26, tel. 76 94 41 20, 46 b.

Norrköping
(Sweden)

Centric (no rest.), Gamla Rådstugugatan 18–20, tel. (011) 18 22 11, 58 b.; Grand Hotel, Tyska Torget 2, tel. 19 71 00, 366 b.; President, Vattengränden 11, tel. 12 95 20, 102 b.; Princess (no rest.), Skomakaregatan 8, tel. 19 72 20, 225 b.; Scandic Hotel Himmelstalund, Utställningsvägen 6, tel. 17 00 20, 180 b.; Scandic Hotel Norrköping, Järngatan 17, tel. 10 03 80; Södra Hotellet, Södra Promenaden 142, tel. 18 99 90, 30 b.

Nyköping
(Sweden)

Blommenhof, Blommenhovsvägen, tel. (0155) 6 20 00, 55 b.; Marsvikens Kursgård (closed July), Emtnäs, tel. 2 42 20, 55 b.; Scandic Hotel Nyköping, Gumsbacken, tel. 8 90 00, 205 b.; Stadshotellet, V. Storgatan 15, tel. 6 90 60, 200 b.

Öland
(Sweden)

In Borgholm: Borgholm, Trädgårdsgatan, tel. (0485) 1 10 60, 55 b.; Halltorps Gästgiveri, Högsrum, tel. 8 50 00, 68 b.; Strand, Villagatan 4, tel. 8 88 88, 360 b.
In Färjestaden: Skansen, tel. 3 05 30, 62 b.

Örebro
(Sweden)

Ansgar (no rest.), Järnvägsgatan 10, tel. (019) 10 04 20, 54 b.; City, Kungs gatan 24, tel. 10 02 00, 230 b.; Good Morning Hotels (no rest.), Stenbackevägen 2, tel. 73 11 22, 207 b.; Grev Rosen (no rest.), Södra Grev Rosengatan 2, tel. 13 02 40, 133 b.; Scandic Hotel Örebro, Västhagagatan 1, tel. 13 04 80, 537 b.; Stora Hotellet, Drottninggatan 1, tel. 12 43 60, 156 b.

Orrefors
(Sweden)

See Småland

Oslo
(Norway)

★ Grand Hotel, Karl Johansgate 31, tel. 22 42 93 90, 500 b.; ★ Nobel, Karl Johansgate 33, tel. 22 42 74 80, 145 b.; ★ Royal Christiania, Biskop Gunnerus'gate 3, tel. 22 42 94 10, 1000 b.; ★ Scandic Crown, Parkveien 68, tel. 22 44 69 70, 320 b.; ★ Ambassadeur, Camilla Collettsveien 15, tel. 22 44 18 35, 71 b.; Anker, Storgate 55, tel. 22 11 40 05, 230 b.; Bondeheimen, Rosen-

krantzgate 8, tel. 22 42 95 30, 135 b.; Bristol, Kristian IV's gate 7, tel. 22 41 58 40, 225 b.; Carlton, Parkveien 78, tel. 22 69 61 70, 86 b.; City, Skippergate 19, tel. 22 41 36 10, 90 b.; Continental, Stortingsgate 24–26, tel. 22 82 40 00, 290 b.; Europa, St Olavsgate 31, tel. 22 20 99 90, 220 b.; Fønix & Postcaféen, Dronningensgate 19, tel. 22 42 59 57, 99 b.; Gabelshus, Gabelsgate 16, tel. 22 55 22 60, 85 b.; Inter Nor Savoy Hotel, Universitetsgate 11, tel. 22 20 26 55, 134 b.; IMI Oslo, Staffeldtsgate 4, tel. 22 20 53 30, 115 b.; Linne Hotel, Statsråd Mathiesensveien 12, tel. 22 64 22 22, 168 b.; Rainbow Cecil, Stortingsgate 8, tel. 22 42 70 00, 196 b.; Rainbow Hotel Gyldenløve, Bogstadveien 20, tel. 22 60 10 90, 284 b.; Rainbow Hotel Spectrum, Brugt 7, tel. 22 17 60 30, 198 b.; Rainbow Hotel Stefan, Rosenkrantzgate 1, tel. 22 42 92 50, 210 b.; Rainbow Hotel Astoria, Dronningensgate 21, tel. 22 42 00 10, 170 b.; Rainbow Hotel Munch, Munchsgate 5, tel. 22 42 42 75, 225 b.; Reso Oslo Plaza, Sonja Henie Plass 3, tel. 22 17 10 00, 1250 b.; Rica Helsfyr, Strømsveien 108, tel. 22 65 70 00, 225 b.; Rica Travel, Arbeidergaten 4, tel. 22 00 33 00, 206 b.; Rica Victoria, Rosenkrantz'gate 13, tel. 22 42 99 40, 321 b.; Ritz, Frederik Stangsgate 3, tel. 22 44 39 60, 90 b.; Saga, Eilert Sundtsgate 39, tel. 22 43 04 85, 62 b.; Smestad, Sørkedalsveien 93, tel. 22 14 64 90, 50 b.; Vika Atrium, Munkedamsveien 45, tel. 22 83 33 00, 91 b.; West, Skovveien 15, tel. 22 55 40 30, 110 b.; Westside Bed & Breakfast, Eilert Sundtsgate 43, tel. 22 56 87 70, 54 b.; White House, President Harbitzgate 18, tel. 22 44 19 60, 36 b.
On Holmenkollen: Holmemkollen Park Hotel Rica, Kongveien 26, tel. 22 92 20 00, 360 b.
In Jessheim: Quality Airport Hotel Gardermoen, tel. 63 97 30 11, 225 b.
In Nesbu: Holmen Fjordhotell, Slemmestadveien 64, 151 b.

Britannia (no rest.), Prästgatan 26, tel. (063) 11 78 40, 45 b.; Jämteborg (no rest.), Storgatan 54, tel. 11 01 01, 37 b.; Linden (no rest.), Storgatan 64, tel. 11 73 35, 63 b.; Östersund, Kyrkgatan 70, tel. 11 76 40, 280 b.; SARA Hotel Winn, Prästgatan 16, tel. 12 77 40, 346 b.; Scandic Hotel Östersund, Krondikesvägen 97, tel. 12 75 60, 288 b.

Östersund
(Sweden)

See Gudbrandsdal

Otta
(Norway)

Apollo, Asemakatu 31–33, tel. (981) 37 43 44, 137 b.; Arina, Pakkahuoneenkatu 16, tel. 3 11 42 21, 110 b.; Cumulus, Kajaaninkatu 17, tel. 316 71 11, 336 b.; Eden Spa, Vellamontie 10, tel. 550 41 00, 308 b.; Lanamäki, Rautatienkatu 8, tel. 37 95 55, 88 b.; Rivoli Oulu, Kirkkokatu 3, tel. 313 91 11, 320 b.; Vaakuna, Hallituskatu 1, tel. 22 46 66, 386 b.
Summer hotel: Välkkylä (June 1st–Aug. 31st), Kajaanintie 36, tel. 311 65 22, 96 b.

Oulu
(Finland)

Amado, Keskusaukio 2, tel. (939) 33 85 00, 106 b.; Cumulus, Itsenäisyydenkatu 37, tel. 82 80 00, 172 b.; Juhana Herttua, Itäpuisto 1, tel. 33 18 41, 110 b.; Vaakuna, Gallén-Kallelankatu 7, tel. 82 01 00, 437 b.
At Yyteri Beach: Meri-Yyteri, tel. 34 53 00, 286 b.
South of town: Raumantien Motelli, Valtatie 8, tel. 8 36 20, 26 b.

Pori
(Finland)

Haikko Manor Spa and Congress Centre, tel. (915) 1 22 01, 450 b.; Seurahovi, Rauhankatu 27B, tel. 1 88 61, 100 b.; Sparre, Piispankatu 34, tel. 1 88 66, 79 b.
Summer hotel: Springhill (June 1st–July 31st), Lohentie 13B, tel. (summer) 14 52 25, (winter) 14 90 11, 58 b.

Porvoo
(Finland)

Bergstadens Turisthotell, Osloveien 2, tel. 72 41 11 11, 150 b.; Fjellheimen Turistasjon, Rv. 30, tel. 72 41 14 68, 36 b.; Inter Nor Hotel Røros, An-Magrittsvei, tel. 72 41 10 11, 226 b.
In Brekkebygd: Vauldalen Fjellhotell, tel. 72 41 31 00, 123 b.

Røros
(Norway)

City Hotel, Pekankatu 9, tel. (960) 31 45 01, 224 b.; Gasthof, Koskikatu 41, tel. 2 32 22, 78 b.; Lapinportti, Pohjolankatu 19–21, tel. 2 25 55, 90 b.; Rantasipi Pohjanhovi, Pohjanpuistikko 2, tel. 3 37 11, 410 b.

Rovaniemi
(Finland)

Hotels

Out of town: Ounasvaara Pirtit, Hiihtokeskus, tel. 36 21 00, 192 b.
Summer hotels: Ammattioppilaitoksen Kesähotelli (June 15th–Aug. 8th),
Kairatie 75, tel. 39 26 51, 108 b.; Oppipoika, Korkalonkatu 33, tel. 2 03 21,
90 b.

Savonlinna
(Finland)

Spa Hotel Casino, Kasinonsaari, tel. (957) 5 75 00, 216 b.; Pietari Kylliäinen,
Olavinkatu 15, tel. 2 29 01, 102 b.; Seurahuone, Kauppatori 4–6, tel. 57 31,
170 b.; Tott, Satmakatu 1, tel. 51 45 00.
Summer hotels: Malakias Summer Hotel (June 1st–Aug. 15th), Pihlajave-
denkuja 6, tel. (summer) 2 32 83, (winter) 2 28 64, 430 b.; Rauhalinna (June
1st–Aug. 19th), Lehtiniemi, tel. (summer) 52 31 19, (winter) 2 28 64, 14 b.;
Vuorilinna Summer Hotel (June 1st–Aug. 31st), Kasinonsaari, tel. 575 04 95
and 2 49 08, 460 b.

Lake Siljan
(Sweden)

In Mora: Mora, Strandgatan 12, tel. (0250) 1 17 50, 206 b.; Moraparken,
Parkgatan 1, tel. 1 78 00, 216 b.; Scandic Hotel Mora, Kristineberg, tel.
1 50 70, 109 b.

Skellefteå
(Sweden)

★Malmia, Torget 2, tel. (0910) 7 73 00, 250 b.; Aurum, Gymnasievägen 12,
tel. 8 83 30, 160 b.; Scandic Hotel Skellefteå, Expolaris Center, Kanalgatan
73, tel. 3 83 00, 282 b.; Stadshotellet Skellefteå, Stationsgatan 8–10, tel. 1 41
40, 174 b.; Stiftsgården, Brännavägen 25, tel. 7 72 72, 54 b.; Victoria (no
rest.), Trädgårdsgatan 8, tel. 1 74 70, 36 b.

Skövde
(Sweden)

Billingen Plaza, Trädgårdsgatan 10, tel. (0500) 1 07 90, 168 b.; Majoren
Home Hotel (no rest.), Torggatan 7, tel. 1 06 10, 67 b.; Prisma, Ekedalsgatan
2, tel. 8 80 00, 141 b.; SARA Hotel Billingehus, Alphyddevägen, tel. 8 30 00,
515 b.; Västerhöjdsgården (no rest.), Vennerbergsgatan 9, tel. 1 38 32, 32 b.

Småland
(Sweden)

In Orrefors: Orrefors, Kantavägen 29, tel. (0481) 3 00 35, 18 b.

Sognefjord
(Norway)

In Balestrand: Bøyum Pensionat, tel. 57 69 11 14, 24 b.; Dragsvik Fjordhotel,
tel. 57 69 12 93, 80 b.; Kvikne's Hotel, Balholm (May 1st–Sept. 30th), tel.
57 69 11 01, 365 b.; Midtnes Pensjonat, tel. 57 69 15 84, 60 b.; Syga Som-
marhotell, tel. 57 69 11 58, 112 b.

Spitzbergen
(Norway)

In Longyearbyen: Spitzbergen Travel Hotel, tel. 79 02 24 50, 71 b.; Svalbard
Kro & Motell, tel. 79 02 13 00, 30 b.; Svalbard Polar Hotel (originally built in
Lillehammer for the 1994 Olympic Games, then dismantled piece by piece
and rebuilt on Spitzbergen), tel. 79 02 35 00, 134 b.
  Information from Info-Svalbard in Longyearbyen (see Information).

Stavanger
(Norway)

★Radisson SAS Royal Hotel, Løkkeveien 26, tel. 51 56 70 00, 293 b.;
★Scandic Hotel Stavanger, Eiganesveien 181, te. 51 52 65 00, 282 b.; Alstor,
Tjensvollveien 31, tel. 51 87 08 00, 150 b.; Commandør, Valberggate 9, tel.
51 89 53 00, 50 b.; Grand Hotel, Klubbgate 3, tel. 51 89 58 00, 132 b.; Inter
Nor Victoria, Skansegate 1. tel. 51 89 60 00, 200 b.; Mosvangen Parkhotel,
Henrik Ibsensgate 21, tel. 51 87 09 77, 106 b.; Reso Atlantic Hotel, Olav V's
gate 3, tel. 51 52 75 20, 545 b.; Reso KNA Hotellet, Lagårdsveien 61, tel. 51 52
85 00, 354 b.; Skagen Brygge, Skagenkaien 28–30, tel. 51 89 41 00, 142 b.
At airport: Quality Airport Stavanger, Sømmeveien 1, tel. 51 65 66 00,
228 b.
In Sola: Sola Strand Hotel, Axel Lundsveien 27, tel. 51 65 02 22, 140 b.

Stockholm
(Sweden)

On Brunkebergstorg: ★RESO Sergel Plaza (No. 9), tel. (08) 22 66 00, 768 b.
On Blasieholmen: ★Grand Hotel, Södra Blasieholmshamnen 8, tel. 22 10
20, 523 b.
In Gamle Stan: ★Lord Nelson (no rest.), Västerlånggatan 22, tel. 23 23 90,
40 b.; ★SARA Hotel Reisen (view), Skeppsbron 12–14, tel. 22 21 60, 212 b.
On Riddarholmen: Mälardrottningen Hotel (ship; with restaurant), tel.
24 36 00, 109 b.

In Norrmalm: ★ Sheraton Stockholm, Tegelbacken 6, tel. 14 26 00, 920 b.; RESO Anglais, Humlegårdsgatan 23, tel. 24 99 00, 360 b.; RESO Continental, Vasagatan/Klara Vattugränd 4, tel. 24 40 20, 550 b.; Stockholm, Norrmalmstorg 1, tel. 6 78 13 20, 197 b.
In Drottninggatan: Queen's (No. 71A; no rest.), tel. 24 92 60, 40 b.
In Vasagatan: ★ SAS Royal Viking Hotel (No. 1), tel. 14 10 00, 614 b.; Terminus (No. 20), tel. 22 26 40, 230 b.; Central (No. 38; no rest.), tel. 22 08 40, 120 b.
On Kungsholmen: Kristineberg (no rest.), Hjalmar Söderbergsvägen 10, tel. 13 03 00, 159 b.; RESO Palace, St. Eriksgatan 115, tel. 24 12 20, 459 b.; SARA Hotel Amarantan, Kungsholmsgatan 31, tel. 6 54 10 60, 730 b.
In Östermalm: ★ Diplomat, Strandvägen 7C, tel. 6 63 58 00, 205 b.; ★ Stockholm Plaza, Birger Jarlsgatan 29, tel. 14 51 20, 230 b.; Eden Terrace Hotel, Sturegatan 10, tel. 22 31 60, 110 b.; Esplanade (no rest.), Strandvägen 7A, tel. 6 63 07 40, 44 b.; Karelia, Birger Jarlsgatan 35, tel. 24 76 60, 143 b.; Kung Carl, Birger Jarlsgatan 23, tel. 6 11 31 10, 180 b.; Mornington, Nybrogatan 53, tel. 6 63 12 40, 140 r.; Wellington, Storgatan 6, tel. 6 67 09 10, 73 b.
In Vasastaden: Birger Jarl, Tulegatan 8, tel. 15 10 20, 427 b.; Oden, Karlbergsvägen 24, tel. 34 93 40, 270 b.
In Södermalm: Aston, Mariatorget 3, tel. 44 05 90, 130 b.; RESO Hotel Malmen, Götgatan 49–51, tel. 22 60 80, 499 b.; RESO Sjöfartshotellet, Katarinavägen 26, tel. 22 69 60, 380 b.
In Solna: Flamingo, Hotellgatan 11, tel. 83 08 00, 172 b.
In Sundbyberg: ★ RESO Park Hotel, Karlavägen 43, tel. 22 96 20, 368 b.
At Arlanda Airport (in Märsta, N of city centre): Flyghotellet Arlanda, Bristagatan 16, tel. (0760) 1 11 00, 124 b.
At Bromma Airport (W of city centre): RESO Hotel Bromma, Brommaplan, tel. (08) 25 29 20, 229 b.; Flyghotellet (no rest.), Brommaplan, tel. 26 26 20, 136 b.
In Älvsjö (S of city): ★ Royal Starhotel, Mässvägen, tel. (08) 99 02 20, 200 b.
In Sollentuna (N of city): ★ Starhotel Sollentuna, Aniaraplatsen 8, tel. 92 01 00, 816 b. (suites only).

★ Bore, Trädgårdsgatan 31–33, tel. (060) 15 06 00, 262 b.; Grand Hotel (no rest.), Nybrogatan 13, tel. 15 72 05, 80 b.; RESO Hotel Sundsvall, Esplanaden 29, tel. 17 16 00, 450 b.; SARA Hotel Strand, Strandgatan 10, tel. 12 18 00, 325 b.; Scandic Hotel Sundsvall, Värdshusbacken 6, tel. 56 68 60, 159 r.

Sundsvall
(Sweden)

See Lofoten

Svolvær
(Norway)

Cumulus Hämeenpuisto, Hämeenpuisto 47, tel. (931) 2 42 42 42, 382 b.; Cumulus Koskikatu, Koskikatu 5, tel. 2 42 41 11, 351 b.; Grand Hotel Tammer, Satakunnankatu 13, tel. 12 53 80, 166 b.; Jäähovi, Sammonvaltatie 2, tel. 55 99 00, 120 b.; Lapinniemi Spa, Lapinniemenranta 12, tel. 59 71 11, 99 b.; Ponja, Satakunnankatu 10, tel. 2 41 51 11, 120 b.; Rivoli Tampere, Yliopistonkatu 44, tel. 2 45 51 11, 282 b.; Rosendahl, Pyynikintie 13, tel. 11 22 33, 450 b.; Tampere, Hämeenkatu 1, tel. 12 19 80, 480 b.; Victoria, Itsenäisyydenkatu 1, tel. 2 42 51 11, 170 b.
Summer hotel: Domus Summer Hotel (June 1st–Aug. 31st), Pellervonkatu 9, tel. (summer) 55 00 00, (winter) 13 32 22, 388 b.

Tampere
(Finland)

Kaupunginhotelli, Itäranta 4, tel. (9698) 4 33 11, 190 b.

Tornio
(Finland)

Standard, Österbrogatan 4, tel. (0410) 1 04 38, 30 b.

Trelleborg
(Sweden)

Grand Nordic Hotel, Storgate 44, tel. 77 68 55 00, 166 b.; Havna Hotell, Breivika Havn, tel. 77 67 59 99, 75 b.; Rainbow Polar Hotell, Grønnegate 45, tel. 77 68 64 80, 101 b.; Rainbow Tromsø Hotell, Grønnegate 50, tel. 77 68 75 20, 70 b.; Saga Hotell Tromsø, Richard Withsplass 2, tel. 77 68 11 80, 100 b.; Scandic Hotel, Heiloveien 23, tel. 77 67 34 00, 315 b.

Tromsø
(Norway)

Hotels

Trondheim
(Norway)

★Ambassadeur, Elvegate 18, tel. 73 52 70 50, 85 b.; ★Radisson SAS Hotel, Kjøpmannsgate 48, tel. 73 53 53 10, 202 b.; ★Residence, Torvet, tel. 73 52 83 80, 113 b.; ★Royal Garden, Kjøpmannsgate 73, tel. 73 52 11 00, 700 b.; ★Scandic Hotel, Brøsetveien 186, tel. 73 93 95 00, 330 b.; Astoria, Nordre Gate 24, tel. 73 52 95 50, 100 b.; Augustin, Kongensgate 26, tel. 73 52 80 00, 135 b.; Bakeriet Home Hotel, Brattørgate 2, tel. 73 52 52 00, 130 b.; Gilde-vangen Rainbow Hotel, Søndregate 22B, tel. 73 51 01 00, 130 b.; Inter Nor Britannia Hotel, Dronningensgate 5, tel. 73 53 53 53, 280 b.; Inter Nor Hotell prinsen, Kongensgate 30, tel. 73 53 06 50, 156 b.; Trondheim Hotell, Kon-gensgate 15, tel. 73 50 50 50, 178 b.

Turku
(Finland)

★Hamburger Börs, Kaupiaskatu 6, tel. (921) 63 73 81, 360 b.; ★Marina Palace, Linnankatu 32, tel. 65 12 11, 310 b.; ★Park, Rauhankatu 1, tel. 51 96 66, 47 b.; Cumulus, Eerikinkatu 28, tel. 63 82 11, 420 b.; Hansa, Kristii-nankatu 9, tel. 63 73 81, 107 b.; Keskushotelli, Yliopistonkatu 12A, tel. 33 73 33, 119 b.; Rantasipi Ikituuri, Pispalantie 7, tel. 36 61 11, 300 b.; Ritz, Humaliistonkatu 7, tel. 65 11 11, 275 b.; Scandic Hotel Turku, Matkustajasa-tama, tel. 30 26 00, 175 b.; Seurahuone, Humaliistonkatu 2, tel. 03 73 01, 131 b.; Turun Karina, Itäinen Pitkäkatu 30B, tel. 33 66 66, 54 b.
Summer hotels: Domus Aboensis (June 1st–Aug. 31st), Piispankatu 10, tel. 32 04 21, 130 b.; Ikituuri Summer Hotel (June 1st–Aug. 31st), Piispalantie 7, tel. 37 61 11, 288 b.

Umeå
(Sweden)

Blå Aveny, Rådhusesplanaden 14, tel. (090) 13 23 00, 258 b.; Blå Dragonen, Norrlandsgatan 5, tel. 13 23 80, 134 b.; Motell Björnen, Björnvägen 3, tel. 13 71 10, 123 b.; SARA Hotel Umeå, Vasaplan, tel. 12 20 20, 299 b.; Scandic Hotel Umeå, Yrkesvägen 8, tel. 13 52 50, 365 b.; Stora Hotellet, Storgatan 46, tel. 11 88 70, 158 b.; Strand Hotell (no rest.), Västra Strandgatan 11, tel. 12 90 20, 64 b.; Wasa, Vasagatan 12, tel. 11 85 40, 170 b.

Uppsala
(Sweden)

Grand Hotel Hörnan, Bangårdsgatan 1, tel. (018) 13 93 80, 70 b.; Linné, Skolgatan 45, tel. 10 20 00, 220 b.; SARA Hotel Gillet, Dragarbrunnsgatan 23, tel. 15 53 60, 269 b.; Scandic Hotel Uppsala, Gamla Uppsalagatan 50, tel. 20 02 80, 402 b.; Uplandia, Dragarbrunnsgatan 32, tel. 10 21 60, 214 b.

Vaasa
(Finland)

★Royal Waasa, Hovioikeudenpuistikko 18, tel. (961) 27 81 11, 650 b.; Fenno, Niemeläntie, tel. 12 10 55, 300 b.; Tekla, Palosaarentie 58, tel. 11 78 50, 314 b.; Waskia, Lemmenpolku 3, tel. 25 71 11, 565 b.

Lake Vänern
(Sweden)

In Vänersborg: Scandic Hotel Vänersborg, Nobbensberg, tel. (0521) 6 21 20, 287 b.; Strand Hotell (no rest.), Hamngatan 7, tel. 1 38 50, 45 b.

Vantaa
(Finland)

★Vantaa, Hertaksentie, tel. (90) 85 78 51, 290 b.; Airport Hotel Rantasipi, Takamaantie 4, tel. 8 70 51, 480 b.; Pilotti, Vermäentie 1, tel. 8 79 21 00, 224 b.

Varberg
(Sweden)

Fregatten, Hamnplan, tel. (0340) 7 70 00, 180 b.; Gästis (no rest.), Borg-mästaregatan 1, tel. 1 80 50, 60 b.; SARA Hotel Statt, Kungsgatan 24–26, tel. 1 61 00, 242 b.; Varberg, Norrgatan 16, tel. 1 61 25, 40 b.

Västerås
(Sweden)

Arkad (no rest.), Östermalmsgatan 25, tel. (021) 12 04 80, 69 b.; Astoria Fenix (no rest.), Kopparbergsvej 29A, tel. 11 00 80, 137 b.; Grand Aros Hotel & Tower, Karlsgatan 9, tel. 10 10 10, 346 b.; Park Hotell, Gunnilbogatan 2, tel. 11 01 20, 210 b.; Scandic Hotel Västerås, Pilgatan/Änggärdsgatan, tel. 18 02 80, 450 b.; Stadshotellet, Stora Torget 7, tel. 18 04 20, 216 b.

Västervik
(Sweden)

Centralhotellet (no rest.), Brunnsgatan 23, tel. (0490) 3 01 40, 90 b.; Hotell Nore, Bredgatan 13, tel. 1 32 95, 35 b.; Västervik Stadshotellet, Storgatan 3, tel. 1 31 00, 110 r.

Växjö
(Sweden)

★Royal Corner, Liedbergsgatan 11, tel. (0470) 1 00 00, 280 b.; Cardinal, Storgatan/Bäckgatan, tel. 1 34 30, 120 b.; Esplanad (no rest.), N. Esplanaden 21A, tel. 2 25 80, 50 b.; SARA Hotel Statt, Kungsgatan 6, tel. 1 34 00, 178 b.; Scandic Hotel Växjö, Hejaregatan 19, tel. 2 20 70, 287 b.; Scandic Hotel Österleden, Sandviksvägen 1, tel. 2 90 50, 239 b.; Värend, Kungsgatan 27, tel. 1 04 85, 54 b.

In Harstad: Grand Nordic Hotell, Strandgate 9, tel. 77 06 21 70, 149 b.; **Vesterålen**
Viking Nordic Hotell, Fjordgate 2, tel. 77 06 40 80, 170 b. (Norway)

See Gotland **Visby**
(Sweden)

Continental du Sud, Hamngatan 13, tel. (0411) 1 37 00, 95 b.; Prins Carl I **Ystad**
Ystad, Hamngatan 8, tel. 7 37 50, 42 b.; RESO Ystads Saltsjöbad, Salts- (Sweden)
jöbadsvägen 6, tel. 1 36 30, 195 b.

Information

National Tourist Offices in Britain and North America

Norwegian Tourist Board   Norway
5 Lower Regent Street
London SW1Y 4LR
tel. (0171) 839 6255, fax (0171) 839 6014

Norwegian Tourist Board
655 Third Avenue, Suite 8110
New York NY 10017; tel. (212) 949 2333

Swedish Travel and Tourism Council   Sweden
11 Montagu Place
London W1H 2AL; tel. (0171) 724 5868

Swedish Travel and Tourism Council
655 Third Avenue (18th floor)
New York NY 10017; tel. (212) 697 0835

Finnish Tourist Board   Finland
UK Office (3rd floor)
30–50 Pall Mall
London SW1Y 5LP
tel. (0171) 930 5871, fax (0171) 321 0696

Finnish Tourist Board
655 Third Avenue (18th floor)
New York NY 10017; tel. (212) 949 2333

National Tourist Offices in Scandinavia

Norwegian Tourist Board (Nortra)   Norway
Drammensveien 40
Box 2893, Oslo Sentrum
N–0230 Oslo
tel. 22 92 52 00
fax 22 56 05 05

Next Stop Sweden   Sweden
Box 10134
S–12128 Stockholm-Globen
tel. (08) 7 25 55 00
fax (08) 6 49 88 82

Information

Finland

Finnish Tourist Board
Töölönkatu 11
FIN–00101 Helsinki
tel. (90) 40 30 300
fax (90) 40 30 13 33

Tourist Information
Eteläesplanadi 4
FIN–00130 Helsinki
tel. (90) 40 30 300
fax (90) 40 30 13 01

Regional and Local Tourist Information Offices

Abisko

See Kiruna

Åland Islands

Ålands Turistförbund
Storagatan 11
FIN–22100 Mariehamn
tel. (928) 2 73 00, fax (928) 2 73 15

Ålesund

Turistkontor
Rådhuset
N–6025 Ålesund; tel. 70 12 12 02

Alingsås

Alingsås Turistbyrå
Kungsgatan 14
S–44181 Alingsås
tel. (0322) 7 52 00, fax (0322) 7 57 30

Alta

Alta Turistinformasjon
Postbox 80
N–9500 Alta

Ängelholm

See Helsingborg

Atlantic Highway

Kristiansund Reiselivslag
Kong Olavsgate 1
Postboks 401
N–6501 Kristiansund
tel. 71 67 72 11

Bergen

Bergen Reiselivslag
Slottsgate 1
Postboks 4055
N–5023 Bergen; tel. 55 31 38 60

Bodø

Bodø Turistinformasjon
Postboks 514
N–8000 Bodø; tel. 75 52 60 00

Bohuslän

BohusTurist
Box 182
S–45116 Uddevalla; tel. (0522) 1 40 55

Borås

Borås Turistbyrå
Hallbergsgatan 14
S–50115 Borås
tel. (033) 16 70 87, fax (033) 16 85 66

Eskilstuna

Eskilstuna Turistbyrå
Hamngatan 19, S–63220 Eskilstuna
tel. (016) 11 45 00, fax (016) 11 45 75

Falkenbergs Turistbyrå
Holgersgatan 22B
S–31123 Falkenberg
tel. (0346) 1 74 10, fax (0346) 1 45 26

Falu Turistbyrå
Stora Torget
S–79183 Falun
tel. (023) 8 36 37, fax (023) 8 33 14

Filipstads Turistbyrå
Box 303
Kyrkogatan 2
S–68201 Filipstad; tel. (0590) 1 47 40

See Joensuu, Jyväskylä, Kajaani, Kuopio, Lahti, Lappeenranta, Mikkeli and
Oulu

Frederikstad Touristkontor
N–1632 Frederikstad
tel. 69 32 03 30

Gällivare Ekförening
Storgatan 16
S–97200 Gällivare
tel. (0970) 1 66 60, fax (0970) 1 47 81

Gävle Turistbyrå
N. Strandgatan 11–13
S–80135 Gävle
tel. (026) 10 16 00, fax (026) 10 78 31

Geiranger Turistinformasjon
N–6216 Geiranger; tel. 70 26 30 99

Rederi AB Göta Kanal
Box 272
S–40124 Göteborg; tel. (031) 17 76 15

Göteborgs Turistbyrå
Kungsportsplatsen 2
S–41110 Göteborg
tel. (031) 10 07 40, fax (031) 11 21 77

Gotlands Turistförening
Burmeisterska Huset
Box 2081
S–62102 Visby
tel. (0498) 4 70 65, fax (0498) 7 89 40

A/L Oppland Reiseliv
Kirkegate 76
N–2600 Lillehammer; tel. 61 28 91 84

Sel-Rondane Reiselivslag
Nygate 4
N–2671 Otta
tel. 61 23 03 65

A/L Fron Reiseliv
Nedregate 5a
N–2640 Vinstra; tel. 61 29 01 66

Information

Hallingdal

Hallingdal Informasjonssenter AS
N–3540 Nesbyen
tel. 32 07 01 70

Halmstad

Halmstads Turistbyrå
Lilla Torg
S–30102 Halmstad
tel. (035) 10 93 45, fax (035) 15 81 15

Hämeenlinna

Hämeen Matkailu
(Municipal Tourist Office)
Palokunnankatu 11
SF–13100 Hämeenlinna
tel. (917) 14 23 88, fax (917) 14 27 16

Hamina

Haminan Matkailupalvelu
(Municipal Tourist Office)
Pikkuympyränkatu 5
FIN–49400 Hamina
tel. (952) 49 52 50, fax (952) 4 04 57

During the summer there is also a tourist information office in the market
square.

Hammerfest

Hammerfest Turist AS
Postboks 460
N–9601 Hammerfest; tel. 78 41 21 85

Hanko

Municipal Tourist Office
Bulevardi 15
FIN–10901 Hanko
tel. (911) 80 34 10, fax (911) 80 34 12

During the summer there is also a tourist information office on the East
Harbour

Hardangerfjord

Hordaland og Bergen Reiselivsråd
Slottsgate 1
N–5003 Bergen
tel. 55 31 66 00, fax 55 31 52 08

Reiselivslag
Postboks 91
N–5730 Ulvik
tel. 56 52 63 60

Hardangervidda

See Hardangerfjord

Härjedalen

Härjedalsfjälls Turistbyrå
Rörosvägen 17
S–84095 Funäsdalen
tel. (0684) 2 14 20, fax (0684) 2 90 26

Härnösand

Turistbyrån Härnösand
Kanaludden, Simhallen
S–87100 Härnösand
tel. (0611) 2 83 88
(Open May–Sept.)

Helsingborg

Helsingborgs Turistbyrå
Rådhuset
S–25661 Helsingborg
tel. (042) 12 03 10

Helsingin Kaupungin Matkailutoimisto
(Helsinki Municipal Tourist Office)
Pohjoisesplanadi 19
FIN–00100 Helsinki
tel. (90) 1 69 37 57, fax (90) 1 69 38 39

Helsinki

Fjell og Fjord Ferie AS
N–3550 Gol
tel. 32 07 45 44, fax 32 07 55 09

Hønefoss

Hudiksvalls Turistbyrå
Box 149 (Möljen)
S–82401 Hudiksvall
tel. (0650) 1 39 20, fax (0650) 9 60 61

Hudiksvall

OVDS
Postekspedisjon
N–8450 Storkmarknes
tel. (088) 5 14 22, fax (088) 5 24 69

Hurtigrute

Tourist Information Office
Piiskuntie 6
(Bus Station)
FIN–99801 Ivalo
tel. (9697) 1 25 21, fax (9697) 1 23 14

Lake Inari

Jämtlands/Härjedalens Turistinformation
S–83182 Östersund
tel. (063) 14 40 01, fax (063) 12 70 55

**Jämtland,
Härjedalen**

Kaupungin Matkailutoimisto
(Municipal Tourist Office)
Koskikatu 1
FIN–80100 Joensuu
tel. (973) 1 67 53 00, fax (973) 12 39 33

Joensuu

Jönköpings Turistbyrå
Djurläkartorget 2
S–55189 Jönköping
tel. (036) 10 50 50, fax (036) 12 83 00

Jönköping

See Nordfjord

Jostedalsbre

Luster Reiselivslag
Rådhuset
N–5820 Gaupne
tel. 57 68 12 11

Jotunheimen

Kaupungin Matkailutoimisto
(Municipal Tourist Office)
FIN–40100 Jyväskylä
tel. (941) 62 49 03, fax (941) 21 43 93

Jyväskylä

Kainuun Matkapalvelu
(Municipal Tourist Office)
Pohjolankatu 16
FIN–87100 Kajaani
tel. (986) 15 58 45, fax (986) 15 55 10

Kajaani

Kalmar Turistbyrå
Larmgatan 6
S–39120 Kalmar
tel. (0480) 1 53 50

Kalmar

Information

Karasjok	Karasjok Opplevelser Postboks 192 N–9730 Karasjok tel. 78 46 73 60
Karlskrona	Karlskrona Kommun Turistinformation Stadsbiblioteket S–37183 Karlskrona tel. (0455) 8 34 90, fax (0455) 8 30 00
Karlstad	Karlstads Turistbyrå Tingvallagatan 1D tel. (054) 19 59 01, fax (054) 19 50 10
Kemi	Kaupungin Matkailutoimisto (Municipal Tourist Office) Kauppakatu 22 FIN–94100 Kemi tel. (9698) 19 94 65, fax (9698) 19 94 68
Kirkenes	AS Grenseland Postboks 8 N–9901 Kirkenes tel. 78 99 25 01
Kiruna	Kiruna Turistbyrå Hjalmar Lundbomsvägen 42 S–98185 Kiruna tel. (0980) 1 88 80, fax (0980) 8 02 91
Kokkola	Kokkolan Matkailu Oy (Municipal Tourist Office) Mannerheiminaukio FIN–67100 Kokkola tel. (968) 31 19 02, fax (968) 31 03 06
Koli Hills	See Joensuu
Kongsberg	Kongsberg Turistkontor Storgate 36 N–3600 Kongsberg tel. 32 73 50 00
Kristiansand	Kristiansand Informasjon Dronningensgate 2 N 4601 Kristiansand tel. 38 02 60 65, fax 38 02 52 55
Kristianstad	Kristianstads Turistbyrå Stora Torg S–29132 Kristianstad tel. (044) 12 19 88, fax (044) 12 08 98
Kuopio	Kaupungin Matkailutoimisto (Municipal Tourist Office) Haapaniemenkatu 17 FIN–70110 Kuopio tel. (971) 18 25 84, fax (971) 12 40 04

Matkailukeskus Karhuntassu
(Municipal Tourist Office)
Torangintaival 2
FIN–93600 Kuusamo
tel. (989) 8 50 29 10, fax (989) 8 50 29 01

Kaupungin Matkailutoimisto
(Municipal Tourist Office)
Torikatu 3B
FIN–15111 Lahti
tel. (918) 8 18 25 80, fax (918) 8 18 25 75

Landskrona-Vens Turistbyrå
Rådhusgatan 3
S–26131 Landskrona
tel. (0418) 1 69 80

Lappland Reisen
Maakuntakatu 10
FIN–96100 Rovaniemi
tel. (960) 34 60 52, fax (960) 31 27 43

Kaupungin Matkailutoimisto
(Municipal Tourist Office)
Box 113
Bus Station
FIN–53101 Lappeenranta
tel. (953) 56 08 60, fax (953) 56 01 40

Larvik Reiselivsforening
Postboks 200
N–3251 Larvik
tel. 33 13 01 00

Lillehammer Turistkontor
Lilletorget
N–2600 Lillehammer
tel. 61 25 92 99

Linköpings Turistbyrå
Ågatan 39
S–58101 Linköping
tel. (013) 20 68 35, fax (013) 10 16 50

Destination Lofoten
Postboks 210
N–8301 Svolvær
tel. 76 17 30 00

Luleå Turistbyrå
Rådstugatan 9
S–95185 Luleå
tel. (0920) 9 37 46, fax (0920) 8 75 53

Lunds Turistbyrå
Kattesund 6
S–22100 Lund
tel. (046) 15 50 40, fax (046) 12 59 63

See Tromsø

Information

Lake Mälar   See Stockholm

Malmö

Malmö Turistbyrå/Destination Malmö
Skeppsbron 1
S–21120 Malmö
tel. (040) 34 12 70, fax (040) 34 34 47

Mikkeli

Mikkelin Matkailu Oy
(Municipal Tourist Office)
Hallituskatu 3A
FIN–50100 Mikkeli
tel. (955) 15 14 44, fax (955) 15 16 25

Lake Mjøsa

Hedmark Reiselivsråd
Grønnegaten 11
N–2300 Hamar
tel. 62 52 90 06, fax 62 52 21 49

Mo i Rana

Polarsirkelen
Reiselivslag, Boks 225
N–8601 Mo i Rana
tel. 75 15 04 21

Molde

Reiselivsforeningen i Molde
Postboks 484
N–6401 Molde
tel. 71 21 92 00

Narvik

Narvik Reiselivsindustri
Postboks 318
N–8501 Narvik
tel. 76 94 60 33

Nordfjord

Reisemål Nordfjord
N–6880 Stryn
tel. 57 87 23 33

Norrköping

Norrköpings Turistbyrå/Destination Norrköping
Rådhuset
S–60181 Norrköping
tel. (011) 15 15 00, fax (011) 10 20 33

North Cape   See Hammerfest

Nyköping

Sörmanlandskustens Turistbyrå
Nyköpingsbro
S–61195 Nyköping
tel. (0155) 5 85 00, fax (0155) 5 84 63

Öland

Ölands Turistförening
Box 74
S–38600 Färjestaden
tel. (0485) 3 90 20, fax (0485) 3 90 30

Borgholms Turistbyrå
Box 115
S–38700 Borgholm
tel. (0485) 8 90 00, fax (0485) 3 90 30

Örebro

Örebro Turistbyrå
Drottninggatan 9
S–70135 Örebro
tel. (019) 21 10 80' fax (019) 21 11 04

Norwegian Information Centre
Vestbaneplassen 1
N–0250 Oslo
tel. 22 83 00 59

Oslo

Tourist Information
Central Station, N–0154 Oslo
tel. 22 17 11 24

See Oslo

Oslofjord

Östersunds Turistbyrå
Rådhusgatan 44
S–83182 Östersund
tel. (063) 14 40 01, fax (063) 12 70 55

Östersund

Kaupungin Matkailutoimisto
(Municipal Tourist Office)
Torikatu 10
FIN–90100 Oulu
tel. (981) 3 14 12 95, fax (981) 3 14 13 10

Oulu

Sodankylä Tourist Office
Jääremente 9
FIN–99600 Sodankylä
tel. (9693) 1 34 74, fax (9693) 1 34 78

Pallastunturi

Kaupungin Matkailutoimisto
(Municipal Tourist Office)
Hallituskatu 9A
FIN–28100 Pori
tel. (939) 33 57 80, fax (939) 33 25 09

Pori

Kaupungin Matkailutoimisto
(Municipal Tourist Office)
Rauhankatu 20
FIN–06100 Porvoo
tel. (915) 17 01 45, fax (915) 18 43 25

Porvoo

During the summer there is a tourist information office in Old Town Hall
Square.

Nordland Reiseliv AS
Storgaten 4a III
N–8001 Bode
tel. 75 52 44 06, fax 75 52 83 28

**Rago
National Park**

Åndalsnes og Romsdal Reiselivslag
Postboks 133
N–6301 Åndalsnes; tel. 71 22 16 22

Romsdal

See Lillehammer

Rondane

Røroa Reiselivsing
Postboks 123
N–7461 Røros
tel. 72 41 00 00

Røros

Kaupungin Matkailutoimisto
(Municipal Tourist Office)
Aallonkatu 1, FIN–96200 Rovaniemi
tel. (960) 34 62 70

Rovaniemi

Information

During the summer there is also a tourist information office in the station: tel. (960) 2 22 18, fax (960) 3 43 51

Lake Saimaa See Savonlinna

Saltfjell See Bodø

Savonlinna
Savonlinna Matkailupalvelu
(Municipal Tourist Office)
Puistokatu 1
FIN–57100 Savonlinna
tel. (957) 1 34 92, fax (957) 51 44 49

Schonen
Skånes Turistråd
Stora Södergatan 8C
S–22223 Lund
tel. (046) 12 43 50, fax. (046) 12 23 72

Setesdal See Kristiansand

Lake Siljan
Siljan Turism Mora
Ångbåtskajen
S–79200 Mora
tel. (0250) 2 65 50, fax (0250) 1 52 51

Skellefteå
Skellefteå Turistbyrå
Storgatan 46
S–93185 Skellefteå
tel. (0910) 5 88 80, fax (0910) 1 41 14

Skövde
Skövde Turistbyrå
Sandtorget
S–54127 Skövde
tel. (0500) 8 05 17, fax (0500) 1 54 15

Småland
Smålands Turistråd
P. G . Vejdesväg 17
S–35252 Växjö
tel. (0470) 7 85 20, fax (0470) 7 89 40

Sognefjord
Balestrand og Fjærland Reiselivslag
Postboks 53
N–5850 Balestrand
tel. 57 69 12 55

Spitsbergen (Svalbard)
Info Svalbard
Postboks 323
N–9170 Longyearbyen
tel. 79 02 23 03

Stavanger
Stavanger Reiselivslag
Postboks 11
N–4005 Stavanger
tel. 51 89 66 00

Stockholm
Tourist Centre
Kungsträdgården (Sverigehuset)
Box 7542
S–10393 Stockholm
tel. (08) 7 89 20 00, fax (08) 7 89 24 50

At Arlanda Airport:
S–19045 Stockholm-Arlanda
Arrivals: tel. (08) 7 97 60 00
Departures: tel. (08) 7 97 61 00

Sundsvall Turistbyrå
Torget
S–85230 Sundsvall
tel. (060) 11 42 35

Sundsvall

Sunndal Reiselivolag
Postboks 62
N–6601 Sunndalsøra
tel. 71 69 25 52

Sunndal

Municipal Tourist Office
Verkatehtaankatu 2
FIN–33211 Tampere
tel. (931) 12 66 52, fax (931) 19 64 63

Tampere

Syd Norge AS
Postboks 91
N–4601 Kristiansand
tel. 38 07 10 08, fax 38 07 11 01

Telemark

Skien Reiselivslag
Postboks 493
N–3701 Skien
tel. 35 53 49 80

Kaupungin Matkailutoimisto
(Municipal Tourist Office)
Lukiokatu 10
FIN–95400 Tornio
tel. and fax (9698) 4 00 48

Tornio

Trelleborgs Turistbyrå
Hamngatan 4
S–23142 Trelleborg
tel. (0410) 5 33 22, fax (0410) 4 41 90

Trelleborg

Tromsø Arrangement AS
Postboks 311
N–9001 Tromsø
tel. 77 61 00 00

Tromsø

Trondheim Aktivum
Postboks 2102
N–7001 Trondheim
tel. 73 92 93 94

Trondheim

Turun Kaupungin Matkailutoimisto
(Turku Municipal Tourist Office)
Käsityöläiskatu 3
FIN–20100 Turku
tel. (921) 33 63 66, fax (921) 33 64 88

Turku

Umeå Turistbyrå
Renmarkstorget 15
S–90247 Umeå
tel. (090) 16 16 16, fax (090) 16 34 23

Umeå

Insurance

Uppsala	Uppsala Turistbyrå Fyristorg 8 S–75320 Uppsala tel. (018) 11 75 00, fax (018) 13 28 95
Vaasa	Kaupungin Matkailutoimisto (Municipal Tourist Office) Raastuvankatu 30 FIN–65101 Vaasa tel. (961) 25 11 45, fax (961) 25 36 20
Valdres	Valdres Turistkontor N–2900 Fagernes tel. 61 36 04 00
Lake Vänern	See Värmland
Varberg	Varbergs Turistbyrå Brunnsparken S–43225 Varberg tel. (0340) 8 87 70, fax (0340) 1 11 95
Värmland	Värmlands Turistråd Box 323, S–65108 Karlstad tel. (054) 10 21 60, fax (054) 18 05 30
Västerås	Västerås Turistbyrå Stora Torget 5 S–72215 Västerås tel. (021) 16 18 30
Västervik	Västerviks Turistbyrå/Blå Kusten Strömsholmen S–59300 Västervik tel. (0490) 8 87 04, fax (0490) 8 87 09
Lake Vättern	Östergötland Länsturustnämnd Kungsgatan 34 S–58102 Unköping tel. (013) 22 76 00, fax (013) 12 00 36 Västergötland Turistråd Box 213, S–54125 Skövde tel. (0500) 1 00 50, fax (0500) 8 40 86
Växjö	Växjö Turistbyrå Kronobergsgatan 8 S–35112 Växjö tel. (0470) 4 14 10
Vesterålen	Vesterålen Reiselivslag Boks 243, N–8401 Sortland tel. 70 12 15 55
Ystad	Ystads Turistbyrå St. Knuts Torg, S–27142 Ystad tel. (0411) 7 72 79, fax (0411) 1 15 85

Insurance

General	Visitors are strongly advised to ensure that they have adequate holiday insurance, including loss or damage to luggage, loss of currency and jewellery.

See Medical Aid   Health

Visitors travelling by car should be ensure that their insurance is compre-   Vehicles
hensive and covers use of the vehicle in Scandinavia

Language

English is widely spoken in the Scandinavian countries, and English-speaking visitors are unlikely to have any language difficulties in the popular
tourist areas or in hotels and travel agencies. In the remoter areas, however, particularly in central and northern Scandinavia, it is helpful to know
something of the language of the country, extending at least to a few
common words and phrases. This section can do no more than give a
minimum of information about each language and a brief selection of
useful vocabulary. Those who want to known more of a particular language
will find no shortage of good grammar books and dictionaries.

A knowledge of either Norwegian or Swedish will enable a visitor to
make himself understood in any of the Scandinavian countries.

Swedish and Norwegian belong to the North Germanic or Scandinavian
language group. Common to all the languages in the group is the use of
suffixes to form the definite article (Swedish *kyrkan,* "the church"), the
plural (*-ar, -er,* etc.) and the passive forms of verbs (Swedish *jag kallas,* "I
am called"). The characteristic Scandinavian vowels *æ* or *ä, ø* and *å* appear
at the end of the alphabet, after *z*.

Finnish is totally different from Norwegian and Swedish; it belongs to
the Finno-Ugrian language group, found in central and eastern Europe and
in western Siberia.

Norwegian has two forms – Bokmål, the official written language, which is   Norwegian
closely related to Danish, and Nynorsk (New Norwegian), a language
constructed from various Norwegian dialects which until 1929 was also
known as Landsmål. After Norway broke free from Denmark in 1814 the
growth of national feeling led to an increased interest in the national
language. Nynorsk (Landsmål) is spoken mainly in southern and western
Norway, Bokmål om the eastern part of the country and in the towns; the
two languages have equal status.

Pronunciation: *æ* is like *a* in "take"; *ø* is like *eu* in French "deux"; *å* has
the vowel sound of "awe"; *y* is like the French *u* in "lune"; *o* is frequently
like *oo; d* is usually mute before *s* and after *n* and *l,* and also when in final
position after *r; g* is usually hard as in "go", but before *j* and *y* has the sound
of consonantal *y;* in the word *jeg* ("I") the *g* forms a diphthong pronounced
somewhere between the diphthongs in English "pay" and "pie"; *j* has the
sound of English *y,* either consonantal or, after a vowel, vocalic; *k* before *i, j*
or *y* is softened to a sound like the German *ch* in "ich", almost like *sh*.

Swedish is perhaps the most sonorous of the Scandinavian languages. As   Swedish
in Norwegian, there are differences between the colloquial language, Tal-
språk, which is often influenced by dialects, and the written or official
language, Riksspråk. In southern Sweden a certain Danish influence can be
detected; in the west and north-west the language shows affinities with
Norwegian.

Pronunciation: *ä* is an open *eh* sound; *ö* is much like Norwegian *ø; a* and
y much the same as in Norwegian; *o* is sometimes like *oo; u* is almost the
same as *y; c* before *e, i* or *y* is pronounced *s,* otherwise *k; ch* before *e, i, y, ä*
or *ö* is like *sh;* in *och* ("and") the *ch* is pronounced *k; d* before *j* at the
beginning of a syllable is mute; *f* at the end of a syllable is pronounced *v; g*
before *ä, e, i, ö* and *y* and after *l* and *r* is like consonantal *y,* as is *gj* before *o*
and *u; k* before *æ, e, i, ö* and *y* and in the combination *kj* has a sound almost
like English *ch; lj* is like consonantal *y; sj* is pronounced *sh; sk, skj* and *stj*
(sti) before *æ, e, i, ö* and *y* are like *sh,* and *tj* before these vowels like *ch.*

Language

Finnish has no relationship to the other Scandinavian languages. It has two main dialects, West Finnish and East Finnish, which are broken up into a number of sub-dialects. Some 6% of the population of Finland, particularly on the south and south-west coasts, speak Swedish.

Finnish is a language of many vowels. It has an alphabet of 21 letters; *b, c, d, f, g, w, x* and *z* are found only in foreign words or proper names.

With a few exceptions, the pronunciation corresponds to the spelling. The stress is always on the first syllable; in words of more than three syllables the third, fifth and seventh syllables – but never the last syllable – have a lighter stress. Single vowels are short (*y* being pronounced like French *u*); double vowels are very long. In a sequence of two vowels in which the second one is *i* the first vowel has a light stress. The letter *h* after a vowel and before a consonant is pronounced like the *ch* in "loch". Double consonants do not shorten the preceding vowel as in English, but are themselves given double length or pronounced with particular distinctness.

There is no definite article in Finnish.

Numbers and Time

Cardinal Numbers	Norwegian	Swedish	Finnish
0	null	noll	nolla
1	en, ett	en, ett	yksi
2	to	två	kaksi
3	tre	tre	kaksi
4	fire	fyra	neljä
5	fem	fem	viisi
6	seks	sex	kussi
7	syv, sju	sju	seitsemän
8	åtte	åtta	kahdeksan
9	ni	nio, nie	yhdeksän
10	ti	tio, tie	kymmenen
11	elleve	elva	yksitoista
12	tolv	tolv	kaksitoista
13	tretten	tretton	kolmetoista
14	fjorten	fjorton	neljätoista
15	femten	femton	viisitoista
16	seksten	sexton	kuusitoista
17	sytten	sjutton	seitsemäntoista
18	atten	aderton	kahdeksantoista
19	nitten	nitton	yhdeksäntoista
20	tjue, tyve	tjugo	kaksikymmentä
21	tjue en	tjugo en	kaksikymmentäyski
22	tjue to	tjugo två	kaksikymmentäkaksi
30	tretti	trettio	kolmekymmentä
40	førti	fyrtio	neljäkymmentä
50	femti	femtio	viisikymmentä
60	seksti	sextio	kuusikymmentä
70	sytti	sjuttio	seitsemänkymmentä
80	åtti	åttio	kahdeksankymmentä
90	nitti	nittio	yhdeksänkymmentä
100	hundre	hundra	sata
101	hundre og en	hundra en	satayksi

Cardinal Numbers	Norwegian	Swedish	Finnish
200	to hundre	två hundra	kaksisataa
300	tre hundre	tre hundra	kolmesataa
1000	tusen	tusen	tuhat

Ordinal Numbers

1st	første	förste	ensimmäinen
2nd	annen	andre	toinen
3rd	tredje	tredje	kolmas

Fractions

½	en halv	en halv	puoli
⅓	en tredjedel	en tredjedel	kolmasosa

Months

January	januar	januari	tammikuu
February	februar	februari	helmikuu
March	mars	mars	maaliskuu
April	april	april	huhtikuu
May	mai	maj	toukokuu
June	juni	juni	kesäkuu
July	juli	juli	heinäkuu
August	august	augusti	elokuu
September	september	september	sysskuu
October	oktober	oktober	lokakuu
November	november	november	marraskuu
December	desember	december	joulukuu

Days of Week

Sunday	søndag	söndag	sunnuntai
Monday	mandag	måndag	maanantai
Tuesday	tirsdag	tisdag	tiistai
Wednesday	onsdag	onsdag	keskiviiko
Thursday	torsdag	torsdag	torstai
Friday	fredag	fredag	perjantai
Saturday	lørdag	lördag	lauantai

Useful Words and Phrases

English	Norwegian	Swedish	Finnish
Britain	Storbritannia	Storbritannien	Iso-Britannia
British	britisk	britisk	brittiläinen
England	England	Englanti	
English	engelsk	engelsk	englantilainen
Scotland	Skottland	Skottland	Skotlanti
Scottish	skotsk	skotsk	skotlantilainen
Wales	Wales	Wales	Wales
Welsh	valisisk	valisisk	
Ireland	Irland	Irland	Irlanti
Irish	irsk	irsk	irlantilainen
United States	De Forente Stater	Förenta Staterna	Yhdysvallat
American	amerikansk	amerikansk	amerikkalainen
Canada	Canada	Kanada	Kanada
Denmark	Danmark	Danmark	Tanska
Danish	dansk	dansk	tanskalainen

Language

English	Norwegian	Swedish	Finnish
Finland	Finland	Finland	Suomi
Finnish	finsk	finsk	suomalainen
Norway	Norge	Norge	Norja
Norwegian	norsk	norsk	norjalainen
Sweden	Sverige	Sverige	Ruotsi
Swedish	svensk	svensk	ruotsalainen
do you speak . . . English?	snakker De . . . engelsk?	talar ni . . . engelska?	puhutteko . . . englantia?
I don't understand	Jeg forstår ikke	Jag förstår inte	En ymmärrä
yes	ja, jo	ja (ha), jo, ju	niin, kyllä
no	nei	nej, nej då	en, ei
please	vær så god	var så god	oikaa hyvä
excuse me	unnskyld	ursäkta mig förlåt	pyydän ankteesi
thank you	takk	tack	kiitos
thank you very much	mange takk	tack så mycket	kiitoksia paljon
good morning	god morgen	god morgon	hyvää huomenta
good day	god dag	god dag	hyvää päivää
good evening	god aften	god afton	hyvää iltaa
good night	god natt	god natt	hyvää yöta
goodbye	farvel	adjö, hej då	näkemiin
man	herre	herre	herra
woman, lady	dame	dam, kvinna	nainen, rouva
girl	trøken	fröken	neiti
where is . . .	hvor er . . .	var är . . .	missä on . . .
. . . Street	. . . gaten	. . . gatan	. . . katu
. . . Square	. . . plassen	. . . platsen, torget	. . . tori
the way to . . .	veien til . . .	vägen till . . .	tie . . .
the church	kirken	kyrkan	kirkko
the museum	museum, museet	museum, museet	museo
the town hall	rådhuset	rådhuset	kaupungintalo
the post office	postkontoret	postkontoret	postikonttori
postage stamp	frimerke	frimärke	postimerkki
the station	jernbane-stasjonen	järnvägs-stationen	rautatieasema
a bank	bank	bank	pankki
a hotel	hotell	hotell	hotelli
accommodation	overnatting	övernatting	yöpyä
I should like	jeg ville gjerne ha	jag skulle vilja ha	haluaisin mielelläni
a room	et værelse	ett rum	huoneen
with one bed (single room)	med en seng	med en bädd (enkelrum)	yhden hengen huone
with two beds (double room)	med to senger	med två bädder (dubbelrum)	kahder hengen huone
with bath	med bad	med bad	kypyhuoneella
without a bath	uten bad	utan bad	ilman kylpä
the lavatory	toalettet	toaletten	vessa
the key	nøkkelen	nyckelen	avain
a doctor	lege	läkare, doktor	lääkäri
when?	når?	när?	milloin?
open	åpen/åpet	öppen/öppet	avoinna
right	til høyre	till höger	oikealla
left	til venstre	till vänster	vasemmalla

English	Norwegian	Swedish	Finnish
straight ahead	rett fram	rakt fram	souraan eteenpäin
above	oppe, ovenpå	uppe, ovanpå	ylhäälä, päällä
below	nede	nedanför, nere	alhaalla, alapuolella
old	gammel	gammal	vanha
new	ny	ny	uusi
what does it cost?	hva koster?	vad kostar?	paljonko maksaa?
dear	dyr	dyr	kallis
newspaper	avis, blad	tidning	(sanoma)lehti

Road Signs and Warnings

Stop	Stopp	Stopp, Halt	Stopp, Seis
Customs	Toll	Tull	Tulli
Caution	Pas på	Se upp, Giv akt	Varokaa
Slow	Sakte	Sakta	Hitaasti, Hiljaa
One-way street	Envegskjøring	Enkelriktad	Yksisuuntainen liikenne
No entry	Gjennomkjøring forbudt	Infart förbjuden	Läpikulku kielletty
Road works	Veiarbeid	Vägarbete, Gatuarbete	Tietyö, Katutyo

Motoring Terms

air	luft	luft	ilma
battery	batteri	batteri	paristo, akku
brake	bremse	broms	jarru
breakdown	motorstopp	motorstopp	konerikko
car	bil	bil	auto
carburettor	forgasser	förgasare	kaasutin
cylinder	sylinder	cylinder	sylinteri
driving licence	førerkort	körkort	ajokortti
fuse	sikring	säkring	proppu
garage (for repairs)	bilverksted	bilverkstad	autokorjaamo
headlight	lys	strålkastare	valonheittäjä
horn	signalhorn	signalhorn, tuta	autotorvi, sireeni
ignition	tenning	tändning	sytytys
indicator	blinklys	blinkljus	vilkkuri
motorcycle	motorsykkel	motorcykel	motska
oil	olje	olja	öljy
oil change	skifte olje	oljebyte	vaihtaa öljy
parking place	parkeringplass	parkeringplats	pysäköintipaikka
petrol	bensin	bensin	bensiini
petrol station	bensinstasjon	bensinstation	bensiiniasema
puncture	punktering	punktering	
radiator	kjøler	kylare	jäähdyttäjä
spare part	reservedel	reservdel	varaosa
sparking plug	tennplugg	tändstift	tulppa
tow away	ta på slep	ta på släp	hinata
tyre	ring	däck	rengas
valve	ventil	ventil	venttiili
wash	vaske	tvätta	pestä
wheel	hjul	hjul	pyörä
windscreen wiper	vinduspusser	vindrutetorkare	tuulilasin pyyhkijä

Glossary of Geographical Terms

Norwegian

ås	hill ridge
bakke	hill
berg	hill, mountain
bre, bræ	glacier plateau
bru	bridge
by	town
dal	valley
elv	river
ferje	ferry
fjell	mountain, fell
fonn	snowfield (névé)
foss	waterfall
gate	street
gjel	ravine, mountain pass
hage	garden, park
hammer	promontory
hø, høi	peak
jernbane	railway
jøkul	glacier
juv	gorge, ravine
kirke	church
kleiv, klev	rock wall
klint	cliff
koll, kolle	knoll, rounded hilltop
landevei	country road
li, lid	hillside
myr	moorland
nut	mountain, peak
øy	island
plass	square
rådhus	town hall
skarv	rocky mountain
skog	wood
slott	castle
strand	beach, coast
sump	bog, marsh
sund	sound, channel
tårn	tower
tind	peak, pinnacle
torg	(market) square
vann, vatn	water, lake
vei	road
vidda	high plateau

Swedish

å	stream, small river
älv	river
ås	hill ridge
backe	hill
berg	hill
bergvägg	rock face
bro	bridge
dal	valley
färja	ferry
fjäll	mountain, fell
fors	waterfall
gata	street

glaciär	glacier
höjd	peak
järnväg	railway
kärr	bog, marsh
klint	cliff
klyfte	gorge, ravine
kulle	hill
kyrka	church
landsväg	country road
mosse	moorland
myr	moorland
ö	island
plan	square
plats	square
rådhus	town hall
skog	wood
skreva	gorge, ravine
slott	castle
spets	peak, pinnacle
stad	town
strand	beach, coast
sund	sound, channel
topp	peak
torg	(market) square
torn	tower
träsk	bog, marsh
trädgård	garden, park
väg	road
vatten	water, lake

Finnish

harju	hill ridge
huippu	peak
joki	river
kallio	rock face
katu	street
kauppatori	market square
kaupungintalo	town hall
kaupunki	town
kirkko	church
koski	rapids
laakso	valley
lautta	ferry
linna	castle
lossi	ferry
maantie	country road
mäki	hill
metsä	wood
puisto, puutarha	garden, park
ranta	beach, coast
rautatie	railway
saari	island
salmi	sound, channel
selkä	hill ridge
silta	bridge
suo	moorland
tie	road
tori	square
torni	tower
tunturi	hill

vaara	hill
vesi	water, lake
vuori	hill

Food and Drink

See entry

Maps

In addition to the general map of Scandinavia at the end of this guide it is helpful, particularly for visitors travelling by car, to have more detailed maps on larger scales. The following is a selection.

Scandinavia

AA/Baedeker: Scandinavia, 1:750,000

AA Road Map: 1:1,500,000

Bartholomew World Travel Map: Scandinavia, 1:2,500,000

Cappelens Bilatlas Norden (in book form): 1:500,000

GeoCenter International: Scandinavia, 1:2,000,000

Kümmerly + Frey: Scandinavia North and South (double map), 1:1,000,000
Scandinavia North, 1:1,000,000
Scandinavia South, 1:1,000,000

Hallwag: South Scandinavia, 1:1,000,000

Lantmäteriet, Gävle: Scandinavia, 1:2,000,000

Norway

Hallwag: Norway, 1:1,000,000

Kümmerly + Frey: Norway, 1:1,000,000
Regional Maps (5 sheets), 1:325,000 and 1:400,000

Cappelen: Regional Maps (5 sheets), 1:325,000

Terrac: Norge (7 sheets), 1:300,000

Sweden

Hallwag: Sweden, 1,000,000

Kümmerly + Frey: Sweden (double map), 1: 800,000
Regional Maps (8 sheets), 1:300,000 and
1:400,000

Terrac: Sverige (8 sheets), 1:300,000

Finland

Bartholomew/RV: Finland, 1:800,000

Hallwag: Finland, 1:1,000,000

Kümmerly + Frey: Finland, 1:1,000,000
Regional Maps (3 sheets), 1:400,000

Lascelles: Finland, 1:800,000

Terrac: Suomi, 1:1,000,000

Medical Aid and Chemists

Norway, Sweden and Finland have reciprocal health agreements with Britain under which British citizens can get certain services free and can obtain reimbursement of part of the cost of other services. Even so it is worth while taking out comprehensive insurance cover before leaving home; and citizens of countries which have no reciprocal health agreement should certainly do so.

Under the reciprocal health agreement hospital in-patient treatment and ambulance travel are provided free. Doctors and dentists are paid in cash. Some of the cost of treatment at a hospital or doctor's surgery may be reimbursed. When seeking treatment a UK passport must be produced; a receipt for any payment should be obtained, and this should be taken, along with the passport, to the local social insurance office (*trygdekasse*). Reimbursement must be claimed before leaving Norway.
    The telephone numbers of doctors are shown on the second page of local telephone directories under the heading Legevakten; dentists under Tannleger.
    Hospital = *sykehus* or *sjukehus,* health centre = *helsestasjon.*
    Chemists' shops (*apoteker*) are open at normal times.

Norway

Under the reciprocal health agreement on admission to hospital or at a doctors, a fee is payable in addition to some medicine charges. When seeking treatment a UK passport must be produced.
    Hospital = *sjukhus,* casualty department = *akutmottagning, doctor = läkare,* dentist = *tandläkare.*
    For medical aid in emergency and emergency doctor dial 9 00 00; for an emergency dentist (in Stockholm) dial 44 92 00.
    Chemists' shops (*apoteker*) are open at normal times, and in the larger towns also at weekends.

Sweden

On presentation of a UK passport visitors can obtain free treatment in doctors' surgeries and restricted charges for medicine and hospital treatment on the same basis as Finnish citizens.
    In a medical emergency for an ambulance dial 112; for a house visit by a doctor dial 008.
    Pharmacies (*apteekki*) are open at normal times, some stay open later; some provide an out-of-hours service.

Finland

N.B. Chemists (*kemikaalikauppa*) only sell cosmetics.

Midnight Sun

North of the Arctic Circle (latitude 66°33' north) the sun remains above the horizon for a number of days in the year which increases towards the North Pole. See Sights from A to Z, Arctic Circle.

Motoring in Scandinavia

Rule of the road	In Norway, Sweden and Finland traffic goes on the right, with overtaking on the left. At junctions and intersections of roads of equal status vehicles coming from the right have priority. Trams always have priority.
Parking	Parking is prohibited on all main roads marked as having priority. In Norway, particularly in the larger towns, there is a general ban on parking except in marked parking-places with meters.
Lights	Dipped headlights must be used even during the day.
City tolls	In Norway cars entering the city limits of Oslo, Bergen and Trondheim must pay tolls (*bompenger*) of 5 or 10 kr.
Traffic signs	The usual international traffic signs are in use in all the Scandinavian countries, but there are some special signs not found elsewhere (e.g. a white M on a blue ground, indicating a passing place on a narrow road; Indkørsel Forbudt = No Entry). Leaflets showing the traffic signs in use can be obtained from motoring organisations.
Seat-belts	The wearing of seat-belts is obligatory.
Use of horn	The use of the horn should be kept to a minimum.
Blood alcohol	The blood alcohol limit is 0.05% in Norway and Finland, 0.02% in Sweden. There are severe penalties for driving with excess alcohol.
Speed limits	Norway: motorways 90kph/56mph, ordinary roads 80kph/50mph, built-up areas 50kph/31mph, cars with trailers 80kph/50mph (braked), 60kph/37mph (unbraked)
	Sweden: motorways 110kph/65mph, ordinary roads 90kph/55mph or 70kph/43mph, built-up areas 50kph/31mph, cars with trailers 70kph/43mph (braked), 40kph/25mph (unbraked)
	Finland: motorways 120kph/75mph, ordinary roads 80kph/50mph, built-up areas 50kph/31mph, cars with trailers 80kph/50mph (braked), 50kph/31mph (unbraked)
	There are heavy penalties on exceeding the speed limit.
Spiked or studded tyres	Spiked or studded tyres may be used in Scandinavia during the winter months: in Norway from Oct. 15th to Apr. 30th, in Sweden from Nov. 1st to the first Monday after the Easter Holiday, in southern and central Finland from Oct. 16th to Apr. 15th, in northern Finland from Oct. 1st to Apr. 30th.
Winter tyres	The use of winter tyres is obligatory throughout Finland in December, January and February.

Breakdown Assistance

Norway	The Norwegian motoring club, Norges Automobil-Forbund (NAF), has road patrols operating a limited service from approximately June 20th to August 20th. All patrols are equipped with mobile telephones, but since each patrol has to cover an extensive stretch of road a motorist should not rely on getting help. If unable to obtain local assistance, therefore, the nearest NAF centre should be contacted: Oslo: tel. 22 60 73 27 Bergen: tel. (05) 29 24 62 Stavanger: tel. (04) 58 25 00 24hr emergency service: 51 58 25 00

The Oslo centre operates a 24-hour service, the regional centres from 6am to 10pm.

The Swedish motoring organisation, Motormännens Riksförbund (M), which is allied to the AA, operates a limited road service on main (E) roads during the summer months. There are also Alarm Centres run by Larmtjänst AB (Alarm Services Ltd), open day and night (English-speaking): tel. (020) 91 00 40 (free phone).

Sweden

The AA is associated with Autolitto, the Automobile and Touring Club of Finland (ATCF), which operates a voluntary patrol service at weekends and on public holidays. Assistance can be obtained from anywhere in Finland by dialling (90) 77 47 61.

Finland

From Monday to Friday, 24 hours a day, the ATCF operates an English-speaking enquiry service which provides information about garages, towing and lock and windscreen services

The new AA Continental Emergency Centre has been established at Lyon in France.

AA Continental Emergency Centre

Motoring Organisations

Norges Automobil-Forbund (NAF)
Storgate 2
N–0155 Oslo
tel. 22 34 14 00, fax 22 33 13 73

Norway

Kongelig Norsk Automobilclub (KNA)
Drammensveien 20C
N–0254 Oslo
tel. 22 56 19 00

Motormännens Riksförbund (M)
Box 5855
S–10248 Stockholm
tel. (08) 7 82 38 00
fax (08) 6 63 89 21

Sweden

Kungliga Automobil-Klubben (KAK)
Gyllenstiernsgatan 4
S–11526 Stockholm
tel. (08) 6 60 00 55
fax (08) 6 62 74 84

Trafiksäkerhetsverket
S–78186 Borläge
tel. (0243) 7 80 00
fax (0243) 7 82 20

MHF
Box 476
S–12604 Hägersten
tel. (08) 7 44 88 00, fax (08) 7 44 88 35

Autolitto
Kansakoulukatu 10
FIN–00101 Helsinki
tel. (90) 6 94 00 22
fax (90) 6 93 25 78

Finland

See entry

Emergencies

See entry

Petrol

See entry

Roads

Safety and
Security

See entry

Museums

The most important museums in Norway, Sweden and Denmark are mentioned in the entries for the various towns in the "Sights from A to Z" section of this guide.

It is advisable to enquire of local tourist information offices (see Information) about current opening times.

National Parks

National Parks are specially designated areas, under state management, in which the natural landscape with its flora and fauna is as far as possible left undisturbed. There are numerous National Parks in Norway, Sweden and Finland, offering a variety of interest for nature-lovers and walkers, with ski trekking in the fell regions in winter. In some of them accommodation is available in huts or cabins.

In northern Scandinavia there are very marked differences between the seasons. The *ruska* period when plants take on their autumn colouring usually begins in Lapland in the second week in September.

National Parks
in Norway

1 Øvre Pasvik
(63sq.km/24½sq. miles; Finnmark)

2 Stabbursdalen
(96sq.km/37sq. miles; Finnmark)

3 Øvre Anarjåkka
(1290sq.km/498sq. miles; Finnmark)

4 Reisadalen
(803sq.km/310sq. miles; Troms)

5 Ånderdalen
(68sq.km/26sq. miles; Troms)

6 Øvre Dividalen
(741sq.km/286sq. miles; Troms)

7 Rago
(171sq.km/66sq. miles; Nordland)

8 Saltfjell
(2250sq.km/869sq. miles; Nordland)

9 Børgefjell
(1087sq.km/420sq. miles; Nordland)

10 Gressåmoen
(180sq.km/69sq. miles; Nord-Trøndelag)

11 Fremundsmarka
(385sq.km/149sq. miles; Hedmark)

12 Gutulia
(19sq.km/7sq. miles; Hedmark)

National Parks
in Scandinavia

National Parks

13 Dovrefjell
   (265sq.km/102sq. miles; Oppland)

14 Rondane
   (572sq.km/221sq. miles; Oppland)

15 Jotunheim
   (1140sq.km/440sq. miles; Oppland and Sogn og Fjordane)

16 Hardangervidda
   (3430sq.km/1324sq. miles; Hordaland, Telemark and Buskerud)

17 Ormtjernkampen
   (9sq.km/3½sq. miles; Oppland)

National Parks
in Sweden

18 Vadvetjåkko
   (26sq.km/10sq. miles; Lapland)

19 Abisko
   (77sq.km/30sq. miles; Lapland)

20 Stora Sjöfall
   (1380sq.km/533sq. miles; Lapland)

21 Sarek
   (1940sq.km/749sq. miles; Lapland)

22 Padjelanta
   (2010sq.km/776sq. miles; Lapland)

23 Muddus
   (493sq.km/190sq. miles; Lapland)

In Tiveden National Park: Fagertärn, with water-lillies

24 Paljekaise
(153sq.km/59sq. miles; Lapland)

25 Skuleskogen
(25sq.km/9½sq. miles; Ångermanland)

26 Töfsingdalen
(16sq.km/6sq. miles; Dalarna)

27 Sånfjäll
(104sq.km/40sq. miles; Härjedalen)

28 Hamra
(0.3sq.km/0.1sq. mile; Dalarna)

29 Ängsö
(0.7sq.km/0.3sq. mile; Uppland)

30 Garphyttan
(1.1sq.km/0.4sq. mile; Närke)

31 Tiveden
(13.6sq.km/5.3sq. miles; Närke)

32 Norra Kvill
(0.3sq.km/0.1sq. mile; Småland)

33 Gotska Sandön
37sq.km/14sq. miles; Gotland)

34 Blå Jungfrun
0.7sq.km/0.3sq. mile; Småland)

35 Stora Mosse
(77.6sq.km/30sq. miles; Småland)

36 Stenshuvud
(3.9sq.km/1.5sq. miles; Skåne)

37 Dalby Söderskog
(0.4sq.km/0.15sq. miles; Skåne)

38 Lemmenjoki
(2855sq.km/1102sq. miles; Lapland)

39 Urho Kekkonen National Park
(2550sq.km/985sq. miles; Lapland)

40 Pallas-Ounastunturi
(506sq.km/195sq. miles; Lapland)

41 Pyhätunturi
(42sq.km/16sq. miles; Lapland)

42 Oulanka
(269sq.km/104sq. miles; Oulu)

43 Riisitunturi
(77sq.km/30sq. miles; Lapland)

44 Rokua
(4sq.km/1½sq. miles; Oulu)

45 Hiidenportti
(43sq.km/17sq. miles; Oulu)

46 Tiilikkajärvi
(25sq.km/10sq. miles; Kuopio)

47 Patvinsuo
(100sq.km/39sq. miles; Northern Karelia)

48 Petkeljärvi
(6sq.km/2½sq. miles; Northern Karelia)

49 Salamajärvi
(60sq.km/23sq. miles; Central Finland)

50 Pyhä-Häkki
(12sq.km/4½sq. miles; Central Finland)

51 Lauhanvuori
(26sq.km/10sq. miles; Vaasa)

52 Kauhaneva-Pohjankangas
(32sq.km/12sq. miles; Vaasa)

53 Helvetinjärvi
(22sq.km/8½sq. miles; Häme)

54 Seitseminen
(41sq.km/16sq. miles; Häme)

55 Isojärvi
(19sq.km/7½sq. miles; Häme)

56 Linnansaari
(28sq.km/11sq. miles; Mikkeli)

57 Liesjärvi
(17sq.km/6½sq. miles; Häme)

58 Kolovesi
(23sqkm/9sq. miles; Savo)

59 Torronsuo
(26sq.km/10sq. miles; Häme)

60 Eastern Gulf of Finland
(5sq.km/2sq. miles; Kymi)

61 Tammisaari-Ekenäs Skerries
(39sq.km/15sq. miles; South-Western Finland)

62 South-Western Skerries
(17sq.km/6½sq. miles; south of Turku)

Newspapers and Periodicals

The principal British newspapers and periodicals and the European edition of the "Herald-Tribune" are usually available during the season on the evening of the day of publication or on the following day.

Major newspapers in the Scandinavian countries have a brief news summary in English.

The newspapers with the largest circulations are "Aftenposten" in Norway, "Dagens Nyheter" in Sweden and "Hufvudstadsbladet" in Finland.

Opening Times

See Business Hours

Petrol

Petrol is relatively dear in the Scandinavian countries. Petrol in spare cans can be taken into Norway duty free; in Sweden and Finland duty is payable.

Lead-free (Norwegian and Swedish *blyfri*) petrol, 95 and/or 98 octane, is available at all filling stations in Norway and Sweden. In Finland diesel vehicles can fill up with duty-free heating oil (*polttoöljy*).   Lead-free petrol
   Information from motoring organisations and tourist information offices.

Postal Services

Postage, letters up to 20 g and postcards: inland 3.20 kr, Europe 4 kr   Norway
   Opening times of post offices: Mon.–Fri. 8 or 8.30am to 4 or 5pm, Sat. 8am–1pm

Postage, letters up to 20 g and postcards: inland 2.50 kr, Europe 4 kr   Sweden
   Opening times of post offices: Mon.–Fri. 9am–6pm, Sat. 9am–noon

Postage, letters up to 50 g and postcards: Scandinavia 2.10 mk, Europe (up   Finland
to 20 g) 2.90 mk
   Opening times of post offices: Mon.–Fri. 9am–5pm; closed Sat.

Public Holidays

The Scandinavians take full advantage of their public holidays. Many shops and offices also close on the day before a holiday or are open only in the morning.
   The following are the statutory public holidays in Norway, Sweden and Finland:

January 1st   Norway
Maundy Thursday
Good Friday
Easter Monday
May 1st
May 17th (National Day)
Ascension Day
Whit Monday
December 25th and 26th

January 1st   Sweden
January 6th
Good Friday
Easter Monday
Labour Day May 1st
Ascension Day
Whit Monday
All Saints (last Saturday in October or first Saturday in November)
December 24th to 26th
New Year's Eve

Radio and Television

Finland
January 1st
January 6th or following Saturday (Epiphany)
Good Friday
Easter Monday
May Day Eve and May Day Apr. 30th–May 1st
Ascension Day
Whitsun May 30th
All Saints (last Saturday in October or first Saturday in November)
December 6th (Independence Day)
December 24th to 26th

Midsummer
Midsummer Day is celebrated in Norway, Sweden and Finland on the second-last Friday/Saturday in June.

Radio and Television

The Scandinavian broadcasting organisations have regular radio programmes in English (mainly news). Films shown on television are usually in the original language, with subtitles. Of interest to visitors are the weather forecasts after the evening television news programmes, which use internationally understood symbols such as the sun, clouds or an umbrella (note that H in Norwegian or Swedish and K in Finnish mean an area of high pressure, L in Norwegian or Swedish and M in Finnish low pressure).

Railways

Rail travel in Scandinavia is a pleasure. The coaches are modern, clean and tidy. The railway network is not particularly dense, but is supplemented by bus and boat services, providing good connections to all parts of Scandinavia.

Scanrail Card
The Scanrail Card (Nord-Turist Railpass) is a monthly ticket which entitles visitors to discount rail travel in Norway, Sweden, Denmark and Finland and to discounts on certain ferry routes.

Norway

Norway's railway system, run by the Norwegian State Railways (Norges Statsbaner, NSB) is relatively thin on the ground. The principal lines are from Oslo to Stavanger (via Kristiansand), Bergen, Åndalsnes, Trondheim (via Dombås or Røros) and Bodø (with bus connection to Kirkenes).

Bodø is the most northerly station in the Norwegian system. The only railway line farther north is the Swedish State Railways line from Narvik to Sweden. There is thus no direct link between Bodø and Narvik.

Particular scenic attractions are offered by the Bergen, Dovre, Nordland and Flåm lines.

Seat reservation tickets are required on express trains. Such trains do not carry bicycles.

Reductions
There are 10% reductions for groups of 2 to 9 persons, 25% reductions for groups of 10 or more, "mini-prices" valid on less busy days, 50% reduction for senior citizens (over 67) and 50% reduction for holders of Rail Europ card (over 60).

Information
Norwegian State Railways
21–24 Cockspur Street
London SW1Y 5DA
tel. (0171) 930 6666, fax (0171) 321 0624

Scandinavia
Railways
—— Main lines
—— Branch lines

Hammerfest
Kirkenes
Tromsø
Narvik
Kiruna
Bodø
Arctic Circle
Rovaniemi
Luleå
Oulu
SWEDEN
FINLAND
Vaasa
Trondheim
Sundsvall
Tampere
NORWAY
HELSINKI
ÅLAND
ISLANDS
Turku
Bergen
OSLO
STOCKHOLM
Stavanger
Karlstad
GOTLAND
Göteborg
DENMARK
Ålborg
ÖLAND
Århus
KØBEN-
HAVN
Malmö
Odense
BORNHOLM

© Baedeker

Norwegian State Railways (NSB: Norges Statsbanen)
NSB Reisesenter, Oslo Sentralstasjon
N–0154 Oslo
tel. 22 36 80 00, fax 22 36 64 84

Sweden

Swedish State Railways (Svenska Statens Järnvägar, SJ) provides an efficient network of train services, mostly electrified, covering the whole country.
Single tickets are valid for 15 days, returns for 30 days.

Reductions
Two children under 12 accompanied by adults travel free; other children under 16 pay half fare. There is a reduction of 25% for groups of 10 or more. On certain services (*röd avgång*, "red departure"), marked with a red symbol in the timetable, there is a 50% reduction in the fare.

Motorail
Motorail car-sleeper services are operated from the beginning of June to the beginning of August on the long-distance routes from Malmö and Göteborg to Kiruna and Luleå.

Special services
Inlandsbanan: Kristinehamn to Gällivare (beginning of June to August); ticket valid 14 days.
Lapplandspilen: Malmö to Narvik (daily in July and August, at weekends only in the months before and after).
Nordpilen: Stockholm to Narvik (daily).

Information
Norwegian State Railways office in London (see above)

Finland

Finnish State Railways (Valtion Rautatiet, VR) run fast and efficient services on the main north–south routes and between Helsinki and Turku; east–west services are fewer in number and less frequent.

Reductions
Senior citizens can buy a Senior Citizen's railcard entitling them to a 50% reduction on the ordinary fare. Up to two children under 6 accompanied by an adult travel free; children from 6 to 17 pay half fare. Groups of at least 3 people, including one paying the full adult fare, get a reduction of 20%, groups of 10 or more 20–50%.
The Finnrail Pass, which must be obtained before arriving in Finland, allows unlimited travel for 3, 5 or 10 days.
Other international reductions are available to holders of a Rail Europ card (senior citizens), Interrail card, Eurail pass, Eurail Youth pass, Eurail Flexipass, Eurail Drive pass or Scanrail card and to groups of students and schoolchildren.

Sleeping cars
There are sleeping cars daily on the following lines, in both directions: Helsinki to Joensuu, Kontiomäki, Oulu, Savonlinna (summer only), Kemijärvi, Kuopio and Rovaniemi; and Turku to Rovaniemi and Kuopio.

Motorail
There are Motorail services between Helsinki and Oulu, Kolari, Kontiomäki and Rovaniemi, between Tampere and Rovaniemi and Kolari, and between Turku and Rovaniemi.

There are twice-daily services from Helsinki to St Petersburg and Moscow in Russia.

Information
Finnish State Railways
Vilhonkatu 13
FIN–00101 Helsinki
tel. (90) 70 71, fax (90) 7 07 37 00

Information and booking from abroad:
VR Matkapalvelu
(Finnish State Railways Ticket Office)
Rautatieasema
FIN–00100 Helsinki
tel. (90) 7 07 25 56, fax (90) 7 07 41 77

Restaurants (A Selection)

See Food and Drink

General

If you want alcohol with your meal you should check whether the restaurant has a licence to serve alcohol – either a full licence or one that allows them to serve only wine and beer.

Restaurants in Norwegian hotels are open to non-residents as well as residents. Thus holidaymakers living in a hut or cabin who do not want to cater for themselves can have their evening meal in a hotel restaurant.

Norway

Most restaurants in Sweden serve a fixed-price meal (the *dagens rätt,* "dish of the day") between 11am and 2pm. In addition to the main course this includes a salad, a soft drink and coffee.

Sweden

Three "gourmet routes" through Lapland have been organised under the designation "Lappi à la carte". An information leaflet is available from the Finnish Tourist Board.

Finland

Brasserie Normandie, in Hotel Rica Parken, Storgate 16, tel. 70 12 50 50; China City, Parkgate, tel. 70 12 91 26; Fjellstua, on the Aksla, tel. 70 12 65 82; Gullix Bistro, Rådhusgate 5B, tel. 70 12 05 48; Hydranten Kro, in Hotel Rica Skansen, Kongensgate 27, tel. 70 12 29 38; Sjøbua Fish Restaurant, Brunholmgate 1, tel. 70 12 71 00.
Cafés: Kafé Vesle Kari, Apotekergate 2, tel. 70 12 84 04; Kafé Balkongen, in Kremmergaarden shopping centre, tel. 70 12 25 80.

Ålesund
(Norway)

Bellevue (on hillside with panoramic views of hills; 10 min. by taxi or bus from city centre), Bellevuebakken 9, tel. 55 31 02 40; Bryggeloftet and Bryggestuen, both Bryggen 11, tel. 55 31 06 30; Bryggen Tracteursted (oldest inn in Norway; Norwegian cuisine), Bryggen, tel. 55 31 40 46; Caroline (main railway station), tel. 55 31 96 76; China Palace (Chinese cuisine and lobsters), Strandgate 2, tel. 55 32 66 55; Enhjørningen (fish), Bryggen, tel. 55 32 79 19; Fiskekrogen (fish specialities), on Fishmarket, Zachariasbryggen, tel. 55 31 75 66; Holbergstuen, Torgalmenningen 6, tel. 53 31 80 15; Kjøttbørsen (meat dishes), Vaskerelven 6, tel. 55 23 14 59; Michelangelo (Italian), Neumannsgate 25, tel. 55 90 08 25; Spisestedet Kornelia (vegetarian), Fosswinkelsgate 9, tel. 55 32 34 32; Wesselstuen, Engen 14, tel. 55 90 08 20. There are also restaurants in most hotels.
Cafés: Bergenhus, Strandkaien 4, tel. 55 23 09 94; Ervingen, Strandkaien 2, tel. 55 32 30 30; Kløver Café, Kløverhuset, Strandgaten 13, tel. 55 32 21 50; Terminus Café, Zander Kaaesgate 6, tel. 55 31 26 95.

Bergen
(Norway)

Restaurants in Borgholm and Strand Hotels (see Hotels, Öland); also China, tel. (0485) 1 18 68; Glada Katten, tel. 1 18 00; Pizzeria Verona, 1 15 28; Pimo's Pizzabutik, tel. 1 32 50.
Open only in summer: Borgholms Baren, tel. 1 04 53; Herman's, tel. 1 20 20; Robinson Crusoe, tel. 1 17 58.

Borgholm
(Öland; Sweden)

Restaurant in Skansen Hotel (see Hotels, Öland); also Café Sundet, tel. (0485) 3 41 27; Pizzeria Shiponja, tel. 3 07 13; Bo Pensionat (8km/5 miles south of Färjestaden), tel. 3 60 01.
Open only in summer: Bojen (also café), tel. 3 19 37; Restaurant Saxnäs Camping, tel. 3 52 77.

Färjestaden
(Öland; Sweden)

Restaurants

Göteborg
(Sweden)

★Johanna, Södra Hamngatan 47, tel. (031) 11 22 50; ★Råda Säteri, Mölnlycke, tel. 88 48 00; ★Stallgården (French cuisine, etc.), Kyrkogatan 33, tel. 11 59 57; ★Victors, Skeppsbroplatsen 1, tel. 17 41 80; 28+ (cellar restaurant; cheese specialities, fish, wine), Götabergsgatan 28, tel. 20 21 61; Bistro Chez Amis, Parkgatan 7, tel. 11 56 06; Centralens Restaurant (Swedish cuisine), Central Station, tel. 15 20 81; Fiskekrogen (fish), Lilla Torget 1, tel. 13 07 30; Gamle Port (Swedish cuisine), Östra Larmgatan 18, tel. 11 07 02; Janeiro (South American cuisine), Majorsgatan 4, tel. 14 47 14; Källarkrogen (Swedish cuisine), Östra Larmgatan 20, tel. 11 85 40; Långedrågs Värdshus (fish and crustaceans), Talattagatan 14, tel. 29 14 12; Le Chablis (fish restaurant), Aschebergsgatan 22, tel. 20 35 45; Ming (Chinese), Kristinelundsgatan 9, tel. 18 04 79; Räkan (fish and crustaceans), Lorensberggatan 16, tel. 16 98 99; Sjömagasinet (fish and crustaceans), Klippans Kulturreservat, tel. 24 65 10 (★view of Vinga and the sea); Victoria (Swedish cuisine), Viktoriagatan 3, tel. 13 14 02.

Gotland
(Sweden)

See Visby

Helsinki
(Finland)

There are restaurants in most of the hotels listed in this guide (see Hotels). Particularly recommended are those on the top floors of the Vaakuna, Palace and Torni Hotels, from which there are good views of the city.
★Capitol, Kasarmikatu 23, tel. (90) 6 22 15 00; ★Havis Amanda (fish specialities), Unioninkatu 23, tel. 66 68 82; Adlon (also café), Fabianinkatu 14, tel. 66 46 11; Alexander Nevski (Russian cuisine), Pohjoisesplanadi 17, tel. 63 96 10; Amadeus, Sofiankatu 4, tel. 62 66 76; Aurinkotuuli (vegetarian), Lapinlahdenkatu 25, tel. 6 94 25 63; China Garden (Chinese), Eteläesplanadi 4, tel. 66 22 89; Casa Andalucia (Spanish), Töölöntorinkatu 2, tel. 44 13 26; El Greco (Greek), Eteläesplanadi 22, tel. 60 75 65; Empire, Wanha Satama, Mastokatu 4, tel. 17 33 44 51; George, Kalevankatu 17, tel. 64 76 62; Happy Days (with garden restaurant), Pohjoisesplanadi 2, tel. 62 40 23; Kabuki (Japanese), Lapinlahdenkatu 12, tel. 6 94 94 46; Kala Rivoli (crabs, etc.), Albertinkatu 38, tel. 64 34 55; Karelia (Karelian cuisine), Käpylänkuja 1, tel. 79 90 88; Katajonakan Kasino, Laivastokatu 1, tel. 65 34 01; Kluuvi (Food and Fashion) Shopping Center, with several restaurants and cafés, Aleksanterinkatu 9–Kluuvikatu 5; König (cellar restaurant, café and bar), Mikonkatu 4, tel. 17 12 71; Kulosaaren Casino, Hopeasalmenpolku 1, tel. 6 84 82 02; Kultainen Sipuli/Gyllene Löken, Kanavaranta 3, tel. 17 09 00; Mamma Rosa (cellar restaurant), Runeberginkatu 55, tel. 49 90 50; Margona (ship restaurant), Kauppatori, tel. 66 64 41; Mexikana (Mexican cuisine), Pusimiehenkatu 5, tel. 66 67 97; Mikadon Salonglt, Mannerhelmlntie 6, tel. 60 74 63; Ossian (Svenska Klubben), Maurinkatu 6, tel. 62 87 06; Ostrobotnia (Finnish cuisine), Dagmarinkatu 2, tel. 44 69 40; Paprika (Hungarian), Salomonkatu 19, tel. 6 94 90 30; Piekka (Finnish cuisine), Mannerheimintie 68, tel. 49 35 91; Rivoli Chéri (seafood), Albertinkatu 38, tel. 64 34 55; Säkkipilli, Kalevankatu 2, tel. 60 56 07; Savoy, Eteläesplanadi 14, tel. 17 65 71; Valkoinen Valas (fish), Vuorimiehenkatu 3, tel. 66 36 56.
Cafés: Senaatti, Aleksanterinkatu 28, tel. 60 24 62; Socis (café-restaurant), Koivokatu 12, tol. 17 04 11; Torrooo Café (oafé rootaurant), Stockmann, Pohjoisesplanadi 41, tel. 66 55 66; Torpanranta (café-restaurant), Munkkiniemenranta 2, tel. 48 42 50.

Kalmar
(Sweden)

Restaurants in some of the hotels listed (see Hotels); also Calmar Hamnkrog, Skeppsbron 30, tel. (0480) 1 10 20; Costa's Krog, Larmgatan 6, tel. 1 15 70; Matisse, Kaggensgatan 1, tel. 2 72 86.

Lillehammer
(Norway)

Bjørns Kro, Vingnes, tel. 61 25 83 00; Bøndernes Hus, Kirkegate 68, tel. 61 25 30 35; Bryggerikjelleren, Elvegate 19, tel. 61 25 23 30; Fossekroa, Hunderfossen, tel. 61 27 71 65; Jensens Spiseri, Lilletorget 1, tel. 61 25 36 75; Kanten Kro, Olympiaparken, tel. 61 26 29 70; Storgatens Landhandleri, Storgate 40, tel. 61 26 38 25; Strand Kro, Strandgate 11, tel. 61 27 00 51; Terrassen (garden restaurant), Storgate 82–84, tel. 61 25 00 49; Thorvald's

Spiseri, Jernbanegate 3, tel. 61 26 95 00; Victoriastuen, Storgate 84, tel. 61 25 00 49; Vertsjuset Solveig, Storgate 68B, tel. 61 26 27 87.

Restaurants in some of the hotels listed (see Hotels); also Fiskaregatan, L. Fiskaregatan 13, tel. (046) 15 16 20; Saint-Michel, Ö. Martensgatan 15, tel. 11 43 00; Sandra, St. Södergatan 42, tel. 15 72 00.

Lund
(Sweden)

Don Quijote (Spanish), Bergsgatan 10, tel. (040) 97 12 26; Kockska Krogen, Stortorget, tel. 7 03 20; Kronprinsen (also cabaret), Mariedalsvägen 32, tel. 7 72 40; Olgas Restaurang (restaurant, bar, garden), Pildammsvägen, tel. 12 55 26 and 12 85 09; The Golden Days, Stora Nygatan 59, tel. 7 85 85. Café: Maritza, Södergatan 16 (pedestrian zone), tel. 11 06 97.

Malmö
(Sweden)

Åhlens, Kyrkogatan 18, tel. (0250) 1 30 15; China House, Moragatan 1, tel. 1 52 40; King's Inn, Kristinebergsgatan 1, tel. 1 50 70; Lilla Björn, Kyrkogatan 5, tel. 1 16 80; Mastes Pizza Kebab House, Älvgatan 73, tel. 1 83 90; Pizza Primo, Fridhemsplan 2D, tel. 1 20 11; Strand, Strandgatan 11, tel. 1 09 98; Wasa Källjare, Kyrkogatan 31, tel. 1 32 98.

Mora/Lake Siljan
(Sweden)

See Borgholm and Färjestaden

Öland
(Sweden)

Babettes Gjestehus, Rådhuspassasjen, tel. 22 41 64 64; Bagatelle, Bygdøy Allé 3, tel. 22 44 63 97; Brasserie Costa (Italian cuisine), Klingenberggatan 4, tel. 22 42 41 30; Blom (artists' restaurant; with notable interior), Karl Johansgate 41B, tel. 22 42 73 00; Den Lille Havfrue, Oscarsgate 81, tel. 22 55 55 45; Det Blå Kjøkken, Drammensveien 39, tel. 22 44 26 50; Fjordflower Havrestaurant, Stranden 30, Aker Brygge, tel. 22 83 68 97; Frascati Rotisserie, Stortinsgate 20, tel. 22 33 65 85; Gamle Rådhus Restaurant, Nedre Slottsgate 1, tel. 22 42 01 07; Håndverkeren, Rosenkrantzgate 7, tel. 22 42 07 50; La Guitarra (Spanish cuisine), Fredensborgveien 44, tel. 22 20 09 28; Harlekin Mat & Vinhus, Hegdehaugsveien 30B, tel. 22 60 75 90; Le Canard, Oscarsgate 81 (entrance on Frognerveien), tel. 22 43 40 28; Lofotstua, Kirkeveien 40, Majorstua, tel. 2 46 93 96; Mona Lisa, Grensen, tel. 22 42 89 14; Peppe's Pizza (American cuisine), Drammensveien 40, Stortinggate 4, Aker Brygge (and other addresses), tel. 22 55 55 55; Presidenten (French cuisine), President Harbitzgate 4, tel. 22 55 87 70; Romani Tar (Yugoslavian), Pilestredet 17, tel. 22 11 03 34; Smedens Grill, Bernt Ankersgate 4, tel. 22 20 56 28; Spisestedet Feinschmekker, Balchensgate 5, tel. 22 44 17 77; Statholdergården, Rådhusgaten 11, tel. 22 41 88 00; Sydvesten, Kirkegaten 30, tel. 22 42 19 82; The Scotsman, Karl Johansgate 17, tel. 22 42 97 43; Tre Brødre, Øvre Slottsgate 14, tel. 22 42 39 00; Vertshus (vegetarian), Munkedamsveien 3B, tel. 22 83 40 20; Zorbas (Greek), Torggate 32, tel. 22 20 78 56; Warehouse Diner & Music Bar, Stranden 1, Aker Brygge, tel. 22 83 03 30. Viewpoint restaurants with Norwegian cuisine: Frognerseteren, Holmenkollveien 200, tel. 22 14 08 90; Holmenkollen Restaurant, Holmenkollveien 119, tel. 22 14 62 26.
Cafés: Cappuccino, Dronningensgate 27, tel. 22 33 34 30; Grand Café, Karl Johansgate 31, tel. 22 42 93 90; Schous Comer, Trondheimveien 2, tel. 22 20 49 45; Steamen, Stortingsgaten 24–26, tel. 22 41 90 60; Von Angels, Karl Johansgate 41B, tel. 22 42 73 22l. 22 41 90 60; Von Angels, Karl Johansgate 41B, tel. 22 42 73 22.

Oslo
(Norway)

Albert, Isokatu 36, tel. (981) 22 57 11; Arina (also steakhouse), Pakkahuoneenkatu 16, tel. 1 42 21; Hovinarri, Isokatu 35, tel. 1 54 32; Iloinen Tori, Isokatu 18, tel. 1 42 21; Kaarlenholvi, Kauppurienkatu 6, tel. 22 37 75; Merikoski, Merikoskenkatu 2, tel. 34 43 76; Pomfelis, Uusikatu 22, tel. 22 40 64; Zakuska, Hallituskatu 13–17, tel. 22 93 69; Zivago, Saaristonkatu 12, tel. 22 38 86.

Oulu
(Finland)

Andalucia, Mikonkatu 6, tel. (939) 4 10 49; Café Anton (café-restaurant), Antinkatu 11, tel. 41 41 44; Kasari and Kasarinna, Satakunnankatu 33, tel.

Pori
(Finland)

Restaurants

33 48 03; Sarpi Oy Be POP (restaurant on upper floor, café on lower floor of shopping centre), Yrjönkatu 22, tel. 33 64 36.
At Airport: Airport Restaurant, tel. 41 27 57.
On Yyteri beach: Yyteri Restaurant, tel. 34 37 07.
1km/³⁄₄ mile from beach: Kaanaa Café (★view of sea), tel. 34 39 50.
On Reposaari (32km/20 miles NW of Pori): Reposaari, tel. 34 40 44.
38km/24 miles north of Pori: Lankoski Coffee Mill, Lankoski, Merikarvia, tel. 51 41 91.

Savonlinna
(Finland)

Bella Ristorante, Tulliportinkatu 2, tel. (957) 2 12 86; Casino, Kasinonsaari, tel. 2 28 64; Kahvila-Ravintola Terazza, Olavinkatu 44, tel. 2 29 41; Lounas-Café San Martin, Tulliportinkatu 10, tel. 2 27 21; Musta Pässi, Tulliportinkatu 2, tel. 2 22 28; Pietari Kylliäinen, Olavinkatu 15, tel. 2 29 01; Pizzeria Capero, Olavinkatu 51, tel. 2 39 55; Seurahuone, Kauppatori 4, tel. 57 31; Snellman, Olavinkatu 31, tel. 1 31 04; Steakhouse San Martin, Olavinkatu 46, tel. 1 30 04; Wanha Kasino, Kasinonsaari, tel. 2 25 72.
Cafés and cafeterias: Café Konditoria, Olavinkatu 35, tel. 1 27 80; Grilli Carlos, Olavinkatu 19–21, tel. 2 33 57; Grilli Murkina, Olavinkatu 17, tel. 1 26 52; Kahvila Sirena, Olavinkatu 41, tel. 1 21 21; Lounaskahvila Annukka, Olavinkatu 33, tel. 51 43 42; Simpukka Grilli, Olavinkatu 39, tel. 2 23 25.

Stavanger
(Norway)

★Jans Mat & Vinhus (gourmet restaurant), Breitorget, tel. 51 89 47 73; Cardinal Skagen 21, tel. 51 92 97 33; China Town, Skagen 14, tel. 51 89 52 54; City Bistro / Vålandstuen, Madlaveien 18–20, tel. 51 53 95 70; Galeien Bistro (fish dishes), Hundvågveien 18–20, tel. 51 54 91 44; India Tandoori (Indian cuisine), Valberggate 14, tel. 51 89 39 35; Mikado & Hong Kong Garden (Chinese and Japanese cuisine), Østervåg 9, tel. 51 89 33 88; Moon House (Chinese), Sølvbergate 9, tel. 51 89 41 90; Nilsen & Wold, Skagen 42, tel. 51 89 60 50; Robertino, Nedre Holmgate 14, tel. 51 89 50 99; Patrioten Bistro (Norwegian speciality dishes), Hikkevågsveien 100, tel. 51 58 20 20; Sjøhuset Skagen (old barn), Skagenkaien, tel. 51 89 51 80; Straen Fiske-restaurant, Strandkaien, tel. 51 52 62 30.
Cafés: Café Arkaden, Klubbgate 5, tel. 51 89 31 22; Caroline Café, Jerne-baneveien 3, tel. 51 52 87 47; Café Sting, Valberggate 3, tel. 51 53 24 40.

Stockholm
(Sweden)

★Arena, Arenaslingan 7, tel. (08) 6 00 20; ★Coq Blanc (Swedish and French cuisine), Regeringsgatan 111, tel. 11 61 55; ★Djurgårdsbrunns Värdshus, Djurgårdsbrunnsvägen 68, tel. 6 67 90 97; ★Kajplats 9 (Swedish and French cuisine; fish), Norr Mälarstrand/Kungsholmstorg, tel. 52 45 45; ★L'Escargot (one of the best French brasseries in Sweden; closed mid July to mid Aug.), Scheelegatan 8, tel. 53 05 77; ★Mälardrottningen (★view of Riddarfjärgen and Town Hall; fish dishes and international cuisine; bar on Barbara Hutton's luxurious yacht), Riddarholmen, tel. 24 36 00; ★Operakällaren (smörgåsbord, Swedish home cooking; French cuisine), Operahuset, tel. 24 27 00 and 11 11 25; ★Stadshuskällaren (Swedish and international cuisine), Stadshuset, tel. 50 54 54; ★Teatergrillen, Nybroga-tan 3, tel. 10 70 44 and 23 68 42; ★Wärdshuset Stallmästaregården (Swedish and international cuisine; barbecue, grill and café), Norrtull, Haga parken, tel. 24 39 10 and 33 79 15; August Strindberg (Swedish home cooking), Tegnérgatan 38, tel. 30 92 83; Bamboo Palace (Cantonese), Kungsgatan 17, tel. 21 82 41; Centralens Restaurang Orientexpressen (pub and bar, interesting atmosphere), Central Station, tel. 20 20 49; Diplomat Teahouse (fixed-price menu, salads, sandwiches; afternoon tea), Strand-vägen 7, tel. 6 67 18 98; Fem Små Hus (Swedish and international cuisine; cellar restaurant), Nygränd 10, tel. 10 87 75; Fratis (Italian pizzeria and restaurant), Stortorget 7, tel. 20 86 77; Grands Veranda (smörgåsbord), S. Blasieholmshamnen 8, tel. 24 52 12; Kalitka (Russian cuisine), Snickar-backen 2, tel. 24 76 60; Kashmir (Indian and Pakistani cuisine), Nybrogatan 42, tel. 6 61 57 66; Martini (Italian), Norrmalmstorg 4, tel. 20 04 20; Örtagår-den (vegetarian), Östermalmshallen, Nybrogatan 31, tel. 6 62 17 28; Riche (specialities from charcoal grill), Birger Jarlsgatan 4, tel. 23 68 40; Seikoen (Japanese), Tegelbacken 2, tel. 10 03 10 and 20 61 85; Stortorgskällaren (Swedish and vegetarian cuisine, fish; cellar restaurant), Stortorget 7, tel.

10 55 33; Vau-de-Ville (sauerkraut à l'alsacienne, onion soup, pâté de foie, bouillabaisse), Hamngatan 17, tel. 21 25 22.
Cafés: Butiken Operakällaren (desserts, cakes, sweets), Operahuset, tel. 24 27 06; Fjäderholmarnas Café (also restaurant), Fjäderholmarna, tel. 7 18 33 55.

Bistro Tavastia, Hämeenkatu 18, tel. (931) 12 27 94; Coussicca, Nyyrikintie 2, tel. 55 21 00; Myllärit, Åkerlundinkatu 4 (behind station), tel. 14 96 66; Rapukka (also vegetarian), Tammelanpuistokatu 34, tel. 11 00 86; Salud, Otavalankatu 10, tel. 3 59 96; Tiiliholvi, Kauppakatu 10, tel. 12 12 20; Wanhat Roomeot, Kuninkaankatu 24A, tel. 11 07 77. **Tampere** (Finland)

11km/7 miles from centre on Jyväskylä road: Aitolahden Rustholli, tel. 62 01 11.

Bryggen Restaurant (fish dishes), Ø. Bakklandet 66, tel. 73 52 02 30; Dickens, Kjøpmannsgate 57, tel. 73 51 57 50; Havfruen (fish dishes), Kjøpmannsgate 7, tel. 73 53 26 26; Hos Magnus, Kjøpmannsgate 63, tel. 73 52 41 10; Lysthuset Hadrian, Kongsgärden, tel. 73 52 20 06. **Trondheim** (Norway)
Restaurants with late-night licence: Pizzakjelleren, Fjordgate 7, tel. 73 51 38 38; Restaurant Pub (student union), Eigesetergate 1, tel. 73 89 95 10.

Brahen Kellari, Puolalankatu 1, tel. (921) 32 54 00; China City (Chinese cuisine), Hansa-kortteli, tel. 50 11 89; Green Frog, Yliopistonkatu 29B, tel. 33 77 01; Haarikka, Eerikinkatu 19, tel. 50 29 12; Kaskenahde, Kaskenkatu 6, tel. 31 55 52; Myllärimatti, Eerikinkatu 16, tel. 51 50 15; Nikolai Gogol (Russian cuisine), Eerikinkatu 17C, tel. 33 31 52; Parthenon (Greek), Aninkaistenkatu 3, tel. 31 01 01; Pikkumylläri, Vähä-Hämeenkatu 1, tel. 31 96 15; Pinella, Porthaninpuisto, tel. 31 11 02; Pippurimylly, Stålarminkatu 2, tel. 35 95 01; Pizzeria Ristorante Bassi, Aurakatu 1, tel. 31 13 08; Taj Mahal (Indian), Itäinen Pitkäkatu 5, tel. 31 45 95. **Turku** (Finland)
Summer restaurants: Le Pirate (French cuisine), Borenpuisto, tel. 51 14 43; Samppalinna, Itäinen Rantakatu, tel. 31 11 65.
Cafés and snack bars: Aschan, Eerikinkatu 15, Antintalo, tel. 50 11 41; Café Emilia, Wiklundin Tavaratalo, Eerikinkatu 11, tel. 69 87 60; Café Katarina, Vihermaailma, Eteläkaari, tel. 42 17 00; Citycafé, Aninkaistenkatu 6, tel. 50 02 42.

Alexander (also pizzeria), Östra Ågatan 59, tel. (018) 13 50 52; Barowiak (vegetarian), Nedre Slottsgatan 3/Svandammen, tel. 12 40 30; Cavallino, Dragarbrunnsgatan 15, tel. 15 80 65; Chez Pierre, Suttungsgränd 3, tel. 12 85 33; China Garden (Chinese cuisine), Kungsgatan 55, tel. 14 57 30; Classique, Kungsängsgatan 30, tel. 12 38 37; Domtrappkällaren, St Eriksgränd, tel. 13 09 55; Drabanten (home cooking; also café), Bangårdsgatan 13, tel. 12 61 70; Fellini (also café and pub, with music), Svartbäcksgatan 7/Plaza St. Per, tel. 10 06 00; Happy Days, Drottninggatan 12, tel. 13 70 13; Kungsgrillen (lunches; home cooking), Kungsgatan 23, tel. 13 86 36; La Colombe (French cuisine), Svartbäcksgatan 26, tel. 10 10 55; La Comedia (Italian), Skolgatan 31, tel. 11 55 40; Lucullus, Roslagsgatan 2–4, tel. 11 48 00; Queen's (also pizzeria), Drottninggatan 7, tel. 13 72 71; Saluhallsbaren (lunches; pasta), St. Erikstorg/Saluhallen, tel. 12 23 23; Svenssons (also brasserie and pub), Sysslomansgatan 15, tel. 55 33 10; Uplandia, Dragarbrunnsgatan 32, tel. 10 21 60; Vegetariana (vegetarian), Östra Ågatan 11, tel. 11 82 42; Wermlandskällaren, Nedre Slottsgatan 2, tel. 13 57 56; William's (also pub), Åsgränd 5, tel. 14 09 20. **Uppsala** (Sweden)
Cafés: Alma, Universitetshuset, tel. 69 50 55; Fågelsången, Munkgatan 3, tel. 14 52 65; Günther's, Östra Ågatan 31, tel. 13 01 39; Kaffekorgen, St Johannesgatan 25, tel. 13 22 45; Linné, Svartbäcksgatan 24, tel. 10 70 17; Ofvandahl's, Sysslomansgatan 3, tel. 13 42 04; Storkens Kafferum, Stora Torget 3, tel. 15 05 22.

Gutekällaren (international cuisine), Stora Torget, tel. (0498) 1 00 43; Rosengården (Swedish, Italian and French cuisine), Stora Torget, tel. 1 81 **Visby** (Gotland, Sweden)

90; Toftagården (also café), tel. 6 54 00; Värdshuset Lindgården (Gotland specialities), Strandgatan 26, tel. 1 87 00.

Roads

Roads play an important part in the transport systems of the Scandinavian countries, since the railway network is relatively sparse, particularly in Norway, northern Sweden and northern Finland. The road network is steadily being expanded and developed.

The condition of the roads is relatively good. The main roads and important secondary roads have been improved in recent years and given dust-free surfaces. Where the surface is still grit or gravel it is kept as smooth as possible by the use of graders and chemical dust-binding substances. Even so it is advisable to stay a safe distance behind the car in front in order to avoid the risk of a shattered windscreen.

After heavy rain, roads without a hard surface become slippery or muddy, and extra care is required.

Because of the long northern winter some roads in the mountain regions of southern Norway and in northern Norway, Sweden and Finland are open only from about June to October.

The amount of traffic on the roads of Scandinavia has increased considerably in recent years, and in the south is comparable with traffic on the roads of western Europe.

Although in Sweden and Finland no specialised driving skills are generally required, the mountain roads of Norway – sometimes very narrow and frequently with blind corners – call for a high standard of driving and road discipline.

Norway

The most important elements in the Norwegian road system are the numbered national highways (*riksveg*), the stretches of motorway or expressway (*motorveg*) round some of the larger towns and the numbered county roads (*fylkesveg*).

In the mountains of southern Norway and on the rocky shores of fjords the roads have been improved in recent years by widening and the construction of tunnels; but great care is still required, particularly on secondary roads, since there are many blind corners. When two vehicles meet at a narrow or difficult spot the one going uphill always has priority. Some mountain roads still have an alternating one-way system. Owners of trailer caravans or large motor caravans should enquire of one of the Norwegian motoring organisations (see Motoring in Scandinavia) or of the Directorate of Roads (Vegdirektoratet, Grenseveien, 0604 Oslo) about the practicability of their proposed route for their vehicle.

Because of heavy snowfalls some mountain roads are open only from the middle of May.

Sweden

In Sweden the main through roads are the European highways (identified by the letter E followed by a number) and the national highways (*riksväg*), numbered from 10 to 99. These are supplemented by the county roads (*länsväg*), with numbers over 100. In addition there are short stretches of motorway or expressway (*motorväg*), which are constantly being extended. In the southern part of the country the main roads are in general excellent, with firm surfaces; in the far north, however, some roads are surfaced with grit, gravel or sand. The mountain roads near the border with Norway are frequently narrow.

Foreign motorists are subject to special regulations in restricted military areas (*skyddsområde*), which are indicated by warning signposts. There are extensive restricted areas around Kalix, Boden, Luleå, Sundsvall, Gävle and Karlskrona. In these areas foreigners may use the roads only for direct transit, and they are not allowed, except with special permission, to stay at

Öland Bridge (Sweden)

any particular place for more than 24 hours (in some cases 72 hours). Camping, leaving the road and taking photographs are prohibited.

In Finland the numbered main roads are divided into first- and second class roads (*valtatie* and *kantatie*). Trunk roads and national highways are indicated by numbers on a red ground. Around some of the larger towns there are stretches of motorway or expressway (*moottoritie*). Some minor roads and roads north of the Arctic Circle have surfaces of sand, grit or oil-bound gravel. Most roads, however, are wide enough to permit easy passing.

Finland

The Nordic countries are traversed by a number of European highways, the most important of which is E 45 in Denmark, running from the frontier near Flensburg to Frederikshavn.

European highways

In Norway E 6 runs through almost the entire length of the country (Oslo–Trondheim–Narvik–Tromsø; last section E 8).

In Sweden E 20 runs from Göteborg to Stockholm, where it joins E 4, coming from Helsingborg, which continues along the Gulf of Bothnia to the Finnish frontier at Tornio.

In Finland E 75 begins in the Market Square of Helsinki, runs through the interior of the country to Oulu and continues to the frontier town of Tornio, from which E 8 follows the Finnish–Swedish frontier and ends at Tromsø, beyond the Norwegian frontier.

Two important east–west links are E 14, which runs from Sundsvall in Sweden by way of Östersund to Trondheim in Norway, and E 12, from Umeå in Sweden to Mo i Rana in Norway.

The sign shown in the margin is frequently seen on the roads of the Nordic countries. It indicates a tourist attraction or feature of interest (e.g. a castle, a stave church or interesting rock carvings).

Safety and Security

Safety on the Road

Seat-belts	Make sure that you have your seat-belt on and that your passengers, in both the front and the rear seats, have theirs on too. The belts should be properly adjusted – taut and not twisted. A loosely fitting belt can cause additional injury in an accident. Seat-belts are most effective when used with properly adjusted head-restraints. These should have their upper edge at least as high as the level of the eyes: only then do they give protection to the cervical vertebrae.
Equipment	Strongly recommended are a warning triangle, a first aid kit and, if the view through the rear window is blocked by luggage or you are trailing a caravan, an additional external mirror. However, these items are not compulsory Such items as the first aid kit should be carefully stowed and not left loose, for example on the rear shelf, since they might become dangerous projectiles if you have to brake sharply.
Other useful equipment	Other items that it is advisable to have: tow rope; spare light bulbs, fuses and fan-belt; tools; jump leads; woollen rug; gloves; torch.
Fire extinguisher	A fire extinguisher of at least 2 kilograms capacity should be carried. In the case of a car fire there is usually time to get the passengers and luggage out: experiments have shown that when a fire starts in the carburettor it takes between five and ten minutes to spread to the interior of the car. Extreme caution is required, however, if the petrol tank is damaged and there is a leak of petrol: when this happens fire can rapidly envelop the whole car.
Camera	It is useful to have a camera (with flash) to record the circumstances of an accident. What is important is not the damage to the vehicles involved but the general situation. In particular photographs should be taken from some distance away in the direction of travel (in both directions).
Laminated windscreen	A laminated windscreen is an important safety precaution. When hit by a stone, for example, it will not break into dangerous fragments: the outer skin will shatter but will remain in place, and you will still be able to see through the windscreen.
Spare fuel	A spare can of fuel is a useful precaution in the remoter parts of the Scandinavian countries, where there may be considerable distances between petrol stations.
Brakes	The effectiveness of brake fluid is reduced over time by dust, water condensation and chemical decomposition: it should, therefore, be renewed at least every two years. It is advisable before going on a long journey to check the whole braking system: when you go on holiday – with a heavily laden car, and perhaps driving in hilly country – the brakes have more work to do.
Tyres	Tyres should have at least 2 millimetres of tread to hold the road properly and maintain their grip even in wet weather. Wide sports tyres should have 3 millimetres, winter tyres at least 4 millimetres. Tyres at the proper pressure hold the road better and save fuel. Pressures should be checked when the tyres are cold, not when they are hot after driving. All tyres are required by law to be of the same type (i.e. either radial or cross-ply). For maximum safety all tyres should have the same depth of tread.

Drivers who alternate between summer and winter tyres should store the tyres not in use on their rims. This lengthens their life and saves time and money when fitting them to the car.

Lights should be regularly checked. If your lights are working properly you not only see better but are seen better by other drivers.

Lights

You can easily check the rear lights and brake lights for yourself when you pull up at traffic lights in front of a bus or van, which will reflect the lights like a mirror. You can check whether the headlights and front indicators are working after dark in your garage or when parked in front of a shop window.

When driving at night or on wet roads you should wipe your headlights and rear lights every 50–100km/30–60 miles. Even a thin layer of dirt on the headlights can reduce their strength by half; if they are very dirty they can lose anything up to 90% of their power.

With increasing age lights decline markedly in efficiency, as tungsten from the coil is deposited on the glass. Bulbs which are defective should be replaced in pairs, so that they are equally bright on both sides.

Spectacle-wearers drive more safely at night if they have special non-reflective glasses. Tinted glasses should not be worn after dark. Since all glass reflects part of the light reaching it, even a clear windscreen lets through only some 90% of the available light; and spectacle-wearers lose another 10%. Tinted windscreens and tinted glasses allow only about half the available light to reach the eye, and safe driving is no longer possible.

Spectacle-wearers

Fog-lights should be mounted symmetrically, in pairs and at the same height. The best place for them is on the front bumper: at that height they give best visibility without dazzling oncoming drivers.

Fog-lights

It is illegal to use fog-lights except when visibility is seriously reduced by fog, rain or snow.

Up to two rear fog-lights may be mounted, not less than 10cm/4in. from the brake-lights and no higher than 100cm/40in. above the road. They may be used only when visibility is reduced to 50m/55yd.

When driving in fog:

Driving in fog

Rear fog-lights should be switched off when you see the outline of a vehicle following you in your rear mirror.

Adjust your speed according to the visibility.

Keep a safe distance behind the vehicle in front of you. Do not overtake.

Use your windscreen-wipers: heavy fog deposits a film of water on the windscreen.

Organising your Trip

Good organisation, starting before you leave home, is important. If you know that everything is in order at home this will allow you to enjoy a relaxed holiday.

It is helpful to draw up a check list of what requires to be done and thought of, ticking off each item as it is dealt with.

Don't forget:
passports;
driving licence and car registration document;
green card;
AA membership card and 5-Star Service documents;
tickets (air, rail, ferry) and confirmation of bookings;
photocopies of important documents (in luggage);
traveller's cheques, Eurocheques, credit and cheque cards, cash;
road maps;
first aid kit, and any medicine which you take regularly;
spare glasses if worn, and sun-glasses.

Insurance

Make sure that you have adequate insurance cover (car insurance, health insurance, insurance against loss and theft of property). Full cover matched to your requirements is provided by the AA 5-Star service (which is available also to non-members).

If you have an accident

However carefully you drive, accidents can happen. If you are involved in an accident, the first rules are: whatever the provocation, don't get angry; be polite; and keep calm. Then take the following action:

1. Warn oncoming traffic by switching on your car's warning lights if you have them and setting your warning triangle (and, if you have one, a flashing light) some distance before the scene of the accident.

2. Look after anyone who has been injured, calling an ambulance if necessary.

3. In Finland any accident should be reported to the police and also to the Finnish Motor Insurers Bureau, Bulevardi 28, 00120 Helsinki; tel. (90) 19 25 1. In Sweden the police take particulars and make a report on any accident other than a minor one, and their report can be made available to the parties concerned. The Norwegian police make a report only in the case of a serious accident.

4. Record full particulars of the accident. These should include:
(a) names and addresses of witnesses (independent witnesses are particularly important);
(b) damage to the vehicles involved;
(c) name and address of the other driver, and of the owner if different;
(d) name and address of the other party's insurance company and, if possible, the number of the insurance certificate;
(e) registration number of the other vehicle;
(f) damage or injury to yourself or other persons;
(g) number of policeman or address of police station if involved;
(h) date, time and location of the accident;
(i) speed of the vehicles involved;
(j) width of the road, any road signs and the condition of the road surface;
(k) any marks on the road relevant to the accident;
(l) the weather and the manner of the other driver's driving.

5. Write down the names and addresses of witnesses. Draw a sketch of the accident, showing the layout of the road, the direction in which the vehicles were travelling and their position at the time of impact, any road signs and the names of streets or roads. If you have a camera, take photographs of the scene.

6. Fill in a European Accident Statement if you have one (it is supplied by most insurers and is included in the AA 5-Star Service pack. It is also provided with the Green Card), have it signed by the other driver and give him a copy.
Make no admission of responsibility for the accident, and above all do not sign any document in a language you do not understand.
On your return home you should of course report the accident to your insurance company and send them the European Accident Statement along with the form which they will ask you to complete.

Sauna

With almost 1½ million saunas – roughly one for every four of the population – Finland is the land of the sauna *par excellence*. The original form was the "smoke sauna", which later gave place to the stove-heated sauna.

The typical Finnish sauna is in a log cabin, with windows and a view of a lake. A sauna bath is a social occasion, in which beer cooled in the lowest layer of water and sausages roasted on the heat-retaining stones on top of the oven also play a part.

When water is thrown on the hot stones a wave of dry steam (*löyly*) is given off, and this stimulates perspiration. To increase the perspiration the bathers brush themselves, or each other, with bunches of soft birch twigs, which opens the pores still further and increases the blood circulation. The best temperature is between 80° and 100°C (176° and 212°F): a relatively moderate temperature leaving sufficient humidity in the air is healthier than very hot and dry air. The best way of cooling off after a sauna is a swim in the lake. In winter a hole is made in the ice, the *avanto*, through which to dip into the water. After a wash and a gradual cooling off period comes a feeling of complete relaxation and wellbeing.

As a rule, except in a family group, men and women take their sauna separately. The party gets together after the bath, when, in the evening twilight, the bathers sit in front of the stove, on the veranda or on the boat landing-stage, with their legs dangling in the water.

Visitors can enjoy a sauna at most hotels, holiday villages and camping sites, where there are separate saunas for men and women.

Information about the sauna can be obtained in the Sauna Village near Jyväskylä in central Finland – Muuramen Saunakylä, FIN–40950 Muurame, tel. (941) 73 26 70 – where there are 24 saunas dating from the 18th and 19th centuries.

Shipping

See Car and Passenger Ferries; Ferries within Scandinavia

Shopping, Souvenirs

All the Nordic countries excel in the field of design. Their designers not only produce the fine furniture of light-coloured wood for which these countries are famous, but also give a wide variety of everyday objects and craft products a modern and yet timeless stamp with their simple and functional lines. It is worth remembering that the high Scandinavian value-added taxes can be recovered by foreign visitors when they leave the country. See Tax-Free Service.

Knitwear (in colourful Norwegian patterns), wooden objects, pewter, enamels, brassware, tapestries, toys, reindeer skins and antlers.   Norway

Glass (Orrefors, Kosta & Boda), wooden objects, textiles, stoneware, ceramics, pewter, reindeer skins, hand-made articles, mostly of wood, in traditional Sami (Lapp) style.   Sweden

Silver and bronze jewellery (sometimes based on ancient models), porcelain, ceramics, hand-woven Ryijy carpets, glass, reindeer skins and antlers.   Finland

Silver jewellery from Telemark (Norway)

Sport

The Scandinavian countries offer ideal conditions for active holidays of all kinds. On access to the countryside and behaviour in the country see "Everyman's Right".

Following are addresses from which information may be obtained about the most popular kinds of sport and recreation in Norway, Sweden and Finland.

Archery

The Finnish Archery Association has 70 member clubs. The best places for archery are in the sports centres of Helsinki, Lahti, Oulu, Pori and Tampere; there are no facilities for the hiring of equipment.
Information:

Finnish Archery Association
Radiokatu 20
FIN–00240 Helsinki
tel. (90) 1 58 24 46, fax (90) 14 52 37

Ballooning

In 1897 S. A. Andrée died during an attempt to fly over the North Pole in a balloon. He is commemorated by a balloonists' meet held twice a year at Gränna.
Information:
Ballonkonsulterna, Per E. Johansson
Blomsterkungsvägen 362
S–16243 Vällingby
tel. (08) 38 28 74

The best and healthiest way to explore the natural landscapes of Scandinavia is by cycling. It is easy to hire bicycles, and they can be carried on trains and boats. Maps and suggested routes can be obtained from tourist information offices.
Information:
Den Rustne Eike
Vestbaneplassen 2
N–0250 Oslo
tel. 22 83 72 31, fax 22 83 63 59

Cycling

Tip: In Norway, areas specially suited to cyclists include the National Parks and the valley regions such as Setesdal, Gausdal and Gudbrandsdal. The Lofoten Islands also lend themselves to being explored on bicycle.

Cykelfrämjandet
Box 6027
S–10231 Stockholm
tel. (08) 32 16 80, fax (08) 31 05 03

Svenska Cykel Sällskapet
Box 606, S–16406 Krista
tel. (08) 7 51 62 04, fax (08) 7 51 19 35

Finnish Youth Hostel Association
Yrjönkatu 28B
FIN–00100 Helsinki
tel. (90) 6 94 03 77, fax (90) 6 93 13 49

Driving a team of huskies over the ice, with snow-clouds lowering overhead, is a very special kind of holiday experience. Information:

Dog-sleigh driving

Den Norske Turistforening (DNT)
Postboks 1963 Vika
N–0125 Oslo
tel. 22 83 25 50

Domän Turist AB
Box 521, S–18215 Danderyd
tel. (08) 7 55 27 30

Forestry Office
Erottajankatu 2
FIN–00121 Helsinki
tel. (90) 6 16 31

The national Tourist Boards issue free brochures and leaflets on fishing in their respective countries. Further details can be obtained from local tourist information offices and the following bodies:

Fishing

Statens Fiskefond
Direktoratet for Vilt og Ferskvannsfisk
Elgesetergate 10
N–7000 Trondheim

Sportfiskarna
Box 11501, S–10061 Stockholm
tel. (08) 7 43 07 90

Ageba Travel Agency
Pohjoisranta 4
FIN–00170 Helsinki
tel. (90) 66 11 12, fax (90) 15 53 88

Sport

Flying and parachuting	Twenty clubs run beginners' courses during the summer. Information: Finnish Aeronautical Association Malmi Airport FIN–00700 Helsinki tel. (90) 37 80 55, fax (90) 3 74 15 51
Gold-panning	Gold-panning will never make you rich, but it is fun. Information about guided safaris and camping holidays: Karasjok Opplevelser A/S Postboks 45 N–9730 Karasjok tel. 78 46 73 60 Norrbottens Turistråd Kungsgatan 5 S–951 84 Luleå tel. (0920) 9 40 70 Wildmarkzentrum Kiilopää FIN–99800 Ivalo tel. (9697) 8 71 01 Suomen Latu FIN–00130 Helsinki tel. (90) 17 01 01, fax (90) 66 33 76
Golf	The season lasts from May to September/October. Information about golf courses and charges in Norway: Norges Golfforbund Hauger Skolevei 1 N–1351 Rud tel. (67) 15 46 00, fax (67) 13 86 40 There are 180 golf courses in Sweden. Information: Svenska Golfförbundet Kevingestrand 20 S–18211 Danderyd tel. (08) 6 22 15 00, fax (08) 7 75 84 39 Finland has 72 golf clubs. Information: Finnish Golf Association Radiokatu 20 FIN–00240 Helsinki tel. (90) 1 58 22 44, fax (90) 14 71 45
Hang-gliding	This sport is not yet widely practised in the Scandinavian countries, though Sweden offers plenty of scope for it, with good thermal conditions. Information: Norsk Aeroclub Møllesvingen 2 N–0854 Oslo tel. 22 69 03 11 Svalbard Polar Travel A/S Næringsbygget N–9170 Longyearbyen tel. 79 02 23 03, fax 79 02 10 20

Racing is very popular in Finland, with almost 700 race meetings in a year.
Information:
Suomen Hippos ry
Tulkinkulja 3
FIN–02600 Espoo
tel. (90) 5 12 14 11, fax (90) 5 12 17 91

Finnish Equestrian Federation
Radiokatu 20
FIN–00240 Helsinki
tel. (90) 1 58 23 15, fax (90) 14 52 37 and 14 68 64

There are orienteering competitions all over Norway (200 courses) and
Finland between spring and autumn.
Information:
Østfold Orienteringskrets
O. G. Gate 41
N–1700 Sarpsborg
tel. 69 14 01 31

DNT (Norwegian Training Association)
Stortingsgaten 28
Postboks 1963 Vika
N–0125 Oslo
tel. 22 83 25 50, fax 22 83 24 78

Finnish Orienteering Association
Radiokatu 20
FIN–00240 Helsinki
tel. (90) 15 81, fax (90) 14 52 37

The friendly Norwegian fjord horses are popular riding animals. They can
be hired all over Norway, and there are numerous riding centres with riding
instructors.
Information:
Norsk Rytterforbund
Hauger Skolevei 1
N–1351 Rud
tel. 67 56 99 00

There are more than 100 riding centres in Sweden, and "wilderness treks"
are organised.
Information:
Sveriges Ridlägerarrangörers Riksförbund (SRR)
Box 30013
S–10425 Stockholm

In southern Scandinavia the game animals are similar to those found in
Central Europe (deer, small game, wildfowl). Farther north there are also
elks. The elk season is normally confined to only a few weeks in the year,
and the sportsman must be accompanied by a local "gillie"; the cost of an
elk-shooting permit is also quite high.
  Information from tourist information offices.

Skiing in summer is a typically Norwegian experience. The glaciers have a
permanent snow cover, and skiing is possible in July, even in a bathing
suit.
Information:
Galdhøppigen Sommerskisenter
N–2687 Bøverdalen
tel. (61) 21 17 50, fax (61) 21 12 86

Sport

Survival training

For those who want a more strenuous holiday there is survival training on Finland's eastern frontier – travelling on foot, in a canoe or by jeep.
Information:
Ilomantsin Matkailu Oy
Mantsintie 8
FIN–82900 Ilomantsi
tel. (974) 2 17 07, fax (974) 2 32 70

Tennis

Many Norwegian hotels have their own tennis courts; it is best to bring your own equipment.
Information:
Norges Tennisforbund
Hauger Skolovei 1
N–1351 Rud
tel. 67 56 88 00

All over Sweden there are tennis courts open to visitors (club membership unnecessary).
Information:
Svenska Tennisförbundet
Lidingövägen 75
S–11537 Stockholm
tel. (08) 6 67 97 70, fax (08) 6 64 66 06

In Finland there are well over 1500 tennis courts, either open-air or indoor, throughout the country.
Information:
Finnish Tennis Association
Radiokatu 20
FIN–00240 Helsinki
tel. (90) 15 81

Walking and climbing

From the point of view of weather the best months for walking in any of the Scandinavian countries are June, August and September.

The Norwegian mountain regions offer endless scope for hill, glacier and fell walking and climbing. Proper clothing and equipment and advance planning are essential. Information and advice can be obtained from local tourist information offices and from the following:

Den Norske Turistforening (DNT)
Postboks 1963 Vika
Stortingsgaten 28
N–05161 Oslo
tel. 22 83 25 50

There are well waymarked footpaths and trails, running through beautiful country, all over Sweden.
Information:
Swedish Touring Club (STF)
Box 25
S–10120 Stockholm
tel. 4 63 21 00, fax (08) 6 78 19 58

Friluftsfrämjandet
Box 708
S–10130 Stockholm
tel. (08) 23 43 50

Svenska Gångförbundet
Box 104
S–83121 Östersund
tel. (063) 10 68 00

Walkers, well equipped for the trail

Canoeing on the Jægervatn (northern Norway)

Sport

The finest time for walking in Finnish Lapland is autumn with its colourful display of foliage. Brochures on waymarked footpaths and trails are issued by the Finnish Tourist Board, and information about guided walks can be obtained from local tourist information offices.

Water sports
Canoeing and rafting

Canoeists have a choice between the pleasure of gliding easily over one of Scandinavia's many lakes and – at the other extreme – trying the exciting sport of canoeing or rafting over rapids or on rapidly flowing mountain streams, accompanied by a local guide. There are also numerous regattas.
Information:
Norges Padleførbund
Brynsveien 100
N–1352 Kolsäs
tel. 67 13 77 00

Norges Padloførbund
Hauger Skolevei 1
N–1351 Rud
tel. 67 15 46 00, fax 67 13 33 35

Svenska Kanotförbundet
Skeppsbron 11
S–61135 Nyköping
tel. (0155) 6 95 08, fax (0155) 1 87 80

Finnish Canoe Association
Radiokatu 2
FIN–00240 Helsinki
tel. (90) 1 58 23 63, fax (90) 14 52 37

Diving

There are excellent diving grounds, in very clear water, in the coastal skerries.
Information:
Norges Dykkerforbund
Hauger Skolevei 1
N–1251 Rud
tel. 67 58 88 00

Swedish Diving Association
Box 14232
S–10440, Stockholm
tel. (08) 4 59 09 90, fax (08) 4 59 09 99

Finnish Diving Association
Radiokatu 2
FiN–00240 Helsinki
tel. (90) 1 58 22 57, fax (90) 1 58 25 18

Sailing

Few countries have coasts better suited for sailing than Norway and Sweden.
Information:
Kongelig Norsk Seilerforening (KNS)
Huk Aveny 3
N–0287 Oslo
tel. 22 42 74 10

Svenska Seglarförbundet
Idrottens Hus
S–12387 Farsta
tel. (08) 6 05 60 00, fax (08) 6 05 63 31

Finnish Yachting Association
Radiokatu 20
FIN–00240 Helsinki
tel. (90) 15 81, fax (90) 14 52 37

Surfing is becoming increasingly popular in Scandinavia. Surf-boards can
be rented at many resorts.
Information:
Sea-Sport Windsurfingcenter
Bygdøy Allé 60A
N–0265 Oslo
tel. 22 44 79 28

Swedish Windsurfer AB
Box 1329
S–18125 Lidingö

Finnish Wind-Surfing Association
Pentti Mäkinen
Tuohimäentie 86B
FIN–00670 Helsinki
tel. (90) 37 11 33

Information:
Norges Vannskiforbund
Hauger Skolevei 1
N–1351 Rud
tel. 67 56 88 00

The Swedish Water Skiing Association
Idrottens Hus
S–12387 Farsta
tel. (08) 6 05 60 00, fax (08) 93 80 09

Finnish Water-Skiing Association
Radiokatu 20
FIN–00240 Helsinki
tel. (90) 1 58 25 95, fax (90) 14 52 37

Skiing is a sport widely practised in Norway, Sweden and Finland, mostly
in the form of cross-country (langlauf) skiing, ski treks over considerable
distances are also popular. Norway in particular, with its extensive mountain regions, is a stronghold of winter sports, and the province of Telemark
played a part in the development of skiing techniques.
   Information from the tourist information offices of the winter sports
centres listed below.

Winter Sports Centres (see map on page 574)

Norway has cross-country skiing, ski trekking and downhill skiing. In the
larger skiing areas there are several winter sports resorts.

1 Oslo and surrounding area
   (Oslo, Eggedal, Hurdal, Norefjell, Ringerike, Vikersund-Modum)

2 Kongsberg and Numedal
   (Kongsberg, Flesberg and the eastern Blefjell, the Numedal as far as
   Dagali, Uvdal)

3 Telemark and Setesdal
   (Telemark: Bolkesjø and Blefjell, Gautefall, Haukelifjell, Lifjell, Marge-
   dahl, Rauland, Vinje, Rjukan area; Setesdal: Byglandsfjord, Vrådal-
   Kviteseid, Hovden, Vråliosen, Åserdal)

Winter Sports Centres in Scandinavia

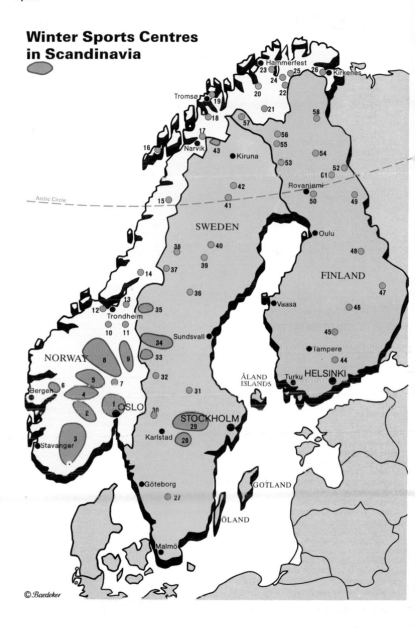

4 Hallingdal and Bergen Railway
(Dagli-Skurdalen, Geilo-Ustaoset, Gol, Golsfjell, Hemsedal)

5 Valdres
(Fagernes area: Aurdal-Tonsåsen, Fagernes, Fjellstølen, Hovda-Sanderstølen, Vaset-Nøsen; Beitostølen area; Vang-Filefjell area: Tyin and surrounding area, Eidsbugaren-Tyinholmen-Jotunheim)

6 Western Norway
(Finse, Mjølfjell, Vatnahalsen, Voss, Oppheim, Seljestad, Standa, Sykkylven, Ørsta, Utvikfjell)

7 Vestoppland–Gjøvik
(Gjøvik, Toten, Lygnaseter, Synnfjell)

8 Gudbrandsdal and Dovre Railway
(Hamar and surrounding area; Lillehammer and surrounding area, Nordseter, Sjusjøen, Øyerfjell, Tretten; middle Gudbrandsdal, with Espedal, Kvam, Ringebu, Gausdal and Vinstra; northern Gudbrandsdal and Jotunheim, with Bøverdalen, Sjodalen and Vågå; northern Gudbrandsdal and Rondane, with Høvringen, Mysuseter and Otta; northern Gudbrandsdal and Dovrefjell, with Bjorli, Dombås and Hjerkinn)

9 Østerdal
(Atna, Engerdal, Elverum, Folldal, Os, Rena, Rendalen and Tynset)

10 Oppdal

11 Røros

12 Trondheim and surrounding area

13 Meråker

14 Grong

15 Lønsdal

16 Svolvær

17 Narvik

18 Bardu

19 Tromsø

20 Alta

21 Kautokeino

22 Karasjok

23 Skaidi

24 Skoganvarre

25 Levajok

26 Kirkenes

Sweden: Skiing is possible from Skåne in the south to the far north of Lapland from November until mid May.

27 Isaberg

Sport

28 Närke

29 Västmanland

30 Sunne

31 Lake Siljan, with Leksand, Rättvik and Tällberg

32 Sälen

33 Idre and Gröveljön

34 Härjedalen, with Vemdalsfjäll, Funäsdalen, Bruksvallarna, Tänndalen, Tännas and Fjällnäs

35 Sylarna, Storulvån and Blåhammaren; Øre, Duved and Trillevallen

36 Strömsund

37 Gäddede and Stora Blåsjön

38 Borgafjäll and Saxnäs

39 Vilhelmina

40 Storuman

41 Jokkmokk

42 Dundred

43 Abisko, Björkliden and Riksgränsen

Finland offers ample scope for cross-country skiing (35 centres) and ski trekking. The following is a selection of areas with facilities for both cross-country and downhill skiing.

44 Lahti

45 Jyväskylä, with Laajavuori

46 Kuopio, with Puijomäki

47 Koli Hills, with Lieksa

48 Sotkamo, with the Vuokatti Sports Institute

49 Kuusamo–Ruka

50 Rovaniemi, with Ounasvaara

51 Kemijärvi, with Suomutunturi and Pyhätunturi

52 Salla, with Sallatunturi

53 Kolari–Yllästunturi

54 Sodankylä, with Luostotunturi

55 Muonio, with Olostunturi

56 Pallastunturi area

57 Kilpisjärvi, with Saanafjäll

58 Saariselkä–Kaunispää

Summer Time

See Time

Tax-Free Shopping Service

When making purchases of some value visitors should take advantage of the Tax-Free Shopping service which operates in Norway, Sweden and Finland. The service, offered by the numerous shops which display a special blue and yellow sign, gives a reduction of over 11 per cent on the normal price to foreign visitors, who pay the full amount in the shop but recover the amount of value-added tax when leaving the country. The scheme does not apply to foodstuffs, sweets, tobacco goods or services.

The visitor must produce a passport when making a purchase and pay the normal price, and will then be given a "tax-free cheque" (the reverse side of which is best filled in giving name, address and passport number when in the shop). The goods will be packed and sealed, and must not be opened before leaving Scandinavia.

The tax-free cheque must be stamped at the airport check-in, and the tax paid (less a service charge) will then be reimbursed by a Tax-Free Shopping representative in the departures hall. On international ferries the cheque will be stamped by the ticket inspector, and the tax will be reimbursed either by the purser's office or at the customs.

Telephoning

Local dialling codes in Sweden begin with 0, in Finland with 9. When dialling from abroad the 0 or 9 should be omitted. In Norway telephone area codes ceased to exist from 1993, and were incorporated into the customer number, which now has eight digits instead of six as before.

Telephone calls can be made from public telephone boxes or from tele-graph offices (the postal and telephone services are separate institutions). In most telephone boxes it is possible to be called back. Payphones accept 1, 5 and often 10 kr coins.

Norway

International dialling codes:
Norway to the United Kingdom: 095 44
Norway to the United States or Canada: 095 1
United Kingdom to Norway: 00 47
United States or Canada to Norway: 011 47

Telephone, telegraph, telex and fax services are available in telegraph offices (marked Tele or Telebutik). There are numerous payphones using either cash (1 or 5 sek) or prepaid phone cards or credit cards.

Sweden

International dialling codes:
Sweden to the United Kingdom: 009 44
Sweden to the United States or Canada: 009 1
United Kingdom to Sweden: 00 46
United States or Canada to Sweden: 011 46

Payphones accept 1 and 5 mk coins.

Finland

International dialling codes:
Finland to the United Kingdom: 990 44
Finland to the United States or Canada: 990 1
United Kingdom to Finland: 00 358
United States or Canada to Finland: 011 358

Time

Norway and Sweden observe Central European Time (one hour ahead of Greenwich Mean Time), Finland observes Eastern European Time (two hours ahead of GMT).

Summer Time (one hour ahead of normal time) is in force from the end of March to the end of September.

Travel Documents

For a stay of up to three months in Scandinavia only a passport is required. A visa is needed only for a longer stay or for visitors taking up paid work.

Under the Nordic Passport and Customs Union there are no passport controls between the Scandinavian countries.

National driving licences and car registration documents are accepted, and must be carried. It is advisable to have an international insurance certificate ("green card"). Cars must bear an oval nationality plate.

When to Go

The best months of the year in the Scandinavian countries are June, July or August, when the weather is at its warmest and in the far north the sun never disappears below the horizon or sets only for a very brief period. Even in northern Scandinavia it can be surprisingly warm, and temperatures above 20°C/68°F are not uncommon. The best season varies from country to country: southern Sweden May to October, central and northern Sweden June to September, Norway June to August, Finland July and August.

The best months for winter sports are March and April, when the days are beginning to grow longer.

Youth Hostels, Holiday Houses and Cabins

A holiday in Scandinavia can be an expensive matter, since hotel tariffs tend to be higher than in other European countries. There are, however, cheaper forms of accommodation, such as youth hostels (which are not confined to young people) and the holiday houses or cabins, often situated on the shores of a fjord or a lake, which are a typically Scandinavian type of holiday accommodation. The following are some sources of information.

Norway

Youth hostels

Norske Vandrerhjem
Dronningensgate 26
N–0154 Oslo
tel. 22 42 14 10, fax 22 42 44 76

Holiday houses
and cabins

Den Norske Hytteformidling A/S
Postboks 3404 Bjølsen
N–0406 Oslo
tel. 22 35 67 10, fax 22 71 94 13
(Booklet "Norsk Hytteferie")

De Norske Hytteformidling A/S
Lille Markvejen 13
N–5005 Bergen
tel. 55 23 20 80, fax 55 23 24 04
(Booklet "Fjordhytter")

A holiday house in Sweden

Sweden

Svenska Turistföreningen (STF)
Box 25
Drottningsgatan 31–33
S–10120 Stockholm
tel. (08) 4 63 21 00, fax (08) 6 78 19 58

Youth hostels

Information about holiday houses, cabins and accommodation in private houses can be obtained from local tourist information offices.
    For cheap overnight accommodation, look out for the signs "stuga" (cabin, holiday house), "stugor", "stugby" (cabin village), "rum" or "rum att hyra" (room to let). In accommodation of this kind, however, visitors must provide their own bed linen.

Holiday houses and cabins

Information about farmhouse holidays can be obtained from local tourist information offices.

Farmhouse holidays

Finland

Youth Hostel Stadionin Maja
P. Stadiontie 3b
Helsinki
tel. (90) 49 60 71

Youth hostels

Reservations of holiday houses, holiday villages and farmhouse holidays:
Lomarengas ry
Malminkaari 23C
FIN–00700 Helsinki
tel. (90) 35 16 13 21, fax (90) 35 16 13 70

Holiday houses, etc.

Youth Hostels, Holiday Houses and Cabins

Holiday houses:
Lomaliiton Myyntipalvelu
Toinenlinja 17
FIN–00530 Helsinki
tel. (90) 71 64 22, fax (90) 71 37 13

Farmhouse holidays

Brochure in English available from:
Suomen 4H-Liitto
Abrahaminkatu 7
FIN–00180 Helsinki
tel. (90) 64 22 33, fax (90) 62 22 74

Bed and breakfast

"Bed and breakfast" accommodation on the British model is also available in Finland. Information from Lomarengas ry (see above).

Index

Index

Index

Principal Sights of Tourist Interest

Note: The places listed above are merely a selection of the principal sights in Norway, Sweden and Finland – scenic attractions and other places of interest. There are, of course, innumerable other sights to which attention is drawn in the A to Z section of the guide by one or two stars.

Imprint

274 illustrations, 40 town plans, 3 ground-plans, 8 drawings, 16 general maps, 6 special maps, 1 large map of Scandinavia

Original German text: Waltraud Andersen, Therese Apelkrans, Barbara Conrad, Dr Johannes Gamillscheg, Reiner Gatermann, Prof. Hans-Dieter Haas, Prof. Wolfgang Hassenpflug, Jens-Uwe Kumpch, Dr Walter Thauer, Johannes Wendland, Christine Wessely, Vera Beck

Editorial work: Baedeker-Redaktion (Gisela Bockamp)

General direction: Dr Peter H. Baumgarten, Baedeker Stuttgart

Cartography: Gert Oberländer, Munich; Hallwag AG, Berne (large map of Scandinavia)

Source of illustrations: Amberg (5); Baedeker-Archiv (1); Bohnacker (27); Finnish Tourist Office (14); Fotoagentur Lade (BAV, 2); Bergmann (1); Bramaz (3); Dass (4); Grossmann (2); Hahn (1); Hinrichs (1); Krecichwost (3); Kürtz (1); Lorenz (1); Mathis (1); Morell (3); Rohr (2); von Girard (18); Görtz (5); Grube (2); Haafke (2); Hauken (1); Historia-Photo (3); Hokkinen (1); Jansen (14); Jyväskylä Municipal Tourist Office (1); Kumpch (1); Lantmäteriet, Gävle (1); Lochstampfer (20); Molander (1); Müller (50); Nahm (1); Nationalmuseet, Stockholm (1); Neumeister (6); Nordis Picture Pool (Bünte, 11); Hermansen (1); Marschel (4); Puntschuh (1); Schmidt (1); Storvik (1); Popow (1); Pott (7); SAS (1); Scheiper (3); Swedish Tourist Office (14); Spitta (1); Studio Esko, Keuruu (1); Trobitzsch (14); TT-Line (Brusius, 1); Turesson (1); Ullstein Bilderdienst (6); Wendland (2); ZEFA (Damm, 1; Eugen, 1).

English language edition: Alec Court

Original English translation: James Hogarth

Revised text: David Cocking

2nd English edition 1996

© Baedeker Stuttgart
Original German edition 1994

© 1996 Jarrold and Sons Limited
English language edition worldwide

© 1996 The Automobile Association
United Kingdom and Ireland

Published in the United States by:
Macmillan Travel
A Simon & Schuster Macmillan Company
1633 Broadway
New York, NY 10019–6785

Macmillan is a registered trademark of Macmillan, Inc.

Distributed in the United Kingdom by the Publishing Division of the Automobile Association, Fanum House, Basingstoke, Hampshire RG21 2EA

A CIP catalogue record of this book is available from the British Library

Licensed user:
Mairs Geographischer Verlag GmbH & Co.,
Ostfildern-Kemnat bei Stuttgart

Printed in Italy by G. Canale & C.S.p.A – Borgaro T.se –Turin

Notes